Lecture Notes in Computer Science 10572

Commenced Publication in 1973
Founding and Former Series Editors:
Gerhard Goos, Juris Hartmanis, and Jan van Leeuwen

Editorial Board

Tolga Bektaş · Stefano Coniglio
Antonio Martinez-Sykora · Stefan Voß (Eds.)

Computational Logistics

8th International Conference, ICCL 2017
Southampton, UK, October 18–20, 2017
Proceedings

 Springer

Editors
Tolga Bektaş (iD)
University of Southampton
Southampton
UK

Stefano Coniglio
University of Southampton
Southampton
UK

Antonio Martinez-Sykora (iD)
University of Southampton
Southampton
UK

Stefan Voß (iD)
University of Hamburg
Hamburg
Germany

ISSN 0302-9743   ISSN 1611-3349   (electronic)
Lecture Notes in Computer Science
ISBN 978-3-319-68495-6   ISBN 978-3-319-68496-3   (eBook)
https://doi.org/10.1007/978-3-319-68496-3

Library of Congress Control Number: 2017954978

LNCS Sublibrary: SL1 – Theoretical Computer Science and General Issues

Printed on acid-free paper

This Springer imprint is published by Springer Nature
The registered company is Springer International Publishing AG
The registered company address is: Gewerbestrasse 11, 6330 Cham, Switzerland

Preface

Logistics is central to world trade. It encompasses a wide range of activities, including the production, handling, storage, and distribution of goods, as well as the use of communication technologies needed for the flow of information to meet consumer demand. In order for these activities to be run in an efficient manner, good, or optimal, decisions are to be taken in relation to various aspects of a logistics system, including the design of the physical and the digital infrastructure on which the logistics network will operate, the interaction between various entities in the network, and the flow of products and information. The breadth and the range of tasks involved in logistics make the management and coordination of the activities complex and challenging, and require advanced methods for the design, planning, and control of the system. This is where computational tools are of competitive advantage, offering ways to capture, store, visualize, and share information to solve complex problems employing optimization techniques, to evaluate systems and policies using simulation, and to enable collaborative schemes through the use of algorithmic mechanisms. The use of computational technology facilitates addressing these challenges within reasonable amounts of computational time and supports decision-making.

The International Conference on Computational Logistics (ICCL) is a forum where recent advances on the topic are presented and discussed. This volume offers a selection of 38 peer-reviewed papers submitted to the 8th International Conference on Computational Logistics (ICCL 2017), held in Southampton during October 18–20, 2017. The papers are indicative of the recent work that is being undertaken in computational logistics, categorized in what emerged as four sufficiently distinct but interrelated areas within computational logistics, and which appear as four sections in the volume:

1. Vehicle Routing and Scheduling: The papers in this area address planning problems arising in road transportation, and, in particular, various extensions of the vehicle routing problem describing algorithmic advances as well as applications in route planning for truck drivers, disaster logistics, snow plowing, offshore petroleum wells, and collaborative logistics.
2. Maritime Logistics: As a recurring and a popular theme within computational logistics, the papers that fall in this area relate to fleet deployment, routing, scheduling, and inventory problems arising in maritime shipping and in offshore wind farms. This section also presents two survey papers, one in the area of autonomous surface vessels structured in two parts, and the other in the use of fuzzy techniques in maritime shipping operations.
3. Synchromodal Transportation: Being an emerging area of research, synchromodal transportation has its unique advantages and challenges. One of the papers that appear in this section presents a framework to classify the problems in this area, whereas another paper reviews the particular aspects of synchromodal

transportation when used within global cold chains. The third paper in this section presents computational tools to solve a scheduling problem arising in the same area.

4. Transportation, Logistics, and Supply Chain Planning: The papers that appear in this section relate to a range of topics concerning various planning problems in transportation, warehouse operations, perishable goods, bike-sharing systems, construction projects, road traffic, container packing, and airport emissions. The section also includes a paper with a tutorial flavor on the use of stochastic programming in supply chains.

ICCL 2017 was the eighth edition of this conference series, following those held in Shanghai (2010, 2012), Hamburg (2011), Copenhagen (2013), Valparaiso (2014), Delft (2015), and Lisbon (2016).

The editors thank all the authors for their contributions and the reviewers for their invaluable support and feedback. We hope that the present volume will help to continue the dialogue within computational logistics and inspire further developments in this exciting area of research.

October 2017

Tolga Bektaş
Stefano Coniglio
Antonio Martinez-Sykora
Stefan Voß

Organization

The 8th International Conference on Computational Logistics 2017 (ICCL 2017) was organized by the Centre for Operational Research, Management Sciences and Information Systems (CORMSIS) spanning the Southampton Business School and Department of Mathematical Sciences at the University of Southampton, in association with the Universität Hamburg.

Organizing Committee

Program Committee

Tolga Bektaş	University of Southampton, UK
Stefano Coniglio	University of Southampton, UK
Antonio Martinez-Sykora	University of Southampton, UK
Stefan Voß	University of Hamburg, Germany

Local Committee

Silvia Gonzato	University of Southampton, UK
Rahimeh Neamatian-Monemi	University of Southampton, UK
Chris Potts	University of Southampton, UK

Scientific Committee

Panagiotis Angeloudis	Imperial College London, UK
Khalid Bichou	Imperial College, UK
Miguel Ayala Botto	Instituto Superior Técnico, Portugal
Jürgen W. Böse	TU Hamburg-Harburg, Germany
Buyang Cao	Tongji University, China and ESRI, USA
Rafael Carmona	Universidad Anahuac Mexico Norte, Mexico
José Ceroni	Católica de Valparaíso, Chile
Marielle Christiansen	Norwegian University of Science and Technology, Norway
Francesco Corman	Delft University of Technology, The Netherlands
Joachim Daduna	University of Economics and Law, Germany
Rommert Dekker	Erasmus University, The Netherlands
Karl F. Doerner	Johannes Kepler University, Austria
Wolfgang Domschke	TU Darmstadt, Germany
Roberto Domínguez Cañizares	Universidad de Sevilla, Spain
Kjetil Fagerholt	Norwegian University of Science and Technology, Norway
Enzo Frazzon	Universidade Federal de Santa Catarina, Brazil
Monica Gentili	University of Salerno, Italy

Additional Reviewers

Douglas Alem
Henrik Andersson
Panagiotis Angeloudis
Christopher Bayliss
Marton Benedek
Julia Bennell
Patrick Beullens
Marta Cabo
Bülent Çatay
Karl Doerner
Jan Fabian Ehmke
Kjetil Fagerholt
Juan José
  Salazar González
Stefano Gualandi
Richard F. Hartl
Leonard Heilig
Sin C. Ho

Ola Jabali
Angel Juan
Jörg Kalcsics
Herbert Kopfer
Eduardo Lalla-Ruiz
Gilbert Laporte
Philip Le
Fabien Lehuédé
Janny Leung
Martijn Mes
Rahimeh Neamatian
  Monemi
Tri-Dung Ngyuen
Julia Pahl
Ana Paias
Dimitris Paraskevopoulos
Meltem Peker
Edgar Possani

Jakob Puchinger
Günther Raidl
Jana Ries
Ruben Ruiz
Mario Ruthmair
Frederik Schulte
Frank Schwartz
L. Douglas Smith
Sven Spieckermann
Magnus Stålhane
Kevin Tierney
Juan G. Villegas R.
Stein W. Wallace
Tony Wauters
Bart Wiegmans
David Woodruff
Yuan Zhang
Shiyuan Zheng

Sponsoring Institutions

Southampton Marine and Maritime Institute

Contents

Maritime Logistics

Synchromodal Transportation

Transportation, Logistics and Supply Chain Planning

Vehicle Routing and Scheduling

An Effective Large Neighborhood Search for the Team Orienteering Problem with Time Windows

Verena Schmid[1] and Jan Fabian Ehmke[2]

[1] CD Laboratory for Efficient Intermodal Transport Operations, Department of Business Administration, University of Vienna, Vienna, Austria
[2] Management Science Group, Otto-von-Guericke University Magdeburg, Magdeburg, Germany, jan.ehmke@ovgu.de

Abstract. We propose an effective metaheuristic for the Team Orienteering Problem with Time Windows. The metaheuristic is based on the principle of Large Neighborhood Search and can outperform the performance of algorithms available in the literature. We provide computational experiments for well known benchmark instances and are able to compute new best solutions for 17 of these instances. On average, the gap between our results and best known solutions so far is below 1%, and our solution approach yields 70% of the best known solutions available in the literature. The new results can serve as benchmarks for future computational studies.

1 Introduction

Traditional routing problems such as the vehicle routing problem (VRP) or the vehicle routing problem with time windows (VRPTW) aim at cost-efficient service to a given number of customers. They consider a fixed fleet of vehicles and minimize total costs while guaranteeing feasibility of the resulting routes with respect to side constraints such as customer time windows, vehicle capacities, and total route durations. In this paper, we tackle a related problem: the Team Orienteering Problem with Time Windows (TOPTW). The TOPTW is a generalization of the well studied VRPTW, which tries to service a *subset* of potential customers. As opposed to the VRPTW, the complexity of the problem is extended by an additional degree of freedom, namely the choice to service a customer (or not). Every customer is associated with a profit, which may be collected upon visiting her. The goal is to maximize the total collected profit as opposed to minimizing total costs in the traditional VRP or VRPTW.

Possible applications of the TOPTW include, but are not limited to home fuel delivery [5], athlete recruiting from high schools [1], and the sport game of orienteering [2]. [22] consider the case of routing technicians to service customers in geographically distributed locations. Leisure related applications are discussed in [24], who present a personalized mobile tour guide for tourists in need for finding a plan to visit the most interesting sights. In [19] and [18], two approaches for selecting bars to be visited during a bar crawl are discussed.

© Springer International Publishing AG 2017
T. Bektaş et al. (Eds.), ICCL 2017, LNCS 10572, pp. 3–18, 2017.
https://doi.org/10.1007/978-3-319-68496-3_1

Since orienteering problems belong to the class of NP-hard problems, it is unlikely that proven optimal solutions for the TOPTW can be found within polynomial time. Even when neglecting the quest for optimality, finding high-quality solutions within a reasonable amount of time remains a challenging task. For this reason, heuristics or more sophisticated metaheuristics seem to be a feasible way of tackling this problem. As pointed out in [4], despite the apparent simplicity of the orienteering problems, it is rather difficult to devise consistently good heuristics for these types of problems. This is partly due to the fact that profits and their locations and distances between locations are independent, and a good solution with respect to one criterion is often unsatisfactory with respect to the other. Hence, it is usually challenging to select the proper nodes albeit its feasible sequence that should be part of a (near-)optimal solution.

The sheer simplicity and the embedded computational complexity has attracted many researchers to investigate orienteering problems. [8] provide an excellent overview on the literature about orienteering problems and its applications. They give a formal description of the OP and present several relevant variants thereof. Within their survey, they extensively discuss and compare published exact and (meta)heuristic approaches presented so far. According to [8], the algorithms developed by [7] and [6] provide the largest proportion of current best known solutions so far. [7] present an iterated local search approach, which starts from an initial solution built with a greedy construction heuristic. The initial solution is improved by well-known local search components such as 2-OPT, SWAP and MOVE. They are able to improve a significant number of best known solutions from standard instances. [6] embed the iterated local search into a simulated annealing framework, which helps overcoming local optima.

Given related work, our aim is to provide a rather simple framework that solves the TOPTW effectively. We build our framework on an LNS-based metaheuristic. We embed the concept of forward time slack in the evaluation of adding or removing nodes from solutions in a smart way. We also investigate the pairwise removal of nodes, which turns out to be very effective for certain problem instances. Overall, by keeping the set of operators clear and manageable, we avoid the algorithm to be tuned and tailored to a specific set of instances. The contributions of this paper can be summarized as follows: i) We present an effective metaheuristic for solving the TOPTW, ii) we present innovative ways of choosing nodes to be added into any given solution, and iii) our approach is applied to a wide range of different types of instances for which the proposed algorithm performs exceptionally well and outperforms algorithms available in the literature.

The paper is structured as follows. We provide a mathematical formulation of the problem (Sect. 2) and describe the proposed solution approach in detail (Sect. 3). The performance of the algorithm is demonstrated on various sets of instances available in the literature (Sect. 4). We also provide a sensitivity analysis for the chosen parameter setting and compare our obtained results against the best ones available in the literature. We then conclude the main findings of this paper in Sect. 5.

2   Mathematical Problem Formulation

To formulate the TOPTW mathematically, we introduce the following notation: We consider a total number of n (potential) customers, where $\mathcal{C} = \{1, \ldots, n\}$ denotes the set of customers. The fleet of m homogeneous vehicles is referred to as set $\mathcal{K}$. Vehicles may start their routes from a central depot, which we will refer to as node 0. For modeling purposes, we also define an identical copy of that node as $n + 1$. Hence, the set of all nodes is denoted as $\mathcal{V}$, where $\mathcal{V} = \mathcal{C} \cup \{0, n + 1\}$. A time window $[e_i, a_i]$ is associated with every node $i \in \mathcal{V}$. Upon visiting node $i \in \mathcal{V}$, a profit of p_i may be collected and it takes d_i time units to do so. For depot nodes (i.e. for $i \in \{0, n + 1\}$) $p_i = d_i = 0$. The time required to travel to node j after i is referred to as t_{ij} $(\forall i, j \in \mathcal{V})$. The maximum route length is denoted as T^{max}. Let M denote a sufficiently large number.

We introduce binary decision variables y_i^k which evaluate to one if and only if node $i \in \mathcal{V}$ is visited by vehicle $k \in \mathcal{K}$. Additionally, we define binary decision variables x_{ij}^k, which will be equal to one if and only if vehicle $k \in \mathcal{K}$ attends node j immediately after i, where $i, j \in \mathcal{V}$. Decision variables s_i^k model the start of service of vehicle $k \in \mathcal{K}$ at node $i \in \mathcal{V}$. Then, the problem can be formulated as follows:

$$Z = \sum_{i \in \mathcal{V}} p_i \sum_{k \in \mathcal{K}} y_i^k \to \max \tag{1}$$

s.t.

$$\sum_{j \in \mathcal{V}} x_{ij}^k = y_i^k \qquad\qquad \forall i \in \mathcal{V} \backslash \{n+1\}, k \in \mathcal{K} \tag{2}$$

$$y_i^k = 1 \qquad\qquad \forall i \in \{0, n+1\}, k \in \mathcal{K} \tag{3}$$

$$\sum_{j \in \mathcal{V}} x_{ji}^k = y_i^k \qquad\qquad \forall i \in \mathcal{V} \backslash \{0\}, k \in \mathcal{K} \tag{4}$$

$$s_i^k + d_i + t_{ij} \le s_j^k + M(1 - x_{ij}^k) \qquad\qquad \forall i, j \in \mathcal{V}, k \in \mathcal{K}, \text{ where } i \ne j \tag{5}$$

$$s_i^k \ge e_i y_i^k \qquad\qquad \forall i \in \mathcal{V}, k \in \mathcal{K} \tag{6}$$

$$s_i^k \le a_i \qquad\qquad \forall i \in \mathcal{V}, k \in \mathcal{K} \tag{7}$$

$$\sum_{i \in \mathcal{V}} d_i y_i^k + \sum_{i \in \mathcal{V}} \sum_{j \in \mathcal{V}} t_{ij} x_{ij}^k \le T^{max} \qquad\qquad \forall k \in \mathcal{K} \tag{8}$$

$$x_{ij}^k \in \{0, 1\} \qquad\qquad \forall i, j \in \mathcal{V}, k \in \mathcal{K} \tag{9}$$

$$y_i^k \in \{0, 1\} \qquad\qquad \forall i \in \mathcal{V}, k \in \mathcal{K} \tag{10}$$

$$s_i^k \ge 0 \qquad\qquad \forall i \in \mathcal{V}, k \in \mathcal{K}. \tag{11}$$

The objective function (1) maximizes the total collected profit. Constraints (2) and (4) ensure that nodes have a successor and predecessor along the route. Constraints (3) ensure that every route contains and consequently starts from and returns to the depot. Constraint (5) guarantees that the routes of all vehicles are feasible and that sub tours are avoided. Due to Constraints (6) and (7), it is ensured that nodes may only be (started to be) serviced within the given time window. Constraints (8) ensure that the maximum duty time per vehicle is not exceeded. Finally, Constraints (9)–(11) restrict the feasible domain of the decision variables.

3   Solution Approach

As outlined above, the TOPTW can be seen as a generalization of a classical routing problem such as the VRPTW and hence is NP-hard. We propose to solve the problem with a metaheuristic based on Large Neighborhood Search (LNS), a metaheuristic which originally has been proposed by [15] for solving a pickup and delivery problem with time windows (PDPTW). Below, their ideas are extended, and additional problem specific operators are presented. LNS itself is an iterative metaheuristic which destroys and repairs a given solution consecutively. This concept has been proposed by [20], who describe the general idea of iteratively destroying (*ruin*) and repairing (*recreate*) solutions. Within the PDPTW and classical routing problems such as the VRPTW, all customers or requests need to be served. This is no longer the case for the TOPTW. Hence, specific operators are required to take care of the *choice* of customers to be visited.

Our algorithm works as follows. We generally employ the main ideas underlying the concept of LNS as proposed by [20] and [15]. First, an initial feasible solution S is generated. Then, the initial or, from the second iteration, current solution is destroyed and repaired. This is done until a given number of iterations N has been reached. Solutions are compared based on their objective function value. Any solution improving (or tying with) the best solution obtained so far is stored in a pool of best solutions S^{best}. The pool of best solutions is updated whenever a new improving solution has been found. Otherwise, a solution is chosen randomly from the set of best solutions found. To include some degree of diversity within the search process and avoid being stuck in a local optimum, after R iterations without improving the current best solution, the current best solution is replaced through a randomly selected solution from the pool of best solutions. A technical outline of the proposed solution approach is depicted in Algorithm 1. Details on the operators are provided below.

The sketched components and procedures are described in more detail within the following subsections. In particular, we introduce several problem-specific operators to be used within this framework.

3.1   Solution Representation

To represent a solution within the algorithm, we encode the individual routes of all vehicles in use. To this end, we focus on the specific customers visited and their sequence within the route. The latter allows us to derive additional information with respect to the timing of visits, the waiting times that may occur in between, and any buffer time (slack) between any two customer nodes on a route that allows for rapid feasibility checks upon inserting new customers.

Algorithm 1 A Large Neighborhood Search for the TOPTW

1:   $\mathcal{S} \leftarrow$ GenerateInitialSequence   ▷ generate initial solution
2:   $Z^{best} \leftarrow Z(\mathcal{S})$ ▷ save objective of best solution so far
3:   $\boldsymbol{S}^{best} \leftarrow \{\mathcal{S}\}$ ▷ initialize pool of best solutions
4: **while** termination criterion not reached **do**
5:     $\mathcal{S}' \leftarrow$ Destroy$(\mathcal{S})$ ▷ destroy solution
6:     $\mathcal{S}' \leftarrow$ Repair$(\mathcal{S}')$ ▷ repair solution (& apply local search within)
7:     **if** $Z(\mathcal{S}') \geq Z^{best}$ **then**   ▷ (new) best solution found?
8:        $Z^{best} \leftarrow Z(\mathcal{S}')$ ▷ update objective of best solution so far
9:        update $\boldsymbol{S}^{best}$ ▷ update pool of best solutions
10:     **else**
11:        $\mathcal{S} \leftarrow$ any solution from $\boldsymbol{S}^{best}$ ▷ pick solution from pool
12:     **end if**
13: **end while**

3.2 Destroy Operators

In every iteration, we destroy the current solution by *removing* a number of customer nodes n_D from the current set of routes, where n_S denotes the total number of customers currently scheduled. Note that $n_D \leq n_S \leq n$. We remove up to $d\%$ of all customer nodes currently scheduled to be visited. The actual number of customer nodes to be selected for removal is chosen randomly from a discrete uniform distribution $n_D \sim U(1, d * n_S)$.

Traditionally, nodes are removed individually. This approach may lead to a suboptimal solution, which may be hard to improve. Imagine a route where a subsequence of nodes is far away from the remainder of the route (e.g. see nodes i_s and i_{s+1} in Figure 1a). Typically, the removal of a single node of the subsequence would neither lead to a significant reduction in travel time nor would there result a sufficient amount of slack upon removal for insertion of alternative nodes. Hence, we allow to remove *sequences of nodes*: rather than removing them individually, we remove several nodes simultaneously.

In particular, sequences of nodes are removed until the total number of nodes to be removed n_D has been reached. The actual length evolves *iteratively*, i.e., the length of the sequence under consideration is extended gradually as long as the average savings in travel time increase. Note that, contrary to classical routing problems, not all customers need to be part of the solution for it to become feasible. Instead, only a subset of customers may be visited if beneficial for the objective function given that we are still able to satisfy all constraints.

More formally, we consider a route defined as a sequence of nodes $(0, i_1, i_2, \ldots, i_{n_k}, 0)$, where n_k denotes the number of customers currently scheduled on route k.[3] The length l of the sequence of nodes to be removed starting from node i_s is extended as long as the following condition holds or the end of

---

[3] For improved readability we refrain from using an index referring to the actual route. The following considerations will be made independently for every route.

the route has been reached:

$$\frac{1}{l}(\sum_{p=s}^{s+l} t_{i_{p-1},i_p} - t_{i_{s-1},i_{s+l}}) < \frac{1}{l+1}(\sum_{p=s}^{s+l+1} t_{i_{p-1},i_p} - t_{i_{s-1},i_{s+l+1}}). \qquad (12)$$

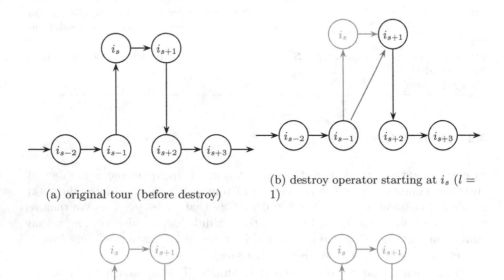

(a) original tour (before destroy)

(b) destroy operator starting at i_s ($l = 1$)

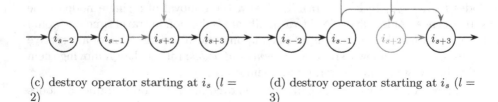

(c) destroy operator starting at i_s ($l = 2$)

(d) destroy operator starting at i_s ($l = 3$)

Fig. 1: Estimating consequences for detouring nodes within the Destroy Operator

This approach has shown to be especially useful when the considered nodes are geographically clustered. The following Fig. 1 illustrates the underlying idea. Fig. 1a shows a subsequence of the original route before being destroyed. Fig. 1b-1d show the resulting changes if l is set to 1, 2 and 3, respectively. Nodes and arcs that are about to be removed are shown in gray, new arcs to be added are highlighted in red. Assuming that the travel time along all horizontal (vertical) arcs in Fig. 1a equals 1 (2) and all travel times are to scale, the average savings are $2 - \sqrt{2}$ ($l = 1$), 1 ($l = 2$) and $0.\dot{6}$ ($l = 3$). As $1 > 0.\dot{6}$, the dynamic length l would be set to 2, and the route would be destroyed as shown in Fig. 1c.

Once the number of nodes to be removed has been determined, a *destroy operator* is selected to identify consequences upon removal of particular nodes. We have developed the following five destroy operators, which focus on different important characteristics of a customer node with regard to solution quality:

- **Profit (P)** calculates the impact the removal of a node has upon the total profit as quantified by the objective function.
- **Travel Time (T)** calculates the impact the removal of a node has upon total travel time.
- **Potential (POT)** calculates the potential that the removal of a node yields for the insertion of another node. Details are given below.
- *POT/TT* denotes the potential of a removal of a node relative to the travel time reduction.
- *POT²/TT* Alternative variant of *POT/TT*, i.e., the squared potential relative to travel time.

Upon removal of nodes, slack time as defined by [17] may appear within a route. The slack time may result from arriving before the start of a time window and hence causes waiting time. Additionally, it may correspond to additional delays that could feasibly be considered, e.g. by postponing the start of a service within the time window without making the remainder of the route infeasible. The idea of operator **POT** is as follows: upon removal of a node, we investigate the possibility of inserting other nodes instead at the same position of the route. The potential is determined by the sum of the maximum profit of up to o additional nodes to be inserted within the available slack time. Similar ideas are considered upon insertion of a node. Here, there might still be some additional slack left which is used to investigate the potential of o additional nodes to be inserted thereafter.

Having quantified the impact of a node's removal on the solution quality, the particular nodes or node sequences are selected for removal. The removal of nodes is implemented according to one of the three following variants:

- **Random (R)** We randomly pick the node (sequence) from the set of candidates available for removal.
- **Greedy (G)** We delete the best node (sequence) according to the above destroy operators.
- **Bias (B)** We randomly pick the node (sequence), and the probabilities are defined according to the above measures of the destroy operators. For instance, when picking nodes based on their profit, the selection probabilities would reflect the relative proportions of the individual nodes' profits.

3.3 Repair Operators

Following a destroy operation, routes are reconstructed by a repair operator. In particular, in every iteration, customer nodes that are not part of the current solution are inserted back into the destroyed solution. To this end, we analyze the current routes in random order and compute the consequences of insertion of each removed node at its best insertion position, which is derived according to smallest increase of travel time. From all possible nodes available for insertion, we select the one for insertion that fits best according to a particular repair operator. Following the ideas of the destroy operators, the repair operators evaluate the consequence of insertion of a customer node with regard to the quality of the current solution (P, T, POT, POT/TT, POT^2/TT). This procedure is finalized for a route once there are no more candidate nodes that could be inserted feasibly into the route, and we can continue with the next route. Note again that we can conduct the required feasibility checks quickly thanks to efficient slack computation as described by [17].

The generation of an initial solution for the TOPTW is trivial. We create an initial solution starting from an empty solution where no customer nodes are currently included. Then, we use the repair operators presented above to fill the initial solution.

4   Results

In this section, we investigate the performance of the proposed algorithm, compare it against benchmark results available in the literature, and justify the chosen parameter settings.

4.1   Benchmark Data and Computational Setup

We tested our algorithm on various sets of instances available in the literature. We present results for instances of both the TOPTW and OPTW (which is a special case of the TOPTW where $m = 1$). [16] propose two sets of instances for the TOPTW: The first set comprises 29 instances (which from now on will be referred to as *Solomon1* in general and c1*, r1*, rc1* in particular), which are based on the Solomon's instances for the VRPTW ([21]). Additionally, they propose 10 instances developed by [3] for the multi-depot vehicle routing problem (pr01-pr10). [13] were among the first to use a second test set of 27 instances from the Solomon set (*Solomon2*, c2*, r2*, rc2*). Finally, [14] proposed to use another set of 10 instances from the Cordeau data set (pr11-pr20). We well refer to pr01-10 and pr11-20 as *Cordeau1* and *Cordeau2*, respectively.

The number of customers corresponds to 100 for instances derived from the Solomon data set and is between 48 and 288 for instances derived from the Cordeau data set. Instances within *Solomon2* have wider time windows than those in *Solomon1*. As a consequence, the resulting routes tend to become longer. Distances between locations for Solomon instances were rounded down to the first decimal point and rounded down to the second decimal point for the instance set *Cordeau1* and *Cordeau2* as originally reported in [16].

For the TOPTW, [14] suggest to vary the number of vehicles in *Solomon1*, *Solomon2*, *Cordeau1* and *Cordeau2* between 1 and 4. No optimal solutions are available for those instances mentioned so far. Hence, we will compare our results against the best known solutions so far (BKS).

Additionally, we consider the set of instances proposed in [24], which we will refer to as set *VanSteenwegen*: These instances correspond to the data sets provided in *Solomon1, Solomon2* and *Cordeau1*. For these instances, the number of vehicles was set to the minimum number of vehicles required to serve all customers. Hence, the optimal value of the objective function can be derived in a straightforward way.

Our solution approach was implemented in C++. All experiments where carried out on a Xeon CPU at 3.1 GHz with 32 GB of RAM, which was shared with 7 other CPUs. If not noted otherwise, all reported CPU times are in seconds. Due to the stochastic nature of our algorithm, we report both the best and average solution found within five independent runs.

In the following, we will provide a comprehensive sensitivity analysis with respect to different parameter settings and proposed operators. We then compare the results against the following state-of-the-art algorithms available in the literature: the ant colony (ACO) system developed by [14], the iterated local search (ILS) algorithm proposed in [24], a variable neighborhood search (VNS) by [23], a hybrid evolutionary local search algorithm which has been combined with a greedy randomized adaptive search procedure (GRASP, see [11]), the slow version of the heuristic based on SSA by [12], the LP-based granular variable neighborhood search (GVNS) developed by [10], the iterative three-component heuristic (I3CH) by [9], the iterative local search as presented by [7] and the iterative local search combined with SA as discussed by [6]. Detailed results for the latter are available from the Orienteering Problem Library at http://centres.smu.edu.sg/larc/orienteering-problem-library/.

4.2   Overall Results

First, we present aggregated results across the various sets of instances. For these instances, our LNS has been parameterized as follows. In every iteration, we destroy up to $d = 40\%$ of the current solution. Nodes to be removed are evaluated according to the resulting reduction in travel time upon removal (*TT-based destroy operator*). We evaluate the consequences upon removal of *sequences* of nodes. Then, the sequence is selected for removal in a *biased* way, the probability of being selected for removal being proportional to the resulting reduction in travel time. In the following repair step, we add nodes depending on a combination of their *squared potential* with a lookahead of $l = 1$ and the corresponding increase in travel time (POT^2/TT-based repair operator). The node to be inserted is selected in a *greedy* way, thereby selecting the node with the highest potential (*POT operator*). The run time limit has been set to $N = 100,000$ iterations, and we perform $R = 100$ iterations without improved solutions before we reinitialize the current solution. Justification of all parameter settings is provided in Sect. 4.3. Note that we have investigated combinations of all reasonable parameter settings in a preliminary study to derive the optimal settings.

In Tables 1 and 2, the *set* column denotes the type of instances that have been aggregated. *BKS* reports the average of the best known solutions available so far, *Best* reports the average of the best solution found per instance across the entire set of instances, and *Avg* gives the average objective function value found by our algorithms. The latter are shown in bold if they meet or are superior to the BKS. CPU_f and CPU_t give the average run times required (in seconds) to find the solution and the run time in total, respectively. Detailed results for each underlying instance can be found in the electronic appendix at `https://goo.gl/jjOvU2`.

For the case of one vehicle (OP, Table 1, $m = 1$), we can find the BKS for all of the *Solomon1* instances and for most of the *Solomon2* instances. Average CPU times are very reasonable: about 1-2 seconds for the *Solomon1* instances, 16-30 seconds for the *Solomon2* instances, 12 seconds for *Cordeau1* and 33 seconds for the *Cordeau2* instances on average. Generally, the *Cordeau* instances are more challenging to solve than the *Solomon* instances. For instances considering two vehicles ($m = 2$), the best solutions obtained by our algorithm are the same as BKS for RC1, C2 and R2. They are quite close for the remaining *Solomon* instances. The average gap is 0.1-0.2% for the *Solomon* and 1.0-2.6% for the *Cordeau* instances. Run times are between about 20 seconds (RC1) and 135 seconds (*Cordeau2*) on average.

Table 1: Aggregated Results Averaged over Various Instance Sets

set	BKS	Best	Avg	CPU_f	CPU_t	set	BKS	Best	Avg	CPU_f	CPU_t
Solomon1, m = 1						*Solomon2*					
C1	366.67	**366.67**	366.67	1.4	19.0	C2	932.50	**932.50**	931.75	3.4	47.0
R1	281.92	**281.92**	281.73	2.1	15.2	R2	1002.36	**1003.45**	1001.00	30.8	65.6
RC1	265.38	**265.38**	264.60	0.6	10.5	RC2	959.25	957.38	954.88	16.0	47.2
Cordeau1						*Cordeau2*					
1-10	462.90	462.30	461.82	11.9	40.1	11-20	534.10	525.10	521.14	33.4	67.5
Solomon1, m = 2						*Solomon2*					
C1	673.33	672.22	672.00	5.6	30.6	C2	1478.75	**1478.75**	1475.75	6.4	63.5
R1	510.83	510.08	509.27	8.0	25.5	R2	1410.45	**1413.55**	1410.40	22.9	42.2
RC1	510.50	**510.50**	510.25	3.2	20.6	RC2	1566.25	1569.25	1563.20	30.2	52.5
Cordeau1						*Cordeau2*					
1-10	850.00	844.60	840.12	50.1	85.0	11-20	952.70	934.70	925.04	85.9	135.1
Solomon1, m = 3						*Solomon2*					
C1	921.11	920.00	916.44	11.5	40.5	C2	1810.00	**1810.00**	**1810.00**	0.3	0.3
R1	717.17	716.58	715.38	12.5	35.3	R2	1456.45	1456.36	1456.16	1.2	4.9
RC1	736.25	736.13	733.58	10.9	30.2	RC2	1720.13	1719.13	1718.25	5.8	14.8
Cordeau1						*Cordeau2*					
1-10	1159.60	1147.80	1139.00	81.6	124.2	11-20	1271.80	1244.30	1233.78	111.4	191.7
Solomon1, m = 4						*Solomon2*					
C1	1136.67	1128.89	1123.33	18.6	48.5	C2	1810.00	**1810.00**	**1810.00**	0.0	0.0
R1	892.42	891.50	889.35	18.3	42.7	R2	1458.00	**1458.00**	**1458.00**	0.0	0.0
RC1	944.25	943.50	941.15	12.1	37.7	RC2	1724.00	**1724.00**	**1724.00**	0.0	0.1
Cordeau1						*Cordeau2*					
1-10	1407.10	1379.00	1366.10	92.7	156.1	11-20	1526.00	1481.00	1467.22	137.7	234.8

With increasing number of vehicles ($m = 3$), we can still determine the BKS for all *Solomon* and C2 instances. For the remaining *Solomon* instances, the gap is negligible. *Cordeau* instances show a gap that is similar to results with two vehicles. Run times increase for *Solomon1*, *Cordeau1* and *Cordeau2* instances, but decrease heavily for *Solomon2* instances. For instances considering four vehicles ($m = 4$), all BKS of *Solomon2* could be found in a very short run time. The average gap for *Solomon1* remains small (about 0.6%), while the gap for *Cordeau1* and *Cordeau2* increases up to 3.3%. Again, the *Cordeau* instances are harder to solve and require more run time for the same number of iteration.

Table 2 presents the average results for the *VanSteenwegen* instances. Note that for these instances, the number of vehicles was set to the minimum number of vehicles required to service all customers. For the majority of instances, we are able to determine the BKS – except for *Cordeau1* instances, where we observe an average gap of 1.2%.

Table 2: Aggregated Results Averaged over *Vansteenwegen* Instance Sets with Minimum Number of Vehicles

set	BKS	Best	Avg	CPU_f	CPU_t	set	BKS	Best	Avg	CPU_f	CPU_t
C1	1810.00	**1810.00**	1810.00	1.50	1.52	C2	1810.00	**1810.00**	**1810.00**	0.00	0.03
R1	1449.58	**1449.58**	1447.32	24.04	45.38	R2	1458.00	**1458.00**	1457.91	5.91	9.68
RC1	1719.00	**1719.00**	1717.28	25.34	39.08	RC2	1724.00	**1724.00**	**1724.00**	2.59	2.62
1-10	2270.40	2259.00	2255.90	89.12	154.86						

4.3 Parameter Settings

In the following, we investigate and justify the parameter settings obtained for the computation of above results.

Selection of Destroy and Repair Operators We proposed five different destroy and repair operators (see Sect. 3.2 and 3.3). They differ in the way consequences upon removal or insertion of nodes are evaluated. We tested all resulting 25 combinations of destroy and repair operators in order to identify the best possible combination for the given benchmark instances (see Table 3). We show average objective function values of the best solutions found (columns "best") as well as averages of all solutions obtained (columns "Avg"). For both cases, the combination of a **TT-based destroy operator** and POT^2/TT-**based repair operator** yields the best overall results.

Procedure of Selection Operator When selecting the nodes to be inserted into or removed from the current solution, we tested three variants on how to choose them based on the estimated consequences. Table 4 presents the average results of all combinations of selection procedure of destroy and repair operators. For both average solution values of best solutions obtained and all solutions, the **biased selection** of customer nodes for removal and the **greedy** repair yield the best results.

Table 3: Identifying the Best Combination of Destroy and Repair Operators

	Best					Avg				
Destroy / Repair	P	TT	POT	POT/TT	POT^2/TT	P	TT	POT	POT/TT	POT^2/TT
Profit (P)	999.13	1001.29	1000.50	1002.45		1002.95	995.09	997.70	998.08	999.75	1000.36
Travel Time (TT)	1000.50	1001.50	1002.09	1002.79		**1003.36**	997.41	997.85	1000.32	1000.19	**1001.20**
Potential (POT)	999.00	1001.02	1000.55	1002.73		1003.20	995.66	997.76	998.26	1000.12	1001.07
POT/TT	999.11	1001.61	1001.04	1002.73		1003.09	995.94	998.10	998.51	1000.12	1000.81
POT^2/TT	999.20	1001.43	1000.68	1002.79		1003.05	995.28	997.28	998.35	1000.11	1000.48

Table 4: Identifying the Best Selection Procedure when Using Destroy and Repair Operators

	Best			Avg		
Destroy / Repair	Random (R)	Greedy (G)	Biased (B)	Random (R)	Greedy (G)	Biased (B)
Random (R)	987.71	1003.04	1000.41	981.20	1000.50	996.79
Greedy (G)	983.25	995.27	994.63	973.58	988.11	987.08
Biased (B)	991.43	**1003.36**	1001.41	985.56	**1001.20**	997.84

Degree of Destruction An important issue for the parameterization of our LNS is the degree of destruction of a solution for further improvement. We investigated the resulting solution quality and run time when varying the degree of destruction d between 10% and 100%. Table 5 shows the corresponding results. As can be observed from the table, CPU times increase significantly with increasing degree of destruction, since this requires increasing efforts of repairing a solution. As can be seen from the table, for the given instances, the **optimal degree of destruction is at 40%.** For this value, the obtained solution quality is best in terms of the average solution quality as well as the average best solution per instance found, while run times still remain at an acceptable level (on average: 12.8 seconds until the solution could be found/38.2 total run time).

Table 5: Effects of Varying d when Destroying Solutions

d	10%	20%	30%	40%	50%	60%	70%	80%	90%	100%
Best	1001.04	1002.57	1002.86	**1003.36**	1002.93	1003.29	1002.86	1002.50	1002.64	1002.32
Avg	997.26	999.89	1000.52	**1001.20**	1001.11	1000.89	1001.15	1000.58	1000.60	1000.23
CPU_f	7.8	8.1	10.7	12.8	15.0	19.0	23.1	26.8	27.2	33.6
CPU_t	19.3	24.6	30.6	38.2	45.0	53.0	63.9	73.0	82.5	91.6

Length of Removal As described in Sect. 3.2, we propose to remove sequences of nodes rather than individual nodes. To prove the effectiveness of this approach, we designed the following experiment: Rather than removing subsequences (of dynamic length) of nodes, we also removed them individually. With a slightly superior solution quality than removing single nodes, removing sequences of nodes leads to better results, both in terms of average and best solutions found, and also reduces the required run time (avg: 1001.20 vs. 999.26; best: 1003.36 vs. 1002.41; CPU_t: 38.2 vs. 51.0).

Lookahead of Potential For the operator POT, we propose to identify the potential of inserting up to o nodes additionally upon destroying or repairing the current solution. In order to identify how many nodes o should be considered, we varied our lookahead parameter between $o = 1$ and $o = 3$. Table 6 shows the corresponding results of this experiment. The variant with $o = 1$ works best. Note that the run time increases significantly when we consider $o > 1$ due to the increasing number of subsets of nodes to be investigated. We have not investigated $o = 0$, since this would correspond to the profit of a single node (and the proposed operator **P**).

Table 6: Effects of Varying Lookahead o of Potential

o	1	2	3
Best	**1003.36**	1003.09	1001.77
Avg	**1001.20**	1000.94	1000.43
CPU_f	38.2	137.9	747.9
CPU_t	12.8	36.3	154.6

4.4   Comparison with other Algorithms

Many related TOPTW papers base their experiments on the same set of instances, which allows for a comparison of the number of BKS obtained by the corresponding algorithm. Table 7 shows the percentage of BKS obtained by most recent TOPTW algorithms at the time they were published compared to the number of BKS our algorithm could obtain. For the cited papers, all *Solomon* and *Cordeau* instances have been considered with a fixed number of vehicles ($m = 1/2/3/4$). We can see from the table that our LNS framework can provide the largest proportion of BKS for the benchmark instances compared with most recent algorithms. Our algorithm seems to be especially beneficial for the instances with two vehicles ($m = 2$). Although our algorithm can provide good solutions in a very short runtime, note that we could not compare the runtimes here due to varying computational environments.

5   Conclusion & Outlook

In this paper, we proposed a simple but effective LNS framework including neighborhood operators especially developed for the characteristics of the TOPTW. We presented smart ideas of destroying and repairing solutions, which turned out to be quite effective for the majority of well-known benchmark instances. In particular, we were able to provide 17 new BKS, and our algorithm was able to

Table 7: Percentage of BKS obtained by Different Algorithms, extending [8]

Reference	Algorithm	Percentage of best known solutions				Average
		m=1	m=2	m=3	m=4	
Labadie et al. (2011)	GRASP-ELS	50.0	21.1	32.9	46.1	37.5
Lin and Yu (2012)	SSA		51.3	34.2	39.5	56.6	45.4
Labadie et al. (2012)	GVNS	36.8	30.3	40.8	44.7	38.2
Souffriau et al. (2012)	GRILS	51.3	15.8	22.4	39.5	32.3
Hu and Lim (2014)	I3CH	43.4	34.2	57.9	55.3	47.7
Cura (2014)	ABC	48.7	36.8	46.1	48.7	45.1
Gunawan et al. (2015b)	ILS	68.4	51.3	56.6	55.3	57.9
Gunawan et al. (2015a)	SAILS	67.1	50.0	57.9	53.9	57.2
Schmid & Ehmke (2017)	LNS	82.9	71.1	65.8	60.1	70.0

provide about 70% of current BKS at reasonable run times. For future research, we would like to consider a variant of the metaheuristic that automatically tunes the parameter d, i.e., a framework that automatically balances between diversification and intensification. Furthermore, we think it would be fruitful to extend our solution framework to a parallel version. Considering GPU computing techniques might also be worthwhile in order to improve the efficiency and effectiveness of our LNS. Finally, it would be interesting to compare the performance of the metaheuristic with commercial solvers like CPLEX.

References

[1] Butt, S.E., Cavalier, T.M.: A heuristic for the multiple tour maximum collection problem. Computers & Operations Research 21, 101–111 (1994)

[2] Chao, I., Golden, B., Wasil, E.: The team orienteering problem. European Journal of Operational Research 88, 475–489 (1996)

[3] Cordeau, J.F., Gendreau, M., Laporte, G.: A tabu search heuristic for periodic and multi-depot vehicle routing problems. Networks 30, 105–119 (1997)

[4] Gendreau, M., Laporte, G., Semet, F.: A tabu search heuristic for the undirected selective travelling salesman problem. European Journal of Operational Research 106, 539–545 (1998)

[5] Golden, B., Levy, L., Vohra, R.: The orienteering problem. Naval Research Logistics 34, 307–18 (1987)

[6] Gunawan, A., Lau, H.C., Lu, K.: Sails: hybrid algorithm for the team orienteering problem with time windows. Proceedings of the 7th multidisciplinary international scheduling conference (MISTA 2015), Prague, Czech Republic pp. 276–295 (2015)

[7] Gunawan, A., Lau, H.C., Lu, K.: Well-tuned ils for extended team orienteering problem with time windows. LARC Technical Report Series (2015), http://centres.smu.edu.sg/larc/files/2015/09/Well-Tuned-ILS-for-Extended-Team-Orienteering-Problem-with-Time-WindowsTR-01-15.pdf

[8] Gunawan, A., Lau, H.C., Vansteenwegen, P.: Orienteering problem: A survey of recent variants, solution approaches and applications. European Journal of Operational Research 255(2), 315 – 332 (2016)

[9] Hu, Q., Lim, A.: An iterative three-component heuristic for the team orienteering problem with time windows. European Journal of Operational Research 232, 276–286 (2014)

[10] Labadie, N., Mansini, R., Melechovsky, J., Wolfler Calvo, R.: The team orienteering problem with time windows: An lp-based granular variable neighborhood search. European Journal of Operational Research 220, 15–27 (2012)

[11] Labadie, N., Melechovsk, J., Wolfler Calvo, R.: Hybridized evolutionary local search algorithm for the team orienteering problem with time windows. Journal of Heuristics 17, 729–753 (2011)

[12] Lin, S.W., Yu, V.F.: A simulated annealing heuristic for the team orienteering problem with time windows. European Journal of Operational Research 217, 94–107 (2012)

[13] Mansini, R., Pelizzari, M., Wolfler Calvo, R.: A granular variable neighborhood search heuristics for the tour orienteering problem with time windows. Technical Report 2008-02-52, Dipartimento di Elettronica per l'Automazione, Università di Brescia (2008)

[14] Montemanni, R., Gambardella, L.: Ant colony system for team orienteering problems with time windows. Foundations of Computing and Decision Sciences 34 (2009)

[15] Pisinger, D., Ropke, S.: Large neighborhood search. In: M, G., J-Y, P. (eds.) Handbook of metaheuristics, pp. 399–419. Springer (2010)

[16] Righini, G., Salani, M.: Decremental state space relaxation strategies and initialization heuristics for solving the orienteering problem with time windows with dynamic programming. Computers & Operations Research 36, 1191–1203 (2009)

[17] Savelsbergh, M.: The vehicle routing problem with time windows: Minimizing route duration. INFORMS Journal on Computing 4, 146–154 (1992)

[18] Schmid, V.: Hybrid metaheuristic for the team orienteering problem with time windows and service time dependent profits (2014), presentation at VeRoLog 2014, Oslo, Norway

[19] Schmid, V., Gómez Rodríuez, J.S.: On solving routing problems with time windows given dynamic service times and profits (2013), presentation at 26th European conference on operational research, Rome, Italy

[20] Schrimpf, G., Schneider, J., Stamm-Wilbrandt, H., Dueck, G.: Record breaking optimization results using the ruin and recreate principle. Journal of Computational Physics 159, 139–171 (2000)

[21] Solomon, M.: Algorithms for the vehicle routing and scheduling problems with time window constraints. Operations Research 53, 254–265 (1987)

[22] Tang, H., Miller-Hooks, H.: A tabu search heuristic for the team orienteering problem. Computers & Operations Research 32, 1379–1407 (2005)

[23] Tricoire, F., Romauch, M., Doerner, K.F., Hartl, R.F.: Heuristics for the multi-period orienteering problem with multiple time windows. Computers & Operations Research 37, 351–367 (2010)
[24] Vansteenwegen, P., Souffriau, W., Vanden Berghe, G., Van Oudheusden, D.: Iterated local search for the team orienteering problem with time windows. Computers & Operations Research 36, 3281–3290 (2009)

Hybrid Heuristic for the Clustered Orienteering Problem

Ala-Eddine Yahiaoui, Aziz Moukrim and Mehdi Serairi

Sorbonne universités, Université de technologie de Compiègne, CNRS
Heudiasyc UMR 7253, CS 60 319, 60 203 Compiègne cedex
{ala-eddine.yahiaoui, aziz.moukrim, mehdi.serairi}@hds.utc.fr

Abstract. This paper addresses the Clustered Orienteering Problem, a
recent variant of the Orienteering Problem. In this variant, customers are
grouped into subsets called *clusters*. A profit is assigned to each cluster
and is collected only if all customers belonging to the cluster are served.
The objective is to visit the customers of a subset of clusters in order to
maximize the total collected profit with respect to a travel time limit. Our
solution method is based on the *order first-cluster second* approach. It
incorporates a *split* procedure that converts a *giant tour* into an optimal
solution. Experiments conducted on benchmark instances show that our
algorithm outperforms the existing methods in the literature. Actually,
we have found the best known solution for 916 instances from 924 with
strict improvement of 82 instances.

Keywords: Clustered Orienteering Problem · Adaptive Large Neighborhood Search . Split · Branch and Bound · Knapsack Problem

1 Introduction

The Orienteering Problem (OP) is a well studied variant of the Traveling Salesman Problem (TSP). In the OP, a profit is associated with every customer to
represent the value of service, and the aim is to select a subset of customers to
visit in order to maximize the total collected profit without exceeding a predefined travel time limit.

Recently, a new generalization of the OP was introduced by Angelelli et al.
[1] called the Clustered Orienteering Problem (COP). In this problem, customers
are grouped into subsets called *clusters*. Unlike the OP, profits are associated
with the clusters instead of the customers. The profit of a given cluster is gained
only if all of its customers are served.

A COP instance, that we denote by I_{COP}, is modeled as a complete undirected graph $G = (V, E)$ where $V = \{1, \ldots, n\} \cup \{0\}$ is the set of vertices representing customers and the depot, and E is the set of edges. A cost $c(e)$ is assigned
to each edge $e \in E$ which represents the travel time needed to cross e. We assume
that travel times satisfy the triangle inequality. A cover $S = \{S_1, S_2, \ldots, S_K\}$ is
a set of K clusters where $\cup_{i=1}^{K} S_i = V \backslash \{0\}$. Each customer can belong to more
than one cluster. A profit P_i is associated with each cluster S_i which is collected

© Springer International Publishing AG 2017
T. Bektaş et al. (Eds.), ICCL 2017, LNCS 10572, pp. 19–33, 2017.
https://doi.org/10.1007/978-3-319-68496-3_2

only if customers belonging to cluster S_i are all served. One vehicle is available to serve customers with a maximum travel time T_{max}. It is noteworthy to mention that there is no requirement on the order of visits, i.e. a vehicle can alternate the visits between customers belonging to different clusters.

Fig.1 shows a feasible COP solution for an instance where $|S| = 3$, $|V| = 9$. Customers with two circles means that they belong to two clusters. In this solution, only the customers of cluster S_2 and cluster S_3 are served.

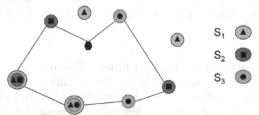

Fig. 1: Example of COP solution

The interest in the COP arises in many real-life applications that can be modeled as variants or generalizations [1]. One of the applications of the COP is when customers are grouped into clusters according to their geographical locations, and a profit is gained only if all customers belonging to a particular area are served. Another example is in the distribution of mass products, where customers are supply chains that contain many retailers. In the case where a contract is made between a carrier and a supply chain, the carrier should serve all the retailers of that supply chain.

Angelelli et al. [1] proposed an exact and a heuristic method to solve the COP. The exact method is a branch and cut algorithm based on the OP formulation proposed in Fischetti et al. [4]. Angelelli et al. [1] solved a linear relaxation of the model without subtour elimination constraints. These constraints are added to the model once violated. The branch and cut algorithm is able to solve optimally small and medium-sized instances. To tackle large-scale instances, Angelelli et al. [1] proposed a heuristic method based on tabu search (TS). TS used an ordered set of insertion and removal moves. Each time a cluster is inserted, TS used a TSP heuristic called Lin-Kernighan heuristic [5] to check the move feasibility.

In this paper, we propose a hybrid heuristic scheme based on the *order first-cluster second* approach [8] to solve the COP. The first component is a metaheuristic scheme called Adaptive Large Neighborhood Search (ALNS) heuristic, whose aim is to generate *giant tours* with good quality. The *giant tours* are then provided to the second component which is a split procedure in order to extract solutions with better profit. The split is based on a branch and bound algorithm that incorporates a knapsack-based upper bound to fathom inferior nodes.

The remainder of this paper is as follows. The global scheme of the proposed heuristic is introduced in Section 2. The ALNS heuristic is detailed in Section 3.

Our split algorithm is presented in Section 4. Computational results are presented in Section 5. Finally, we conclude by some remarks in Section 6.

2   Heuristic global scheme

In the last decade, numerous heuristics based on the *order first-cluster second* approach have been proposed for the VRP and its variants [8]. This approach consists of two phases: the ordering phase in which a giant tour covering all customers is constructed. In the second phase, a split procedure is used to extract the optimal solution while respecting the predefined order of customers. The first split method was introduced by Beasley in [2] for the CVRP. Then, this method was incorporated within a genetic algorithm by Prins in [7].

For selective VRP, in most cases it is impossible to serve all the customers due to the travel time limit. Thus, the objective of a split procedure is to select a subset of customers that satisfies the objective function. Vidal et al. [10] and Vargas et al. [9] studied some selective problems like the Team Orienteering Problem, Capacitated Profitable Tour Problem, Covering Tour Problem, etc. while considering the giant tour. Vidal et al. [10] modeled the problem as a resource constrained shortest path. To solve the problem, they proposed an efficient split procedure based on dynamic programming in order to maximize the total collected profit. Vargas et al. [9] used also in their heuristic a dynamic programming based split to minimize the total travel time. For more detailed literature on the *order first-cluster second* approach, we reffer the reader to [8].

Our solution method adopts also the *order first-cluster second* approach. Algorithm 1 describes the global scheme of our heuristic. It is composed of two main components: an ALNS metaheuristic and a split procedure. The ALNS generates solutions with good quality in a short time (line 4). From a given solution, a giant tour is constructed by randomly inserting the unrouted customers (line 5). Then, the giant tour is given to the split procedure in order to extract a solution with better profit (line 6). We use in Algorithm 1 $Eval(X)$ to denote the profit of a solution X. This process is iterated until a stop condition is reached. In our algorithm, we consider two conditions: the first one is the maximum number of iterations which is fixed at n, where n is the number of customers. The second stop condition is the maximum number of iterations without improvement, which is fixed at the average number of customers per cluster.

3   Adaptive large neighborhood search

The main feature of the ALNS is the use of multiple neighborhoods in parallel during the search process [6]. These different neighborhoods are identified by a set of competing removal and insertion operator. An operator is defined as a fast heuristic that explores a large part of the neighborhood in a polynomial time. In each iteration, the algorithm selects a removal and an insertion operator based

---

Algorithm 1: GLOBAL SCHEME

Input: *Solution X*
Output: *Solution* X_{best}
1 $X_{best} \leftarrow X$
2 $LB \leftarrow Eval(X)$
3 **repeat**
4 | $ALNS(X)$(see Section 3)
5 | Construct a giant tour GT from X
6 | $X \leftarrow SPLIT(GT, LB)$(see Section 4)
7 | **if** $(Eval(X) > Eval(X_{best}))$ **then**
8 | | $X_{best} \leftarrow X$
9 | | $LB \leftarrow Eval(X)$
10 **until** *(stop condition is reached)*
11 **return** X_{best}

---

on statistics gathered during the search process. This characteristic improves the flexibility of the heuristic to tackle a wide variety of instances.

Our ALNS scheme includes one removal operator and a set of three insertion operators. We use a local search operator called 2-opt to improve the travel time of the current solution. This operator is called at each iteration between the removal and the insertion operator.

Random removal operator

This operator selects a random number of clusters between 1 and d_{max} and removes their customers from the current solution. Note that customers which are shared with other clusters in the solution are not removed. The worst-case complexity of this operator is $O(n * K)$.

The parameter d_{max} is a diversification/intensification parameter. If it is small, the heuristic tries to intensify the search in a limited neighborhood. On the other hand, if d_{max} is large, it helps the heuristic to modify a large part of the solution in order to escape from local optima. In our heuristic, d_{max} is set to initial value equal to 3, then it is increased by 1 after each iteration without improvement. Note that d_{max} must not exceed the current number of routed clusters. Once the current solution is improved, d_{max} is set to 3.

Insertion operators

Insertion operators are incorporated in a global scheme that inserts unrouted clusters one by one in the current solution. A cluster is unrouted if and only if at least one of its customers is unrouted. At each iteration, an unrouted cluster is randomly selected, then its unrouted customers are identified (probably some of its customers have been already inserted) and given to one of the insertion operators. The process is iterated until either no further insertions are possible or all the clusters are inserted.

Best insertion operator (BIO): This operator evaluates all feasible insertions for each unrouted customer. Then the best insertion with the smallest
travel time gap is selected. The process is iterated until either all customers are
inserted or the solution cannot accept other customers. The complexity of this
operator is $O(n^3)$.

Insertion with regret Operator (IRO): IRO evaluates all feasible insertions
for each unrouted customer. Then, it calculates the gap in terms of travel time
between the two best insertions of each customer. We call this gap as *regret*. Then
it selects the customer with the highest *regret* and inserts it in the solution. The
process is iterated until either all customers are inserted or no customer can be
added to the solution. The complexity of this operator is $O(n^3)$.

Random Best Insertion Operator (RBIO): RBIO randomly selects one
unrouted customer then evaluates all of its feasible insertions that respect the
travel time limit. The best insertion is then selected. The process is iterated until
either all customers are inserted or no customer can be added to the solution.
The complexity of this operator is $O(n^2)$.

Adaptive weight adjustment

An important aspect of the ALNS is the dynamic weight adjustment carried out
during the search process. Weights are associated with insertion operators and
are initialized using the same value. Then, these weights are dynamically changed
during the search progress according to the performance of each operator. The
aim is to give larger weights to operators which have contributed better to the
solution process. The criteria used to measure how much an operator contributes
during the search process is based on the quality of the solution found after each
iteration:

- if it is a new best solution, it gives a large weight to the operator.
- if it is better than the current solution, it gives a medium weight to the
  operator.
- if it is worse than the current solution, it gives a small weight.

For more details about the update procedure, the reader is referred to Pisinger
and Ropke [6].

4   Split procedure

We propose in the following a split procedure based on a branch and bound
scheme. The aim of the split is to find the subset of clusters that maximizes the
collected profit while respecting the order of customers in π and the travel time
limit. Before detailing our split procedure, let us first introduce a preliminary
result. This result is used afterwards in the upper bound.

Algorithm 2: ALNS

Input: *Solution* X
Output: *Solution* X_{best}

1 $d_{max} \leftarrow 1 + rand()\%3$
2 $X_{best} \leftarrow X$
3 **repeat**
4 | Remove d_{max} clusters from X
5 | Apply 2-opt on X
6 | Select an insertion operator i
7 | Apply i on X
8 | **if** $(Eval(X) > Eval(X_{best}))$ **then**
9 | | $X_{best} \leftarrow X$
10 | | $d_{max} \leftarrow 1 + rand()\%3$
11 | **else** $d_{max} \leftarrow d_{max} + 1$
12 |
13 | Update weights using the adaptive weight adjustment procedure
14 **until** (*stop condition is reached*)
15 **return** X_{best}

4.1   Preliminary result

In this subsection, we present a relaxation scheme for the COP based on the OP.

Definition 1. *Given a COP instance I_{COP}. We define an OP associated instance I_{OP} composed of the same set of vertices $V = \{0, 1, \ldots, n\}$ and the same set of edges E. Profits of customers in I_{OP} are computed as follows: $\rho_j = \sum_{i:j \in S_i} \frac{P_i}{|S_i|}$. In fact, the ratio $\frac{P_i}{|S_i|}$ could be interpreted as the contribution of the customer j to the cluster S_i. Finally, the maximal travel time is T_{max}.*

Proposition 1. *For any COP instance I_{COP}, the optimal objective value of the associated OP instance, I_{OP}, represents an upper bound on the profit of I_{COP}.*

Proof. We prove in the following that the optimal solution of a given I_{COP} is a feasible solution for I_{OP} with a profit lower than or equal to the optimal objective value of the I_{OP}.

Assume that S^* is the set of clusters of the optimal solution of I_{COP} with a total collected profit $P_{cop}(S^*) = \sum_{i:S_i \in S^*} P_i = P_{cop}^*(I_{COP})$. Let V^* be the set of customers belonging to S^*. It is obvious that this optimal solution is a feasible solution for the I_{OP} and its profit is $P_{op}(V^*) = \sum_{j \in V^*} \rho_j$. We denote by $P_{op}^*(I_{OP})$ the optimal objective value for I_{OP}.

$$P_{op}(V^*) = \sum_{j \in V^*} \rho_j = \sum_{j \in V^*} \sum_{i:j \in S_i} \frac{P_i}{|S_i|}$$

$$= \sum_{j \in V^*} \sum_{i:j \in S_i \text{ and } S_i \in S^*} \frac{P_i}{|S_i|} + \sum_{j \in V^*} \sum_{i:j \in S_i \text{ and } S_i \notin S^*} \frac{P_i}{|S_i|}$$

$$= P_{cop}(S^*) + \sum_{j \in V^*} \sum_{i:j \in S_i \text{ and } S_i \notin S^*} \frac{P_i}{|S_i|}$$

$$= P_{cop}^*(I_{COP}) + \sum_{j \in V^*} \sum_{i:j \in S_i \text{ and } S_i \notin S^*} \frac{P_i}{|S_i|} \qquad (1)$$

We conclude that an optimal solution for I_{COP} is feasible for the I_{OP}. Furthermore, $P_{cop}^*(I_{COP}) = P_{cop}(S^*) \leq P_{op}(V^*) \leq P_{op}^*(I_{OP})$. □

Let us consider now a giant tour $\pi = (\pi_1, \pi_2, ..., \pi_n)$ that covers all the customers of I_{COP}. The giant tour π imposes an order of visit among all the customers of I_{COP}. This can be seen as a derived instance I'_{COP}, in which arcs that do not respect this ordering are not considered. The following corollary holds.

Corollary 1. *Given a COP instance I_{COP}, its associated instance I_{OP} and a giant tour π. The optimal objective value of I_{OP} while considering π represents an upper bound on the optimal objective value of I_{COP} w.r.t. to π.*

4.2   Principle of the split

The goal is to calculate a partial sequence σ that visits the customers of a subset of clusters in order to maximize the total collected profit while preserving the original order of customers in π. To that end, the branch and bound algorithm explores a search tree generated according to decisions made on clusters.

In the root node, an arbitrary order of branching is established among clusters. In each node of the search tree, the possible decision that can be made regarding a given cluster is whether it is selected or rejected. This leads to a binary search tree with at most $2^{K+1} - 1$ nodes.

Several components are embedded within the branch and bound algorithm in order to achieve high performance. These components include in addition to the branching scheme, a suitable node selection strategy, an upper bound to fathom inferior nodes, a feasibility test to discard unfeasible nodes. In what follows, we describe the different components implemented in our branch and bound algorithm.

Before proceeding further, we distinguish in each node η three subsets of clusters: the selected clusters denoted by S_s^η, the removed clusters denoted by S_r^η and the potential clusters denoted by S_p^η representing the remainder set of clusters on which decision has not been made yet.

4.3   Knapsack-based upper bound

Vargas et al. [9] proposed a dynamic programming split procedure that incorporates a lower bound based on the Fractional Knapsack Problem (FKSP). We propose in this paper an upper bound that is also based on the FKSP. We make use of the cluster constraint in order to improve this upper bound.

Given a giant tour π and a node η in the branch and bound tree. We consider the Knapsack instance I_{FKSP} in which we associate an item to each potential customer. A customer is considered as potential if it belongs at least to one of the potential clusters S_p^η and does not belong to any of the selected clusters S_s^η.

The profit of a given item/potential customer π_j is calculated using Definition 1. Note that to calculate these profits in a node η, we consider only contributions related to potential clusters S_p^η and we discard those related to removed clusters S_r^η. Consequently, in a given node η and for a given potential customer π_j, we have: $\rho_{\pi_j}^\eta = \sum_{i:\pi_j \in S_i \text{ and } S_i \in S_p^\eta} \dfrac{P_i}{|S_i^\eta|}$, where $|S_i^\eta|$ is the number of potential customers belonging to cluster S_i in the node η.

The weight $w_{\pi_j}^\eta$ of the item/potential customer π_j in a given node η is modeled by the minimal insertion cost. Assume that I_j^η is the set of all valid insertion positions composed of a predecessor and a successor of π_j in π, i.e. $I_j^\eta = \{(\pi_l, \pi_r) | l < j < r, \pi_l, \pi_r \in S_s^\eta \cup S_p^\eta\}$. Thus the minimal insertion cost is calculated as $w_{\pi_j}^\eta = min\{c(\pi_l, \pi_j) + c(\pi_j, \pi_r) - c(\pi_l, \pi_r) | (\pi_l, \pi_r) \in I_j^\eta\}$, where $c(\pi_l, \pi_r)$ is the travel time between customers π_l and π_r.

To model the knapsack size W^η, we proceed as follows. We consider the partial sequence that contains the customers of the selected clusters S_s^η. Assume D is the travel time needed to go from the depot, visit all these customers and return back to the depot. W^η is modeled as the residual distance, i.e. $W^\eta = T_{max} - D$.

Proposition 2. *Given a giant tour π and a node η in the branch and bound tree, the optimal objective value of the I_{FKSP} previously defined represents an upper bound on the profit of the I_{COP} while considering π and η.*

Proof. Given a giant tour π covering all the customers of I_{COP} and a node η. We construct $FKSP$ instance I_{FKSP} in which, each item/ potential customer π_j has a weight w_j^η and a profit $\rho_{\pi_j}^\eta$. According to Corollary 1, an upper bound on I_{OP} is also an upper bound on the I_{COP} while considering π and η. In the following, we prove that the optimal solution of I_{FKSP} is an upper bound on I_{OP} while considering π and η.

Assume σ^η is the optimal partial sequence in the node η and $\delta^\eta(\pi_j)$ is the insertion cost of the customer π_j in σ^η. According to the definition of the minimal cost insertion, we observe that $w_j^\eta \le \delta^\eta(\pi_j)$ for any potential customer π_j in S_p^η. Consequently, the optimal solution for the I_{FKSP} is an upper bound on the profit of I_{OP} while considering π and η. $\square$

Each customer can have n^2 possible insertion positions. In the following, we propose to reduce this number. Assume that π_j is a potential customer and $(\pi_l, \pi_r) \in I_j^\eta$ is a possible insertion position. This couple of customers must satisfy the following rules.

- The first rule is that (π_l, π_r) must not skip any visited customer, i.e. (π_l, π_r) is considered only if:

$$\nexists j'/(l < j' < j \text{ or } j < j' < r) \quad and \quad \pi_{j'} \in S_s^{\eta} \tag{2}$$

- The second rule is that for any skipped customer, its cluster set must not include the cluster set of any of the involved customers in the insertion (π_l, π_r or π_j). Let us define $\Omega(i)$ as the set of clusters which customer i is included in, i.e. (π_l, π_r) is considered only if:

$$\nexists j'/(l < j' < j \text{ or } j < j' < r)$$
$$and \quad (\Omega(\pi_l) \subseteq \Omega(\pi_{j'}) \text{ or } \Omega(\pi_r) \subseteq \Omega(\pi_{j'}) \text{ or } \Omega(\pi_j) \subseteq \Omega(\pi_{j'})) \tag{3}$$

For computational efficiency, the best insertion for each customer is pre-computed beforehand and saved. Each time a cluster is selected or rejected, this list of possible insertions is updated.

4.4   Feasibility check

Feasibility check (FC) is done every time a potential cluster is selected. This is done by computing the length of the partial sequence that contains only the customers of the selected clusters while considering the given order of the giant tour. If the length of this partial sequence exceeds T_{max}, and due to the triangle inequality, node η can be pruned. The complexity of this test is $O(n)$.

4.5   Local search procedure

We propose to improve the split procedure by integrating a Local Search heuristic (LS). The LS uses some relevant information from the enumeration tree in order to explore efficiently the search space alongside with the branch and bound. The solution value obtained by LS is used also as a lower bound in the branch and bound.

Each time the LS is called in a given node η, it considers only the selected and the potential sets of clusters $S_s^{\eta} \cup S_p^{\eta}$. The LS consists of two phases: a destruction phase which is used as a perturbation technique. It removes a small number of clusters from the current solution. This number is chosen randomly between 1 and 3.

The second phase is a constructive heuristic which tries to insert clusters one by one until either the solution cannot accept additional clusters or there is no clusters left. It randomly selects in each iteration one unrouted cluster and tries to insert its customers in the current solution. To check the feasibility of a cluster insertion, this procedure calls an Iterative Destructive Constructive Heuristic (IDCH) proposed in [3]. If IDCH fails to insert the customers, the Lin-Kernighan TSP heuristic [5] is used (see Algorithm 3).

Algorithm 3: ITERATIVE INSERTION

Input: Solution X
Output: Solution X

1 $\Delta \leftarrow$ unrouted clusters of X
2 $insert \leftarrow true$
3 **while** $(\Delta \neq \emptyset$ **and** $insert = true)$ **do**
4 $\quad$ $insert \leftarrow false$
5 $\quad$ **foreach** $(k \in \Delta)$ **do**
6 $\quad\quad$ **if** $(IDCH(X, k) = true)$ **then**
7 $\quad\quad\quad$ $\Delta \leftarrow \Delta \backslash \{k\}$
8 $\quad\quad\quad$ $insert \leftarrow true$
9 $\quad\quad\quad$ **break**
10 $\quad\quad$ **else if** $(LinKernighan(X, k) = true)$ **then**
11 $\quad\quad\quad$ $\Delta \leftarrow \Delta \backslash \{k\}$
12 $\quad\quad\quad$ $insert \leftarrow true$
13 $\quad\quad\quad$ **break**
14 $\quad\quad$ $\Delta \leftarrow \Delta \backslash \{k\}$

15 **return** X

4.6   Beam search

When the number of clusters becomes large, computational time dramatically increases. To cope with this problem, we propose to limit the number of nodes generated during the search process. The main idea is to explore the search tree using a breath-first search (BFS) and impose a limit on the number of nodes expanded in each level of the tree. Consequently, this scheme does not guarantee that the solution found is optimal. It is important to select in each level the most promising nodes to be expanded, so that a good-quality solution could be found. To this end, we use the knapsack upper bound described in Section (4.3) as a selection criteria. Another important aspect is the number of nodes selected at each level. This parameter was fixed after experimentation at K nodes per level.

Algorithm 4 describes the whole split procedure. We use in Algorithm 4 two ordered lists, one is the active list, and the second is temporary. The lower bound LB is initialized by the best objective value obtained by the global heuristic.

5   Computational results

Our heuristic is coded in C++ using the Standard Template Library (STL) for data structures. Experiments were conducted on a computer with Intel Xeon X7542 CPU@2.66 GHz and a Linux OS 64 bits.

In order to verify the efficiency of our approach, we used benchmark instances designed in [1]. The benchmark is derived from 57 instances of TSPLIB with the number of vertices ranging from 42 to 532. For each base instance of TSPLIB, a

---

Algorithm 4: SPLIT

   Input: giant tour GT, Lower bound LB
   Output: best solution X_{best}
   Data: Ordered lists of size K: $actList$, $tmpList$

1 **Initialization**: ordered list of the clusters $Order$ used as branching strategy,
   current level $L \leftarrow 0$, current node $e \leftarrow 0$, $actList \leftarrow e, tmpList \leftarrow \emptyset$
2 **while** *(actList $\neq \emptyset$ and $L < K$)* **do**
3   Select the best node e in $actList$ based on Knapsack UB (See Section 4.3)
4   Expand e to two nodes e_1 and e_2 based on $Order(L)$ (See Section 4.2)
5   **foreach** *($e \in \{e_1, e_2\}$)* **do**
6   **if** *(e is infeasible)* **then continue** (See Section 4.4)
7   **if** *(Knapsack UB of (e)* $\leq LB$) **then continue** (See Section 4.3)
8          $tmpList \leftarrow tmpList \cup \{e\}$
9   Extract solution X from e
10   Apply Local Search on X (See Section 4.5)
11   **if** *(Eval(X) $>$ Eval(X_{best}))* **then**
12            $X_{best} \leftarrow X$
13   **if** *(Eval(X) $> LB$)* **then** $LB \leftarrow Eval(X)$
14   **if** *(actList $= \emptyset$)* **then**
15          $actList \leftarrow tmpList$
16          $tmpList \leftarrow \emptyset$
17      $L + +$
18 Select the best node e in $actList$ based on Knapsack UB (See Section 4.3)
19 Extract solution X from e
20 **if** *(Eval(X) $>$ Eval(X_{best}))* **then** $X_{best} \leftarrow X$
21 **return** X_{best}

---

set of derived instances for the COP is constructed according to different values
assigned to the following parameters:

1. Number of clusters: It varies between the values 10, 15, 20 and 25.

2. Profits of clusters: Two models are used, the first is deterministic while the
   second is random.

3. T_{max}: Given TSP^* the optimal value of TSP over all vertices of the base
   instance, T_{max} is set to the values $\frac{1}{2}TSP^*$ and $\frac{3}{4}TSP^*$.

As a result, 16 different instances are derived from each TSP instance. Furthermore, 12 other instances are added to the biggest class with 532 vertices. These
instances have a larger number of clusters (50, 75 and 100). Thus, the total
number of instances is 924. The instances can be found at the following URL:
http://or-brescia.unibs.it/. For detailed description of instance generation, the
reader can refer to Angelelli et al. [1].

5.1   Parameter setting

The execution of the LS procedure inside the branch and bound algorithm seems to be expensive in terms of computational time. In order to reach the best performance of our algorithm in terms of solution quality and computational time, we propose to tune the number of calls of the LS procedure inside the branch and bound algorithm. We call this parameter N_{LS}. In our experiments, N_{LS} takes different values of $k \times C_{avg}$ where $(k = 1, 10, 20, 30, 40)$. C_{avg} represents the average number of customers per cluster. We carried out these experiments on a representative sample composed of 22 instances. These instances are chosen between the most difficult ones for which high values of N_{LS} are needed to obtain solutions with good quality.

To measure the performance of each configuration, we used the relative gap to the best solution found in the literature, denoted by RPE and the average CPU time. To calculate the RPE, we recorded the Best Known Solution for each instance (Z_{best}), and also we recorded the maximal score (Z_{max}) realized by our heuristic. The relative percentage error RPE of a given instance using (4).

$$RPE = \frac{Z_{best} - Z_{max}}{Z_{best}} \times 100 \qquad (4)$$

According to Fig. 2, the value $20 \times C_{avg}$ gives the best compromise in terms of RPE and CPU time. In fact, the RPE tends to stabilize at a value near to zero when the N_{LS} exceeds $20 \times C_{avg}$, whereas the CPU time continues to increase. As a result, we set N_{LS} at $20 \times C_{av}$.

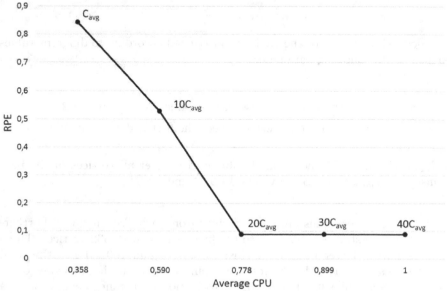

Fig. 2: Performance of our heuristic with different values of N_{LS}

5.2   Performance comparison

Results achieved by our algorithm are compared to the different versions of tabu heuristics proposed in [1]. Three versions of tabu were presented: COP-TABU-Basic, COP-TABU-Multistart and COP-TABU-Reactive.

Table 1. shows the results organized per class of instances. As described earlier, each class is composed of 16 instances, except the last one (att532), which is composed of 28 instances. We run our algorithm 10 times per instance as in [1]. For each method, we provide the number of instances per class for which the Best Known Solution was found (BKS). We report also the relative percentage error per class ($CRPE$) which is the average RPE per class of instances. The average CPU time (CPU) for each class is compared to the best results of each heuristic.

The results show clearly that our algorithm outperforms existing methods in the literature. It succeeds to reduce the $CRPE$ to less than 0.011 against 1.498 for COP-TABU-Basic, 0.841 for COP-TABU-Multistart and 0.327 for COP-TABU-Reactive. Our heuristic found up to 916 BKS against 656, 720 and 816 for the three tabu versions. Furthermore, new BKS were found for 82 instances. In terms of CPU time, our heuristic consumes lower computational time than the three tabu versions. In fact, our heuristic has an average CPU time of $136.33s$, against $153.71s$ for COP-TABU-Basic, $174.37s$ for COP-TABU-Multistart and $223.88s$ for COP-TABU-Reactive.

Table 1: PERFORMANCE OF OUR HEURISTIC

Class	COP-TABU-Basic			COP-TABU-Multistart			COP-TABU-Reactive			Our Contribution		
	BKS	CRPE	CPU	BKS	CRPE	CPU	BKS	CRPE	CPU	BKS	CRPE	CPU
dantzig42	16	0	13.27	16	0	17.77	16	0	38.95	16	0	0.55
swiss42	13	0.719	15.38	14	0.281	23.09	15	0.013	31.93	16	0	0.56
att48	16	0	18.24	16	0	26.08	15	0.062	38.76	16	0	1.51
gr48	11	5.709	13.74	12	3.184	26.02	16	0	37.96	16	0	0.78
hk48	15	1.250	20.58	16	0	30.76	15	0.315	37.68	16	0	1.05
eil51	11	2.181	15.92	11	2.181	24.46	15	0.242	36.83	14	0.228	1.11
berlin52	15	0.548	38.88	15	0.120	53.39	15	0.120	60.41	16	0	2.42
brazil58	13	0.573	58.99	14	0.115	75.72	16	0	83.97	16	0	4.51
st70	11	1.303	23.18	11	1.012	38.95	12	0.639	48.01	16	0	2.44
eil76	9	6.407	24.50	10	4.050	33.74	15	0.125	45.84	16	0	2.41
pr76	11	1.014	21.40	13	0.105	30.88	15	0.009	54.76	16	0	4.79
gr96	12	0.612	44.07	13	0.116	51.35	14	0.025	68.19	16	0	5.49
rat99	12	1.752	32.99	12	0.127	52.03	15	0.034	63.65	15	0.079	7.03
kroA100	11	6.013	44.65	14	0.123	50.98	14	0.429	52.62	16	0	3.92
kroB100	15	0.714	47.96	16	0	58.94	16	0	62.20	16	0	3.87
kroC100	10	3.687	37.55	15	0.269	48.74	14	0.452	59.42	16	0	3.73
kroD100	10	1.879	36.85	11	1.247	56.70	13	0.520	69.57	16	0	4.94
kroE100	12	2.889	46.59	12	1.374	48.83	14	0.270	62.77	16	0	3.69
rd100	12	1.431	36.51	13	1.030	47.81	15	0.568	82.29	16	0	4.89
eil101	7	2.495	32.97	12	0.729	44.62	16	0	79	16	0	5.87
lin105	11	1.393	36.06	13	0.461	52.48	14	0.348	105.21	16	0	11.42
pr107	13	6.350	72.19	15	0.203	86.35	15	0.160	135.39	16	0	36.10
gr120	10	2.917	50.87	11	2.856	66.36	14	0.185	105.25	16	0	10.43
pr124	14	1.180	80.33	16	0	88.26	16	0	150.15	16	0	18.7
bier127	12	0.873	63.05	14	0.108	94.57	15	0.005	149.64	16	0	14.65
ch130	7	4.016	49.79	9	2.949	64.58	12	1.376	106.57	16	0	10.91
pr136	12	1.588	59.86	14	0.949	71.37	15	0.694	121.5	16	0	14.83
gr137	15	0.156	82.07	16	0	104.45	16	0	181.54	16	0	14.25
pr144	16	0	168.25	16	0	175.28	16	0	247.29	16	0	29.07

continued on next page

Table 1 – continued from previous page

Class	COP-TABU-Basic			COP-TABU-Multistart			COP-TABU-Reactive			Our Contribution		
	BKS	CRPE	CPU	BKS	CRPE	CPU	BKS	CRPE	CPU	BKS	CRPE	CPU
$ch150$	8	2.684	34.19	8	2.543	53.97	14	0.554	101.37	**16**	0	13.87
$kroA150$	9	1.002	36.84	13	0.228	50.6	14	0.074	102.11	**16**	0	13.13
$kroB150$	8	2.456	40.06	10	2.127	56.69	14	0.621	107.93	**16**	0	12.31
$pr152$	15	0.545	120.08	16	0	164.81	16	0	248.1	16	0	26.30
$u159$	6	3.300	113.36	9	2.373	125.51	8	1.447	184.68	**16**	0	48.45
$si175$	16	0	47.69	16	0	63.36	16	0	126.80	16	0	227.71
$brg180$	12	0.656	54.29	13	0.578	72.18	15	0.091	127.74	**16**	0	166.41
$rat195$	12	0.531	68.18	10	0.209	78.52	14	0.401	172	**16**	0	48.04
$d198$	15	0.062	172.56	16	0	217.29	16	0	368.98	16	0	40.15
$kroA200$	11	1.130	55.09	12	1.093	76.17	14	1.052	139.43	**15**	0.035	30.45
$kroB200$	8	2.610	71.45	10	1.978	87.73	13	0.129	142.43	**16**	0	29.4
$gr202$	11	1.256	88.17	12	1.001	121.27	16	0	236.24	16	0	56.19
$ts225$	12	0.259	162.94	12	0.158	189.13	15	0.019	234.81	**16**	0	65.60
$tsp225$	9	1.583	87.78	9	0.495	102.99	11	0.142	180.26	**16**	0	64.19
$pr226$	12	0.872	244.84	12	0.787	268.33	15	0.042	331.10	**16**	0	84.61
$gr229$	15	0.023	109.99	15	0.023	121.07	15	0.023	170.85	**16**	0	34.08
$gil262$	7	8.107	57.09	6	4.296	84.20	10	2.441	135.48	**15**	0.032	70.85
$pr264$	11	4.230	151.96	10	4.243	208.51	14	0.323	304.70	**16**	0	100.79
$a280$	11	0.159	99.98	12	0.156	150.54	10	0.255	191.39	**15**	0.003	249.43
$pr299$	10	1.097	105.14	10	1.089	125.98	12	0.614	205.23	**16**	0	221.36
$lin318$	8	1.009	247.01	9	0.870	260.81	11	0.492	311.25	**16**	0	309.03
$rd400$	10	2.014	100.44	11	1.435	147.13	12	1.413	203.08	**16**	0	322.72
$fl417$	11	1.055	518.97	12	0.397	577.53	13	0.079	708.57	**16**	0	362.65
$gr431$	12	0.788	236.75	15	0.009	252.35	16	0	280.53	16	0	251.45
$pr439$	11	0.685	180.16	13	0.074	221.23	14	0.058	324.17	**16**	0	316.19
$pcb442$	11	0.390	151.28	11	0.610	199.82	13	0.593	274.18	**16**	0	499.62
$d493$	7	1.157	418.35	9	1.208	419.66	12	1.051	515.84	**16**	0	638.77
$att532$	16	3.218	3815.65	19	2.684	3927.68	24	1.769	4082.2	**26**	0.275	3343.6
$Total$	656	1.498	153.719	720	0.841	174.37	816	0.327	223.88	**916**	0.011	136.338

6   Conclusion and future work

In this paper, we proposed a hybrid heuristic for the Clustered Orienteering Problem. This heuristic is composed of a split procedure that evaluates efficiently *giant tours* and an Adaptive Large Neighborhood Search heuristic. The split procedure is based on a branch and bound scheme, in which an efficient upper bound based on the Knapsack Problem is used. A Local Search procedure is also incorporated inside the split procedure. The LS is applied each time on a subset of clusters in order to find better combination of clusters quickly. The computational results show clearly the efficiency of our method compared to the existing heuristic methods. Many improvements have been achieved as well as new Best Known Solutions.

As future work, our aim is to propose different extensions for the COP, including the case of multiple vehicles. Also, additional constraints like time windows or vehicle capacity should be considered.

Acknowledgements

The authors would like to thank the Hauts-de-France region and the European Regional Development Fund (ERDF) 2014/2020 for the funding of this work.

This work was carried out in the framework of ANR project TCDU (Collaborative Transportation in Urban Distribution ANR-14- CE22-0017) and of Labex MS2T funded through the program "Investments for the Future" managed by the National Agency for Research (Reference ANR-11-IDEX-0004-02).

References

1. Enrico Angelelli, Claudia Archetti, and Michele Vindigni. The clustered orienteering problem. *European Journal of Operational Research*, 238(2):404–414, 2014.
2. John E Beasley. Route first-cluster second methods for vehicle routing. *Omega*, 11(4):403–408, 1983.
3. Hermann Bouly, Duc-Cuong Dang, and Aziz Moukrim. A memetic algorithm for the team orienteering problem. *4OR*, 8(1):49–70, 2010.
4. Matteo Fischetti, Juan Jose Salazar Gonzalez, and Paolo Toth. Solving the orienteering problem through branch-and-cut. *INFORMS Journal on Computing*, 10(2):133–148, 1998.
5. Shen Lin and Brian Kernighan. An effective heuristic algorithm for the traveling-salesman problem. *Operations Research*, 21(2):498–516, 1973.
6. David Pisinger and Stefan Ropke. Large neighborhood search. In *Handbook of metaheuristics*, pages 399–419. Springer, 2010.
7. Christian Prins. A simple and effective evolutionary algorithm for the vehicle routing problem. *Computers & Operations Research*, 31(12):1985–2002, 2004.
8. Christian Prins, Philippe Lacomme, and Caroline Prodhon. Order-first split-second methods for vehicle routing problems: A review. *Transportation Research Part C: Emerging Technologies*, 40:179–200, 2014.
9. Leticia Vargas, Nicolas Jozefowiez, and Sandra Ulrich Ngueveu. A dynamic programming operator for tour location problems applied to the covering tour problem. *Journal of Heuristics*, 23(1):53–80, 2017.
10. Thibaut Vidal, Nelson Maculan, Luiz Satoru Ochi, and Puca Huachi Vaz Penna. Large neighborhoods with implicit customer selection for vehicle routing problems with profits. *Transportation Science*, 50(2):720–734, 2015.

An Adaptive Large Neighborhood Search for the Periodic Vehicle Routing Problem

Sandra Zajac

Ruhr University Bochum, Faculty of Management and Economics
Universitätsstraße 150, 44801 Bochum, Germany
sandra.zajac@rub.de

Abstract. In this paper, an Adaptive Large Neighborhood Search (ALNS) is proposed for the Periodic Vehicle Routing Problem (PVRP). Each customer requires service on one or more days on a pre-defined time horizon. They must be assigned to feasible visit options and Vehicle Routing Problems (VRP) need to be solved for each day. In the proposed ALNS, destroy and repair operators work on the two levels of the problem. Those heuristics are rewarded which explore the search space in the beginning of the algorithm. A concept to measure if a heuristic contributes to exploring or exploiting the search space based on the dissimilarity between solution alternatives is proposed. It is investigated whether following this strategy is beneficial in terms of performance on selected instances of the PVRP. Moreover, the impact of the chosen dissimilarity measure is studied. The results show that the proposed algorithm is a promising approach for the PVRP. It pays off to reward the exploration of the search space but it is not worthwhile to use dissimilarity measures of a higher level of detail due to the increased computational effort.

1 Introduction and problem description

Vehicle routing problems have been intensively studied in both theoretical research and real world applications as the associated costs are significant. The periodic vehicle routing problem is a natural extension of the classical VRP and occurs e.g. in raw material supply [1] or waste collection [13]. In the PVRP, a planning period of several days is considered in which each customer $i = 1, \ldots, n$ requires a certain number of visits but the exact service days are to some extent flexible. A non-negative cost proportional to the travel time from customer i to customer j is given by $c_{i,j}$. The objective is to assign customers to a feasible visit day combination (to a so-called *pattern*) and determine a routing for each day of the planning horizon so that the sum of costs $c_{i,j}$ is minimized and constraints are met. Each customer i needs to be assigned to one of its patterns $p \in P_i$ with P_i as the set of patterns for customer i. This results in different subsets of customers to be routed on each day $l = 1, \ldots, t$ for which a VRP needs to be solved. Each customer is associated with a service duration d_i as well as a demand q_i. For each day, the served customers need to be assigned to a vehicle $k = 1, \ldots, m$ which starts and ends at the depot at vertex 0. The vehicle capacity

© Springer International Publishing AG 2017
T. Bektaş et al. (Eds.), ICCL 2017, LNCS 10572, pp. 34–48, 2017.
https://doi.org/10.1007/978-3-319-68496-3_3

Q needs to be respected. A sequence is to be determined so that each route's total duration (sum of driven distances and required service duration) does not exceed the time duration limit D.

Due to the complexity of the problem, exact methods are limited in the size of the instance they can solve in an adequate time. Noteworthy is the exact approach of [2] which provides optimal solutions for both the PVRP and the multi-depot vehicle routing problem (MDVRP). These two problems are strongly related as is shown by [5]: The MDVRP can be viewed as a special case of the PVRP by considering each of the t depots to be a day on a t-day planning horizon, and each customer to require a delivery on exactly one day over that horizon. Several successful heuristics have been developed for the PVRP. A tabu search heuristic is presented by [5]. In [6] a parallel evolutionary method is developed while in [18] a hybrid genetic algorithm is proposed that uses a couple of mechanisms to enhance diversity during the search to avoid being stuck in a local optimum. Dissimilarity is measured by comparing pattern assignments of the customers. A scatter search procedure is presented in [1] for solving a problem of periodic pick-up of raw materials for a manufacturer of auto parts. The method is especially designed for PVRPs with a large number of periods. A variable neighborhood search was suggested by [9]. [8] propose a record-to-record travel approach which combines local search and integer-programming based large neighborhood search. The interested reader is referred to [3, 7] for a more detailed overview on the PVRP.

Despite some promising approaches in literature, the PVRP remains a complex problem which needs to be further studied. In particular, data sets with a high number of customers, number of days and/ or time duration constraints are still difficult to solve. Developing an ALNS for the practical PVRP is a natural choice as a solution alternative can be destroyed and repaired in various ways. Moreover, the basic solution concept is easily understandable by a decision maker. We contribute to this research area as follows: First, an adaptive large neighborhood search is presented for the PVRP which includes local search. It shows first promising results on selected instances. Second, an approach to classify a move to a neighboring solution into "exploring" or "exploiting" the search space is suggested and is taken into account during the ALNS. For this, a dissimilarity measure needs to be defined. We suggest several ones with various levels of detail for the PVRP and study the impact the chosen measure has on the performance of the approach. Lastly, it is shown how the split procedure introduced in [11] can be reinterpreted as a local search neighborhood.

2 Solution approach

The adaptive large neighborhood search was proposed in [12] and tested for several variants of the vehicle routing problem in [10]. A set of destroy and repair operators is defined. Each destroy/ repair heuristic is assigned a weight that controls how often a method is applied during the search. The weights are adjusted dynamically during the execution of the algorithm so that the heuristic adapts to the instance at hand. As a result, a number of simple algorithms compete to modify the current solution. A pseudo-code for the developed ALNS for the PVRP is shown in Algorithm 1. The ALNS is embedded in a simulated annealing framework and is enhanced with a local search procedure to improve the solution quality of promising candidates. It additionally makes use of a concept of exploration, for which an archive Ω is maintained.

The developed algorithm starts with a randomly constructed solution alternative s to which the best found solution alternative s^{best} is set (line 1). While a stop criterion is not met, lines 2–18 repeat and finally return s^{best}. The temporary alternative s' is copied from the incumbent one s (line 3), destroyed and repaired again (line 4). In line 5, the move from s to s' is classified into either *exploring* or *exploiting* the search space $\mathcal{S}$. The idea is to promote the usage of exploring operators towards the beginning of the algorithm. $\mathcal{S}$ is defined as a set of feasible and infeasible solutions $s \in \mathcal{S}$. A solution alternative may only be infeasible with respect to the number of vehicles m_l operating on day l, the load $q_{k,l}$ transported by a vehicle k on day l and the total travel time $dur_{k,l}$ in a route. These infeasibilites are taken into account when evaluating an alternative. Let χ^m, χ^q and χ^{dur} represent the penalties for exceeding the number of available vehicles on a day, the route vehicle capacity and the route maximum duration, respectively. A solution s is evaluated by the penalized function $\Psi(s)$:

$$
\begin{aligned}
\Psi(s) = \sum_{l=1}^{t}\sum_{k=1}^{m}\sum_{i=0}^{n}\sum_{j=0}^{n} c_{ij}x_{ijkl} + \sum_{l=1}^{t}\chi^m \cdot max\{0, m_l - m\} \\
+ \sum_{l=1}^{t}\sum_{k=1}^{m}\left(\chi^q \cdot max\{0, q_{k,l} - Q\} + \chi^{dur} \cdot max\{0, dur_{k,l} - D\}\right)
\end{aligned}
\tag{1}
$$

Here, x_{ijkl} is 1 if there is a direct connection between customer i and j of vehicle k during day l, 0 otherwise. The relative quality $\Psi'(s)$ of a solution s is then given by setting it into relation to the function value of s^{best}, that is $\Psi'(s) = \frac{\Psi(s)-\Psi(s^{best})}{\Psi(s^{best})}$. If s' is feasible, the penalization factors are divided by 1.001, otherwise, they are multiplied by it (line 6). This applies provided that lower and upper bounds are not violated [9]. While χ^{dur} and χ^q can alternate between 10 and 1,000, χ^m varies between 100 and 10,000. The penalties are initialized to their respective upper bounds to quickly determine feasible solution alternatives in the beginning. In case of infeasibility, procedures to restore feasibility are applied with a probability of 50% (lines 7– 8). If successful and s' not yet included, the archive Ω is updated. A local search procedure is applied on a feasible solution alternative if either s' is promising (indicated by $\Psi'(s') \leq \alpha_1$) or the move was exploring *and* s' reveals a sufficiently good solution quality (that is $\Psi'(s') \leq \alpha_2$). The archive is updated with the improved s' and s^{best} is replaced by s' if applicable (lines 9–13). s' is accepted as the new incumbent alternative s with probability $e^{-(\Psi(s')-\Psi(s))/T}$ where $T > 0$ is the *temperature* and initialized to T^{start} (line 14). It is decreased every 10 seconds so that it reaches zero in the end (line 15). In the next line, the scores σ_1, σ_2 or σ_3 are added to the total scores of the used destroy and repair operator if applicable. An exploration score

---

Algorithm 1: Adaptive large neighborhood search for the PVRP

---

input: temperature $T = T^{start}$; archive $\Omega \leftarrow \emptyset$; initialize penalization parameters;

1 get random solution s; $s^{best} = s$
2 **while** *stop criterion not met* **do**
3 | $s' = s$
4 | destroy and repair s'
5 | **if** Ω *updated with* s' **then** classify move from s to s' in search space $\mathcal{S}$
6 | update penalty parameters according to feasibility of s' and evaluate s'
7 | **if** s' *infeasible* **then**
8 | | restore feasibility with a probability of 50% and update archive Ω if restored
9 | **if** s' *feasible* **then**
10 | | **if** $\Psi'(s') \leq \alpha_1$ **or else** (*move was exploring* and also $\Psi'(s') \leq \alpha_2$) **then**
11 | | | improve s' with local search
12 | | | update Ω with s'
13 | | **if** $\Psi(s') < \Psi(s^{best})$ **then** $s^{best} = s'$
14 | **if** s' *is accepted considering s and temperature T* **then** $s = s'$
15 | **if** 10 *seconds passed* **then** cool down temperature T
16 | assign scores σ_1, σ_2 or σ_3 as well as σ_4 (if applicable)
17 | **if** 100 *iterations passed* **then** update ALNS weights and statistic of Ω
18 | **if** *maximum archive size is reached* **then** reduce archive size
19 **return** s^{best}

σ_4 is additionally attributed if the move was classified as exploring. The application weights of the individual operators are updated every 100 iterations and a statistic of the archive Ω used within the exploration concept is recomputed (line 17). Finally, the archive is reduced to 300 solution alternatives whenever a maximum archive size of 500 is reached in line 18. Here, solutions with a high number of neighbors are preferably deleted.

The following subsections go into detail of the described ALNS. Subsection 2.1 shows how a random alternative is constructed for the PVRP with help of the Split procedure [18] (line 1). The used destroy and repair operators are explained in the following subsection (line 4). A concept of exploration (line 5) as well as the assignment of scores and update of the operator weights (line 17) are presented in Subsection 2.3. The last subsection illustrates the local search as well as the thereon resting procedure to regain feasibility (lines 7 and 11).

2.1 Constructing a random alternative for the PVRP

An initial solution for the PVRP is generated by first randomly choosing a pattern for each customer. For each day, a giant tour is constructed by serving all customers to be visited on this day in a random order. Then, routes are obtained by the *Split* procedure introduced in [11]. Vidal illustrated in [17] how the Split algorithm can be performed in linear time. This dynamic programming algorithm determines an optimal routing sequence given the customers are approached in the order the giant tour specifies. An optimal segmentation of the giant tour into routes consists in identifying a minimum-cost path from 0 to n in an auxiliary graph. It only possesses the edges between the depot and the customers in the giant tour as well as the edges of the giant tour. In each iteration, the next customer of the giant tour is included optimally in the routing by keeping track of non-dominated predecessors and the associated costs of the shortest routes containing the customers included so far. Note that in our implementation, Split tries to construct feasible routes by taking into consideration maximum m vehicles, capacity and time duration constraints. If this is not possible, the m-th+1 route includes the remaining customers and the solution alternative is infeasible with respect to driven routes. For further details on how to adapt the Split algorithm to a limited fleet with a total complexity of $\mathcal{O}(nm)$ see [17]. However, note that the pseudo code does not consider time duration constraints and therefore slightly was adapted. The procedure repeats until either a feasible solution alternative was found or 60 seconds have passed.

2.2   Obtaining a new solution alternative by destroy and repair

A set of destroy and repair operators is implemented to move to neighboring solution alternatives. Some operators modify the subset of customers to be visited on each day (by using a "complete removal") while others focus on the routes of a given subset (in "partial removal"). In that way, the operators are able to both slightly and strongly modify an alternative. Figure 1 illustrates this procedure.

The destroy operator is selected by applying a roulette wheel selection. With Φ heuristics and weights $w_\varphi, \varphi = 1, \ldots, \Phi$, heuristic φ' is selected with probability

$$\frac{w_{\varphi'}}{\sum_{\varphi=1}^{\Phi} w_\varphi} \tag{2}$$

If the corresponding operator invokes a complete removal, all customers of the instance are candidates for elimination. The selected ones are removed from all days of their current pattern. The randomly determined parameter ε with $5 \leq \varepsilon \leq \min(100; 0.4 \cdot n)$ indicates how many customers will be removed from the current solution alternative. In case of partial removal, a subset of days is randomly selected. Each chosen day is treated separately and all customers served on that day represent the candidates. With n_l as the number of customers served on the chosen day l, ε_l candidates with $5 \leq \varepsilon_l \leq \min(100; 0.4 \cdot n_l)$ are removed. In each case, the candidates are sorted with respect to a criterion dictated by the destroy operator. Candidates in the beginning of this sorted list are preferably eliminated but some variation is introduced. The destroyed solution is fixed with a repair operator which is again chosen by roulette wheel selection within the heuristics for complete and partial removal. Note that in the last case, the removed customers are reinserted on the same days and no pattern change takes place. The solution is fixed by again sorting the removed customers according to the criterion of the chosen repair operator, i.e. by some sort of costs. To prevent the algorithm to repeatedly generate the same alternatives, these costs are modified by adding a random noise in the interval $-0.025 \cdot dist_{max} \leq$

$noise \leq 0.025 \cdot dist_{max}$ with a probability of 50%. Here, $dist_{max}$ represents the maximum distance between two vertices in the data set. The ALNS keeps track of the success of using noise and also adapts this application probability.

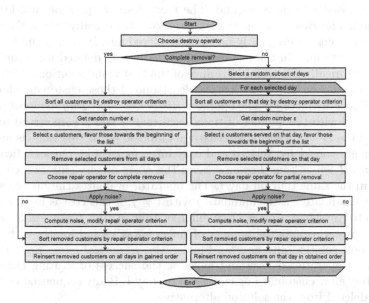

Fig. 1. Schematic illustration of applying a destroy and a repair operator

The depicted destroy operators appear in both complete and partial removal if not stated otherwise and are based on [10, 12]. The most simple operator is the *Random Removal* which randomly selects the customers to be eliminated. The aim of the *Shaw Removal* is to choose "similar customers" as those are easier to interchange in a solution with regard to satisfying the load and time duration constraints of the respective routes [14, 15]. For that, a relatedness matrix $R(i, j, s)$ is computed for all candidates i and j with $i \neq j$ in solution s. Their similarity in s is measured as a weighted sum of various measures. The distance similarity $sim^c_{i,j}$ takes the geographical distance between i and j into account and sets it in relation to the highest distance between two customers in the data set. The temporal similarity $sim^l_{i,j,s}$ is measured by counting the number of different day assignments of the candidates i and j in solution s and divide the value by the total number of days. Lastly, the demand similarity $sim^q_{i,j}$ is computed as the ratio between the absolute demand difference of i and j and the highest demand of a customer in the instance. Following literature, $R(i, j, s)$ is obtained by applying the weighted sum function $R(i, j, s) = 9 \cdot sim^c_{i,j} + 3 \cdot sim^l_{i,j,s} + 3 \cdot sim^q_{i,j}$. The Shaw Removal randomly selects a seed candidate and sorts the remaining ones according to their relatedness to it. The destroy operators *Location Oriented Removal* and *Time Oriented Removal* work analogously to the Shaw Removal except that only $sim^c_{i,j}$ and $sim^l_{i,j,s}$ are used for determining $R(i, j, s)$, respectively. The *Worst Removal* computes the cost savings achieved when removing the candidate i from s and sort the candidates accordingly. Those customers are removed which will result in high cost savings as they seem to be badly positioned. Lastly, *Small Removal* chooses customers which reveal a small demand as those are easier to move around. The next destroy operators use historical information. The *Historical Same Day Removal* strategically tracks the success of visiting two customers jointly on the considered day. It aims to find the best customer partitioning in the instance and thus is only defined for complete removal. If historically the average distance of the best found solution which served customer i and j on day l was long, at least one of those customers should be reassigned to a distinct day. The operator *Historical Same Day Removal (B best)* works instead with the number of times customers i and j were served together on day l in the B best solution alternatives found so far. If this value is high, the customers are considered related and easy interchangeable. On a tactical level, the *Historical Same Tour Removal* saves the costs of servicing two customers together in the same tour on day l. The operator evaluates the historical costs of visiting candidate i with candidate j with $i \neq j$. If this cost is high, it can be beneficial to reassign customer i to a different tour. Again, *Historical Same Tour Removal (B best)* counts the number of times i was visited jointly with $j, i \neq j$ in the B best solution alternatives. Finally, the *Historical Same Edge Removal* works on an operational level and looks at the success of visiting customer j immediately after customer i or vice versa on day l. Badly sequenced customers are then deleted from the solution alternative.

There are several ways to repair a destroyed solution. In the *Parallel Best Insertion*, the least-cost pattern over all removed customers and their feasible patterns is identified. The corresponding customer is inserted on the least-cost position on the associated days of the pattern. The procedure repeats until all deleted customers are reassigned. In the *Sequential Best Insertion*, the least-cost pattern is determined for a randomly selected customer instead. Again, the customers are inserted on their best position on each day of the chosen pattern. The repair operators *Random Patterns* as well as *Regret Heuristic Pattern (β)* are solely used in case of complete removal. Random Patterns both randomly selects a customer and one of its patterns. It is then reinserted on its best position. Thus, it can be seen as a counterpart to Random Removal. In the PVRP, multiple regret heuristics can be defined which incorporate some kind of lookahead in the insertion procedure. Regret Heuristic Pattern (β) computes for each customer the cost difference – that is the *regret* – of selecting the β-th best pattern instead of the best pattern for customer i. If this cost is high, customer i should be assigned to its best pattern. If a partial removal took place, the repair operators *Regret Heuristic Routes(β)* and *Regret Heuristic Position(β)* may be applied. In the first case, the regret consists of putting the considered customer on the best position of its β-th best route instead of being visited by its best route. A finer approach is taken in the latter case which computes the regrets of not choosing the best but the β-th best position over all routes on the considered day. Note that this position may be in the same or in a different route.

2.3 Adaptive weight adjustment and the concept of exploration

In the ALNS, the destroy and repair heuristics are evaluated after each application and scores are assigned. The score of a heuristic is increased by either σ_1, σ_2 or σ_3. The highest score σ_1 is given if s' improves s^{best}. Two cases are distinguished if s' is accepted by the ALNS considering the current temperature T. If s' is (currently) not in the archive Ω, the score is increased by σ_2, otherwise σ_3 applies. Note that it is also possible to compare s' to all solutions found until this point which is however computationally demanding. Naturally, $\sigma_1 > \sigma_2 > \sigma_3$ holds. Additionally, a score is attributed for following the currently desired search space strategy. In literature, it is typically distinguished between *exploration* and *exploitation*. However, it is not clear how to measure which search space strategy is currently pursued. Let $\mathbf{1}$ (*cond*) be a valuation function that returns 1 if the condition *cond* is true, 0, otherwise. In this paper, s' is exploring the search space $\mathcal{S}$ given s if the following two conditions hold:

$$\delta(s, s') \geq \delta^{Th} \tag{3}$$

$$\sum_{s'' \in \Omega, s' \neq s''} \mathbf{1}\left[\delta(s', s'') \leq \delta^{Th}\right] \leq \frac{1}{|\Omega|} \sum_{s'' \in \Omega} \sum_{s''' \in \Omega, s'' \neq s'''} \mathbf{1}\left[\delta(s'', s''') \leq \delta^{Th}\right] \tag{4}$$

The Inequality (3) requires that s' is at least δ^{Th} dissimilar to s using the dissimilarity measure δ, i.e. s' is not "in the vicinity" of s. Additionally, Inequality (4) demands that the search space of s' is "sparsely covered". The left term counts the solutions inside the archive Ω which are less than δ^{Th} dissimilar to s' (so-called "neighbors"). This value is compared with the average number of neighbors of the solutions in Ω (right term). This statistic of Ω is updated every 100 iterations. If the two inequalities are true, the search space in the vicinity of s' has been explored little so far and therefore the move of the operators can be classified as *exploring*. Otherwise, the search space has been *exploited*. Note that, due to the lacking information of the true distribution of all possible solutions in the instance at hand, it is assumed that the distribution is fairly even over the search space. An adaptation to the actual landscape of the search space could be topic of future research. Figure 2.3 illustrates the concept of exploration on a simplified example. Assume that the search space is put together by determining the values for the x and y coordinate with $x, y \geq 0$. All solutions s'' inside the radius of a solution (represented as a circle) are its neighbors. In the left case, for instance, s has two neighbors and s' one. The average number of neighbors given the illustrated solution alternatives is ~ 1.67. Since s' is outside the radius of s and has one neighbor, s' has *explored* the search space. In the right case, *exploitation* occurred since s' is inside the radius of s and the number of its neighbors exceeds the average number of neighbors in Ω ($2 > 1.67$).

Inequalities (3) and (4) require the definition of a dissimilarity measure. We suggest the four measures δ_1, δ_2, δ_3 and δ_4 for the PVRP which increase by the level of detail and by needed computation time. First, the solutions s_1 and s_2 can differ in the pattern assignments of the customers [18]. With y_{ip} assuming

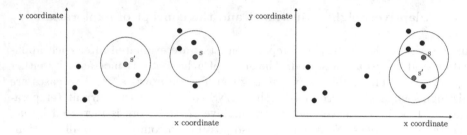

Fig. 2. Left: s' explores the search space given s. Right: s' exploits it given s.

1 if customer i is served following pattern p and 0 otherwise, δ_1 is defined as:

$$\delta_1(s_1, s_2) = \frac{1}{n} \sum_{i=1}^{n} \sum_{p \in P_i} \mathbf{1}(y_{ip}(s_1) \neq y_{ip}(s_2)) \tag{5}$$

Second, the subset of customers served on each day can be compared, i.e. the number of different day assignments of the customers in s_1 and s_2 is studied for each day. With a_{pl} being equal to 1 if and only if day l belongs to pattern p, $\delta_2(s_1, s_2)$ is computed by:

$$\delta_2(s_1, s_2) = \frac{1}{n \cdot t} \sum_{i=1}^{n} \sum_{l=1}^{t} \sum_{p \in P_i} \mathbf{1}(a_{pl} y_{ip}(s_1) \neq a_{pl} y_{ip}(s_2)) \tag{6}$$

Third, $\delta_3(s_1, s_2)$ checks on each day whether the customers i and j are served by the same vehicle k. That is, the dissimilarity increases if customer i and j were served in the same route in s_1 but in different ones in s_2 or vice versa. Let z_{ijl} take 1 if both customers i and j are served by the same vehicle on day l and 0 otherwise. Then, $\delta_3(s_1, s_2)$ is defined as:

$$\delta_3(s_1, s_2) = \frac{1}{\frac{n(n-1)}{2} \cdot t} \sum_{i=1}^{n-1} \sum_{j=i+1}^{n} \sum_{l=1}^{t} \mathbf{1}(z_{ijl}(s_1) \neq z_{ijl}(s_2)) \tag{7}$$

Finally, δ_4 compares the driven customer order in the routes:

$$\delta_4(s_1, s_2) = \frac{1}{\frac{n(n-1)}{2} \cdot t} \sum_{i=1}^{n-1} \sum_{j=i+1}^{n} \sum_{k=1}^{m} \sum_{l=1}^{t} \mathbf{1}(x_{ijkl}(s_1) \neq x_{ijkl}(s_2)) \tag{8}$$

By intuition, it is more important in an early stage of the algorithm to explore the search space while exploiting it towards the end. Note, however, that exploitation is not desired per se, but only in the vicinity of promising solution alternatives. Let ϑ increase by one after each 10 seconds and let Θ^{max} be the maximum time an exploration score is awarded. Then, the following weighted exploration score σ_4 is given:

$$\sigma_4 \cdot \left(1 - \frac{\vartheta \cdot 10}{\Theta^{max}}\right) \tag{9}$$

So, the given score is gradually decreasing until Θ^{max} is reached. Let ι be the current segment where each segment comprises 100 iterations. The weight $w_{\varphi,\iota+1}$ of heuristic φ for segment $\iota + 1$ is computed by:

$$w_{\varphi,\iota+1} = w_{\varphi,\iota}(1 - r) + r\frac{\pi_\varphi}{\theta_\varphi} \tag{10}$$

π_φ is the score of heuristic φ obtained during the current segment ι and θ_φ is the number of times φ has been applied in it weighted by its needed computation time. $r \in [0, 1]$ denotes the reaction factor and controls how much the weight of the current segment influences the weight in the next one. Following [12], $r = 0.1$ was used in the computational experiments.

2.4 The local search procedure

Promising solution alternatives are further investigated by applying a local search procedure based on [18]. It consists of a split improvement procedure (SI), a route improvement procedure (RI) and a pattern improvement procedure (PI). The procedures are called in the sequence SI-RI-PI-SI-RI. Both SI and RI dedicate to optimize the VRP subproblem for each day of the planning horizon. SI reinterprets the Split procedure introduced in [11] as a neighborhood. After shuffling the sequence of the routes and inverting some routes at random, a giant tour representation is extracted. SI returns an optimally split list of routes with respect to the given giant tour as well as fleet, load and time duration constraints. The procedure terminates after 5 unsuccessful repetitions.

Seven classical neighborhoods are used within RI which are investigated in a random order following a first-improvement strategy. The neighborhoods are restricted by applying the granular approach suggested in [16] in which only "promising" moves are evaluated, i.e. those moves which add at least one "good" edge. Such an edge either connects to the depot or has a length lower than the granularity threshold value $\lambda \cdot \frac{\Psi^{Sav}}{n+m^{Sav}}$ with Ψ^{Sav} and m^{Sav} as the length and the number of routes of a routing alternative generated by the Savings approach [4] and λ as the sparsification parameter. In the computational experiment, $\lambda = 2.5$ was chosen. The neighborhood *Relocate(1)* removes a customer i from its route and tries to reinsert it before or after j, that is the edge connecting i to j is either "short" or includes the depot. In the related neighborhood *Relocate(2)*, two succeeding customers i and $i + 1$ are relocated together accordingly. *Exchange(1,2)* switches a single customer i with two customers j and $j + 1$. The neighborhoods *Exchange(1,1)* and *Exchange(2,2)* are defined analogously. All described route improvement neighborhoods are investigated both inter- and intra-route. Finally, the classical *TwoOptInter* and *TwoOptIntra* exchange two edges with two different ones inter-route and intra-route, respectively.

PI improves the visit assignments of customers. It iterates on routes and customers in random order and computes for each customer i the costs of all its patterns $p \in P_i$. The customer i is first removed from the solution. The pattern costs emerge by putting customer i in its best route and best position on all days a_{pl} of pattern p. The customer is then reinserted on the least-cost position on the days of the least-cost pattern. Note that it is possible that i is assigned to the same pattern as before but to different routes or positions.

The local search procedure is also used to restore an infeasible solution alternative with a probability of 50%. The procedure *Reduce* first checks if the total load of the customers visited on each day exceeds the total available vehicle capacity. If so, PI is applied. If the solution remains infeasible and the total load to be transported by the limited fleet is still too high, the procedure exits without success. Otherwise, on each day two routes are randomly selected and merged until the number of used vehicles is smaller m. The least-cost position is chosen. Note that the merge may result in infeasible routes with respect to load or time duration. If this is the case, a further investigation is excecuted in the procedure *Intensify*. As in [18], the penalization factors χ^m, χ^{dur} and χ^k are increased by factor 10 and the described local search is applied. The procedure repeats with a further multiplication by factor 100 if the solution alternative remains infeasible. In a last attempt, *Reduce* is applied and the procedure terminates. In summary, the sequence Reduce-Intensify(factor 10)-Intensify(factor 100)-Reduce is implemented and the procedure is exited whenever a feasible solution is obtained.

3   Computational study

The proposed algorithm was tested on the PVRP benchmark instances of [5] which contain between 50 and 417 customers to be routed on 2 to 10 days by 1 to 12 vehicles. Note that the data sets pr01–pr10 (the "new" data set) impose time duration constraints while instances p01–p32 (the "old" data set) do not. The solution approach has been coded in Visual Basic .NET and was tested on a machine with an Intel Xeon processor E5-2690. The 8 gigabytes RAM were shared by eight parallel single threads. To obtain insight into the average behavior of the algorithm, 10 runs were conducted.

First, it is investigated if the chosen dissimilarity measure has an impact on the performance of the algorithm. As a stop criterion, a run time of maximum 10 minutes and 10,000 iterations without improving s^{best} was chosen ("short run"). The parameters were calibrated for a test set of instances comprising the data sets p05, p08, p23, pr02, pr05 and pr08. For all experiments, $(\sigma_1, \sigma_2, \sigma_3, \alpha_1, \alpha_2) = (30, 9, 3, 0.05, 0.1)$ were set. For each regret repair heuristic, $\beta = 2$, $\beta = 3$ and $\beta = 4$ were applied. According to [9], an initial temperature $T^{start} = 125$ is appropriate for instances with a high average distance (i.e. instances p27–p32) while $T^{start} = 7$ was chosen for the remaining ones. Table 1 shows which values have been selected within a full-factorial experiment for the dissimilarity threshold δ^{Th}, the exploration score σ_4 and Θ^{max} (the maximum time exploration is rewarded) in the short run. Table 2 presents the average results over all instances with various dissimilarity measures. The first row clearly demonstrates that the chosen dissimilarity measure indeed has an impact on the performance of the algorithm. The measure δ_1 with the lowest level of detail (that is measuring dis-

Table 1. Best parameter configuration for all dissimilarity measures in the short run

parameter	tested values	best configuration δ_1	δ_2	δ_3	δ_4
δ^{Th}	$0.001, 0.005, 0.01, 0.05, 0.1$	0.01	0.05	0.05	0.001
σ_4	$3, 9, 30$	3	3	3	9
Θ^{max} (in mins)	$3, 7, 10$	3	10	7	3

Table 2. Results for various dissimilarity measures (short run)

	δ_1	δ_2	δ_3	δ_4
gap overall (in %)	1.38	1.55	2.11	1.90
# iterations range	[1139, 40870]	[1081, 38795]	[442, 23074]	[567, 29619]
# iterations avg.	13861	11898	6961	9316
explored range (in %)	[1.6, 67.4]	[2.5, 31.0]	[0, 34.5]	[0, 71.8]
explored avg. (in %)	23.4	15.2	5.1	26.4
avg. dissim. range	[0.0173, 0.1019]	[0.0067, 0.0628]	[0.0016, 0.103]	[0.0003, 0.029]
avg. dissim.	0.0461	0.0238	0.0225	0.0043
gap old data set (in %)	1.01	1.19	1.67	1.47
gap new data set (in %)	2.59	2.68	3.54	3.30
gap $n \leq 150$ (in %)	0.54	0.67	0.88	0.72
gap $n > 150$ (in %)	3.50	3.75	5.2	4.85

similarity via common pattern assignments) obtained the lowest gap overall. The gap is determined by taking into account the best known solutions (BKS) of the respective PVRP data sets reported in [18] and is computed by $\frac{\Psi(s^{best}) - \Psi(BKS)}{\Psi(BKS)}$. A possible explanation for these significant differences is the increased running time associated with a higher level of detail. The rows "# iterations range" and "# iterations avg." present the total number of iterations of the outer loop conducted in the experiments (see Algorithm 1). On average, the highest number of iterations was obtained using δ_1 while the smallest one was achieved applying δ_3. Note that for both δ_3 and δ_4, the number of used iterations on average was smaller than the stopping criterion 10,000. Therefore, the run time using δ_3 or δ_4 is potentially higher than the one applying δ_1 or δ_2.

The next two lines show the range as well as the average of how often an exploration was detected. A significant gap can be noticed between the respective minimum and maximum values. For δ_3 and δ_4 there were even instances in which no single move from s to s' was classified as exploring in one run. Taking δ_4 and data set p13 as an example, s' was on average 0.003 dissimilar to s so that Inequality (3) was never satisfied. This can be attributed to the fact that in p13 417 customers need to be served over a planning horizon of 7 days and the number ε of to be removed customers in one move is maximum 100. For δ_3, the smallest number of moves was qualified as exploring and thus potentially local search was executed to a lesser extent. The rows "avg. dissim. range" and "avg.

dissim." show that on average the dissimilarity of s' to s was higher than the respectively set dissimilarity threshold for δ_2, δ_3 and δ_4. Therefore, many moves were not classified as exploring as the vicinity of the search space of s has been exploited. The results suggest that it is vital to select δ^{Th} wisely. An adaptation to specific instance characteristics seems reasonable. The last lines present the results for specific subsets of instances. For each measure, a significant gap can be noticed comparing the performance of the algorithm on the old data set (without time duration constraints) and on the new one (including them). An even stronger difference can be observed comparing the gaps of instances with lower than 150 customers with those serving more than 150 ones.

Table 3. Impact of exploration on performance using δ_1

	short run						long run					
	w/ exploration			w/o exploration			w/ exploration			w/o exploration		
	gap	rt	rt^{best}	gap	rt	rt^{best}	gap	rt	rt^{best}	gap	rt	rt^{best}
overall	1.38%	6.8	4.8	1.43%	6.7	4.6	1.15%	12.8	9.5	1.17%	12.8	9.5
old data set	1.01%	6.2	4.0	1.07%	6.1	3.8	0.85%	9.7	6.4	0.86%	9.6	6.5
new data set	2.59%	9.0	7.5	2.57%	8.9	7.4	2.09%	22.7	19.6	2.14%	22.8	19.3
$n \leq 150$	0.54%	5.6	3.4	0.60%	5.4	3.2	0.56%	7.0	4.1	0.55%	6.8	3.7
$n > 150$	3.50%	10.0	8.2	3.51%	10.0	8.3	2.61%	27.1	23.2	2.69%	27.6	24.1

Proceeding with the dissimilarity measure δ_1 which yielded the best results on average, the algorithm was rerun with no exploration consideration. In particular, no exploration score was given and therefore the local search was only applied if the considered solution s' was short enough ($\Psi'(s') \leq \alpha_1$). In total 21 instances revealed a run time which was 8 minutes or longer. Those were rerun for maximum 30 minutes as well as maximum 10,000 unsuccessful repetitions ("long run"). Using a smaller test set comprising data sets p08, pr02, pr08 and pr05, the best parameter configuration for the long run was determined. For δ^{Th} and σ_4, the tested values presented in Table 1 were used while for Θ^{max}, the values $9, 21$ and 30 were inspected. The best parameter configuration was determined as $(\delta^{Th}, \sigma_4, \Theta^{max}) = (0.005, 9, 30)$. Table 3 shows that for the short run, explicitly considering the exploration of the search space (indicated by "w/ exploration") is advantageous for both short and long run. In the short run, this is particularly true for the old data set and instances with a smaller number of customers. The columns "rt" indicate the actual running time of the algorithm while "rt^{best}" shows when the reported s^{best} has been obtained. It is evident that around 2 minutes were spent on average to either conduct 10000 unsuccessful iterations or reach the time limit in the short run. In the long run, this figure even amounts to around 3.3 minutes. Thus the maximum number of unsuccessful iterations has a significant impact on the reported run time of the algorithm and should be carefully chosen. However, note that the PVRP can be considered a tactical problem as a planning horizon including several days is part of the problem definition. As a result, the run time of an algorithm is of secondary priority. In the long run, the results have been further improved. In the version with exploration consideration, the overall gap decreased by 0.23% while both rt and rt^{best} nearly doubled. It is up to the decision maker to evaluate this trade-off between run time and solution quality.

Finally, Table 4 compares the obtained results with δ_1 in the short run to state-of-the-art heuristics presented in literature, that is with the tabu search heuristic of [5] (CGL), the scatter search of [1] (ALP), the variable neighborhood search of [9] (HDH), the record-to-record approach of [8] (GGW) as well as the hybrid genetic algorithm of [18] (VCGLR). The presented run times are taken from [18]. While VCGLR outperforms our proposed approach, it is clearly competitive to the other state-of-the-art solution methods for the PVRP. With the best alternative determined after around 4.8 minutes on average the run times are comparable. The suggested ALNS obtained lower gaps compared to CGL, ALP and GGW in every category, while HDH outperformed it in the new data set as well as on instances with a high number of customers. Concretely, the ALNS outperformed CGL in 74% of the data sets by 1.07% on average, ALP in 50% of the cases by 1.06%, HDH in 64% of the data sets by 0.86% and GGW in 38% of the instances by around 0.77%.

Table 4. Results of the short run in comparison to literature

	CGL	ALP	HDH	GGW	VCGLR	ALNS
avg. time (in mins)	4.28	3.64	3.34	10.36	5.56	4.8
gap overall (in %)	+2.04	–	+1.66	–	+0.41	+1.38
gap old data set (in %)	+1.80	+1.57	+1.60	+1.11	+0.31	+1.01
gap new data set (in %)	+2.82	–	+1.86	–	+0.71	+2.59
gap $n > 150$ (in %)	+3.63	–	+3.34	–	+1.02	+3.50

4   Conclusions

This paper developed an adaptive large neighborhood search for the periodic vehicle routing problem that rewards exploring movements of the algorithm in the search space. We propose a novel concept of exploration as well as four dissimilarity measures for the PVRP. A heuristic contributed to exploration if the newly generated solution alternative is sufficiently dissimilar to the incumbent one and its close search space is sparsely covered. A computational study showed that dissimilarity measures with a lower level of detail yield better results, possibly because of the interconnected saving in run time. The results indicated that it is beneficial to take into account the currently followed search space strategy. In general, the first computational results are promising and proved competitive with state-of-the-art solution approaches for the PVRP. Future research should investigate in more detail under which circumstances and until which point it is promising to further promote the exploration of the search space.

References

1. Alegre, J., Laguna, M., Pacheco, J.: Optimizing the periodic pick-up of raw materials for a manufacturer of auto parts. European Journal of Operational Research 179(3), 736–746 (2007)
2. Baldacci, R., Bartolini, E., Mingozzi, A., Valletta, A.: An exact algorithm for the period routing problem. Operations Research 59(1), 228–241 (2011)
3. Campbell, A.M., Wilson, J.H.: Forty years of periodic vehicle routing. Networks 63(1), 2–15 (2014)
4. Clarke, G., Wright, J.W.: Scheduling of vehicles from a central depot to a number of delivery points. Operations Research 12(4), 568–581 (1964)
5. Cordeau, J.F., Gendreau, M., Laporte, G.: A tabu search heuristic for periodic and multi-depot vehicle routing problems. Networks 30, 105–119 (1997)
6. Drummond, L.M.A., Ochi, L.S., Vianna, D.S.: An asynchronous parallel metaheuristic for the period vehicle routing problem. Future Generation Computer Systems 17(4), 379–386 (2001)
7. Francis, P.M., Smilowitz, K.R., Tzur, M.: The period vehicle routing problem and its extensions. In: Golden, B., Raghavan, S., Wasil, E. (eds.) The Vehicle Routing Problem: Latest Advances and New Challenges, pp. 73–102. Springer US, Boston, MA (2008)
8. Gulczynski, D., Golden, B., Wasil, E.: The period vehicle routing problem: New heuristics and real-world variants. Transportation Research Part E: Logistics and Transportation Review 47(5), 648–668 (2011)
9. Hemmelmayr, V., Doerner, K., Hartl, R.: A variable neighborhood search heuristic for periodic routing problems. European Journal of Operational Research 195(3), 791–802 (2009)
10. Pisinger, D., Ropke, S.: A general heuristic for vehicle routing problems. Computers & Operations Research 34(8), 2403–2435 (2007)
11. Prins, C.: A simple and effective evolutionary algorithm for the vehicle routing problem. Computers & Operations Research 31(12), 1985–2002 (2004)
12. Ropke, S., Pisinger, D.: An adaptive large neighbourhood search heuristic for the pickup and delivery problem with time windows. Transportation Science 40, 455–472 (2006)
13. Russell, R., Igo, W.: An assignment routing problem. Networks 9(1), 1–17 (1979)
14. Shaw, P.: A new local search algorithm providing high quality solutions to vehicle routing problems. Tech. rep., Department of Computer Science, University of Strathclyde, Scotland (1997)
15. Shaw, P.: Using constraint programming and local search methods to solve vehicle routing problems. In: Maher, M., Puget, J.F. (eds.) Principles and Practice of Constraint Programming. Lecture Notes in Computer Science, vol. 1520, pp. 417–431. Springer Berlin Heidelberg (1997)
16. Toth, P., Vigo, D.: The Granular Tabu Search and its application to the vehicle routing problem. INFORMS Journal on Computing 15(4), 333–346 (2003)
17. Vidal, T.: Technical note: Split algorithm in $\mathcal{O}(n)$ for the capacitated vehicle routing problem. Computers & Operations Research 69, 40–47 (2016)
18. Vidal, T., Crainic, T.G., Gendreau, M., Lahrichi, N., Rei, W.: A hybrid genetic algorithm for multidepot and periodic vehicle routing problems. Operations Research 60(3), 611–624 (2012)

The Vehicle Routing Problem with Dynamic Occasional Drivers

Lars Dahle$^{(\boxtimes)}$, Henrik Andersson, and Marielle Christiansen

Department of Industrial Economics and Technology Management, Norwegian
University of Science and Technology, Trondheim, Norway.
`lars.dahle@ntnu.no`, `henrik.andersson@ntnu.no`, `mc@ntnu.no`

Abstract. Technological advances, such as smart phones and mobile internet, allow for new and innovative solutions for transportation of goods to customers. We consider a setting where a company not only uses its own fleet of vehicles to deliver products, but may also make use of ordinary people who are already on the road. This may include people who visit the store, who are willing to take a detour on their way home for a small compensation. The availability of these occasional drivers is naturally highly uncertain, and we assume that some stochastic information is known about their appearance. This leads to a stochastic vehicle routing problem, with dynamic appearance of vehicles. The contribution of this paper is a mixed-integer programming formulation, and insights into how routes for the company vehicles could be planned in such a setting. The results of the stochastic model are compared with deterministic strategies with reoptimization.

Keywords: Vehicle Routing, Occasional Drivers, Stochastic Programming

1   Introduction and Literature

Transportation can be a significant cost for last-mile and same-day delivery, which has prompted many companies to seek creative and innovative solutions to lower their costs. One such solution, considered by among others Walmart and Amazon, is *crowdshipping*, i.e. getting ordinary people who are already en route to pick up and deliver packages [5, 6]. Better utilization of vehicles that are already on the road can be profitable both for the company and the occasional drivers, and help lower emissions.

Walmarts vision of having in-store customers to help deliver goods ordered by online customers, gives rise to new variants of the dynamic vehicle routing problem (DVRP). In a recent survey and taxonomy of the DVRP [11], the authors state that "some 80% of the problems in the taxonomy involve the dynamic appearance of customers, some 10% involve dynamic travel times and some 3% consider vehicle breakdowns. In our search we were not able to find papers handling other types of dynamic events (...)". Since then, some research has been done on the effects of occasional drivers [3, 4], where [3] introduces crowdshipping and study a static version of the problem, and [4] looks at a deterministic

© Springer International Publishing AG 2017
T. Bektaş et al. (Eds.), ICCL 2017, LNCS 10572, pp. 49–63, 2017.
https://doi.org/10.1007/978-3-319-68496-3_4

approach of matching dynamically appearing customers and drivers. A crowd-shipping platform would naturally contain a lot of uncertainty with respect to the availability of drivers. Our problem is similar to [3, 4], but extends these works by introducing stochasticity and studying how this uncertainty affects the problem.

The related body of literature for this paper can be split into two parts. Firstly, the work done on dynamic vehicle routing problems (see, for instance, the surveys in [10, 11]) is relevant for models and solution methods for the DVRP. Secondly, the various innovative variants of urban logistic problems, such as ride-sharing [1, 7], transporting people and parcels simultaneously through taxi networks [8] or public buses [9], together with the aforementioned papers on crowdshipping, are relevant to put this paper into a larger frame of the environmental direction of our research community.

Here we study a setting in which a company not only uses its own vehicles to deliver a set of small parcels from a warehouse to customers, but may also use dynamically appearing occasional drivers (ODs) that arrive at some point in time during the day. This is a new variant of the DVRP, with one central depot, a set of customers, one set of company vehicles, and a set of stochastically appearing occasional drivers, see Fig. 1 for an illustration. We assume that some stochastic information related to the ODs are known, and exploitable. The objective of the problem is to generate routes for the regular vehicles that minimize the total expected cost throughout the day, with the knowledge that ODs may appear later in the day.

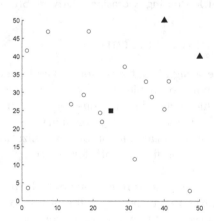

Fig. 1. Example of a stochastic vehicle routing problem with dynamic occasional drivers. The square located in the center of the graph is the warehouse, which also is the origin and destination of the company vehicles, and the origin of the ODs. Customers are circles, and the destinations of ODs are depicted as triangles in the upper right corner. The availability of the ODs is revealed while the routes for regular vehicles are executed.

To model this problem, a two stage stochastic problem is proposed. The first stage models decisions that must be made before information about the ODs become available, and the second stage models decisions after. Customer delivery locations are known in advance, together with a planning horizon starting in T_0 and ending in T_4. At a point in time T_1, information related to ODs arrive, and they may be used between T_2 and T_3. The company vehicles may start to deliver goods before T_1, or wait until the information is revealed. See Fig. 2 for the flow of a day of planning.

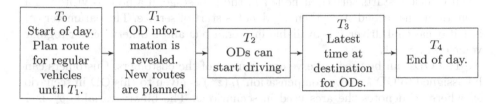

Fig. 2. Structure of the problem for one day of planning. Note that new information is revealed at T_1, so decisions are made at T_0 and T_1.

The purpose of this paper is to study the effects of uncertainty in planning of routes when ODs can appear later in the day. The contribution is a presentation of a new vehicle routing problem, the vehicle routing problem with dynamic occasional drivers. A mathematical formulation is proposed, together with an extended formulation, symmetry breaking constraints and valid inequalities. This allows us to solve large enough instances such that we can show how the uncertainty of this problem affects the routes. The results are compared with the solutions from deterministic models with different risk profiles, showing the strength of a stochastic model.

The remainder of the paper is organized as follows. In Sect. 2, we formally define the stochastic vehicle routing problem with occasional drivers and present a mixed-integer programming formulation. The formulation is strengthened with an extended formulation, valid inequalities and symmetry breaking constraints in Sect. 3, and a computational study is presented in Sect. 4. Finally, in Sect. 5, we present some final remarks and discuss future research directions.

2   Mathematical Formulation

The stochastic vehicle routing problem with dynamic occasional drivers consists of a set of nodes $\mathcal{N} = \{1, \ldots, n\}$. A homogeneous fleet of regular vehicles $\mathcal{K}^R$, and a fleet of occasional drivers $\mathcal{K}^O$, are available to service these nodes. Vehicle $k \in \mathcal{K} = \mathcal{K}^R \cup \mathcal{K}^O$ has an origin $o(k)$ at the depot and a destination $d(k)$. For all regular vehicles, the destination is at the depot, while for the ODs, the destination is at a different location. Let $\mathcal{N}_k \subseteq \mathcal{N} \cup \{o(k), d(k)\}$ be the set of nodes a vehicle k can visit, and $\mathcal{A}_k \subset \mathcal{N}_k \times \mathcal{N}_k$ be the set of possible arcs for vehicle k, and denote the arc from node i to node j as (i, j).

All vehicles have time windows for their origin node $[\underline{T}_{o(k)}, \overline{T}_{o(k)}]$ and destination node $[\underline{T}_{d(k)}, \overline{T}_{d(k)}]$. For the regular vehicles this spans the entire planning horizon, while the ODs are only available for parts of the day. There is a cost of C_{ijk} and travel time of T_{ijk} to travel from node i to node j with vehicle k.

Let $\mathcal{W}$ be the set of all scenarios and let p^ω be the probability of scenario ω. The binary variables x_{ijk} and z_{ijk}^ω denote if vehicle k uses arc (i, j), in respectively the first or second stage in scenario ω. The variable t_{ik} denotes the time when vehicle k starts service at node i in the first stage, if a node is visited in a scenario in the second stage then u_{ik}^ω denotes start of service. The parameter α_k^ω is 1 if occasional driver k is available in scenario ω and 0 otherwise; for regular vehicle k, $\alpha_k^\omega = 1$.

The ODs can be used to serve one or more of the customers. Customers can be assigned to OD k and a compensation $f_k(z^\omega)$ is given to this OD in scenario ω, where z^ω denotes the arcs used in scenario ω. The binary variable y_i^ω is 1 if customer i is not served in scenario ω, and 0 otherwise. If customer i is not served, a penalty γ_i is given. The objective is to design a set of routes, one for each vehicle, such that the average cost, consisting of the routing cost plus the compensation to the ODs and the penalties of not serving a customer, is minimized.

$$\min \sum_{k \in \mathcal{K}^R} \sum_{(i,j) \in \mathcal{A}_k} C_{ijk} x_{ijk} + \sum_{\omega \in \mathcal{W}} p^\omega \Big(\sum_{k \in \mathcal{K}^R} \sum_{(i,j) \in \mathcal{A}_k} C_{ijk} z_{ijk}^\omega$$
$$+ \sum_{k \in \mathcal{K}^O} \alpha_k^\omega f_k(z^\omega) + \sum_{i \in \mathcal{N}} \gamma_i y_i^\omega \Big) \quad (1)$$

subject to

$$\sum_{j \in \mathcal{N} \cup \{d(k)\}} (x_{o(k)jk} + z_{o(k)jk}^\omega) = \alpha_k^\omega \qquad\qquad \omega \in \mathcal{W}, k \in \mathcal{K} \quad (2)$$

$$\sum_{i \in \mathcal{N} \cup \{o(k)\}} (x_{ijk} + z_{ijk}^\omega)$$
$$\omega \in \mathcal{W}, k \in \mathcal{K}, j \in \mathcal{N} \quad (3)$$
$$- \sum_{i \in \mathcal{N} \cup \{d(k)\}} (x_{jik} + z_{jik}^\omega) = 0$$

$$\sum_{i \in \mathcal{N} \cup \{o(k)\}} (x_{id(k)k} + z_{id(k)k}^\omega) = \alpha_k^\omega \qquad\qquad \omega \in \mathcal{W}, k \in \mathcal{K} \quad (4)$$

$$\sum_{k \in \mathcal{K}} \sum_{j \in \mathcal{N} \cup \{d(k)\}} (x_{ijk} + z_{ijk}^\omega) + y_i^\omega = 1 \qquad\qquad \omega \in \mathcal{W}, i \in \mathcal{N} \quad (5)$$

$$(t_{jk} - t_{ik} - T_{ijk}) x_{ijk} \geq 0 \qquad\qquad \omega \in \mathcal{W}, k \in \mathcal{K}^R, (i,j) \in \mathcal{A}_k \quad (6)$$
$$(u_{jk}^\omega - u_{ik}^\omega - T_{ijk}) z_{ijk}^\omega \geq 0 \qquad\qquad \omega \in \mathcal{W}, k \in \mathcal{K}, (i,j) \in \mathcal{A}_k \quad (7)$$
$$z_{ijk}^\omega + x_{jlk} + y_j^\omega \leq 1 \qquad\qquad \omega \in \mathcal{W}, k \in \mathcal{K}^R, (i,j), (j,l) \in \mathcal{A}_k \quad (8)$$

$$u_{ik}^\omega - t_{ik} \geq 0 \qquad\qquad\qquad \omega \in \mathcal{W}, k \in \mathcal{K}^R, i \in \mathcal{N}_k \quad (9)$$

$$u_{ik}^\omega \geq T_1 \qquad\qquad\qquad \omega \in \mathcal{W}, k \in \mathcal{K}, i \in \mathcal{N}_k \quad (10)$$

$$\underline{T}_i \leq t_{ik} \leq \overline{T}_i \qquad\qquad\qquad k \in \mathcal{K}^R, i \in \{o(k), d(k)\} \quad (11)$$

$$\underline{T}_i \leq u_{ik}^\omega \leq \overline{T}_i \qquad\qquad\qquad \omega \in \mathcal{W}, k \in \mathcal{K}, i \in \{o(k), d(k)\} \quad (12)$$

$$z_{ijk}^\omega \in \{0,1\} \qquad\qquad\qquad \omega \in \mathcal{W}, k \in \mathcal{K}, (i,j) \in \mathcal{A}_k | \alpha_k^\omega = 1 \quad (13)$$

$$x_{ijk} \in \{0,1\} \qquad\qquad\qquad k \in \mathcal{K}^R, (i,j) \in \mathcal{A}_k . \quad (14)$$

The objective function (1) minimizes the here-and-now routing costs in the first stage, plus the expected costs of the second stage, namely routing costs, compensations offered to ODs and penalties. The compensation is set to make up for the detour of the occasional driver, times a compensation parameter P, such that $f_k(z^\omega) = P(\sum_{(i,j) \in \mathcal{A}_k} C_{ijk} z_{ijk}^\omega - C_{o(k),d(k),k})$. To increase readability, the sums in constraints (2)-(5) are made over both x_{ijk} and z_{ijk}^ω for all vehicles, even though the first stage variables x_{ijk} do not exist for the ODs. Constraints (2) and (4) make sure that a vehicle exits its origin and enters its destination, and for the company vehicles this may happen in the first or second stage. Constraints (3) ensure that the flow is balanced from origin to destination. Further, (5) force every delivery to be performed either by a regular vehicle in stage one, or any vehicle in stage two, or a penalty is paid if the customer is not served. Constraints (6) and (7) are scheduling constraints, and ensure that time passes when an arc is traversed, and waiting is allowed. Constraints (8) ensure that the first stage arc variables are no longer used, after a second stage arc variable has been used. The term y_j^ω in (8) is added to strengthen the constraints. Constraints (9) and (10) couple the first and second stage time variables. Constraints (10) require that the second stage variables cannot be used before T_1, while (9) enforce that the second stage variables cannot be used for a regular vehicle k that is on its way to a customer i at T_1, before it has visited that customer at $t_{ik} > T_1$. Constraints (11) and (12) set time windows on origin and destination nodes. Finally, the binary restrictions for the arc variables are given in (13) and (14). To increase readability, we have not included that several of the constraints are only necessary when $\alpha_k^\omega = 1$.

3 Strengthening Formulation

In the following we show an extended formulation, symmetry breaking constraints for the homogeneous vehicles and when to shift from first to second stage variables, and valid inequalities. Additionally, as there are time windows on the origin and destination of each vehicle, there are implicitly time windows on all deliveries, which we strengthen to the earliest possible arrival and latest possible departure. This is not further explained.

3.1 Extended Formulation

To exploit the structure of the problem, we extend the formulation. Extended formulations may create tighter relaxations, at the cost of adding more variables and constraints [2]. The flow variable f_{ijdk}^ω is equal to 1 only if vehicle k traverses arc (i,j) on the way to d in scenario ω. Let $\mathcal{F}_k \subset \mathcal{N} \times \mathcal{N} \times \mathcal{N}$ be the set of all possible flows (i,j,d) on arc (i,j) on its way to node d for vehicle k. Then we add the following constraints to obtain an extended formulation,

$$f_{ijdk}^\omega \leq 1 - y_d^\omega \qquad\qquad\qquad \omega \in \mathcal{W}, k \in \mathcal{K}, (i,j,d) \in \mathcal{F}_k \quad (15)$$

$$\sum_{k \in \mathcal{K}} \sum_{j \in \mathcal{N}} f_{o(k)jdk}^\omega = 1 - y_d^\omega \qquad\qquad\qquad \omega \in \mathcal{W}, d \in \mathcal{N} \quad (16)$$

$$\sum_{i \in \mathcal{N} \cup \{o(k)\}} f_{ijdk}^\omega - \sum_{i \in \mathcal{N} \cup \{d(k)\}} f_{jidk}^\omega = 0 \qquad \omega \in \mathcal{W}, k \in \mathcal{K}, j, d \in \mathcal{N} | j \neq d \quad (17)$$

$$\sum_{k \in \mathcal{K}} \sum_{i \in \mathcal{N}} f_{iddk}^\omega = 1 - y_d^\omega \qquad\qquad\qquad \omega \in \mathcal{W}, d \in \mathcal{N} \quad (18)$$

$$f_{ijdk}^\omega \leq x_{ijk} + z_{ijk}^\omega \qquad\qquad\qquad \omega \in \mathcal{W}, k \in \mathcal{K}, (i,j,d) \in \mathcal{F}_k \quad (19)$$

$$f_{ijdk}^\omega \geq 0 \qquad\qquad\qquad \omega \in \mathcal{W}, k \in \mathcal{K}, (i,j,d) \in \mathcal{F}_k . \quad (20)$$

Constraints (15) ensure that no flow for delivery d occurs if d is not serviced. Constraints (16) and (18) ensure that if the delivery is serviced, then the flow of delivery d is one out of the depot and one into the delivery. Constraints (17) make sure that the flow is balanced through all nodes, except the depot and the delivery node. Constraints (19) ensure that there is no flow on arcs that are not used. Constraints (20) define the variables. Note that due to the time windows, several of these variables and constraints may in some instances be excluded from the problem.

3.2 Symmetry Breaking Constraints

As the regular vehicles are homogeneous, the symmetry caused by any permutation of their routes can be broken, and hopefully decrease solution time. This is done by requiring that the lowest indexed delivery that is served by a regular vehicle, is served by the lowest indexed regular vehicle in either the first stage or in the second stage in a chosen scenario ω_1. The following constraints are added,

$$x_{ijk} = 0, z_{ijk}^{\omega_1} = 0, \qquad\qquad k \in \{2 \dots |\mathcal{K}^R|\}, i \in \{1 \dots k-1\}, (i,j) \in \mathcal{A}_k \quad (21)$$

$$\sum_{j \in \mathcal{N}_k} (x_{ijk} + z_{ijk}^{\omega_1}) \leq \sum_{p=k-1}^{i-1} \sum_{s=k-1}^{\min\{p,|\mathcal{K}^R|\}} \sum_{j \in \mathcal{N}_s} (x_{pjs} + z_{pjs}^{\omega_1}), \qquad (22)$$

$$i \in \mathcal{N} \backslash \{1\}, k \in \{2 \dots \min\{i, |\mathcal{K}^R|\}\},$$

where ω_1 can be any scenario. We set ω_1 to be the scenario with no ODs in the computational study. Constraints (21) enforce that the i-th delivery is not done by a higher indexed regular vehicle in the first stage or second stage in ω_1.

Constraints (22) force the set of regular vehicles that can deliver to node i, to be equal to the set of regular vehicles that can deliver to node $i - 1$, plus one extra regular vehicle if available. In effect, the set of possible regular vehicles for a delivery gets smaller if a lower indexed delivery is served by an OD, a lower indexed regular vehicle or not delivered at all.

Different constraints can be used to decide when the first stage variables x_{ijk} and t_{ik} should no longer be used, and the second stage variables z_{ijk}^w and u_{ik}^w should take over. The following constraints make the change directly based on T_1, such that a first stage arc variable x_{ijk} can only be used if $t_{ik} \leq T_1$,

$$t_{ik} \leq T_1 + (T_4 - T_1)(1 - \sum_{j \in \mathcal{N}_k} x_{ijk}) \qquad i \in \mathcal{N}_k, k \in \mathcal{K}^R . \tag{23}$$

Note that this does not enforce that $t_{jk} \leq T_1$. If arc (i, j) is part of an optimal solution, where i is serviced before T_1 and j is serviced after T_1, then (6) together with $t_{jk} \leq T_1$ would make that solution infeasible. Thus we need to allow t_{jk} to be greater than T_1 when there are no first stage arcs out of node j.

An alternative way of changing between stages is to make the change when decisions become different for a vehicle, i.e. if the same arc is traversed in all scenarios with the same vehicle just after the first stage, then this can be forced to be stated with the first stage variables instead. This leads to an alternative way of breaking symmetry,

$$\sum_{w \in \mathcal{W}} z_{ijk}^\omega \leq |\mathcal{W}| - \sum_{l \in \mathcal{N}_k} x_{lik} \qquad (i, j) \in \mathcal{A}_k, k \in \mathcal{K}^R . \tag{24}$$

These constraints enforce that if a first stage arc variable is used into a node i, then all second stage arc variables for (i, j) out of that node cannot be used. This causes x_{ijk} to be one, instead of letting z_{ijk}^ω be one for all scenarios ω. In effect this can cause the first stage variables to be used, even after T_1, as long as all scenarios lead to the use of the same arcs by the same vehicles. This makes (23) and (24) incompatible. Constraints (24) do not apply to the occasional drivers, as they are not modelled with first stage variables.

3.3 Valid Inequalities

To further exploit the structure of the problem, valid inequalities have been developed to strengthen the LP relaxation and in turn reduce the solution time.

Firstly, the total amount of time used in the second stage for each vehicle and scenario can be limited. By studying Figure 2, we see that these limits are different for the regular and occasional drivers, and valid inequalities may be expressed as,

$$\sum_{(i,j) \in \mathcal{A}_k} T_{ijk} z_{ijk}^\omega \leq T_4 - T_1 \qquad \omega \in \mathcal{W}, k \in \mathcal{K}^R$$

$$\sum_{(i,j) \in \mathcal{A}_k} T_{ijk} z_{ijk}^\omega \leq T_3 - T_2 \qquad \omega \in \mathcal{W}, k \in \mathcal{K}^O . \tag{25}$$

Secondly, as the flow balance constraints (3) include both first and second stage variables, the flow is not necessarily balanced in the first and second stage variables separately. Except for through the node where we change from first to second stage, the flow should be balanced in both the first and second stage variables over all nodes in $\mathcal{N}$. As the node where this shift is done is not known in advance, these valid inequalities instead state that the flow of the second stage variables increase through every node, and that the first stage flow through nodes decrease. This is stated as,

$$
\begin{aligned}
\sum_{j \in \mathcal{N}_k} z_{jik}^{\omega} &\leq \sum_{j \in \mathcal{N}_k} z_{ijk}^{\omega} & \omega \in \mathcal{W}, k \in \mathcal{K}, i \in \mathcal{N} \\
\sum_{j \in \mathcal{N}_k} x_{ijk} &\leq \sum_{j \in \mathcal{N}_k} x_{jik} & k \in \mathcal{K}^R, i \in \mathcal{N} \ .
\end{aligned}
\tag{26}
$$

Thirdly, the time windows of the vehicles can lead them to be able to visit two nodes separately, but not in the same route. If this is the case for node i and j, then the following holds,

$$
\sum_{l \in \mathcal{N}_k} (x_{ilk} + z_{ilk}^{\omega} + x_{jlk} + z_{jlk}^{\omega}) \leq 1 \qquad \omega \in \mathcal{W}, k \in \mathcal{K}, i, j \in \mathcal{N}_k \ .
\tag{27}
$$

Lastly, subtour elimination constraints between two nodes are written as,

$$
x_{ijk} + z_{ijk}^{\omega} + x_{jik} + z_{jik}^{\omega} + y_i^{\omega} \leq 1 \qquad \omega \in \mathcal{W}, k \in \mathcal{K}, (i, j) \in \mathcal{A}_k \ .
\tag{28}
$$

4   Computational Study

All instances of our mathematical programming models are solved using Mosel Xpress in Windows 7 Enterprise, on a Dell Precision M4800 with Intel(R) Core(TM) i7-4940MX CPU @ 3.10GHz, 3.30GHz and 32 GB RAM. Note that Xpress solves LP problems integrated with the IP solution procedure. Due to the use of Presolve in Xpress, the LP bounds that are reported in this section may be higher than if the LP relaxation of the IP problem was solved explicitly. All figures of routes in this section break the symmetry between stages by (24), such that equal decisions in all scenarios are assigned to first stage variables.

4.1   Instance Generation

Four main instances with 20 delivery locations each were randomly generated on a square of 50×50, and named A, B, C and D. These are each divided into four sizes of the first 5, 10, 15 and 20 deliveries (S, M, L and XL). A concatenation of these are used as reference, such that AL refers to the instance with the first 15 destinations in A.

The instances have either two or three ODs, with destinations at $(40, 50)$ and $(50, 40)$ for two ODs, and $(30, 50), (50, 50),$ and $(50, 30)$ for three. To show the effect of the location of the destinations of the ODs, these are in some of the examples rotated 90, 180 and 270 degrees around the center of the 50×50 square.

From preliminary tests we have chosen several parameters of the problem that seems to be suitable to demonstrate the effects of ODs and the uncertainty of the ODs. The planning horizon starts at $T_0 = 0$ and ends at $T_3 = T_4 = 100$, and ODs can be used as soon as the information is revealed at $T_1 = T_2 = 50$. The ODs are compensated $P = 1.3$ times the cost of their detour. The penalty of not serving a customer is set to 50, and two regular vehicles are available in all instances. All possible realizations of ODs are used in the scenarios, giving $|\mathcal{W}| = 2^{|\mathcal{K}^O|}$ number of scenarios, with equal probability $p^\omega = \frac{1}{|\mathcal{W}|}$ for each scenario.

4.2   Effect of Strengthening the Formulation

In this section, the results from the testing of the model, the valid inequalities and symmetry breaking constraints are presented. We have tested the valid inequalities and symmetry breaking constraints independently, as well as in some promising combinations. Table 1 shows results from these tests for a subset of the instances. The compact formulation (1)-(14) is noted by C, and the extended formulation (1)-(20) is noted by E. The columns of the table show these formulations with different symmetry breaking constraints and valid inequalities. C+X and E+X give respectively C and E with (21), (24) and all valid inequalities. A maximum of 2 hours CPU time is allowed, and the linear relaxation bound, best bound, best integer solution and used CPU time is reported.

E provides tighter LP bounds than C, but due to the added complexity it struggles to improve the lower bound for larger instances. Even though C has a weaker LP bound, it manages to improve the lower bound more than E during the solution process. Due to this, C outperforms E in solution time for several of the instances, while for the XL instances the bound of C never reaches the LP bound of E. The symmetry breaking constraints and valid inequalities improve the bounds and solution time for most instances, both separately and together, for both C and E. We note that adding constraints (22) to C+(21) did not improve the performance significantly, neither did adding constraints (27) and (28) to the compact formulation. Both formulation C+X and E+X solve up to 15 customers with 2 and 3 ODs, with C+X being slightly faster on the M and L instances. For all instances, we see that E+X gives an LP bound that is at most 12% from the best known integer solution. Thus, E+X may be useful to get a dual bound for larger instances together with heuristics for primal bounds.

4.3   Routes under Uncertainty

In this section two figures are included to show the effect of uncertainty on the routes of the regular vehicles. In Fig. 3, the destinations of the ODs are rotated clockwise to clearly illustrate the effect of uncertainty on the first stage routes of the regular vehicles. The trend is that the regular vehicles wait to serve the

Table 1. Results for a subset of the instances with different methods of strengthening the formulation. z_{LP}, $\underline{z}$ and $\bar{z}$ give objective value of the LP bound, and the best bound and integer solution after two hours, respectively. A - indicates no integer solution was found. Bold font is used to indicate the quickest formulation, or the best bounds for those instances that were not solved to optimality.

Inst.	Info	C	C+(21)	C+(23)	C+(24)	C+(25)	C+(26)	C+X	E	E+X
AS	z_{LP}	60.8	60.8	60.8	60.8	60.8	60.8	79.9	85.6	87.7
2OD	$\underline{z}$	96.2	96.2	96.2	96.2	96.2	96.2	96.2	96.2	96.2
	$\bar{z}$	96.2	96.2	96.2	96.2	96.2	96.2	96.2	96.2	96.2
	t	1.4	1.0	1.1	**0.5**	1.7	1.0	0.6	1.1	0.6
BM	z_{LP}	113.3	114.4	115.4	114.4	113.2	114.7	120.0	124.5	128.7
2OD	$\underline{z}$	134.5	134.5	134.5	134.5	134.5	134.5	134.5	134.5	134.5
	$\bar{z}$	134.5	134.5	134.5	134.5	134.5	134.5	134.5	134.5	134.5
	t	3643.7	52.3	283.0	112.6	71.1	21.1	**8.8**	54.4	26.7
CL	z_{LP}	160.1	160.1	160.1	160.1	160.1	160.1	163.0	198.1	199.1
2OD	$\underline{z}$	197.7	211.4	211.4	211.4	211.4	211.4	211.4	199.9	211.4
	$\bar{z}$	211.4	211.4	211.4	211.4	211.4	211.4	211.4	211.4	211.4
	t	7200.0	1361.0	359.7	2184.4	766.8	100.1	**19.4**	7200.0	185.2
DXL	z_{LP}	104.1	104.8	104.1	104.1	104.1	104.1	105.8	159.6	**162.5**
2OD	$\underline{z}$	119.3	126.7	119.5	120.3	134.2	121.5	139.4	160.1	**163.8**
	$\bar{z}$	273.7	185.9	220.2	-	**173.5**	256.8	176.4	602.8	182.9
	t	7200.0	7200.0	7200.0	7200.0	7200.0	7200.0	7200.0	7200.0	7200.0
AS	z_{LP}	56.8	57.3	56.8	56.8	56.8	56.8	70.5	76.5	78.4
3OD	$\underline{z}$	89.0	89.0	89.0	89.0	89.0	89.0	89.0	89.0	89.0
	$\bar{z}$	89.0	89.0	89.0	89.0	89.0	89.0	89.0	89.0	89.0
	t	3.5	4.7	5.1	16.3	5.4	6.2	4.4	3.2	**1.3**
BM	z_{LP}	106.7	107.6	105.9	109.9	106.0	107.3	106.8	118.3	121.7
3OD	$\underline{z}$	117.6	128.1	114.6	122.4	128.1	118.1	128.1	128.1	128.1
	$\bar{z}$	128.1	128.1	128.1	128.1	128.1	128.1	128.1	128.1	128.1
	t	7200.0	673.8	7200.0	7200.0	765.0	7200.0	**39.7**	6319.2	62.4
CL	z_{LP}	155.1	155.2	155.1	155.1	155.1	155.1	157.6	197.2	197.6
3OD	$\underline{z}$	209.5	209.5	192.9	209.5	209.5	209.5	209.5	197.9	209.5
	$\bar{z}$	209.5	209.5	209.5	209.5	209.5	209.5	209.5	211.1	209.5
	t	3376.6	2933.5	7200.0	3959.7	3460.9	1015.9	**340.9**	7200.0	4985.9
DXL	z_{LP}	102.4	103.1	102.4	102.4	102.4	102.4	104.0	157.0	**158.9**
3OD	$\underline{z}$	112.0	111.8	112.0	112.3	114.2	113.0	115.7	157.7	**161.0**
	$\bar{z}$	299.2	390.9	340.1	-	**175.3**	175.7	278.1	-	180.5
	t	7200.0	7200.0	7200.0	7200.0	7200.0	7200.0	7200.0	7200.0	7200.0

deliveries that can be taken by ODs, until this information gets revealed. We also see that at the end of the first stage, the vehicles tend to position themselves to make good second stage decisions possible. This is especially obvious in the two graphs to the left and the upper right graph. In the upper right graph, only one of the company vehicles is used in the first stage, but this vehicle is well positioned to serve the cluster of customers to the right of the depot if necessary. Finally, in the lower right, we see one of the regular vehicles moving close to the destination of the ODs, which might seem like a bad decision at first glance, but the second stage solutions that follow show this to be a good decision.

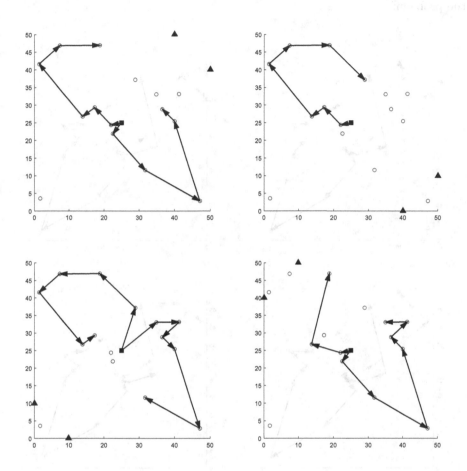

Fig. 3. Four examples of how the first stage routes for the company vehicles change when only the destinations of the ODs are altered, for the instance CL. Notice that the customers are the same in all graphs. Starting in the first graph with the destinations of the two ODs in the upper right corner, and rotating the destinations 90 degrees around the center for each graph.

Second stage solutions for the lower right graph from Fig. 3 is shown in Fig. 4. This shows how the behaviour of the regular vehicles in the first stage fits well with the different scenarios. The route of the regular vehicle that served a delivery close to the destination of the ODs in the first stage now seems more reasonable. All the deliveries in this area are served in all scenarios, with ODs when they are available and through rerouting of the company vehicles when no

ODs appear. Notice also how the route crosses itself when no ODs are available. This would obviously be suboptimal if we knew beforehand that no ODs occur, but this is part of the repositioning that happens due to the information flow of the problem.

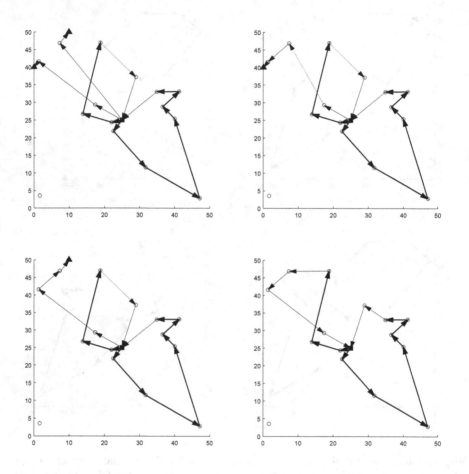

Fig. 4. Comparison of second stage solutions of different scenarios. Notice that the first stage solution is the same in all graphs, and allows for good second stage solutions in all the scenarios.

4.4   Comparison to Deterministic Strategies

To test the quality of the stochastic solutions, we compare them to the solutions of three strategies where deterministic planning and reoptimization are used. The strategies differ in their risk profiles, where the no risk, medium risk and high risk profile relate to planning with respectively zero, one or all ODs available. A plan is created at T_0 for the entire day, with the assumption that either zero, one or all ODs are available. All decisions from the plan that are taken before T_1 are considered fixed, and reoptimization is done at T_1 for each scenario. An average over all scenarios is considered the expected *actual cost* of the strategy for a given instance, while the cost of the initial plan is referred to as the *objective value*.

Table 2 shows that the objective value from the deterministic planning with high risk gives an optimistic value when we compare with the actual cost of that solution, and that the no risk solution gives a pessimistic objective value. The deterministic models never give a better actual cost than the solution from the stochastic model.

The objective values of the no risk profile corresponds to solving the VRP without ODs, and thus give us results for the potential savings by using crowd-shipping in these instances. In a paper with only deterministic models, the objective value of the no risk profile is often compared to the objective values that are found in the medium or high risk profiles. This could for our instances show savings of up to almost 50 %. A more realistic comparison is however to compare the no risk objective value to the objective value of the stochastic models. These savings are on average 13% for our instances and up to 23%. Further, a comparison of the actual costs of the deterministic strategies to the costs of the stochastic solution, gives us the value of solving a stochastic model over a deterministic model. This shows that the stochastic model gives 2-3% better solutions than the medium and high risk deterministic profiles, and 12% better solutions than the no risk profile.

Deterministic planning gives optimal solutions for the scenarios that match their risk profile, while the stochastic solution plans for the uncertainty and thus performs better on average. The table does however also show the problem of the stochastic model, where the XL instances are not solved in reasonable time and therefore omitted. The deterministic models are faster to solve, and can be used as heuristics to solve the stochastic model.

5   Final Remarks

In this paper, we develop a stochastic mixed-integer programming formulation for a new vehicle routing problem, where occasional drivers appear dynamically. Symmetry breaking constraints and valid inequalities are proposed, and some of them are shown to decrease solution time substantially. The LP bounds are strengthened by an extended formulation, while the compact formulation slightly outperforms it with respect to solution time. Several figures are included to show the effects of the uncertainty in the problem. This shows that the company vehicles focus on first delivering to the customers that are unlikely to be served by the ODs. The solutions from the stochastic model are compared to solutions from deterministic models, showing that the stochastic model performs 2-3% better than planning with some ODs and reoptimizing when information became

Table 2. Planned deterministic objective function value for different risk profiles, compared to actual expected cost of implementing the solutions from these profiles. The rightmost column gives the stochastic optimal value. The avg. ratio gives the average ratio between the stochastic solution and the solutions in that column. Italics are used for best integer solution when the optimal solution is not found in 2 hours.

Instance \ Risk	Objective value			Actual cost			Stoch
	No	Medium	High	No	Medium	High	
AS	113.9	78.9	70.0	105.9	102.1	100.2	96.2
AM	169.7	140.5	119.3	169.7	163.7	158.9	158.9
AL	223.1	170.0	163.1	223.1	200.0	195.9	194.8
BS	107.3	96.4	82.4	107.3	93.3	101.6	93.3
BM	160.4	142.8	102.0	159.2	143.4	153.1	134.5
2OD BL	172.6	155.1	123.7	172.6	170.3	180.0	165.5
CS	81.9	68.3	52.0	81.9	68.9	68.9	68.9
CM	134.3	113.7	96.7	134.3	112.7	112.7	112.7
CL	219.3	215.0	204.1	219.3	212.0	212.9	211.4
DS	133.3	112.2	112.0	133.3	118.2	132.0	118.2
DM	171.7	149.1	149.1	171.7	160.5	161.9	156.5
DL	176.5	151.8	151.8	176.5	163.2	163.2	160.1
AS	113.9	73.5	42.7	107.9	94.5	89.0	89.0
AM	169.7	135.1	106.7	169.7	156.2	148.8	148.8
AL	223.1	164.8	152.2	220.1	191.0	196.3	188.1
BS	107.3	90.2	70.5	107.3	85.1	89.7	85.1
BM	160.4	112.4	89.5	160.4	132.7	134.8	128.1
3OD BL	172.6	144.0	104.0	170.8	164.2	157.2	*157.2*
CS	81.9	62.9	45.8	81.9	64.0	63.1	63.1
CM	134.3	108.3	92.6	134.3	107.0	107.0	107.0
CL	219.3	209.6	199.7	219.3	214.7	215.5	209.5
DS	133.3	110.6	100.7	133.3	121.1	131.1	118.4
DM	171.7	147.5	147.5	171.7	158.0	158.0	156.8
DL	176.5	150.3	149.7	160.0	160.8	160.7	*160.0*
Avg. ratio	0.87	1.06	1.26	0.88	0.98	0.97	

available, and 12% better than planning without ODs and reoptimizing. For our instances, the average cost savings of using ODs are 13%. Creating better solution methods, e.g. through scenario generation, heuristics and decomposition algorithms, together with testing on real data, is future research.

Acknowledgments. The work presented in this paper was partly funded by the Research Council of Norway, Distribution Innovation AS, and the Norwegian Public Roads Administration, in the context of the DynamITe project [Contract 246825/O70, SMARTRANS].

References

[1] Agatz, N., Erera, A., Savelsbergh, M., Wang, X.: Optimization for dynamic ride-sharing: A review. European Journal of Operational Research 223(2), 295–303 (2012)

[2] Agra, A., Andersson, H., Christiansen, M., Wolsey, L.: A maritime inventory routing problem: Discrete time formulations and valid inequalities. Networks 62(4), 297–314 (2013)

[3] Archetti, C., Savelsbergh, M., Speranza, M.G.: The vehicle routing problem with occasional drivers. European Journal of Operational Research 254(2), 472–480 (2016)

[4] Arslan, A., Agatz, N., Kroon, L.G., Zuidwijk, R.: Crowdsourced delivery: A dynamic pickup and delivery problem with ad-hoc drivers. ERIM Report Series Reference. Available at http://dx.doi.org/10.2139/ssrn.2726731 (2016)

[5] Barr, A., Wohl, J.: Exclusive: Walmart may get customers to deliver packages to online buyers. REUTERS–Business Week - March 28 (2013)

[6] Bensinger, G.: Amazons next delivery drone: You. The Wall Street Journal - June 16 (2015)

[7] Furuhata, M., Dessouky, M., Ordóñez, F., Brunet, M.E., Wang, X., Koenig, S.: Ridesharing: The state-of-the-art and future directions. Transportation Research Part B: Methodological 57, 28–46 (2013)

[8] Li, B., Krushinsky, D., Reijers, H.A., Van Woensel, T.: The share-a-ride problem: People and parcels sharing taxis. European Journal of Operational Research 238(1), 31–40 (2014)

[9] Masson, R., Trentini, A., Lehuédé, F., Malhéné, N., Péton, O., Tlahig, H.: Optimization of a city logistics transportation system with mixed passengers and goods. EURO Journal on Transportation and Logistics 6(1), 81–109 (2017)

[10] Oyola, J., Arntzen, H., Woodruff, D.L.: The stochastic vehicle routing problem, a literature review, part ii: solution methods. EURO Journal on Transportation and Logistics pp. 1–40 (2016)

[11] Psaraftis, H.N., Wen, M., Kontovas, C.A.: Dynamic vehicle routing problems: Three decades and counting. Networks 67(1), 3–31 (2016)

Maximizing the Number of Served Requests in an Online Shared Transport System by Solving Dynamic DARP

Sven Vallée[1,2]**, Ammar Oulamara[1], and Wahiba Ramdane Cherif-Khettaf[1]

[1] Université de Lorraine, Lorraine Research Laboratory in Computer Science and its Applications - LORIA (UMR 7503), Campus Scientifique, 615 Rue du Jardin botanique, 54506 Vandœuvre-les-Nancy.
[2] Padam, 19 rue des feuillantines 75005, Paris, France

Abstract. The Dial-a-Ride Problem (DARP) consists in serving a set of users who specify their departure or arrival locations using a single vehicle. The aim of DARP is to design vehicle routes satisfying requests of users and minimizing the total traveled distance. In this work, we consider a real case of dynamic DARP service operated by *Padam*[3] in Paris and Bristol. *Padam* offers a high quality transportation service in which users ask for a service either in real time or in advance, and get an immediate answer about whether their requests are accepted or not. The transport activity is outsourced in *Padam*'s service, and contracts are negotiated with third parties firms. Then each day, a fixed set of drivers is available during a working period of time to provide a transportation service of *Padam*. The main goal then becomes to maximize the number of accepted requests during the service. In this work, we develop a two-phase procedure to achieve it. In the first phase an insertion heuristic is used to quickly find out whether a request of a customer can be inserted, then, in the second phase, we run an ALNS algorithm between the occurrence of requests to improve the quality of the solution. The procedure was extensively tested on real data provided by *Padam* with up to 2000 requests and very tight side constraints and time-windows.

Keywords: Dynamic DARP, Insertion Heuristic, Computational experiments, Online heuristic

1 Introduction

The new mobility services are growing with the development of Information and Communications Technology (ICT) and the extension of the Smartphone usage that involves the embedded geolocation devices (Global Positioning System - GPS). For instance, the car-sharing system (Autolib) implemented in Paris shows how the ICT technologies combined with a new service of mobility is enabling

---

** corresponding author: sven.vallee@loria.fr, sven@padam.io
[3] www.padam.io

© Springer International Publishing AG 2017
T. Bektaş et al. (Eds.), ICCL 2017, LNCS 10572, pp. 64–78, 2017.
https://doi.org/10.1007/978-3-319-68496-3_5

new business models. In this growing of services, ICT are at the core of the change from traditional mobility of using private car or public transport to new mobility service in which end-users do not need to own a car to drive one, example of car-sharing, ride-sharing, on-demand transportation, etc. The change is also operated in business model of these services, in which a revenue and cost structure are distributed diversely, where end-users pay a subscription fee that includes all ancillary costs such as insurance, maintenance, and refueling, while the service company bears all of the upstream and downstream risks.

This paper was motivated by the mobility service offered by *Padam*[4] in Paris and Bristol. *Padam* develops a B2B transportation service using a mobile platform on Smartphone. The main purpose of the service is to create dynamic bus lines according to the customer demands. In *Padam*'s system, customers send a demand of transportation via a mobile application either in advance, i.e. booking few days before the service, or in real-time for an immediate service. Customers specify when they wish to be picked up or when the they have to be at their destination and the number of passengers. Such a transportation demand is denoted a request. Furthermore, the transportation service is operated with mini-bus by creating dynamic lines, in which all potential stop locations of buses are predefined. Pickup and destination addresses of customer are then associated to their nearest nodes among predefined locations covering the geographical area, and the customer will be serviced at these nodes. Once a customer has submitted its request, the optimization engine decides whether the request can be accepted or not, i.e. the request can be inserted in the existing rides or not. When solutions exist, several offers are then proposed to the customer around its requested time-window, among he/she will choose the most convenient for himself.

The transport activity is outsourced in *Padam*'s service, and contracts are negotiated with third parties firms. In these contracts are specified, for each day, the number of drivers and mini-bus available as well as the shift of working hours. The number of mini-bus for each day is determined by *Padam* as the result of forecasting calculation based on historical data of transportation demands. Every day, the starting location of each ride is a decision variable fixed by the optimization engine, depending on the number and the localization of requests. Furthermore, as the transport activity corresponds to a fixed cost (i.e. cost of outsourcing), the main objective of *Padam*'s service is to serve as many requests as possible during the service shift.

In this work, we develop methods implemented in optimization engine of mobility service of *Padam*. More precisely, we consider a variant of dynamic dial-a-ride problem with online requests of transportation. Since a solution should be proposed for a user in real time, i.e. in few seconds for each request, a heuristic approach is proposed to dynamic DARP problem. The proposed method is based on fast insertion algorithm to obtain a feasible solution then a metaheuristic-like algorithm based on ALNS to improve the current solution before the appearance of the next request in the system.

---

[4] www.padam.io

The remainder of this paper is structured as follows. In section 2 we provide a selective review on problems related to DARP problem. In Section 3 we give more details on the constraints and characteristics of our problem. In section 4 we describe our two solving algorithms and the way they interact. Experimental results are presented in section 5. The paper concludes with a short summary and an outlook on future research in Section 6.

2   Related work

DARP problems have been investigated in the literature for over 30 years. The basic problem consists of serving a set of users who specify their departure or arrival locations using a single vehicle [17], namely, the static DARP and the dynamic DARP. In the static case, all user requests are known before the start of the route calculation. Therefore the route to be taken by each vehicle is fixed in advance and can not be changed even when a user cancels his reservation or if another user has just requested the service ([5]). In the dynamic case the user requests arrive in real time, or on a sufficiently short time scale, while the routes of vehicles have already been scheduled and their routing have started ([1]).

Several characteristics can be used to classify DARP, such as the number of used vehicles [13]. The problem with multiple vehicles is called multi-vehicle DARP (m-DARP) ([12]). Another characteristic of DARP is related to departure or arrival time, specified as time-window constraints. The presence of time window constraints increases the complexity of the problem and influences the order of visits of the users which implies an increase in the cost of transport. In practice, other constraints may be encountered, namely a fleet of heterogeneous vehicles, medical constraints etc. [6] provides a review on existing models of DARP and solving methods. Given the context of our problem, we will concentrate our review on the dynamic DARP.

Several solving procedures have been proposed in the literature for the dynamic DARP and which can be gathered into two categories : fast heuristics to insert new requests and solving approaches focused on a meta-heuristic search running between the appearance of consecutive requests ([7], [1]). Hybrid methods are proposed in which meta-heuristics is stopped *each time* a new request appears and treats the new request with fast insertion heuristic ([2]). Others approaches rather *periodically check* if news requests have appeared, and if so try to insert it in the current solution via a meta-heuristic ([15]).

[1] uses a parallel tabu search to solve a dynamic DARP with the objective of minimizing the total routing cost. Their algorithm runs between the appearance of consecutive requests. When a new request arises, they perform a feasibility check (limited to 30s) with a tabu search method until a feasible solution is found. In [7] authors consider only one vehicle with the objective of service quality for already planned customers. Authors insert unexpected request, i.e., request which appears when the vehicle is at a stop. A fast heuristic is used to quickly answer unexpected customer, then a local search is performed in the neighborhood of the current solution until the bus reaches it's next stop.

In [2] authors model a German hospital transportation system as a dynamic DARP, with additional constraints to take into account specificities of their medical context. Their objective is to minimize the weighted sum of total travel time, earliness and tardiness. Requests of users are subject to soft time windows and violation of these time windows are penalized in the objective function. An insertion heuristic is run whenever a request needs to be scheduled and an improvement phase using tabu search is performed between the occurrence of two events. [16] adapts 4 meta-heuristics to cope with a dynamic stochastic DARP by using stochastic information on demands of transport to improve solution quality. The objective is a lexicographic function whose first goal is the minimization of total tardiness. In their settings, requests are subject to soft time windows and they never reject any request. They regularly check for the appearance of new requests and incorporate them in their search procedure.

3   Problem description

A road network is represented by a weighted directed graph $G = (V, E)$, where V is the set of nodes, E the set of edges. Nodes model pickup or drop-off locations and edges depict paths between these locations. With each edge (i, j) a weight t_{ij} is associated which depicts the shortest traveling time between nodes i and j. The set of nodes V is partitioned into three subsets: the subset of pickup nodes $P = \{1, \ldots, n\}$, the subset of drop-off nodes $D = \{n + 1, \ldots, 2n\}$ and the subset of departure nodes $DN = \{2n + 1, \ldots 2n + K\}$ at which vehicles start their routes. We denote by K the set of vehicles available during the service. To each vehicle is associated a capacity Q_k, i.e. the number of users that can be transported at the same time. A transportation request is a couple $(i, n + i)$, where $i \in P$ and $n + i \in D$. Each request i is characterized by the service duration u_i at a node i, a load q_i, which represents the number of persons associated with this request ($q_{n+i} = -q_i$). Request i specifies if the demand is pickup (resp. drop-off) oriented PO (resp. DO), and the target time h of service, i.e., desired pickup time (drop-off) if the demand is PO (DO). A time window $[e_i, l_i]$ is associated with the pickup and drop-off node of each request of customers. This time window depends on several parameters and on the business model of Padam. In the rest of the paper we consider it as a data associated to each request.

   Our objective is serving the maximum number of requests during an entire service, and a solution is feasible if all accepted requests are serviced within their time windows. Since requests arrive in real time, only a partial set of requests is known at each time. Thus, we define two objective functions, namely, *duration*, and *max_slack*.

- *duration* is the total duration of all rides, and the duration of a ride being the sum of the travel time between its consecutive stops.
- *max_slack* is the sum of the max slack time of all stops of all rides. For a given stop, a max slack time is defined as the difference between the maximum

arrival time of the stop, (i.e., endpoint l_i of the time window associated to that stop) and its effective arrival time.

duration must be minimized whereas *max_slack* have to be maximized. Minimizing the *duration* is equivalent to serve all requests in the shortest time. Conversely, maximizing *max_slack* ensures that the future insertions will not be limited by the time window constraints, since each stop has a bigger flexibility to be postponed.

4 Solving approaches

In this section, we develop a two-phase heuristic to solve our dynamic DARP. Each time a new request appears, we launch a fast insertion heuristic to get a quick answer for the customer (less than 2 seconds). We call this phase the *online insertion algorithm*. If feasible insertions are found, the heuristic output several proposals to the customer, each one at a different time, as timetable in public transportation system. The idea is to take into account the wishes of the customer while keeping in the foreground the concept of shared transportation. The customer is free to choose one of them or to refuse proposals. In order to improve the feasible solution, we run in phase two an ALNS search algorithm until the next event appears. The next event can be either the appearance of a new request or the arrival of a bus at a stop node. We call this improvement phase the *offline improvement algorithm*. Details about these two phases are given in the following sections.

4.1 Online Insertion Algorithm

The online insertion algorithm is a greedy heuristic which try to insert pickup and drop-off nodes at every possible position of each ride. To take into account the target time h of the customer, we impose a constraint on the tested insertion position, i.e., for each insertion position pair (pickup, drop-off), and if the customer is PO (resp. DO) the resulting pickup time (resp. drop-off time), called the critical time, must be within time interval $[\max(h - DB, t), h + DA]$ where DB (delay before) and DA (delay after) are adjustable parameters and t is the current time (important for real time request). To be feasible, an insertion must also respect constraints imposed on others clients (i.e. the the detour generated by the insertion can't violate time window of other clients) and by the vehicle constraints (max capacity, and service end time). In the case where no feasible insertion is found, the demand is rejected. Otherwise, we get several insertion positions with associated arrival times to pickup and drop-off, among which only the best insertions will be kept to be proposed to the client.

4.2 Offline Improvement Algorithm

As described in section 4, the offline improvement algorithm runs between the occurrence of two events, where an event is either the arrival of a vehicle at its next stop or the appearance of new request. The offline improvement algorithm is based on the Adaptive Large Neighborhood Search (ALNS) method, which has been successfully used in vehicle routing problem ([14], [10]) and in static DARP problem [9]. To the best of our knowledge, it has no yet been used to solve instances of dynamic DARP.

ALNS begins with an initial solution and improves the objective value gradually, by applying a pair of destroy and repair operators randomly chosen from a collection of operators. A reward function is used to promote more efficient pairs of operators. The method is adaptive since the pair of operators chosen at each iteration depends on its previous performance. We now briefly present the characteristics of our ALNS method.

4.2.1 Initial conditions and simulated annealing

Due to the dynamic aspect of our problem, our ALNS works on a set of already existing rides which corresponds to the initial solution. We use a classical simulated annealing framework where c is the cooling rate. The initial temperature is set to $T_0 = \frac{C_0 \times 0.1}{log(2)}$ with C_0 the objective value of the initial solution [3].

4.2.2 Adaptive weight procedure

A roulette-wheel mechanism is used to control the selection of the neighborhood operators. Destroy and repair operators are independently chosen at each iteration according to the current probability distribution. At the beginning, the probability of destroy and repair operators are uniformly assigned. The search strategy is divided in segments of size seg of iterations. At each iteration of a segment, the score of each operator (destroy and repair) is increased according to three parameters, namely, σ_1 which rewards operators when a new best solution is obtained, σ_2 which rewards operators when newly generated solution is better than the current one and σ_3 which rewards operator when a newly generated solution is worse but accepted. In the next segment, the probability of each operator i is updated as follow:

$$p_i^{s+1} = p_i^s (1 - r) + r \frac{\pi_i}{n_i}$$

where π_i is the cumulated weight of operator i during the previous segment s and n_i the number of times the operator is used. r is a parameter called the reaction factor.

4.2.3 Destruction Operators

At each iteration, we choose a number k of requests to remove. Only requests whose pickup has not yet been serviced by its ride can be removed. k is randomly sampled between 1 and $max_r * T_{request}$ where $T_{request}$ is the total number of unserved requests and $max_r \in \ ]0; 1]$ is a free parameter. We use 5 different destruction operators inspired from [14].

Random operator: Select k requests randomly.

Worst operator: Select the k requests with the biggest saving, i.e., the difference between the objective value of the current solution and the objective value of solution once the request is removed. In order to increase the diversification, this operator is randomized as follow: all unserved requests are sorted in decreasing order of saving values in a list L. A random number y is sampled between 0 and 1 and the request at the position $\lfloor y^{p_r} |L| \rfloor$ where $|L|$ is the size of L and p_r a parameter. This is repeated until k requests have been chosen.

Relatedness operator: Choose a request randomly and select $k - 1$ related requests. The relatedness measure between request i and j is defined as follow:

$$\frac{1}{2} \left(t_{p_i, p_j} + t_{d_i, d_j} \right) + \frac{1}{2} \left(|u_{p_i} - u_{p_j}| + |u_{d_i} - u_{d_j}| \right)$$

where p_i and d_i are the pickup and drop-off nodes, respectively, and u_{p_i} and u_{d_i} the service time of pickup and drop-off of request i. This operator is also randomized as in the previous case. The parameter controlling the randomness is called p_w.

Strong Overlap Relatedness operator: Choose a request randomly and remove all the related requests. Given a request i, a request j is related to i if their overlapping ratio exceeds a given ratio r_s. If $T_{p_i} = \left[\underline{p}_i, \overline{p}_i \right]$ is the time window at the pickup of a request i and $T_{d_i} = \left[\underline{d}_i, \overline{d}_i \right]$ the time window of its delivery, the overlapping ratio is computed as follows:

$$r_{ij} = \begin{cases} 0 & \text{if } T_{p_i} \cap T_{p_j} = \emptyset \text{ OR } T_{d_i} \cap T_{d_j} = \emptyset \\ \frac{inter(T_{p_i}, T_{p_j}) + inter(T_{d_i}, T_{d_j})}{(\overline{p}_i - \underline{p}_i) + (\overline{d}_i - \underline{d}_i)} & \text{otherwise} \end{cases}$$

where the $inter(a, b)$ is the length of the intersection of the intervals a and b. This operator selects requests which are similar, and so can be exchanged or inserted on the same ride. This operator is motivated by the fact that time window is the most restrictive constraint in our problem.

Random Ride operator: Select all the requests of k_r randomly chosen rides.

4.2.4   Repair Operators

After selecting the requests to be removed, repair operators are used to reinsert removed requests. Our operators can remove all the selected requests at once and reinsert them one by one or remove them one by one and reinsert each removed request immediately. Our operators are inspired from [14]. Let L be the list of removed requests.

Deep Greedy operator: Remove all requests at once and perform the best insertion among all feasible insertions of all requests still to reinsert. The best insertion is defined as the insertion with the minimal increase in the objective function.

Regret operator: Remove all requests at once and sequentially insert from list L the request with the large regret. The regret computation follows the classic scheme presented in [14].

Modified Regret operator: This operator uses a modified version of regret operators as presented in [8].

Basic Greedy operator: Remove requests of L one by one and reinsert each removed request at its best position.

Since existing requests are already accepted by the system, it is not possible to reject them. When repair operators fail to reinsert all requests, the move is then refused, i.e. the method does not accept infeasible solutions during the search.

4.2.5 Shifting procedure

After each move (destruction & repair operations) we perform, on each ride, a shifting operation that insures the feasibility of time window, i.e., the left side of time windows are not violated. Indeed, due to tight time windows, a violation of left-side of time window could happens after the destruction phase, and not be corrected by repair phase. In such case correcting procedure called *shifting procedure* is used to avoid the left-side violation of time window. It consists in shifting on the right the starting processing times of a block of requests in each ride till all left-side time windows become feasible. If shifting procedure is not able to correct the violation, the solution will be considered infeasible and the move refused.

5 Experiments

In this section we compare our proposed ALNS method with online insertion heuristic by considering several objective functions. All tests in our experiments have been performed on real data provided by *Padam*. For confidentiality issues, we are not able to get into too much details on these instances but we will nevertheless present their main features.

5.1 Instance_type

The data presented here concern 4 real cases coming from partnerships between *Padam* and transport agencies. Each case models a real transport context in a given geographical area including the following information:

– Service data: set of scattered nodes across the territory, matrix of traveling times between nodes, service time span and parameters defining the quality of the service.
– Customer data : stochastic distribution generating customer requests appearance and behavior.

These informations define what we call an 'Instance-type' and allow us to perform real-world simulations to test our algorithms. We have 4 Instance-type: $F95\_1$, $F95\_2$, $F93\_77$ and TH. The 2 following subsections provide more details on their service and requests data.

5.1.1   Service data

Table 1 presents global characteristics of Instance_types. Column 'Nodes' indicates the number of nodes in the territory, column 'Service duration' shows the number of hour during the service, column 'Non zero OD' indicates the number of possible pairs of origin-destination based on real data and column 'Vehicle number' denotes the number of vehicles decided with transport agencies. In our experiments we will change the number of vehicles to see the behavior of our algorithms when the number of vehicle decreases. For each Instance-type, the capacity of each vehicle is 8. Finally, for each Instance-type we calculate matrices of distances and traveling times between nodes using the Google API.

Name	Nodes	Service duration	Non zero OD	Vehicle number
F95_1	286	12	339 (0.42 %)	10
F95_2	286	10	273 (0.33 %)	5
F93_77	286	11	375 (0.45 %)	11
TH	213	4	213 (12.9 %)	75

Table 1: Main service features for each Instance-type

5.1.2   Requests data

Another important part of data is the requests generation context. It determines the temporal and spatial repartition of the requests and the customer's behavior regarding various proposals.Our simulator allows us to use different laws to generate requests. The 4 Instance-type use the same generation law with different values for parameters. Here are the main steps of the customers's generation:

1. Sample the arrival times of requests during the service period using a poisson-level distribution
2. Fix a proportion of the sampled requests to be in advance, and the rest as real time requests.
3. Sample for each request the origin and destination nodes according to origin-destination matrix.
4. Generate the behavior of each client regarding our various trip proposals. In our Instance_type the behavior of clients is as follows: a client selects the proposal which is the nearest to its request time. If the gap between the request time and the nearest proposal is greater than $MWTA$ for advance requests or $MWTR$ for real time requests, the customer reject the proposal.

In Instance_types the values of parameters $MWTA$ and $MWTR$ are fixed to 45 mn and 30 mn respectively, except for TH where $MWTA = MWTR = 30$ mn.

Table 2 presents temporal characteristics of the Instance-types. Instance_types $F95\_1$, $F95\_2$ and $F93\_77$ are very similar and contain mainly requests in advance. Instance_type TH contains more than 2000 requests and has a service duration of 4 hours. 75% of request are in real time which make this instance harder.

Table 2: *Temporal density of instances*

Name	Mean Number Requests	% of Real Time requests
F95_1	486	25 %
F95_2	148	25 %
F93_77	373	25 %
TH	2200	75 %

5.2 Tuning the ALNS parameters

Our ALNS method includes several parameters whose values must be determined (4.2). To fix these parameters, we use an iterated racing algorithm implemented in the R package "irace" [11]. irace is based on statistical concepts and inspired from Machine Learning algorithms. See [4] for more details on technical aspects of racing algorithm for meta-heuristic tuning. The idea of irace is to run several races to discard bad configurations and sample new one similar to the best configurations seen up to now. The best configurations found are then returned at the end of the process. For more details on technical aspects (number of configurations sampled at each iteration, similarity measure etc...) see [11].

In our case, we ran irace for each Instance_type presented in 5.1 separately because each one corresponds to a different probability distribution and so can potentially have a different set of optimal parameters. For each Instance_type, we generated a set of 30 instances, and for each instance, all in advance requests are booked with the online algorithm to create what can be seen as an initial solution for the ALNS method. The number of vehicles used is the default number of the Instance_type. These instances will then be used by irace during the training phase to run ALNS when testing the different parameters configurations. Table 3 exposes the final range for each parameter.

Table 4 gives the best set of parameters found by irace. We will use these values for the experiments.

5.3 Results

For each Instance_type (F95_1, F95_2, F93_77 and TH), we generated 10 instances that will be used in the experiments. This allows us to capture the

Table 3: *Interval of variation of each parameter for the training phase*

c	σ_1	σ_2	σ_3	r
$[0.95, 0.99975]$	$[\![1, 20]\!]$	$[\![1, 20]\!]$	$[\![1, 20]\!]$	$[0.15, 0.7]$

p_r	p_w	seg	r_s	max_r
$[\![1, 10]\!]$	$[\![1, 10]\!]$	$[\![10, 100]\!]$	$[0.3, 0.9]$	$[0.2, 0.5]$

Table 4: *Best values found by irace for each Instance*

Parameter / Instance_type	c	σ_1	σ_2	σ_3	r	p_r	p_w	seg	r_s	max_r
F95_1	0.9854	20	23	11	0.25	10	6	63	0.42	0.38
F95_2	0.9922	8	11	11	0.36	9	4	41	0.38	0.26
F93_77	0.9837	21	14	4	0.48	8	2	71	0.38	0.28
TH	0.9519	24	13	11	0.58	7	3	16	0.88	0.40

stochasticity of the problem while keeping the results reproducible. Integrated in the backend of the solution of Padam, the code of the simulator and the algorithms were implemented in python/cython [5]. The simulations were executed on a server with 16 Intel Processor Core cadenced to 3 GHZ. The purpose of this section is to compare the performance of the insertion heuristic with and without the offline improvement phase using two different objectives described in section 3.

5.3.1 Impact of the objective function on insertion process

For each Instance_type, the default number of vehicle was used. Table 5 provides results of simulations. The *duration* objective is taken as reference for comparison with the *max_slack* objective. Columns *psr* and *tk* represent the percentage of accepted requests and the total number of kilometers, respectively, and columns *diff psr* and *%tk* represent the variation of accepted requests and the number of kilometers in comparison with *psr* and *tk*, respectively.

We observe that the *duration* objective always outperforms the *max_slack* objective, especially in terms of number of kilometers. We also observe that the larger the instance, the better *duration* performs. It shows that the best objective for the online insertion algorithm is the *duration*.

5.4 Comparison online-offline

In this section we study the impact of the two objectives when online insertion heuristic is combined with the off-line improvement algorithm. We ran simulations with and without offline improvement for the 10 sampled instances of each

---

[5] http://cython.org/

Table 5: *Impact of each objective on the online insertion algorithm*

Instance	duration		max_slack	
	psr	tk	diff psr	% tk
F95_1	77.5 %	3082	- 1.96 %	11.62 %
F95_2	85.69 %	1210	- 1.6%	6.94 %
F93_77	87.14 %	3805	- 3.34 %	8.14 %
TH	72.98 %	5759	- 6.33 %	10.52 %

Instance_type. The purpose is to have a global trend on each Instance_type. To speed up simulations, we allowed the offline algorithm to run only between the appearance of 2 requests and not after each vehicle arrival to a stop. Table 6 reports the results of experiments. Column Ve represents the number of vehicles. For both objective, 3 results are reported: %psr is the percentage of served requests with offline improvement minus percentage of served requests without improvement. %tk is defined as $\frac{t_k^{off}-t_k^{on}}{t_k^{on}} \times 100$ where t_k^{off} and t_k^{on} represent the total number of kilometers of all rides with offline and without offline improvement, respectively. %obj is defined in a similar manner, for example, %obj in *duration* is defined as $\frac{t_d^{off}-t_d^{on}}{t_d^{on}} \times 100$ where t_d^{off} and t_d^{on} represent the total duration of the obtained solution with offline and without offline improvement, respectively. For each Instance_type and each vehicle number, the percentage of served requests, total kilometers and the final objective value are mean of simulations on the 10 instances.

Table 6: *Comparison with and without offline improvement*

Instance	Ve	duration			max_slack		
		% psr	% tk	% obj	% psr	% tk	% obj
F95_1	4	3.66	- 5.10	-3.93	3.59	-2.41	17.59
	6	4.30	- 9.60	-7.12	6.23	- 2.68	17.48
	8	5.18	- 9.84	-8.40	5.14	2.52	10.08
	10	4.30	- 9.79	-8.76	4.69	5.67	4.03
F95_2	2	5.36	- 0.79	- 1.01	2.91	0.75	28.22
	3	5.30	- 4.31	- 4.08	3.86	0.36	20.26
	4	4.00	- 9.92	- 8.76	3.39	0.82	10.59
	5	3.58	- 10.00	- 9.24	2.66	4.03	2.43
F93_77	5	4.21	- 6.68	-4.65	6.47	- 2.70	15.65
	7	5.14	- 7.38	-5.47	6.93	- 2.84	21.41
	9	5.45	- 10.48	-8.02	5.44	0.30	8.80
	11	4.97	- 12.22	-9.76	3.78	1.38	6.43
TH	50	8.54	- 5.47	-3.44	5.65	1.76	20.14
	60	8.65	- 4.56	-2.80	5.06	2.00	17.91
	70	7.38	- 4.35	-3.39	4.73	2.07	15.81
	80	6.66	- 5.39	-4.42	3.96	4.56	15.56

In table 6, we observe that simulations with offline improvement always obtain a higher percentage of served requests (PSR) than simulations with only the online insertion algorithm. If we restrict to PSR, we observe that *duration* is the best objective on F95_2 and TH whereas *max_slack* performs better on the 2 others Instances. The best global improvement on the percentage of served requests is on TH, which is the larger and more complex Instance_type. This is probably due to the fact that this is the instance with the smallest geographical area and so ride sharing is easier. For *max_slack*, we observe that TK is improved when few vehicles are used, however the solution is deteriorated when additional vehicles are used. On the other hand, *duration* always decreases TK and the decrease becomes larger when more vehicles are used. This is coherent with the *%obj* column which shows that the improvement on TK increases when the number of vehicles increases.

To summarize this section, we can conclude that the best objective is the *duration*, which provides significant improvements for the company both on PSR and on TK. Indeed, when considering the default number of vehicles, the gain on TK is 10% and the gain on PSR is 5%. Moreover, we show that our 2 phases procedure can cope with highly dynamic and very large Instance_type as TH, which have 75% of dynamic requests. In any case, the percentage of served requests always decreases with the size of the fleet, even for *duration*. We could at first glance conclude that the improvement on served requests percentage and on the duration are negatively correlated. However, the last section tends to indicate that this is not the case.

5.5   Comparison with pure offline

In this section, we evaluate the quality of solutions obtained by ALNS in dynamic environment by comparing them with solutions that will be obtained when applying ALNS method on our problem assuming that all data are known in advance.

Table 7 shows the results. Column *%on* depicts the results of *%obj* of table 6 for each objective and represents the improvement obtained by the ALNS while running during the service. Column *%off* indicates the mean of improvement over the 10 generated solutions, where each solution is obtained with ALNS limited to 10 minutes. The discrepancy between *%on* and *%off* for TH is explained by the fact that TH is a very difficult instance and that 10 minutes of pure offline optimization (*%off*) are not enough to perform as well as continuous optimization during the service (*%on*). Data in column *duration* shows that increasing the number of vehicles prevents the improvement of the ALNS during service and it seems to be far from its possible best performance. On the other hand, the improvement are similar when fewer vehicles are used so it means that we cannot expect a bigger improvement on PSR and TK while using the *duration* objective with few vehicles. It confirms that the duration is a good objective but more effort should be done to get a better improvement during the service.

Table 7: Comparison with pure offline mode

Instance	Ve	duration		max_slack	
		% on	% off	% on	% off
F95_1	4	-3.93	- 4.11	17.59	23.13
	6	-7.12	- 8.19	17.48	26.76
	8	-8.40	- 13.57	10.08	35.02
	10	-8.76	- 17.30	4.03	37.25
F95_2	2	- 1.01	- 1.94	28.22	29.25
	3	- 4.08	- 7.32	20.26	28.18
	4	- 8.76	- 11.08	10.59	34.98
	5	- 9.24	- 15.08	2.43	45.82
F93_77	5	- 4.65	- 4.46	15.65	27.18
	7	- 5.47	- 9.22	21.41	31.83
	9	- 8.02	- 13.64	8.80	40
	11	- 9.76	- 15.97	6.43	47.94
TH	50	-3.44	- 1.70	20.14	1.99
	60	-2.80	- 2.75	17.91	2.34
	70	-3.39	- 4.11	15.81	4.34
	80	-4.42	- 6.34	15.56	7.96

6 Conclusion

In this paper, we have studied hard instances of dynamic Dial-a-Ride Problem (DARP) proposed by Padam. We proposed a two phases optimization procedure. We showed with intense experiments that this procedure offers a real improvement in term of percentage of accepted requests and total traveled kilometers over a simple insertion heuristics. Our algorithms are thus able to cope with highly dynamic and large instances with more than 2000 requests. Among the two objective functions, the *duration* objective is the best which is able to insert the maximum of requests. Also, our analysis showed that the improvement over the insertion algorithm is limited when the number of vehicle increases and we proposed a valid justification of this fact. Future work will focus on the improvement of insertion heuristic by re-ordering existing requests or temporarily allowing infeasible solutions which might be repaired in offline phase.

References

1. Andrea Attanasio, Jean-Francois Cordeau, Gianpaolo Ghiani, and Gilbert Laporte. Parallel tabu search heuristics for the dynamic multi-vehicle dial-a-ride problem. *Parallel Computing*, 30(3):8–15, 2004.
2. Alexandre Beaudry, Gilbert Laporte, Teresa Melo, and Stefan Nickel. Dynamic transportation of patients in hospitals. *OR Spectrum*, 32(1):77–107, 2010.
3. Walid Ben-Ameur. Computing the initial temperature of simulated annealing. *Computational Optimization and Applications*, 29:369–385, 2004.
4. Mauro Birattari. *Tuning Metaheuristics : A Machine Learning Perspective.* Springer, 2009.

5. J-F. Cordeau and G. Laporte. A tabu search heuristic for the static multi-vehicle dial-a-ride problem. *Transportation Research part B : Methodological*, 37(6):579–594, 2003.
6. J-F. Cordeau and G. Laporte. The dial-a-ride problems, models and algorithms. *Annals of Operations Research*, 153:29–46, 2007.
7. Luca Coslovich, Raffaele Pesenti, and Walter Ukovich. A two-phase insertion technique of unexpected customers for a dynamic dial-a-ride problem. *European Journal of Operational Research*, 175(3):1605–1615, 2006.
8. Marco Diana and Maged M. Dessouky. A new regret insertion heuristic for solving large-scale dial-a-ride problems with time windows. *Transportation Research Part B : Methodological*, 38(6):539–557, 2004.
9. Baoxiang Li, Dmitry Krushinsky, Tom Van Woensel, and Hajo A. Reijers. An adaptive large neighborhood search heuristic for the share-a-ride problem. *Computers and Operations Research*, 66:170–180, 2016.
10. Yuan Li, Haoxun Chen, and Christian Prins. Adaptive large neighborhood search for the pickup and delivery problem with time windows, profits, and reserved requests. *European Journal of Operational Research*, 252(1):27–38, 2016.
11. Manuel López-Ibáñez, Jérémie Dubois-Lacoste, Leslie Pérez Cáceres, Mauro Birattari, and Thomas Stützle. The irace package: Iterated racing for automatic algorithm configuration. *Operations Research Perspectives*, 3:43–58, 2016.
12. Oli BG Madsen, Hans F Ravn, and Jens M Rygaard. A heuristic algorithm for a dial-a-ride problem with time windows, multiple capacities, and multiple objectives. *Annals of Operations Research*, 60(1):193–208, 1995.
13. Harilaos Psaraftis. An exact algorithm for the single vehicle many-to-many dial-a-ride problem with time windows. *Transportation science*, 17(3):351–357, 1983.
14. Stefan Ropke and David Pisinger. An adaptive large neighborhood search heuristic for the pickup and delivery problem with time windows. *Transportation Science*, 40(4):455–472, 2006.
15. Douglas O. Santos and Eduardo C. Xavier. Taxi and ride sharing: A dynamic dial-a-ride problem with money as an incentive. *Expert Systems with Applications*, 42(19):6728–6737, 2015.
16. M. Schilde, K.F. Doerner, and R.F. Hartl. Metaheuristics for the dynamic stochastic dial-a-ride problem with expected return transports. *Computers and Operations Research*, 38(12):1719–1730, 2011.
17. N Wilson, J Sussman, H Wang, and B Higonnet. Scheduling algorithms for dial-a-ride systems. *Technical Report USL-TR-71-13*, 1971.

A Polyhedral Study of the Elementary Shortest Path Problem with Resource Constraints *

Jiarui Da, Lanbo Zheng and Xin Tang$^{(\boxtimes)}$
{dajiarui, lanbozheng, tangxin}@whut.edu.cn

School of Logistics Engineering, Wuhan University of Technology, Hubei, China

Abstract. The elementary shortest path problems with resource constraints (ESPPRC) in graphs with negative cycles appear as subproblems in column-generation solution approaches for the well-known vehicle routing problem with time windows (VRPTW). ESPPRC is $\mathcal{NP}$-hard in the strong sense [8]. Most previous approaches alternatively address a relaxed version of the problem where the path does not have to be elementary, and pseudo-polynomial time algorithms based on dynamic programming are successfully applied. However, this method has a significant disadvantage which is a weakening of the lower bound and may induce a malfunction of the algorithm in some applications [9]. Additionally, previous computational studies on variants of VRPs show that labeling algorithms do not outperform polyhedral approaches when the time windows are wide [13] and may not even be applied in some situations [7]. Furthermore, an integer programming approach is more flexible that allows one to easily incorporate general branching decisions or valid inequalities that would change the structure of the pricing subproblem. In this paper we introduce an ILP formulation of the ESPPRC problem where the capacity and time window constraints are modeled using path inequalities. Path inequalities have been used by Ascheuer et al. [1] and Kallehauge et al. [13], respectively, in solving the asymmetric traveling salesman problem with time windows and the VRPTW. We study the ESPPRC polytope and determine the polytope dimension. We present a new class of strengthened inequalities lifted from the general cutset inequalities and show that they are facet-defining. Computational experiments are performed on the same ESPPRC instances derived from the Solomon's data sets [9]. Results compared with previous formulations prove the effectiveness of our approach.

Keywords: Elementary shortest path with resource constraints, Vehicle routing problem with time windows, integer programming, Polyhedral study

1 Introduction

The *elementary shortest path path problem with resource constraints* considered in this paper can be described as follows: for a given directed graph $G = (V, A)$,

---

* This research was supported by the national natural science foundation of China, no. 71501152 and no. 71372202.

© Springer International Publishing AG 2017
T. Bektaş et al. (Eds.), ICCL 2017, LNCS 10572, pp. 79–93, 2017.
https://doi.org/10.1007/978-3-319-68496-3_6

where $V = \{0, \ldots, n + 1\}$ is the set of nodes, $|V| = n + 2$, and A is the set of arcs. Node 0 represents the start node and node $n+1$ represents the target node. The other n nodes represent the set of intermediate nodes $N = V \backslash \{0, n + 1\}$. With each arc $(i, j) \in A$, we associate an arc cost $c_{ij} \in \mathbb{R}$ and an arc travel time $t_{ij} \in \mathbb{Z}_+$. We assume that the triangle inequality on the travel times is satisfied, i.e. $t_{ik} \leq t_{ij} + t_{jk}$, for all $(i, k) \in A$. With each node $i \in N$ we associate a demand $d_i \in \mathbb{Z}_+$, $d_i \leq q$, a *release date* $a_i \in \mathbb{Z}_+$, a *processing time* $p_i \in \mathbb{Z}_+$, and a *deadline* $b_i \in \mathbb{Z}_+$. The parameter q often represents a vehicle capacity in a vehicle routing scenario, and the release date a_i and the deadline b_i, respectively, represent the earliest possible and the latest possible starting time for servicing node $i \in N$. The interval $[a_i, b_i]$ is called the *time window* for node i. The time window is called *active* if $a_i > 0$ or $b_i < \infty$; a time window of the type $[0, \infty]$ is called *relaxed*. In cases where servicing may start before a_i, one need to wait until the node is released. We assume that $d_0 = d_{n+1} = 0$, $a_0 = a_{n+1} = 0$, and $\{(0, n + 1)\} \notin A$. The problem is to find a min-cost elementary path from node 0 to node $n + 1$ such that, for every node i on the path, the start time for processing (visiting) node i lies within the given time window $[a_i, b_i]$, and the overall demand from the nodes on the path does not exceed q. A path is *elementary* if it does not visit any node more than once, i.e., if it does not contain subtours.

Since the ESPPRC is NP-hard in the strong sense, general approaches in addressing the problem as a subproblem in a vehicle routing or crew scheduling scenario often look at a relaxed version of the problem where the path does not have to be elementary, called shortest path problem with resource constraints (SPPRC). In a column generation procedure where the master problem is formulated as a set covering problem, this approach is able to generate valid optimal solutions for a VRPTW provided that the triangle inequality is satisfied. An important group of these approaches is based on dynamic programming (DP) and has pseudo-polynomial complexity. This approach has been successfully applied by Desrochers et al. [6] for the VRPTW and by Graves et al. [10] for the flight crew scheduling problems to mention only a few examples. However, such relaxation leads to weak lower bounds and large branch and bound trees [11]. For a number of other problems, e.g. the Vehicle Routing Problems with Profits, the elementary path restriction has too much impact on the solution to be relaxed or might even be necessary [9].

Feillet et al. [9] evaluate firstly an exact approach for the ESPPRC extended from the labeling algorithm by Desrochers et al. [6]. In their approach, a customer resource is included to indicate if a given customer can be visited or not by extending the current partial path. The algorithm reduces the duality gap compared to the usual approaches that are based on the SPPRC bound and enables the use of a column generation solution methodology for some special problems or with some special branching schemes that cannot rely on SPPRC solutions. More recently, Righini and Salani [16] propose a bidirectional labeling algorithm for the ESPPRC that relies on a state-space relaxation. A similar DP algorithm proposed by Boland et al. [4] achieves good performance on randomly generated instances. Rousseau et al. [17] solve the VRPTW using a branch-and-price approach that handles the ESPPRC subproblem with constraint programming (CP). Although the CP component proved to be flexible, their approach is somewhat slow in comparison with traditional branch-and-price strategies. Baldacci et al. [3] extend the exact algorithm of Righini and Salani by including bounding functions based on state-space relaxation. They introduce the concept of ng-route relaxation that is used to calculate completion bounds for partial paths, thus accelerating the DP algorithm by means of label fathoming. Very recently, Lozano et al. [14] present an exact algorithm based on implicit enumeration with a new bounding scheme that remarkably reduces the search space. For a comprehensive review on resource constrained shortest paths, see the survey paper by Di Puglia Pugliese and Guerriero [15].

Different to the traveling salesman problem, polyhedral studies on the elementary shortest path problems and vehicle routing problems are quite limited. Kallehauge et al. [13] present a formulation for the VRPTW based on the infeasible path inequalities from a study of the ATSP-TW polytope [1]. The authors analyze the dimension of the VRPTW polytope and show that, under certain conditions, a class of infeasible path inequalities is facet-defining. For the elementary shortest path problem without any resource constraints (ESPP), Taccari [19] analyze several integer programming formulations and present some polyhedral results to show the equivalence between polytopes based on two different models. To the best of our knowledge, polyhedral studies of the ESPPRC polytope have not been addressed in the literature.

From a general engineering point of view, integer programming approaches are more flexible to incorporate general branching decisions or valid inequalities that would change the structure of the pricing subproblem and allow a direct use of general-purpose MIP solvers. In this paper, we present a polyhedral study on the ESPPRC polytope and derive valid inequalities useful to the effectiveness of a branch-and-cut based method. Section 2 introduces notation, the standard MIP model for ESPPRC and some new formulations based on infeasible path inequalities. Section 3 investigates the ESPPRC polytope dimension and introduce a set of facet-defining inequalities. Several classes of novel valid inequalities are introduced in Section 4. Section 5 reports computational results where we are in particular aiming at showing the effectiveness of the presented inequalities in improving LP relaxation bounds and reducing the sizes of branch-and-bound search trees. Finally, in Section 6, we give some concluding remarks and discuss further research topics.

2 Notation and Modeling

To make a polyhedral study on this problem, we need to further configure the structure of the directed graph $G = (V, A)$. We assume that for any $i \in \mathbb{N}$, $\max\{t_{0i}, a_i\} + t_{in+1} \leq b_{n+1}$, otherwise, node i can be removed from G without impacting the optimal solution. Given a node set $W \subseteq V$, let

$$A(W) := \{(i, j) \in A | i, j \in W\}$$

denote the set of all arcs with tail and head in W. For any two node sets $U, W \subseteq V$ let,

$$(U : W) := \{(i, j) \in A | i \in U, j \in W\}$$

denote the set of arcs with tail in U and head in W. To simplify notation, we use $(W : j)$ and $(j : W)$ instead of $(W : \{j\})$ and $(\{j\} : W)$, respectively. Given a node set $W \subset V$, $W \neq \emptyset$, we also define

$$\delta^-(W) := \{(i, j) \in A | i \in V \backslash W, j \in W\},$$

$$\delta^+(W) := \{(i, j) \in A | i \in W, j \in V \backslash W\},$$

$$\delta(W) := \delta^-(W) \cup \delta^+(W).$$

The arc set $\delta(W)$ is called a *cut*. For simplicity, we use $\delta^-(v)$, $\delta^+(v)$, and $\delta(v)$ instead of $\delta^-(\{v\})$, $\delta^+(\{v\})$, and $\delta(\{v\})$, respectively. The number of $|\delta^-(v)|$, $|\delta^+(v)|$, and $|\delta(v)|$ are called the *indegree*, *outdegree* and *degree* of node v. In this study, we assume $\delta^-(0) = \delta^+(n+1) = \emptyset$, and $A(N) = \{(i, j) \in A | a_i + p_i + t_{ij} \leq b_j$ and $d_i + d_j \leq q\}$, otherwise, arc (i, j) can be removed from G without impacting the optimal solution. Let $m = |A(N)|$, we have $A = \delta^+(0) \cup A(N) \cup \delta^-(n + 1)$ and $|A| = 2n + m$.

There are a few ways in the literature to model the ESPPRC as integer linear programs. The most comprehensively used one involves binary arc variables x_{ij} as well as node variable τ_i, indicating the time when node i is visited. A standard integer programming formulation to determine an elementary shortest path from node 0 to node $n+1$ satisfying capacity and time window constraints is as follows:

$$z = \min \sum_{(i,j) \in A} c_{ij} x_{ij} \tag{1}$$

$$\sum_{(0,j) \in \delta^+(0)} x_{0j} - \sum_{(j,0) \in \delta^-(0)} x_{j0} = 1 \tag{2}$$

$$\sum_{(n+1,j) \in \delta^+(n+1)} x_{n+1j} - \sum_{(j,n+1) \in \delta^-(n+1)} x_{jn+1} = -1 \tag{3}$$

$$\sum_{(i,j) \in \delta^+(i)} x_{ij} - \sum_{(j,i) \in \delta^-(i)} x_{ji} = 0 \qquad (\forall i \in N) \tag{4}$$

$$x_{ij}(\tau_i + p_i + t_{ij} - \tau_j) \leq 0 \qquad (\forall (i,j) \in A) \tag{5}$$

$$a_i \sum_{j \in \delta^+(i)} x_{ij} \leq \tau_i \leq b_i \sum_{j \in \delta^+(i)} x_{ij} \qquad (\forall i \in V) \tag{6}$$

$$\sum_{i \in V} d_i \sum_{j \in \delta^+(i)} x_{ij} \leq C \tag{7}$$

$$x_{ij} \in \{0, 1\} \qquad (\forall (i,j) \in A) \tag{8}$$

The binary arc variables x_{ij} take value 1 if the arc (i, j) belongs to the path. Constraints (2), (3) and (4) are flow conservation constraints that ensure the path start from node 0 and end at node $n + 1$. Note that, these constraints

alone are not sufficient to guarantee a solution without subtours. And if a subtour disjoint from the elementary path from 0 to $n + 1$ has a negative cost,
the elementary path may not be the true minimum cost path as desired. Constraints (5), (6) and (7) guarantee path feasibility with respect to time window
and capacity constraints. Additionally, the variable set τ generates a precedence
order among the nodes on the path such that subtours can be prevented. The
binary condition (8) allow the nonlinear constraints (5) linking between the x
and τ variables to be linearized via a generalization of the Miller-Tucker-Zemlin
inequalities, namely:

$$\tau_i + p_i + t_{ij} - \tau_j \leq (1 - x_{ij})M_{ij} \qquad\qquad \forall\, (i,j) \in A \qquad (9)$$

where M_{ij} is a sufficiently large positive value and can be replaced by $max\{b_i +
p_i + t_{ij} - a_j, 0\}$, $(i,j) \in A$, and constraints (5) or (9) need only be enforced for
arc $(i,j) \in A$ such that $M_{ij} > 0$; otherwise, these constraints are satisfied for all
variables of τ_i, τ_j and x_{ij}. However, these constraints involve a "big M" term that
is known to cause computational problems. In the computational experiment of
this study, we also introduce a set of valid inequalities to strengthen the time
window constraints.

To avoid the disadvantage caused by the additional time indicating variables
and linking constraints which may lead to poor linear relaxation performance,
Ascheuer et al. [1] introduce a set of *infeasible path constraints* to model the
time window constraints implicitly when addressing the asymmetric traveling
salesman problem with time windows (ATSP-TW). Kallehauge et al. [13] further extend the formulation to solve the VRPTW instances. In this study, our
polyhedral analysis of ESPPRC is based on this type of formulation.

A path P consisting of the arc set $\{(v_i, v_{i+1})|i = 1, \ldots, k - 1\}$ is sometimes
denoted by $P = (v_1, v_2, \ldots, v_k)$. If not stated differently, the path P is always
intended to be open and *simple*, that is, $|P| = k - 1$ and $v_i \neq v_j$ for $i \neq j$. A
path P is *infeasible* if it does not occur as a subproblem in any feasible route,
i.e. if either $\sum_{i=1}^{k} d_i > q$ or $\tau_{v_i} > b_{v_i}$, for some $i \in \{1, \ldots, k\}$. An infeasible path
$P = \{v_i, v_{i+1} \in A|i = 1, \ldots, k - 1\}$ is said to be *minimal infeasible* if the
truncated subpaths $P\backslash\{(v_1, v_2)\}$ and $P\backslash\{(v_{k-1}, v_k)\}$ are feasible. We denote the
set of all minimal infeasible paths in G as $\mathcal{P}_G$. For any $Q \subseteq A$, we write $x(Q)$
for $\sum_{(i,j)\in Q} x_{ij}$. With this notation, the feasible set of solutions in ESPPRC is
the set of those $x \in \mathbb{R}^A$ satisfying the flow conservation constraints (2)–(4) and
constraints (8), together with, the subtour inequalities

$$x(A(W)) \leq |W| - 1 \qquad\qquad \forall \emptyset \neq W \subseteq N, \qquad (10)$$

and the path inequalities

$$x(P) \leq |P| - 1 \qquad\qquad \forall P \in \mathcal{P}_G. \qquad (11)$$

We can therefore define the ESPPRC polytope as

$$P_{\mathsf{ESPPRC}} := conv\{x \in \mathbb{R}^A | x \text{ satisfies } (2)\text{–}(4), (10)\text{–}(11), \text{ and } (8)\} \qquad (12)$$

the characteristic vectors of all feasible elementary shortest paths from node 0 to node $n+1$ on the directed graph $G = (V, A)$. In the next section, we present some results from a polyhedral study of the ESPPRC polytope. To proceed with the theoretical analysis, we need some more notations.

Because of the time windows associated with each node, one can derive precedences among the nodes. For any two vertices i and j, if $a_j + p_j + t_{ji} > b_i$, then vertex i must be visited before vertex j if they are all included in the shortest path. Let $i \prec j$ denote the precedence relationship between i and j and let $G_P = (V, R)$ denote the *precedence digraph* where each arc $(i,j) \in R$ represents a precedence relationship $i \prec j$. In the context of ATSP-TW, the precedence digraph is acyclic and transitive closed. Balas et al. [2] presented the so-called (π, σ)-inequalities and Ascheuer et al. [1] presented strengthened (π, σ)-inequalities by taking time windows into account explicitly. In the context of VRPTW, the graph G_P may contain cycles, e.g. if a 2-cycle exists $(i - j - i)$ it means that the node pair i and j cannot belong to the same path. Also, the precedence relationship is not transitive, i.e., if $i \prec j$ and $j \prec k$ it does not mean that $i \prec k$ because j may not be on the path and therefore, k may precede i. Kallehauge et al. [13] considered two strengthenings of the precedence inequalities, called *weak π-inequality* and *weak σ-inequality*. However, in the context of the ESPPRC, none of the above inequalities is applicable since a node i may or may not be included in any path in a final solution. Therefore, to make use of the precedence information, we put a more restricted definition on the precedence relationship among nodes. Let

$$\pi(i) := \{j \in V | a_i + min(t_{ij} + p_i, b_i - a_i) > b_j\}, \tag{13}$$
$$\sigma(i) := \{k \in V | a_k > b_i\}, \tag{14}$$

represent the set of the *predecessors* and *successors* of a node $i \in V$, respectively. Note that, this definition may narrow down the precedence relationship among nodes, but it ensures that a predecessor of a node i must also be a predecessor of the successors of i, which validates the precedence inequalities for ESPPRC introduced later in section 4.

Moreover, for any feasible path $P = (v_1, \ldots, v_k)$, denote

$$\delta_P^+(k) := \{(k, l) \in \delta^+(k) | P' = (v_1, \ldots, v_k, v_l) \text{ is feasible}\} \tag{15}$$

the set of edges *extendable* from path P.

3 Polyhedral Analysis

In this section, we aim at analyzing the *ESPPRC polytope* defined in (12). We first determine the dimension of the polytope and then present a set of facet-defining inequalities.

Proposition 1. $dim(P_{\mathsf{ESPPRC}}) = n + m - 1$

Proof. Clearly, The equation system (2)–(4) has rank $|V| - 1 = n + 1$. Since $P_{\mathsf{ESPPRC}} \subset \mathbb{R}^A$, $dim(P_{\mathsf{ESPPRC}}) \leq |A| - (n+1) = n + m - 1$. On the other hand, we show P_{ESPPRC} contains $n + m$ affinely independent shortest paths connecting node 0 and node $n + 1$. First, consider the set of n paths

$$P_n := \{(0, i, n+1) | i \in N\}$$

and then consider the set of m paths

$$P_m := \{(0, i, j, n+1) | (i, j) \in A\}.$$

Observe that incidence vectors of paths from P_n and P_m are linearly independent, and we are done. $\qquad\square$

The classical Dantzig-Fulkerson-Johnson subtour elimination constraints (10) [5] can be equivalently written as a set of *generalized cutset inequalities*(GCS).

$$\sum_{(i,j)\in A(S)} x_{ij} \leq \sum_{i\in S\setminus\{k\}} \sum_{(i,j)\in\delta^+(i)} x_{ij} \qquad \forall k \in S, \forall S \subseteq N, |S| \geq 2. \qquad (16)$$

This approach is used for a symmetric version of the elementary shortest path problem with capacity constraints by Jepsen et al. [12] and applied to the asymmetric elementary shortest path problem by Drexl and Irnich [7] and Taccari [19].

Proposition 2. *The generalized cutset inequalities (16) are valid for the ESP-PRC polytope.*

Proof. Consider any subset $S \subseteq N, |S| \geq 2$, for any $k \in S$, $x(\delta^+(k)) \leq x(\delta^+(S))$, and $x(\delta^+(S)) = \sum_{i\in S} x(\delta^+(i)) - x(A(S))$. This proves the claim. $\qquad\square$

Theorem 1. *For any trivial path p in the set $P := \{(0, i) | i \in V\}$, the enhanced GCS inequality in the minimum case where $S = \{i, j\}$,*

$$x_{ij} \leq x(\delta_p^+(j)\setminus\{(j, i)\}) \qquad\qquad \forall(i, j) \in A(N) \qquad (17)$$

defines a facet for the ESPPRC polytope.

Proof. In the minimum case, the GCS inequality looks like

$$x_{ij} + x_{ji} \leq x(\delta^+(j)) \Rightarrow x_{ij} \leq x(\delta^+(j)\setminus\{(j, i)\})$$

Consider any feasible solution of the ESPPRC, if $x_{ij} = 0$, the right hand side of inequality (17) is 0 (restricted by the flow conservation constraints); if $x_{ij} = 1$, clearly $x(\delta^+(j)\setminus\delta_p^+(j)) = 0$. Therefore, inequality (17) is valid for the ESPPRC polytope.

It is easily observed that there are feasible solutions whose incidence vectors do not satisfy (17) with equality. We are only left to show that there are $n+m-1$ linearly independent solutions of ESPPRC satisfying (17) with equality.

First, consider the set of $n - 1$ paths

$$P_n := \{(0, i, n + 1)|i \in N \setminus \{j\}\}$$

Second, for any arc $(k, l) \in A(N) \setminus \delta_p^+(j)$, consider the set of $m - |\delta_p^+(j)|$ paths

$$P_{m1} := \{(0, k, l, n + 1)|(k, l) \in A(N) \setminus \delta_p^+(j)\}$$

Last, consider the set of $|\delta_p^+(j)|$ paths

$$P_{m2} := \{(0, i, j, l, n + 1)|(j, l) \in \delta_p^+(j)\}$$

Paths from $P_n \cup P_{m1} \cup P_{m2}$ are linearly independent, and $|P_n \cup P_{m1} \cup P_{m2}| = m + n - 1$. $\qquad\square$

4   Classes of Valid Inequalities

In this section, we present several other sets of valid inequalities applied within a branch and cut procedure in the computational tests.

4.1   Strengthened time window constraints

Through the computational analysis, we observe that there exists a large amount of cases where for an arc (i, j), the linear relaxation has $x_{ij} > 0$ but $\tau_i \geq \tau_j$. We call x_{ij} a *reverse flow* on the path which may cause many infeasible solutions satisfying the linear relaxation constraints. Moreover, we observe that the existence of *reverse flows* may lower the effectiveness of some subtour elimination constraints. In this situation, we introduce a new set of time window constraints to avoid *reverse flows*.

Proposition 3. *For $\forall j \in \pi(i)$, if it is satisfied that $a_i - b_j - p_j - t_{ji} \leq 0$, the strengthened time window constraint*

$$
\begin{aligned}
(1 - x(\delta^+(i)))(b_j - a_i + p_i + t_{ij}) + \tau_i \geq \\
\tau_j + p_j + t_{ji} + (1 - x(\delta^+(j)))(a_i - b_j - p_j - t_{ji}) \, \forall i \in N
\end{aligned}
\tag{18}
$$

is valid for the ESPPRC polytope.

Proof. To prove proposition (3), we consider the following four cases:

- If both i and j are on the path, then constraint (18) is converted to $\tau_i \geq \tau_j + p_j + t_{ji}$ which ensures that i is visited after j, valid;
- If i is on the path, and j is not, then the constraint is $\tau_i \geq \tau_j + a_i - b_j$, valid;
- If j is on the path, and i is not, then the constraint is $\tau_i \geq \tau_j + a_i - b_j$, valid;
- If both i and j are not on the path, then the constraint is $(b_j - a_i + p_i + t_{ij}) + \tau_i \geq \tau_j + p_j + t_{ji} + (a_i - b_j - p_j - t_{ji})$, since $a_i - b_j - p_j - t_{ji} \leq 0$, the constraint is valid.

This proves the claim. $\qquad\square$

4.2   Precedence constraints

As introduced in section 2, time windows introduce precedences among nodes. For any node $i \in V$, if there is a path connecting a node $k \in \pi(i)$ and a node $l \in \sigma(i)$, and i is on the path, then there is only one possibility as shown in Figure 1. Therefore, we have the following results.

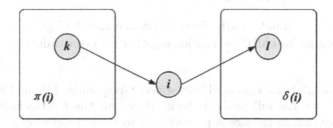

Fig. 1. An example of precedence relationship in the ESPPRC context

Proposition 4. *The precedence constraint*

$$x(\pi(i) : \sigma(i)) \leq 1 - x(\delta^+(i)) \qquad\qquad \forall i \in V \qquad (19)$$

is valid for the ESPPRC polytope.

Proof. Obvious from the statement.   □

5   Computational Results

In order to evaluate the effectiveness of the facet-defining inequalities through our polyhedral analysis, as well as the new valid strengthened inequalities derived particularly for the ESPPRC polytope, we perform extensive experiments. In this section, we report the results and compare them to the standard integer programming formulation testing with the same data sets used by Feillet et al. [9].

These instances are generated from the Solomon's data sets [18]. These data sets are classified into three categories:

– The r-instances where the customers are located randomly;
– The c-instances where the customers are located in clusters;
– The rc-instances with some random and some clustered structures.

Each instance is represented by a directed graph $G = (V, A)$ where arcs not satisfying the primal time window and capacity constraints as described in section 2 are removed in a preprocessing procedure. In the context of ESPPRC, each arc is associated with a cost $c_{ij} = dist_{ij} - \alpha(i)$, where $dist_{ij}$ is calculated as the Euclidean distance between customer nodes and $\alpha(i)$ is a random integer variable, uniformly distributed in $\{0,\ldots,20\}$. The limit value 20 has been chosen to generate a reasonable number of arcs having a negative cost. The reason to include arcs with negative costs is because in the context of column generation, the ESPPRC, as a subproblem, often contains negative costs. The same approach was used in [9] to generate test instances for the ESPPRC.

In our experiments, we compare the behavior of a state-of-the-art MIP solver using two formulations, namely:

- standard - the standard MIP formulation of constraints (2)-(8)
- new - the standard MIP formulation together with constraints (17), (18) and (19)

For the polynomial–size enhanced time window inequalities (18) and precedence inequalities (19), the full model is built. While for the facet-defining general cutset inequalities, as the size is proportional to the number of edges, the MIP solver spent too much time in solving an LP relaxation, if all of the inequalities are included in the model. Therefore, we randomly selected a proportion of the inequalities to add in the model. And our experiments showed that the algorithm has the best performance when the proportion is close to 50%.

Computational experiments were carried out on a PC with an Intel dual core processor running at 2.50GHz, with 12GB of RAM and 64-bit Windows operating system. Algorithms were implemented in Java (compiler version 1.7) with IBM Ilog Cplex/Concert 12.6, using default settings for the branch-and-cut. The time limit to find a solution was set to 500 seconds.

The MIP model with the newly added valid and facet-defining inequalities is able to find optimal solutions for 70 instances out of 87 in less than 500 seconds, while the standard model permits only to solve 57 instances. Table 1 highlights the significant reduction of computing times resulting from this improvement. Note that, for the r-instances which show high complex due to the randomness on time windows, the strengthened time window constraints are very effective that the new running time is 20 times faster. Details of the computational results for the three sets of instances are reported in table 3, 4 and 2 respectively in the appendix. It is observed that, for some median size instances, namely, the 50 nodes random and random clustered instances, the linear relaxation gaps are largely closed, and the problem is even solved at the root node.

Table 1. Summary of average computation times (on the 57 instances solved by both models)

Instance type	Standard	New
r-instances	24.399	1.216
c-instances	11.141	1.441
rc-instances	9.431	0.752

6   Conclusion and Future Work

The elementary shortest path problem with resource constraints (ESPPRC) is a very important basic network optimization model for scheduling and routing applications. When solving as a subproblem in a column-generation procedure for the VRPTW, the ESPPRC reduces the duality gap compared to the usual approaches that are based on the SPPRC bound. It also enables the use of a column generation methodology for some special problems or with some special branching schemes that cannot rely on SPPRC solutions. Previous computational studies show that standard labelling algorithms based on dynamic programming approaches are not at all competitive if resource constraints required to limit the state space are absent in some situations. These all motivate the study.

In this paper, we performed a polyhedral analysis of the ESPPRC polytope, and determined the polytope dimension. We presented enhanced generalized cutset inequalities for $|S| = 2$ and showed that the new set of inequalities is facet defining. To our knowledge, these are the first polyhedral results for the ESPPRC. We next presented a set of strengthened time window constraints as well as a set of precedence constraints in the context of ESPPRC and proved their validity. It is also important to understand how effective the formulations are from a computational point of view. In this regard, we report a set of extensive computational experiments, suggesting that the newly added inequalities are effective in closing linear relaxation gaps and fasten running times.

Future research is stimulated in a few directions. From the polyhedral study, more facet-defining inequalities might be derived from strong inequalities with respect to the resource and path-structural constraints, e.g. the 0–1 knapsack cover inequalities, the GCS inequalities, and the infeasible path inequalities. Following similar ideas, a thorough polyhedral study of the ESPP without any resource constraints might be possible. From the computational study, the facet-defining inequalities presented in this paper worth a further study within a branch-and-cut routine. And to prove the effectiveness of polyhedral approaches, more sets of effective inequalities, like subtour elimination inequalities inherited from ASTP should be implemented within an advanced branch-and-cut framework and compared with the state-of-art dynamic programming approaches. Furthermore, all approaches should be utilized to tackle the solution of VRPTW instances within a column generation procedure.

References

1. N. Ascheuer, M. Fischetti, and M. Grötschel. A polyhedral study of the asymmetric traveling salesman problem with time windows. *Networks*, 36(2):69–79, 2000.
2. E. Balas, M. Fischetti, and W. R. Pulleyblank. The precedence-constrained asymmetric traveling salesman polytope. *Mathematical Programming*, 68(1–3):241–265, 1995.
3. R. Baldacci, A. Mingozzi, and R. Roberti. New route relaxation and pricing strategies for the vehicle routing problem. *Operations Research*, 59(5):1269–1283, 2011.
4. N. Boland, J. Dethridge, and I. Dumitrescu. Accelerated label setting algorithms for the elementary resource constrained shortest path problem. *Operations Research Letters*, 34(1):58–68, 2006.
5. G. Dantzig, R. Fulkerson, and D. S. Johnson. Solution of a large-scale traveling salesman problem. *Operations Research*, 2(4):393–410, 1954.
6. M. Desrochers, J. Desrosiers, and M. Solomon. A new optimization algorithm for the vehicle routing problem with time windows. *Operations Research*, 40(2):342–354, 1992.
7. M. Drexl and S. Irnich. Solving elementary shortest-path problems as mixed-integer programs. *OR Spectrum*, 36(2):281–296, 2014.
8. M. Dror. Note on the complexity of the shortest path models for column generation in vrptw. *Operations Research*, 42(5):977–978, 1994.
9. D. Feillet, P. Dejax, M. Gendreau, and C. Gueguen. An exact algorithm for the elementary shortest path problem with resource constraints: Application to some vehicle routing problems. *Networks*, 44(3):216–229, 2004.
10. G. W. Graves, R. D. Mcbride, I. Gershkoff, D. Anderson, and D. Mahidhara. Flight crew scheduling. *Management Science*, 39(6):657–682, 1993.
11. S. Irnich and D. Villeneuve. The shortest path problem with resource constraints and k-cycle elimination for $k \geq 3$. *INFORMS J. Computing*, 18(3):391–406, 2006.
12. M. K. Jepsen, B. Petersen, and S. Spoorendonk. A branch-and-cut algorithm for the elementary shortest path problem with a capacity constraint. Technical report, Department of Computer Science, University of Copenhagen, 2008.
13. B. Kallehauge, N. Boland, and O. Madsen. Path inequalities for the vehicle routing problem with time windows. *Networks*, 49(4):273–293, 2007.
14. L. Lozano, D. Duque, and A. L. Medaglia. An exact algorithm for the elementary shortest path problem with resource constraints. *Transportation Science*, 50(1):348–357, 2016.
15. L. Di Puglia Pugliese and F. Guerriero. A survey of resource constrained shortest path problems: exact solution approaches. *Networks*, 62(3):183–200, 2013.
16. M. Righini and M. Salani. New dynamic programming algorithms for the resource constrained elementary shortest path problem. *Networks*, 51(3):155–170, 2008.
17. L-M. Rousseau, M. Gendreau, G. Pesant, and F. Focacci. Solving vrptws with constraint programming based column generation. *Annals of Operations Research*, 130(1):199–216, 2004.
18. M. M. Solomon. *Vehicle routing and scheduling with time window constraints: Models and Algorithms*. PhD thesis, Department of Decision Sciences, University of Pennsylvania, 1983.
19. L. Taccari. Integer programming formulations for the elementary shortest path problem. *European Journal of Operational Research*, 252(1):122–130, 2016.

A   Computational Results

The key evaluation factors are as follows:

- rt: root relaxation solution time, we round the number down to 0 if it is less than 0.005 seconds;
- gap: is measured as $(z_{incumbent} - z_{lowerbound})/z_{incumbent}$
- node: the number of nodes in a branch-and-bound tree explored in obtaining an optimal solution;
- CPU: total running time in seconds if an optimal solution can be found within the time limit.

Table 2. Solution of the ESPPRC for rc-instances

Problem	Standard				New			
	rt	gap	node	CPU	rt	gap	node	CPU
rc101.25	0	0.00%	0	0.072	0	0.00%	0	0.066
rc101.50	0	126.74%	0	0.331	0.02	0.00%	0	0.176
rc101.100	0.02	84.39%	71	1.734	0.23	0.00%	0	2.009
rc102.25	0	107.15%	9022	0.983	0	0.00%	0	0.164
rc102.50	0.02	192.77%	54472	10.024	0	0.00%	0	0.68
rc102.100	0.02	–	–	–	0.17	187.36%	54649	269.956
rc103.25	0	120.32%	66990	8.932	0	0.00%	0	0.724
rc103.50	0	221.93%	–	–	0.03	436.84%	10254	6.003
rc103.100	0.03	–	–	–	0.14	–	–	–
rc104.25	0	140.26%	92754	8.663	0	135.67%	1646	0.716
rc104.50	0.02	246.78%	–	–	0.02	540.27%	–	–
rc104.100	0.03	–	–	–	0.11	–	–	–
rc105.25	0.02	121.10%	6106	0.503	0	0.00%	0	0.149
rc105.50	0	496.55%	51224	8.038	0.03	0.00%	0	0.623
rc105.100	0.03	–	–	–	0.11	136.41%	15093	62.188
rc106.25	0	106.86%	2000	0.565	0	0.00%	0	0.149
rc106.50	0	445.56%	50275	10.394	0.02	–	434	1.664
rc106.100	0.02	–	–	–	0.19	204.45%	34642	151.795
rc107.25	0	157.02%	125156	12.005	0	0.00%	0	0.144
rc107.50	0	335.38%	–	–	0.03	466%	423663	294.043
rc107.100	0.02	–	–	–	0.16	330.25%	–	–
rc108.25	0	160.38%	483791	60.354	0	195%	21275	2.508
rc108.50	0.02	247.47%	–	–	0.01	289.82%	–	–
rc108.100	0.05	–	–	–	0.11	–	–	–

Table 3. Solution of the ESPPRC for r-instances

Problem	Standard				New			
	rt	gap	node	CPU	rt	gap	node	CPU
r101.25	0	0.00%	0	0.021	0	0.00%	0	0.009
r101.50	0	0.00%	0	0.041	0	0.00%	0	0.135
r101.100	0	0.00%	0	0.146	0.03	0.00%	0	0.807
r102.25	0	0.00%	0	0.038	0	0.00%	0	0.014
r102.50	0	0.00%	0	0.191	0	0.00%	0	0.135
r102.100	0.02	150.84%	–	–	0.08	74.79%	39620	71.892
r103.25	0	0.00%	0	0.098	0	0.00%	0	0.041
r103.50	0.02	419.32%	27623	10.791	0	0.00%	0	0.381
r103.100	0.03	–	–	–	0.09	42.84%	–	–
r104.25	0	0.00%	0	0.108	0	0.00%	0	0.081
r104.50	0.02	845.07%	–	–	0.02	177.40%	8811	4.519
r104.100	0.03	–	–	–	0.09	97.99%	–	–
r105.25	0	0.00%	0	0.023	0	0.00%	0	0.009
r105.50	0	0.00%	0	0.069	0.02	0.00%	0	0.104
r105.100	0.02	40.85%	201	2.029	0	0.00%	0	2.522
r106.25	0	0.00%	0	0.108	0	0.00%	0	0.031
r106.50	0.02	133.51%	0	0.93	0.02	0.00%	0	0.376
r106.100	0.02	182.52%	–	–	0.13	90.00%	–	–
r107.25	0	0.00%	0	0.089	0	0.00%	0	0.046
r107.50	0	576.08%	69764	320.96	0.02	127.59%	445	1.376
r107.100	0.03	–	–	–	0.13	249%	–	–
r108.25	0	0.00%	0	0.094	0	0.00%	0	0.049
r108.50	0.02	812.59%	–	–	0.01	553.62%	90068	62.137
r108.100	0.03	–	–	–	0.11	–	–	–
r109.25	0	0.00%	0	0.06	0	0.00%	0	0.032
r109.50	0.02	242.16%	1738	1.792	0.02	0.00%	0	0.413
r109.100	0.02	89.43%	–	–	0.13	33.71%	54544	208.631
r110.25	0	0.00%	0	0.132	0	0.00%	0	0.051
r110.50	0.02	750.82%	231016	92.664	0.02	598.86%	11947	6.585
r110.100	0.03	314.95%	–	–	0.17	156.76%	–	–
r111.25	0	0.00%	0	0.083	0	0.00%	0	0.046
r111.50	0.02	578.40%	106461	40.941	0.02	184.79%	588	1.551
r111.100	0.02	–	–	–	0.17	76.09%	82356	490.401
r112.25	0	128.29%	211	0.153	0	0.00%	0	0.098
r112.50	0.02	846.29%	257762	114.003	0.02	747.43%	22996	14.297
r112.100	0.05	–	–	–	0.09	–	–	–

Table 4. Solution of the ESPPRC for c-instances

Problem	Standard				New			
	rt	gap	node	CPU	rt	gap	node	CPU
c101.25	0.02	0%	0	0.076	0	0.00%	0	0.034
c101.50	0	0.00%	0	0.048	0	0.00%	0	0.118
c101.100	0.02	0.00%	0	0.134	0.05	0.00%	0	0.95
c102.25	0	92.11%	21296	2.567	0	0.00%	0	0.038
c102.50	0	190.90%	497282	108.925	0.02	55.33%	425	1.049
c102.100	0.03	827.18%	–	–	0.06	57.58%	91023	92.37
c103.25	0	–	100327	14.005	0	55.51%	9195	1.863
c103.50	0.02	938.79%	–	–	0.02	148.01%	–	–
c103.100	0.03	–	–	–	0.11	196.39%	–	–
c104.25	0	652.33%	405889	60.402	0	100.64%	19962	3.766
c104.50	0.02	975.51%	–	–	0.02	929.28%	–	–
c104.100	0.03	–	–	–	0.13	–	–	–
c105.25	0.02	0.00%	0	0.03	0	0.00%	0	0.038
c105.50	0	0.00%	0	0.064	0.02	0.00%	0	0.231
c105.100	0	0.00%	0	0.251	0.09	0.00%	0	1.613
c106.25	0	0.00%	0	0.019	0	0.00%	0	0.033
c106.50	0.02	0.00%	0	0.071	0	0.00%	0	0.208
c106.100	0	134.07%	3944	4.489	0.02	0.00%	0	2.957
c107.25	0	0.00%	0	0.059	0	0.00%	0	0.055
c107.50	0	0.00%	0	0.072	0	0.00%	0	0.233
c107.100	0	0.00%	0	0.338	0.11	0.00%	0	1.511
c108.25	0	40.08%	0	0.384	0.02	0.00%	0	0.163
c108.50	0	70.58%	6626	5.115	0.02	33.85%	328	1.968
c108.100	0.03	44.06%	30320	24.794	0.09	35.15%	1341	11.517
c109.25	0	93.98%	3459	0.975	0	15.62%	3	0.475
c109.50	0	254.00%	–	–	0.02	135.47%	90609	44.107
c109.100	0.03	119.22%	–	–	0.11	86.27%	107928	301.095

Vehicle Routing with a Heterogeneous Fleet of Combustion and Battery-Powered Electric Vehicles under Energy Minimization

Herbert Kopfer[1], Benedikt Vornhusen[1], and Jan Dethloff[2]

[1] University of Bremen, Chair of Logistics, Bremen, Germany
kopfer@uni-bremen.de, bvornhusen@uni-bremen.de
[2] Hochschule Bremen, Bremen, Germany
Jan.Dethloff@hs-bremen.de

Abstract. This paper compares energy minimization with minimizing distance and travel time in vehicle routing. The focus is on the influence of the objective chosen when deploying homogeneous and heterogeneous vehicle fleets. To achieve that, vehicles with different capacities and ranges as well with combustion engines as with battery-powered electric engines are taken into consideration. Results show that when deploying homogeneous fleets there are no significant differences between the optimal solutions when using energy minimization instead of distance or time minimization. Hence, the potential for reducing energy consumption of distance or time optimal solutions is very small with homogeneous fleets. By contrast, when deploying a heterogeneous fleet, a significant reduction of energy consumption in the double-digit percentage order can be achieved. On the other hand the total travel distance as well as total travel time increases. Comprehensive computational experiments show that certain fleets can be identified that consume only small amounts of additional energy compared to an idealized fleet consisting of an arbitrarily large number of vehicles of all different types. Furthermore, numerical experiments show that minimizing both the energy consumption as well as the distance, only a small number of Pareto-optimal solutions exist. The most attractive of those can be chosen easily according to practical preferences.

Keywords: Vehicle routing, Heterogeneous vehicle fleet, Electric versus combustion engine, Pareto optimization, Ecological objective

1 Introduction

In addition to traditional objectives that are typically used in vehicle routing, in recent years more work relating to ecological objectives in vehicle routing has been published in the literature on transport logistics. Most of the ecological criteria of "green vehicle routing" [6] are based on the energy consumption required to fulfill a given set of transportation requests [3]. The immediate CO_2 emission and the total global warming potential (i.e. the CO_2 equivalents, measured in CO_2e) depend on the amount of energy consumed for a transportation

© Springer International Publishing AG 2017
T. Bektaş et al. (Eds.), ICCL 2017, LNCS 10572, pp. 94–109, 2017.
https://doi.org/10.1007/978-3-319-68496-3_7

process and can be determined solely based on this amount of energy. Other external effects of transportation processes are not considered in this paper (see e.g. [4]). The global warming effects of energy consumption are assessed using different methods [13]. The WTW (Well-to-Wheel) analysis method takes into consideration the total energy chain required to instantiate a locomotion, i.e. from energy generation to provision of energy at the point of consumption on to transformation into kinetic energy. By contrast, the TTW (Tank-to-Wheel) analysis method focuses only on the greenhouse gas emitted locally through transformation of stored energy (in a fuel tank or battery) into kinetic energy.

In the literature, several articles are dedicated to a comparison of energy-minimizing objectives and distance-minimizing objectives in vehicle routing (e.g. [7,10]). [14] consider energy minimization for homogeneous fleets and conclude that different types of VRPs should be remodeled by considering fuel consumption.

[5] consider a time- and load-dependent problem of minimizing CO_2 emissions in the routing of vehicles in urban areas. In their paper [5] present experiments on using different objective functions like minimizing distance, minimizing time-dependent travel times, minimizing time-dependent emissions based on the gross weight of a vehicle, and minimizing time-dependent emissions based on the actual weight (i.e. empty weight plus weight of the cargo) of a vehicle. In contrast to our paper, only vehicles with combustion engines and no battery-powered electric vehicles are considered by [5]. Moreover, most of the experiments are performed on TSP instances with one single vehicle which is able to serve all customers, while only a very small part of [5] refers to results obtained for fleets with multiple vehicles. Two homogeneous fleets and only one single configuration of a mixed fleet are considered. The pickup quantities are adjusted to the specific fleet capacity so that always three vehicles are required. Consequently, the test instances used in [5] vary for different fleet compositions. That is why, in contrast to our paper, a direct comparison of the solutions generated for different fleets is not possible in [5].

Results shown in [7] and [10] demonstrate that in the case of homogeneous vehicle fleets energy minimization compared to distance minimization results in very small energy savings of only a few percentage points (1% - 2%). However, in the case of heterogeneous fleets the potential to save energy is much larger. The deployment of suitably composed heterogeneous fleets can result in energy savings in the order of double-digit percentages [12]. Due to the fact that time, distance and energy are the main contributing factors to the variable cost of transport processes, the existing literature does not treat time and distance minimization as alternatives to energy minimization but as components of more comprehensive objective functions that comprise time and distance as well as energy consumption [1,9].

This paper addresses WTW-energy-oriented criteria and the traditional criteria of time and distance in vehicle routing relating to different types of vehicles. An interesting insight derived from the study of [11] is that using a heterogeneous fleet without speed optimization allows for a further reduction in total

cost than using a homogeneous fleet with speed optimization. As opposed to
the paper of [12], not only vehicles with a combustion engine but also vehicles
equipped with a battery-powered electrical engine will be taken into consideration. Battery-powered electric vehicles are more energy-efficient but they have a
reduced driving range and a reduced payload compared to combustion-powered
vehicles with the same gross weight. Particularly the following research questions
will be addressed:

1. How large is the difference between energy-optimal solutions compared to
   time- and distance-optimal solutions concerning the following criteria: energy
   consumed, total travel time and total travel distance needed to perform all
   transportation requests?
2. Are the impressive energy savings by deploying idealized heterogeneous fleets
   with a flexible number of vehicles [12] instead of homogeneous fleets only
   achieved by exploiting the degrees of freedom given by the choice of vehicles
   from an unlimited vehicle pool; in other words: can fixed fleet configurations be identified that yield high energy savings for all instances of a given
   planning scenario?
3. How can an efficient heterogeneous fleet with a small number of available
   vehicles be determined and how large is the loss of efficiency compared to
   an idealized fleet with an arbitrarily large number of vehicles of each type?
4. What are the properties of the Pareto set in multi objective optimization,
   particularly in Pareto optimization concerning the two objectives energy and
   distance minimization?

2   Planning Scenarios and Vehicle Properties

As a basis for the specification of planning scenarios used to conduct an analysis
to answer the above research questions the well-known CVRP is chosen [2]. The
CVRP has a distance-oriented objective that minimizes the total travel distance
of all vehicles dispatched. In addition to the capacity restrictions concerning the
maximum payload, the planning scenarios analyzed in this paper take into consideration the range of the vehicles. The maximal length of a tour is limited by
a given parameter. The CVRP with additional range limitations shall be called
distance-based vehicle routing problem TP-D. The TP-D is transformed into a
time-based vehicle routing problem TP-T by using the objective of minimizing
total time needed for all tours instead of total distance. The constant vehicle
specific average speed v_k of vehicle k converts travel distance into travel time.
For the energy-oriented vehicle routing problem TP-E the energy consumption
for the execution of tours is estimated as a function of the mass moved and the
distance the mass is moved. It is generally accepted that the following equation (1) is a suitable approximation for a simplified estimation of the energy
consumption $F_k(i,j)$ of vehicle k, that transports goods of the mass q_{ij} from
location i to location j (see e.g. [14]).

$$F_k(i,j) = (a_k + b_k \cdot q_{ij}) \cdot d_{ij} \tag{1}$$

The symbol d_{ij} denotes the distance between location i and location j, while a_k and b_k denote vehicle specific parameters for energy consumption. As a result, the objective criterion of the optimization problem TP-E consists of the total estimated energy consumption for all tours.

This paper considers four different types of vehicles: two smaller types with a gross weight of 7.5 metric tons each and two larger types with a gross weight of 18 tons each. Two vehicle types are equipped with a conventional combustion engine, one of them with 7.5 tons (sCV) and the other with 18 tons (lCV) gross weight. The other two vehicle types are equipped with a battery-powered electrical engine, one with 7.5 tons (sEV) and the other with 18 tons (lEV) gross weight. Those types of vehicles are available on the commercial vehicle market and are typically used for local pickup or delivery. The characteristic parameters for payload and energy consumption shown in Table 1 can be found in technical specifications of vehicle manufacturers or derived from descriptions provided by manufacturers. The maximal daily tour length of 600 km limits the range of all vehicles; for vehicles equipped with an electrical engine, the maximal energy available (i.e. the battery capacity) additionally limits the range. Smaller vehicles of type sEV have a battery capacity of 601 MJ and larger vehicles of type lEV have a battery capacity of 2,425 MJ. The actual range of those vehicles depends on the load while en route. Table 1 shows a lower and an upper value, where the lower value corresponds to a vehicle fully loaded and the upper value corresponds to an empty vehicle. For all vehicles with more than 3.5 tons gross weight, the legal speed limit on German highways (i.e. BAB or Kraftfahrstraßen) is 80 km/h; on all other ordinary non-urban roads the speed limit is 60 km/h for vehicles of more than 7.5 tons gross weight. Assuming that this difference in speed limits is incurred for one third of any tour, the smaller vehicles (sCV und sEV) are approximately 10% faster than the larger vehicles (lCV und lEV).

Table 1. Characteristics of the vehicle types considered

Vehicle type	Payload [t]	Range [km]	a_k [MJ/km]	b_k [MJ/km]	v_k [km/h]
sCV	4.0	600	5.77	0.36	55
sEV	3.5	98 – 140	4.27	0.53	55
lCV	9.0	600	7.99	0.29	50
lEV	6.0	253 – 300	7.80	0.24	50

3   Model

The mathematical model for the energy-oriented vehicle routing problem TP-E is an extension of the CVRP [2]. The important extensions address on the one hand the objective function of the model in order to introduce and minimize vehicle specific values concerning the load-based energy consumption. On the other hand, the constraints have to ensure the maximal tour length, concerning the electric vehicles caused by the limited battery capacity.

Indices:

i,j Nodes: $i,j \in N = \{0,1,...,n,n+1\}$, where 0 and $n+1$ represent the depot and $C = \{1,...,n\}$ represents the customers

k Vehicle $k \in K = \{1,...,m\}$

Parameters:

d_{ij} Distance between nodes i and j

tt_{ijk} Travel time of vehicle k on the arc from i to j

π_j Customer's demand in node $j = 1,...,n$

s_j Service time at customer $j = 1,...,n$

Constants:

a_k Energy consumption of the empty vehicle k per kilometer

b_k Energy consumption for the load of vehicle k per ton and kilometer

E_k Energy supply of vehicle k when leaving the depot

T_k Maximal tour length of vehicle k

Q_k Maximal payload capacity of vehicle k

Variables:

e_{ijk} Energy content available for vehicle k traversing the arc from i to j

q_{ijk} Weight of load in vehicle k on the arc from i to j

x_{ijk} 1, if vehicle k uses the arc from i to j
         0, else

y_{jk} 1, if customer j is serviced by vehicle k
         0, else

$$\min \sum_{i=0}^{n+1} \sum_{j=0}^{n+1} \sum_{k=1}^{m} d_{ij} \cdot (a_k \cdot x_{ijk} + b_k \cdot q_{ijk}) \tag{2}$$

subject to

$$\sum_{j=1}^{n+1} x_{0jk} = 1 \qquad\qquad \forall k \in K \tag{3}$$

$$\sum_{i=0}^{n} x_{in+1k} = 1 \qquad\qquad \forall k \in K \tag{4}$$

$$\sum_{j=0}^{n+1} x_{n+1jk} = 0 \qquad\qquad \forall k \in K \tag{5}$$

$$\sum_{i=0}^{n} x_{ijk} - \sum_{i=1}^{n+1} x_{jik} = 0 \qquad\qquad \forall j \in C, \forall k \in K \tag{6}$$

$$\sum_{k=1}^{m} y_{jk} = 1 \qquad\qquad \forall j \in C \qquad (7)$$

$$\sum_{i=0}^{n} x_{ijk} = y_{jk} \qquad\qquad \forall j \in C, \forall k \in K \qquad (8)$$

$$\sum_{j=0}^{n+1} \pi_j \cdot y_{jk} \le Q_k \qquad\qquad \forall k \in K \qquad (9)$$

$$x_{iik} = 0 \qquad\qquad \forall i \in N, \forall k \in K \qquad (10)$$

$$\sum_{i=0}^{n+1} q_{ijk} - \sum_{i=0}^{n+1} q_{jik} = \pi_j \cdot y_{jk} \qquad\qquad \forall j \in C, \forall k \in K \qquad (11)$$

$$q_{ijk} \le Q_k \cdot x_{ijk} \qquad\qquad \forall i,j \in N, \forall k \in K \qquad (12)$$

$$\sum_{i=0}^{n+1}\sum_{j=0}^{n+1} d_{ij} \cdot x_{ijk} \le T_k \qquad\qquad \forall k \in K \qquad (13)$$

$$\sum_{i=0}^{n+1} d_{ij} \cdot (a_k \cdot x_{ijk} + b_k \cdot q_{ijk}) = \sum_{i=0}^{n+1} e_{ijk} - \sum_{i=1}^{n+1} e_{jik} \qquad \forall j \in C, \forall k \in K \qquad (14)$$

$$d_{ij} \cdot (a_k \cdot x_{ijk} + b_k \cdot q_{ijk}) \le e_{ijk} \qquad\qquad \forall i,j \in N, \forall k \in K \qquad (15)$$

$$E_k \cdot x_{0jk} = e_{0jk} \qquad\qquad \forall j \in N, \forall k \in K \qquad (16)$$

$$e_{ijk} \le E_k \cdot x_{ijk} \qquad\qquad \forall i,j \in N, \forall k \in K \qquad (17)$$

$$q_{ijk} \ge 0 \qquad\qquad \forall i,j \in N, \forall k \in K \qquad (18)$$

$$x_{ijk} \in \{0,1\} \qquad\qquad \forall i,j \in N, \forall k \in K \qquad (19)$$

$$y_{ik} \in \{0,1\} \qquad\qquad \forall i \in N, \forall k \in K \qquad (20)$$

The objective function (2) minimizes the total energy required for all tours. The equations / inequalities (3) through (10) represent the usual constraints for modeling the CVRP. Equations (11) guarantee that the required demand π_j is unloaded at customer j and the load of the vehicle k is reduced accordingly. Inequalities (12) ensure that the loads q_{ijk} are zero if vehicle k does not use arc (i,j). Inequalities (13) limit the maximal tour length for each vehicle k. Equalities (14) determine the remaining energy supply at customer j in vehicle k. Equalities / inequalities (15), (16), and (17) ensure that the remaining energy supply in vehicle k to cover the arc from i to j is between the maximal possible and the minimal required energy supply. Relations (18), (19), and (20) define the domains of variables q_{ijk}, x_{ijk} and y_{jk}.

$$\min \sum_{i=0}^{n+1}\sum_{j=0}^{n+1}\sum_{k=1}^{m} d_{ij} \cdot x_{ijk} \qquad\qquad (21)$$

$$\min \sum_{i=0}^{n+1} \sum_{j=0}^{n+1} \sum_{k=1}^{m} (tt_{ijk} + s_j) \cdot x_{ijk} \tag{22}$$

The MIP formulation of TP-E above aims at minimizing the total energy consumption. In order to minimize total travel distance in the model of the distance-based vehicle routing problem TP-D objective function (21) replaces objective function (2). To minimize total travel time in the time-based vehicle routing problem TP-T the objective function (22) replaces (2).

4   Generating Test Instances

The analysis regarding the research questions listed above is conducted using specific problem instances with short travel distances corresponding to inner city transportation or pickup / delivery tours in rural areas. To solve the problem instances of the vehicle routing problems TP-D, TP-T and TP-E, the commercial solver IBM ILOG CPLEX 12.6.1 is used. To obtain reliable results for the further analysis, only small instances are generated that can be expected to be solved to optimality using CPLEX on a PC. Initially, generic problem instances with eight customers are generated. Customers' demands are measured in tons and evenly distributed over the interval $[1, 3]$; i.e., the values for customers 1 through 8 are: 1.0 / 1.3 / 1.6 / 1.9 / 2.1 / 2.4 / 2.7 / 3.0. Altogether, 50 different generic problem instances with the above-mentioned eight customers are generated. The coordinates of the eight customer locations are determined randomly for each generic instance. Coordinates are within a geographic area of 30 km × 30 km; i.e. they are randomly located within a grid square of $[0, 30] \times [0, 30]$. The depot of the vehicle routing problem is located in the middle of the grid square, i.e. at coordinates $(15, 15)$.

Based on the previously generated 50 generic random problem instances, concrete test instances are generated by the following two additional problem specifications:

(a) First of all, the available vehicle fleet is specified. Five different fleet configurations will be considered: one homogeneous fleet sC-HOM with eight vehicles of type sCV, one homogeneous fleet sE-HOM with eight vehicles of type sEV, one homogeneous fleet lC-HOM with eight vehicles of type lCV, one homogeneous fleet lE-HOM with eight vehicles of type lEV and one heterogeneous fleet HET, that consists of all of the above-mentioned homogeneous fleet configurations, i.e. eight vehicles of type sCV, sEV, lCV, lEV each.

(b) Secondly, a gauge factor g is introduced that varies the distances between all relevant locations of the test instances. The factor g has the values 1, 2, 3, and 4, which are used to scale the original grid square. By scaling, the grid square is enlarged and all distances between relevant locations (depot, customers) are multiplied with the gauge factor. The depot remains in the original location in the middle of the grid square in all instances.

The size of the vehicle fleets in (a) was chosen such that the total available pay-load is definitely sufficient to service all customers. The accumulated weight of all eight customer demands is 16 tons; when deploying eight vehicles of a homogeneous fleet, a maximal demand between 28 and 72 tons can be transported, depending on the vehicle type. More than eight vehicles will never be dispatched because all test instances feature exactly eight customers. The heterogeneous fleet HET is an idealized fleet composed in such a way that the solution space when using HET is larger than with any of the homogeneous fleets. The values of the gauge factor g in (b) are chosen in such a way that the range of the vehicles in fleet sE-HOM is sufficient to reach all customers in the grid square in a pendulum tour for $g \leq 2$. If $g > 2$ it is to be expected that some test instances are infeasible due to the limited range of the vehicles in fleet sE-HOM. The range of the vehicles in fleet lE-HOM is sufficiently large to ensure feasibility of all test instances with $1 \leq g \leq 4$. For instances with $g > 4$ that are not considered in this paper, the range of vehicles of type lEV may not be sufficient in all instances. In this case, the deployment of vehicles with combustion engine cannot be avoided.

Service times for all scenarios and instances are chosen to be $s_0 = 0$ (depot) and $s_j = 15$ min (each customer).

5   Analysis of Optimal Transportation Plans

In this section, research questions (1) through (3) are investigated. All 3,000 test instances (50 generic problem instances, 3 planning scenarios, i.e. objectives, 4 values of the gauge factor, 5 different vehicle fleets) can be solved to optimality using CPLEX. As was to be expected, deploying fleet sE-HOM optimal solutions for all test instances with $g \leq 2$ can be found. For $g = 3$ feasible solutions exist for 47 out of 50 instances. Due to the limited range of vehicles of type sEV, experiments show that only 10 out of 50 test instances with $g = 4$ are feasible. Let oTP-E, oTP-D and oTP-T denote an attribute (#Tours, Time, Distance, Energy) of the optimal solution of TP-E, TP-D and TP-T, respectively. Table 2 lists the relative differences ((oTP-E − oTP-T) / oTP-E, and (oTP-E − oTP-D) / oTP-E), respectively, that can be achieved by energy minimization instead of time respectively distance minimization concerning the number of vehicles

Table 2. Energy minimization versus time and distance minimization

Fleet	Time minimization			Distance minimization		
	Δ#Tours	ΔTime	ΔEnergy	Δ#Tours	ΔDistance	ΔEnergy
sC-HOM	2.0%	0.0%	-0.1%	2.0%	0.03%	-0.1%
sE-HOM	2.7%	0.1%	-0.3%	2.3%	0.1%	-0.2%
lC-HOM	8.9%	0.3%	-0.4%	8.9%	0.4%	-0.4%
lE-HOM	5.9%	0.1%	-0.2%	5.9%	0.1%	-0.2%
HET	51.5%	21.3%	-13.3%	54.2%	21.4%	-14.7%

deployed, total travel time, total distance traveled, and energy consumed. As a matter of course, the values in Table 2 for the fleet sE-HOM only include test instances, that are guaranteed to be feasible, i.e. test instances with $g = 1$ or $g = 2$.

The results in Table 2 provide an answer to research question (1). They show that significant differences between optimal solutions that are found minimizing on the one hand distance or time and on the other hand energy can only be observed with a heterogeneous vehicle fleet. The differences between time and distance minimization caused by the differing average speed of the vehicles are very small. In detail, the differences when using the fleet HET are the following: Independent of the value of the gauge factor g distance-minimizing solutions to TP-D need on average 0.1% more travel time than corresponding time-minimized solutions to TP-T. Reciprocally, optimal solutions to TP-T independent of the value of g result on average in 0.16% longer tours compared to TP-D. Furthermore, results show that distance-minimized solutions compared to time-minimized solutions consume on average 1.2% more energy but require a 5.9% smaller number of vehicles, independent of the value of g. For homogeneous fleets no differences between time-oriented and distance-based optimization can be observed concerning distance traveled, time needed and energy consumed. Larger differences concerning required energy, time and distance are only to be expected in extended scenarios where electric vehicles can recharge batteries en route at external charging stations.

A detailed analysis of the optimal solutions to the test instances generated for HET will contribute to answering research question (2). The analysis will focus on the use of different vehicle types in the solutions. This will provide insight into the question whether certain vehicle configurations are optimal for a larger number of test instances. Among the 200 test instances solved under energy optimization, 34 instances have an optimal solution that deploys a homogeneous vehicle fleet. Furthermore, a great variety of different fleets yields optimal solutions. For each value of g each vehicle type is deployed in at least one of the 50 test instances, i.e. none of the vehicle types is dispensable when generating optimal solutions. A cursory analysis does not provide any indication that for a certain value of g a specific fleet configuration or specific properties of fleets deployed are advantageous to yield optimal solutions. However, an in-depth analysis shows that in some cases certain fleet configurations are optimal for all values of g for some of the generic test instances. This indicates that the properties of an optimal heterogeneous fleet are mainly dependent on the customers' locations and on their demands, but little on the distances between the customers, as long as the distances vary only within a given spectrum of factor 4.

The idealized fleet HET comprises eight vehicles per vehicle type, thus 32 vehicles. Optimal solutions to the planning scenario TP-E require maximal 3, 6, 2, 1 vehicles of the types sCV, sEV, lCV and lEV, respectively. Consequently, a fleet configured accordingly with 12 vehicles would be sufficient to find the same optimal solutions as to the idealized fleet.

To address research question (3): Optimal solutions to the planning scenario TP-E using the idealized fleet HET require in the test sets on average $(0.6/3.1/0.6/0.1)$ vehicles of types (sCV/sEV/lCV/lEV). Rounding the average number of vehicles to the next integer and using at least one vehicle of each type, the result is a heterogeneous fleet of six vehicles (HET6), comprising $(1/3/1/1)$ of the vehicle types specified above. Promising fleets of five vehicles can be developed by either surrendering the vehicle lEV or the vehicle sCV contained in HET6. Hence, the fleets HET5-A $= (1/3/1/0)$ and HET5-B $= (0/3/1/1)$ with five vehicles each are derived. The relative differences ((oTP-E $-$ oTP-T) / oTP-E, and (oTP-E $-$ oTP-D) / oTP-E), respectively, that are achieved by energy minimization instead of distance minimization concerning the energy consumption are -9.0% (for HET6), -5.7% (for HET5-A), and -8.5% (for HET5-B). For a comparison of these values with the relative differences that have been computed for the other fleets, Table 2 can be consulted. Table 3 compares the energy consumption of different fleets. The reference value is the energy consumed by HET; i.e. the table lists the relative differences in energy consumption (on average over all values of g) of the homogeneous and heterogeneous fleets considered in relation to the energy consumption of the idealized fleet HET (i.e. the additional energy consumption of these fleets compared to HET). For sE-HOM the comparison is only performed for $g \leq 2$, because for test instances with $g = 3$ and $g = 4$ not all of the instances are feasible. Therefore, the value for sE-HOM in Table 3 is displayed in parenthesis. A comparison of sE-HOM with HET6, HET5-A, and HET5-B, respectively, shows that sE-HOM (on average over all values of $g \leq 2$) consumes on average 3.36%, 3.14%, and 2.38%, respectively, more energy than the respective heterogeneous fleets.

Table 3. Increase of energy consumption compared to HET

sC-HOM	sE-HOM	lC-HOM	lE-HOM	HET6	HET5-A	HET5-B
17.98%	(4.92%)	13.73%	23.14%	1.13%	1.60%	3.22%

6   Energy-Efficient Fleets and Multi Criteria Analysis

This section is dedicated to an intensified investigation of research question (3); and research question (4) will be investigated in-depth. Based on the outcomes of Section 5 concerning research question (3), it suggests itself to investigate test instances using fleets consisting of exactly five vehicles when trying to identify efficient fleets and Pareto-optimal solutions. F(5) denotes the set of all five-element vehicle fleets that consist of the four vehicle types defined in Section 2. To determine energy-efficient fleets and to perform multi criteria analysis concerning energy and distance-efficient solutions, the test instances of Section 4 will be used. The test instances of Section 4 represent a transportation scenario for less-than-truckload shipments with weights between one and three tons in a distribution area characterized by distances of up to 21 km for $g = 1$ (length of half the diagonal of the grid square). For greater values of the gauge factor g, the maximum distances within the distribution area are increased correspondingly. To determine the most efficient fleets consisting of five vehicles (research question (3)) and to determine the properties of Pareto sets under multi criteria vehicle routing for heterogeneous fleets, a brute-force approach is chosen. Systematically, all eligible fleets consisting of five vehicles are tested and the corresponding vehicle routing problems are solved.

When generating a fleet out of the set $F(5)$, five elements have to be chosen out of a basic set of four vehicle types. The elements (vehicle types) may be chosen multiple times and the sequence is irrelevant. Hence, there are $((5 + 4 - 1)/5) = 56$ different possibilities to configure a fleet out of the set $F(5)$. Using the brute-force approach to determine the energy efficiency of all possible five-element fleets out of $F(5)$ for all 200 test instances (50 generic problem instances, 4 values for the gauge factor), the energy-optimized solutions to the vehicle routing problem TP-E have been computed for each of the 56 different fleets. Consequently, applying the brute-force approach 11,200 (56 x 200) vehicle routing problems were solved. Numerical experiments show that the fleet $(1/3/1/0)$ actually is the most energy-efficient fleet out of all 56 fleets in $F(5)$. The fleet $(1/3/1/0)$ was already considered in Section 5 and denoted by HET5-A (see also Table 3). Concerning the energy efficiency on average over all gauge factors g, HET5-A is the only fleet that is only less than 2% worse than the idealized fleet HET. Only three other fleets $((1/2/0/2), (1/2/1/1),$ and $(2/2/1/0),$ respectively) show differences of less than 3% compared to HET with 2.19%, 2.19%, and 2.35%, respectively. The above-mentioned fleet $(1/2/0/2)$ consists of four electric vehicles and one conventional vehicle with a diesel engine. In the fleet configurations $(1/3/1/0)$ and $(1/2/1/1)$ three electric vehicles and two conventional vehicles with a combustion engine are deployed, and the fleet $(2/2/1/0)$ uses two electric vehicles and three conventional vehicles. Half of all the fleets in $F(5)$ result in a relatively poor energy consumption with a difference above 8% compared to HET. The average difference over all fleets in $F(5)$ where all instances with all gauge factors could be solved is 8.96%. Poorest performance of all heterogeneous fleets could be observed at fleet $(1/0/0/4)$ with a difference of 18.44%. Homogeneous fleets result in particularly large differences. They are 23.15% for $(0/0/0/5)$, 13.73% for $(0/0/5/0)$, and 18.1% for $(5/0/0/0)$. Comparing homogeneous fleets, the performance of conventional vehicles is superior to electric vehicles. Hence, the homogeneous fleet of vehicles of type lCV consumes considerably less energy than the homogeneous fleet with small conventional vehicles, which again consumes considerably less energy than the homogeneous fleet consisting of large electric vehicles. For the homogeneous fleet $(0/5/0/0)$ with small electric vehicles a comparison of energy consumption with HET is not possible, because feasible solutions do not exist for all test instances using such a homogeneous fleet. The variation of the gauge factor g has only a small influence on the energy efficiency of the best fleets. HET5-A is the best fleet for the values $g = 1$, $g = 2$, and $g = 3$. For $g = 4$ the fleet $(1/2/2/0)$ yields slightly better results. Note that this fleet is very similar to HET5-A, because it evolves by exchanging one vehicle of type sEV by type lCV.

A detailed analysis of the optimal solutions obtained with HET5-A shows that only 16.5% of all 200 test instances have solutions actually using all five vehicles in HET5-A. All the other test instances yield better solutions deploying only four and in one case even only three vehicles than any five-element fleet configuration. For 46% of all test instances, the fleet $(0/3/1/0)$ can be identified as the best possible fleet to obtain optimal vehicle routes, i.e. the vehicle of type sCV is not used. For 29.5% of all instances the third vehicle of type sEV is not used (fleet $(1/2/1/0)$), and for another 8% of all instances only one of the three vehicles of type sEV is actually deployed (fleet $(1/1/1/0)$). It is remarkable that the fleet yielding the best results for nearly half of all test instances (i.e. $(0/3/1/0)$) deploys as well electric as combustion engine vehicles, namely three small electric vehicles and one large combustion engine vehicle.

The analysis of the solutions obtained with the idealized fleet HET shows that for after all 38 out of 200 test instances the best results could be found with fleets consisting of six vehicles. Insofar it is remarkable that HET5-A with only five vehicles yields results that are only 1.6% inferior to HET. The reason may be that for 56 out of 200 test instances the fleet $(0/3/1/0)$ and for 28 out of 200 instances the fleet $(1/2/1/0)$ is the most energy-efficient one. Both fleets are included in HET5-A.

By means of the brute-force approach, it could be achieved to identify particularly energy-efficient heterogeneous fleets for the planning scenario introduced in Section 2, extended to an application scenario in Section 4 (research question (3)). It could be shown that heterogeneous fleets with a small number of vehicles exist that are nearly as energy-efficient as the idealized fleet HET. Hence, the large potential for energy savings through heterogeneous instead of homogeneous fleets is not caused by the large variety and flexibility of an idealized fleet (research question (2)), but can also be put into effect using a specific small vehicle fleet with an appropriate number of vehicles. To investigate research question (4), all elements of the Pareto set in a bicriteria optimization for three selected fleets shall be determined, again using a brute-force approach. Whether this is possible at all depends on the cardinality of the Pareto sets.

Due to the fact shown in Section 5 that the differences between objective function values comparing optimal solutions to distance minimization with time minimization are very small, it can be assumed that a Pareto optimization comparing energy- and time-optimal solutions on the one hand and comparing energy- and distance-optimal solutions on the other hand will result in similar values. Hence, the analysis conducted in this section in the framework of a multi criteria optimization will be limited to the comparison of energy minimization and distance minimization; i.e. the comparison of the optimization criteria energy minimization and time minimization will not be undertaken. In order to determine the Pareto sets to be investigated, for the idealized fleet HET, for the best known heterogeneous fleet with five vehicles HET-5A, and for the most energy-efficient homogeneous fleet (0/0/5/0) all 200 test instances (with 50 generic problem instances and 4 different gauge factors) are considered. Altogether 600 Pareto sets will be determined.

To determine the Pareto set of a test instance, at first the energy-optimal solution P1 is computed by solving the vehicle routing problem TP-E for this test instance. Thus, the first element of the Pareto set is found. Subsequently, an additional constraint R1 is inserted into TP-E that ensures that the sum of all distances traveled has to be by 0.01 km smaller than in solution P1, and, if it exists, a second element P2 of the Pareto set can be found by solving the problem that has been extended with R1. All other Pareto-optimal solutions are determined iteratively by requiring that any additional solution has a total travel distance that is at least 0.01 km shorter than the immediately preceding solution. This is repeated until the optimization problem to be solved does not have a feasible solution due to the latest of the inserted constraints.

Among the 200 Pareto sets that have been determined for the idealized fleet HET, there are two sets consisting of 17 Pareto-optimal solutions. All other Pareto sets have a smaller number of Pareto-optimal solutions, and some Pareto sets consist of only one element. On average, the 200 Pareto sets of the fleet

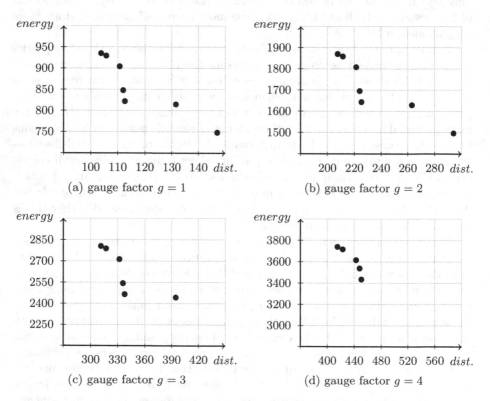

Fig. 1. Pareto frontiers of fleet HET

HET possess a cardinality of 6, 6, 6, and 5, for $g = 1$, $g = 2$, $g = 3$, and $g = 4$, respectively. Thus to determine the Pareto sets of HET, approximately 1,200 vehicle routing problems were solved. The Pareto sets computed for the fleet HET-5A possess a maximal cardinality of 8 and a minimal cardinality of 1. The average values of cardinality are 3, 3, 3, and 2, for $g = 1, 2, 3$, and 4, respectively. For the most energy-efficient homogeneous fleet $(0/0/5/0)$ the maximal, average, and minimal cardinality is 3, 1, and 1, respectively.

Overall, it can be observed that the Pareto sets are relatively small. Due to the small cardinality of the Pareto sets, it is entirely reasonable and easily possible to utilize the Pareto sets for a subsequent selection process where the most attractive Pareto-optimal solution is chosen to match specific decision criteria according to a given purpose. Figures 1 and 2 display the Pareto frontiers of fleets HET and HET5-A at different values of the gauge factor g for one selected generic problem instance. In order to obtain as large a distance as possible between the extreme values in the Pareto sets, the particular instance out of all 50 generic problem instances that shows the largest differences of all instances between solutions to TP-E and TP-D for HET-5A is selected for display in Figures 1 and 2.

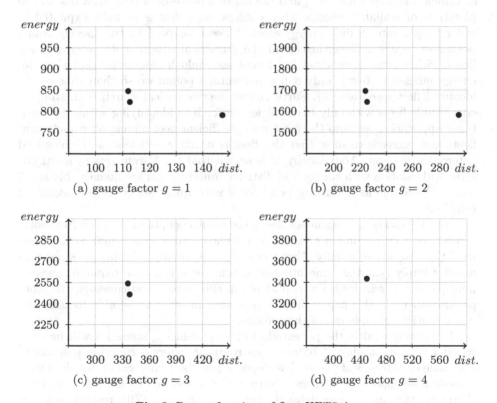

(a) gauge factor $g = 1$

(b) gauge factor $g = 2$

(c) gauge factor $g = 3$

(d) gauge factor $g = 4$

Fig. 2. Pareto frontiers of fleet HET5-A

7   Results and Future Research

The numerical experiments were deliberately performed using small instances in order to be able to obtain optimal solutions as a basis for the analysis. Because generating suboptimal solutions, as they will typically be found when applying heuristics to larger instances, and then using those to perform comparisons and draw conclusions carries the considerable risk of false conclusions (see already [8]). This particularly holds when no knowledge is available about the average- or worst-case behavior of the heuristics applied, which is frequently the case. Hence, the results used for answering the questions (1) to (4) are based solely on the above mentioned small test instances. Since the tests do not exploit any specific attributes of small CVRP test instances, we believe that experiments on large instances would yield similar answers to our questions. In order to prove whether the found answers are not restricted to small CVRP instances, algorithms capable of handling larger instances will be developed in future work.

The experiments show that there are significant differences concerning energy consumption of heterogeneous vehicle fleets between energy-optimal solutions on the one hand and distance-optimal or time-optimal solutions on the other hand (see Table 1). In an idealized heterogeneous fleet with a sufficiently large number of vehicles, all types are used; and the degrees of freedom that exist due to the plenitude of available vehicles when configuring a fleet is actually exploited in order to generate flexibly energy-efficient fleets adapted to the specific transportation requests. Nevertheless, in the numerical experiments heterogeneous fleets with a small number of fixed vehicles could be identified that show an energy efficiency that is only a few percentage points worse than that of the idealized fleet (see Table 3). Furthermore, a systematical search evaluating all conceivable fleets with only five vehicles succeeds in identifying within the analyzed application scenario the most energy-efficient fleet among all five-element fleets and succeeds to show that this fleet is nearly as efficient as the idealized heterogeneous fleet. Additionally, it is shown that the Pareto sets in multi criteria optimization with energy and distance minimization are manageably small and well suitable as a starting point for a subsequent selection of customized solutions.

When utilizing heterogeneous fleets, the resulting optimal solution frequently consists of a large number of tours, particularly when many small vehicles are used that execute especially short tours. A large number of tours does not necessarily imply that the same number of vehicles/drivers are required, because multiple use of vehicles is not considered in this paper. Consequently, the models introduced in this paper shall be amended in order to be able to take into consideration multiple use of the vehicles.

To entirely exploit the potential of electric vehicles, scenarios will be evaluated where recharging of batteries en route at external charging stations or exchange of batteries at the vehicle depot is possible. This will obviously have a considerable impact on the time electric vehicles need to execute a tour and furthermore, this may require detours to charging stations. With respect to a cost analysis it should be noted that energy consumption, time needed to execute tours and total distance traveled are the dominating factors when minimizing the variable cost in vehicle routing.

References

1. Bektaş, T. and Laporte, G.: The pollution-routing problem, Transportation Research Part B: Methodological, 45(8), pp. 1232 – 1250 (2011)
2. Dantzig, G.B. and Ramser, J.H.: The truck dispatching problem, Management Science, 6(1), pp. 80 – 91 (1959)
3. Demir, E. and Bektaş, T. and Laporte, G.: A review of recent research on green road freight transportation, European Journal of Operational Research, 237(3), pp. 775 – 793 (2014)
4. Dethloff, J. and Seelbach, H.: Umweltorientierte Logistik, In: Hansmann, K.-W. (eds.) Umweltorientierte Betriebswirtschaftslehre, pp. 145-190. Gabler, Wiesbaden (1998)
5. Ehmke, J. F. and Campbell, A. M. and Thomas, B. W.: Vehicle routing to minimize time-dependent emissions in urban areas, European Journal of Operational Research, 251(2), pp. 478 – 494 (2016)
6. Eglese, R. and Bektaş, T.: Green vehicle routing, In: Toth, P. and Vigo, D. (eds.) Vehicle routing: problems, methods and applications (2nd edition), pp. 437 – 458 Philadelphia: MOS-SIAM Series on Optimization 18 (2014)
7. Figliozzi, M.: Vehicle routing problem for emissions minimization, Transportation Research Record: Journal of the Transportation Research Board, 2197(1), pp. 1 – 7 (2010)
8. Geoffrion, A. M. and Van Roy, T. J.: Caution: Common sense planning methods can be hazardous to your corporate health, Sloan Management Review, 20(4), pp. 31 – 42 (1979)
9. Goeke D. and Schneider, M.: Routing a mixed fleet of electric and conventional vehicles, European Journal of Operational Research, 245(1), 81 – 99 (2015)
10. Kara, I. and Kara, B.Y. and Yetis, M.K.: Energy minimizing vehicle routing problem, In: Dress, A. and Xu, Y. and Zhu, B. (eds.) Combinatorial optimization and applications, pp. 62 – 71, Springer, Berlin / Heidelberg (2007)
11. Koç, Ç. and Bektaş, T. and Jabali, O. and Laporte, G.: The fleet size and mix pollution-routing problem, Transportation Research Part B: Methodological, 70, pp. 239 – 254 (2014)
12. Kopfer, H.W. and Schönberger, J. and Kopfer, H.: Reducing greenhouse gas emissions of a heterogeneous vehicle fleet, Flexible Services and Manufacturing Journal, 26(1), pp. 221 – 248 (2014)
13. Schmied, M. and Knörr, W.: Calculating GHG emissions for freight forwarding and logistics services in accordance with EN 16258, European Association for Forwarding, Transport, Logistics and Customs Services (CLECAT) (2012)
14. Xiao, Y. and Zhao, Q. and Kaku, I. and Xu, Y.: Development of a fuel consumption optimization model for the capacitated vehicle routing problem, Computers & Operations Research, 39(7), pp. 1419 – 1431 (2012)

Time-Dependent Route Planning
for Truck Drivers

Alexander Kleff[1,2]($\boxtimes$), Christian Bräuer[1,2], Frank Schulz[1], Valentin Buchhold[2],
Moritz Baum[2], and Dorothea Wagner[2]

[1] PTV Group, Karlsruhe, Germany
{alexander.kleff,christian.braeuer,frank.schulz}@ptvgroup.com
[2] Karlsruhe Institute of Technology (KIT), Karlsruhe, Germany
{buchhold,moritz.baum,dorothea.wagner}@kit.edu

Abstract. We study the problem of computing time-dependent shortest
routes for truck drivers. In contrast to conventional route planning, truck
drivers have to obey government regulations that impose limits on non-
stop driving times. Therefore, route planners must plan *break periods* in
advance and select suitable parking lots. To ensure that maximum driving
times are not exceeded, predictable congestion due to, e. g., peak hours
should also be taken into account. Therefore, we introduce the truck
driver routing problem in *time-dependent* road networks. It turns out
that the combination of time-dependent driving times with constraints
imposed by drivers' working hours requires computation of multiple time-
dependent *profiles* for optimal solutions. Although conceptually simple,
profile search is expensive. We greatly reduce (empirical) running times
by calculating bounds on arrival and departure times during additional
search phases to only query partial profiles and only to a fraction of
the parking lots. Carefully integrating this approach with a *one-to-many*
extension of time-dependent contraction hierarchies makes our approach
practical. For even faster queries, we also propose a heuristic variant that
works very well in practice. Excellent performance of our algorithms is
demonstrated on a recent real-world instance of Germany that is much
harder than time-dependent instances considered in previous works.

Keywords: Time-dependent shortest paths · Drivers' working hours · Truck
driver scheduling · Parking locations

1 Introduction

In many countries of the world, truck drivers are legally obligated to take breaks
on a regular basis to obviate drivers' fatigue and hence increase road safety. For
instance, Regulation (EC) No. 561/2006 of the European Union [15] demands a
break of at least 45 minutes after at most 4.5 hours of driving. And according to
the hours-of-service regulation in the United States [16], a 30-minutes-break is
mandatory after at most eight hours have elapsed. Truck drivers must park their
vehicle at a suitable location before taking such a "lunch break". Due to the size

© Springer International Publishing AG 2017
T. Bektaş et al. (Eds.), ICCL 2017, LNCS 10572, pp. 110–126, 2017.
https://doi.org/10.1007/978-3-319-68496-3_8

of their trucks, the drivers are severely limited compared to car drivers when in search of a parking space. For assistance in finding appropriate and available parking lots, truck drivers use mobile apps like Truck Parking Europe [1] that maintain databases of parking lots and display nearby lots to users. In this work, we investigate the following optimization problem: En route from one customer to another, when and where should the driver take a break (if at all) to conform to the provisions on breaks and arrive at the destination earliest possible?

We only consider one drive from a source to a destination. In general, a truck driver may visit multiple customers per day. In this case, the customers' time windows also have to be regarded. Moreover, if a trip takes more than one day, not only lunch breaks have to be scheduled but also longer rest breaks for the driver to sleep. The problem of scheduling breaks in order to comply with regulations while also taking customer time windows into account is known as the *truck driver scheduling problem* [21]. However, the locations of the parking lots remain disregarded in this setting. In this work, we take a major first step towards combining *time-dependent route planning* and *truck driver scheduling*. We determine not only *when* but also *where* to take a break.

We consider time-dependent driving times to model predictable congestion. In this scenario, it might be beneficial to not depart from source right away, or to prolong a break, or to wait at a parking lot for a time that is too short to count as break. As an example of *short-term waiting*, imagine the following: At the time of arrival at a parking lot, the driving time to the destination would be two minutes longer than the remaining allowed driving time. Luckily, the driver just has to wait ten minutes for the congestion to disperse and for the driving time to drop by these two minutes. In contrast to the European Union, short-term waiting does not pay off in the United States because the lunch break becomes mandatory after eight hours have elapsed, and not after a certain accumulated driving time. In the following, we focus on the EU regulation.

Time-dependency makes the problem particularly challenging, and the question arises whether it can be solved efficiently in practice. We are interested both in optimal and in heuristic approaches. There are a couple of parameters to reduce the run-time, and we seek to shed light on their impact on the solution quality. For our experimental analysis, it is sufficient to assume that the driver stops at only one parking lot (if at all). For a planning horizon of one day, this is no substantial limitation in practice as a daily driving time of 9h (US: 11h) should not be exceeded, even though it may be extended to 10h twice a week. For the sake of completeness, we discuss the implications regarding multiple stops.

Related Work. Route planning algorithms have received a large amount of attention in recent years, resulting in a multitude of *speedup techniques* [2]. In the *time-dependent* scenario, *driving time functions* associated with the edges map the time of the day to a driving time [7]. Dijkstra's algorithm [12] can be generalized [14] to answer *earliest arrival* (EA) queries. However, *profile* queries asking for the driving time function between two vertices are not feasible for large road networks [11], as such functions may have superpolynomial complexity [17] and maintaining them for all vertices makes Dijkstra's algorithm impractical.

Several classic speedup techniques have been generalized to the time-dependent scenario [6, 9, 10], typically focusing on fast EA queries. Efficient EA and profile queries at continental scale are provided by TCH [3], a generalization of Contraction Hierarchies (CH) [20]. Batched shored paths in the time-dependent scenario are studied in [19]. Recently, Strasser [30] introduced a simple heuristic for time-dependent routing that is cheap in time and space, but drops optimality and provides no approximation guarantees.

As far as the truck driver scheduling problem is concerned, the interested reader can find descriptions of optimal algorithms for the EU variant of this problem in [21, 13, 26] and for the US variant in [22, 24, 25]. Of these, [26] and [24] propose a *mixed-integer linear programming* formulation. The former even takes time-dependent driving times into account, the latter is the only one to include real-world data of parking lots (here: interstate rest areas) into their experimental analysis. However, in both cases not only the sequence of customers is fixed but also the path in the road graph. So in the former case the path cannot change over time, and in the latter case truck stops aside the path are disregarded. In [27], time-dependent routes for truck drivers subject to government regulations and time windows are solved heuristically. Finally, other lines of research have considered problems that resemble our setting but are $\mathcal{NP}$-hard, such as crew scheduling [29], routing of electric vehicles [5], or time-dependent pollution-routing [18].

Contribution and Outline. We introduce the truck driver routing problem that asks for the fastest route between two customers that complies with legal provisions for truck drivers (Section 2). To the best of our knowledge, we are the first to integrate the choice of routes, breaks and parking lots in one query – unlike previous works that first fix the route and then schedule breaks, possibly missing the optimal solution. Since rush hours severely affect driving times, we consider the time-dependent scenario. We propose a naive approach (Section 3) that would be far too expensive in time and space without at least one of two described acceleration techniques (Sections 3.1 and 3.2): An implementation based on TCHs achieves query times in the order of minutes on the German road network. Sophisticated bounds computations on top of that speed queries up by a factor of 25, yielding running times well below 10 seconds. Finally, a heuristic approach (Section 3.3) enables queries below a second and less. Most of our experiments (Section 4) are performed on a new instance of the German road network, currently used by PTV in production systems. It turns out to be much harder than the ten-year-old instance used in most publications so far. Before we conclude (Section 6), we discuss the implications of allowing multiple stops (Section 5).

2   Problem Statement and Preliminaries

The basic input for every variant of the *truck driver routing problem* is the following: Let a road network be given, modeled as a directed *graph* $G = (V, E)$ with $n = |V|$ *vertices* and $m = |E|$ *edges*, where vertices $v \in V$ typically correspond to intersections and edges $(u, v) \in E$ to road segments. The subset

$P \subset V$ of the vertices contains exactly the *parking locations* that represent the parking lots (or even parking spaces) where the driver may take a break. The *minimum break period* and the *maximum driving time* until such a break is mandatory are denoted by *break* and *limit* respectively. These two parameters are sufficient to handle the Regulation (EC) No. 561/2006 of the European Union [15] for a planning horizon of one day.

We are also given a sequence of exactly two customers to be visited, *source* $s \in V \setminus P$ and *destination* $d \in V \setminus P$. An *s–d-path* $Path_{s,d}$ (in G) is a sequence $[v_1 = s, v_2, \ldots, v_k = d]$ of vertices such that $(v_i, v_{i+1}) \in E$ and $v_i \neq v_j$ for all $1 \leq i < j \leq k$. A *(truck driver) route* $Route_{s,d}$ from s to d in turn is a sequence $[Path_{u_i,v_i}]_{1 \leq i \leq k}$ of paths such that $u_1 = s$ and $u_i \in P$ for $1 < i \leq k$, $v_k = d$ and $v_i \in P$ for $1 \leq i < k$, and $v_{i-1} = u_i$ for $1 < i \leq k$. In this paper, we will only deal with routes with a sequence length $|Route_{s,d}| := k$ of at most two.

In the time-independent case, the weights on the edges are constants and indicate the driving time along the edge. A path is feasible iff the accumulated driving time along the path is no longer than *limit*, and a route is feasible iff all its paths are. The duration of a truck driver route $Route_{s,d}$ is the sum of the accumulated driving times of its paths plus $(|Route_{s,d}| - 1) \cdot break$. In time-independent truck driver routing, we are interested in a shortest feasible route from s to d if such a feasible route exists.

In time-dependent truck driver routing, we are given *time-dependent driving time functions* for every edge instead of constant driving times. That is, for every edge (u, v) there is a function $\Psi_{u,v} \colon \mathbb{R} \to \mathbb{R}^+$ that maps the time of departure from u to the driving time to v. In this work, all functions are supposed to be piecewise-linear. The driver is not allowed to wait at any vertex other than the parking locations or s. In this scenario, it is common to demand that the functions fulfill the *FIFO property* because the shortest-path problem would become $\mathcal{NP}$-hard if it was not satisfied for all edges [28, 8]. We even presume that functions are continuous and fulfill the *strict FIFO property*, i.e., for arbitrary $t < t' \in \mathbb{R}$, the condition $t + \Psi(t) < t' + \Psi(t')$ holds for every edge (later departure leads to later arrival). This way, the *arrival time function* id $+\Psi$ is bijective (id being the identity function) and we can build the inverse $(\mathrm{id} +\Psi)^{-1}$ that maps an arrival time to the appropriate departure time.

To check feasibility of a route $Route_{s,d} = [Path_{u_i,v_i}]_{1 \leq i \leq k}$, we also ask for *departure and arrival times* $dep(u_i)$ and $arr(v_i)$ for all i. This way, the duration of a path $Path_{u,v}$ can easily be computed by $arr(v) - dep(u)$ (must be positive) and the waiting time at a parking location by $dep(u_i) - arr(v_{i-1})$ (must be non-negative). To be feasible, no single path is allowed to be longer than *limit*. In addition, a route $[Path_{s,p}, Path_{p,d}]$ is feasible only if either the sum of the paths' durations does not exceed *limit* or there is a waiting time that counts as break at the parking location p in between. Among all feasible truck driver routes we look for one with the earliest arrival at d. To this end, we are also given a *lower bound* on the *earliest departure* $lbED(s)$ from s, i.e., we demand $dep(s) \geq lbED(s)$. It is only a lower bound because a feasible route with $dep(s) = lbED(s)$ may not exist. In this paper, we call a vertex v *reachable* from u at time t if there is a feasible route $Route_{u,v}$ with $dep(u) = t$.

A *(driving time) profile* between u and v is a time-dependent function $\psi_{u,v}\colon \mathbb{R} \to \mathbb{R}^+$ that maps every departure time at u to the *shortest* driving time to v. If $(u,v) \in E$, the profile is identical to the given driving time function $\Psi_{u,v}$. If not, we can compute the profile $\psi_{u,v}$ recursively either forward or backward using the *link operation* $\odot$ and the *merge operation* $\oplus$:

$$\psi_{u,v} := \bigoplus_{w\colon (w,v)\in E} \psi_{u,w} \odot \Psi_{w,v} \quad \text{or} \quad \psi_{u,v} := \bigoplus_{w\colon (u,w)\in E} \Psi_{u,w} \odot \psi_{w,v} \quad (1)$$

where $\psi \odot \varphi$ is defined to be $\psi + \varphi \circ (\mathrm{id} + \psi)$ and $\psi \oplus \varphi$ defined to be $\min(\psi, \varphi)$. A profile search can be implemented as described in [11].

3   Solution Approach

We first describe a basic and rather naive approach to compute the earliest arrival at destination d. There are three ways in which d may be reachable from s: Either without passing a parking location at all, or by taking a break at a parking location, or by short-term waiting at a parking location. Accordingly, we will now compute three values opt_{none}, opt_{break}, and opt_{short}. The minimum of these is then the overall optimal solution.

At first, we investigate whether d can be reached from s without passing a parking location. To do this, we compute the driving time profile $\psi_{s,d}$ from s to d and then look up the earliest feasible departure time $dep_{s,d}$ from s in this respect: $dep_{s,d} := \min\{t : \psi_{s,d}(t) \leq limit \wedge t \geq lbED(s)\}$. With this, we can conclude: $opt_{none} := dep_{s,d} + \psi_{s,d}(dep_{s,d})$.

To consider the parking locations, we have to search forward and backward in order to compute the driving time profiles $\psi_{s,p}$ and $\psi_{p,d}$ for all $p \in P$. In the case with a break at a parking location, the next step is, similarly as before and for every parking location $p \in P$, to determine the earliest feasible departure time $dep_{s,p}$ from s when going to p as $dep_{s,p} := \min\{t : \psi_{s,p}(t) \leq limit \wedge t \geq lbED(s)\}$, and then to look up the earliest feasible departure time $dep_{p,d}$ from p when going to d after a break as $dep_{p,d} := \min\{t : \psi_{p,d}(t) \leq limit \wedge t \geq dep_{s,p} + \psi_{s,p}(dep_{s,p}) + break\}$. In turn, we can conclude: $opt_{break} := \min_{p\in P}\{dep_{p,d} + \psi_{p,d}(dep_{p,d})\}$.

But maybe the optimal solution consists in just waiting at a parking location for a short time that does not necessarily count as break. To take this case into account, we determine the earliest feasible departure time $dep_{s,p,d}$ from p when going from s to d for every parking location $p \in P$ as follows: $dep_{s,p,d} := \min\{t : \exists t' : \psi_{s,p}(t') + \psi_{p,d}(t) \leq limit \wedge lbED(s) \leq t' \leq t - \psi_{s,p}(t')\}$. Again, we conclude: $opt_{short} := \min_{p\in P}\{dep_{s,p,d} + \psi_{p,d}(dep_{s,p,d})\}$.

This description is only a sketch. It is meant to give an overview. A naive implementation would certainly be far too slow for any practical use. This motivates the following three acceleration approaches: by narrowing down profile searches, by time-dependent contraction hierarchies, and heuristically.

3.1 Acceleration by Narrowing Down Searches

Some computations can be performed faster than others. The idea is to spend little extra time on quick computations in order to gain bounds that help us speed up the expensive calculations such as the profile search.

We define $ubMax(\psi)$ as an upper bound on the maximum value of the profile ψ, i.e., $ubMax(\psi) \geq \max_{t \in \mathbb{R}} \psi(t)$. Analogously, $lbMin(\psi)$ is a lower bound on the minimum value of ψ. A query for these bounds, called a *profile bounds query* here, can be answered by applying Dijkstra's algorithm [14] on a graph where the constant edge weights are the minimum (maximum) values of the respective driving time functions. Given a departure time t in addition, an earliest arrival (EA) query asks for the earliest arrival at d when departing at time t. Both queries can be processed rapidly and are described in greater detail in [3]. In our context, a usual EA query only gives a lower bound $lbEA(d)$ on the earliest arrival if $lbEA(d) > t + limit$. To highlight this, we call it an *lbEA query*.

Computing Partial Profiles. One of the key acceleration techniques in this paper is to only compute a *partial profile*. A partial profile maps a departure time $t \in \mathbb{R}$ to a driving time in $\mathbb{R}^+ \cup \{\bot\}$, where $\bot$ can be read as *undefined*. We have to distinguish a *partial forward profile* from a *partial backward profile*. More precisely, the following holds for a partial forward profile ψ^f given a *departure time range* $[t^{begin}, t^{end}] \subset \mathbb{R}$: $\psi^f(t) \in \mathbb{R}^+$ for $t^{begin} \leq t \leq t^{end}$ and $\psi^f(t) = \bot$ otherwise. An analog statement holds for a partial backward profile ψ^b given an *arrival time range* $[t^{begin}, t^{end}] \subset \mathbb{R}$: $\psi^b(t) \in \mathbb{R}^+$ for $(id + \psi^b)^{-1}(t^{begin}) \leq t \leq (id + \psi^b)^{-1}(t^{end})$ and $\psi^b(t) = \bot$ otherwise.

A partial (forward or backward) profile for a given (departure or arrival time) range can be computed similar to before. If $(u, v) \in E$, we set

$$\psi^f_{u,v}(t) := \begin{cases} \Psi_{u,v}(t), & \text{if } t \text{ in range} \\ \bot, & \text{otherwise} \end{cases} \qquad \psi^b_{u,v}(t) := \begin{cases} \Psi_{u,v}(t), & \text{if } t + \Psi_{u,v}(t) \text{ in range} \\ \bot, & \text{otherwise} \end{cases}$$

If not, we use the same (forward or backward) recursion formula as before in (1). But we have to adjust the definitions of the link and merge operations and distinguish the forward from the backward case. The forward and backward link operations for a partial profile and a driving-time function of some edge are now defined as follows:

$$(\psi^f_{u,v} \odot^f \Psi_{v,w})(t) := \begin{cases} \psi^f_{u,v}(t) + \Psi_{v,w}(t + \psi^f_{u,v}(t)), & \text{if } \psi^f_{u,v}(t) \neq \bot \\ \bot, & \text{otherwise} \end{cases}$$

$$(\Psi_{u,v} \odot^b \psi^b_{v,w})(t) := \begin{cases} \Psi_{u,v}(t) + \psi^b_{v,w}(t + \Psi_{u,v}(t)), & \text{if } \psi^b_{v,w}(t + \Psi_{u,v}(t)) \neq \bot \\ \bot, & \text{otherwise} \end{cases}$$

The forward and backward merge operations for two partial profiles for the same vertex pair and range are now defined as follows:

$$(\psi^f \oplus^f \varphi^f)(t) := \begin{cases} \min\{\psi^f(t), \varphi^f(t)\}, & \text{if } \psi^f(t) \neq \bot \wedge \varphi^f(t) \neq \bot \\ \bot, & \text{otherwise} \end{cases}$$

$$(\psi^b \oplus^b \varphi^b)(t) := \begin{cases} \psi^b(t), & \text{if } \psi^b(t) \neq \bot \wedge (\text{id} + \varphi^b)^{-1}(t + \psi^b(t)) \leq t \\ \varphi^b(t), & \text{if } \varphi^b(t) \neq \bot \wedge (\text{id} + \psi^b)^{-1}(t + \varphi^b(t)) < t \\ \bot, & \text{otherwise} \end{cases}$$

Given a source, a destination, and a range, we call a query for a partial profile a *profile range query*.

One-to-one queries. At first, we perform a *one-to-one* lbEA query for s and d and departure time $lbED(s)$, that is, we compute the earliest arrival at d as if there was no break to take when leaving s earliest possible. If this lower bound $lbEA(d)$ on the earliest arrival is no later than $lbED(s) + limit$, it is tight, and we have found the requested earliest arrival at d.

The second step is to compute a lower bound $lbMin(\psi_{s,d})$ on the driving time from s to d. If this bound is already greater than $2 \cdot limit$, we stop here because d is considered to be not reachable from s as we only take one break into account.

If $lbMin(\psi_{s,d}) \leq limit$, then an optimal solution may incorporate short-term waiting at a parking location. We store this information by setting $lbWaiting := 0$. Otherwise we set $lbWaiting := break$ because it is certain that the driver will have to take a break at one of the parking locations.

One-to-many-to-one queries. We perform both an lbEA search and a profile bounds search from s to all potentially reachable parking locations, that is, we compute $lbMin(\psi_{s,p})$, $ubMax(\psi_{s,p})$ and $lbEA(p)$ for all $p \in P$ with $lbMin(\psi_{s,p}) \leq limit$. We insert all those parking locations p with $lbEA(p) \leq lbED(s) + limit$ into a set $Blue_1$. So for all $p \in Blue_1$, the lower bound $lbEA(p)$ is tight and equals the earliest arrival $EA(p)$ at p. We add the other potentially reachable parking locations p, i.e. with $lbEA(p) > lbED(s) + limit$ (and also $lbMin(\psi_{s,p}) \leq limit$ by construction), to a set Red_1. These are the ones for which the lower bound is known to be not tight. The set Red_1 may remain empty, especially if waiting at s was not allowed. An empty set Red_1 helps to speed up computation as we can omit the forward profile range query later. If both sets are empty, there is no feasible solution. $Blue_1$ and Red_1 are each the first element of a sequence of subsets of P that we will construct in the following. An illustration is shown in figure 1.

The next step is to conduct a profile bounds search from d backwards to all potentially reachable parking locations in $Blue_1 \cup Red_1$, i.e., we compute $lbMin(\psi_{p,d})$ and $ubMax(\psi_{p,d})$ for all $p \in Blue_1 \cup Red_1$ with $lbMin(\psi_{p,d}) \leq limit$. Let $Blue_2$ (resp. Red_2) be the subset of parking locations in $Blue_1$ (resp. Red_1) that are also potentially reachable backwards. Again, if $Blue_2 \cup Red_2$ is empty, there is no feasible solution. With the bounds on the driving time we get (better) bounds on the earliest arrival at d. We can set the upper bound $ubEA(d)$ to $\min\{EA(p) + break + ubMax(\psi_{p,d}) : p \in Blue_2 \wedge ubMax(\psi_{p,d}) \leq limit\}$, where the minimum over the empty set is considered to be infinite. If $lbWaiting = break$ and improving, we can update the lower bound $lbEA(d)$ to $\min\{lbEA(p) + break + lbMin(\psi_{p,d}) : p \in Blue_2 \cup Red_2\}$.

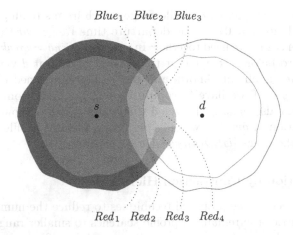

Fig. 1. The set sequences $Blue_1 \supset Blue_2 \supset Blue_3$ and $Red_1 \supset Red_2 \supset Red_3 \supset Red_4$. The two sets $Blue_1$ and Red_1 are disjoint.

A profile range search backwards from d in the range $[lbEA(d), ubEA(d)]$ to all $p \in Blue_2 \cup Red_2$ yields a partial profile $\psi_{p,d}$ for all these p. It is defined for exactly those departure times t from p for which $t + \psi_{p,d}(t) \in [lbEA(d), ubEA(d)]$ holds. For all $p \in Blue_2$ we can now determine an upper bound $ubED(p)$ on the earliest departure from p as the earliest point in time t such that $t \geq EA(p) + break$ and $\psi_{p,d}(t) \leq limit$. In case $lbWaiting = break$, this bound is tight. In the other case, we may be able to improve it by the earliest point in time t for which $t \geq EA(p)$ and $\psi_{p,d}(t) \leq limit - (EA(p) - lbED(s))$ holds. However, we might not be able to find such an upper bound because neither of the conditions are met. So let $Blue_3 \subset Blue_2$ be the set of parking locations for which $ubED(p)$ can be determined. Then, we may improve the upper bound $ubEA(d)$ on the earliest arrival at d by $\min\{ubED(p) + \psi_{p,d}(ubED(p)) : p \in Blue_3\}$.

On the other hand, we calculate a lower bound $lbED(p)$ on the earliest departure from p for all $p \in Red_2$ as the earliest point in time t with $t \geq lbEA(p) + break$ and $\psi_{p,d}(t) \leq limit$. If $lbWaiting = 0$, we may have to lower this bound to the earliest point in time t with $t \geq lbEA(p)$ and $\psi_{p,d}(t) \leq limit - lbMin(\psi_{s,p})$. And, again, let $Red_3 \subset Red_2$ be the set of parking locations for which $lbED(p)$ can be determined.

Let $Red_4 \subset Red_3$ be the set of parking locations p for which $lbED(p) + \psi_{p,d}(lbED(p)) < ubEA(d)$ holds. So Red_4 contains those parking locations for which a forward profile range search is inevitable. If this set is empty and $lbWaiting = break$, then $ubEA(d)$ is tight, so we are done. If not, we need to compute an upper bound $ubED(p)$ on the departure time from p for all $p \in Red_4$ (and $p \in Blue_2$ if $lbWaiting = 0$): It is the point in time t with $t + \psi_{p,d}(t) = ubEA(d)$. With the upper bound for all p, we can obtain an upper bound $ubED(s)$ on the departure from s: It is $\max\{ubED(p) - lbWaiting - lbMin(\psi_{s,p})\}$ over all $p \in Red_4$ (and $p \in Blue_2$ if $lbWaiting = 0$).

Finally, we conduct a forward profile range search from s to all $p \in Red_4$ (and $p \in Blue_2$ if $lbWaiting = 0$) for the departure time range $[lbED(s), ubED(s)]$. Now we have everything we need together: In case $lbWaiting = break$, we compute opt_{break} similar to before, except that the earliest arrival at d via the parking locations in $Blue_3$ is already known and has to be determined only for Red_4. In case $lbWaiting = 0$, we have to compute opt_{short} in addition, but only for $Blue_2 \cup Red_4$, and also opt_{none} (provided that waiting at s is allowed). To speed up the computation of opt_{none}, we only perform a forward profile range search from s to d for the range $[lbED(s), ubEA(d) - lbMin(\psi_{s,d})]$.

3.2 Acceleration by Contraction Hierarchies

In the previous section, we proposed techniques to reduce the number of profile searches and restrict the remaining profile searches to smaller ranges. We accelerate our approach even further by speeding up the profile searches (and EA queries) themselves using *time-dependent contraction hierarchies* [3]. (T)CHs were originally proposed for point-to-point queries, whereas we also need to compute a variant of one-to-many queries (from a source vertex to all parking lots). In this section we recap the (time-dependent) contraction hierarchies algorithm and describe our modifications of it.

A contraction hierarchy (CH) [20] is built by *contracting* the vertices of a graph in increasing order of importance. Intuitively, vertices that lie on many shortest paths (such as vertices on highways) are considered important. To contract a vertex v, it is (temporarily) removed from the graph, and *shortcuts* are added between its neighbors in order to preserve distances in the remaining graph. *Witness searches* are performed to determine whether a shortcut is necessary or can be discarded. For each pair of neighbors u, w with $(u, v) \in E, (v, w) \in E$, we run a Dijkstra search from u to w. Only if the path via v is the *unique* shortest u–w-path, we add the shortcut between u and w. In the time-dependent case, we need to run a profile search from u to w. A shortcut can only be omitted if it is not needed *at any point in time*.

CH queries are a modified variant of bidirectional Dijkstra, where both forward and reverse search relax only upward edges, i. e., edges going from less to more important vertices. In the time-dependent scenario, the reverse search is particularly difficult, because the time of arrival at the target is unknown. In a basic query variant, the reverse search only marks all edges in the reverse search space from d, and the forward search is allowed to additionally relax all marked arcs. More sophisticated query variants compute bounds during the reverse search that guide the forward search into the direction of d.

The obvious approach to compute EA queries or profiles from a source to all parking lots P runs $|P|$ point-to-point TCH queries. However, we can do better with the following modification. During the contraction process, we *block* all vertices representing parking lots, i. e., we disallow to contract them. After contraction, there remains a *core graph* at the top of the hierarchy, consisting of all parking lots and (shortcut) arcs between them. Queries from a source s to all parking lots now boil down to a forward search from s that relaxes no edges to less important vertices. As long as the query has not yet reached the core, it behaves like a normal forward CH search. On the core graph, it behaves like a standard Dijkstra search. We can accelerate the search using the *stall-on-demand* optimization [20] and stop it as soon as all parking lot vertices are settled, or a certain time limit is reached. Since blocking arbitrary vertices can lead to suboptimal contraction orders, we do not contract all vertices but the parking lots, but rather stop contraction as soon as the remaining graph becomes too dense.

3.3   Heuristic Acceleration

In our study, we schedule waiting times on the assumption that the time-dependent driving times are deterministic. This is not the case in real-life. So it is questionable whether a route with, for instance, scheduled short-term waiting would be acceptable in practice. This is the motivation for the *restricted waiting policy* that disallows waiting at s, short-term waiting at any parking location, and the prolongation of a break. To conform to this policy, the driver must depart immediately at time $lbED(s)$ and may take a break of exactly 45 minutes if inevitable. In this scenario, it is not necessary to query any profiles, even if d cannot be reached directly without break. Then, the *Red* sets are ignored, and instead of computing partial profiles backwards from d to $Blue_2$, we conduct multiple $lbEA$ searches forward from the parking locations in $Blue_2$, getting a better and better upper bound on the earliest arrival at d.

4   Experiments

In this section, we first describe the data and the test setup and then analyze run-time and solution quality of the described approaches. Our experiments are based on two versions of the road network of Germany with time-dependent driving time functions, see Table 1. The older network from the year 2006 has been used by several other studies related to time-dependent routing (see Section 1) and contains car driving times based on a traffic model. The very recent data from 2017 is quite different: The new data is more detailed with respect to time dependency, there are more edges with driving time functions that are not constant, and the total number of breakpoints representing the functions is larger. The driving times are based on historic data provided by TomTom which is post-processed by PTV such that it models truck driving times.

We use the database of PTV Group's Truck Parking Europe app [1]. It contains currently more than 25 000 parking lots all over Europe. Some parking lots cannot be linked to the old road network of 2006. Therefore, the number of parking locations is a bit lower than in the road network of 2017. The database does not only contain rest areas with fuel stations, restrooms, and restaurants but also parking areas without any facilities. It is not clear if or under what circumstances the choice of a parking area without facilities would be acceptable in practice. We will take this into account by also testing our algorithm with a

120   A. Kleff et al.

Table 1. Key figures of the input data used for the experiments. TD Edges denotes the relative number of edges with a time-dependent and not constant driving time function.

Road network	Vertices	Edges	TD Edges	Breakpoints	Parking set	Parking subset
Germany 2017	7.2 M	15.7 M	28.6 %	136.9 M	6 596	759
Germany 2006	5.1 M	12.6 M	3.7 %	20.9 M	6 447	731

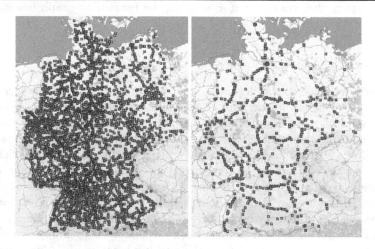

Fig. 2. The left image shows all available parking lots in Germany, the right image shows the reduced set with only big parking lots.

smaller subset of parking lots that offer 30 parking bays or more each. Figure 2 shows these two sets of parking lots.

Test Setup. We run our experiments on a VMware ESX cluster. Our machine has four cores of a 2.2 GHz Intel Xeon E5-2698 v4, 64 GB main memory, and runs Ubuntu 16.04. Besides the construction of the contraction hierarchies the algorithms use only one core. Our code is written in C++ and compiled with gcc 5.4, optimization level -O3. Our CH implementation is based on the code by Batz [3, 4] and has been extended as described in Section 3. We set the size of the CH cores to 0.2 % of the vertices in case of the whole parking set and 0.02% in case of the subset. This results in a CH search graph size of 38.90 GB in the former and 37.28 GB in the latter case (and 2.03 GB in the case of the 2006 road network).

Since our test data is the road network of Germany, we consider the EU regulation, i.e., *break*=45 min and *limit*=4.5 h. We generate 10 000 truck driver route queries for both versions of the road network. To this end, we randomly select vertices s and d and (a lower bound on) the earliest departure from s between 6 am and 9 am. Since the run-time of these queries can differ a lot, we assign each of them to one of five categories: Category C1 comprises the queries for which the *lbEA* query suffices, i.e., $lbEA(d) \leq lbED(s) + limit$. Category

Table 2. Number of truck driver route queries per category.

	C1	C2	C3	C4	C5	Over all
Query set 2017	4278	210	4943	165	404	10000
Query subset 2017	877	36	980	31	76	2000
Query set 2006	7109	126	2754	1	10	10000

Table 3. Mean run-time per category in seconds for different scenarios.

Scenario	C1	C2	C3	C4	C5	Over all
Default scenario	0.0038	18.1756	5.9549	121.9516	0.0053	5.3392
Restricted waiting	0.0033	0.2925	0.2187	0.1163	0.0910	0.1212
Parking subset	0.0041	5.8109	1.0646	7.8424	0.0057	0.7796
Naive approach	2.8018	287.1991	227.5335	228.4150	195.4254	128.8562
Query subset 2017	0.0039	18.5811	5.8160	121.5858	0.0056	5.0708
Germany 2006	0.0013	0.9829	0.3932	23.8170	0.0021	0.1239

C2 contains the ones with $lbEA(d) > lbED(s) + limit$ and $lbMin(\psi_{s,d}) \leq limit$, category C3 the ones with $lbMin(\psi_{s,d}) > limit$ and $ubMax(\psi_{s,d}) \leq 2 \cdot limit$, and category C4 the ones with $ubMax(\psi_{s,d}) > 2 \cdot limit$ and $lbMin(\psi_{s,d}) \leq 2 \cdot limit$. Finally, category C5 holds the instances with $lbMin(\psi_{s,d}) > 2 \cdot limit$ that cannot be solved.

Table 2 lists how these queries are distributed among the five categories. In case of the *query set 2006*, there are far more queries in C1 because with car driving times the vehicle's range is larger. Also in this list is the *query subset 2017*. We need this smaller subset of queries to measure the run-time of the long running naive approach.

Results on Run-Time. Table 3 shows the mean run-time for different scenarios, broken down into the five categories. The categories themselves are not part of the input of the algorithm. For the *default scenario*, we use the 2017 road graph, all described acceleration techniques, all parking locations, and allow waiting of any duration. The other scenarios deviate from this in one aspect each. In the default scenario, the run-time varies a lot with the category. A query from category C4 takes more than 30 000 times longer than one from C1. Since there are far more queries in C1 than in C4, the mean run-time over all 10 000 queries is still less than 6 seconds. Queries from C4 take so long because in 106 cases no upper bound on the earliest arrival at d can be determined, so a full backward profile search is necessary. Figure 3 illustrates the run-time distribution among the 10 000 queries.

In case of the *restricted waiting* policy, waiting at s is not allowed and waiting at any parking location is only allowed if the waiting time equals exactly the time for a break. This speeds the calculation up by a factor of 40 over all queries. In the *parking subset* scenario, we allow waiting only at larger parking lots. We

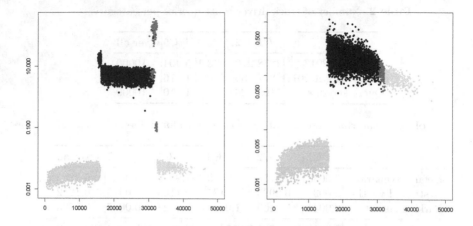

Fig. 3. Run-time of each s-d-query in the default scenario (left) and according to restricted waiting policy (right), $lbMin(\psi_{s,d})$ on abscissa and run-time in seconds on ordinate (on a logarithmic scale). Points are colored by category. Scales differ.

run the algorithm on the Germany 2017 network but the search graphs differ. Compared to the default setting, the smaller size of the core graph leads to faster one-to-many profile range queries (approx. by a factor of 7.5) but slower one-to-one profile range queries (approx. by a factor of 1.2). In both of these scenarios, not all queries can be solved. Solution quality is discussed later.

The *naive approach* does not make use of the acceleration based on partial profiles as described in Section 3.1 but still CH as in Section 3.2. Because of the long run-time of the naive approach, the run-times are based on the reduced query subset 2017 (see Table 2). For better comparability, we also give the run-times of the default scenario for the reduced query subset. An achieved speed-up of 25 over all queries proves the effectiveness of our described acceleration in general. The main aspect of it is the computation of only partial profiles that concerns category C3 primarily. Here, we even achieve a speed-up of almost 40.

In case of the *Germany 2006*, we run the accelerated approach on the 2006 road graph that was used in the original TCH publication [3]. The run-time is smaller by an order of magnitude compared to our recent data.

Some more numbers are of interest. A crucial issue of our bounds-based acceleration is to find a (good) upper bound $ubEA(d)$. In the default scenario, there are 113 cases in which such a bound cannot be determined and so a complete profile needs to be searched for backwards. A complete profile search backwards takes 138.7 s on average. In contrast, a profile range search is performed in 5168 cases and takes 5.8 s on average. The mean length of these ranges, i.e. $ubEA(d) - lbEA(d)$, is 604 s. A second important aspect of the acceleration is to avoid the profile (range) search forward if the set Red_4 is empty. This set contains elements only in 50 cases and then only a few, most often just one. Figure 4 shows a sample query with empty set Red_4.

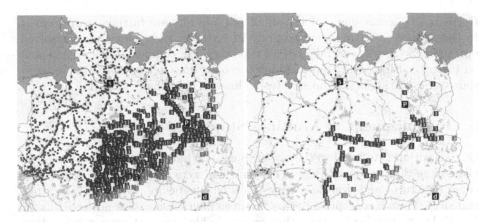

Fig. 4. Sample query from Hamburg to Dresden in the default scenario (left) and in the parking subset scenario (right). Different parking lots (P) are selected. The largest squares represent the sets $Blue_3$ and Red_3.

Results on Quality. Table 4 compares the solution quality of the default scenario to the *restricted waiting* and the *parking subset* scenario. The results of the *naive approach* are identical to the default, and the results of *Germany 2006* are hardly comparable, particularly since the driving times in this setting are based on a car model.

In the default setting, 9558 of 10 000 queries can be solved. We observe that the travel time, i.e., the driving time plus all waiting time (at s and at parking), exceeds 15 hours in some cases, presumably to exploit the short driving times during the night. Such a solution is feasible according to our problem statement but most likely it would neither be acceptable in practice nor legal as truck drivers have to take a sleep rest daily. In the following, we call a solved query legal if the travel time does not exceed 15 hours. In case of the restricted waiting policy, a solved query is always legal.

We also state how many queries are solved (legally and) optimally, i.e., how often is the calculated earliest arrival at d identical to the default scenario. In the parking subset scenario, this happens in 58% of the cases, even though there are less than 12% of the parking lots in the subset. Parking lots with more than 30 parking bays are most often located right next to a freeway (Autobahn in

Table 4. Comparison of solution quality for different scenarios. Mean and maximum deviation is in seconds over all queries that are legal but not optimal.

Scenario	solved	legal	optimal & legal	mean dev	max dev
Default scenario	9558	9512	9512	0	0
Restricted waiting	9474	9474	9453	1211	2265
Parking subset	9518	9470	5518	127	17559

Germany), whereas many of the small parking lots are further away from it. In the restricted waiting scenario, only 21 of the solved queries are not solved optimally. So in the vast majority of the cases, the computational effort spent on taking waiting of any duration into account does not pay off. For instance, short-term waiting is scheduled only 11 times in the default scenario.

5   Enhancement to Multiple Stops

Our algorithm is tailored to the one-stop case. What are the implications if we allow more than one stop? For instance, if there were two drivers on board, they could take turns and stop three times for a change before they must take a rest and sleep. From a conceptual perspective, the multi-stop case is not too difficult. Let P_s be the parking locations that are reachable from s at some point in time without taking a break along the path, and let P_d be the parking locations that are potentially reachable backwards from d, i.e., $lbMin(\psi_{p_d,d}) \leq limit$ for all $p_d \in P_d$. Moreover, suppose we had precomputed a $|P| \times |P|$ matrix M of travel time profiles such that for two parking locations p_s and p_d, $M[p_s, p_d]$ maps the departure time from p_s (where the driver is expected to have taken a break) to the shortest travel time to p_d, including as many breaks as needed and also one at p_d (unless $p_s = p_d$). With this, a truck driver route query boils down to three steps: First, we compute the earliest arrival at every $p_s \in P_s$. Then, we determine the earliest departure from every $p_d \in P_d$ with the help of M as follows:

$$ED(p_d) = \min_{p_s \in P_s} EA(p_s) + break + M[p_s, p_d](EA(p_s) + break)$$

Having done that, we can finally calculate the earliest arrival at d, also checking if d could be reached without any break.

We could easily adapt the restricted waiting policy heuristic to this general case. It is short-term waiting that makes the computation of the earliest arrival at every $p_s \in P_s$ challenging. In order to do so, we could propagate a time-dependent function forward (here: mapping an arrival time to the minimum accumulated driving time). But as we have seen, propagating a time-dependent function is expensive. So from a practical point of view, it would be important to again find ways of narrowing down the search, like finding good bounds and only propagating partial functions as we have demonstrated before. In addition to this challenge, our assumption that we have a matrix M in memory is not realistic. Due to the superpolynomial complexity of the travel time profiles, we would most likely need hundreds of GB of main memory for the parking lots in Germany. So the question is raised what a good trade-off would be between memory consumption and computational effort (and solution quality).

6   Conclusion and Outlook

We have introduced the truck driver routing problem and described an exact algorithm for it. While a naive approach would be far too costly in time and space, it can be made feasible using our two proposed acceleration methods. One is a modification of TCH. Additionally narrowing down TCH searches by several fast bounds computations and queries of only partial profiles results in an extra speed-up of 25 and practical run-times. We have also suggested a heuristic based on the policy of restricted waiting and analyzed its effect. In this setting, truck driver route queries take well below one second without losing too much solution quality. Similarly effective is the restriction of the parking set to the more relevant parking locations.

In this paper, we have left out our experiments with approximated driving time functions. Using the algorithm of Imai and Iri [23] to approximate the functions of both original and shortcut edges further reduces the run-time, especially of profile (range) queries. In doing so, we only sacrifice a precision that is not justified in practice. Future work includes a solution to the combined truck driver routing and scheduling problem for a given sequence of customers by using the results of this paper as a building block. Moreover, it would be interesting to reevaluate the existing work on algorithms for time-dependent route planning on the new benchmark instance. We conjecture that other shortcut-based methods such as TD-CRP [6] also suffer significantly from the new instance. It could be promising to further investigate shortcut-free approaches like the ALT algorithm [10].

Our algorithm will also be evaluated in the EU research projects AEOLIX and Clusters 2.0.

References

1. Truck Parking Europe, https://truckparkingeurope.com/
2. Bast, H., Delling, D., Goldberg, A.V., Müller–Hannemann, M., Pajor, T., Sanders, P., Wagner, D., Werneck, R.F.: Route Planning in Transportation Networks. LNCS, vol. 9220, pp. 19–80. Springer (2016)
3. Batz, G.V., Geisberger, R., Sanders, P., Vetter, C.: Minimum Time-Dependent Travel Times with Contraction Hierarchies. ACM J. Exp. Algorithmics 18, 1.4:1–1.4:43 (2013)
4. Batz, G.V.: KaTCH, https://github.com/GVeitBatz/KaTCH/
5. Baum, M., Dibbelt, J., Gemsa, A., Wagner, D., Zündorf, T.: Shortest Feasible Paths with Charging Stops for Battery Electric Vehicles. ACM SIGSPATIAL'15, pp. 44:1–44:10. ACM (2015)
6. Baum, M., Dibbelt, J., Pajor, T., Wagner, D.: Dynamic Time-Dependent Route Planning in Road Networks with User Preferences. SEA'16, LNCS, vol. 9685, pp. 33–49. Springer (2016)
7. Cooke, K.L., Halsey, E.: The Shortest Route Through a Network with Time-Dependent Internodal Transit Times. J. Math. Anal. Appl. 14(3), 493–498 (1966)
8. Dean, B.C.: Algorithms for Minimum-Cost Paths in Time-Dependent Networks with Waiting Policies. Networks 44(1), 41–46 (2004)
9. Delling, D.: Time-Dependent SHARC-Routing. Algorithmica 60(1), 60–94 (2011)
10. Delling, D., Nannicini, G.: Core Routing on Dynamic Time-Dependent Road Networks. Informs J. Comput. 24(2), 187–201 (2012)
11. Delling, D., Wagner, D.: Time-Dependent Route Planning, LNCS, vol. 5868, pp. 207–230. Springer (2009)

12. Dijkstra, E.W.: A Note on Two Problems in Connexion with Graphs. Numer. Math. 1(1), 269–271 (1959)
13. Drexl, M., Prescott-Gagnon, E.: Labelling Algorithms for the Elementary Shortest Path Problem with Resource Constraints Considering EU Drivers' Rules. Logistics Research 2(2), 79–96 (2010)
14. Dreyfus, S.E.: An Appraisal of Some Shortest-Path Algorithms. Oper. Res. 17(3), 395–412 (1969)
15. European Parliament, Council of the European Union: Regulation (EC) No. 561/2006 of the European Parliament and of the Council of 15 March 2006 on the harmonisation of certain social legislation relating to road transport and amending Council Regulations (EEC) No. 3821/85 and (EC) No. 2135/98 and repealing Council Regulation (EEC) No. 3820/85. OJ L 102(1), 1–13 (2006)
16. Federal Motor Carrier Safety Administration: Hours of Service of Drivers. Fed. Reg. 76(248), 81133–81188 (2011)
17. Foschini, L., Hershberger, J., Suri, S.: On the Complexity of Time-Dependent Shortest Paths. Algorithmica 68(4), 1075–1097 (2014)
18. Franceschetti, A., Honhon, D., Van Woensel, T., Bektaş, T., Laporte, G.: The Time-Dependent Pollution-Routing Problem. Transportation Res. B - Meth. 56, 265–293 (2013)
19. Geisberger, R., Sanders, P.: Engineering Time-Dependent Many-to-Many Shortest Paths Computation. ATMOS'10, OASIcs, vol. 14, pp. 74–87 (2010)
20. Geisberger, R., Sanders, P., Schultes, D., Vetter, C.: Exact Routing in Large Road Networks Using Contraction Hierarchies. Transport. Sci. 46(3), 388–404 (2012)
21. Goel, A.: Truck Driver Scheduling in the European Union. Transport. Sci. 44(4), 429–441 (2010)
22. Goel, A.: Hours of Service Regulations in the United States and the 2013 Rule Change. Transp. Policy 33, 48–55 (2014)
23. Imai, H., Iri, M.: An Optimal Algorithm for Approximating a Piecewise Linear Function. Journal of Information Processing 9(3), 159–162 (1987)
24. Koç, C., Bektaş, T., Jabali, O., Laporte, G.: A Comparison of Three Idling Options in Long-Haul Truck Scheduling. Transportation Res. B - Meth. 93, Part A, 631 – 647 (2016)
25. Koç, Ç., Jabali, O., Laporte, G.: Long-Haul Vehicle Routing and Scheduling with Idling Options. J. Oper. Res. Soc. (forthcoming)
26. Kok, A., Hans, E., Schutten, J.: Optimizing Departure Times in Vehicle Routes. Eur. J. Oper. Res. 210(3), 579 – 587 (2011)
27. Shah, V.D.: Time Dependent Truck Routing and Driver Scheduling Problem with Hours of Service Regulations. Master's thesis, Northeastern University (2008)
28. Sherali, H.D., Ozbay, K., Subramanian, S.: The Time-Dependent Shortest Pair of Disjoint Paths Problem: Complexity, Models, and Algorithms. Networks 31(4), 259–272 (1998)
29. Smith, O.J., Boland, N., Waterer, H.: Solving Shortest Path Problems with a Weight Constraint and Replenishment Arcs. Comput. Oper. Res. 39(5), 964–984 (2012)
30. Strasser, B.: Intriguingly Simple and Efficient Time-Dependent Routing in Road Networks. CoRR abs/1606.06636 (2016)

A Combinatorial Auction for Transportation Matching Service: Formulation and Adaptive Large Neighborhood Search Heuristic

Baoxiang Li and Hoong Chuin Lau

Fujitsu-SMU Urban Computing and Engineering Corporate Lab, Singapore
Management University, 71 Stamford Road, 178895, Singapore
{bxli,hclau}@smu.edu.sg

Abstract. This paper considers the problem of matching multiple shippers and multi-transporters for pickups and drop-offs, where the goal is to select a subset of group jobs (shipper bids) that maximizes profit. This is the underlying winner determination problem in an online auction-based vehicle sharing platform that matches transportation demand and supply, particularly in a B2B last-mile setting. Each shipper bid contains multiple jobs, and each job has a weight, volume, pickup location, delivery location and time window. On the other hand, each transporter bid specifies the vehicle capacity, available time periods, and a cost structure. This double-sided auction will be cleared by the platform to find a profit-maximizing match and corresponding routes while respecting shipper and transporter constraints. Compared to the classical pickup-and-delivery problem, a key challenge is the dependency among jobs, more precisely, all jobs within a shipper bid must either be accepted or rejected together and jobs within a bid may be assigned to different transporters. We formulate the mathematical model and propose an Adaptive Large Neighborhood Search approach to solve the problem heuristically. We also derive management insights obtained from our computational experiments.

Keywords: Pickup-and-Delivery Problem with Jobs Dependency, Winner Determination Problem, Logistics

1 Introduction

In this paper, we study the winner determination problem (WDP) for an online auction platform for B2B less-than-truckload transport matching. In such platforms, we have multiple shippers with job bundles and multiple transporters with a heterogeneous fleet participating in an auction market, and the platform operator (auctioneer) is to perform a match of jobs with vehicles that maximizes profits at periodic (say hourly) intervals. Such platforms are rapidly emerging in a sharing economy with the rise of Uber-like business models.

The problem we present in this paper arises from a real-world implementation for a large urban logistics platform operator. It is a variant of the standard

© Springer International Publishing AG 2017
T. Bektaş et al. (Eds.), ICCL 2017, LNCS 10572, pp. 127–142, 2017.
https://doi.org/10.1007/978-3-319-68496-3_9

pickup-and-delivery problem with time windows (PDPTW), with additional dependencies among jobs and a number of side constraints between cargo, locations and vehicle types, as well as profitability as the objective function. Each shipper's delivery request may include a group of pickup-and-delivery jobs, and such grouping is called a shipper bid, which must either be accepted or rejected together. There are three reasons for the grouping of delivery jobs as a shipper bid: firstly, some jobs may be unprofitable and very difficult to find a matching transporter (due to low profit margins). But if such low-profit jobs would combine with high-profit jobs as a bundle, then the bid could be more ready to find matching transporters; secondly, some shipper companies may like to bundle delivery jobs themselves based on their own consideration (e.g., reverse logistics); thirdly, some shippers may prefer a one-stop solution rather than having to manage separate delivery requests.

In addition, arising from grouped jobs, a shipper bid may be split in terms of deliveries; that is, the different jobs in the shipper bid can be served by more than one transporter bid (assuming one transporter bid includes one vehicle in this paper). Our goal is to maximize the profit, which is calculated as total revenues associated with served bids minus the total transportation costs incurred correspondingly.

2 Literature Review

Transportation auctions are considered in the context where shippers compete with each other in order to purchase transport services at the lowest possible price from transporters aiming to sell their service at the highest possible price (see [5]). [1] first proposed a transportation auction to reduce logistics costs. Subsequently, a good number of transportation auction papers were published, which mainly considered full truckload (FTL, i.e. one bid uses all available space in a vehicle auction), e.g., [13]. However, not all pickup/delivery jobs could be formed as FTL bids, and under such case, FTL auction cannot fulfill both shipper and transporter requirements. During the last decade, practitioners started to test the more challenging settings of less-than-truckload (LTL) auction platforms. [7] for example proposed an LTL transportation auction, where auctioneers generate bundles of shipper requests and offers them to the transporters, and transporters place their bids for the offered bundles.

The research topics for transportation auctions mainly focus on two aspects: the bundle generation problem and WDP. For example, [9] formulated the bundle generation problem as a PDPTW in an iterative bid generation auction problem. On winner determination, the interesting aspect is in coping with uncertainty. [8] presented a double auction model for transportation service procurement in a spot market with stochastic demand and supply. [12] proposed a tractable two-stage robust optimization approach to solve the WDP under shipment volume uncertainty. In addition to the standard desirable properties for auctions, transport logistics auction designers must deal with the specific challenge on the economic sustainability of the auction platform. [15] for instance discussed a bi-criteria auction mechanism to achieve environmental sustainability while ensuring economic sustainability.

The above-mentioned papers focus on improving the service quality of the auction, whether from the strategic viewpoint (e.g., [5]) or operational viewpoint (e.g., [9]). From the computational perspective, [6] addressed the concerns of transporters bidding on an exponentially large set of bundles, and solving the corresponding exponentially large WDP. In this paper, we focus on a computationally efficient solution for an online auction platform for LTL matching. Unlike past research, we allow multiple vehicles to serve one bundle (consisting of multiple jobs) and each vehicle may serve jobs from different bundles (i.e. many-to-many matching). Moreover, to avoid too many rounds of bidding (e.g., [10]), we propose a simple single-shot auction where each shipper submits the bundles, each transporter submits the truck availability and cost structure; and the auctioneer will decide the winning shippers and transporters.

3   Mathematical model

The G-PDPTW integrates the pickup and delivery problem (PDP) and the group bundle constraints, aims to select a subset of bundled shipper jobs (bids) and design service itineraries, and maximize the profit obtained from shipper revenue minus transporter cost, at same time respecting shipper and transporter constraints. We formulate the problem as a mixed-integer programming (MIP) model in this section. First, we present notations used throughout the paper as shown in Table 1. Jobs within a bid are defined by a set of nodes.

G-PDPTW can be defined on a complete undirected graph $\mathcal{G} = (V, E)$ where $V = V^p \cup V^d \cup \{0\} \cup \{2n + 1\}$. Subsets V^p and V^d correspond to pickup and delivery nodes, respectively, while nodes 0 and $2n + 1$ represent the dummy depots (distance to other nodes, service time, and weight/volume are all equal to 0). While in the real-life auction platform there is no tracking for each vehicle's/carrier's origin, and each vehicle/carrier needs to start serving the shipper jobs within the jobs time window. For ease of reference, we arrange all nodes in V in such a way that all origins precede all destinations, and the destination of each job can be obtained as its origin offset by a fixed constant n.

Let K be the set of transporter vehicles. Each vehicle $k \in K$ has a weight capacity Q_k and volume capacity H_k. The hourly cost of vehicle k is p_k. Let O be the set of shipper bids. The revenue (i.e. bid price) for delivering a shipper bid o is represented by r_o, while z_o is a binary decision variable indicating whether shipper bid o is served or not. Each shipper bid includes one or more jobs, each job is defined by two nodes (a pickup node and a delivery node). A time window $[e_i, l_i]$ is associated with node $i \in V$, where e_i and l_i represent the earliest and latest arrival time, respectively. Each edge $(i, j) \in E$ has a travel time t_{ij}. In addition, let λ_i be the loading/unloading time, w_i be the weight, and c_i be the volume of node i (for a given pickup and delivery pair, $w_i = -w_{i+n}$, and $c_i = -c_{i+n}$).

For each arc $(i, j) \in A$ and each vehicle $k \in K$, $x_{ij}^k = 1$ if vehicle k travels from node i directly to node j. For each node $i \in V$ and each vehicle $k \in K$, let τ_i^k be the time for which vehicle k begins to serve node i, and W_i^k / C_i^k be the weight/volume load of vehicle k after visiting node i. The integer variable y_k indicates the hours traveled by vehicle k.

Table 1: Parameters and variables for the G-PDPTW model

n	Number of jobs, one job includes two nodes (one origin and one destination)
K	Set of vehicles, $K = \{1, 2, \ldots, |K|\}$, and $k \in K$
V^p	Set of origins $V^p = \{1, 2, \ldots, n\}$
V^d	Set of destinations $V^d = \{n + 1, n + 2, \ldots, 2n\}$
V	Set of nodes $V = V^p \cup V^d \cup \{0\} \cup \{2n + 1\}$
	$\{0\}$ and $\{2n+1\}$ represent the vehicle dummy origin and destination points, and $i \in V$
O	Set of bids (each bid includes a group of jobs), $O = \{1, 2, \ldots, |O|\}$, and $o \in O$
$|O_o|$	Number of jobs inside bid o
r_o	Revenue obtained from serving bid o
w_i	Weight of node i
c_i	Volume of node i
$[e_i, l_i]$	Time window for node i
λ_i	Service time at node i
t_{ij}	Travel time between nodes i and j
Q_k	Weight capacity of vehicle k
H_k	Volume capacity of vehicle k
$[\iota_k, \hbar_k]$	Time window associated with dummy depot for vehicle k
p_k	Hourly cost of vehicle k
x_{ij}^k	Binary decision variables indicating if vehicle k goes directly from node i to node j, it is equal to 0 if vehicle k does not travel from node i to node j direct
y_k	Integer variables indicating the number of hours traveled by vehicle k
z_o	Binary decision variables indicating if bid o is served; it is 0 if bid o is not served
τ_i^k	Time point when vehicle k leaves node i
W_i^k	Weight load of vehicle k after visiting node i
C_i^k	Volume load of vehicle k after visiting node i

Given these notations, the formulation of the G-PDPTW is as follows:

$$\max \sum_{o \in O} r_o z_o - \sum_{k \in K} p_k y_k \tag{1}$$

Subject to:

$$\sum_{i \in O_o} \sum_{j \in V} \sum_{k \in K} x_{ij}^k = |O_o| z_o, \quad \forall o \in O \tag{2}$$

$$\sum_{j \in V} \sum_{k \in K} x_{ij}^k \leq 1, \quad \forall i \in V^P \tag{3}$$

$$\sum_{i \in V} x_{0,i}^k = \sum_{i \in V} x_{i,2n+1}^k = 1, \quad \forall k \in K \tag{4}$$

$$\sum_{i \in V} x_{i,0}^k = \sum_{i \in V} x_{2n+1,i}^k = 0, \quad \forall k \in K \tag{5}$$

$$\sum_{j \in V} x_{ij}^k = \sum_{j \in V} x_{ji}^k, \quad \forall i \in V^p \cup V^d, \ k \in K \tag{6}$$

$$\sum_{i \in V} x_{i,j+n}^k = \sum_{i \in V} x_{ij}^k, \quad \forall j \in V^P, \ k \in K \tag{7}$$

$$\tau_j^k + t_{j,j+n} + \lambda_j \leq \tau_{j+n}^k, \quad \forall\, j \in V^P,\, k \in K \tag{8}$$

$$(\tau_i^k + t_{ij} + \lambda_i)x_{ij}^k \leq \tau_j^k, \quad \forall\, i,\, j \in V,\, k \in K \tag{9}$$

$$(W_i^k + w_j)x_{ij}^k \leq W_j^k, \quad \forall\, i,\, j \in V,\, k \in K \tag{10}$$

$$(C_i^k + c_j)x_{ij}^k \leq C_j^k, \quad \forall\, i,\, j \in V,\, k \in K \tag{11}$$

$$e_i \leq \tau_i^k \leq l_i, \quad \forall\, i \in V^P \cup V^d,\, k \in K \tag{12}$$

$$0 \leq W_i^k \leq Q_k, \quad \forall\, i \in V^P \cup V^d,\, k \in K \tag{13}$$

$$0 \leq C_i^k \leq H_k, \quad \forall\, i \in V^P \cup V^d,\, k \in K \tag{14}$$

$$\tau_0^k \geq \iota_k, \quad \forall\, k \in K \tag{15}$$

$$\tau_{2n+1}^k \leq \hbar_k, \quad \forall\, k \in K \tag{16}$$

$$(\tau_{2n+1}^k - \tau_0^k)/60 \leq y_k, \quad \forall\, k \in K \tag{17}$$

$$x_{ij}^k, \tau_i^k, W_i^k \in \mathbb{R}_+, \quad \forall\, i,\, j \in V,\, k \in K \tag{18}$$

$$z_o \in \{0,1\}, \quad \forall\, o \in O \tag{19}$$

$$y_k, \in \mathbb{Z}_+ \quad \forall\, k \in K \tag{20}$$

The objective function (1) maximizes the total profit that corresponds to the revenue obtained from bids minus the transporter costs. The cost is calculated based on travel time (with hourly unit) and is calculated as the difference between the departure time and return time at the dummy depot. The objective function is set for the auction platform operator, and the profit will be rebated to the platform owner, shipper and transporter after delivery based on various performance indicators.

Constraints (2) show that the nodes belong to the same bid o is considered to be a bundle, i.e., they must be served or reject together. Constraints (3) indicate that every node can be served at most once by one vehicle. Constraints (4) and (5) are imposed to fix the origin and destination points (which are dummy nodes, with distance to all nodes equal to 0) of vehicles. Note that an empty route will be represented by a path with 2 stops, which starts at 0 and ends at (2n+1). Every node except the origin and the destination of a vehicle must have same number of preceding and one succeeding node, which is defined in Constraints (6). Constraints (7) and (8) ensure that the job origin is visited before the destination. Constraints (9), (10) and (11) compute the travel times and loads of vehicles (both weight and volume dimension). The shipper node time window constraints are defined in (12). Constraints (13) and (14) represent the vehicle capacity constraint in both weight and volume dimension. The time window associated with dummy depot for each vehicle is defined in Constraints (15) and (16). Moreover, Constraints (17) define the vehicle travel time in hours (translate from minutes based to hourly based). Finally, Constraints (19)-(20) specify the domains of the variables.

4   ALNS Approach

4.1   The ALNS Framework

Our heuristic is based on the ALNS described in [4,14] with simulated annealing as the local search framework, and the pseudo-code is presented in Algorithm 1. In the algorithm, each iteration includes two subroutines: job selection and perturbation. In particular, the request in the ALNS are treated independently and not as a bundle in most of the job selection and perturbation operators.

Algorithm 1: Adaptive Large Neighborhood Search

Input: Initial solution s, solution $s_{best} := s$, initial probabilities associated with the operators

1 **while** *stopping criteria not reached* **do**
2 $\quad$ $s' := s$
3 $\quad$ Apply operator P1 for pre-process of neighborhood search
4 $\quad$ Apply selection operator (R1-R3) to select jobs for removal
5 $\quad$ Apply perturbation operator (I1-I5) to remove selected jobs from s' and reinsert as many unserved jobs as we can into s'
6 $\quad$ **if** $f(s') > f(s_{best})$ **then**
7 $\quad\quad$ $s := s'$, $s_{best} := s'$
8 $\quad$ **else**
9 $\quad\quad$ **if** $f(s') > f(s)$ **then**
10 $\quad\quad\quad$ $s := s'$
11 $\quad\quad$ **else**
12 $\quad\quad\quad$ $s := s'$ with probability $p(s', s)$ defined in Equation (21)

13 **end while**
14 Remove the bids that are partly served in s_{best}

Output: s_{best};

Let s be the current solution, s' be the new solution, and $f(s)$, $f(s')$ – the corresponding objective values. If $f(s')$ is worse than $f(s)$, we accept the solution s with probability $p(s', s)$:

$$p(s', s) = \min\{1, e^{(f(s') - f(s))/\overline{T}}\}, \tag{21}$$

where $\overline{T} \geq 0$ is the "temperature" that starts at $\overline{T_0}$ and decreases every iteration using the expression $\overline{T} := 0.9999 \cdot \overline{T}$, $\overline{T_0}$ is defined in such a way that objective value of the first iteration is accepted with a probability 0.5. The simulated annealing structure is the same as in [4]. The search continues until the stopping criteria is met (20000 iterations or no improvement for the last 2000 iterations).

4.2 Solution Evaluation

Two solution evaluation approaches are used for the ALNS:
(1) $ALNS_F$: only feasible solutions are allowed during the search;
(2) $ALNS_I$: infeasible solutions are considered and a penalty of the violated constraints is added to the objective.

Let $c(s)$ be the routing profit, The solution is evaluated by $c(s)$ plus the penalty of timw window violation $\bar{t}(s)$ and load violation $\bar{q}(s)$:

$$f(s) = c(s) + \alpha_t \bar{t}(s) + \alpha_q \bar{q}(s) \tag{22}$$

For the $ALNS_F$, $f(s) = c(s)$ holds, because all constraints must be satisfied and $\bar{t}(s)$ and $\bar{q}(s)$ are equal to zero.

At the end of each iteration, the values of the parameters α_t, and α_q are modified by a factor $1 + \delta$, with $0 < \delta \leq 1$. If the current solution is feasible with respect to load constraints, the value of α_q is divided by $1 + \delta$. Otherwise, it is multiplied by $1 + \delta$.

To compute the profit of each route, we need to compute the revenue minus the cost of the route. However, since a shipper bid may be assigned to multiple vehicles, it is impossible to precisely calculate the revenue of a single route during search. As a heuristic, we break the bundles and split the price of a bid to the jobs according to their weights/volumes. For the route cost, which is a function of the route duration in hours, we first set the vehicle k to depart from the depot at ι_k, and compute the total waiting time $\overline{W}$ along the route. If no violation of time window can be found, we postpone the departure time by adding $\overline{W}$. After that, we check the feasibility of the route, once an upper time window violation is found, the departure time is adjusted by deducting the upper time window violation value. The algorithm iterates until no time window violations can be found. Finally, we recalculate the route duration. For details we refer to Algorithm 2.

Algorithm 2: Travel time duration calculation

Input: Route $R := (0, 1, \ldots, 2n + 1)$, departure time $\tau_0 := \iota_k$, whole route
waiting time $\overline{W}$, index $m \leftarrow 1$, and postponed time
$u_0 \leftarrow \overline{W} + 1$, $u_1 \leftarrow \overline{W}$

1 **while** $u_m < u_{m-1}$ **do**
2 $\quad \tau_0 \leftarrow \iota_k + u_m$
3 $\quad$ **for each** $i \in R$ **do**
4 $\quad\quad \tau_i \leftarrow \max\left(\tau_{i-1} + \lambda_{i-1} + t_{(i-1,i)}, e_i\right)$
5 $\quad\quad$ **Until** $\tau_i > \min(l_i, \hbar_k)$, $u_{m+1} \leftarrow (u_m - \tau_i + \min(l_i, \hbar_k))$
6 $\quad m \leftarrow m + 1$
7 **end while**

Output: $\tau_{2n+1} - \tau_0$;

4.3   Initial Solution

An initial solution is constructed by a basic greedy insertion heuristic. The heuristic randomly chooses a job, and inserts it to the best position in the routes (with the highest profit added). Afterwards, the ALNS heuristic is implemented to improve the initial solution. Simulated annealing is applied during the ALNS update process.

4.4   Adaptive weight adjustment procedure

The choice of the selection and perturbation heuristics is governed by a roulette wheel mechanism. We have three selection operators and six perturbation operators. On the one hand, we diversify the search by combining different operators. On the other hand, a good balance between the quality of the solution and the running time can be reached by choosing a suitable operator at every iteration.

We define P_d^t as the probabilities of choosing operator d at iteration t. Starting from a predefined value, they are updated as $P_d^{t+1} := P_d^t(1-\rho) + \rho\chi_i/\zeta_i$, where ρ is the roulette wheel parameter, χ_i is the score of operator i, and ζ_i is the number of times it was used during the last 200 iterations. The score of an operator is updated as follows. If the current iteration finds a new best solution, the scores related to the used operators are increased by π_1; if it finds a solution better than the previous one, their scores are increased by π_2; if it finds a non-improving yet accepted solution, their scores are increased by π_3. Every 200 iterations, new weights are calculated using the scores obtained, and all scores are reset to zero.

4.5   Pre-process for neighborhood search (P1)

Once a new best solution been found and without partly served bid, we optimize the route (s_{best} and $f(s_{best})$) by sequentially removing job from the route and reinserted in the best position so as to maximize the profit.

For some instances, there always exist some bids may never be fully served during all the iterations, remain them in the selection sets seldom lead to better served solution. Therefore, from the 100 iterations of the ALNS, there is a 50% of chance for low win probability bids involved for the next iteration search, the low win probability criteria is set as below: shipper bid that has been served less than 45 times in the last 100 iterations, and transporter bid (vehicle) that serve less than 2 jobs on average in the last 100 iterations.

4.6   Jobs Selection

At each iteration, jobs are selected and added to a perturbation set C (set C initially includes the unserved jobs). Three selection operators are used, details shown as follows:

- **Random job based (R1)**: This operator randomly selects a number of jobs.

- **Random bid based (R2)**: This operator random selects a number of bids.
- **Partly served bid based (R3)**: Let U be the set of all partly served bid jobs (only part of jobs in a bid been served by vehicles), then, this operator randomly selects 50% – 70% jobs from set U.

4.7 Jobs Perturbation

After the procedure of jobs selection, five perturbation heuristics have been implemented.

- **1-by-1 (I1)**: The selected jobs are sequentially removed one by one and reinserted into the best position (the highest improvement for the current objective value).
- **Global all-at-once (I2)**: The operator repeatedly inserts jobs in the best position of all the routes. The difference with **I1** is that all jobs are removed at once, then inserted again one by one.
- **Balanced all-at-once (I3)**: All jobs are removed out from the route at once. Then, for every job, we choose a route with the lowest profit value to insert. It tends to generate a relatively balanced solution.
- **Tabu 1-by-1 (I4)**: This operator implements a diversification strategy similar to the tabu search. Suppose that job i is removed from some route k, the job is then prohibited to be reinserted into route k. The ban can only be canceled if insertion into route k leads to a better routing profit compared to the best-known routing profit of route k with i inside. For the job that has never been served before, skip the removal step and only do the insertion.
- **Local all-at-once (I5)**: Suppose, job i is removed from some route k, it tries to insert the job i into the same route k again but in a better position.

5 Computational Experiments

In this section, we first test our algorithm on benchmark instances, and then analyse the result for instances of moderate size. Our ALNS approach is implemented in Java, and executed on an Intel Xeon E5-2667v4 8C/16T (3.2GHz) 16 core CPU 32 GB RAM machine. The parameters used in the ALNS are shown in Table 2, chosen by the tuning strategy proposed by [4]. Each time only one single parameter is adjusted, while the rest are fixed. The setting with the best average behavior (in terms of average deviation from the best-known solutions) is chosen. This process iterates through all parameters once.

5.1 Performance Comparison on PDPTW Benchmark instances

To evaluate the effectiveness of the proposed ALNS approach, we first apply it to solve the PDPTW benchmark instances.[1] For detailed descriptions, we refer the reader to [3]. Due to the difference between G-PDPTW and PDPTW, essential

---

[1] See https://www.sintef.no/projectweb/top/pdptw/li-lim-benchmark.

changes must made to the ALNS and instances: 1) we assume every job stands for a bid in the benchmark instances; 2) we change the objective to minimize the travel distances and the number of used vehicles; 3) $ALNS_I$ is used, penalty is added to the objective value to ensure all the jobs must be served. The overall performance of the ALNS shows as Table 3, the results show 0.55-7.85% gap (best results of 16 runs) to the best benchmark results. Main reason is that the ALNS is tailored for G-PDPTW, and slight changes of the model may lead to quite different solution, e.g., if we only minimize the travel distance (without minimizing the number of vehicles as benchmark instance settings), we observe 149 improved solutions.

Table 2: Parameters used in the ALNS

Description	values
Number of selection jobs	5%-25%
Roulette wheel parameter, ρ	0.50
Score of a global better solution, π_1	6.00
Score of a better solution, π_2	1.00
Score of a worse solution but accept, π_3	2.00
$P_{d_R}^0$ used for selection operators	0.33
$P_{d_I}^0$ used for perturbation operators	0.17

Table 3: Results comparison against the benchmark instances in [3]

# Nodes	Gaps	Running times (minutes)
100	0.55%	1
200	0.82%	3
400	3.09%	17
600	5.86%	42
800	6.87%	79
1000	7.85%	106

5.2 Relationship between bid features and win probability

Moving from computational performance, we next present our insights that give shippers and transporters some indication of the factors that may affect their probability of winning a bid. For this purpose, we run three groups of auctions. Each group includes 1000 instances. In the first group, one vehicle can serve 22 nodes on average. While in the second group, each vehicle may visit 11 nodes on average, and the ratio reduces to 7 for the third group. Bids with different prices, time windows, sizes, weights, and volumes are generated; for more details, we refer the reader to Table 4. All the test instances can be found at https://unicen.smu.edu.sg/pickup-and-delivery-problem-time-window-g-pdptw. Moreover, for the sake of notational consistency, we use "SBid" / "TBid" to represent shipper bid and transport "bid" (which is simply the capacity, availability and cost associated with a vehicle) respectively.

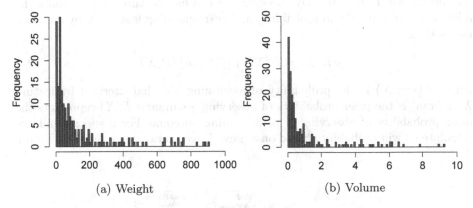

(a) Weight   (b) Volume

Fig. 1: Histogram for weight (kg) and volume (m^3)

Table 4: Design of experimental instances

Number of instances	3000, 3 groups, each group includes 1000 instances, in the first group instances, the ratio between number of nodes and vehicles equals to 22, while the ratio equals to 11 and 7 for the second and third group instances, respectively
Shipper jobs time windows	Randomly choose from 1, 2, 3 and 9 hours
SBid size (number of jobs inside a SBid)	Randomly choose from (1-6)
Base price per SBid, ζ	Randomly chosen from $15, $30, $45, $60
SBid weight&volume	Weight value randomly choose from (0-1000) kg, then, find the corresponding volume, histogram graphs show as Figure 1a and 1b
Shipper job service time	15 minutes
Number of vehicles	Randomly choose a number from (2-21)
Vehicles capacity	2500 kg, 7 m^3
Vehicles available time period	9:00-18:00
Vehicles unit cost	Randomly choose from $10, $20, $30, $40 per hour

Additionally, we calculate the bid price using equation (23), which is mainly based on the number of jobs, and adjusted according to the weight/volume of the cargo. Let ζ and α be the per job price and number of jobs within a shipper bid, respectively. β, χ, and δ denote the number of small size (with cargo lighter than 10 kg), medium size (with cargo lighter than 100 kg but heavier than 10 kg), and large size (with cargo heavier than 100 kg) jobs inside a bid. In addition, the total weights of medium and large size cargo are represented as ϕ and φ.

$$price = \zeta\alpha - 1.71\beta - 4\chi + 4.7\delta + 0.09\phi + 0.007\varphi \qquad (23)$$

Considering that running 3000 instances is time-consuming, we only apply the ALNS once with 5000 iterations for each instance, and $ALNS_F$ is applied. We analyze the effect of the shipper bid size (the number of jobs inside a bid), shipper bid unit price, shipper job time window, and transporter bid unit (hourly) cost on the win probability. By checking the win bids features, we calculate the relationship of the bid win probability and corresponding feature X by applying Bayes theorem:

$$P(win|X) = P(X|win)P(win)/P(X) \qquad (24)$$

where $P(win|X)$ is the probability of a winning bid characterized by feature X, $P(win)$ is the prior probability of observing a win, and $P(X)$ represents the prior probability of observing X as a winning outcome. For a specific bid, we calculate its win probability based on a naive Bayes network, as shown in Figure 2.

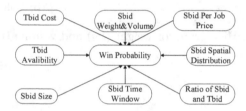

Fig. 2: Naive Bayes network

One can observe from Figure 3 that the SBid median win probability ranges from 25% to 87%, depends on the total number of SBid involved in an auction, the lower the ratio, the higher the win probability. On the contrary, the TBid median win probability varies from 56% to 100%, the higher the ratio, the higher the win probability.

In Figure 4a, we check the SBid win probability versus bid size, it addresses that the SBid include 1 or 2 jobs tend to win regardless other factors (e.g., price, time window, cost). However, if the ratio between SBid and TBid is high, the win probability is always low due to high demand and low supply. Assuming that the number of shipper bids is fixed, an unassigned SBid may win with an increasing the number of transporter bids.

Figure 4b shows the SBid win probability against the per job price of SBid (named "SBid Unit Price"), it indicates that the SBid win probability is not sensitive to per job price. Take "Nodes/Vehicles = 11" as an example, even if the price increases from 15 to 60, the SBid win probability only increases from 50% to 59%. The reason is that the SBid win probability is a determining by multiple factors, and the price is not a main factor. However, in real-life context, high bid price may attract more TBid to involve in the platform, subsequently, the SBid win probability will improve.

Figure 4c depicts the shipper job win probability against the time window. Suppose that the shipper submit a job with one hour time window for "Nodes/Vehicles = 7" group, the result is not so promising. However, if the time window width increases to 9 hours, the shipper bid win probability increases from 30% to around 40%. Moreover, the win probability of groups that "Nodes/Vehicles = 11" and "Nodes/Vehicles = 22" seems not affected by the time window. The reason is that different shipper jobs with different time windows are randomly bundled together, so the win probability not only depends on single job time window, but also relies on the groups time window. For instance, if the time window of all jobs in a given bid are 3 hours, then, the results are totally different from the situation that the half jobs time window equal to 1 hour and another half jobs time window equal to 5 hours.

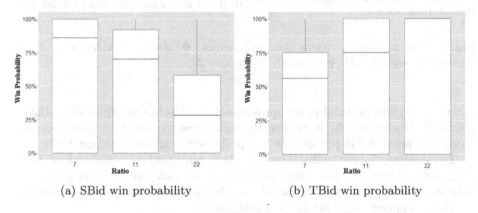

(a) SBid win probability   (b) TBid win probability

Fig. 3: Overall win probability

From Figure 4d, one can see the vehicles win probability seems not affected by unit cost under the case of "Nodes/Vehicles = 22". However, with the increasing of the vehicles number, the cheap vehicles (with low unit cost) have higher win probability compare to expensive vehicles (with high per unit cost). At the same time, even if the vehicles number is much lower than the shipper jobs number, the vehicle win probability does not reach to 100%, an explanation is that some vehicles cost is too high comparing to the shipper bid price, it is better to fail those bids as unprofitable to serve them.

As the objective function is based on profit, we cannot use the win probability as criteria to evaluate the performance the algorithm. However, the win probability can be used to provide suggestions for both shippers and transporters, which is one means to improve the auction platform financial sustainability. For instance, a shipper bid with one job (time window equals 2 hours, unit price

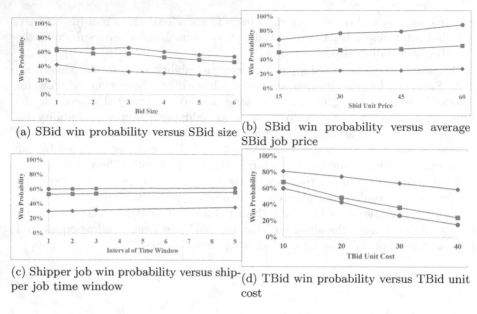

(a) SBid win probability versus SBid size

(b) SBid win probability versus average SBid job price

(c) Shipper job win probability versus shipper job time window

(d) TBid win probability versus TBid unit cost

Fig. 1. Win probability versus different factors, ● #Nodes/#Vehicles = 7, ■ #Nodes/#Vehicles = 11, ◆ #Nodes/#Vehicles = 22

equals to 15) win probability is approximately 50% (obtained from naive Bayes network). In contrast, by increasing the tight time window to 9 hours, and increase the price to $45 per job, the win probability can reach almost 100%.

In summary, the win probability depends on multiple factors drawn from both demands and supplies. Generally, most factors are independent of one another. Where some factor may depend on others, advanced machine learning techniques should be applied to predict the win probability.

6   Conclusion

In this paper, we investigate the winner determination problem with bundled jobs, which is an variant of the PDPTW. From the academic perspective, this work raises many new challenges. From a data analytics point of view, we find that the win probability may not be high when shippers/transporters randomly submit bids. Therefore, mechanisms should be properly designed to improve the win probability, such as moving from single-shot to multi-round iterative auctions, allowing the failed bid owner increase/decrease their bid price or relax some constraints. Besides that, we see the following broad areas for future research: 1) extending the current model by addressing heterogeneous vehicle routing with a mixture of cost structures (e.g., some traditional logistic companies prefer cost structure based on weight, volume, number of visited locations, or travel distance); 2) extending the current model to multi-objective, for example, the platform may need to achieve high match rate in addition to maximizing profit; 3) evaluating the impact of relaxing some constraints; for example, imposing a penalty cost for violating some rules instead of rejecting an order completely may benefit all stakeholders (shipper, transporter, and sharing platform owner); 4) profit sharing with the stakeholders in the form of rebates post-auction, which may incentivise more users to participate in the platform. In this regard, a fair and stable profit sharing mechanism was proposed in [11] that encourages coalition formation among multiple logistics providers for vehicle routing.

Acknowledgment

This research is funded by the National Research Foundation Singapore under its Corp Lab @ University scheme and Fujitsu Limited as part of the A*STAR-Fujitsu-SMU Urban Computing and Engineering Centre of Excellence.

References

1. Ledyard, J.O., Olson, M., Porter, D., Swanson, J.A. and Torma, D.P.: The first use of a combined-value auction for transportation services. Interfaces, **32**(5), 4–12 (2002)
2. Cordeau, J.F. and Laporte, G.: A tabu search heuristic for the static multi-vehicle dial-a-ride problem. Transportation Research Part B: Methodological, **37**(6), 579–594 (2003)
3. Li, H. and Lim, A.: A metaheuristic for the pickup and delivery problem with time windows. International Journal on Artificial Intelligence Tools, **12**(2), 173–186 (2003)
4. Ropke, S. and Pisinger, D.: An adaptive large neighborhood search heuristic for the pickup and delivery problem with time windows. Transportation Science, **40**(4), 455–472 (2006)
5. Mes, M.: Sequential auctions for full truckload allocation. PhD thesis, University of Twente, The Netherlands (2008)
6. Chen, R.L.Y., AhmadBeygi, S., Cohn, A., Beil, D.R. and Sinha, A.: Solving truckload procurement auctions over an exponential number of bundles. Transportation Science, **43**(4), 493–510 (2009)
7. Berger, S. and Bierwirth, C.: Solutions to the request reassignment problem in collaborative carrier networks. Transportation Research Part E: Logistics and Transportation Review, **46**(5), 627–638 (2010)
8. Xu, S.X. and Huang, G.Q.: Transportation service procurement in periodic sealed double auctions with stochastic demand and supply. Transportation Research Part B: Methodological, **56**, 136–160 (2013)
9. Wang, X. and Kopfer, H.: Collaborative transportation planning of less-than-truckload freight. OR Spectrum, **36**(2), 357–380 (2014)
10. Dai, B., Chen, H. and Yang, G.: Price-setting based combinatorial auction approach for carrier collaboration with pickup and delivery requests. Operational Research, **14**(3), 361–386 (2014)
11. Agussurja, L., Lau, H.C. and Cheng, S.F.: Achieving stable and fair profit allocation with minimum subsidy in collaborative logistics. In Proceedings of the 13th AAAI Conference, Phoenix, Arizona, USA., 3785–3792 (2016)

12. Zhang, B., Yao, T., Friesz, T.L. and Sun, Y.: A tractable two-stage robust winner determination model for truckload service procurement via combinatorial auctions. Transportation Research Part B: Methodological, **78**, 16–31 (2015)
13. Kuyzu, G., Akyol, Ç.G., Ergun, Ö. and Savelsbergh, M.: Bid price optimization for truckload carriers in simultaneous transportation procurement auctions. Transportation Research Part B: Methodological, **73**, 34–58 (2015)
14. Li, B., Krushinsky, D., Van Woensel, T. and Reijers, H.A.: An adaptive large neighborhood search heuristic for the share-a-ride problem. Computers & Operations Research, **66**, 170–180 (2016)
15. Handoko, S.D., Lau, H.C. and Cheng, S.F.: Achieving Economic and Environmental Sustainabilities in Urban Consolidation Center With Bicriteria Auction. IEEE Transactions on Automation Science and Engineering, **13**(4), 1471–1479 (2016)

Metaheuristic Framework for a Disaster Logistics Problem with Time-Dependent Demands

Jorge F. Victoria[1], H. Murat Afsar[1], and Christian Prins[1]

ICD-LOSI, Université de Technologie de Troyes,
UMR CNRS 6281, 12 Rue Marie Curie,
CS 42060-10004 Troyes Cedex - France.
{jorge.victoria, murat.afsar, christian.prins}@utt.fr

Abstract. This paper addresses a novel capacitated vehicle routing problem with time-dependent demands (CVRP-TDD) arising in a relief distribution situation in a region struck by the disaster. The locations closest to the epicenter are the ones hit hardest and the natural reaction of survivors is to flee from these points, called critical nodes. Lacks or delays in relief distribution amplify this behavior. To reduce this phenomenon, we aim to maximize the demand satisfied at the critical nodes. We present an optimal splitting procedure and a metaheuristic framework that can execute four different methods, by changing only three parameters. The results shows the good performance of two methods and highlight the efficiency of the splitting procedure.

1 Introduction

Natural and man-made disasters have enormous consequences on the population. In 2015, 376 disasters occurred leaving about 20 thousand dead, 110 million victims worldwide and US$ 70 billion of economic damages [9]. Disaster Management (DM) appears from the efforts of individuals and societies trying to decrease these consequences, developing measures to address initial impact as well as post-disaster response and recovery needs [5].

DM is composed by four phases. *Mitigation phase* refers to plans or mechanisms such as training to reduce people vulnerability, where the government and associations play an important role. *Preparation phase* refers to operations or strategies that must be planned before a disaster occurs. *Response phase* begins immediately after a disaster strikes, all the operations planned in previous phases must be carried on in order to reduce the casualties. Finally, the *Reconstruction phase* refers to the rehabilitation process of infrastructure and the impact generated to the population. The last three phases constitute the humanitarian logistics (HL) stream [6].

Thomas and Kopczak [24] defines HL as a process of planning, implementing and controlling efficiently the flow and storage of goods, materials and information from the point of origin to the point of consumption for the purpose of alleviating the suffering of vulnerable people. The above shows that HL is interested in social more than economical benefits.

© Springer International Publishing AG 2017
T. Bektaş et al. (Eds.), ICCL 2017, LNCS 10572, pp. 143–157, 2017.
https://doi.org/10.1007/978-3-319-68496-3_10

This work is focused on *Response phase*. The CVRP-TDD considers a set of shelters that must be visited after a disaster strikes an area. The affected people go directly to shelters and wait for first aid. If they do not receive them as quickly as expected, they flee away from the shelters seeking necessary resources. This increases the chaos already generated by the catastrophe and makes more difficult to the humanitarian organizations to assist all the victims. So, the objective is to arrive as quickly as possible at shelters to maximize the satisfied demand.

To our best knowledge CVRP-TDD is not studied before except in [26] where, a column generation based heuristic method is used to solve small - medium size instances.

The paper is organized as follows: in the next section we present a literature review, in section 3 we give a formal definition of CVRP-TDD and the solution framework which includes the local search and the split procedure that are tailored for our problem. Computational experiments are presented in section 4 and, followed by some conclusions in section 5.

2   Literature review

Literature is classified taking into account the phases that constitute the HL stream. Gutjahr and Dzubur [10], and Pillac et al. [17] are interested in the *preparation phase*. The first determine the best location of relief distribution centers (DCs) and the last work in evacuation plans. Gutjahr and Dzubur [10] propose a bi-level optimization and an exact algorithm to minimize the opening cost of DCs and the uncovered demand. Pillac et al. [17] considers the number of evacuees solving a sub-problem that generates evacuation paths and a master problem that optimizes the flow of evacuees maximizing the number of evacuees.

The *response phase* has attracted more researchers than other phases. Lu et al. [13] minimize the total time to deliver relief goods to satisfy the demand. They present a rolling horizon-based framework for real-time relief distribution in the aftermath of the disasters. Moshref-Javadi and Lee [15] solve a multi-commodity VRP with split deliveries to minimize the total waiting time at the affected nodes. They propose two mixed-integer linear programs (MILPs) and a hybridization of a variable neighborhood search (VNS) and a simulated annealing (SA) to solve the problem. Ngueveu et al. [16] solve the cumulative capacitated vehicle routing problem (CCVRP) using a memetic algorithm. The CCVRP seeks to minimize the average arrival time to nodes. Lysgaard and Wøhlk [14] also solve the CCVRP, but they implement a branch-and-cut-and-price algorithm. Rivera et al. [22] solve a multi-trip cumulative VRP. This problem is quite similar to the CCVRP, but instead of a homogenous fleet, a single vehicle performs more than one trip to serve all nodes. They propose two MILPs and dynamic programming is used to solve the large instances.

The CCVRP is similar to our problem because both implicitly seek to minimize the arrival times at each node, but the trade-off between the arrival time and the flee rate is only taken into account in the CVRP-TDD. The fairness between the nodes is reinforced by requiring all nodes to be visited so that nobody sacrificed to improve the overall performance.

The most common objectives functions in the *response phase* are the maximization of the satisfied demand, the minimization of the total waiting time and the minimization of the average arrival time. None of the reviewed articles consider a time-dependent demand due to population displacement after a disaster.

In the *reconstruction phase*, Maya et al. [7] address the scheduling and routing of a repair crew, while the accessibility to the towns are optimized. They develop a dynamic programming algorithm and an iterated greedy-randomized constructive procedure to solve the problem. The objective is the minimization of the weighted sum of the moments at which each demand node becomes accessible. Akbari et al. [1] propose an exact MILP and a matheuristic to minimize the maximum time of the walks for the synchronized work schedule for the road clearing teams. A walk is composed by the edge-traversing time, road clearance time and waiting time.

3   Problem definition and solution framework

The CVRP-TDD can be formally defined on a complete undirected graph $G = (N, E)$, where $N = \{0, ...n\}$ is the node set and E is the edge set. Node 0 correspond to the depot while $N' = N \setminus \{0\}$ is the set of critical nodes (shelters). Each node $i \in N'$ has a demand a_i at time zero and a demand variation b_i. This variation corresponds to the number of people per time unit who flee from this node before the arrival of the humanitarian aids. Each arc (i, j) has a travel time c_{ij}.

The objective is to identify a set of feasible routes so that every node is visited exactly once and the number of people attended is maximized. A feasible route begins and ends at node 0. A homogeneous fleet of k vehicles is available and the total tour length of each vehicle should be less than $Tmax$. The satisfied demand at node i has a decreasing behavior equal to $satisfiedDemand_i = a_i - b_i t_i$ where t_i is the arrival time at node i. The total demand serviced by a route should not exceed the vehicle capacity Q.

The mathematical model can be found in Victoria et al. [26]; they prove the importance to develop a method capable to solve larger instances. Thus, we propose a general framework that explores the solution space using a local improvement procedure and different strategies of exploration that can be executed changing a set of three parameters. Among the strategies of exploration, we develop an optimal splitting procedure that allows to alternate between the VRP solution space and the traveling salesman problem (TSP) solution space.

The different combinations of three parameters give as results some of the well-known metaheuristics on the literature: Greedy Randomized Adaptive Search Procedure (GRASP), Iterated Local Search (ILS) [12], Evolutionary Local Search (ELS) [28] and their multi-start versions. The general framework can be seen in Algorithm 1.

Algorithm 1 Metaheuristic Framework

```
1:  Z(S*) ← 0 (S* is the global best solution)
2:  Z(bestChild) ← 0 (bestChild is the local best solution)
3:  for i = 1 to nbOfRestarts do
4:      S ← initialSol()
5:      localSearch(S)
6:      for j = 1 to nbOfIter do
7:          for k = 1 to nbOfChildren do
8:              child ← perturbate(S)
9:              localSearch(child)
10:             if (Z(child) > Z(bestChild) and isFeasible(child)) then
11:                 bestChild ← child
12:             end if
13:         end for
14:         if Z(bestChild) > Z(S) then
15:             S ← bestChild
16:         end if
17:         if (Z(S) > Z(S*) and isFeasible(S)) then
18:             S* ← S
19:         end if
20:     end for
21: end for
22: return S*
```

The ILS starts with an initial solution S obtained by a randomized constructive heuristic explained in subsection 2.1. At each iteration, a local search to improve the solution and a perturbation procedure to escape the local optima are applied successively. The perturbation procedure generates a different solution from S. It is known as a *child* of S.

The number of iterations is denoted by the parameter $nbOfIter$. In one iteration of ELS algorithm, $nbOfChildren$ solutions are generated by the perturbation and each solution is improved by local search. If $nbOfChildren=1$, then the ELS becomes an ILS procedure. Each method can be restarted $nbOfRestarts$ times. If $nbOfRestarts > 0$ and $nbOfIter = 1$, the algorithm is equivalent to a GRASP.

The GRASP, ILS, ELS or their multi start versions can be selected by assigning the parameters $nbOfRestarts$, $nbOfIter$ and $nbOfChildren$.

Additionally, when S^* is updated during the execution of the algorithm, each route that belongs to it is transformed into a zero-one column of size $|N'|$. Each position takes the value 1 if node is visited in the route and 0 otherwise. These columns are added to a columns pool and a set partitioning problem is solved at the end of the framework. It tries to improve the solution (S^*) already found.

3.1 Constructive Heuristic

A parallel randomized best insertion procedure $initialSol()$ is used to find one initial solution of the problem. Iteratively, the procedure randomly chooses one of the unassigned nodes. All positions to insert are evaluated and the three best ones are saved. Then, one of three best positions is randomly selected and the node is assigned to this position. The next unassigned node is randomly chosen and the process continues until all nodes are inserted. If no feasible solution can be obtained, the procedure is aborted and restarted. At the end of a given number of restarts, if a feasible solution is not yet reached, then an infeasible solution with a penalty is accepted (penalty $\times \delta(S)$) where $\delta(S)$ is the difference between the tour length and $Tmax$. In addition, it is possible that when a position is evaluated, the demand of the selected node and/or some of the following nodes already in the route becomes zero due to delayed visits. The humanitarian context of the problem does not allow leaving a node unattended, because the solution must ensure fairness in the distribution of first aid. Then, the nodes with zero demand are allowed in the initial solution, but a solution with positive demands is sought at the end.

3.2 Pre-Computations

The time-dependence between the arrival time at nodes and demand variations complicates the calculations when a sequence of nodes is inserted, removed or inverted by the local search. Silva et al. [23] show for the CCVRP that any move can be expressed by concatenations of node sequences. By pre-computing and updating some relevant information, we can evaluate concatenation and reversing operators in constant time. Therefore, any move using a fixed number of concatenation and reversing operators can be evaluated in constant time as well. For any sequence of nodes σ_x, indexed from 0 to v, define:

- σ_{x_i} the node in position i.
- $T(\sigma_x) = \sum_{i=0}^{v-1} c_{\sigma_{x_i}, \sigma_{x_{i+1}}}$ the duration of the sequence σ_x.
- $\beta(\sigma_x)$ is the total demand change per time unit (delay) in sequence σ_x. It can be calculated as $\beta(\sigma_x) = \sum_{i=1}^{v} b_{\sigma_{x_i}}$, where $b_{\sigma_{x_i}}$ is the demand change per time unit for node at position i. If a node at position i has a demand to satisfy equal to zero due to its position in σ_x, then $b_{\sigma_{x_i}} = 0$.
- $D(\sigma_x)$ is the total demand to satisfy in sequence σ_x. It is calculated as $D(\sigma_x) = a_{\sigma_{x_0}} + \sum_{i=1}^{v} d_{\sigma_{x_i}}$, where $a_{\sigma_{x_0}}$ is the initial demand of node at position 0 and $d_{\sigma_{x_i}}$ is the satisfied demand of each other node at position i in sequence σ_x, assuming that the sequence begins at σ_{x_0} at time 0.
- $Y(\sigma_x)$ is the maximum time slack that sequence σ_x can be shifted while guaranteeing positive demand for each node. $Y(\sigma_x) = \min(y_{\sigma_{x_i}})\ \forall i = 0, \ldots, v$, where $y_{\sigma_{x_i}}$ is calculated as $y_{\sigma_{x_i}} = \max((a_{\sigma_{x_i}}/b_{\sigma_{x_i}}) - t_{\sigma_{x_i}}, 0)$. $t_{\sigma_{x_i}}$ is the arrival time at node σ_{x_i}, assuming a departure at time 0 from σ_{x_0}. This time slack is checked and it helps to define the feasibility of the moves.

Consider any two sequences of nodes $\sigma_1 = (\sigma_{1_0}, ..., \sigma_{1_v})$ and $\sigma_2 = (\sigma_{2_0}, ..., \sigma_{2_w})$ in a solution and their concatenation $\sigma_1 \oplus \sigma_2 = (\sigma_{1_0}, ..., \sigma_{1_v}, \sigma_{2_0}, ..., \sigma_{2_w})$. The information for the new sequence can be derived in $O(1)$ as follows:

$$T(\sigma_1 \oplus \sigma_2) = T(\sigma_1) + c_{\sigma_{1_v}, \sigma_{2_0}} + T(\sigma_2) \tag{1}$$

$$\beta(\sigma_1 \oplus \sigma_2) = \beta(\sigma_1) + \beta(\sigma_2) \tag{2}$$

$$D(\sigma_1 \oplus \sigma_2) = D(\sigma_1) + D(\sigma_2) + \beta(\sigma_2)(T(\sigma_1) + c_{\sigma_{1_v}, \sigma_{2_0}}) \tag{3}$$

$$Y(\sigma_1 \oplus \sigma_2) = min(Y(\sigma_1), (max((Y(\sigma_2) - c_{\sigma_{1_v}, \sigma_{2_0}}), 0))) \tag{4}$$

Equation (1) was proposed by Rivera et al. for the multitrip CCVRP [21]. Equation (2) is the demand variation for $\sigma \oplus \sigma'$, equal to the sum of demand variations for σ and σ'. Equation (3) is the total demand of $\sigma \oplus \sigma'$, equal to the sum of the demands of σ and σ' and the demand variation induced by the shift of the starting time in sequence σ'. Equation (4) is the maximum time that $\sigma \oplus \sigma'$ can be shifted ensuring that all nodes will have positive demand. As the problem is highly asymmetrical, these values must be also pre-computed for the reversal of each sequence, $\overleftarrow{\sigma}$.

3.3 Local Search

After a solution is found, some moves are used to find a local optimum in the solution space. Time dependent behavior of the demand require a careful mechanism to evaluate the objective function as well as to verify of the capacity constraint violations in constant time, during the local search. This mechanism is only possible with the help of some preliminary information, obtained as explained in the previous sub-section. Therefore it is possible to execute the moves : node relocation, swap 1-1, swap 2-2 and 2-opt. All these moves are applied to a single route (intra-routes) and a pair of routes (inter-routes) looking for the best improvement. The infeasible solutions are penalized as in the constructive heuristic.

Node relocation neighborhood: it takes each node of a route and evaluates all possible positions to relocate it. Fig. 1 illustrates the intra-route case using the pre-computations mentioned above. A node sequence (σ_2) is relocated between two others sequences (σ_3 and σ_4) at the same route. The concatenations ($\sigma_1 \oplus \sigma_3 \oplus \sigma_2 \oplus \sigma_4$) must be evaluated. The evaluation of the satisfied demand is shown in Equation (5).

$$\begin{aligned}
D_{(\sigma_1 \oplus \sigma_3 \oplus \sigma_2 \oplus \sigma_4)} &= D[D(\sigma_1 \oplus \sigma_3) \oplus D(\sigma_2 \oplus \sigma_4)] \\
D(\sigma_1 \oplus \sigma_3) &= D(\sigma_1) + D(\sigma_3) + \beta(\sigma_3)(T(\sigma_1) + c_{\sigma_{1_2},\sigma_{3_0}}) \\
D(\sigma_2 \oplus \sigma_4)) &= D(\sigma_2) + D(\sigma_4) + \beta(\sigma_4)(T(\sigma_2) + c_{\sigma_{2_0},\sigma_{4_0}}) \\
D[D(\sigma_1 \oplus \sigma_3) \oplus D(\sigma_2 \oplus \sigma_4)] &= D(\sigma_1 \oplus \sigma_3) + D(\sigma_2 \oplus \sigma_4) + \\
&\quad \beta(\sigma_2 \oplus \sigma_4)(T(\sigma_1 \oplus \sigma_3) + c_{\sigma_{(\sigma_1 \oplus \sigma_3)_2},\sigma_{(\sigma_2 \oplus \sigma_4)_0}})
\end{aligned} \tag{5}$$

Swap 1-1 neighborhood: two distinct nodes are exchanged. An example of the inter-route move is represented in Fig. 2 where nodes σ_2 and σ_5 are exchanged. The node σ_2 is placed between the node sequences σ_4 and σ_6. The node σ_5 is positioned at the position released by node σ_2. The tour length of each route is calculated as the sum of $T(\sigma_i)$ for all σ_i that belongs to the concatenation. Equation (6) evaluates the satisfied demand of the example in Fig. 2.

$$\begin{aligned}
&\textit{Route } i \\
D_{(\sigma_1 \oplus \sigma_5 \oplus \sigma_3)} &= D[D(\sigma_1 \oplus \sigma_5) \oplus \sigma_3] \\
D(\sigma_1 \oplus \sigma_5) &= D(\sigma_1) + D(\sigma_5) + \beta(\sigma_5)(T(\sigma_1) + c_{\sigma_{1_2},\sigma_{5_0}}) \\
D[D(\sigma_1 \oplus \sigma_5) \oplus \sigma_3] &= D(\sigma_1 \oplus \sigma_5) + D(\sigma_3) + \\
&\quad \beta(\sigma_3)(T(\sigma_1 \oplus \sigma_5) + c_{\sigma_{(\sigma_1 \oplus \sigma_5)_3},\sigma_{\sigma_{3_0}}}) \\
&\textit{Route } j \\
D_{(\sigma_4 \oplus \sigma_2 \oplus \sigma_6)} &= D[D(\sigma_4 \oplus \sigma_2) \oplus \sigma_6] \\
D(\sigma_4 \oplus \sigma_2) &= D(\sigma_4) + D(\sigma_2) + \beta(\sigma_2)(T(\sigma_4) + c_{\sigma_{4_2},\sigma_{2_0}}) \\
D[D(\sigma_4 \oplus \sigma_2) \oplus \sigma_6] &= D(\sigma_4 \oplus \sigma_2) + D(\sigma_6) + \\
&\quad \beta(\sigma_6)(T(\sigma_4 \oplus \sigma_2) + c_{\sigma_{(\sigma_4 \oplus \sigma_2)_3},\sigma_{\sigma_{6_0}}})
\end{aligned} \tag{6}$$

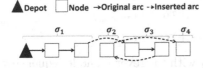

Fig. 1. Intra-route node relocation

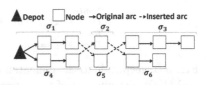

Fig. 2. Inter-route swap 1-1

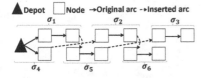

Fig. 3. Inter-route swap 2-2

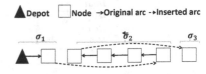

Fig. 4. Intra-route 2-Opt

Swap 2-2 neighborhood: it is quite similar to the previous one. Two distinct pairs of consecutive nodes are exchanged. An example of the inter-route move is presented in Fig. 3 and how the satisfied demand is evaluated is shown in Equation (7). The Fig. 3 shows as the pair-nodes sequence σ_2 is positioned between the nodes sequence σ_4 and σ_6 and the pair-nodes sequence σ_5 between the σ_1 and σ_3.

$$
\begin{aligned}
&\textit{Route } i\\
&D(\sigma_1 \oplus \sigma_5 \oplus \sigma_3) = D[D(\sigma_1 \oplus \sigma_5) \oplus \sigma_3]\\
&D(\sigma_1 \oplus \sigma_5) = D(\sigma_1) + D(\sigma_5) + \beta(\sigma_5)(T(\sigma_1) + c_{\sigma_{1_2},\sigma_{5_0}})\\
&D[D(\sigma_1 \oplus \sigma_5) \oplus \sigma_3] = D(\sigma_1 \oplus \sigma_5) + D(\sigma_3) +\\
&\qquad\qquad \beta(\sigma_3)(T(\sigma_1 \oplus \sigma_5) + c_{\sigma_{(\sigma_1 \oplus \sigma_5)_4},\sigma\sigma_{3_0}})\\
&\textit{Route } j\\
&D(\sigma_4 \oplus \sigma_2 \oplus \sigma_6) = D[D(\sigma_4 \oplus \sigma_2) \oplus \sigma_6]\\
&D(\sigma_4 \oplus \sigma_2) = D(\sigma_4) + D(\sigma_2) + \beta(\sigma_2)(T(\sigma_4) + c_{\sigma_{4_1},\sigma_{2_0}})\\
&D[D(\sigma_4 \oplus \sigma_2) \oplus \sigma_6] = D(\sigma_4 \oplus \sigma_2) + D(\sigma_6) +\\
&\qquad\qquad \beta(\sigma_6)(T(\sigma_4 \oplus \sigma_2) + c_{\sigma_{(\sigma_4 \oplus \sigma_2)_3},\sigma\sigma_{6_0}})
\end{aligned}
\tag{7}
$$

2-Opt neighborhood: two distinct and non-consecutive arcs are deleted and the route or routes are reconnected. Fig. 4 shows the intra-route move where the arcs between σ_1 and σ_2 as well as the arcs between σ_2 and σ_3 are deleted. The node sequence σ_2 is reversed ($\overleftarrow{\sigma_2}$) and reconnected with σ_1 and σ_3. The satisfied demand for this example is evaluated using Equation (8).

$$
\begin{aligned}
&D(\sigma_1 \oplus \overleftarrow{\sigma_2} \oplus \sigma_3) = D[D(\sigma_1 \oplus \overleftarrow{\sigma_2}) \oplus \sigma_3]\\
&D(\sigma_1 \oplus \overleftarrow{\sigma_2}) = D(\sigma_1) + D(\overleftarrow{\sigma_2}) + \beta(\overleftarrow{\sigma_2})(T(\sigma_1) + c_{\sigma_{1_1},\overleftarrow{\sigma}_{2_0}})\\
&D[D(\sigma_1 \oplus \overleftarrow{\sigma_2}) \oplus \sigma_3] = D(\sigma_1 \oplus \overleftarrow{\sigma_2}) + D(\sigma_3) +\\
&\qquad\qquad \beta(\sigma_3)(T(\sigma_1 \oplus \overleftarrow{\sigma_2}) + c_{\sigma_{(\sigma_1 \oplus \overleftarrow{\sigma_2})_5},\sigma_{3_0}})
\end{aligned}
\tag{8}
$$

Additionally, two inter-route moves are used: the inter-route 2-Opt (Fig. 5) and the inter-route 2-Opt* (Fig. 6). In Fig. 5, the concatenation of the node sequence σ_1 with the node sequence σ_4 and node sequence σ_3 with the node sequence σ_2. Equation (9) shows how to evaluate the satisfied demand for this move.

$$\begin{aligned}&\text{Route } i\\&D(\sigma_1 \oplus \sigma_4) = D(\sigma_1) + D(\sigma_4) + \beta(\sigma_4)(T(\sigma_1) + c_{\sigma_{1_2},\sigma_{4_0}})\\&\text{Route } j\\&D(\sigma_3 \oplus \sigma_2) = D(\sigma_3) + D(\sigma_2) + \beta(\sigma_2)(T(\sigma_3) + c_{\sigma_{3_1},\sigma_{2_0}})\end{aligned} \tag{9}$$

Fig. 6 corresponds to the concatenation of σ_1 with the reversed node sequence $\overleftarrow{\sigma_4}$ and the concatenation of the reversed node sequence $\overleftarrow{\sigma_5}$ with the node sequence σ_2. Equation (10) evaluates this move that is represented in Fig. 6.

$$\begin{aligned}&\text{Route } i:\\&D(\sigma_1 \oplus \overleftarrow{\sigma_4}) = D(\sigma_1) + D(\overleftarrow{\sigma_4}) + \beta(\overleftarrow{\sigma_4})(T(\sigma_1) + c_{\sigma_{1_3},\overleftarrow{\sigma}_{4_0}})\\&\text{Route } j:\\&D_{(\sigma_3 \oplus \overleftarrow{\sigma_5} \oplus \sigma_2)}\end{aligned} \tag{10}$$

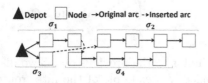

Fig. 5. Inter-route 2-Opt

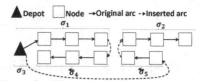

Fig. 6. Inter-route 2-Opt*

3.4 Split Procedure

This procedure is based on the second phase of the route-first cluster-second principle of the VRP introduced by Beasley [2]. In the first phase, a giant tour covering all nodes is built, by eliminating the time limit and capacity constraint. The second phase is to divide the giant tour considering all constraints to find a solution for the original problem. The split procedure divides the giant tour finding the optimal solution for the given sequence.

Prins [18] introduced a memetic algorithm (MA) which incorporates the split procedure to solve the distance-constrained CVRP where the number of vehicles is a decision variable and the objective is to minimize the total cost of the trips. He shows the flexibility of this procedure mentioning three extensions to other objective functions as the minimization of the total cost and the number of vehicles, the minimization of the operating cost plus the fleet cost considering an unlimited and limited fleet size. The last two extensions refer to the vehicle fleet mix problem (VFMP) and the heterogeneous fleet VRP (HFVRP), respectively. The extension to these problems is treated by Prins [19].

Recently, other authors continue to use this procedure in their methods. Among them are Cattaruzza et al. [3] and Lacomme et al. [11]. The Multitrip VRP (MTVRP) is solved by Cattaruzza et al. [3] and the multi-objective VRP with route balancing is presented by Lacomme et al.[11] where the total routing cost and the difference between the largest and smallest route cost are minimized simultaneously. Vidal [27] presents a technical note where the complexity of the procedure for the CVRP is reduced from $O(nB)$ to $O(n)$. The number of customers is given by n and B is the average number of feasible routes that start with a given customer in the giant tour.

The works cited above prove the good performance and the adaptability of the split procedure into different routing problems. These are the reasons to integrate the split procedure in the general framework.

For the classical CVRP, the split procedure starts by constructing an auxiliary directed acyclic graph $H = (V, A)$ where V is a set of numbered nodes from 0 (dummy node) to n. The set of arcs A contains all the feasible arcs such than an arc (i, j), $i < j$, represents a route sequence starting from depot, visiting $v(i+1)$ to $v(j)$ and coming back to the depot. The arc weight D_{ij} is the cost of the route in the real network. Bellman's algorithm is used to find the shortest path from 0 to n in H. This gives as result a set of feasible routes for the original problem and the optimal solution of the given giant tour.

It should be noted that the CVRP-TDD seeks to maximize the satisfied demand with a homogeneous limited fleet. Therefore, a maximum cost path from 0 to n in H should be found. Hence, D_{ij} corresponds to the satisfied demand in the route sequence. d_i^l is the satisfied demand of the longest path from 0 to i with vehicle l and P_i^l store the predecessor of node i on the longest path leading to i with vehicle l.

The split procedure is included to the general framework in Algorithm 1 as follows. A giant tour GT is built, instead of execute the perturbation procedure to S (line 8). The GT is the concatenation of routes in S in a given order seq. Then, a copy of GT is shaken and the split procedure is executed. If after the split procedure, a solution is not found, another copy of GT is shaken and the split procedure is executed again. This is repeated until a solution is found or a number of iterations is fulfilled. If the latter occurs, the order seq changes and a different GT is generated. Additionally, a percentage $xTmax$ that relax the tour length constraint is increased by 0.1. This allows routes that exceed $tMax$ until $tMax \times xTmax$ in H. The process is restarted with the new GT and the updated $xTmax$. All of the above is done until a feasible or relaxed solution (*child*) is found, then the general framework continues at line 9. A feasible solution found is the optimal solution for the given order seq.

Algorithm 2 shows the adapted split procedure. It is based on a compact version of Bellman's algorithm presented by Prins et al. [20]. The complexity of the algorithm is proportional to $O(n^2 k)$, but if γ denotes the average number of nodes of feasible subsequences, H has $n \cdot \gamma \cdot k$ arcs and we get a more precise complexity in $O(n\gamma k)$.

3.5   Perturbation procedure

A perturbation is applied to escape from local optima and to try to explore a different area of the solution space. To escape the local optima, a perturbation

---

Algorithm 2 *Split Procedure*

1: $copyGT = \{v(0), v(1), ..., v(n)\}$ $v(x)$ is the node at position x in the copy of GT
2: $T(\sigma_1)$ is the tour length of node sequence σ_1
3: $P_0^0 \leftarrow \{0\}$
4: **for** $i = 0$ to n **do** $d_i^0 \leftarrow 0$ **end for**
5: **for** $i = 0$ to n **do**
6:     $j \leftarrow i + 1;\ D_{ij} \leftarrow 0;\ time \leftarrow 0; \sigma_1 \leftarrow v(i+1)$
7:     **repeat**
8:         $\sigma_1 = \sigma_1 \cup v(j)$
9:         $time = c_{(0, v(i+1))} + T(\sigma_1)$
10:         $D_{ij} = D_{ij} + \max[(a_{v(j)} - (b_{v(j)} \cdot time), 0]$
11:         $time = time + t_{(v(j),0)}$
12:         $l \leftarrow 1$
13:         **repeat**
14:             **if** $(D_{ij} \leq Q)$ and $(time \leq (tMax \cdot xTmax))$ and $(d_i^l + D_{ij} > d_j^l)$ **then**
15:                 **if** $(time > tMax)$ **then** D_{ij} is penalized **end if**
16:                 $d_j^l \leftarrow d_i^l + D_{ij}$
17:                 $P_j^l \leftarrow i$
18:             **end if**
19:             $l \leftarrow l + 1$
20:         **until** $(l > k)$ or $(D_{ij} > Q)$ or $(time > (tMax \cdot xTmax))$
21:         $j \leftarrow j + 1$
22:     **until** $(j > n)$ or $(D_{ij} > Q)$ or $(time > (tMax \cdot xTmax))$
23: **end for**

---

operator is used as a diversification mechanism. The perturbation operator cannot be one of the moves used during the local search, otherwise it can be easily undone (repaired).

We propose two perturbation operators, one for the giant tour and the other for the complete solution. The complete solution is perturbed by the node ejection chain procedure, introduced by Glover[8]. In each route, a node is randomly selected and relocated in the best position in another route. The node removed from the last route is inserted in the first one. A solution that exceeds the maximum tour length is allowed with a penalization factor.

A dynamic swap procedure is applied as perturbation to the giant tour. Given a giant tour, two subsets $S1$ and $S2$ are chosen. Each subset contains $|S1|$ and $|S2|$ distinct and consecutive nodes ($|S1| = |S2|$). The size of subsets is increased by one if a feasible or relaxed solution is not found by the split procedure. The nodes in $S1$ are swapped with nodes in $S2$ generating a different giant tour.

4   Computational Experiments

The algorithm is coded in JAVA and run on an Intel(R) Core(TM) i7-4800MQ 2.70GHz with 16 GB of RAM running Windows 7 Professional. The set partitioning problem is solved using CPLEX 12.6. To the best of our knowledge, Victoria et al. [26] are the first to propose a MILP and a column generation based heuristic method to solve small - medium size instances for CVRP-TDD. They used adapted Solomon's instances, but as we want to test our framework in larger instances. Then, the 14 instances for the CVRP proposed by Christofides et al. [4] are adapted. These instances can be divided into two groups: those that include the maximum tour length and service time and those that do not

Table 1. Detailed results of ILS and MS-ILS without and with the split procedure

ILS (1-500-1)

			Without split							Split						
			Satisfied Demand			CPU Time (s.)			SSP	Satisfied Demand			CPU Time (s.)			SSP
Inst.	n	k	Best	Avg.	Worst	Min.	Avg.	Max.		Best	Avg.	Worst	Min.	Avg.	Max.	
Set 1 1	50	6	592.62	591.28	590.19	4.43	4.94	6.17	0	592.62	589.86	587.87	3.83	5.43	6.57	0
2	75	11	1006.07	1000.67	993.56	21.70	36.13	61.71	3	1006.03	1002.08	993.63	20.17	49.40	88.41	0
3	100	9	1101.87	1098.11	1094.19	25.90	28.22	30.86	3	1101.78	1098.29	1089.69	31.00	44.47	49.73	0
4	150	14	-	-	-	-	-	-	-	-	-	-	-	-	-	-
5	199	18	-	-	-	-	-	-	-	-	-	-	-	-	-	-
6	120	11	1027.86	1023.80	1020.67	75.31	84.71	131.23	4	1027.37	1020.95	1015.96	40.10	62.88	101.11	0
7	100	11	1434.21	1433.74	1433.38	31.95	34.12	35.80	0	1434.21	1433.76	1433.38	12.87	14.18	16.41	0
Set 2 1	50	7	615.66	615.66	615.66	4.70	4.94	6.26	0	615.66	615.54	614.46	2.71	3.09	4.34	0
2	75	12	1037.04	1036.16	1032.12	15.09	16.03	17.24	2	1037.04	1034.79	1031.66	10.25	12.76	14.79	0
3	100	10	1133.77	1133.23	1130.22	30.20	32.09	33.56	1	1133.98	1132.95	1129.88	20.36	22.66	27.10	0
4	150	15	1743.21	1741.17	1738.07	102.18	105.95	111.97	3	1742.96	1739.92	1736.52	112.18	117.72	126.75	0
5	199	19	2447.86	2444.13	2438.19	252.66	269.71	313.23	4	2449.82	2444.71	2440.95	229.35	259.41	306.51	0
6	120	12	1056.2	1056.14	1056.02	49.38	54.38	57.70	0	1056.20	1055.70	1054.72	20.70	23.77	25.38	0
7	100	12	1467.36	1467.36	1467.36	28.63	30.14	32.00	0	1467.36	1466.88	1465.40	10.30	11.10	12.81	0
Set 3 1	50	8	632.00	631.97	631.75	4.66	5.07	6.40	0	632.00	631.95	631.75	2.59	2.96	4.56	0
2	75	13	1056.39	1056.03	1055.51	16.64	17.73	19.86	0	1056.39	1055.67	1055.03	7.92	8.72	9.84	0
3	100	11	1157.56	1157.06	1155.59	30.75	33.53	35.79	0	1157.56	1157.15	1156.12	14.31	15.50	18.22	0
4	150	16	1769.86	1768.63	1767.38	108.87	116.59	131.61	3	1768.69	1767.69	1766.46	52.36	69.74	88.48	1
5	199	20	2482.97	2479.97	2476.19	285.60	326.63	395.72	1	2481.52	2477.92	2473.94	131.36	169.10	188.92	0
6	120	13	1077.40	1077.23	1077.01	49.00	51.96	55.54	0	1077.53	1077.27	1077.02	21.92	26.16	31.80	0
7	100	13	1494.77	1494.74	1494.73	31.43	33.42	36.04	0	1494.77	1494.27	1492.47	10.06	10.66	12.98	0

MS-ILS (5-100-1)

			Without split							Split						
			Satisfied Demand			CPU Time (s.)			SSP	Satisfied Demand			CPU Time (s.)			SSP
Inst.	n	k	Best	Avg.	Worst	Min.	Avg.	Max.		Best	Avg.	Worst	Min.	Avg.	Max.	
Set 1 1	50	6	592.62	591.72	590.19	4.59	4.87	6.06	0	591.76	590.66	589.39	5.60	6.03	7.88	0
2	75	11	1007.54	1003.05	996.99	45.97	100.72	147.02	5	1006.91	1004.83	1001.08	38.06	112.53	166.08	3
3	100	9	1100.05	1096.90	1093.86	28.56	31.61	34.34	2	1099.05	1097.24	1094.24	46.68	50.81	56.27	0
4	150	14	-	-	-	-	-	-	-	-	-	-	-	-	-	-
5	199	18	-	-	-	-	-	-	-	-	-	-	-	-	-	-
6	120	11	1026.80	1024.84	1021.98	155.53	225.24	286.53	1	1024.38	1021.71	1017.30	194.39	251.33	329.61	0
7	100	11	1434.21	1434.08	1433.7	33.37	33.90	35.38	1	1434.11	1433.74	1433.14	13.64	15.36	16.83	0
Set 2 1	50	7	615.66	615.66	615.66	6.24	6.72	8.53	0	615.66	615.66	615.66	3.96	4.32	5.90	0
2	75	12	1037.04	1036.61	1036.2	21.10	22.32	23.61	2	1036.89	1035.83	1033.23	15.36	18.05	21.58	1
3	100	10	1134.03	1133.71	1133.36	44.86	46.48	50.85	2	1133.77	1132.76	1131.62	29.08	32.77	37.10	0
4	150	15	1742.15	1739.62	1736.8	114.10	119.36	123.24	2	1740.68	1737.64	1733.15	123.57	130.23	137.37	0
5	199	19	2446.53	2442.68	2439.42	283.31	316.65	372.14	3	2445.71	2441.85	2437.73	285.79	316.56	398.77	0
6	120	12	1056.16	1056.11	1055.96	57.02	59.19	61.67	1	1056.13	1055.89	1055.29	23.77	25.63	27.71	0
7	100	12	1467.36	1467.36	1467.33	30.12	31.49	33.66	0	1467.36	1467.18	1466.39	11.36	12.03	13.20	2
Set 3 1	50	8	632.00	632.00	632.00	4.91	5.15	6.24	0	632.00	631.99	631.93	2.68	3.05	4.56	0
2	75	13	1056.39	1056.32	1056.20	16.99	17.75	19.14	0	1056.39	1056.04	1055.36	8.33	9.00	10.70	1
3	100	11	1157.56	1157.39	1157.23	33.68	34.50	35.29	1	1157.56	1157.37	1157.22	16.32	17.43	19.66	0
4	150	16	1769.80	1769.11	1768.11	115.14	117.06	120.10	2	1768.95	1767.41	1764.85	72.70	75.90	78.28	2
5	199	20	2482.43	2480.83	2479.78	285.18	293.31	301.11	3	2480.83	2477.81	2475.14	164.08	179.95	191.24	0
6	120	13	1077.53	1077.36	1077.14	51.48	52.72	53.91	0	1077.52	1077.28	1077.02	24.91	27.73	30.33	1
7	100	13	1494.77	1494.76	1494.74	31.87	32.79	34.40	1	1494.72	1494.54	1494.24	10.67	11.29	13.43	0

include them. We use the seven instances which include them because they are more similar to our problem.

The used instances are known in the CVRP literature as CMT6, CMT7, CMT8, CMT9, CMT10, CMT13 and CMT14 (denoted from 1 to 7 in the following). The customers of the first five instances are randomly distributed, while customers in the other two are grouped by clusters. These instances are adapted including a random β value to each node ("shelter") and adding the given service time to the travel distance between shelter-shelter and shelter-depot pairs.

The number of vehicles is not fixed in Christofides et al. instances, but the minimum number of vehicles in the best-known solutions (BKS) for the CVRP reported in the Uchoa et al. [25] is used for each instance. Based on this information, we generate three different sets of instances and each set has seven

Table 2. Detailed results of ELS and MS-ELS without and with the split procedure

ELS (1-50-10)

| | | | Without split | | | | | | | Split | | | | | | |
| | | | Satisfied Demand | | | CPU Time (s.) | | | SSP | Satisfied Demand | | | CPU Time (s.) | | | SSP |
Inst.	n	k	Best	Avg.	Worst	Min.	Avg.	Max.		Best	Avg.	Worst	Min.	Avg.	Max.	
Set 1	1	50	6	**592.62**	591.02	588.15	4.16	4.84	6.63	0	**592.62**	589.26	584.53	3.18	5.60	7.08	0
	2	75	11	1005.66	1000.86	993.56	22.09	37.13	64.20	3	1005.87	1001.15	993.63	22.98	48.69	88.45	0
	3	100	9	1100.40	1096.55	1092.20	26.28	**28.12**	29.11	2	1101.64	1098.20	1093.13	39.79	45.79	54.73	0
	4	150	14	-	-	-	-	-	-	-	-	-	-	-	-	-	-
	5	199	18	-	-	-	-	-	-	-	-	-	-	-	-	-	-
	6	120	11	**1028.12**	1025.25	1020.67	91.07	129.12	158.76	2	1027.87	1022.34	1017.93	52.57	95.22	156.81	0
	7	100	11	**1434.21**	1433.78	1433.41	39.91	43.97	47.36	1	1434.16	1433.52	1432.99	17.24	18.89	20.91	0
Set 2	1	50	7	**615.66**	615.66	615.66	4.68	4.97	6.07	0	**615.66**	615.66	615.66	2.78	3.17	4.52	0
	2	75	12	**1037.04**	1036.02	1032.02	14.90	16.05	17.58	0	**1037.04**	1035.38	1030.76	9.03	11.93	15.16	0
	3	100	10	**1134.12**	1133.68	1132.93	31.09	32.16	34.79	0	1133.73	1132.88	1131.83	18.91	23.96	30.78	0
	4	150	15	1743.66	1740.70	1738.73	100.73	106.32	111.21	2	**1743.84**	1738.75	1730.28	106.42	117.81	130.60	1
	5	199	19	2448.28	2443.09	2439.60	259.48	274.42	315.79	2	2448.36	2444.24	2438.50	243.28	263.92	286.24	0
	6	120	12	1056.17	1056.06	1055.90	52.52	54.79	57.58	0	1056.16	1055.47	1054.31	21.18	24.65	30.39	0
	7	100	11	**1467.36**	1467.36	1467.36	29.81	30.62	31.87	0	**1467.36**	1466.80	1465.63	10.37	11.21	12.90	0
Set 3	1	50	8	**632.00**	631.99	631.92	4.54	5.01	6.13	0	**632.00**	631.95	631.75	2.62	**2.96**	4.24	0
	2	75	13	**1056.39**	1056.07	1055.61	16.40	17.66	18.61	0	**1056.39**	1055.80	1053.72	7.47	**8.58**	10.33	0
	3	100	11	**1157.59**	1157.15	1156.12	32.31	33.60	35.74	0	1157.45	1157.10	1155.71	14.70	16.59	19.11	0
	4	150	16	**1770.20**	1768.56	1766.92	122.04	124.75	129.06	0	1769.53	1768.01	1766.36	50.83	**67.80**	83.62	0
	5	199	20	2482.60	2480.58	2477.57	297.37	309.95	324.28	2	2480.00	2477.16	2470.83	137.42	**161.56**	179.93	1
	6	120	13	1077.44	1077.25	1077.07	48.33	53.57	58.20	0	**1077.53**	1077.35	1077.15	21.23	27.49	32.48	0
	7	100	13	**1494.77**	1494.68	1494.39	32.34	33.24	34.59	0	**1494.77**	1494.59	1494.37	10.05	10.80	13.04	0

MS-ELS (5-20-5)

| | | | Without split | | | | | | | Split | | | | | | |
| | | | Satisfied Demand | | | CPU Time (s.) | | | SSP | Satisfied Demand | | | CPU Time (s.) | | | SSP |
Inst.	n	k	Best	Avg.	Worst	Min.	Avg.	Max.		Best	Avg.	Worst	Min.	Avg.	Max.	
Set 1	1	50	6	**592.62**	591.78	590.19	5.90	6.29	8.29	2	591.51	590.56	589.53	6.79	8.03	9.06	0
	2	75	11	1006.04	1003.43	997.43	60.09	130.98	177.16	4	**1007.90**	1004.00	999.11	114.72	145.01	181.59	1
	3	100	9	1100.10	1097.92	1095.26	39.13	42.52	47.13	1	1099.28	1097.11	1094.59	62.96	66.54	74.09	0
	4	150	14	-	-	-	-	-	-	-	-	-	-	-	-	-	-
	5	199	18	-	-	-	-	-	-	-	-	-	-	-	-	-	-
	6	120	11	1026.25	1024.72	1022.24	144.97	202.18	279.84	0	1024.89	1021.90	1018.95	150.74	205.26	248.86	0
	7	100	11	**1434.21**	1433.89	1433.50	33.29	34.25	36.77	0	1434.17	1433.87	1433.38	14.01	15.12	17.39	0
Set 2	1	50	7	**615.66**	615.66	615.66	4.79	5.13	6.52	0	**615.66**	615.66	615.66	3.05	3.37	5.00	0
	2	75	12	**1037.04**	1036.60	1036.17	16.06	16.92	17.63	2	**1037.04**	1035.28	1032.04	12.17	13.50	14.96	1
	3	100	10	1133.98	1133.75	1133.57	32.58	33.81	36.53	3	1133.98	1133.06	1132.18	20.92	23.82	26.92	0
	4	150	15	1742.15	1739.15	1736.19	115.33	120.20	125.99	1	1741.66	1738.70	1736.38	122.85	130.95	140.76	0
	5	199	19	2445.39	2442.09	2439.55	297.10	328.51	381.14	2	2443.27	2440.11	2436.25	278.96	313.96	372.93	0
	6	120	12	1056.16	1056.09	1055.98	55.93	57.66	59.33	2	1056.16	1055.86	1054.51	23.73	25.60	27.55	1
	7	100	12	**1467.36**	**1467.36**	1467.35	30.90	31.48	33.77	0	**1467.36**	1466.96	1466.20	11.39	11.97	13.54	0
Set 3	1	50	8	**632.00**	632.00	632.00	4.85	5.11	6.18	0	**632.00**	632.00	632.00	2.76	3.02	4.37	0
	2	75	13	**1056.39**	1056.35	1056.27	17.11	17.67	19.28	0	1056.36	1055.89	1055.40	8.28	9.15	10.70	0
	3	100	11	1157.51	1157.35	1157.13	34.40	34.91	36.57	0	1157.46	1157.02	1156.46	16.44	17.99	19.48	0
	4	150	16	1769.71	1768.76	1767.78	124.20	128.39	134.15	1	1768.19	1766.73	1764.23	73.74	81.44	90.09	0
	5	199	20	2480.76	2479.38	2476.07	308.54	315.44	320.87	2	2480.53	2477.71	2474.53	175.26	187.71	204.02	0
	6	120	13	**1077.53**	1077.37	1077.11	56.65	58.61	60.39	0	**1077.53**	1077.31	1077.15	27.38	29.02	31.42	1
	7	100	13	**1494.77**	1494.76	1494.73	33.97	34.80	36.31	0	1494.74	1494.48	1494.08	11.31	11.99	14.05	0

adapted instances for a total of 21. The *set 1* use the same number of vehicles reported in the BKSs for the CVRP, the *set 2* and *set 3* increase by one and two the number of vehicles, respectively.

Each of four methods with ('Split') and without ('-') the split procedure are executed. Each method runs the local search 500 times and each instance was solved ten times.

Table 1 and 2 present the number of nodes (n) and the number of used vehicles (k) by instance as well as the detailed results of each method with its respective set of assigned parameters in parenthesis ($nbOfRestarts$-$nbOfIter$-$nbOfChildren$). The best, average and worst satisfied demand and the minimum, average and maximum CPU time in seconds per run are reported for each

Table 3. Summary of results by set and in total

	ILS (1-500-1)		MS–ILS (5-100-1)		ELS (1-50-10)		MS–ELS (5-20-5)	
	-	Split	-	Split	-	Split	-	Split
Set 1 (5 instances)								
Average GAP	**0.04%**	0.05%	0.07%	0.17%	0.07%	0.05%	0.10%	0.15%
# of BFS	**3**	2	2	0	**3**	1	2	1
Avg. CPU Time (s.)	37.62	**35.27**	79.27	71.41	48.64	42.84	83.24	87.99
Set 2 (5 instances)								
Average GAP	0.01%	**0.00%**	**0.00%**	0.01%	**0.00%**	0.01%	**0.00%**	**0.00%**
# of BFS	4	4	3	2	4	3	3	3
Avg. CPU Time (s.)	27.52	**14.68**	33.24	18.56	27.72	14.98	29.00	15.65
Set 3 (5 instances)								
Average GAP	**0.00%**	**0.00%**	**0.00%**	**0.00%**	**0.00%**	**0.00%**	**0.00%**	**0.00%**
# of BFS	3	4	4	2	4	4	4	2
Avg. CPU Time (s.)	28.34	**12.80**	28.58	13.70	28.62	13.28	30.22	14.23
Set 2 (7 instances)								
Average GAP	0.02%	**0.01%**	0.03%	0.06%	**0.01%**	**0.01%**	0.04%	0.06%
# of BFS	4	**5**	3	2	4	4	3	3
Avg. CPU Time (s.)	73.32	**64.36**	86.03	77.08	74.19	65.24	84.82	74.74
Set 3 (7 instances)								
Average GAP	**0.00%**	0.02%	0.01%	0.02%	**0.00%**	0.02%	0.02%	0.03%
# of BFS	4	4	4	2	**5**	4	4	2
Avg. CPU Time (s.)	83.56	43.26	79.04	46.34	82.54	**42.25**	84.99	48.62
TOTAL (19 instances)								
Average GAP	**0.02%**	0.03%	0.03%	0.08%	**0.02%**	0.03%	0.05%	0.07%
# of BFS	11	11	9	4	**12**	9	9	6
Avg. CPU Time (s.)	67.7	**48.93**	81.68	64.26	70.54	50.87	84.47	68.6

method. The column 'SSP' represents the number of times that solution of the set partitioning problem improves the solution obtained by the framework.

No feasible solution was found in instances 4 and 5 of the *set 1*. So, these are not considered for the following analyzes. The best found solution (BFS) and the minimum average CPU time for each instance are indicated in boldface. The ELS without split and the ILS with and without split found the BFS in 12 and 11 out of 19 instances, respectively. The ILS with split in 12 out of 19 instances obtained the minimum average CPU time. This means that ILS with split gives the best results in terms of quality and execution time.

The maximum number of times that the solution of the set partitioning improves the results obtained by the framework is four and it happens only once. In most cases, this procedure did not improve the results.

In this problem, the number of vehicles plays an important role because the number of vehicles increases or decreases the number of attended people. The best scenario is to have a vehicle to attend each shelter, but this is not possible due to the limited quantity of resources in this context.

The GAP of each instance is calculated as $GAP = ((\frac{BFS - bestSatisfiedDemand}{BFS}) \times 100)$ for all methods. Then, the average GAP by set and in total is computed and it is shown in Table 3. This table also summarizes the number of BFS found by each method and each set as well as the Avg. CPU time. It should be note that Table 3 is divided by three. The first part is to compare the three sets of instances. It only computes the results of the five instances which a feasible solution is found in *set 1*. The second part computes the seven instances for *set 2* and *set 3* and the last part consider the 19 instances. The best value on each row is indicated in boldface.

The average GAP differences between all methods is less than 0.2%. Nevertheless, the differences of methods that include the split procedure converge much faster than those that do not include it. This difference can be up to 50%.

In general, the ILS and ELS without split give the best solutions, but the ILS with split is faster than other methods. The percentage difference with the methods that report the best solutions is only 0.01%.

5   Conclusion

This article addresses the CVRP-TDD in the humanitarian context. A metaheuristic framework able to execute four metaheuristics using or not the split procedure only changing a set of three parameters is proposed. Numerical experiments show that the ILS and ELS give better results than multi-start versions and the faster convergence using the split procedure highlights the efficiency and good performance of this procedure. This procedure converges faster and the number of attended people increases each time that the number of vehicles is greater.

References

1. Akbari, V., Salman, F.S.: Multi-vehicle synchronized arc routing problem to restore post-disaster network connectivity. European Journal of Operational Research 257(2), 625–640 (2017)
2. Beasley, J.E.: Route first cluster second methods for vehicle routing. Omega 11(4), 403–408 (1983)
3. Cattaruzza, D., Absi, N., Feillet, D., Vidal, T.: A memetic algorithm for the multi trip vehicle routing problem. European Journal of Operational Research 236(3), 833–848 (2014)
4. Christofides, N., Mingozzi, A., Toth, P.: The vehicle routing problem. Chichester: Wiley (1979)
5. Coppola, D.P.: The management of disasters. In: Coppola, D.P. (ed.) Introduction to International Disaster Management (Third Edition). Butterworth-Heinemann, (2015)
6. Cozzolino, A.: Humanitarian logistics and supply chain management. In: Humanitarian Logistics, pp. 5–16. Springer Briefs in Business, Springer Berlin Heidelberg (2012)
7. Duque, P.A.M., Dolinskaya, I.S., Sörensen, K.: Network repair crew scheduling and routing for emergency relief distribution problem. European Journal of Operational Research 248(1), 272 – 285 (2016)
8. Glover, F.: Ejection chains, reference structures and alternating path methods for traveling salesman problems. Discrete Applied Mathematics 65(13), 223 – 253 (1996)
9. Guha-Sapir, D., Hoyois, P., Below, R.: Annual disaster statistical review 2015: The numbers and trends (2016)
10. Gutjahr, W.J., Dzubur, N.: Bi-objective bilevel optimization of distribution center locations considering user equilibria. Transportation Research Part E: Logistics and Transportation Review 85, 1 – 22 (2016)

11. Lacomme, P., Prins, C., Prodhon, C., Ren, L.: A multi-start split based path relinking (msspr) approach for the vehicle routing problem with route balancing. Engineering Applications of Artificial Intelligence 38, 237–251 (2015)
12. Lourenço, H.R., Martin, O.C., Stützle, T.: Iterated local search. In: Glover, F., Kochenberger, G. (eds.) Handbook of Metaheuristics, International Series in Operations Research & Management Science, vol. 57, pp. 320–353. Springer US (2003)
13. Lu, C.C., Ying, K.C., Chen, H.J.: Real-time relief distribution in the aftermath of disasters–a rolling horizon approach. Transportation Research Part E: Logistics and Transportation Review 93, 1–20 (2016)
14. Lysgaard, J., Wøhlk, S.: A branch-and-cut-and-price algorithm for the cumulative capacitated vehicle routing problem. European Journal of Operational Research 236(3), 800 – 810 (2014)
15. Moshref-Javadi, M., Lee, S.: The customer-centric, multi-commodity vehicle routing problem with split delivery. Expert Systems with Applications 56, 335–348 (2016)
16. Ngueveu, S.U., Prins, C., Calvo, R.W.: An effective memetic algorithm for the cumulative capacitated vehicle routing problem. Computers & Operations Research 37(11), 1877 – 1885 (2010)
17. Pillac, V., Hentenryck, P.V., Even, C.: A conflict-based path-generation heuristic for evacuation planning. Transportation Research Part B: Methodological 83, 136 – 150 (2016)
18. Prins, C.: A simple and effective evolutionary algorithm for the vehicle routing problem. Computers & Operations Research 31(12), 1985–2002 (2004)
19. Prins, C.: Two memetic algorithms for heterogeneous fleet vehicle routing problems. Engineering Applications of Artificial Intelligence 22(6), 916–928 (2009)
20. Prins, C., Lacomme, P., Prodhon, C.: Order-first split-second methods for vehicle routing problems: A review. Transportation Research Part C: Emerging Technologies 40, 179–200 (2014)
21. Rivera, J.C., Afsar, H.M., Prins, C.: A multistart iterated local search for the multi-trip cumulative capacitated vehicle routing problem. Computational Optimization and Applications 61(1), 159–187 (2015)
22. Rivera, J.C., Afsar, H.M., Prins, C.: Mathematical formulations and exact algorithm for the multitrip cumulative capacitated single-vehicle routing problem. European Journal of Operational Research 249(1), 93–104 (2016)
23. Silva, M.M., Subramanian, A., Vidal, T., Ochi, L.S.: A simple and effective metaheuristic for the minimum latency problem. European Journal of Operational Research 221(3), 513 – 520 (2012)
24. Thomas, A.S., Kopczak, L.R.: From logistics to supply chain management: the path forward in the humanitarian sector. Fritz Institute 15, 1–15 (2005)
25. Uchoa, E., Pecin, D., Pessoa, A., Poggi, M., Vidal, T., Subramanian, A.: New benchmark instances for the capacitated vehicle routing problem. European Journal of Operational Research 257(3), 845–858 (2017)
26. Victoria, J.F., Afsar, H.M., Prins, C.: Column generation based heuristic for the vehicle routing problem with time-dependent demand. IFAC-PapersOnLine 49(12), 526–531 (2016)
27. Vidal, T.: Technical note: Split algorithm in $O(n)$ for the capacitated vehicle routing problem. Computers & Operations Research 69, 40–47 (2016)
28. Wolf, S., Merz, P.: Evolutionary Local Search for the Super-Peer Selection Problem and the p-Hub Median Problem, pp. 1–15. Springer Berlin Heidelberg, Berlin, Heidelberg (2007)

Planning of an Offshore Well Plugging Campaign: A Vehicle Routing Approach

Steffen Bakker[1(✉)], Mats Aarlott[2], Asgeir Tomasgard[1], and Kjetil Midthun[2]

[1] Department of Industrial Economics and Technology Management, Norwegian University of Science and Technology, Trondheim, Norway
steffen.bakker@ntnu.no
[2] Department of Applied Economics, SINTEF, Trondheim, Norway

Abstract. When a petroleum well no longer serves its purpose, the operator is required to plug and abandon (P&A) the well to avoid contamination of reservoir fluids. An increasing number of offshore wells needs to be P&A'd in the near future, and the costs of these operations are substantial. Research on planning methods in order to allocate vessels that are required to perform these operations in a cost-efficient manner is therefore essential. We use an optimization approach and propose a mixed-integer linear programming model based on a variant of the uncapacitated vehicle routing problem that includes precedence and non-concurrence constraints to plan a plugging campaign. P&A costs are minimized by creating optimal routes for a set of vessels, such that all operations that are needed to P&A a set of development wells are executed. In a case study, we show that our proposed optimization approach may lead to significant cost savings compared to traditional planning methods and is well suited for P&A planning purposes on a tactical level.

Keywords: Routing, Plug and Abandonment, Plugging Campaign

1 Introduction

An active petroleum well goes through different phases: exploration, production, and injection. After the well has served its purpose, and is no longer profitable, it must be plugged and abandoned. According to [13, Chapter 9], Plug and Abandonment (P&A) is the process of securing a well by installing required well barriers (plugs) such that the well will be permanently abandoned and cannot be used or re-entered again. We refer to P&A as the permanent abandonment of the well, as opposed to temporary P&A, where the well may be re-entered. Permanently plugged wells shall be abandoned with an eternal perspective taking into account the effects of any foreseeable chemical and geological processes. This definition holds for offshore and onshore wells, but in this paper we consider solely the former. Moreover, we only focus on development wells (consisting of production and injection wells), as exploration wells are P&A'd immediately after drilling.

To give an impression of the magnitude of future P&A work, [12] forecast a total of 1,800 development wells to be P&A'd the next decade on the United

T. Bektaş et al. (Eds.), ICCL 2017, LNCS 10572, pp. 158–173, 2017.
https://doi.org/10.1007/978-3-319-68496-3_11

Kingdom and Norwegian Continental Shelf. The average P&A cost per well in the same period and regions is estimated to be around £5 – 15 million. Currently, approximately 50% of the costs of decommissioning, which also takes into account removal of installations, is related to P&A. On the United States Outer Continental Shelf, which most notably consists of the Gulf of Mexico, there are at present 5,082 production wells and 3,220 temporarily plugged wells, that are in need of permanent plugging [3].

The high costs related to these operations and opportunity costs of the vessels required to perform these operations (e.g. exploration or drilling activities), makes this topic highly relevant for research on efficient resource allocation and scheduling of P&A operations.

In this paper, we look at a tactical time horizon for the planning and scheduling of P&A operations for a number of subsea wells in which the production systems are located on the seabed. In this respect, a *P&A campaign* is an allocation of *vessels* (ships and rigs) to perform plugging operations on a set of wells.

As P&A costs derive mainly from renting vessels, cost savings can be achieved by, e.g., developing new or improving existing techniques such that the durations of the operations are reduced. When taking a system perspective, savings may also be obtained by optimizing routing of vessels and scheduling of operations. These cost savings might result from, for example, decreased sailing time or more use of vessels with a low day-rate. Here lies the basis for developing and demonstrating how an optimization approach based on vehicle routing theory may be used to reap these rewards.

In view of this, we propose an optimization model for the tactical planning problem concerned with P&A campaigns. We refer to this problem as the P&A Campaign Problem (PACP).

Even though optimization has been extensively applied to the petroleum industry (e.g. [10, 6]), literature on the use of optimization in P&A planning is, to the best of our knowledge, scarce. The only application of optimization to P&A that we are aware of is [1].

The planning of a P&A Campaign can be considered to be a vehicle routing problem (VRP). In this context, "routing" can be defined as the assignment of sequences of operations to be performed by vessels. The term "scheduling" is then used when the timing aspect is brought into routing. Therefore, scheduling includes the timing of the various events along a vessel's route. [4] give a review of ship routing and scheduling problems within maritime transportation, categorized on the basis of strategic, tactical and operational planning levels. An optimization model for maintenance routing and scheduling for offshore wind farms, based on a VRP with pick-up and delivery, is proposed in [7]. This model has similar features as the PACP. However, just like most maritime transportation problems, it involves cargo or inventory considerations.

The PACP can be represented as an extension of the Uncapacitated Vehicle Routing Problem (u-VRP) or Multiple Traveling Salesman Problem (m-TSP) with precedence and non-concurrence constraints, a heterogeneous fleet of vessels and the possibility of multiple routes, see [14]. Related work is done in [5] and

[2]. The former paper considers an extension of the traveling salesman problem (TSP) with precedence constraints applied to ship scheduling and presents other related work on TSPs, whereas the latter contains a review of literature on the m-TSP and practical applications.

There are several ways in which the PACP problem can be formulated. We have investigated using a time-indexed mixed-integer programming formulation. However, as P&A campaigns are characterized by both a long time horizon (1-2 years) and a fine time resolution for individual operations (hours/days), this formulation leads to a large number of binary variables. As a result, the model quickly becomes intractable, even for toy-sized problems. Therefore, we formulate the model using an arc-flow formulation, treating time as continuous. This formulation requires significantly less binary variables and is capable of solving larger instances of the problem.

We extend current literature on vehicle routing problems by introducing a new practical application of an u-VRP, besides proposing 'non-concurrence' constraints, which are required when considering multilateral wells.

The remainder of this paper is structured as follows. We start by giving a problem description in Section 2 and provide a model formulation in Section 3. A case study consisting of three wells is then described in Section 4, of which the computational as well as economical results are presented in Section 5. The results are compared with other realistic routing alternatives. The paper concludes with Section 6, which summarizes the main findings from this work as well as suggesting the direction future research could take.

2   Problem Description

Offshore petroleum wells can be distinguished by being connected to either a subsea or platform installation, where the wells are usually clustered in *templates*. In order to P&A an offshore well, several operations have to be performed in a strictly ordered sequence. These operations consist of amongst others preparatory work, the setting of plugs and removal of the wellhead. Subsea wells need vessels to perform these operations. There are several classes of vessels that are able to carry out these operations. In general, Mobile Offshore Drilling Units (MODUs), also called rigs, can conduct all types of operations. This class of vessels includes jackup rigs, semi-submersible rigs (SSRs) and drillships. Another class consisting of lighter vessels such as light well intervention vessels (LWIVs) and light construction vessels (LCVs) can only perform a subset of operations, but have a cheaper day-rate compared to rigs.

A categorization of these different operations into phases is given by [11], which is also extensively used by the industry. Based on this categorization, we define four operation types, or phases, which will be used more explicitly in the case study in Section 4. Phase 0 consists of preparatory work, which can, in general, be executed by all vessels. Phase 1 comprises the cutting and pulling of casing and tubing and setting of primary and secondary barriers, which requires a rig. Phase 2 again requires a rig and includes the setting of a surface plug.

Finally, phase 3, removal of the conductor and well head, might be performed from some lighter vessels. An overview of compatibilities between phases and vessel classes is given in Table 1.

Note that this categorization is constructed for wells in the North Sea, and need not necessarily hold for wells under different regulatory regimes. Still, it is a good representation that is useful in showing the traits of the model.

Table 1. Compatibility of phases and vessel classes

Phase	SSR	LWIV	LCV
0	X	X	X
1	X	-	-
2	X	-	-
3	X	X	-

Besides traditional wells with a single wellbore, there also exist wells with multiple wellbores connected to a common wellhead. These wells are known as multilateral wells. To give an example, Figure 1 shows a multilateral well with three lateral wellbores and a mainbore. The nodes represent operations in the wellbores that have to be performed to P&A the well. Multilateral wells are designed to reduce construction costs and increase production from a reservoir. Operations in different lateral wellbores cannot be performed simultaneously, as these wellbores must be entered through the same mainbore.

P&A operations are in general not time-critical, which means that wells can be left temporarily or partially plugged, as long as the wells are continuously monitored. Nonetheless, there might be reasons to include time windows for the operations. This might be due to legal issues, such as the expiry of a lease contract, or plans made by the operators. Vessel-use can also be limited due to contractual issues, alternative usage such as exploration or drilling, or other conditions like harsh weather.

Based on these different aspects of the P&A process we are able to formulate a general optimization model that minimizes the total costs related to a P&A campaign. The decision variables consist of binary variables determining the routes of the vessels and continuous variables specifying start times of operations. The constraints in the model are related to timing, precedence, non-concurrence and legal routes for vessels. The objective of the model is to minimize total rental costs, which is constructed based on time usage and day-rates of the different vessels.

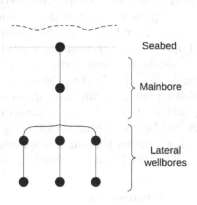

Fig. 1. Diagram of a multilateral well

3   Mathematical Formulation

In this section, we present the Mixed-Integer Linear Programming (MILP) Model for the PACP. We explain the notation (sets, indices, parameters and variables) used in the model and we provide the mathematical formulation of the constraints and objective functions.

3.1   Sets and Indices

To P&A a well, a certain number of operations have to be executed. These operations might be represented by the previously defined phases, but can be more or less detailed. We therefore define the set $\mathcal{N} = \{1, ..., N^{OPS}\}$, which consists of all the operations required to be executed on all wells. The set $\mathcal{K} = \{k_1, ..., k_{N^{VES}}\}$ consists of N^{VES} heterogeneous vessel that are available to perform these P&A operations. For every vessel $k \in \mathcal{K}$, we define $\mathcal{N}_k \subseteq \mathcal{N}$ to be the set of operations that vessel k can perform. We define origin and destination vertices $o(k)$ and $d(k)$, which represent locations such as harbours, where the vessels are situated at the start and end of the planning period, respectively. We model routing options as arcs, and P&A operations as vertices. Let $\mathcal{A}_k = \{(i,j) : i, j \in \mathcal{V}_k\}$ represent the arc set corresponding to vessel $k \in \mathcal{K}$, where $\mathcal{V}_k = \mathcal{N}_k \cup \{o(k), d(k)\}$ is the vertex set of vessel k. The precedence set $\mathcal{P}$, consists of pairs (i,j) with $i, j \in \mathcal{N}$, for which operation i should precede operation j. This set is included to ensure correct sequencing of operations. Some operations are prevented, due to technical reasons, from being executed simultaneously. Therefore, we let $\mathcal{S}$ consist of pairs of operations (i,j) with $i, j \in \mathcal{N}$ that cannot be executed simultaneously.

Moreover, given vertex i, $\delta_k^+(i)$ is defined as the set of vertices j such that arc $(i,j) \in \mathcal{A}_k$. That is, the set of possible vertices j that vessel k can visit after visiting vertex i. Similarly, given vertex i, $\delta_k^-(i)$ is defined as the set of vertices j such that $(j,i) \in \mathcal{A}_k$, i.e. the set of possible vertices j that a vessel k may have visited before visiting vertex i. The term "visit" is used to include operations as well as leaving the origin or entering the destination.

The PACP is now defined on the directed graphs $G_k = (\mathcal{V}_k, \mathcal{A}_k)$ for all $k \in \mathcal{K}$.

3.2   Parameters

For each vessel $k \in \mathcal{K}$, non-negative durations T_{ijk}^S and T_{ik}^{EX} representing sailing and execution times, are associated with each arc $(i,j) \in \mathcal{A}_k$ and vertex $i \in \mathcal{V}_k$, respectively. Sailing times equal zero for arcs between operations in the same well and otherwise consist of (de-)mobilization time and actual sailing time between wells. For every vertex $i \in \bigcup_{k \in \mathcal{K}} \mathcal{V}_k$ we associate a time window $[\underline{T}_i, \overline{T}_i]$, where $\underline{T}_i$ and $\overline{T}_i$ represent earliest start time and latest completion time of the corresponding operation in vertex i, respectively.

Non-negative day-rates C_k are defined for each vessel $k \in \mathcal{K}$. When using an alternative objective function which depends on vessel usage, we make use of varying day-rates C_k^{EX}, C_k^S, C_k^{SB}, for execution, sailing, and stand-by time, respectively.

3.3 Variables

The aim of the PACP is to find a collection of feasible vessel routes that minimizes total cost. We present this problem using an arc-flow formulation. We define a binary flow variable x_{ijk} for each vessel $k \in \mathcal{K}$ and arc $(i, j) \in \mathcal{A}_k$; equaling 1 if vessel k traverses arc (i, j) in the optimal solution, and 0 otherwise. Moreover, we define the continuous time variables t_{ik}, for each $k \in \mathcal{K}, i \in \mathcal{V}_k$, specifying the start-time of operation i by vessel k. We also introduce auxiliary variables, y_{ij}, for all $(i, j) \in \mathcal{S}$, taking the value 1 if operation i is executed before operation j, to deal with non-concurrence in multilateral wells.

3.4 Constraints

The constraints defining the MILP are treated below.

Operations. To P&A all wells under consideration, all corresponding operations have to be executed. This is ensured by the following constraints:

$$\sum_{k \in \mathcal{K}} \sum_{j \in \delta_k^+(i)} x_{ijk} = 1, \quad i \in \mathcal{N}. \tag{1}$$

These constraints also restrict the assignment of each operation to exactly one vessel.

Routing. The following sets of constraints define the possible routes that the vessels are allowed to take. First, we make sure that a vessel's route starts at its origin, and performs only one route:

$$\sum_{j \in \delta_k^+(o(k))} x_{o(k)jk} = 1, \quad k \in \mathcal{K}. \tag{2}$$

The inclusion of an arc between the origin and destination with zero cost gives the option not to make use of a vessel. Then, we assure that each vessel ends its route in its destination:

$$\sum_{i \in \delta_k^-(d(k))} x_{id(k)k} = 1, \quad k \in \mathcal{K}. \tag{3}$$

Finally, we have flow balance constraints ensuring feasible routing, stating that if a vessel is used to perform a P&A operation, it must move to another operation (in the same or any other well), or to the destination:

$$\sum_{i \in \delta_k^-(j)} x_{ijk} - \sum_{i \in \delta_k^+(j)} x_{jik} = 0, \quad k \in \mathcal{K}, j \in \mathcal{N}_k. \tag{4}$$

Multiple Routes. The previous constraints force the number of times a vessel can be used to one, assuming that when a vessel has left its origin to perform P&A operations, it must perform all its planned operations on that one route. This is a reasonable assumption if vessels are committed to a project for a longer time and vessel rent has to be payed throughout this whole period, independent on whether it is executing an operation or remains idle. However, if a vessel is allowed to return to a harbour where rental costs are not incurred, the possibility of multiple trips should be taken into account. This can be done by redefining the set $\mathcal{K}$. We include copies of the vessels if multiple routes are allowed. Formally, this leads to the following. First, we define $\mathcal{R}_k := \left\{1,..,N_k^R\right\}, k \in \mathcal{K}$, where N_k^R equals the maximum allowed number of routes for vessel k. Now, let $\tilde{\mathcal{K}} = \left\{\tilde{k}_{kr} : k \in \mathcal{K}, r \in \mathcal{R}_k\right\}$. To make sure that the routes are then planned in correct order we define the following constraints:

$$t_{d(\tilde{k}_{kr})\tilde{k}_{kr}} \le t_{o(\tilde{k}_{kr'})\tilde{k}_{kr'}}, \quad k \in \mathcal{K}, \quad r,r' \in \mathcal{R}_k \mid r' - r = 1. \tag{5}$$

That is, if we have two subsequent routes for a vessel, then the former route should be finished before the latter can start. The model now allows for multiple routes by replacing $\mathcal{K}$ with $\tilde{\mathcal{K}}$.

Timing. The time constraints ensure schedule feasibility with respect to start times of the operations. If a vessel performs an operation on a well (or enters its destination), it must have completed its previous operation (or left its origin) and travelled to the current location:

$$x_{ijk}\left(t_{ik} + T_{ik}^{EX} + T_{ijk}^S - t_{jk}\right) \le 0, \quad k \in \mathcal{K}, (i,j) \in \mathcal{A}_k. \tag{6a}$$

This can be linearized as

$$t_{ik} + T_{ik}^{EX} + T_{ijk}^S - t_{jk} \le M_{ijk}(1 - x_{ijk}) \quad k \in \mathcal{K}, (i,j) \in \mathcal{A}_k, \tag{6b}$$

where $M_{ijk} = \overline{T}_i + T_{ijk}^S - \underline{T}_j$.

Time windows for operations are defined by the following constraints:

$$\underline{T}_i \sum_{j \in \delta_k^+(i)} x_{ijk} \le t_{ik} \le (\overline{T}_i - T_{ik}^{EX}) \sum_{j \in \delta_k^+(i)} x_{ijk}, \quad k \in \mathcal{K}, i \in \mathcal{N}_k. \tag{7}$$

If a vessel does not perform a certain operation, then these constraints force the corresponding time variable to zero.

We also impose time windows for the origin and destination vertices, representing limitations in vessel use:

$$\underline{T}_i \le t_{ik} \le \overline{T}_i, \quad k \in \mathcal{K}, i \in \bigcup_{k \in \mathcal{K}} \{o(k), d(k)\}. \tag{8}$$

Precedence. As explained in Section 2, there exists a strict ordering in the sequence in which operations have to be performed within a well. This ordering is guaranteed to hold by the following precedence constraints:

$$\sum_{k \in \mathcal{K}} t_{ik} + \sum_{k \in \mathcal{K}} \sum_{l \in \delta_k^+(i)} T_{ik}^{EX} \cdot x_{ilk} - \sum_{k \in \mathcal{K}} t_{jk} \leq 0, \quad (i,j) \in \mathcal{P}. \tag{9}$$

Non-concurrence. The precedence constraints control the order in which operations in the same wellbore are being executed, but they cannot deal with the fact that operations from different lateral wellbores cannot be performed simultaneously. This phenomenon arises when considering multilateral wells. We refer to the constraints that arise in this situation as non-concurrence constraints. The following constraints enforce that for all non-concurrence pairs $(i,j) \in \mathcal{S}$ we have that either operation i is performed before operation j ($y_{ij} = 1$), or vice versa ($y_{ij} = 0$).:

$$\sum_{k \in \mathcal{K}} t_{ik} + \sum_{k \in \mathcal{K}} \sum_{l \in \delta_k^+(i)} T_{ik}^{EX} \cdot x_{ilk} - \sum_{k \in \mathcal{K}} t_{jk} \leq M_{ji}(1 - y_{ij}), \quad (i,j) \in \mathcal{S}, \tag{10a}$$

$$\sum_{k \in \mathcal{K}} t_{jk} + \sum_{k \in \mathcal{K}} \sum_{l \in \delta_k^+(j)} T_{jk}^{EX} \cdot x_{jlk} - \sum_{k \in \mathcal{K}} t_{ik} \leq M_{ij} y_{ij}, \quad (i,j) \in \mathcal{S}, \tag{10b}$$

where $M_{ij} = \overline{T}_j - \underline{T}_i$.

Alternatively, one can represent multilateral wells in a more restricted way, such that constraints (10) are not necessary. We can obtain this by either bundling operations that have the same phase but are in different wellbores or imposing an order for the execution of operations in the different lateral wellbores. This approach leads to a reduction in the number of constraints and integer variables, but might lead to sub-optimality.

3.5 Objective Functions

Differences in the construction of P&A contracts leads to the need to model different types of objective functions. To illustrate this, we present two exemplifying objective functions. When service companies perform P&A operations for operators, contracts are usually written on a day rate or turnkey basis [8]. Day rates are made up of, amongst others, vessel rent and personnel and equipment costs. Specification of turnkey contracts needs a precise breakdown of P&A costs, which leads to an analysis of the same cost factors. Therefore, we formulate the objective function in its most basic form as the sum of individual day-rates multiplied by total time the vessels are used offshore:

$$\min \sum_{k \in \mathcal{K}} C_k (t_{d(k)k} - t_{o(k)k}). \tag{11}$$

Some contracts specify varying day rates, such as operating, sailing and stand-by rates (C_k^{EX}, C_k^S, C^{SB}, respectively), which can easily be taken into account by the following objective function:

$$\min \sum_{k \in \mathcal{K}} \left(C_k^{EX} t_k^{EX} + C_k^S t_k^S + C_k^{SB} t_k^{SB} \right), \tag{12}$$

with:

$$t_k^{EX} = \sum_{i \in \mathcal{N}_k} T_{ik}^{EX} \sum_{j \in \delta_k^+(i)} x_{ijk}, \qquad\qquad k \in \mathcal{K}, \tag{13}$$

$$t_k^S = \sum_{(i,j) \in \mathcal{A}_k} T_{ijk}^S x_{ijk}, \qquad\qquad k \in \mathcal{K}, \tag{14}$$

$$t_k^{SB} = t_{d(k)k} - t_{o(k)k} - t_k^S - t_k^{EX}, \qquad\qquad k \in \mathcal{K}, \tag{15}$$

where t_k^{EX}, t_k^S and t_k^{SB} denote the execution, sailing, and stand-by time, respectively.

In some cases, large operating companies perform the P&A operations themselves. They usually have entered into long-term contracts with ship companies to rent vessels, which are used for multiple purposes. In this situation, the objective function might reflect opportunity costs arising from alternative uses of the vessel, such as exploration or well development.

3.6   Variable Domains

The domains of the variables used in the aforementioned constraints and objective functions are declared below:

$$x_{ijk} \in \{0,1\}, \quad k \in \mathcal{K}, (i,j) \in \mathcal{A}_k, \tag{16}$$

$$t_{ik} \in \mathbb{R}_0^+, \quad k \in \mathcal{K}, i \in \mathcal{N}_k, \tag{17}$$

$$y_{ij} \in \{0,1\}, \quad (i,j) \in \mathcal{S}. \tag{18}$$

Thus, the PACP model used in the case study in this paper consist of constraints (1) - (10b), variables (16) - (18), and objective function (11).

4   Case Study

To test the functioning and show possible benefits of the model, we run the model under several scenarios. We then compare these results with the results resulting from the use of simple plugging strategies, reflecting different ways in which plugging campaigns currently are, or could be, executed. The scenarios consist of one base case scenario, and five alternative scenarios that are derived by changing some parameters of the base case scenario. In the base case, we consider three subsea wells (denoted by W1, W2 and W3) on which operations have to be performed such that all wells will be permanently P&A'd. We assume that the vessels under consideration are located at the same harbour at the beginning of the planning period, and that this harbour is also the destination. The wells have a single wellbore and are located on the same field, of which W2 and W3 are located on the same template. We assume that all wells are at a distance of 150 kilometers from the harbour and W1 is 5 kilometers apart from W2 and W3. The locations and distances between wells are taken from existing wells on the Alvheim field in the North Sea. We use the four phases as described in Section 2 as a categorization of the P&A operations for each well. We assume that two different vessels are available to carry out the operations: a Semi-Submersible Rig (SSR), that can perform operations in all phases, and a Light Well Intervention Vessel (LWIV), that can perform operations in phase 0 and 3. Both vessels have a fixed day-rate, independent of the activity (executing P&A operations, sailing, or stand-by). Input data to the model, retrieved from the P&A database as described in [9], is given in Table 2. Note that the execution

Table 2. Summary of input data for SSR and LWIV.

	Execution time (days)				Day Rate	Speed	(de-) Mobilization
Phase:	0	1	2	3	(k$)	(knots)	(days)
SSR	11.9	8.85	5.63	0.75	700	5	2.5
LWIV	11.9	-	-	0.75	450	15	0.2

times are the same for all wells, as we assume that all wells are similar. However, the model allows for unique values for execution times in the case where well specific duration estimates are available. Sailing times consist of actual sailing times (calculated based on distances between the wells and speeds of the different vessels), as well as mobilization and de-mobilization time. As opposed to LWIVs, some SSRs require anchor handling, which leads to a significant difference in (de-)mobilization time. We note that when a vessel moves between wells on the same template, no anchor handling is required.

4.1 Scenarios

We perform a sensitivity analysis in which we, ceteris parabus, change some of the parameters of the base case as defined above (*SCEN1*). As an LWIV is more sensitive to bad weather than a SSR, we look at the scenarios where we increase the execution times for the LWIV. To investigate this effect we multiply the duration of phase 0, when using a LWIV, by arbitrary factors 1.5 and 2 given in scenarios *SCEN2* and *SCEN3* respectively. In the fourth and fifth scenario (*SCEN4* and *SCEN5*), we multiply the duration of phase 3 by factors 1.5 and 2 as well, when executed by a LWIV.

Finally, in the sixth scenario (*SCEN6*) the execution time of phase 3 for both LWIV and SSR is multiplied by a factor of 2. This scenario is chosen to reflect a case where it is optimal to perform all possible operations using a LWIV in two separate trips.

4.2   Strategies

We now define five different strategies that might be employed to perform a plugging campaign. The first strategy is simply the optimal outcome suggested by the model (*OPT*), whereas the last four strategies are examples of how different P&A campaigns can be planned manually. Traditionally, P&A operations are performed by a single rig, which is characterised by *STRAT1*. The optimal solution in this case is to execute all operations in a well consecutively and find the optimal sequence of wells to visit for the rig. More recently, cheaper light vessels are being used to perform light P&A operations that do not require a drilling rig. This might be optimal from a well perspective, but not necessarily from a system perspective. Different variations of vessel use are given in *STRAT2*, *STRAT3* and *STRAT4*. We refer to these strategies as manual strategies, even though we solve restricted versions of the optimization model. The five strategies are now given by:

- *OPT*: In this case, we allow the model to find the optimal allocation of vessels to P&A operations. The SSR may perform all operations in all phases (but must perform all operations in phases 1 and 2. The LWIV may perform any operations in phases 0 and 3. Finally, the LWIV is allowed to perform two routes. That is, it can return to the harbour once, where it does not incur rental costs.
- *STRAT1:* We restrict the model only to make use of the SSR to perform all the P&A operations on the wells.
- *STRAT2:* We require that all phase 0 operations are performed by the LWIV, and that the remaining operations are done by the SSR. The LWIV is only allowed to perform one route.
- *STRAT3:* Same as *STRAT2*, but we also require that all operations in phase 3 are performed by the LWIV.
- *STRAT4:* Same as *STRAT3*, however this strategy allows the LWIV to perform two routes. This reflects the possibility to do all preparatory work with a light vessel (after which the vessel goes back to the harbour), then use a rig to perform the cutting and pulling operations in phase 1 and 2, and finally use the light vessel to perform phase 3.

5   Results

In this section, we present results from running the model for the different strategies and scenarios set out in Section 4. The model has been implemented in the Mosel programming language, and solved with FICO Xpress version 8.0.4. The analyses have been carried out on a HP dl165 G5 computer with an AMD Opteron 2431, 2,4 GHz processor, 24Gb RAM running Red Hat Linux v4.4.

Table 3. Cost increase (in percentage) for the different strategies compared to the optimal cost (in million dollars) and start- and end-times for the routes in the optimal strategy (second route in parenthesis).

			Scenario					
			1	2	3	4	5	6
Cost (M$) Optimal			55.32	63.16	63.65	55.41	55.42	56.55
Cost increase (%)	Strategy	1	15.06	0.77	0.00	14.87	14.86	15.34
		2	0.17	0.44	12.30	0.00	0.00	0.77
		3	15.79	8.80	20.59	15.90	16.20	13.87
		4	0.39	0.64	12.49	1.14	2.06	0.00
Start- and end-times (days)	SSR	start	9.1	19.4	0	9.1	9.1	9.1
		end	63.5	73.2	90.9	64.3	64.3	62.0
	LWIV	start	0	0	-	0	0	0 (54.7)
		end	38.2	56.8	-	37.2	37.2	37.2 (60.7)

Table 3 shows numerical results for the different strategies and scenarios, whereas Figure 2 illustrates the optimal routes for each of the five scenarios.

There are several observations we can make based on these figures. To begin with, we see from Figure 2 that each scenario results in a different optimal routing (except for *SCEN4* and *SCEN5*), despite the differences between the scenarios being small. As the LWIV cannot perform operations in phases 1 and 2, the main differences between the optimal routing strategies become apparent in the choice of vessel to perform phased 0 and 3. Looking at Table 3, in the first two scenarios, none of the defined manual strategies is optimal (even though strategies 2 and 4 result in objective function values that are close to the optimal value). For each of the last four scenarios, one of the manually defined strategies is optimal, however none of these strategies performs well under all scenarios. Based upon the data input, the performance might even get arbitrarily bad. *STRAT3* performs worst under all scenarios. In this strategy we commit the LWIV to perform the operations in phases 0 and 4. But, since the LWIV cannot start operations in phase 4 before the SSR is done with phase 3, this strategy leads to an increase in costs due to idle time of the LWIV.

The dynamics in scenarios 1 to 3 are also worth mentioning. In the base case, the LWIV only performs phase 3 on one well. When it takes more time (factor 1.5, scenario 2) to perform phase 0, the LWIV no longer has to wait to perform an additional phase 3 operation. However, when the duration of phase 0 doubles (scenario 3), using the LWIV is no longer optimal at all.

The differences between scenario 4 and 5 are small as phase 3 has a relatively short duration

We conclude that the optimal routes depend heavily on differences in travel distance, execution times and day rates for the different vessels. Based on our inputs, assumptions, and choice of case study, we see that the optimal solution

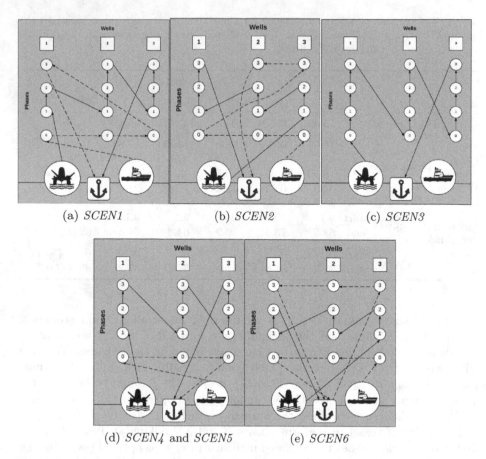

(a) *SCEN1*   (b) *SCEN2*   (c) *SCEN3*

(d) *SCEN4* and *SCEN5*   (e) *SCEN6*

Fig. 2. Optimal vessel routes for the six different scenarios. The solid and dashed routes correspond to the SSR and LWIV respectively.

might represent cost savings in the order of magnitude of US$ million compared to other and more conventional planning methods, represented by the manually defined strategies. This shows the strength of the application of an optimization model in planning of a P&A campaign.

Considering that the scenario in question consists of three wells, it is reasonable to assume that cost savings will be significant when including more wells.

The case study we considered consisted of three wells that needed to be P&A'd, which is a realistic sized problem. However, depending on the case, P&A campaigns on larger sets of wells can be planned, and might result in other system effects. We therefore perform a computational study, to investigate the scalability of the model. We take the previously defined case study with two vessels (SSR and LWIV) and three wells as base case. We then add wells that are located on the same field and are in need of P&A, and try to solve the model to optimality. The results are given in Table 4. The maximum run time is set to 24 hours, which is reached in the case with 7 wells. Since the addition of one extra well implies adding four different operations or vertices, we clearly see an exponential increase in the solution time. Moreover, we observe very slow convergence of the lower bound.

Non-concurrence in Multilateral Wells. In the following example we show the importance of including the non-concurrence constraints (10) as opposed to using a simplification. We consider a multilateral well that needs to be P&A'd. The well has one mainbore and three lateral wellbores, as represented in Figure 1. We assume that the well is located on the same field as in the case study, and we make use of the same vessels (i.e. a LWIV and SSR). Now assume that the LWIV is only available in the first month. Embracing the formulation with non-concurrence constraints, this leads to an optimal solution where the LWIV performs phase 0 operations in two lateral wellbores, after which the SSR performs the remaining operations. This results in an objective value of 47.806 million dollars. In a more restricted version of the model with an imposed order for the execution of operations in the different lateral wellbores, in the optimal solution, the SSR performs all operations and the LWIV is not being used. This leads to an objective function value of 53.116 million dollars. So, in this example, not including the non-concurrence constraints leads to an additional cost of approximately 5 million dollars. The simplified model consists of 61 binary variables and 124 constraints. Inclusion of non-concurrence constraints leads to an additional number of binary variables equal to the cardinality of the set S (denoted by $|S|$) and $2 \cdot |S|$ extra constraints. In the example above we have $|S| = 12$, which does not lead to a significant increase in solution time.

6   Conclusions

The main contribution in this paper is a novel formulation of an optimization model for a P&A campaign. This is a field where, to the extent of our knowledge, optimization techniques so far have not been applied. In the case study, we show that there might be significant benefits from using this optimization model in monetary terms. Small changes in the data basis may lead to highly differing optimal routes. The manually defined planning strategies are therefore not robust to such changes in the data. Moreover, we

Table 4. Computational results

Wells	Time (sec)	MIP-Gap (%)
3	0.51	0
4	2.52	0
5	46.14	0
6	900.74	0
7	86401.50	0.48

show that the inclusion of non-concurrence constraints is preferred over a simplified representation of multilateral wells. As a result, the model may serve as decision support to decision makers. Nonetheless, we recommend to run more extensive case analyses, to evaluate alternative campaigns and discover general rules that can be used when planning P&A campaigns. The model can then also be used to run different scenario analyses to evaluate the effect of changes in parameters or definition of phases due to, for example, new technology.

The major challenge is related to scalability of the model. In order to solve more realistic cases, future research might therefor be conducted into several directions. To begin with, the literature suggests the implementation of decomposition techniques, such as column-generation, and inclusion of valid inequalities. Alternatively, when taking a non-exact approach, heuristics mights be developed for the problem, which however cannot guarantee that the obtained solution is optimal. Still, routes obtained from a heuristic approach might perform significantly better than existing planning approaches. Moreover, the case study in this paper did not define specific start and completion times for the individual operations and vessels. Inclusion of such time-windows might decrease computation time as well.

Another aspect worth looking at is the possible inclusion of a learning effect. Industry actors have observed that dedicated vessels performing operations during a P&A campaign have a significant reduction in execution times. The inclusion of such an effect is however challenging, and would lead to endogenous execution times.

Finally, there is a lot of uncertainty in the execution times of operations, due to unknown well conditions. Schedules and routes resulting from the deterministic model formulated in this paper might therefore be non-optimal when uncertainty is taken into account. Future work might therefore also focus on the application of stochastic programming to this problem.

References

1. Aarlott, M.M.: Cost Analysis of Plug and Abandonment Operations on the Norwegian Continental Shelf Mats Mathisen Aarlott. Master thesis, Norwegian University of Science and Technology (2016)
2. Bektas, T.: The multiple traveling salesman problem: An overview of formulations and solution procedures. Omega 34(3), 209–219 (2006)
3. Bureau of Safety and Environmental Enforcement: BSEE Well Database (2017), https://www.data.bsee.gov/homepg/data_center/well/borehole/master.asp
4. Christiansen, M., Fagerholt, K., Ronen, D.: Ship Routing and Scheduling: Status and Perspectives. Transportation Science 38(1), 1–18 (2004)
5. Fagerholt, K., Christiansen, M.: A travelling salesman problem with allocation, time window and precedence constraints an application to ship scheduling. International Transactions in Operational Research 7(3), 231–244 (2000)
6. van den Heever, S.A., Grossmann, I.E., Vasantharajan, S., Edwards, K.: A Lagrangean Decomposition Heuristic for the Design and Planning of Offshore Hydrocarbon Field Infrastructures with Complex Economic Objectives. Industrial & Engineering Chemistry Research 40(13), 2857–2875 (2001), http://pubs.acs.org/doi/abs/10.1021/ie000755e

7. Irawan, C., Ouelhadj, D., Jones, D., Stålhane, M., Sperstad, I.: Optimisation of maintenance routing and scheduling for offshore wind farms. European Journal of Operational Research 39(1), 15–30 (2015)
8. Kaiser, M.J.: Offshore Decommissioning Cost Estimation in the Gulf of Mexico. Journal of Construction Engineering and Management 132(March), 249–258 (2006)
9. Myrseth, V., Perez-Valdes, G.A., Bakker, S.J., Midthun, K.T., Torsæter, M.: Norwegian Open Source P&A Database. In: SPE Bergen One Day Seminar, 20 April, Grieghallen, Bergen, Norway. Society of Petroleum Engineers (2016)
10. Nygreen, B., Christiansen, M., Haugen, K., Bjørkvoll, T., Kristiansen, Ø.: Modeling Norwegian petroleum production and transportation. Annals of Operations Research 82, 251–268 (1998)
11. Oil & Gas UK: Guidelines for the Abandonment of Wells. Tech. rep. (2015)
12. Oil & Gas UK: Decommissioning Insight 2016. Tech. rep. (2016)
13. Standards Norway: NORSOK Standard D-010: Well integrity in drilling and well operations (2013)
14. Toth, P., Vigo, D. (eds.): The Vehicle Routing Problem. Society for Industrial and Applied Mathematics (2002)

Arc Routing with Precedence Constraints: An Application to Snow Plowing Operations

Anders H. Gundersen[1], Magnus Johansen[1], Benjamin S. Kjær[1], Henrik Andersson[1], and Magnus Stålhane[1]

1) Norwegian University of Science and Technology,
Department of Industrial Economics and Technology Management
Alfred Getz veg 3, Trondheim, Norway

Abstract. In this paper we present an arc routing problem with precedence constraints, with a focus on its application to snow plowing operations in Norway. The problem studied considers the clearing of snow from a network of roads, where there exists precedence relations between the driving lanes and the sidewalks. The goal is to minimize the total time it takes for a heterogeneous fleet of vehicles to clear all the snow from the road network. We describe a mathematical model of the problem and present symmetry breaking constraints to improve the computational performance. We present a computational study where the performance of the model is tested. Further, we study the effect of forbidding or penalizing U-turns along the route, something the snow plowing vehicles struggle to do. The computational experiments show that it is possible to generate solutions without U-turns with only a marginal increase in the objective value.

Keywords: Arc routing; Snow plowing; vehicle routing;

1 Introduction

In this paper we study an extension of the capacitated arc routing problem ([3]), where there exist precedence constraints on the traversal of given pairs of arcs, and where U-turns are undesirable. The problem is inspired by the planning of snow plowing operations in urban areas of Norway, during, or immediately after, a snowfall.

The problem under consideration can be described as clearing all the snow from a network of roads. This network consists of a set of road segments, where each segment consists of one or more lanes, in one or two directions, and/or one or more sidewalks. Whenever the characteristics of the road changes, such as at intersections, places where two lanes merge into one, or one splits into two, ramps on or off a highway, and so on, we assume that one road segment ends and another begins. We define the term *lane* for each driving lane on a road segment, and *sidewalk* for a sidewalk associated with the road segment. A map showing a small area of downtown Trondheim together with the corresponding road network is shown in Figure 1.

© Springer International Publishing AG 2017
T. Bektaş et al. (Eds.), ICCL 2017, LNCS 10572, pp. 174–188, 2017.
https://doi.org/10.1007/978-3-319-68496-3_12

 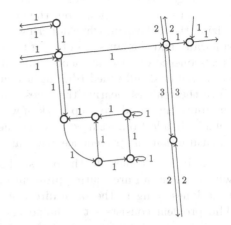

Fig. 1: Map and the corresponding road network from a small part of downtown Trondheim. Arrows and numbers indicate the driving direction and the number of lanes in each direction, respectively. Sidewalks and pedestrian pathways are not included.

To service the road network, two types of vehicles are available: heavy trucks for plowing the lanes, and smaller vehicles for clearing the sidewalks. All vehicles are associated with one depot where they begin and end their route. Each heavy truck has a large plow attached to the front, capable of clearing one lane at a time. However, when clearing a lane, the snow is pushed to the right hand side of the vehicle, pushing it from the middle toward the side of the road segment. Therefore, if there are multiple lanes in the same direction, a general requirement is the need to service the innermost lane first. Where there is a sidewalk beside a lane, some, or all, of the snow may be shoved on to it, and therefore the sidewalk must be serviced after the corresponding lane(s). This creates a precedence relation, all lanes must be cleared before the sidewalk can be cleared. The vehicles plowing the sidewalks are smaller and cannot be used to plow the lanes. However, the smaller vehicles can traverse the lanes without plowing. This is often a necessity, as the network of sidewalks may not be connected. Sometimes the only way to make sure that the sidewalks are serviced after the lanes, is for the vehicles to wait for the truck to plow the specific lane. It is therefore allowed for vehicles to wait at intersections.

Due to the large size of the heavy trucks plowing the lanes, U-turns is a rather problematic, time consuming, and often impossible maneuver for them in urban areas. For the smaller vehicles clearings the sidewalk, U-turns are possible, but time consuming since it has to cross all the driving lanes to reach the sidewalk on the opposite side of the road. Information regarding extra time spent at an intersection when taking a U-turn, and which intersections where U-turns are prohibited, is assumed to be known to the planner.

The goal is to determine one route for each vehicle so that the total time it takes to clear the snow from the entire road network is minimized, i.e. minimizing the makespan, while adhering to the precedence constraints between the sidewalks and the lanes, and trying to avoid U-turns. A route for a given vehicle is a sequence of road segments, and information of whether the road segment is plowed or deadheaded (driving a road segment without plowing). Note that since the vehicles clearing the lanes cannot clear the sidewalks and vice versa, the route only needs to keep track of which road segments are traversed for each vehicle. In addition, we need to know the time each lane and sidewalk is plowed, to ensure that the precedence constrains are respected at each road segment.

A similar problem to the one studied in this paper was introduced in [11] which studies an arc routing problem for snow plowing operations, where multiple lanes going in the same direction have to be serviced at the same time. The problem consists set of homogeneous vehicles, where each vehicle has a maximum number of arcs it can traverse, and the objective is to minimize the makespan. The problem is solved by a two-phase Adaptive Large Neighborhood Search heuristic (ALNS). Another similar snow plowing problem is studied in [2], where the time it takes to deadhead an arc before plowing it is longer than after it has been serviced. The problem is defined for a single vehicle, and the objective is to minimize costs associated with the route. To solve the problem they introduce a local search heuristic. In contrast to the problem studied in this paper, [11] and [2] consider a homogeneous fleet of vehicles, and a single vehicle, respectively.

In [4] a vehicle routing problem for snow plowing operations that considers heterogeneous vehicle fleets is introduced. The presented model is designed to consider both plowing and salt-spreading operations. The problem is defined on a mixed multigraph representing unidirectional and bidirectional plow jobs. Unlike the problem studied in this paper they consider replenishment of consumed resources such as fuel and salt along a route. However, they do not consider any type of temporal dependencies, such as precedence, between the different vehicles. They compare a MIP model, a constraint programming model, and a two-phase heuristic procedure for solving the problem.

Another paper that considers a heterogeneous fleet for snow plowing operations is [6], which studies a problem where the set of arcs is divided into non-overlapping subsets called priority classes, and each class can only be serviced by a subset of the available vehicles. The vehicles can vary both with respect to size, and service- and deadheading speed. The problem includes penalties on U-turns, and synchronization of plowing operations. A mathematical model, and two constructive methods are presented to solve the problems. A difference between [6] and this paper is that the model in [6] assumes that all arcs in one priority set is serviced before the first arc in a lowered priority set (though the model allows arcs to be upgraded to a higher priority class), while the problem studied in this paper has precedence relations between pairs of arcs. Thus, the mathematical formulation presented below explicitly models the service time of each arc, and allows waiting times before an arc is serviced, while in [6] they compare the completion time of the last arc in one priority set to the first arc in another set.

For a complete overview of earlier papers studying optimization of the routing of snow plowing vehicles, we refer to the survey presented in [10], while for a thorough review of other winter road maintenance operations we refer to [7, 8, 9]. For a comprehensive discussion of the capacitated arc routing problem and its variants, we refer to [1].

The purpose of this paper is to study a new variant of the capacitated arc routing problem, where there is precedence between when pairs of arcs may be serviced. We present a new mathematical formulation of the problem, and several ways in which the computational efficiency of the model may be improved. Further, we conduct a computational study to inspect the effect of the suggested improvements to the model, and to study the effect of U-turns on the solution quality of the problem.

The remainder of the paper is organized as follows: In Section 2 we present a mathematical model of the problem, before conducting a computational study of this model in Section 3. Finally, we give some concluding remarks in Section 4.

2   Mathematical Model

The most intuitive way of formulating the arc routing problem with precedence relations is to extend the capacitated arc routing problem presented by [3], with the necessary sets and constraints needed for plowing operations. The formulation is a mixed-integer program (MIP).

Let $G = (\mathcal{V}, \mathcal{A})$ be a directed multigraph where the vertex set $\mathcal{V}$ represents the nodes in the road network (geographic locations with changes in service criteria), and the arc set $\mathcal{A}$ represents the lanes and sidewalks. If there is a lane and a sidewalk between the same two nodes, this is represented with two separate arcs. If there are two lanes in one direction, this is represented by just one arc. Figure 2 illustrates an example of such a directed multigraph.

We have a set of vehicles $\mathcal{K}$, which is separated into two fleets. Let $\mathcal{K}^L \subset \mathcal{K}$ be the set of plowing trucks for the lanes, and $\mathcal{K}^S \subset \mathcal{K}$ be the set of vehicles that service the sidewalks. The trucks can only drive on and service lanes, while the vehicles for sidewalks can drive on both lanes and sidewalks, but only service the sidewalks. Let $\mathcal{A}^S \subseteq \mathcal{A}$ represent the arcs that the vehicles for sidewalks can traverse, and $\hat{\mathcal{A}}^S \subseteq \mathcal{A}^S$ be the set of arcs that have sidewalks with service needs. Similarly, let $\mathcal{A}^L \subseteq \mathcal{A}^S$ represent the arcs that can be traversed by the plowing trucks, and $\hat{\mathcal{A}}^L \subseteq \mathcal{A}^L$ be the set of lanes which have to be serviced.

To fulfill the service demands on different arcs, each vehicle $k \in \mathcal{K}$ has to drive a defined route. Each route starts and ends at the depot, and each traversal of an arc corresponds to a leg, numbered by n, in a route. Since a route can pass through the depot, D, several times, we define the vertices $o(k)$ and $d(k)$ as the artificial origin and destination of vehicle k, which are only connected to the original depot D. An upper bound on the number of legs included in a route

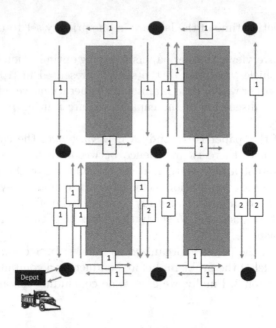

Fig. 2: An illustration of a directed multigraph. The black dots represent the nodes, while the blue and green arrows represent the lanes and sidewalks, respectively. The number on each arrow indicates how many lanes and sidewalks there are on that arc.

is given by $\overline{n}$, and we define the set of possible legs, $\mathcal{N} = \{1, ..., \overline{n}\}$. As seen in Figure 2 an arc can have a number of lanes or sidewalks in the same direction. Let R_{ij}^L and R_{ij}^S be the number of lanes and sidewalks on arc (i, j), respectively. Further, let T_{kij} be the time vehicle k uses to service arc (i, j), and T_{kij}^D be the time vehicle k uses to deadhead arc (i, j). In general, the plowing trucks use shorter time to service an arc (i, j), compared with the smaller vehicles for service the corresponding sidewalk, therefore $T_{kij} \leq T_{\hat{k}ij}$, given $k \in \mathcal{K}^L$ and $\hat{k} \in \mathcal{K}^S$. This means that we only need to consider the start of service a lane and the corresponding sidewalk in the precedence relation. Let T^{Max} be an upper bound on the maximum time a vehicle can use on its route.

To penalize U-turns, T_{kij}^U is the time it takes to do a U-turn from arc (j, i) to arc (i, j) for vehicle k, and u_{kijn} is a binary variable that states whether vehicle k made a U-turn before it traversed arc (i, j) as leg n, or not. Let the binary variable x_{kijn} be 1 if vehicle k service arc (i, j) as the nth of its route, and 0 otherwise. Similarly, let y_{kijn} be 1 if arc (i, j) is traversed by vehicle k and appears as the nth leg of the route while deadheading, and 0 otherwise. The variable τ_{kn} tracks the end time of service or traversal of leg n in the route of vehicle k, while t_{ij}^L and t_{ij}^S tracks the end time of service of the lanes and sidewalks on arc (i, j), respectively. Finally, the variable t^{MS} defines the total makespan of the solution. For shorthand notation, we denote $\mathcal{A}_k$ as the set of arcs vehicle k can traverse, and for a given vehicle k the sets $\delta_k^+(i) = \{j|(i,j) \in \mathcal{A}_k\}$, and $\delta_k^-(i) = \{j|(j,i) \in \mathcal{A}_k\}$. Using this notation the mathematical model of the problem can be described as follows:

$$\min t^{MS} \tag{1}$$

s.t.

$$x_{ko(k)D1} + y_{ko(k)D1} = 1 \qquad\qquad k \in \mathcal{K} \tag{2}$$

$$\sum_{n \in \mathcal{N}} \left(x_{kDd(k)n} + y_{kDd(k)n} \right) = 1 \qquad\qquad k \in \mathcal{K} \tag{3}$$

$$\sum_{k \in \mathcal{K}^L} \sum_{n \in \mathcal{N}} x_{kijn} = R_{ij}^L \qquad\qquad (i,j) \in \hat{\mathcal{A}}^L \tag{4}$$

$$\sum_{k \in \mathcal{K}^S} \sum_{n \in \mathcal{N}} x_{kijn} = R_{ij}^S \qquad\qquad (i,j) \in \hat{\mathcal{A}}^S \tag{5}$$

$$\begin{aligned} &\sum_{i \in \delta_k^-(j)} \left(x_{kijn} + y_{kijn} \right) - \\ &\sum_{i \in \delta_k^+(j)} \left(x_{kji(n+1)} + y_{kji(n+1)} \right) = 0 \end{aligned} \quad \begin{aligned} &k \in \mathcal{K}, j \in \mathcal{V}\backslash\{o(k),d(k)\}, \\ &n \in \mathcal{N}|n < \overline{n} \end{aligned} \tag{6}$$

$$\sum_{(i,j) \in \mathcal{A}_k} \left(x_{kijn} + y_{kijn} \right) \leq 1 \qquad\qquad k \in \mathcal{K}, n \in \mathcal{N} \tag{7}$$

$$\begin{aligned} &x_{kij(n-1)} + y_{kij(n-1)} + \\ &x_{kjin} + y_{kjin} \leq u_{kjin} + 1 \end{aligned} \quad \begin{aligned} &k \in \mathcal{K}, (i,j) \in \mathcal{A}_k, \\ &n \in \mathcal{N}|(j,i) \in \mathcal{A}_k, n > 1 \end{aligned} \tag{8}$$

$$\begin{aligned} &\tau_{kn} - \tau_{k(n-1)} \geq \\ &\sum_{(i,j) \in \mathcal{A}_k} \left(T_{kij} x_{kijn} + T_{kij}^D y_{kijn} + T_{kij}^U u_{kijn} \right) \end{aligned} \quad k \in \mathcal{K}, n \in \mathcal{N}|n > 1 \tag{9}$$

$$\tau_{kn} - T^{Max}\left(1 - x_{kijn} \right) \leq t_{ij}^L \qquad\qquad k \in \mathcal{K}, (i,j) \in \hat{\mathcal{A}}^L, n \in \mathcal{N} \tag{10}$$

$$\tau_{kn} - T^{Max}\left(1 - x_{kijn} \right) \leq t_{ij}^S \qquad\qquad k \in \mathcal{K}, (i,j) \in \hat{\mathcal{A}}^S, n \in \mathcal{N} \tag{11}$$

$$\tau_{kn} \leq T^{Max} \qquad\qquad k \in \mathcal{K}, n \in \mathcal{N} \tag{12}$$

$$\begin{aligned} t_{ij}^L - T_{kij} \leq t_{ij}^S - T_{\hat{k}ij} \end{aligned} \quad \begin{aligned} &k \in \mathcal{K}^L, \hat{k} \in \mathcal{K}^S, \\ &(i,j) \in \hat{\mathcal{A}}^L|(i,j) \in \hat{\mathcal{A}}^S \end{aligned} \tag{13}$$

$$\tau_{kn} \leq t^{MS} \qquad\qquad k \in \mathcal{K}, n \in \mathcal{N} \tag{14}$$

$$x_{kijn} \in \{0,1\} \qquad\qquad k \in \mathcal{K}, (i,j) \in \mathcal{A}_k, n \in \mathcal{N} \tag{15}$$

$$y_{kijn} \in \{0,1\} \qquad\qquad k \in \mathcal{K}, (i,j) \in \mathcal{A}_k, n \in \mathcal{N} \tag{16}$$

$$u_{kijn} \in \{0,1\} \qquad\qquad\qquad k \in \mathcal{K}, (i,j) \in \mathcal{A}_k, n \in \mathcal{N} \quad (17)$$

$$\tau_{kn} \geq 0 \qquad\qquad\qquad k \in \mathcal{K}, n \in \mathcal{N} \qquad\qquad (18)$$

$$t_{ij}^L \geq 0 \qquad\qquad\qquad (i,j) \in \hat{\mathcal{A}}^L \qquad\qquad\qquad (19)$$

$$t_{ij}^S \geq 0 \qquad\qquad\qquad (i,j) \in \hat{\mathcal{A}}^S \qquad\qquad\qquad (20)$$

The objective function (1) is to minimize the total makespan of the solution. Constraints (2) and (3) state that each route starts and ends in each vehicle's depot, while constraints (4) and (5) ensure that all arcs with demands are serviced. Further, constraints (6) make sure that the plowing routes are connected. Each vehicle can only traverse one arc in each leg of its route; this is taken care of by constraints (7). Constraints (8) ensure the U-turn variable to be 1 if a vehicle take a U-turn, while constraints (9) provide that the vehicles behave consistent according to time. Constraints (10) and (11) connect the time variables, and constraints (12) ensure that the time of a route does not exceed the upper bound. Constraints (13) assure that the precedence requirements between the corresponding lanes and sidewalks hold. Finally, constraints (14) ensure that no traversal time of a given leg for a given vehicle can be larger than the makespan of the solution, while constraints (15)–(20) define the domain of the variables in the model.

2.1   Improvements to the model

As the MIP model described has two homogeneous vehicle fleets, the model can produce several mathematically different solutions which are practically equivalent by altering which vehicle drives which route in a solution. E.g. given a fleet of three homogeneous vehicles, and a solution of three vehicle routes, there exist six ways to assign routes to vehicles which are all practically equivalent (since the vehicles are identical). To reduce the number of symmetric solutions we introduce two sets of symmetry breaking constraints based on lexicographic ordering of the vehicle routes based on the consumption of some resource accumulated along the route. Given that the resource consumption along each route is unique, this will remove all permutations except for one, while in the case where the resource consumption along two or more routes are equal, the lexicographic order is arbitrary, and some (or all) symmetry may remain in the problem. However, ffor both sets of constraints there exist (at least one) lexicographic ordering of the routes, and thus we are ensured that all practically different routing solutions are still present in the model. For more details on lexicographic symmetry breaking constraints we refer to [5].

The first set of symmetry breaking constraints proposed are based on the number of arcs traversed by each vehicle along its route. We here formulate constraints to force the vehicle with the lowest index number to service at least as many arcs as the vehicle with the second lowest index and so on. The constraints are given in constraints (21) and (22).

$$\sum_{n\in\mathcal{N}}\sum_{(i,j)\in\hat{A}^L} x_{kijn} \geq \sum_{n\in\mathcal{N}}\sum_{(i,j)\in\hat{A}^L} x_{(k+1)ijn} \qquad k\in\mathcal{K}^L \big| k < |\mathcal{K}^L| \qquad (21)$$

$$\sum_{n\in\mathcal{N}}\sum_{(i,j)\in\hat{A}^S} x_{kijn} \geq \sum_{n\in\mathcal{N}}\sum_{(i,j)\in\hat{A}^S} x_{(k+1)ijn} \qquad k\in\mathcal{K}^S \big| k < |\mathcal{K}^S| \qquad (22)$$

The second set of symmetry breaking constraints proposed are based on the total duration of the route of each vehicle. We here formulate constraints to force the vehicle with the lowest index number to drive a route with at least the same duration as the vehicle with the second lowest index and so on. The constraints are given in constraints (23) and (24).

$$\sum_{n\in\mathcal{N}}\sum_{(i,j)\in\hat{A}^L} \left(T_{kij}x_{kijn} - T_{(k+1)ij}x_{(k+1)ijn}\right) \geq 0 \qquad k\in\mathcal{K}^L \big| k < |\mathcal{K}^L| \qquad (23)$$

$$\sum_{n\in\mathcal{N}}\sum_{(i,j)\in\hat{A}^S} \left(T_{kij}x_{kijn} - T_{(k+1)ij}x_{(k+1)ijn}\right) \geq 0 \qquad k\in\mathcal{K}^S \big| k < |\mathcal{K}^S| \qquad (24)$$

Note that these two sets of lexicographic ordered constraints cannot be implemented at the same time in the model, and still guarantee optimality. It is hard to say which symmetry breaking constraints are the best and how well they will perform. This is further studied in Section 3.

To reduce the solution time when the MIP model is solved by a commercial software, we may tighten the range of the variables, thus improving the lower bound - and thereby decrease the solution space for the relaxed formulation. We know that the earliest time an arc is serviced is the shortest time it takes to travel from the depot to the start of the arc, plus the service time of the arc. We therefore introduce the parameters α_j^L and α_j^S, which state the shortest travel time from the depot to node j for vehicles in $\mathcal{K}^L$ and $\mathcal{K}^S$, and obtain the following constraints:

$$t_{ij}^L \geq min_{k\in\mathcal{K}^L}\{\alpha_i^L + T_{kij}\} \qquad\qquad (i,j)\in\mathcal{A}^L \qquad (25)$$
$$t_{ij}^S \geq min_{k\in\mathcal{K}^S}\{\alpha_i^S + T_{kij}\} \qquad\qquad (i,j)\in\mathcal{A}^S \qquad (26)$$

Constraints (19) and (20) in the initial formulation can now be replaced with constraints (25) and (26), which improves the lower bound of the time variables, and likely reduce the solution time.

3 Computational Study

In this section we present a computational study of the mathematical model described in Section 2. We first present the set of test instances used, before testing the computational effect of adding the different improvements of the model suggested in Section 2.1. Finally, we study the impact of adding U-turn penalties or forbidding U-turns in the model, both when it comes to computational efficiency and solution quality.

The model has been implemented in the commercial optimization software Xpress Optimization Suite and run on a computer with a 3.4 GHz Intel Core i7 processor and 32 GB of RAM, running Windows 10 Education. Version 1.24.08 of Xpress IVE was used, with version 3.10.0 of Xpress Mosel, and version 28.01.04 of Xpress Optimizer.

3.1   Test instances

The test instances are based on fictitious road networks that are set to mimic those found in urban areas. These generally involve road segments with one lane in each direction, and 4-way intersections where two perpendicular roads meet. Additionally, there often exists a sidewalk on one or both sides of the traffic lanes. The numerical values of the traversing times are based on proportionality, such that there is a difference between road segments, while they all lie in the same order of magnitude. All instances have an average traversal time of $5 - 6$ time units per arc. Equally, the service time for a sidewalk is longer than that of the associated lane, if such a lane exist.

A set of 25 test instances have been generated to test the model. These are grouped into test instances $1 - 10$, presented in Table 1, and $11 - 25$, presented in Table 2. For each instance, Table 1 and 2 presents the number of trucks ($|\mathcal{K}^L|$) and smaller vehicles ($|\mathcal{K}^S|$) in each instance, as well as the number of nodes (# Nodes), lanes (# Lanes) and sidewalks (# SW) in the graph representing the road network. All arcs need to be serviced only once. Further, the number of arcs with precedence constraints (# Prec), the upper bound on the number of legs used (# Legs) and the maximum time a vehicle can use on its route (T^{Max}) is given. Test set 1 is smaller and only used to test the symmetry breaking constraints and improved bounds, while test set 2 is larger, and used to test the capabilities of the model.

3.2   Testing the effect of the suggested improvements to the model

To compare the different variations of the models, we have run each of the test instances in Table 1, without considering U-turn penalties, for a maximum of $1,000$ seconds. The results can be found in Table 3. The column *Original model* is the mathematical model with none of the suggested improvements from Section 2.1. In *Symmetry Breaking 1 (SB1)* we have included constraints (21) and (22) to the model, while *Symmetry Breaking 2 (SB2)* includes constraints (23) and (24). In *Increased Bound (IB)*, the lower bound of the time variables have been increased. That is, we have replaced constraints (19) – (20) with (25) – (26). In addition we have tested combining each of the symmetry breaking constraints with the increased bound. For each variant of the model we report the computing time (Time) in seconds and the optimality gap (Gap) in percent.

Table 1: Characteristics of the test instances in *Test set 1*.

Instance	$|\mathcal{K}^L|$	$|\mathcal{K}^S|$	# Nodes	# Lanes	# SW	# Prec	# Legs	T^{Max}
1	1	1	6	10	3	3	17	50
2	2	1	6	10	3	3	17	50
3	2	1	8	18	5	5	17	50
4	3	2	13	32	16	14	17	90
5	2	2	17	42	24	18	28	150
6	3	2	17	42	24	18	28	150
7	3	2	20	48	29	21	35	150
8	4	2	20	48	29	21	35	150
9	3	3	30	78	42	30	45	250
10	4	3	30	78	42	30	45	250

Table 2: Characteristics of the test instances in *Test set 2*.

Instance	$|\mathcal{K}^L|$	$|\mathcal{K}^S|$	# Nodes	# Lanes	# SW	# Prec	# Legs	T^{Max}
11	1	1	7	14	3	3	17	50
12	2	1	7	14	3	3	17	50
13	2	1	11	24	8	6	17	90
14	2	2	11	24	8	6	17	90
15	2	2	15	36	24	18	22	90
16	3	2	15	36	24	18	22	90
17	2	2	20	48	29	21	35	150
18	3	3	20	48	29	21	35	150
19	2	2	30	78	42	30	45	250
20	3	2	30	78	42	30	45	250
21	4	2	30	78	42	30	45	250
22	3	2	40	112	60	46	65	350
23	3	3	40	112	60	46	65	350
24	4	2	40	112	60	46	65	350
25	4	3	40	112	60	46	65	350

Table 3: Results from running test instance 1–10 with different symmetry breaking constraints and valid inequalities added to the model formulation.

Instance	Original model		SB1		SB2		Inc. Bound		SB1 + IB		SB2 + IB	
	Time(s)	Gap(%)	Time(s)	Gap(%)	Time(s)	Gap(%)	Time(s)	Gap(%)	Time(s)	Gap(%)	Time(s)	Gap(%)
1	0	0	0	0	0	0	0	0	0	0	0	0
2	0.2	0	0	0	0.2	0	0.2	0	0.2	0	0.1	0
3	1.1	0	0.8	0	0.4	0	0.8	0	0.1	0	0.8	0
4	12.5	0	18.3	0	13.3	0	10.8	0	11.8	0	9.5	0
5	938.3	0	120.4	0	59.1	0	181	0	79.7	0	118.7	0
6	526.1	0	304.7	0	157.9	0	761	0	215.8	0	262.6	0
7	1000	0.56	694.1	0	1000	0.56	1000	0.56	1000	0.56	1000	0.56
8	332.6	0	235.5	0	1000	2.38	1000	2.03	759.5	0	200.3	0
9	480.6	0	1000	7.26	1000	3.36	1000	3.36	1000	6.5	1000	14.18
10	1000	38.51	1000	27.78	1000	33.09	1000	27.78	1000	32.59	1000	29.46
Average	429.14	3.91	337.38	3.50	423.09	3.94	495.38	3.37	406.71	3.97	359.2	4.42

On average, *Symmetry Breaking 1* yields the best results, with respect to computational time, and the second best with respect to the optimality gap. It is also the only improved model that solves 8 out of 10 instances to optimality within 1,000 seconds. The *Increased Bound* model has the lowest gap on average and although not performing better than the original model in all test instances, we conclude that the initial bound on the time variables in general contribute positively to better bounds on the obtained solutions. It shall be noted, that when merging *Increased Bound* and *Symmetry Breaking 1*, this constitutes a model that, on average, perform worse than each of them applied separately. The original model, which, on average, perform among the worst models with respect to solution time, was the only model to prove optimality on instance 9 within the 1,000 seconds limit.

We conclude that the *Symmetry Breaking 1* model is the best performing, and have chosen to continue with these lexicographically ordered symmetry breaking constraints. In the analysis that follows we refer to the *Symmetry Breaking 1* model as the *Basic model*. try to minimize the fleet size, it is not clever to say that we have an infinite fleet size in the initiate state. It is better to start with a realistic amount of vehicles, and increase iterative if it should not exist any feasible solution for the given size within the maximum time for a schedule.

3.3   Effect of penalizing or forbidding U-turns

We now study how forbidding or penalizing U-turns affect the computational performance and the solution quality of the test instances. When penalizing a U-turn the cost is given in time units, which in this case is set to 2, a bit less than half of the average service time for a lane. In the case where U-turns are forbidden, they are only forbidden for the plowing trucks. Since the vehicles plowing the sidewalks are smaller, they are allowed to make U-turns, which corresponds to crossing a lane after plowing a sidewalk, to reach the sidewalk on the other side. Although allowed, a penalty cost of 2 time units is given for this maneuver. The results, and a comparison with the *Basic model* are presented in Table 4 where all instances have been run for 1,000 seconds. For each version of the model, the computational time (Time) in seconds as well as the optimality gap (Gap) in percent, is given. For the instances with an n/a in the Gap column, no feasible solution was found within the time limit.

The results show that the computational time is roughly the same for all three versions of the problem. However, while the *Basic model* is able to provide a feasible solution within the time limit on all but one instance (24), penalizing and forbidding U-turns do not provide a feasible solution within the time limit on 3 and 4 instances, respectively. Forbidding U-turns reduce the number of feasible solutions to the problem which may explain why Xpress struggles more to find feasible solutions in this case. In case of U-turn penalties the explanation may be related to increased fractionality in the solutions, since the u-variables now indirectly affect the objective value. It is also interesting to note that for instance 24, Xpress is able to find a feasible solution when adding U-turn penalties to the model, while no feasible solution is found for the two other versions.

Table 4: Comparison of the computational performance of forbidding U-turns and penalizing U-turns to the *Basic model*.

	Basic model		With U-turn penalty		U-turns forbidden	
Instance	Time(s)	Gap(%)	Time(s)	Gap(%)	Time(s)	Gap(%)
11	0	0.00	0	0.00	0	0.00
12	0	0.00	1	0.00	1	0.00
13	1	0.00	2	0.00	1	0.00
14	3	0.00	11	0.00	9	0.00
15	10	0.00	32	0.00	102	0.00
16	13	0.00	102	0.00	43	0.00
17	397	0.00	1000	3.00	219	0.00
18	1000	3.48	1000	11.42	1000	34.01
19	1000	0.29	1000	4.14	1000	10.62
20	1000	4.55	1000	19.36	1000	22.50
21	1000	1.09	1000	25.40	1000	1.76
22	1000	21.89	1000	n/a	1000	n/a
23	1000	49.12	1000	n/a	1000	n/a
24	1000	n/a	1000	42.08	1000	n/a
25	1000	55.13	1000	n/a	1000	n/a
Average	562	9.68	610	8.78	558	6.26

Table 5 compares the optimal solution of the *Basic model* on instance 11–21 to the optimal solutions of the model when forbidding and penalizing U-turns, respectively. For each instance and version of the model we give the change in the number of U-turns performed by trucks (Δ lanes), by small vehicles (Δ SW), and the change in the makespan (Δ Makespan). The optimal solutions to each instance was obtained by running the model for several days, however, for the instances marked with a * and **, we only managed to obtain results within 2 % and 6 % of optimum, respectively.

As shown in Table 5, on average, the number of U-turns performed by the two vehicle fleets is reduced quite significantly both when penalizing and forbidding U-turns. This comes at an average increase in the total makespan of less than three time units. Even in the worst case, the increase in the makespan is only six time units (instance 18), equal to the maximum traversal time of a single arc. An interesting anomaly in the results in the case of penalizing U-turns is instance 16, where the number of U-turns performed by the larger trucks increase. This may be explained by the fact that any vehicle that drives a route that is significantly shorter than the route defining the makespan, may perform U-turns without it affecting the objective value. However, the total makespan of the instance is increased by 5, indicating that the route defining the makespan has changed from the *Basic model*.

The results presented in Table 5 indicate that it is possible to design vehicle routes for the plowing trucks that does not perform any U-turns, without significantly increasing the total time it takes to clear the road network of snow.

Table 5: Comparing how the U-turn constraints influence the makespan and the number and U-turns in the different models.

	Time penalty for U-turns			U-turns forbidden		
Instance	Δ lanes	Δ SW	Δ Makespan	Δ lanes	Δ SW	Δ Makespan
11	-2	0	0	-2	-2	0
12	-1	0	2	-4	0	2
13	-2	0	4	-6	0	4
14	-7	0	0	-7	2	0
15	3	-7	5	-8	-7	5
16	1	-4	5	-11	-4	5
17	-7	-1	0	-7	-3	0
18	-3	0	4**	-5	-1	6**
19	-16	-10	1	-16	-3	1
20	-14	0	3	-28	0	4*
21	-13	-2	3*	-27	-2	3*
Average	-5.55	-2.18	2.45	-11.00	-1.82	2.73

4 Concluding remarks

In this paper we have studied an arc routing problem inspired by a snow plowing problem faced by planners in Norway. The objective is to minimize the total time of clearing a road network of snow, but it is complicated by the fact that there is precedence between pairs of arcs in the network. To solve the problem we have introduced a mathematical model, and suggested symmetry breaking constraints to improve the computational performance when solving the model using commercial software. In addition, we have tested the effect of penalizing or forbidding U-turns in the model, something which is difficult for the snow plowing vehicles to do in many urban areas. The results of these tests show that we can eliminate the need for U-turns in the vehicle routes, with only a marginal increase in the total time it takes to clear the road network.

Since the mathematical model presented in this paper is unable to solve realistic instances of the problem, future research should look into heuristic solution methods for the problem. In addition, it would be interesting to test the model presented in this paper on graphs generated from real road networks to corroborate the findings regarding the influence of U-turns on the makespan of a solution.

References

[1] Corberán, Á. and Laporte, G. (2013). *Arc routing: problems, methods, and applications*. SIAM.

[2] Dussault, B., Golden, B., Groër, C., and Wasil, E. (2013). Plowing with precedence: A variant of the windy postman problem. *Computers & Operations Research*, 40(4):1047–1059.

[3] Golden, B. L. and Wong, R. T. (1981). Capacitated arc routing problems. *Networks*, 11(3):305–315.

[4] Kinable, J., van Hoeve, W.-J., and Smith, S. F. (2016). Optimization models for a real-world snow plow routing problem. In Quimper, C.-G., editor, *International Conference on AI and OR Techniques in Constriant Programming for Combinatorial Optimization Problems*, Lecture Notes in Computer Science, pages 229–245. Springer.

[5] Margot, F. (2010). Symmetry in integer linear programming. In Jünger, M., Liebling, T. M., Naddef, D., Nemhauser, G. L., Pulleyblank, W. R., Reinelt, G., Rinaldi, G., and Wolsey, L. A., editors, *50 Years of Integer Programming 1958-2008: From the Early Years to the State-of-the-Art*, pages 647–686. Springer Berlin Heidelberg, Berlin, Heidelberg.

[6] Perrier, N., Langevin, A., and Amaya, C.-A. (2008). Vehicle routing for urban snow plowing operations. *Transportation Science*, 42(1):44–56.

[7] Perrier, N., Langevin, A., and Campbell, J. F. (2006a). A survey of models and algorithms for winter road maintenance. part I: system design for spreading and plowing. *Computers & Operations Research*, 33(1):209–238.

[8] Perrier, N., Langevin, A., and Campbell, J. F. (2006b). A survey of models and algorithms for winter road maintenance. part II: system design for snow disposal. *Computers & Operations Research*, 33(1):239–262.

[9] Perrier, N., Langevin, A., and Campbell, J. F. (2007a). A survey of models and algorithms for winter road maintenance. part III: Vehicle routing and depot location for spreading. *Computers & Operations Research*, 34(1):211–257.

[10] Perrier, N., Langevin, A., and Campbell, J. F. (2007b). A survey of models and algorithms for winter road maintenance. part IV: Vehicle routing and fleet sizing for plowing and snow disposal. *Computers & Operations Research*, 34(1):258–294.

[11] Salazar-Aguilar, M. A., Langevin, A., and Laporte, G. (2012). Synchronized arc routing for snow plowing operations. *Computers & Operations Research*, 39(7):1432–1440.

Analysis of the Partner Selection Problem in Horizontal Collaboration Among Shippers

Hanan Ouhader[✉] (orcid.org/0000-0001-9694-9242) , Malika El Kyal

National School of Applied Sciences,
Ibn Zohr University, Agadir , Morocco
ouhader@gmail.com

Abstract. Besides network design and defining objectives, successful horizontal collaboration among shippers requires another important strategic decision: identifying compatible partners. To focus on the problem of coalition formation, we exploit a bi-objective mathematical model for a two echelon location routing problem (2E-LRP) to test if partners fit for the collaboration or not and if opportunity for each partner to make economic and environmental benefits exists. Extended known instances reflecting the real distribution in urban area are regenerated to evaluate several goods' delivery strategies. Shapley value method, belonging to the field of cooperative game theory, is used to allocate cost and CO_2 emissions to partners of the coalition. This approach proposes a coalition formation mechanism allowing the decision makers to measure the sustainability performance of partners during the design phase of the coalition.

Keywords. Horizontal collaboration. Coalition formation problem. Sustainable urban road transport. Two-echelon Location Routing problem. Multi-objective optimization. Cost allocation

1 Motivation and description of the problem

Experts estimate that urban goods movements account for 20 % to 30% of total vehicle kilometers driven [1]. Accordingly, the urban road transport sector can play a considerable role in reducing emissions. Today, environmental concerns oblige every city to think in how it will be able to meet the increased demand for urban road transportation without underestimating the impact on the environment or even the quality of life. To ensure that environmental, social, and economic considerations are factored into decisions affecting urban transportation activity is the goal of sustainable urban transportation [2]. Several strategies with the aim of improving efficiency and sustainability from urban road transport have been suggested both in practice and in the academic literature. Logistics collaboration is gaining traction as a one of the key policies to assure this mission [3] [4].

We talk about collaborative supply chain when two players (or more) of the "Supply Chain" seek to optimize together the logistics of the distribution circuit in which they are linked [5]. Logistics collaboration was studied in two main areas: Ver-

© Springer International Publishing AG 2017
T. Bektaş et al. (Eds.), ICCL 2017, LNCS 10572, pp. 189–204, 2017.
https://doi.org/10.1007/978-3-319-68496-3_13

tical and horizontal collaboration. The vertical collaboration occurs between members of the same chain value (industrial and distributor) while the horizontal collaboration occurs between companies (may be competitors or not) that can provide goods or complementary services [6]. Vertical cooperation has already led to an abundant literature. Nevertheless, less attention has given to research on horizontal logistics collaboration [7], [8], [9],[10]. Horizontal cooperation can be a means to share risk, save costs, increase investments, pool know-how, enhance product quality and variety, and launch innovation faster [11]. Also, this type of collaboration contributes in the reduction of environmental impact of distribution activities [12] [13].

From the literature of supply chain management, horizontal cooperation was applied to logistics for the first time in Cruijssen & Salamon [14] who used a case study of flower transport in the Netherland [15]. A good recent reviews on horizontal collaboration can be found in [8],[16], and [17].

The importance of the potential economic and environmental benefits of horizontal collaboration has been acknowledged in several collaborative projects. In 2014, the horizontal collaboration community between shippers (Nestlé & PepsiCo) has won the price of "Best European Horizontal Collaboration Project " as part of The EU-funded project 'Collaboration Concepts for Co-modality', or 'CO3' in short[1]. In this project, Nestlé and PepsiCo have bundled the warehousing, co-packing and outbound distribution of their fresh and chilled food products to retail customers in Belgium and Luxembourg. This coalition can generate 10-15% transport cost savings and even more significant CO2 reductions.

There are several ways for horizontal cooperation: carriers can collaborate with each other and shippers can collaborate among themselves [18]. In existing literature, there are few studies on the problem of collaboration between shippers in comparison with carriers [16] [19].

From transportation management view, few works studying the environmental impact in horizontal collaboration between shippers was found in literature. Ballot & Fontane [13] used logistical data from real firms on the retail industry to demonstrate the potential saving of CO2 emissions in horizontal collaboration supply chain. Pan [20] optimized separately the total transportation cost and the CO2 emission by developing transportation problem models based on a mixed linear integer programming (MILP). Pérez-Bernabeu et al. [18] adapted a set of well-known benchmarks for the Multi-depot Vehicle Routing Problem (MDVRP) to illustrate an example of horizontal cooperation between shippers owning the vehicle fleet and to quantify routing costs savings both in terms of distance-based costs as well as in terms of environmental costs due to greenhouse gas emissions. Juan et al. [12] studied the same example as [18] but discussed backhaul horizontal collaboration to evaluate the relevance of this way in saving routing and environmental costs. Danloup et al. [21] analyzed the potential for improving sustainability performance in collaborative distribution by measuring the potential improvements regarding the reduced total number of running by delivery trucks and also regarding the reduced amount of CO2 emissions.

Recently, Montoya-torres et al. [3] used the multi-depot vehicle routing problem (MDVRP) for horizontal collaborative delivery between firms and a variant of the location–allocation problem to design the transport infrastructure and to quantify the

---

[1] http://www.co3-project.eu/

benefits that can be achieved when collaborative logistics operations are implemented, represented in transportation costs and CO_2 reduction. Soysal et al. [10] were interested in analyzing the benefits of horizontal collaboration related to perishability, energy use (CO_2 emissions) from transportation operations and logistics costs in the Inventory Routing Problem (IRP) with multiple suppliers. Muñoz-villamizar et al. [22] studied the implementation of an electric fleet of vehicles in collaborative urban distribution of goods, in order to reduce environmental impacts while maintaining a level of service. They proposed an approach using mathematical modeling with multiple objectives, for tactical and operational decision-making to explore the relationship between the delivery cost and the sustainability impact.

In existing literature, the optimization of supply chain under horizontal collaboration between shippers was mainly stand on single objective mathematical modeling approach dealing with economic concern and the integration of sustainability is accordingly in his infancy. Thereby, very few papers discussed horizontal cooperation using multi-objective decision- making models. Also, the majorities of papers were consisting of vehicle routing problem and its variants assuming that strategic facility location decisions have met in a prior step and cannot be modified. Daskin et al. [23] affirmed that for the location/routing problem, the facility location decisions that would be made in isolation are different from this that would be made taking into account routing. The overall system cost may be excessive if the two decisions are tackled separately [24].

To overcome this drawback, we quantified in our previous work [25] the aggregated economic benefit of horizontal collaboration basing on a single-objective two echelons Location Routing problem (2E-LRP) model and we performed a posterior evaluation of the impact of collaboration in CO_2 emissions based on travelled distances. In [26] and [27] we investigated the potential economic, environmental and social effects of combining depot location and vehicle routing decisions in urban road freight transportation under horizontal collaboration. We adopted a quantitative approach based on multi-objective mathematical modeling as a two echelon location routing problem (2E-LRP). We have shown that this combination provides significant gains on studied metrics than separate decisions. Also decision making about the location of depots and the routes of distribution is of great importance and can affect the collaborative supply chain. For interested readers, Drexl & Schneider [28] and Prodhon & Prins 2014 [29] published two exhaustive literature reviews of LRP and these variants. In particular, Cuda et al. [30] provides an overview of 2E-LRP.

Besides network design and defining objectives of collaboration, successful horizontal collaboration requires another important strategic decision: identifying compatible partners. Several methodologies for logistics partner selection were proposed in the literature: multi-criteria decision making (MCDM) approaches, optimization approaches, empirical studies, simulation and/or clustering based approaches, and hybrid approaches combining two or more of above [31]. As stated by Amer & Eltawil [8], the Analytic Hierarchy Process (AHP), examples of MCDM methods approach, is often used for partner selection problem in horizontal collaboration.

To focus on the problem of partner selection, we exploit the mathematical model developed in our previous works, cited above, to test if partners fit for the collaboration or not and if opportunity for each partner to make economic and environmental benefits exists. These conflicting interests of stakeholders drive to a multi-objective decision-making problem.

We are interested to the case of horizontal cooperation between several suppliers (shippers) who decide to joint deliveries to their customers located in urban area subcontracting the truck service to a private transportation company. We assume that authorities prohibit large vehicle to entry to congested areas in the aim of reducing the GHG emissions of freight distribution, congestion and accidents. Goods are delivered to customers via intermediate depots (e.g Urban Consolidation Centre (UCC)) rather than direct shipments. Large trucks are used to transport directly goods to intermediate depots where consolidation takes place. After that, products are transferred to customers using small vehicles. Delivery to different clients is done in multi-drop. The partners' objective is to minimize, simultaneously, the transportation cost and the amount of CO_2 emissions of upstream and downstream transportation in a two-echelon distribution system.

The main decisions involved in problem described above are: (1) which depots/satellites out of a finite set of potential ones should be used (2) How to assign each customer to one open depot (3) How to determine routes to perform distribution. The goal is to identify the best coalition to form so that profit and sustainability of each collaborating partner are increased. Both collaborative and non-collaborative scenarios are compared by the adaptation of known instances of the 2E-LRP reflecting real distribution urban area.

This is a problem of City Logistics network design. According to Crainic et al. [4], this problem focuses in most case on decisions on the number, characteristics, layout, and location of facilities such as CDCs and also the vehicle fleets composition and size. Fleischmann [32] was the first to consider multi-trip VRP (vehicle routing problem) for delivering goods in urban areas [33]. Sterle [34], Boccia et al. [35] and Crainic et al.[36] were the first to study the proper two echelon location routing problem on two-tier City Logistics systems [4]. Implementing a two-echelon distribution system could be an effective response to nuisances associated to freight transportation in urban areas [30]. Consolidation is the fundamental concepts of City Logistics [37]. Traditional consolidation strategies are becoming limited in providing significant improvements as supply chains are independently designed for an industry or a retailer. Therefore, new logistics organizations like horizontal collaboration are necessary. This strategy aims at medium/long-term strategic collaboration, compared with the various opportunistic, local approaches of consolidation [15] [13].

The proposed mechanism facilitates analysis in that only a single model needs to be developed and can then be run for various coalitions. Also, this model has the advantage in showing explicitly how a change in partners also changes the generated gains as well the configuration of the collaborative network. The goal is to present to decision makers a preliminary mechanism to gain general insights into beneficial coalitions and to determine for each company which coalition to joint.

As in any collaboration, dividing the coalition gains in a fair manner between the participants constitutes a key issue [38]. We investigate the well-known Shapley value, commonly considered as a possible best practice by the industry [39], especially, after that the method is gaining popularity as it was put forward by the European CO3-project [40] [41].

The logistics network studied in this paper is a multistage logistics network including factories (F), depots or possible satellites (W) and customers (S). Our modeling approach consist of a bi-objective mathematical model for a two echelon location routing problem (2E-LRP). The first objective function is the minimization of the transportation cost consisting of the sum of satellites opening cost, the handling cost in the satellites, the fixed costs of trucks and vehicles and the traversal costs of the arcs in the two distribution levels. The second objective function minimizes CO_2 emissions of transportation induced by the heavy trucks in the first echelon and light vehicles in the second echelon. The estimation of CO_2 emissions was referring to European studies as [42] , [43] and [44]. These emissions depend on the weight carried by the vehicle , on the capacity of the vehicle that is used , on the distance traveled and the average speed of the vehicle. The full mathematical program formulation is detailed in [26].

We solve the presented bi-objective model by the ε -constraint method by optimizing one of the most preferred objective functions (cost), and considering the other objective (CO_2 emissions) as constraints. Mavrotas [45] provide the basic definitions to better understand this method. We will discuss the problem by establishing an example in the next section.

The remainder of this paper is organized as follows. The second Section discusses the results of numerical experiments, whereas the last Section deals with our conclusions for the sake of providing a new perspective.

2   Numerical Experiments

2.1   Instances Description

In order to make the problem as close to real life as possible, we reused Sterle's instances [34] which reproduce a reel schematic representation of a multi-level urban area. The performance of the developed model is addressed using 6 data sets ranging from small-scale instances to large ones. The constructed sets have the following features: number of customers {15,25,40,75,100,200}, number of factories {2,3,4,5} ,number of satellites {3,4,5,8,10,20}, demands in the range [1,100], capacities of satellites in the range [550; 950] , opening costs are in the range [45; 75] and transshipment costs are in the range [0.02; 0.07], the costs are the Euclidean distances and they are doubled in the first level. Origin-destination matrixes are regenerated according to the specifications of instances I1 explained in [35] (see Figure 1). For interested readers, these instances are available in http://claudio.contardo.org/instances/). The model is implemented by using commercial solver (MATLAB 2014) and tested on a 2.67 GHz Core i5 with 4 GB RAM under Windows 7 environment. In order to replicate the experiments, full origin-destination matrices, demand sets and the other parameters are available upon request to the corresponding author of this paper.

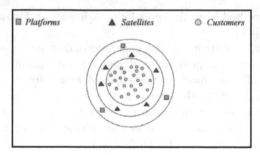

Fig. 1. Satellite distribution in the I1 instances (from [35])

2.2 Optimization Approach

In order to provide a useful tool for decision-makers addressing such issues, we present two decision-making scenarios: (i) Non collaborative scenario NCS in which horizontal collaboration does not exist between the suppliers, (ii) collaborative scenario CS in which horizontal collaboration exists between the suppliers. The 2E-LRP models can be implemented to analyze both scenarios.

In the NCS scenario, each manufacturer must define its own distribution scheme and solve the model separately. The CS scenario is modeled as a multi-source LRP-2E (F= {2,3,4,5}).The anticipation of a profitable coalition implies that partners share some logistical information (demands, delivery dates, locations of all the customers) to develop common distribution patterns. The two scenarios are evaluated under single-objective and multi-objective approach.

Single-objective Approach

First, we opt for a single objective approach to discuss the partner selection problem. Two cases are analyzed. Cost minimizing case (C_min) in which the model is solved considering only the objective function that minimizes cost and emissions minimizing case (Em_min) where the model is solved for optimal levels of CO2 emissions. The proposed evaluation process consists of a comparison between the performance of the non-collaborative scenario and the collaborative one. The performance of the considered coalitions in terms of generated gains is shown in Table 1 and Fig. 2

Computational results show that the collaborative cost and CO2 emissions are always smaller than stand-alone values (see Figure 2).Therefore, the gaps between collaborative and non collaborative scenarios are positive ranged in [10,10%;39,98%] for cost in C_min case and in [33,88%; 78,45%] for CO2 emissions in Em_min case. These gains are mainly realized by the reduction in the shipments distances and the number of used vehicles due to the new allocation of customers to satellites and the increase of the load rates of vehicles. Results confirm that jointly and optimally deciding on the location of depot and route of distribution can reduces total logistics costs and have a positive environmental impact under the scenario of collaboration. Numerical examples also show that gains improve as the number of partner's coalition increase meaning that more partners create more savings.

We note that solving larger-sized instances requires much computation time. As the LRP-2E is an NP-hard problem combining location and routing decisions, specific heuristic and meta-heuristics approach must be used in order to tackle the problem on large size instances.

Table 1. Generated gains in different sets after collaboration

Coalitions			Non collaboration		Collaboration		Gap	
			Cost (€)	CO_2 (g/km)	Cost (€)	CO_2 (g/km)	Cost (€)	CO_2 (g/km)
Set	F	W	S	C_min	Em_min	C_min	Em_min	C_min	Em_min
1	2	3	15	517	5576	465	3687	10.10%	33.88%
2	3	4	25	1383	48740	1143	25803	17.37%	47.06%
3	3	5	40	2245	66714	1726	31422	23.12%	52.90%
4	4	8	75	5319	190213	3735	73118	29.78%	61.56%
5	5	10	100	9088	359401	5846	109725	35.67%	69.47%
6	5	20	200	22934	1740580	13765	375095	39.98%	78.45%

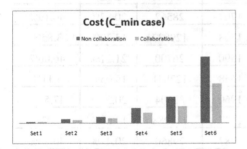
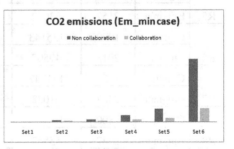

Fig. 2. Gap values for collaborative and non collaborative scenarios

In practice, the majority of horizontal coalitions are formed with two or three partner [46]. So, we focus on the case of a network of 3 possible partners, 5 satellites and 40 costumers. As firms aim to select the appropriate partners who can sustain their competitive advantage [38], It will be interesting to decisions makers to evaluate the sustainability performance of all possible coalitions that can be formed by the three partners.

We assume that suppliers have different sizes in terms of the volume of shipped products and number of customers: F1(big size/20 customers), F2(medium size/12 customers) and F3(small size/8 customers).

The studied set includes 10 instances generated according to the specifications described in Section 2.1. We simulate any possible coalition that can be formed by three suppliers from de network: F1 and F2, F2 and F3,F1 and F3 in addition to the grand coalition F1,F2 and F3. An extract of the obtained results for coalition F1 and F2 is reported in Table 2 for each instance .The average of generated gains after collaboration for all possible coalition are illustrated in Fig. 3.

Table 2. Comparison between collaborative and non collaborative scenarios in coalition F1 & F2

Inst	Case	Non Collaboration		Collaboration F1 & F2		Gap	
		Cost(€)	CO2(g/km)	Cost(€)	CO2(g/km)	Cost(€)	CO2(g/km)
R1	C_min	1695	114497	1450	111021	14.46%	3.04%
	Em_min	2372	56548	1888	30616	20.40%	45.86%
R2	C_min	2016	139077	1794	134688	11.00%	3.16%
	Em_min	2315	57056	1842	30850	20.43%	45.93%
R3	C_min	1894	128066	1615	124083	14.75%	3.11%
	Em_min	2134	52083	1660	28440	22.21%	45.39%
R4	C_min	1759	118935	1502	112344	14.63%	5.54%
	Em_min	2434	60040	1929	32300	20.75%	46.20%
R5	C_min	1911	129946	1668	124841	12.72%	3.93%
	Em_min	2152	53082	1704	28562	20.82%	46.19%
R6	C_min	1970	135143	1708	129937	13.30%	3.85%
	Em_min	2018	49502	1590	26700	21.21%	46.06%
R7	C_min	1952	131947	1658	127841	15.05%	3.11%
	Em_min	2467	61033	1960	32004	20.55%	47.56%
R8	C_min	1800	121674	1537	117988	14.60%	3.03%
	Em_min	2247	55567	1787	29860	20.47%	46.26%
R9	C_min	2003	130110	1726	129333	13.83%	0.60%
	Em_min	2080	51720	1650	27724	20.67%	46.40%
R10	C_min	1807	122131	1513	119922	16.25%	1.81%
	Em_min	2305	57056	1840	30400	20.17%	46.72%
AVR	C_min	1881	127153	1617	123196	**14.02%**	**3.11%**
	Em_min	2251	55369	1785	29747	**20.70%**	**46.28%**

Results confirm the profitability of cooperation in all cases and for all possible coalitions. When considering an objective of minimizing transportation cost (C_min case), the number of coalition partners affects the total amount of collaborative in a positive way for both cost and carbon emissions. When considering an objective of minimizing CO2 emissions (Em_min case), the grand coalition generates the greater emissions gain and coalition (F3 & F2) generates the greater cost gain.

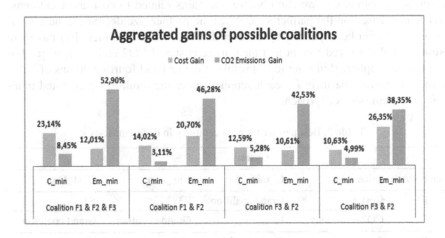

Fig. 3. Comparison between the aggregated gains generated by all possible coalitions

The partners are not, generally, interested in the profits generated by the entire alliance, but in the impact of the cooperation on their own P&L (profit and lost) instead. Then, before the companies agree to participate in a horizontal cooperation scheme, both an estimation of the individual cost and CO2 emissions savings must be available. According to (Cruijssen & BV 2013) [41], one of the main challenges in horizontal collaboration is to ensure a fair allocation of synergy estimated to all partners. Many cost allocation mechanisms were proposed in the literature. Recently, Guajardo [47] provided a survey on cost allocation methods found in the literature on collaborative transportation and also described the theoretical basis for the main methods as well as the cases where they are used. Several of these methods come from previous work on cooperative game theory. Defryn et al. [48] stated that no single cost allocation method works best in all situations and many researchers acknowledge the need for a case-specific approach. In this work, we use the well-known Shapley value, belonging to the field of cooperative game theory. The Shapley value method [49] takes into account the partners' contribution to all possible (sub)coalitions. Vanovermeire et al. [50] explained the calculation method. The allocation methods are primarily formulated to distribute gains (cost) among members in collaborative scenarios but they are in principle useful for allocating emissions [51]. So, the Shapley value can be used to divide CO2 emissions.

To be able to divide the two metrics according to the Shapley value, we created lists that contain orders of these sub-coalitions and repeating precedent calculation for the two cases C_min and Em_min. Results are presented in Fig. 4.

Results show the profitability of cooperation in all cases for all partners. In C_min case, the best gains generated by individual partners range in [8,84% ; 36,99%] for cost and in [26,74% ; 74,04%] for CO2 emissions. In Em_min case, these gains range in [4,24% ; 51,57%] for cost and in [23,93% ; 89,31%] for CO2 emissions. In both cases, we can observe that gains related to cost and CO2 emissions change based on the partner size. When the partner size decreases, these gains increase .This can be explained by the fact that the big size partner (F1) has more customers and delivered freight and then, more cost and CO2 emissions were allocated to this supplier. Referring to last results, the third and fourth columns of Table 3 indicates the best partners for each supplier under the minimizing cost and minimizing CO2 emissions approaches.

Table 3. Best partner for each company in different cases

suppliers	gains	Cases		
		C_min	Em_min	C_st_Em
F1	Cost	Grand coalition	F3	F3
	CO2 emissions	F2	Grand coalition	Grand coalition
F2	Cost	Grand coalition	F1	F1
	CO2 emissions	F1	F1	F1
F3	Cost	Grand coalition	F1	F1
	CO2 emissions	F1	F1	F1

In C_min case, the grand coalition is the most profitable for all suppliers in term of cost but in term of CO2 emissions and collaborating with F2 maximize generated gains for F1 and collaborating with big size supplier F1 maximize generated gains for F2 and F3. In Em_min case, F1 prefers F3 to maximize cost gains and the grand coalition to maximize CO2 emissions ones. F2 and F3 prefer to collaborate with F1 to maximize the two metrics.

Multi-objective Approach

Conflicting interests of stakeholders drive to a multi-objective decision-making problem. In our problem, decision makers don't completely known the importance of each objective and want to study the sensitivity of the total transportation cost versus CO2 emissions reduction (C_St_Em case). Thereby, a set of efficient solutions can be generated. The goal is giving to decision makers a tool for evaluating the solutions provided by the model and choosing the appropriate one to their objectives in terms of the CO2 emissions and transportation cost. We used ε-constraint method to solve this problem. In this method, one objective is selected for optimisation and the others are reformulated as constraints [52]. By progressively changing the constraint values ε, which represent the limit on CO2 emissions in our case, different points on the Pareto-front could be sampled. By calculating the extremes of the Pareto-front, the range of different objective functions could be calculated and constraint values selected accordingly. Efficient solutions and the Pareto frontier are presented in [53]. The multi-objective optimization helps decision makers to decide about the best trade-off by determining the cost of being sustainable from the point of reducing transportation emissions. Then, one of the generated solutions can be selected. We select the solution corresponding to the constraint value ε is slightly higher than the optimum emission level obtained in Em_min case which seems to be an ambitious sustainable solution.

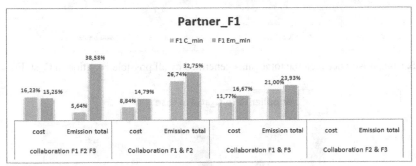

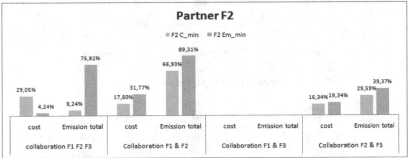

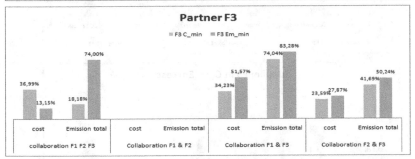

Fig. 4. Comparison between gains allocated to each supplier in all possible coalitions under single-objective approach

For the members of coalitions, it's also important to estimate the impact of solution selected on their cost and emissions in the case of multi-objective approach (C_st_Em). As the same way, like single-objective approach, for each instance, we simulate any possible coalition that can be formed by the three suppliers from de network. Averages of generated gains are summarized in Fig. 5.

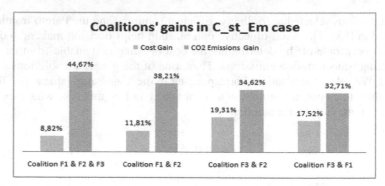

Fig. 5. Comparison between the total gains generated by all possible coalition in C_st_Em

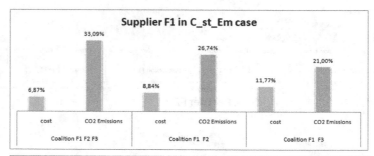

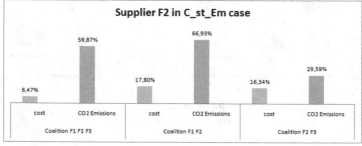

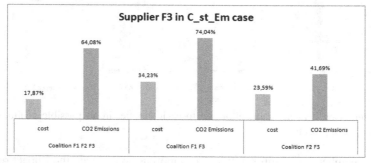

Fig. 6. Comparison between gains allocated to each supplier in all possible coalitions under the multi-objective approach

When considering an objective of minimizing cost under environment constraint (C_St_Em case), coalition that including more partners increases the total savings achieved for carbon emissions but affects the total amount of collaborative cost gains in a negative way. As such, a two-partner coalition make economic gains that are on average between 3% and 10,5% higher than those of a coalition with three partners.

Analyzing the gains allocated to each partner in all possible coalitions (see Fig. 6 and Table 3), we remark that the benefits of collaboration are not uniform but depend on the participating partners. Cooperation with supplier F1 was the most advantageous for suppliers F2 and F3. For F1, Supplier F3 and the grand coalition were, respectively, more beneficial in term of cost and emissions reduction.

3   Conclusions and Future Work

Horizontal collaboration between shippers is an important research area given the highly competitive environment in which shippers need to operate. This paper presents to decision makers a coalition formation mechanism to preliminary evaluate the economic and environmental effects of collaborative freight delivery in urban areas before that companies agree to participate in a horizontal cooperation scheme. This quantitative analysis is based on multi-objective mathematical model for a two echelon location routing problem (2E-LRP) to test if partners fit for the collaboration or not and if opportunity for each partner to make economic and environmental benefits exists. Extended known instances reflecting the real distribution in urban area are regenerated to evaluate several goods' delivery strategies. Shapley value method, belonging to the field of cooperative game theory, is used to allocate cost and CO_2 emissions to partners of the coalition. The obtained results confirm that horizontal collaboration leads to a reduction in transport costs and enhances the ecologic performance of partners in such coalitions. Also firms tend to further collaborate when the size of the coalitions formed are larger. Shippers differing in average order size leads to important results in terms of collaborative profit and smallest companies can increase the performance of the network, achieving improvements for generated gains in the horizontal collaboration.

We highlight that the evaluation of a profitable coalition imply to share some information about demands, delivery dates and customers' locations. To guarantee the neutrality and confidentiality of the information sharing, an external logistics service provider can pilot this process. Sensitive information including customer payments and cost structures is unexposed during the collaboration.

These conclusions underline the value of using operational research models such as the 2E LRP to help shippers investigate the value of careful partner selection. Eventually, evaluation and selection of partners for horizontal collaboration is a complex process related to other different factor than profit.

We acknowledge the limitations of our experimental study in terms of general validity of these findings. Reviewing current literature reveals that the results presented in this article display clear similarities with the conclusions drawn in other logistics horizontal collaboration contexts.

As an extension of this work, we can opt for other allocation mechanism to extend the analysis and consider additional objectives besides cost and CO2 emissions minimization as customer service level or preference of each partner. Also, to address uncertainty in decision makers' preferences and the lack of information we can combine our mathematical approach with fuzzy set theory.

References

[1]   Economic World Forum, "World Economic Forum White Paper Digital Transformation of Industries : In collaboration with Accenture Electricity Industry," no. 8, 2016.

[2]   X. Zhang and X. Hu, "Enabling sustainable urban road transport in China : A policy and institutional perspective Enabling sustainable urban road transport in China.Working Paper-CICERO," 2003.

[3]   J. R. Montoya-Torres, A. Muñoz-Villamizar and C.A. Vega-Mejía, "On the impact of collaborative strategies for goods delivery in city logistics," *Prod. Plan. Control*, vol. 27, pp. 443–455, 2016.

[4]   T. G. Crainic, T. Bekt, T. G. Crainic, and T. Van Woensel, "From Managing Urban Freight to Smart City Logistics Networks From Managing Urban Freight to Smart City Logistics Networks.Working paper-CIRRELT," 2015.

[5]   J. Juvien, "Club Défis Logistiques en Champagne-Ardenne : La mutualisation logistique," *Club Défis Logistiques en Champagne-Ardenne*, pp. 1–8, 2011.

[6]   N. H. Taieb and H. Affes, "Approaches to improve the performance of the collaborative supply chain management: Literature review," *2013 Int. Conf. Adv. Logist. Transp.*, pp. 440–445, 2013.

[7]   R. Leitner, F. Meizer, M. Prochazka, and W. Sihn, "Structural concepts for horizontal cooperation to increase efficiency in logistics," *CIRP J. Manuf. Sci. Technol.*, vol. 4, no. 3, pp. 332–337, 2011.

[8]   L. E. Amer and A. B. Eltawil, "Analysis of quantitative models of horizontal collaboration in supply chain network design: Towards 'green collaborative' strategies," *2015 Int. Conf. Ind. Eng. Oper. Manag.*, pp. 1–10, 2015.

[9]   A. Moutaoukil, R. Derrouiche, G. Neubert, E. S. C. Saint-etienne, and F. Bp, "Modeling a pooling logistics strategy for agri-food SMEs Acknowledgments," *14th IFIP WG 5.5 Work. Conf. Virtual Enterp. PRO-VE 2013*, pp. 2–3, 2013.

[10]   M. Soysal, J. M. Bloemhof-, R. Haijema, and J. G. A. J. Van Der Vorst, "Modeling a green inventory routing problem for perishable products with horizontal collaboration," *Comput. Oper. Res.*, 2016.

[11]   European commission, "Guidelines on the applicability of Article 101 of the Treaty on the Functioning of the European Union to horizontal co-operation agreements," 2011.

[12]   A. a. Juan, J. Faulin, E. Pérez-Bernabeu, and N. Jozefowiez, "Horizontal Cooperation in Vehicle Routing Problems with Backhauling and Environmental Criteria," *Procedia - Soc. Behav. Sci.*, vol. 111, pp. 1133–1141, 2014.

[13]   E. Ballot and F. Fontane, "Reducing transportation CO2 emissions through pooling of supply networks: perspectives from a case study in French retail chains," *Prod. Plan. Control*, vol. 21, no. 6, pp. 640–650, 2010.

[14]   F. Cruijssen and M. Salamon, "Empirical study : Order sharing between transportation companies may result in cost reductions between 5 to 15 percent Empirical study : Order sharing between transportation companies may result in cost reductions between 5 to 15 percent *," *SSRN Electron. J. 80(2004-80)*, 2004.

[15]   S. Pan, E. Ballot, F. Fontane, and D. Hakimi, "Environmental and economic issues arising from the pooling of SMEs' supply chains: Case study of the food industry in western France," *Flex. Serv. Manuf. J.*, vol. 26, no. 1–2, pp. 92–118, 2014.

[16]   L. E. Amer and A. B. Eltawil, "Collaborative sustainable supply chain network design: State of the art and solution framework," *CIE 2014 - 44th Int. Conf. Comput. Ind. Eng. IMSS 2014 - 9th Int. Symp. Intell. Manuf. Serv. Syst. Jt. Int. Symp. "The Soc. Impacts Dev. Informat*, no. January, pp. 479–493, 2014.

[17]   L. Okdinawati and T. M. Simatupang, "Modelling Collaborative Transportation Management : Current State And Opportunities For Future Research," *J. Oper. Supply Chain Manag.*, vol. 8, no. 2, pp. 96–119, 2015.

[18]   E. Pérez-Bernabeu, A. A. Juan, J. Faulin, and B. B. Barrios, "Horizontal cooperation in road transportation : a case illustrating savings in distances and greenhouse gas emissions," *Int. Trans. INOPERATIONAL Res.*, vol. 0, pp. 1–22, 2014.

[19]   N. Danloup, H. Allaoui, and G. Goncalves, "Literature review on or tools and methods for collaboration in supply chain," *Proc. 2013 Int. Conf. Ind. Eng. Syst. Manag. IEEE - IESM 2013*, 2013.

[20]   S. Pan, "Contribution à la définition et à l'évaluation de la mutualisation de chaînes logistiques pour réduire les émissions de CO2 du transport : application au cas de la grande distribution.Thesis," MINES ParisTech, 2010.

[21]   N. Danloup, V. Mirzabeiki, H. Allaoui, G. Goncalves, D. Julien, and C. Mena, "Reducing transportation greenhouse gas emissions with collaborative distribution:A case study," *Manag. Res. Rev.*, 2015.

[22]   A. Muñoz-villamizar, J. R. Montoya-torres, and J. Faulin, "Impact of the use of electric vehicles in collaborative urban transport networks : A case study," *Transp. Res. Part D J.*, vol. 50, pp. 40–54, 2017.

[23]   M. S. Daskin, L. V Snyder, and R. T. Berger, "Facility Location in Supply Chain Design," *Syst. Eng.*, no. 3, pp. 39–65, 2003.

[24]   C. Prodhon and C. Prins, "A survey of recent research on location-routing problems," *Eur. J. Oper. Res.*, vol. 238, no. 1, pp. 1–17, 2014.

[25]   H. Ouhader and M. El Kyal, "A Two-Echelon Location-Routing Model for Designing a Pooled Distribution Supply Chain," in *3rd International Conference on Logistics Operations Management (GOL), Fez, Morocco*, 2016, pp. 1–9.

[26]   H. Ouhader and M. El Kyal, "Combining facility location and routing decisions in sustainable urban freight distribution under horizontal collaboration : How shippers can be benefited ?," *Math. Probl. Eng.*, pp. 1–27, 2017.

[27]   H. Ouhader and M. El Kyal, "The impact of horizontal collaboration on CO2 emissions due to road transportation," in *Proceedings of the International Conference on Industrial Engineering and Operations Management*, 2017.

[28]   M. Drexl and M. Schneider, "A survey of variants and extensions of the location-routing problem," *Eur. J. Oper. Res.*, vol. 241, no. 2, pp. 283–308, 2015.

[29]   C. Prodhon and C. Prins, "A survey of recent research on location-routing problems," *Eur. J. Oper. Res.*, vol. 238, no. 1, pp. 1–17, 2014.

[30]   R. Cuda, G. Guastaroba, and M. G. Speranza, "A survey on two-echelon routing problems," *Comput. Oper. Res.*, vol. 55, pp. 185–199, 2015.

[31]   A. Awasthi, T. Adetiloye, and T. Gabriel, "Collaboration partner selection for city logistics planning under municipal freight regulations," *Appl. Math. Model.*, 2015.

[32]   Fleischmann, "The vehicle routing problem with multiple use of vehicles.," *Tech. report, Fachbereich Wirtschaftswissenschaften, Univ. 't Hambg. Fleischmanne*, 1990.

[33]   D. Cattaruzza, N. Absi, and D. Feillet, "Vehicle routing problems for city logistics," *EURO J Transp Logist*, 2015.

[34]   C. Sterle, "Location-Routing models and methods for Freight Distribution and Infomobility in City Logistics.Thesis," Universit` a degli Studi di Napoli "Federico II" Dipartimento di Informatica e Sistemistica Dottorato di Ricerca in Ingegneria Informatica ed Automatica, 2009.

[35]   M. Boccia, T. G. Crainic, A. Sforza, and C. Sterle, "Location-Routing Models for

Two-Echelon Freight Distribution System Design Location-Routing Models for Two-Echelon Freight," *CIRRELT Work. Pap.*, p. 28, 2011.

[36]   T. G. Crainic, a. Sforza, and a. Sterle, "Tabu Search Heuristic for a Two- Echelon Location-Routing Problem," *CIRRELT Work. Pap.*, 2011.

[37]   T. G. Crainic, N. Ricciardi, and G. Storchi, "Models for Evaluating and Planning City Logistics Systems," *Transp. Sci.*, vol. 43, no. 4, pp. 432–454, 2009.

[38]   L. Verdonck, P. Beullens, A. Caris, K. Ramaekers, and G. K. Janssens, "Analysis of collaborative savings and cost allocation techniques for the cooperative carrier facility location problem," *J. Oper. Res. Soc.*, pp. 1–19, 2016.

[39]   M. A. Krajewska, H. Kopfer, G. Laporte, S. Ropke, and G. Zaccour, "Horizontal cooperation among freight carriers: request allocation and profit sharing," *J. Oper. Res. Soc.*, vol. 59, no. 11, pp. 1483–1491, 2007.

[40]   C. Defryn, K. Sörensen, and T. Cornelissens, "The selective vehicle routing problem in a collaborative environment," *Eur. J. Oper. Res.*, 2015.

[41]   F. Cruijssen and A. BV, "CO^3 POSITION PAPER: FRAMEWORK FOR COLLABORATION," 2012.

[42]   A. Moutaoukil, Derrouich, R. E, G. Neubert, I. Fayol, and C. Fauriel, "Modélisation d'une stratégie de mutualisation logistique en intégrant les objectifs de Développement Durable pour des PME agroalimentaires," *13e Congrés Int. G´énie Ind. (CIGI'13), Jun 2013, LA ROCHELLE, Fr.*, 2013.

[43]   S. Pan, E. Ballot, and F. Fontane, "The reduction of greenhouse gas emissions from freight transport by pooling supply chains," *Int. J. Prod. Econ.*, vol. 143, no. 1, pp. 86–94, 2013.

[44]   A. Moutaoukil, G. Neubert, R. Derrouiche, and I. F.-U. M. R. Evs, "Urban Freight Distribution: The impact of delivery time on sustainability," *IFAC-PapersOnLine*, vol. 48, no. 3, pp. 2455–2460, 2015.

[45]   G. Mavrotas, "Effective implementation of the e -constraint method in Multi-Objective Mathematical Programming problems," *Appl. Math. Comput.*, vol. 213, no. 2, pp. 455–465, 2009.

[46]   M. Senkel and B. Durand, "Entre Théories Et Pratiques," *Logistique Manag.*, vol. 21, pp. 19–30, 2013.

[47]   M. Guajardo, "A review on cost allocation methods in collaborative transportation," vol. 23, pp. 371–392, 2016.

[48]   C. Defryn, C. Vanovermeire, and Kenneth Sörensen, "Gain Sharing in Horizontal Logistic Co-operation: A Case Study in the Fresh Fruit and Vegetables Sector," in *Sustainable Logistics and Supply Chains Innovations and Integral Approaches*, Sustainabl., Springer International Publishing, 2016, pp. 75–89.

[49]   L. S. Shapley, "Notes on the n-person game--II: the Value for n-Person Games," *U.S.AIR FORCE Proj. RAND Res. Memo.*, 1952.

[50]   C. Vanovermeire, K. Sörensen, A. Van Breedam, B. Vannieuwenhuyse, and S. Verstrepen, "Horizontal logistics collaboration: decreasing costs through flexibility and an adequate cost allocation strategy," *Int. J. Logist. Res. Appl.*, vol. 17, no. 4, pp. 339–355, 2014.

[51]   F. Kellner and A. Otto, "Allocating CO2 emissions to shipments in road freight transportation," *J. Manag. Control*, vol. 22, no. 4, pp. 451–479, 2012.

[52]   A. Chaabane, A. Ramudhin, and M. Paquet, "Designing supply chains with sustainability considerations," *Prod. Plan. Control Manag. Oper.*, no. August 2013, pp. 37–41, 2011.

[53]   H. Ouhader and M. El Kyal, "A decision support model for sustainable urban freight delivery under horizontal collaboration.," *Submitt. Manuscr.*, 2017.

A Simple Mechanism for the Disaster Emergency Unit Scheduling Problem

P.J. Araya-Córdova and Óscar C. Vásquez

Industrial Engineering Department
Universidad de Santiago de Chile
Av. Ecuador 3769, Estación Central, Chile.
{patricio.arayac,oscar.vasquez}@usach.cl

Abstract. In this paper, we study the optimization and mechanism design for the disaster emergency unit (DEU) scheduling problem motivated by the 2017 Chile wildfires, which is described as the worst in Chile's modern history. We consider a DEU to control wildfires and n forestry companies. Each forestry company j is located in town j. We assume these companies do not satisfy all safety conditions in order to reduce the wildfires impact and then, an emergency induces a damage function $D_j(\ell_j)$ to the town j, with ℓ_j the working time of DEU to control wildfires in town j. Each forestry company j has private information about the forest density, which in addition to the feedrate of wildfires determines its marginal waiting cost p_j due to forest working area to be recovered. In practice, it generates a waiting cost for each forestry company j, $p_j \sum_{\sigma(i) \leq \sigma(j)} \ell_i$, where $\sigma(j)$ is the position of forestry company j in the sequence σ. The goal is to determine a schedule defined by a sequence σ and the working time of DEU $\boldsymbol{\ell} = (\ell_1, \ldots, \ell_n)$ for minimizing of the sum of the total damage and the total waiting cost of the forestry companies subject to constraints on the damage and use of the working time of DEU. We show that the centralized problem can be solve Karush-Kuhn-Tucker (KKT) conditions and design an easy-to-implement truthful mechanism for decentralized problem, charging in some way the damage to the forestry companies based on the optimal solution properties obtained from the centralized problem. A numerical example to illustrate the problem and the usefulness of our contributions is described.

Keywords: scheduling, disaster emergency unit, mechanism design, truthfulness

1 Introduction

The scheduling problems in the disaster operation management (DOM) are highlighted as an important factor into policies of national security [9] and considered as the opportunity to re-visit and re-define operation research, being a likely and worthwhile growing area in the next 50 years [22]. Indeed, there is increasing recognition of the need for applying centralized and decentralized resolution

© Springer International Publishing AG 2017
T. Bektaş et al. (Eds.), ICCL 2017, LNCS 10572, pp. 205–215, 2017.
https://doi.org/10.1007/978-3-319-68496-3_14

methods in DOM, because it develops a scientific approach to help decision making before, during and after a disaster [1,7].

In this paper, we are focused on the disaster emergency unit scheduling problem from both centralized and decentralized perspectives. The goal is to determine a schedule defined by a sequence of the emergency points to be visited and the working time on these points aiming at minimizing the total damage [26]. We are motivated by the 2017 Chile wildfires, which is described as the worst in Chile's modern history as it destroyed many towns in the central Maule Region, displacing thousands of people.

Specifically, we consider n forestry companies and a single disaster emergency unit (DEU) to control wildfires, which supposes a scenario with a limited number of personnel and specialized equipment. Each forestry company j is located in town j. We assume these companies do not satisfy all safety conditions in order to reduce the wildfires impact and then, an emergency induces a damage to the town j defined by the isoelastic function $D_j(\ell_j) := 4d_j/(\pi\ell_j^{\gamma_j})$, $1 < \gamma_j < 2$, with ℓ_j the working time of DEU to control wildfires in town j, d_j the damage cost associated to the inhabited area in town j affected by wildfires and, $\pi\ell_j^{\gamma_j}/4$ the area controlled by DEU in town j. Notice that an isoelastic damage function makes sense as the percentage change of DEU working time by increasing of area control implies a decreasing percentage change in the town area where the damage is induced. Formally, we consider $\pi\ell_j^{\gamma_j}/4 := \epsilon_j\pi\ell_j^2/4$ with $\epsilon_j \in (0,1)$ decreasing in ℓ_j.

Each forestry company j has private information about its forest density, which in addition to the feedrate of wildfires determines its marginal waiting cost p_j due to forest working area to be recovered. The DEU requests the marginal waiting costs $\hat{p}_j$ from each forestry company j and chooses an arbitrary sequence σ that indicates the order to visit the towns by DEU, with $\sigma(j)$ being the position of town j in the sequence σ.

For convenience, we denote $\tau(k)$ the town in the position k in the sequence σ. Given sequence σ, we have a transfer time $r_{\tau(\sigma(j)-1),j}$ between the town $\tau(\sigma(j)-1)$ and town j. We assume an initial point from DEU arrives to the towns, which could determine a set of towns to be visited in the first position in sequence σ.

The total cost damage and damage cost of each town j are constrained by $\overline{D}$ and $\overline{D_j}$, respectively. Similarly, the total and the particular DEU working time in each town j are constraint by $\overline{L}$ and $\overline{\ell_j}$. These constraints aim to state (i) lower bounds on total damage and the particular damage of town communities; and (ii) upper bounds on the total and particular waiting times for DEU of towns, whose values could be estimated according to the operative constraints of the DEU (e.g. equipment capacity, working shift, geographic, whether and environmental conditions, among others) and/or a potential maximum collateral damage of town communities in this emergency setting. Note that for a working time $\ell_j \leq a$, a constant, $D_j(\ell_j) \geq D_j(a)$.

We want to compute the optimal *social cost* given a sequence σ for working time of DEU, which is given by

$$\sum_j D_j(\ell_j) + \sum_j \hat{p}_j \left(\sum_{\sigma(i) \leq \sigma(j)} \ell_{\sigma(i)} + r_{\tau(\sigma(j)-1),j} \right),$$ (1)

subject to

$$\sum_j \ell_j \leq \overline{L}$$ (2)

$$\ell_j + r_{\tau(\sigma(j)-1),j} \leq \overline{\ell_j} \quad \forall j$$ (3)

$$\sum_j D_j(\ell_j) \leq \overline{D}$$ (4)

$$D_j(\ell_j) \leq \overline{D}_j \quad \forall j$$ (5)

In this social cost, we consider the conversion of damage and waiting cost into monetary values and assume for simplification that the conversion factors are hidden in the damage function.

In this situation, the assumption of centralized problem that the DEU would know the real waiting cost from the forestry companies, i.e., $\hat{p} = p$, would compute the *optimal social cost* and consequently, charge directly the damage generates by each forestry company j may not be feasible. In fact, the implementation of the optimal allocation could be not possible because the DEU knows only the announced values $\hat{p}$, which are not necessary the real values p, and then a truthful mechanism for the decentralized problem would of interest.

Our Contribution. We show that the centralized problem can be solved by Karush-Kuhn-Tucker (KKT) conditions and design an easy-to-implement truthful mechanism for the decentralized problem, charging in some way the damage to the forestry companies based on the optimal solution properties obtained from centralized problem. A numerical example to illustrative the problem and the usefulness of our contributions is described.

Related work. In literature, an important problem of fire management is to decide when and where to suppress wildfires and when and where to light prescribed fires or allow wildfires to burn [11]. This problem has been studied by several authors from a centralized perspective, considering various assumptions in its formulation and different resolution methods for solving, such as: simulation and stochastic integer programming approach to wildfire initial attack planning [19], mixed-integer programming model for spatially explicit multi-period landscape level fuel management to mitigate wildfire impacts [15], survival analysis methods to model the control time of forest fires [16], chance-constrained programming model to allocate wildfire initial attack resources for a fire season [25], among others. However, few have tackled the complex social, economic and ecological issues that complicate modern forest fire management [20]. In particular, our work addresses both centralized and decentralized perspectives in a scenario with a limited number of personnel and specialized equipment, which implies the sequential work of the single DEU available in this emergency situation.

2   Optimizing social cost

We consider the centralized problem consisting in minimizing the sum of the damage functions and the waiting costs, under the assumption that the DEU knows the real waiting cost from the forestry companies. Theorem 1 defines the unique optimal working time of DEU for the town j in the sequence σ.

Theorem 1. *Fix a sequence σ and consider the minimization of the social cost (1) subject to constraints on the working time of DEU (2)- (3), and the damage (4)- (5). The unique optimal working time of DEU for the town j in the sequence σ satisfies*

$$\ell_j^* = \left(\frac{\gamma_j d_j 4 \left(1 + \lambda_2 + \lambda_{2j}\right)}{\pi \left(\sum_{\sigma(i) \geq \sigma(j)} \hat{p}_i + \lambda_1 + \lambda_{1j}\right)} \right)^{\frac{1}{1+\gamma_j}},$$

where $\lambda_1, \lambda_{1j}, \lambda_2$ and λ_{2j} are the KKT multiplier associated to the (2), (3),(4) and (5), respectively.

Proof. First, we show that the minimization of the social cost subject to the damage and working time of DEU constraints for a given sequence σ is a convex programming problem.

We fix a sequence σ. We claim that the minimization of social cost subject to the constraints on the damage and working time of DEU has convex and affine constraints and a convex objective function (1). The former statement is trivial and follows the working time of DEU and damage function definition, i.e., $D_j''(\ell_j) = \frac{4(1+\gamma_j)\gamma_j d_j}{\pi(\ell_j)^{\gamma_j}} > 0$, for $1 < \gamma_j < 2$ and the latter statement follows from the first derivative of the objective function (1) in ℓ_j

$$D_j'(\ell_j^*) + \sum_{\sigma(i) \geq \sigma(j)} \hat{p}_i,$$

which is independent of ℓ_i for any $i \neq j$, and so its Hessian has zero non-diagonal terms, whereas the second derivative of the objective function (1) in ℓ_j is $D_j''(\ell_j) > 0$. Thus, we have that the diagonal terms of the Hessian are positive, the Hessian is positive definite and the objective function (1) is convex.

Second, we have that for the above problem the Karush-Kuhn-Tucker (KKT) conditions give necessary and sufficient conditions on an optimal solution [3]. We write the Lagrangian associated to the problem, apply the KKT conditions and have:

$$D_j'(\ell_j) = -\frac{\sum_{\sigma(i) \geq \sigma(j)} \hat{p}_i + \lambda_1 + \lambda_{1j}}{1 + \lambda_2 + \lambda_{2j}} = -\frac{4\gamma_j d_j}{\pi (\ell_j)^{1+\gamma_j}},$$

where $\lambda_1, \lambda_{1j}, \lambda_2$ and λ_{2j} are the KKT multiplier associated to the (2), (3),(4) and (5), respectively.

Third, we obtain the optimal working time of DEU for the town j in the sequence σ from the above equalities and have

$$\ell_j^* = \left(\frac{\gamma_j d_j 4 \left(1 + \lambda_2 + \lambda_{2j}\right)}{\pi \left(\sum_{\sigma(i) \geq \sigma(j)} \hat{p}_i + \lambda_1 + \lambda_{1j}\right)} \right)^{\frac{1}{1+\gamma_j}},$$

Finally, the uniqueness of ℓ_j^*, $\forall j$ follows from the strict monotonicity of $D_j'(\ell_j)$, concluding the proof.   □

Note that the minimization of the social cost subject to the damage and use of working time of DEU constraints for a given sequence σ is a convex programming problem, which can be solved in polynomial time up to an arbitrary precision with the Ellipsoid method [17].

3   The mechanism

We study the decentralized problem, in which the DEU knows only the announced marginal waiting costs $\hat{p}$ by the forestry companies, which are not necessarily the real values p.

We introduce our mechanism for the decentralized problem, which charges a_j to every forestry company j depending on the announced marginal waiting cost $\hat{p}$ and the use of the optimal working time of DEU ℓ^* minimizing the social cost for a given sequence σ from Theorem 1 by applying Karush-Kuhn-Tucker (KKT) conditions [3].

We consider that every player j wants to minimize the sum of the waiting cost and the cost share defined by the mechanism $p_j \sum_{\sigma(i) \leq \sigma(j)} \ell_i^*(\hat{p}_j, \hat{p}_{-j}) + a_j$, where a_j is defined as follows

$$\sum_{\sigma(i) \leq \sigma(j)} (1 + \gamma_i)(1 + \lambda_2 + \lambda_{2i}) \left(D_i(\ell_i^*(\hat{p}_j, \hat{p}_{-j})) - D_i(\ell_i^*(0, \hat{p}_{-j})) - \hat{p}_j \ell_i^*(\hat{p}_j, \hat{p}_{-j})\right)$$

or equivalently

$$\sum_{\sigma(i) \leq \sigma(j)} (1 + \gamma_i)(1 + \lambda_2 + \lambda_{2i}) \left(\frac{d_i 4}{\pi}\right)^{\frac{1}{1+\gamma_i}} \left(\frac{\left(\sum_{\sigma(k) \geq \sigma(i)} \hat{p}_k + \lambda_1 + \lambda_{1i}\right)}{\gamma_i (1 + \lambda_2 + \lambda_{2i})}\right)^{\frac{\gamma_i}{1+\gamma_i}}$$

$$- \sum_{\sigma(i) \leq \sigma(j)} (1 + \gamma_j)(1 + \lambda_2 + \lambda_{2j}) \left(\frac{d_j 4}{\pi}\right)^{\frac{1}{1+\gamma_j}} \left(\frac{\left(\sum_{\sigma(k) \geq \sigma(i)} \hat{p}_k - \hat{p}_j + \lambda_1 + \lambda_{1i}\right)}{\gamma_i (1 + \lambda_2 + \lambda_{2i})}\right)^{\frac{\gamma_i}{1+\gamma_i}}$$

$$- \sum_{\sigma(i) \leq \sigma(j)} \hat{p}_i \left(\frac{\gamma_i d_i 4 \left(1 + \lambda_2 + \lambda_{2i}\right)}{\pi \left(\sum_{\sigma(k) \geq \sigma(i)} \hat{p}_k + \lambda_1 + \lambda_{1i}\right)}\right)^{\frac{1}{1+\gamma_i}}$$

This mechanism is *truthful*, which is a desirable property, meaning that every firm j minimizes its total cost defined as the sum of the waiting cost and the established cost share by announcing his true value, i.e., $\hat{p}_j = p_j$, as shown in Theorem 2, and then the strategy profile $\hat{\boldsymbol{p}}$ is an unique pure Nash equilibrium.

Theorem 2. *The mechanism is truthful.*

Proof. We derive the objective function of player j, which is to minimize the sum of waiting cost and the defined cost share and have

$$
\frac{\partial(p_j \sum_{\sigma(i) \leq \sigma(j)} \ell_i^*(\hat{p}_j, \hat{p}_{-j}) + a_j)}{\partial \hat{p}_j} = p_j \sum_{\sigma(i) \leq \sigma(j)} \frac{\partial \ell_i^*(\hat{p}_j, \hat{p}_{-j})}{\partial \hat{p}_j}
$$

$$
+ \sum_{\sigma(i) \leq \sigma(j)} \ell_i^*(\hat{p}_j, \hat{p}_{-j}) - \sum_{\sigma(i) \leq \sigma(j)} \ell_i^*(\hat{p}_j, \hat{p}_{-j})
$$

$$
- \hat{p}_j \sum_{\sigma(i) \leq \sigma(j)} \frac{\partial \ell_i^*(\hat{p}_j, \hat{p}_{-j})}{\partial \hat{p}_j}
$$

$$
= (p_j - \hat{p}_j) \sum_{\sigma(i) \leq \sigma(j)} \frac{\partial \ell_i^*(\hat{p}_j, \hat{p}_{-j})}{\partial \hat{p}_j}
$$

We have

$$
\frac{\partial \ell_i^*(\hat{p}_j, \hat{p}_{-j})}{\partial \hat{p}_j} = - \frac{\gamma_j d_j 4 (1 + \lambda_2 + \lambda_{2j})}{1 + \gamma_j} \left(\frac{\pi \left(\sum_{\sigma(i) \geq \sigma(j)} \hat{p}_i + \lambda_1 + \lambda_{1j} \right)}{\gamma_j d_j 4 (1 + \lambda_2 + \lambda_{2j})} \right)^{\frac{\gamma_j}{1 + \gamma_j}} < 0,
$$

which implies that $\hat{p}_j = p_j$ minimizes the firm's total cost, concluding the proof. $\qquad\square$

4   A numerical example

We perform a numerical example based on 2017 Chile wildfires, which destroyed many towns in the central Maule Region, displacing thousands of people. We consider $n = 4$ towns called Aquelarre ($j = 1$), Culenmapu ($j = 2$), Llico ($j = 3$) and Tilicura ($j = 4$), which are located in the affected zone around the Vichuquén Lake. The route access to these towns is from the freeway J-820, which constrained to Aquelarre and Tilicura as the first town to visit by DEU in any sequence. Figure 1 shows the zone of central Maule Region, Chile, in where the towns are located.

The parameters values and time between towns are estimated from [10,4,5,8] such as shown Table 1 and 2, respectively.

Later, we compute the optimal solution of the centralized problem by using the Optimization Tool provided by MATLAB, with a unitary vector initial solution and the following general configuration: (i) Solver: fmincon-Constrained

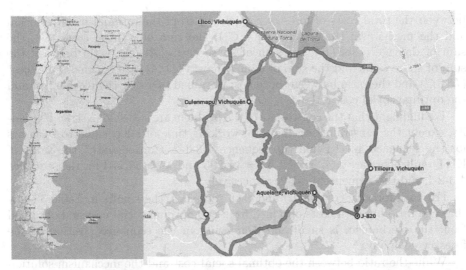

Fig. 1: Map of Central Maule Region, Chile, in where the towns are located.

j	1	2	3	4
γ_j	1.99	1.95	1.80	1.90
d_j (USD\$ $\cdot$ km^2)	4,535,497	4,069,315	73,991,611	7,346,182
p_j (USD\$/h)	23,292	76,575	187,961	94,716
$\ell_j(h)$	9.99	11.47	16.45	12.27
$\overline{D}_j$ (USD\$)	60,152	45,114	615,059	80,905
$\overline{L}$ (h)	24			
$\overline{D}$ (USD\$)	12,000,000			

Table 1: Parameters of problem

$r_{i,j}(h)$	1	2	3	4
0 (Freeway J-820)	0.15	-	-	0.08
1	-	0.42	0.75	0.22
2	0.42	-	0.15	0.37
3	0.75	0.15	-	0.35
4	0.22	0.37	0.35	-

Table 2: Time between towns

nonlinear minimization; (ii) Algorithm: Interior point; (iii) Derivatives: Approximated by solver; (iv) Function tolerance: 1e-20; (v) Constraint tolerance: 1e-20; (vi) Max iterations: 50000; (vii) Max function evaluations: 10e6.

Table 3 provides the obtained results from MATLAB for all sequences in a total execution time less than 60 seconds. The values reported are: the working time of DEU in each town (ℓ_j), the total working time of DEU ($\sum_i \ell_i$), the damage cost associated to each town (D_j), the ratio between cost share and damage cost of each town (a_j/D_j), the waiting time cost of each forestry company (C_j), the total cost associated to each forestry company and town ($D_j + C_j$), the ratio between the total costs of forestry company j from the optimal social solution and the mechanism $((a_j + C_j)/(D_j + C_j))$, the sum of waiting costs (C), the sum of damage costs (D), the sum of share costs (A), the ratio between the sum of share costs and the sum of damage costs (D/A), the optimal social cost $(D + C)$ and the ratio between social cost obtained by using the mechanism and the optimal social cost $((A + C)/(D + C))$.

We highlight that the constraints of the problem are satisfied in strict inequality, except the constraints on the total working time of DEU equal to 24 hours for the sequence 4-3-2-1 and the sequence 4-3-1-2. Consequently, the value of KKT multipliers are zero, except $\lambda_1 = 38,295$ and $\lambda_1 = 25,984$ for the sequence 4-3-2-1 and the sequence 4-3-1-2, respectively.

For each forestry company j and each sequence, the results in Table 3 show that the ratio between costs obtained from the optimal social cost and obtained from the mechanism is small and decreasing in the sequence position of the forestry company.

While the ratio between the optimal social cost and the mechanism solution value is bounded by a factor less than 1.5 for all sequences, the ratio between the total damage cost and the total cost shares is small in comparison to the upper bound associated to the maximum elasticity value of damage functions.

We highlight that the sequence with the minimum damage and the minimum social cost could not necessarily have the minimum ratios. Indeed, the sequence with the minimum social cost is 4-3-1-2, but its ratios D/A=2.21 and $(A + C)/(D + C)$=1.46 are third and fourth value in decreasing order, respectively.

5   Final remarks

The minimization of the social cost subject to the damage and use of a type of resource constraints by finding an optimal sequence could be very difficult to computed. An interesting approach is the reformulation of the sequencing problem in another equivalent scheduling problem, for which some computational complexity results and resolution methods are known from the literature. For instance, Dürr et al. [6] and Megow and Verschae [13] showed an equivalence between the single machine scheduling problem $1|| \sum_j w_j C_j^{\frac{\gamma}{\gamma+1}}$ and the minimization of the social cost for a damage function $D_j(\ell_j) = w_j^{1+\gamma} \ell_j^{-\gamma}$ with $\gamma \in [1, 2]$. For the above problem, no polynomial algorithm for finding an optimal schedule is known. However, a PTAS in [13] and dominance properties in [2] for solving this problem have been established.

We highlighted that our mechanism address to a new emergence challenge in fire management, improving the analytic solutions to predict and sometimes evaluate the consequences of implementing alternatives courses the action from a decentralized perspective [12]. In practice, our approach could be easily integrated in a fire management decision support system, giving an easy-to-implement alternative to the classical axiomatic and hard to compute approach of the cooperative games in generalized characteristic function form to model situations

sequence	1-3-2-4	1-3-4-2	4-3-2-1	4-3-1-2
ℓ_1 (h)	3.12	3.12	5.75	4.53
ℓ_2 (h)	3.98	5.24	4.28	4.74
ℓ_3 (h)	9.02	9.02	9.33	9.46
ℓ_4 (h)	6.09	4.96	3.63	3.67
$\sum_i \ell_i$ (h)	23.63	23.95	24.00	24.00
D_1 (USD\$)	599,327	599,853	177,883	286,220
D_2 (USD\$)	349,621	205,506	303,560	249,287
D_3 (USD\$)	1,797,524	1,799,345	1,690,842	1,649,528
D_4 (USD\$)	302,848	446,838	805,225	789,713
a_1/D_1	2.87	2.87	2.22	2.47
a_2/D_2	2.19	2.25	2.01	1.69
a_3/D_3	1.90	1.89	2.18	2.13
a_4/D_3	1.36	1.98	2.47	2.46
C_1 (USD\$)	76,207	76,175	351,910	355,453
C_2 (USD\$)	2,451,453	2,450,241	2,518,272	2,549,577
C_3 (USD\$)	1,315,355	1,737,313	415,349	1,442,688
C_4 (USD\$)	2,238,118	1,833,634	1,837,800	559,008
$D_1 + C_1$ (USD\$)	675,534	676,028	2,015,683	1,728,908
$D_2 + C_2$ (USD\$)	1,664,976	2,039,140	718,909	808,295
$D_3 + C_3$ (USD\$)	4,248,977	4,249,586	4,209,114	4,199,105
$D_4 + C_4$ (USD\$)	2,540,966	2,184,151	1,157,135	1,145,167
$(a_1 + C_1)/(D_1 + C_1)$	2.66	2.66	1.11	1.24
$(a_2 + C_2)/(D_2 + C_2)$	1.25	1.13	1.43	1.21
$(a_3 + C_3)/(D_3 + C_3)$	1.38	1.38	1.47	1.44
$(a_4 + C_4)/(D_4 + C_4)$	1.04	1.20	2.02	2.01
C (USD\$)	6,081,134	6,097,363	5,123,330	4,906,726
D (USD\$)	3,049,320	3,051,542	2,977,510	2,974,748
A/D	2.07	2.12	2.25	2.21
$D + C$ (USD\$)	9,130,454	9,148,905	8,100,841	7,881,475
$(A + C)/(D + C)$	1.36	1.37	1.46	1.46

Table 3: Results for illustrative case grouped by sequence. The values reported are: the working time of DEU in each town (ℓ_j), the total working time of DEU ($\sum_i \ell_i$), the damage cost associated to each town (D_j), the ratio between cost share and damage cost of each town (a_j/D_j), the waiting time cost of each forestry company (C_j), the total cost associated to each forestry company and town ($D_j + C_j$), the ratio between the total costs of forestry company j from the optimal social solution and the mechanism ($(a_j + C_j)/(D_j + C_j)$), the sum of waiting costs (C), the sum of damage costs (D), the sum of share costs (A), the ratio between the sum of share costs and the sum of damage costs (D/A), the optimal social cost ($D + C$), the ratio between social cost obtained by using the mechanism and the optimal social cost ($(A + C)/(D + C)$).

where the total cost/utility can be distributed among firms, which depend not only on its members but also on the order/sequence of formation [18,21,24,14].

For future research, we propose to study this problem with uncertainty where the input data is initially not known precisely. In particular, we refer to take into account the inherent stochastic nature of wildfire phenomena [23]; for example, considering the constant elasticity coefficient of the damage functions into a bounded interval or defined by a probability distribution.

Finally, we leave open the question about an truthfulness and bound for the overcharging in our mechanism for an arbitrary damage function into a general setting where the use sequential of a resource is assumed. Here, two interesting insights for exploring are: (1) the study of a possible bound for the overcharging of mechanism by the constant elasticity coefficient of this type damage functions based on the obtained results in this work; and (2) the definition of the *good features* for the damage functions in order to preserve the *truthfulness* of the mechanism.

Acknowledgement The authors would like to thank the anonymous referees who spotted errors in previous versions of this paper. This work is partially supported by FONDECYT grant 11140566.

References

1. N. Altay and W. G. Green III. OR/MS research in disaster operations management. *European Journal of Operational Research*, 175(1):475–493, 2006.
2. N. Bansal, C. Dürr, N. K. Thang, and Ó. C. Vásquez. The local–global conjecture for scheduling with non-linear cost. *Journal of Scheduling*, 20(3):239–254, 2017.
3. S. Boyd and L. Vandenberghe. *Convex optimization*. Cambridge University Press, 2004.
4. CONAF. Fija costos de forestacion, recuperacion de suelos degradados, estabilizacion de dunas, poda y raleo, por hectarea, y establecimiento de cortinas cortavientos por kilometro, al 31 de julio de 2011, para los efectos del Decreto Ley 701 de 1974 y sus modificaciones posteriores, 2011.
5. CONAF. Informe de riesgo de ocurrencia de incendios forestales en la comuna de Vichuquén, 2016.
6. C. Dürr, Ł. Jeż, and Ó. C. Vásquez. Scheduling under dynamic speed-scaling for minimizing weighted completion time and energy consumption. *Discrete Applied Mathematics*, 196:20–27, 2015.
7. G. Galindo and R. Batta. Review of recent developments in OR/MS research in disaster operations management. *European Journal of Operational Research*, 230(2):201–211, 2013.
8. INE. División Político Administrativa y Censal, 2007.
9. B. A. Jackson, K. S. Faith, and H. H. Willis. Evaluating the reliability of emergency response systems for large-scale incident operations. Technical report, DTIC Document, 2010.
10. G. Julio and G. Giroz. Notas sobre el comportamiento del fuego y su aplicacion en el control de incendios forestales. *Bosque (Valdivia)*, 1(1):18–27, 1975.
11. D. L. Martell. Forest fire management. *Handbook of operations research in natural resources*, pages 489–509, 2007.
12. D. L. Martell. The development and implementation of forest and wildland fire management decision support systems: reflections on past practices and emerging needs and challenges. *Mathematical and Computational Forestry & Natural Resource Sciences*, 3(1):18, 2011.

13. N. Megow and J. Verschae. Dual techniques for scheduling on a machine with varying speed. In *International Colloquium on Automata, Languages, and Programming*, pages 745–756. Springer, 2013.
14. T. P. Michalak, P. L. Szczepański, T. Rahwan, A. Chrobak, S. Brânzei, M. Wooldridge, and N. R. Jennings. Implementation and computation of a value for generalized characteristic function games. *ACM Transactions on Economics and Computation*, 2(4):1–35, 2014.
15. J. P. Minas, J. W. Hearne, and D. L. Martell. A spatial optimisation model for multi-period landscape level fuel management to mitigate wildfire impacts. *European Journal of Operational Research*, 232(2):412–422, 2014.
16. A. A. Morin, A. Albert-Green, D. G. Woolford, and D. L. Martell. The use of survival analysis methods to model the control time of forest fires in ontario, canada. *International Journal of Wildland Fire*, 24(7):964–973, 2015.
17. Y. Nesterov, A. Nemirovskii, and Y. Ye. *Interior-point polynomial algorithms in convex programming*, volume 13. SIAM, 1994.
18. A. S. Nowak and T. Radzik. The shapley value for n-person games in generalized characteristic function form. *Games and Economic Behavior*, 6(1):150–161, 1994.
19. L. Ntaimo, J. A. Gallego-Arrubla, J. Gan, C. Stripling, J. Young, and T. Spencer. A simulation and stochastic integer programming approach to wildfire initial attack planning. *Forest Science*, 59(1):105–117, 2013.
20. M. Rönnqvist, S. D'Amours, A. Weintraub, A. Jofre, E. Gunn, R. G. Haight, D. L. Martell, A. T. Murray, and C. Romero. Operations research challenges in forestry: 33 open problems. *Annals of Operations Research*, 232(1):11–40, 2015.
21. E. Sanchez and G. Bergantiños. On values for generalized characteristic functions. *Operations-Research-Spektrum*, 19(3):229–234, 1997.
22. N. Simpson and P. Hancock. Fifty years of operational research and emergency response. *Journal of the Operational Research Society*, 60(1):S126–S139, 2009.
23. S. W. Taylor, D. G. Woolford, C. Dean, and D. L. Martell. Wildfire prediction to inform management: Statistical science challenges. *Statistical Science*, pages 586–615, 2013.
24. R. van den Brink, E. González-Arangüena, C. Manuel, and M. del Pozo. Order monotonic solutions for generalized characteristic functions. *European Journal of Operational Research*, 238(3):786–796, 2014.
25. Y. Wei, M. Bevers, E. Belval, and B. Bird. A chance-constrained programming model to allocate wildfire initial attack resources for a fire season. *Forest Science*, 61(2):278–288, 2015.
26. F. Wex, G. Schryen, S. Feuerriegel, and D. Neumann. Emergency response in natural disaster management: Allocation and scheduling of rescue units. *European Journal of Operational Research*, 235(3):697–708, 2014.

Maritime Logistics

Survey on Autonomous Surface Vessels: Part I - A New Detailed Definition of Autonomy Levels

Matteo Schiaretti, Linying Chen, and Rudy R. Negenborn

Department of Maritime and Transport Technology, Delft University of Technology,
Delft, The Netherlands
L.Chen-2@tudelft.nl,R.R.Negenborn@tudelft.nl

Abstract. Autonomous Surface Vessels (ASVs) have been involved in numerous projects since the 1990s. Many ASV projects have been successfully realized, and as many are still under development. Together with the development of those new autonomous vessels, the research on classification about ASVs has become important. The classifications provide clarity to researchers, designers, shipbuilders, equipment manufacturers, ship owners and operators, enabling accurate specification of the desired level of autonomy in design and operations. Moreover, the involved research paves the way to a clearer understanding of the opportunity and challenges of research on autonomous vehicles.
In this paper, we introduce the emerging concept of autonomous vessels. A multi-layer multi-agent control architecture of cooperative transport systems from the perspective of ASVs is proposed. Moreover, we provide an overview of existing research on the classification of autonomy. Based on the analysis, a detailed definition and categorization of autonomy levels for ASVs is proposed starting from the characteristics of ASVs and existing classification of autonomy. The proposed autonomy levels categorization assesses the overall autonomy level of a vessel by analyzing the automated sub-systems: Decision, Actions, Exceptions, and Cooperation. This categorization can be used to analyze existing ASV prototypes to gain insight into the status and trend of ASV research.

Keywords: Autonomous Surface Vessels; Autonomy level; ASV; Cooperative transport systems

1 Introduction

Autonomous Surface Vessels (ASVs) have been involved in numerous projects since the 1990s. Typically, the goal is to achieve fully autonomous navigation. The concept of ASV has been well known at an academic level for a while. Recently, industry has began developing full scale vessels for the container and bulk sectors [3, 15, 27, 26]. Together with the development of those new autonomous

© Springer International Publishing AG 2017
T. Bektaş et al. (Eds.), ICCL 2017, LNCS 10572, pp. 219–233, 2017.
https://doi.org/10.1007/978-3-319-68496-3_15

vessels, the research on classification about ASVs becomes important. The classifications provide clarity to researchers, designers, shipbuilders, equipment manufacturers, ship owners and operators, enabling accurate specification of the desired level of autonomy in design and operations. Moreover, the relative research paves the way to a clearer understanding of the opportunity and challenges of research on autonomous vehicles. Lloyd's Register [13], has published a categorization of vessels based on the level of autonomy. This is a step forward in the process to make ASVs a common means of transportation. Other types of categorization have been adopted by different autonomous applications, like the one proposed by SAE International, about the level of autonomy in vehicles [2]. However, above mentioned categorizations are not considering all the aspects subject to automation and the characteristics of vessels.

This paper is organized as follows. An introduction to the concept of ASV and their role in transport systems is given in Section 2. Following this, three existing autonomy level categorizations are explained in Section 3. A new autonomy level categorization is proposed, together with the additional sub-categories in Section 4. The conclusions of this paper are presented in Section 5

2   Autonomous Surface Vessels

An ASV is a vessel that has achieved a level of autonomy in its employment. For example, the human operator is helped or completely replaced by systems on board or at a remote location.

ASVs have started being developed at an academic level in 1993, when MIT presented its first vessel called ARTEMIS [18]. The goal of this ship was to collect bathysphere data along a river. Following this first vessel, many more institutes have started researching the field of autonomy on board of increasingly big vessels, up to the more recent proposal by Rolls-Royce and Man Diesel, to automate cargo and bulk ships [15, 26].

In order to clearly understand the main concept of ASVs, the following part presents the role of ASVs in a multi-agent, multi-layer cooperative transport system. Subsequently, the architecture of an ASV is introduced and the subsystems found on board are explained.

2.1   Cooperative transport system

The existing vessels are currently used to transport any kind of cargo, from bulk material, to containers, to people. Being part of a transportation system means the vessels are not the only actors in the transport environment. The components in the transport systems are controlled by agents. It is therefore interesting to analyze the control architecture with extensive communication and cooperation between the involved agents. Based on the three level planning and control architecture for transport over water proposed by Zheng et al. [29], we design a four level multi-layer multi-agent control architecture. Figure 1 shows those levels, from the point of view of a single agent ASV:

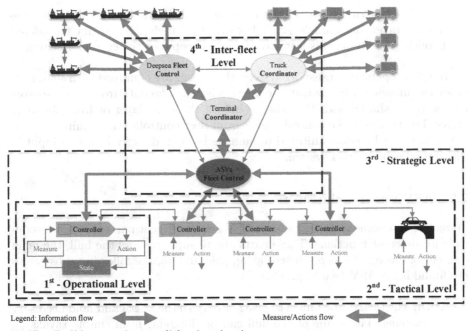

Figure 1. Multilayer environment for autonomous ASVs

1. **Operational level.** This is the single agent level. The autonomy of the vessel is directly related to the dynamics of the vessel. Additionally, it can exchange information, measurements and actions with the agents found in the same layer or in the layers above. There must be an enhanced communications capability.

2. **Tactical level.** This level comprehends a single layer, considering all the agents active in a direct connection. For example, as in Figure 1, information is exchanged between ASVs and infrastructures (locks, bridges, sluices, etc.). The decision control level of the single ASVs can receive important data about future disturbances or incoming conditions, adopting different control strategies based on this information.

3. **Strategic level.** The ASVs fleet control strategy in the second layer is connected to all the ASVs and infrastructures found in the first layer. The entire fleet must be considered and extensive planning must be achieved analyzing the multiple actions of every agent.

4. **Inter-fleet level.** The last level in Figure 1 connects the different coordinators found in the shipping environment. The goal of this level is to actively exchange information, cooperating in order to achieve the optimum controls of every agent involved in the shipping of goods. The first layers are not

considered anymore, so the data exchanged will not directly influence the actions taken on a single ASV. Because the single ASV is not considered explicitly anymore, this last layer is out of scope for the current research.

In this cooperative transport system, the vessels are equipped with sensors in order to autonomously navigate or take decisions. The data from those sensors can easily be shared with the other agents in the same layer or from the layer above. Furthermore, the control inputs from fleet controller or terminal coordinator must not be communicated to humans but can directly be set as input in the autonomous control system.

2.2 ASV vessel architecture

To realize autonomous navigation, an ASV needs different parts that are responsible for different functions. These parts are all supported by the hull, the main element of the vessel. As discussed by [5], [29], and [6], the following subsystems are found in an ASV (see Figure 2):

- **Hull.** The task of the hull is to give stability to the vessel and hold necessary subsystems. The shape of the hull can be different; from simple kayaks [8] to huge cargo vessels [15, 26], moving through many catamarans [7, 10, 4, 28, 11], sailing boats [21, 24, 14, 9, 20] and an unusual "flying saucer" [12].
- **Engine system.** Main component of the vessel, gives the ability to move. Combined with the propeller and the rudder gives direction. The automation

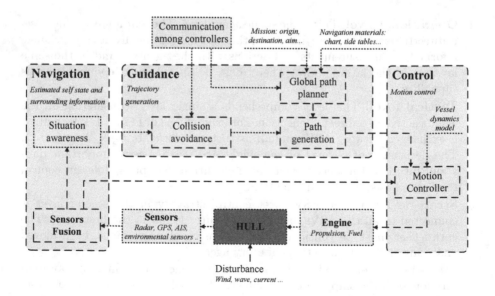

Figure 2. Subsystems in an ASV [6]

of this component is related to navigation, control and guidance system. Further engine monitoring systems can be implemented.

- **Communications system.** The connection between ship and shore or other ships. Key point in the automation of the vessel, gives the ability to remotely control the current situation and act on future states of the vessel. Autonomous exchange of data can be implemented.
- **Sensors.** Sensors are important to retrieve data from environment and the vessel itself. This inputs are elaborated and transformed in following controls of the actuators. Standard sensor found on board of many vessels are the GPS, together with the Inertia Measurement Unit (IMU). Further experiments have been performed using stereo vision cameras, laser vision, LiDARS and Automatic Identification Systems (AIS).
- **Navigation, Guidance and Control system.** The Navigation, Guidance and Control system is mainly software based. The task of the system is to obtain data from the sensors, calculate the desired output that comply with the optimal solution of the algorithm, and send the outputs to the actuators or to another module.

3   Existing autonomy level categorizations

In the previous section, the different components of an ASV have been presented. In this section, the systems and sub-systems will be related to the autonomy levels. The existing categorization of ASVs, introduced by Lloyd's Register [13], is discussed. The solution adopted by autonomous vehicles [1] is then introduced, building on longer development. Finally, the influence of the the interaction between human and machine is discussed, as described by Sheridan [23, 16].

3.1   Lloyd's Register autonomous ship guidance document

According to Lloyd's Register [13], an Autonomy level can be assigned to cyber-enabled ships. Three main tasks have been identified in the levels description: decisions making, actions taking, exceptions handling. The categorization is focused on the cyber safety of the vessel, where the hacking of the communication system is the worst risk. The summary of autonomy levels is given in Table 1.

3.2   SAE International automated driving levels

The SAE Level for autonomous vehicles have been redacted by the Society of Automotive Engineering to define clear boundaries for autonomous drive. The levels have been issued for vehicles on wheels, but the solution can easily be compared with the marine environment. The 6 autonomy levels are characterized by four tasks, each task is performed either by human or by system or by a collaboration of both. The summary is found in Table 2.

	Decision	Actions	Exceptions
AL 0	I. Manual	I. Manual	I. Manual
AL 1	II. Human in the loop (On-board data)	I. Manual	I. Manual
AL 2	III. Human in the loop (On- and off-board data)	I. Manual	I. Manual
AL 3	IV. Human supervision (Ship level)	IV. Human supervision (Ship level)	IV. Human supervision (Ship level)
AL 4	V. Human supervision (Broad level)	V. Human supervision (Broad level)	V. Human supervision (Broad level)
AL 5	VI. Rarely supervised	VI. Rarely supervised	VI. Rarely supervised
AL 6	VII. Unsupervised	VII. Unsupervised	VII. Unsupervised

Table 1. Autonomy Level illustrated as in Lloyd's Register document [13]

	Execution of Steering and Acceleration/ Deceleration	Monitoring of Driving Environment	Fallback Performance of Dynamic Driving Task	System Capability (Driving Modes)
SAE 0	I. Human Driver	I. Human Driver	I. Human Driver	n/a
SAE 1	II. Human driver and system	I. Human Driver	I. Human Driver	Some driving modes
SAE 2	III. System	I. Human driver	I. Human driver	Some driving modes
SAE 3	III. System	III. System	I. Human driver	Some driving modes
SAE 4	III. System	III. System	III. System	Some driving modes
SAE 5	III. System	III. System	III. System	All driving modes

Table 2. SAE Level for autonomous vehicles [1]

HIGH X. The computer decides everything, acts autonomously, ignoring the human.

IX. Informs the human only if it, the computer, decides to.

VIII. Informs the human only if asked.

VII. Executes automatically, then necessarily informs the human.

VI. Allows the human a restricted time to veto before automatic execution.

V. Execute a suggestion if the human approve.

IV. Suggests one alternative.

III. Narrows the selection down to a few.

II. The computer offers a complete set of decision/action alternatives.

LOW I. The computer offers no assistance: human must take all decisions and actions.

Table 3. Different levels of autonomy as suggested by [23] and [16]

3.3   Sheridan types and levels of human interaction with automation

Sheridan and Parasuraman [23, 16] have defined a set of 10 levels of interaction between human and autonomous system, from the computer decides everything to the computer offers no assistance (see Table 3). The levels are based on the classic four control concepts:

- **Information acquisition:** sensing and acquiring input data through the continuous monitoring of the environment around, or through a communication channel.
- **Information analysis:** elaborating received data, trying to create predictive algorithms or integrating different input variables together.
- **Decision selection:** evaluating different proposals, selecting decision and action.
- **Action implementation:** receiving the inputs from the decision made and has the goal to execute the actions.

3.4   Comparison of existing autonomy level categorizations

In the categorizations proposed by Lloyd's Register, SAE International and Sheridan, a system is subdivide in smaller functions or subsystems. Each of these subsystems is analyzed and labeled with a specific autonomy level. SAE International and Lloyd's Register propose an overall classification, based on the smaller subsystems. However, a overall classification can not give an explicit insight into subsystems. For example, Lloyd's register considers the possibility that a vessel has an autonomous decision making system and all the actions are human driven (AL 1 and AL 2). On the opposite side, SAE 1 and SAE 2 leave the decision task mainly to the human driver while taking care of the path following function as most important autonomy parameter. With these categorizations, the existing autonomous vessels usually fall in the SAE 1 or SAE 2 category, having autonomous actions implemented. The current cargo ships are within the AL 1 or AL 2 from Lloyd's Register, since decision making support can already be found on board.

Furthermore, as mentioned in Section 2.2, vessels are not the only actors in the transport environment. The communication and cooperation between agents are important functions that should be realized. The previous classifications are all lacking the explicit concept of cooperation between different agents. Lloyd's Register categorization is the only proposal that considers communications and data coming from the vessel only, or shared by a remote location. This seems like an hint to a collaboration with the central coordinator, but no explicit reference is made. If the communication and cooperation is implemented in the current ASV domain, then information could flow between ships, shore and infrastructures. Connecting those three data sources can lead to the creation of smart collaborating multi-agent networks, where information is exchanged to achieve an overall, more efficient, environment, instead of only optimizing the individual agent [17].

Additionally, the categorization proposed by [23] and [16] is quite flexible, but not directly useful for an overall ASV division.

A key component has been found to contrast between Lloyd's Register solution and SAE International division. The main topic of the former is the decision making task, which must be addressed before being able to rely on an autonomous action subsystem. On the other side, the latter, proposes an autonomy level that only considers the driving part (equivalent to the actions taking) of the autonomous vehicle. Furthermore, [23] and [16] seems to support the choice used in Lloyd's Register document [13]. The scale defined in the two research is considering first the achievement in autonomy at a decision making level, and then further considers the possibility to expand the autonomy by automatically actuating the physical components.

4   Definition and classification of autonomy levels for ASVs

Comparing the previous categorizations proposed by Lloyd's Register, SAE International and Sheridan, when defining the autonomy level for ASVs, we can look in both the subsystems and overall functions. In this section, we propose a new autonomy level categorization that considers both subsystems and overall systems.

Our new categorization system considers four main subsystems: decision making, actions taking, exceptions handling and cooperation. The levels assessed in each subsystem are going from a lack of interaction between human and computer to a full control of the computer that ignores the human actions. The levels of first three subsystems scale from 1 to 10. This scale is taken from [23]. For the newly introduced concept of cooperation in the autonomy scale, the levels are made by giving an increasing level of cooperation based on the number of agents the system is able to communicate with. For example, a vessel that is able to share data (not cooperate) with other agents will have a cooperation level of 2. A vessel that is better interfaced and can cooperate with vessels and a remote coordinator will have a cooperation level of 4. The level of cooperation ranges from 1 to 5. Detailed descriptions are presented in Tables 4 and 5.

The decision making subsystem is the first and easiest to automate; routing and planning tasks can be autonomously optimized, together with the maintenance schedule. *The actions taking subsystem* is more complex than the decision making subsystem, since physically actuated mechanical components are involved in the control loop. *The exceptions handling system* is a key part to obtain an overall high autonomy level, different solutions are being studied to detect and avoid obstacles. Finally, *the cooperation subsystem* considers the cooperation between the vessel and the surrounding environment. Information is exchanged with other vessels, infrastructures or remote control locations.

Once autonomy levels of the subsystems have been determined, the next move is to create a general autonomy level classification for the overall system

Decision making subsystem

The decision making subsystem is in charge of defining the overall trip (from origin to destination), considering long term data, electronic nautical charts, weather forecast and, if available, the shared information incoming from cooperative vessels.

1. The computer offers no assistance: human must take all decisions.
2. The computer offers a complete set of decision alternatives.
3. The computer narrows the selection down to a few.
4. The computer suggests one alternative.
5. The computer executes that suggestion if the human approve.
6. The computer allows the human a restricted time to veto before automatic execution.
7. The computer executes automatically, then necessarily informs the human.
8. The computer informs the human only if asked.
9. The computer informs the human only if it, the computer, decides to.
10. The computer decides everything, ignoring the human.

Actions taking subsystem

The actions taking subsystem is in charge to interpret higher level inputs and transform those data in actions, directly related to the motion of the vessel.

1. The computer offers no assistance: human must take all actions.
2. The computer offers a complete set of action alternatives.
3. The computer narrows the selection down to a few.
4. The computer suggests one alternative.
5. The computer executes either steering or acceleration suggestion if the human approve.
6. The computer executes steering and acceleration suggestion if the human approve.
7. The computer allows the human a restricted time to veto before automatic execution.
8. The computer executes automatically, then necessarily informs the human.
9. The computer informs the human only if it, the computer, decides to.
10. The computer acts autonomously, ignoring the human.

Table 4. Scale used to assess the autonomy level in different subsystems – Part 1

Exceptions handling subsystem

The exception handling subsystem is in charge of always monitoring the surrounding of the vessel, detect unexpected obstacles and, if implemented, compute a new local path to avoid the impediment.

1. The computer offers no assistance: human must detect, decide and act.
2. The computer offers a reduced set of possible obstacles.
3. The computer offers a complete set of possible obstacles.
4. The computer detect possible obstacles and suggests a local rerouting.
5. The computer detect possible obstacles and executes a local rerouting if the human approve.
6. The computer allows the human a restricted time to veto before automatic execution.
7. The computer executes automatically, then necessarily informs the human.
8. The computer informs the human only if asked.
9. The computer informs the human only if it, the computer, decides to.
10. The computer acts everything, ignoring the human.

Cooperative subsystem

The cooperative system is in charge of exchanging information between the vessel and other agents, acting in the same domain. The data exchanged is then passed and integrated in the decision making, actions taking and exceptions handling subsystems. The communication are always exchanged in an autonomous way. For cooperation is intended the process of working together toward the same goal.

1. The vessel does not exchange any information and does not cooperate with any agent.
2. The vessel exchange information with one or more agents but does not actively cooperate.
3. The vessel exchange information with one or more agents but does only cooperate with one type of agent.
4. The vessel exchange information with one or more agents and does cooperate with two types of agents.
5. The vessel exchange information with one or more agents and does cooperate with three types of agents or more.

Table 5. Scale used to assess the autonomy level in different subsystems – Part 2

of the ASVs. The overall autonomy level is determined by the autonomy levels of the subsystems.

Many different subsystem autonomy combinations are found in prototypes and even more could be defined by combining existing technology and working models. To create a general ASV scale that is able to cover all the possible combinations, we adopt sub-levels to consider different variations. However, some ASVs may have high level autonomy on the decision making system, but a low level on the action taking. Consequently, a priority is given to a certain subsystem. By analyzing the existing ASV prototypes, we find that not all ASVs consider all the four subsystems. For example, the cooperation subsystems have not been considered in most prototypes. Among the four subsystems, decision making or actions taking subsystems can be found in almost all the existing. Therefore, the autonomy level of decision making or actions taking are considered as the candidates of the priority. As seen in [23] and [13], the decision making subsystem can easily be integrated in the existing and future vessels. Hence, the automation of decision making system is considered less important than the one of the action subsystem. For the same reason, the capability of autonomous exception handling and cooperation are also regarded as the sign of higher autonomy.

Besides, many projects and prototypes are considering a variable level of autonomy, depending on the situation or task being executed by the vessel. This concept is called "Dynamic autonomy" in [19]. In the our categorization, the maximum level of autonomy reachable on the vessel will be classified.

In addition, the combination of the autonomy level of the four subsystems is not randomly. The four subsystems are closely linked. Observed from existing ASV prototypes, when one of the subsystems has a high autonomy level, the autonomy level of the other subsystems will not be very low. For example, when the autonomy level of decision making and action taking is 5, the lowest level of cooperation is 1; when the autonomy level of decision making and action taking increase to 6, the lowest level of cooperation is 2. Therefore, when design the sub-levels, we take the possible combinations of subsystems in existing ASV projects.

Table 6 defines the main levels. The name of the levels describes their function. In each levels, there are several sub-levels. The relation between main levels and sub-level of the overall system and autonomy scales of the subsystems are explained in Table 7. With these two tables, the overall autonomy level of an ASV and the autonomy level of its subsystems can be determined. Here, we use an ASV developed by TU Delft, Delfia-1 [25], as an example. It is able to make decisions, take acts and handle exceptions autonomously, and inform human when it is requested. It has the capability to cooperate with other ASVs and infrastructures. Correspondingly, the Delfia-1 reaches decision making level 8, action taking level 8, exception handling level 8, and cooperation level 5. Therefore, it has an overall autonomy level 9, sub-level 2.

Autonomy Level	Name
0.	*Human is alone*
1.	*Human is helped by systems*
2.	*Human is helped by the systems and other agents*
3.	*Autonomous path following vessel*
4.	*Autonomous trajectory tracking vessel*
5.	*Human in the loop*
6.	*Human supervise the decisions making system*
7.	*Human supervise the actions making system*
8.	*Human supervise the exceptions handling system*
9.	*Human supervise actions, decision and exceptions*
10.	*Fully autonomous*

Table 6. Main autonomy level classes for ASVs

5 Conclusion and further research

ASVs have seen an increasing development in recent years. The rising number of projects leads to an increasingly higher autonomy level. To have a better understanding of autonomy of ASVs, the existing autonomy level categorizations related to the ASV domain have been presented and analyzed. The solutions proposed by Lloyd's Register [13] and by SAE International (related to the Autonomous Surface Vehicles) [2] assess the autonomy level of a specific sub-system of the ASV only. Even more, the solution proposed by Sheridan [23], which describe 10 levels of autonomy based on the amount of interactions required to the human operator, can be a viable alternative to describe the autonomy. However, an overall level to categorize the future vessels is lacking. Additionally, none of existing classifications considers the communication and cooperation between different agents in the transport system.

In this paper, a detailed definition and categorization of autonomy levels for ASVs are proposed based on the characteristics of ASVs and existing classification of autonomy. This new scale uses three subsystems proposed by Lloyd's Register and SAE International: Decision Making, Actions Taking and Exceptions Handling; a fourth newly added system takes care of the Cooperative Communication. This last aspect of the autonomy of a vessel has been actively researched through projects but only a few prototypes have implemented the solution. The integration of the cooperative sub-system in the new autonomy categorization wants to be an hint for the future development. The Decision, Actions and Exceptions subsystems are assessed by means of a scale from 1 to 10, where 1 is completely human operated and 10 is fully autonomous. The last subsystem, Cooperative, is evaluated from 1 to 5 based on the number of agents it is able to communicate with. After evaluating the subsystems, an overall autonomy level of the entire system can be determined. the overall autonomy level ranged from 0-10. In each autonomy level, sub-levels are designed consider different combinations of the four subsystems. In [22], we provide an extensive overview of existing ASV prototypes according to this innovative categorization. The tendency and

Autonomy Level	Sub level	Decision	Action	Exception	Co-operation	Autonomy Level	Sub level	Decision	Action	Exception	Co-operation
0	1	1	1	1	1	6	1	7-8	5	1	1
1	1	1	1	1	2	6	2	7-8	5	2	2
1	2	2-4	1	1	1	6	3	7-8	5	2	3-5
1	3	1	2-4	1	1	6	4	7-8	5	3	2
1	4	1	1	2	1	6	5	7-8	5	3	3-5
2	1	2-4	1	1	3-5	6	6	7-8	5	4	2
2	2	1	2-4	1	3-5	6	7	7-8	5	4	3-5
2	3	1	1	2	3-5	6	8	7-8	5	5-6	2
2	4	1	1	1	3-5	6	9	7-8	5	5-6	3-5
3	1	1	5	1	1	6	10	7-8	6	1	1
3	2	1	5	1	2	6	11	7-8	6	2	2
3	3	2-4	5	1	1	6	12	7-8	6	2	3-5
3	4	2-4	5	1	2	6	13	7-8	6	3	2
3	5	2-4	5	1	3-5	6	14	7-8	6	3	3-5
3	6	2-4	5	2	2	6	15	7-8	6	4	2
3	7	2-4	5	2	3-5	6	16	7-8	6	4	3-5
4	1	1	6	1	1-2	6	17	7-8	6	5-6	2
4	2	1	6	1	3-5	6	18	7-8	6	5-6	3-5
4	3	2-4	6	1	1	7	1	5-6	7-8	1	1
4	4	2-4	6	1	2	7	2	5-6	7-8	1	2
4	5	2-4	6	1	3-5	7	3	5-6	7-8	1	3-5
4	6	2-4	6	2	2	7	4	5-6	7-8	2	2
4	7	2-4	6	2	3-5	7	5	5-6	7-8	2	3-5
5	1	5-6	5	1	1	7	6	5-6	7-8	3	2
5	2	5-6	5	2	2	7	7	5-6	7-8	3	3-5
5	3	5-6	5	2	3-5	7	8	5-6	7-8	4	2
5	4	5-6	5	3	2	7	9	5-6	7-8	4	3-5
5	5	5-6	5	3	3-5	7	10	5-6	7-8	5-6	2
5	6	5-6	5	4	2	7	11	5-6	7-8	5-6	3-5
5	7	5-6	5	4	3-5	8	1	5-6	5	7-8	2
5	8	5-6	5	5-6	2	8	2	5-6	5	7-8	3-5
5	9	5-6	5	5-6	3-5	8	3	5-6	6	7-8	2
5	10	5-6	6	1	1	8	4	5-6	6	7-8	3-5
5	11	5-6	6	2	2	9	1	7-8	7-8	7-8	2
5	12	5-6	6	2	3-5	9	2	7-8	7-8	7-8	3-5
5	13	5-6	6	3	2	10	1	9-10	9-10	9-10	2
5	14	5-6	6	3	3-5	10	2	9-10	9-10	9-10	3-5
5	15	5-6	6	4	2						
5	16	5-6	6	4	3-5						
5	17	5-6	6	5-6	2						
5	18	5-6	6	5-6	3-5						

Table 7. Main autonomy level classes and corresponding sub-level

possible future developments of ASVs are analyzed according to the divisions obtained.

References

1. Levels of driving automation are defined in new SAE International standard J3016 (2016), https://goo.gl/gCIFCm
2. Taxonomy and Definitions for Terms Related to Driving Automation Systems for On-Road Motor Vehicles (2016), https://goo.gl/AnXwcj
3. Bertram, V.: Towards Unmanned Ships. Presentation (2013), https://goo.gl/YrOgFb
4. Caccia, M., Bono, R., Bruzzone, G., Bruzzone, G., Spirandelli, E., Veruggio, G., Stortini, A.M.: Design and Exploitation of an Autonomous Surface Vessel for the Study of Sea-Air Interactions. In: Proceedings of the 2005 IEEE International Conference on Robotics and Automation. pp. 3582–3587. Shatin, N.T., China (2005)
5. Campbell, S., Naeem, W., Irwin, G.W.: A Review on Improving the Autonomy of Unmanned Surface Vehicles Through Intelligent Collision Avoidance Manoeuvres. Annual Reviews in Control 36(2), 267–283 (2012)
6. Chen, L., Negenborn, R.R., Lodewijks, G.: Path planning for autonomous inland vessels using A*BG, pp. 65–79. Springer International Publishing, Cham (2016)
7. Codiga, D.L.: A Marine Autonomous Surface Craft for Long-Duration, Spatially Explicit, Multidisciplinary Water Column Sampling in Coastal and Estuarine Systems. Journal of Atmospheric and Oceanic Technology 32(3), 627–641 (2014)
8. Curcio, J., Leonard, J., Patrikalakis, A.: SCOUT - A Low Cost Autonomous Surface Platform for Research in Cooperative Autonomy. In: Proceedings of OCEANS 2005 MTS/IEEE. vol. 1, pp. 725–729. Washington, D.C., USA (2005)
9. Giger, L., Wismer, S., Boehl, S., Busser, G., Erckens, H., Weber, J., Moser, P., Schwizer, P., Pradalier, C., Yves, R.S.: Design and Construction of the Autonomous Sailing Vessel AVALON. In: Proceedings of The World Robotic Sailing Championship and International Robotic Sailing Conference. pp. 17–22. Matosinhos, Portugal (2009)
10. Hitz, G., Pomerleau, F., Garneau, M.E., Pradalier, C., Posch, T., Pernthaler, J., Siegwart, R.Y.: Autonomous Inland Water Monitoring: Design and Application of a Surface Vessel 19(1), 62–72 (2012)
11. Holler, J., Striz, A., Bretney, K., Kavett, K., Bingham, B.: Design, Construction, and Field Testing of an Autonomous Surface Craft for Engineering and Science Education. In: Proceedings of OCEANS 2007. pp. 1–6. Aberdeen, Scotland, United Kingdom (2007)
12. Idland, T.K.: Marine Cybernetics Vessel CS Saucer: Design, Construction and Control. Master's thesis, NTNU (2015)
13. Lloyds Register: ShipRight Procedure - Autonomous Ships (2016), https://goo.gl/ROyXyD
14. Miller, P., Beal, B., Capron, C., Gawboy, R., Mallory, P., Ness, C., Petrosik, R., Pryne, C., Murphy, T., Spears, H.: Increasing Performance and Added Capabilities of USNA Sail-Powered Autonomous Surface Vessels (ASV). Tech. rep., DTIC Document (2010)
15. MUNIN: Research in Maritime Autonomous Systems Project Results and Technology Potentials. Tech. rep., Maritime Unmanned Navigation through Intelligence in Networks (2016)

16. Parasuraman, R., Sheridan, T.B., Wickens, C.D.: A Model for Types and Levels of Human Interaction with Automation. IEEE Transactions on Systems, Man, and Cybernetics - Part A: Systems and Humans 30(3), 286–297 (2000)
17. Polvara, R., Sharma, S., Sutton, R., Wan, J., Manning, A.: Toward a Multi-agent System for Marine Observation. In: Advances in Cooperative Robotics: Proceedings of the 19th International Conference on Clawar 2016. p. 225. World Scientific, London, UK (2016)
18. Rodriguez-Ortiz, C.D.: Automated Bathymetry Mapping Using an Autonomous Surface Craft. Master's thesis, Massachusetts Institute of Technology (1996)
19. Rolls-Royce: Remote and Autonomous Ships: The next steps. White paper (2016), https://goo.gl/GJTMaZ
20. Santos, D., Silva Junior, A.G., Negreiros, A., Vilas Boas, J., Alvarez, J., Araujo, A., Aroca, R.V., Gon?alves, L.M.G.: Design and Implementation of a Control System for a Sailboat Robot. Robotics 5(1), 1–5 (2016)
21. Sauze, C., Neal, M., others: An autonomous sailing robot for ocean observation. In: Proceedings of Towards Autonomous Robotic Systems 2006 (TAROS-06). vol. 2006, pp. 190–197. Guildford, United Kingdom (2006)
22. Schiaretti, M., Chen, L., Negenborn, R.R.: Survey on autonomous surface vessels: Part II - categorization of 60 prototypes and future applications. In: Proceedings of 8th International Conference on Computational Logistics (ICCL2017), October 18-20, Southampton, UK (2017)
23. Sheridan, T.B., Verplank, W.L.: Human and computer control of undersea teleoperators. Tech. rep., DTIC Document (1978)
24. Sliwka, J., Reilhac, P., Leloup, R., Crepier, P., Roncin, K., Aizier, B., Jaulin, L.: Autonomous robotic boat of ENSIETA. In: Proceedings of 2nd International Robotic Sailing Conference. pp. 1–7. Matosinhos, Portugal (2009)
25. TU Delft: Tu Delfia-1 in action (2017), https://www.youtube.com/watch?v=yqAfWIkEGUI\&feature=youtu.be
26. Tvete, H.A.: ReVolt : The Unmanned, Zero Emission, Short Sea Ship of the Future. Dnv Gl Strategic Research & Innovation (2015)
27. Tvete, H.A., Engelhardtsen, Ø.: DNV GL's research within Autonomous Systems. Presentation (2014), https://goo.gl/Uz44zJ
28. Wang, J., Gu, W., Zhu, J.: Design of an Autonomous Surface Vehicle Used for Marine Environment Monitoring. In: Proceedings of International Conference on Advanced Computer Control, 2009. pp. 405–409. Singapore, Singapore (2009)
29. Zheng, H., Negenborn, R.R., Lodewijks, G.: Model Predictive Control of a Waterborne AGV at the Operational Level. In: Proceedings of the International Maritime and Port Technology and Development Conference (MTEC 2014). pp. 99–108. Trondheim, Norway (2014)

Survey on Autonomous Surface Vessels:
Part II - Categorization of 60 Prototypes and Future Applications

Matteo Schiaretti, Linying Chen, and Rudy R. Negenborn

Department of Maritime and Transport Technology, Delft University of Technology,
Delft, The Netherlands
L.Chen-2@tudelft.nl, R.R.Negenborn@tudelft.nl

Abstract. Autonomous Surface Vessels (ASVs) have been developed for more than 20 years. Many ASV projects have been successfully realized, and as many are still under development. In literature there is a lack of research on the different applications and suitable environments for the deployment of ASV.
Recently, a detailed definition and categorization of autonomy levels for ASVs has been proposed based on the characteristics of ASVs and existing classifications of autonomy. With this innovative autonomy level classification, this paper presents an extensive overview of existing ASV prototypes. The tendency and possible future developments of ASVs are analyzed according to the divisions obtained.

Keywords: Autonomous Surface Vessels; Autonomy level; ASV projects; ASV prototypes

1 Introduction

Autonomous Surface Vessels (ASVs) have been involved in numerous projects since the 1990s. The goal is typically to achieve fully autonomous navigation. The concept of autonomous surface vessel is well known at an academic level, and is now gaining attention also in full scale vessel development for the container and bulk sectors [8, 51, 67, 68].

In literature, a lack of research about current development of ASVs has been observed. Therefore, in this paper, we present an overview of existing projects to gain knowledge about the emerging concepts and techniques that have been applied in ASV research. The tendency and possible future developments of ASVs are analyzed according to the overview.

The remainder of this paper is organized as follows. An overview of existing ASVs found in literature is presented in Section 2. Detail informations about the ASV prototypes are introduced in Section 3 according to their autonomy levels. The tendency and unknown future developments of ASVs are analyzed according to the divisions in Section 4. Conclusions are discussed in Section 5.

© Springer International Publishing AG 2017
T. Bektaş et al. (Eds.), ICCL 2017, LNCS 10572, pp. 234–252, 2017.
https://doi.org/10.1007/978-3-319-68496-3_16

2   Overview of existing ASV projects

To gain insight into the ASVs prototypes, the existing projects are analyzed in this section. Different components of the ASVs are compared to obtain a full picture of the current technologies used in ASV research.

Existing ASV prototypes (includes those under development) that have been mentioned in literature are presented in Table 1, Table 2 and Table 3. We review the ASV prototypes based on the components as discussed in [61]. An ASV is divided in four control subsystems: engine system, communication system, sensors and navigation, guidance and control (NGC) system. The common element that supports all the those components is the hull. The dimensions, scope and the deployment year of the ASVs are also presented in the tables.

Most existing ASVs are scaled models. Mainly two types of hull are used, i.e., single hull and double hull (as catamaran). The main solution in the engine compartment is the adoption of electric motors together with batteries. If the vessel should endure in the operations, solar panels or methanol fuel cells are implied. Another common option, which requires higher level of navigation control, is using sails as a propulsion system (Project 11, 17, 18, 19, etc.). Several projects also considered heavy fuel treatment systems, such as Project 51.

Focusing on the NGC system, almost all the prototypes rely on a path following control, coupled with compass, IMU and GPS. The most advanced prototypes are able to detect obstacles, with stereo cameras, LiDAR or ARPA, and recompute the route in order to avoid them. Some vessels have the function of dynamic positioning, such as as Project 3, 20, 21, etc.

The communication system in the prototypes is arranged for the information exchange between vessel and controllers, or to take remote control of the vessels or with other agents. Wi-Fi and Radio are two main methods.

Detailed descriptions regarding the projects can be found in Section 3, structured according to the autonomy level they achieved.

3   Autonomy levels of ASV prototypes

3.1   Autonomy level categorization for ASVs

In [61], we proposed an innovative autonomy levels categorization based on the characteristics of ASVs and existing classification of autonomy. As shown in Table 4, the categorization gives an overall autonomy level of a vessel by analyzing the automated sub-systems: Decision, Actions, Exceptions, and Cooperation. The Decision, Actions and Exceptions subsystems are assessed by means of a scale from 1 to 10, where 1 is completely human operated and 10 is fully autonomous. The last subsystem, Cooperative, is evaluated from 1 to 5 based on the number of agents it is able to communicate with. After evaluating the subsystems, an overall autonomy level of the entire system can be determined. the overall autonomy level ranged from 0-10. In each autonomy level, sub-levels are designed consider different combinations of the four subsystems. Subsequently, these existing prototypes are classified based on the autonomy level.

Table 1. Overview of ASV projects – Part 1

No.	Prototype Name	Institution	Hull Si	Hull Ca	Engine EM	Engine Sa	Engine CE	Fuel Ba	Fuel FF	Fuel So	Steering Dp	Steering Pr	Steering Ru	NGC PF	NGC OA	NGC DP	Comm.	Sensors	Dim. L (m)	Dim. W (m)	Dim. H (m)	Scope Geo.	Scope App.	Year	Ref.
1	Proteus	Marine Advanced Research, Inc.		•	2			†			▲			Human					30.48	15.24	-	Off-shore	Military	2007	[1]
2	ASV MUN	MUN (Uni)		•	2			†			▲						Radio	GPS, AHRS	1.5	1	0.5	On-shore	Scientific	2013	[43]
3	ASV SMU	SMU (Uni)		•	2			†				▲		✓		✓	Wi-Fi	GPS	2.7	1.48	0.36	On-shore	Scientific	2008	[72]
4	Seabax	TU Delft (Uni)	•		4			†				▲		QR-codes			Wi-Fi	GPS, IMU, Camera, accelerometer, gyroscope, rpm sensors	1.4	0.28	0.38	Off-shore, Waterways[1]	Commercial	2015	[22, 53]
5	Rolls Royce ASV	Rolls Royce	•																60	-	-	On-shore	Commercial	2020	[42, 58]
6	ASV Prototype	UNIVPM (Uni)			1		1	†	G			▲		Set of commands			Wi-Fi	GPS, IMU, Camera	3.05	1.4	-	On-shore	Scientific	2015	[19]
7	Circe	Olin College (Uni)		•	2			†						✓				GPS, Compass	1.98	1.37	-	Inland[2]	Recreational	2007	[38]
8	ALANIS	CNR-ISSIA	•				1		G			▲		✓			Radio	GPS, Compass, Clinometer	4.5	2.2	-	On-shore	Scientific	2009	[9, 11]
9	ERON	Frederick (Uni)	•		4			†			▲			✓				GPS, Compass, Accelerometer	2.86	0.7	-	On-shore	Scientific	2016	[24, 25]
10	CaRoLIME	HTWG (Uni)		•	2			†			▲							GPS, Compass, IMU	2.5	1.2	-	Inland	Scientific	2012	[73]
11	ENSIETA	ENSIETA (Uni)	•					†						Heading following			Radio	GPS, Wind, Compass	1.2	-	-	On-shore	Recreational	2009	[2, 63]
12	DELFIM	ISR-Lisboa		•	2			†				▲		✓			Radio	GPS, Acoustic transducer, Sonar	3.5	2	-	On-shore	Scientific	2006	[3]
13	MARV	SCU (Uni)		•	2			†				▲		✓			Wi-Fi	GPS, Sonar	1.37	2	0.25	Inland	Scientific	2016	[5]
14	WAM-V	UC Berkeley (Uni)		•	2			†				▲		✓			Radio, Cellular	GPS, IMU, Camera, Hydrophone	4.3	2.1	1.23	Off-shore	Military	2012	[54, 15]
15	SCOAP	URI (Uni)		•	2			†	D		▲			✓			Radio, Satellite	GPS, AIS, ADCP, winched CTD, Weather station	11	5	-	On-shore	Scientific	2014	[18]
16	Zarco	U.Porto (Uni)		•	2			†			▲			✓			Wi-Fi	2x DGPS, Compass, Sensor	1.5	-	-	Waterways	Scientific	2007	[20]
17	A-TIRMA G2	ULPGC (Uni)	•			2							▲						2	0.48	-	Off-shore	Recreational	2015	[26]
18	A-TIRMA G1	ULPGC (Uni)	•			2		†					▲	✓			Radio	GPS, Compass, Wind, Inclinometers	1	0.245	1.6	On-shore	Recreational	2014	[10]
19	SailBuoy	MET Norway	•			1		†					▲	✓			Satellite	GPS, Temperature, Oxygen Sensor	2	-	-	Off-shore	Scientific	2012	[32]
20	OASIS	Emergent Space Technologies, Inc.	•		1			†					▲	✓		✓	Radio, Satellite	GPS, Compass, Inclinometers, IMU, Weather	5.48	1.5	1.82	Off-shore	Scientific	2005	[35]

Hull: Si: Single, Ca: Catamaran

Fuel: Ba: Battery, FF: Fossil Fuel, So: Solar panel, D: Diesel, G: Gasoline

NGC: PF: Path following, OA: Obstacle Avoidance, DP: Dynamic Positioning

Institution: abbreviation with (Uni) are universities

Engine: EM: Electric Motor, Sa: Sail, CE: Combustion engine

Steering: Dp: Differential propeller, Pr: Propeller Rotation, Ru: Rudder

Scope: Geo.: Geographic, App.: Application

[1] 'Waterways' denotes inland waterways (rivers and canals).

[2] 'Inland' denotes lakes.

Table 2. Overview of ASV projects – Part 2

No.	Prototype Name	Institution	Hull Si	Ca	Engine EM	Sa	CE	Fuel Ba	FF	So	Steering Dp	Pr	Ru	NGC PF	OA	DP	Comm.	Sensors	Dim. L (m)	W (m)	H (m)	Scope Geo.	App.	Year	Ref.
21	WaveGlider	Liquid Robotics	•	•	1			†		†						✓	Radio, Satellite	GPS, Compass, Hydrophone	3.05	-	-	Off-shore	Scientific	2005	[36]
22	Lizhbeth	ETH Zurich (Uni.)	•		2			†			◄			✓			Wi-Fi	GPS, Compass, Winched probe, Sonar	2.5	1.8	-	Inland	Scientific	2012	[37]
23	Artemis	MIT (Uni.)	•		1			†					◄	✓			Radio	DGPS, Compass, Depth sounder	1.4	0.4	-	Inland	Scientific	1993	[57, 46]
24	ACES	MIT (Uni.)		•			1		G				◄	✓			Radio	DGSP	1.9	1.3	-	Inland	Scientific	1997	[46]
25	Swordfish	ISEP (Uni.)		•	2			†			◄			✓			Radio, Wi-Fi, Cellular	GPS, Compass, IMU, Camera	4.5	2.2	0.5	On-shore	Scientific	2007	[29]
26	ASV	RMUTT (Uni.)	•				1		G				◄	✓			Cellular	GPS, IMU, Sonar	3.5	1.52	0.6	Inland	Scientific	2015	[56]
27	N-Boat	UFRN(Uni.)	•					†				◄		✓			Wi-Fi	GPS, Wind	0.9	-	-	Inland	Scientific	2015	[40, 59]
28	Proto 1	Aberystwyth (Uni.)	•			2		†					◄		Heading following			GPS, Compass, Wind	1.5	-	-	Inland	Scientific	2005	[60]
29	Proto 2	Aberystwyth (Uni.)	•			2		†					◄		Heading following			GPS, Compass, Wind	1.5	-	-	Inland	Scientific	2006	[60]
30	ASV ROBOAT³	INNOC	•			2		†		†			◄				Wi-Fi, Cellular, Satellite	GPS, compass	3.72	-	-	Off-shore	Scientific	2012	[65]
31	WAM-V USV16	FAU (Uni.)	•		2			†				◄		✓			Radio	GPS, IMU, Sonar	4.05	2.44	-	Inland	Scientific	2016	[71]
32	VAIMOS	IFREMER	•			1		†		†			◄	✓			Wi-Fi, Satellite	GPS, Compass, Wind	3.65	-	-	On-shore	Scientific	2013	[6]
33	CRW	CMU (Uni.)		•	1			†				◄		✓			Cellular, Wi-Fi, Bluetooth	Phone (GPS, Compass, Gyroscope, Camera), Water sampler	1.5	-	-	Inland	Scientific	2014	[70]
34	USNA	USNA (Uni.)	•			1		†		†			◄		✓		Wi-Fi	GPS, Compass, Wind, Ultrasonic Range Finder	2	0.3	-	On-shore	Recreational	2010	[50]
35	IMOCA 60		•			2	1	†				◄			✓		Satellite	GPS, AIS, ARPA	18	-	-	Off-shore	Recreational	2000	[62]
36	Tito Neri	TU Delft (Uni.)	•		3			†								✓	Wi-Fi	Webcam, two sensors for azimuth thruster speeds	0.97	0.32	0.12	Off-shore, Waterways	Scientific	1993	[23, 53]
37	SeaWASP	SCU (Uni.)	Submerged Catamaran		2			†				◄		✓			Wi-Fi	GPS, Velocimetry, AHRS, Sonar	1.5	1.5	-	Waterways	Scientific	2008	[7, 45]
38	Charlie USV	CNR-ISSIA		•	2			†		†	◄				Vessel following capabilities		Wi-Fi, Radio	GPS, Compass	2.4	1.7	0.6	On-shore	Scientific	2004	[9, 12, 13, 14]
39	Electric boat	Northrop Grumman Corporation	•		1			†					◄	✓			Radio	GPS, Compass, IMU, 6xCameras	4	-	-	Waterways	Scientific	2004	[64]
40	Rolls Royce ASV 2	Rolls Royce	•					†							✓				60	-	-	Off-shore	Commercial	2030	[42, 58]

³ Prototype 30 has Methanol Fuel Cell as fuel.
⁴ Prototype 41 has Methanol Fuel Cell as fuel.

Table 3. Overview of ASV projects – Part 3

No.	Name	Institution	Si	Ca	EM	Sa	CE	Ba	FF	So	Dp	Pr	Ru	PF	OA	DP	Comm.	Sensors	L (m)	W (m)	H (m)	Geo.	App.	Year	Ref.
41	AVALON[4]	ETH Zurich (Uni.)	•			1		†		†			▲	√			Satellite	GPS, IMU, Wind, AIS	3.95	0.7	0.4	Off-shore	Recreational	2009	[33]
42	MAINAMI	MARITEC	•		2			†	D				▲	Path and AUV following			Wi-Fi, Radio, Inmarsat	GPS, Camera, Compass, ADCP, Acoustic device	6	2.6	3.2	Off-shore	Scientific	2015	[52]
43	iNav-I	WUT (Uni.)	•		1			†				▲		√			Radio	GPS, IMU, RTK, Camera, MMW, compass, Wind	4.0	1.5	0.6	Inland, Waterways	Scientific	2014-⁵	[75]
44	ROAZ	ISEP (Uni.)	•		2			†			▲			√			Wi-Fi	GPS, Compass, IMU, Video Camera	1.5	1	0.52	On-shore	Scientific	2006	[28, 48, 49]
45	ROAZ II	ISEP (Uni.)	•		2			†				▲		Path and target following			Wi-Fi	GPS, IMU, Camera	4.5	2.2	0.5	On-shore	Scientific	2007	[49]
46	SCOUT	MIT (Uni.)	Single Kayak		1			†				▲		√			Wi-Fi, Radio	GPS, Compass	3	-	-	Inland	Scientific	2004	[21]
47	Challenger 2000	SPAWAR					1					▲			√			GPS, ENC, Radar, Stereo vision, Monocular vision	6	2.4	-	On-shore	Military	2006	[41]
48	WUT-1	WUT (Uni.)	•		1			1				▲			√	√	Wi-Fi	GPS, Lidar, Radar, INS, Fathometer, Camera	3.2	0.65	0.5	Inland, Waterways	Scientific	2014-	[17, 44]
49	ReVOLT	DNV GL	•		2			†				▲							60	14.5	12.18	Off-shore	Commercial	2018	[8, 67, 68]
50	CS Saucer	NTNU (Uni.)	Spherical		3			†				▲		√	√		Wi-Fi	Accelerometer, Lidar	0.548	0.548	-	Inland	Scientific	2015	[69, 39]
51	MUNIN	MUNIN Consortium	•					†	D			▲		√	√		Satellite	GPS, Radar, AIS, Weather	-	-	-	Off-shore	Commercial	2016	[51]
52	ASAROME⁶	ISIR	•			2		†		†			▲	√	√		Wi-Fi	GPS, IMU, 360° Camera, Sonar, Hydrophones, WindVane, Water Speed	3.5	-	-	Inland	Scientific	2015	[55]
53	PROPAGATOR 2	UF (Uni.)		•		2		†				▲		√	√		Radio, Wi-Fi	GPS, Camera, Lidar	1.8	-	-	Inland	Recreational	2015	[30, 31]
54	PROPAGATOR 1	UF (Uni.)		•	3			†			▲			√	√		Wi-Fi	GPS, IMU, Camera, Lidar, Infrared Thermometer	1.8	0.76	0.7	Inland	Recreational	2013	[34]
55	Rolls Royce ASV 3	Rolls Royce	•															Camera, 6 infrared sensors, 8 ultra-sonic sensors	60	-	-	Off-shore	Commercial	2035	[42, 58]
56	Delfia-1	TU Delft (Uni.)		•		2		†				▲		√	√		Radio, Wi-Fi	Camera, 6 infrared sensors, 8 ultra-sonic sensors	0.375	0.184	0.11	Waterways, port	Commercial	2015-	[53, 66]
57	Delfia-1 Star	TU Delft (Uni.)		•		2		†				▲		√	√	√	Radio, Wi-Fi	Camera, 6 infrared sensors, 8 ultra-sonic sensors	0.375	0.184	0.11	Waterways, port	Commercial	2016-	[53]
58	ROBOAT AMS	MIT (Uni.)		•															3	2.5	-	Waterways	Civil	2017-	[4]
59	Barflavento	CINAV	•		2								▲	√			Radio	GPS, Compass, Anemometer	2	0.2	-	On-shore	Recreational	2017	[27]
60	AutoCAT	MIT (Uni.)		•	2			†			▲						Radio	GPS	1.8	1.3	-	Inland	Scientific	2000	[47]

⁵ "2014-" means the project starts from 2014.
⁶ Prototype 52 has Wind Turbine.

Table 4. Autonomy levels for ASVs [61]

	Autonomy Level	Sub level	Decision	Action	Exception	Co-operation
Human is alone	0	1	1	1	1	1
Human is helped by systems	1	1	1	1	1	2
	1	2	2-4	1	1	1
	1	3	1	2-4	1	1
	1	4	1	1	2	1
Human is helped by the systems and other agents	2	1	2-4	1	1	3-5
	2	2	1	2-4	1	3-5
	2	3	1	1	2	3-5
	2	4	1	1	1	3-5
Autonomous path following vessel	3	1	1	5	1	1
	3	2	1	5	1	2
	3	3	2-4	5	1	1
	3	4	2-4	5	1	2
	3	5	2-4	5	1	3-5
	3	6	2-4	5	2	2
	3	7	2-4	5	2	3-5
Autonomous trajectory tracking vessel	4	1	1	6	1	1-2
	4	2	1	6	1	3-5
	4	3	2-4	6	1	1
	4	4	2-4	6	1	2
	4	5	2-4	6	1	3-5
	4	6	2-4	6	2	2
	4	7	2-4	6	2	3-5
Human in the loop	5	1	5-6	5	1	1
	5	2	5-6	5	2	2
	5	3	5-6	5	2	3-5
	5	4	5-6	5	3	2
	5	5	5-6	5	3	3-5
	5	6	5-6	5	4	2
	5	7	5-6	5	4	3-5
	5	8	5-6	5	5-6	2
	5	9	5-6	5	5-6	3-5
	5	10	5-6	6	1	1
	5	11	5-6	6	2	2
	5	12	5-6	6	2	3-5
	5	13	5-6	6	3	2
	5	14	5-6	6	3	3-5
	5	15	5-6	6	4	2
	5	16	5-6	6	4	3-5
	5	17	5-6	6	5-6	2
	5	18	5-6	6	5-6	3-5

	Autonomy Level	Sub level	Decision	Action	Exception	Co-operation
Human supervise the decisions making system	6	1	7-8	5	1	1
	6	2	7-8	5	2	2
	6	3	7-8	5	2	3-5
	6	4	7-8	5	3	2
	6	5	7-8	5	3	3-5
	6	6	7-8	5	4	2
	6	7	7-8	5	4	3-5
	6	8	7-8	5	5-6	2
	6	9	7-8	5	5-6	3-5
	6	10	7-8	6	1	1
	6	11	7-8	6	2	2
	6	12	7-8	6	2	3-5
	6	13	7-8	6	3	2
	6	14	7-8	6	3	3-5
	6	15	7-8	6	4	2
	6	16	7-8	6	4	3-5
	6	17	7-8	6	5-6	2
	6	18	7-8	6	5-6	3-5
Human supervise the actions making system	7	1	5-6	7-8	1	1
	7	2	5-6	7-8	1	2
	7	3	5-6	7-8	1	3-5
	7	4	5-6	7-8	2	2
	7	5	5-6	7-8	2	3-5
	7	6	5-6	7-8	3	2
	7	7	5-6	7-8	3	3-5
	7	8	5-6	7-8	4	2
	7	9	5-6	7-8	4	3-5
	7	10	5-6	7-8	5-6	2
	7	11	5-6	7-8	5-6	3-5
Human supervise the exceptions	8	1	5-6	5	7-8	2
	8	2	5-6	5	7-8	3-5
	8	3	5-6	6	7-8	2
	8	4	5-6	6	7-8	3-5
Human supervise actions, decision and exceptions	9	1	7-8	7-8	7-8	2
	9	2	7-8	7-8	7-8	3-5
Fully autonomous	10	1	9-10	9-10	9-10	2
	10	2	9-10	9-10	9-10	3-5

3.2   Autonomy levels of ASV prototypes

Table 5 shows the score of each subsystem found on board and the overall autonomy level of each prototype. In the last column, the number before the decimal point is the main autonomy level the ASV belongs to, while the number after the decimal point is the sub-level. For example, Level 3.2 means the ASV prototype belongs to sub-level 2 in autonomy level 3.

The most populated main autonomy level is Level 3, which represent an autonomous path following vessel. The first step is to set up an ASV able to follow a predefined path, established using coordinates as the keypoints. The sublevel 3.1 represent the ability to only engage an autopilot, sublevel 3.2 implement the ability to communicate with a remote control, sublevel 3.5 has an updated decision making system and is able to communicate with other vessels, while sublevel 3.6 is an improvement in the exceptions handling system. Level 9 is the highest level that existing prototypes achieve. The sublevel 9.1 has 4 prototypes able to autonomously set up a route, follow it and avoid the obstacles on the way. The limitation is the ability to communicate only with a remote control. This problem is overcome in sublevel 9.2, where the ASVs are able to communicate with additional means of transportation.

Following are the introduction of prototypes at each level:

Level 0 is the lowest achievable autonomy level. PROTEUS [1] is a twin-hull innovative concept, the vessel floats on two articulated inflatables. The command cabin is hanging in between, attached to a dumped structure. The concept has given birth to smaller ASVs like the WAM-V ASV.

Level 1.1 has three remote-controlled vessels, which is regarded as the first step toward an autonomous prototype. In [43] and [72], studies about the hulls, controllers, actuators and dynamic data are accomplished. The Seabax [22, 53] recognizes QR-codes and will be able to respond accordingly. These binary markers can be used for several purposes: they could represent a waypoint, a traffic redirection signal or a building ashore.

Level 1.2 includes a new project sponsored by Rolls Royce [42, 58]. The timeline plans a first deployment of remote controlled ASV with decision making support in 2020.

Level 1.3 is found in the ASV proposed by [19] and Circe from [38]. The controllers onboard are able to store and send time dependent commands to the actuators. The sets of actions are given in an open loop control, which is not autonomous given the limited prediction in a highly disturbed environment.

Level 3.1 refers to the vessels which have path following controllers. ALANIS [11] uses a Line-of-sight guidance technique, combined with a Proportional-Differential (PD) controller. ERON [25] navigate through waypoints with a Proportional-Integral-Differential controller. These prototypes are not able to communicate with remote computers.

Level 3.2 is the level which the largest number of ASVs achieve. Those prototypes have path following controllers and remote connection with computers, but do not have any decision making support system or obstacle detection sys-

Table 5. Autonomy level of ASV prototypes

No.	Proto-type	De	Act	Ex	Co	Auto-nomy	No.	Proto-type	De	Act	Ex	Co	Auto-nomy
1	Proteus	1	1	1	1	0	33	CRW	2	5	1	4	3.5
2	ASV MUN	1	1	1	2	1.1	34	USNA	2	5	2	2	3.6
3	ASV SMU	1	1	1	2	1.1	35	IMOCA 60	2	5	2	2	3.6
4	Seabax	1	1	1	2	1.1	36	Tito Neri	1	6	1	3	4.2
5	Rolls Royce ASV	3	1	1	1	1.2	37	SeaWASP	1	6	1	2	4.4
6	ASV Prototype	1	2	1	1	1.3	38	Charlie USV	4	6	1	3	4.5
7	Circe	1	2	1	1	1.3	39	Electric boat	5	5	5	2	5.8
8	ALANIS	1	5	1	1	3.1	40	Rolls Royce ASV 2	5	6	6	2	5.17
9	ERON	1	5	1	1	3.1	41	iNav-1	6	8	1	4	7.3
10	CaRoLIME	1	5	1	1	3.1	42	AVALON	6	8	2	3	7.4
11	ENSIETA	1	5	1	2	3.2	43	MAINAMI	6	8	2	3	7.5
12	DELFIM	1	5	1	2	3.2	44	ROAZ	6	8	2	3	7.5
13	MARV	1	5	1	2	3.2	45	ROAZ II	6	8	2	3	7.5
14	WAM-V	1	5	1	2	3.2	46	SCOUT	5	5	8	3	8.2
15	SCOAP	1	5	1	2	3.2	47	Challenger 2000	5	6	8	2	8.3
16	Zarco	1	5	1	2	3.2	48	WUT-1	6	6	8	2	8.3
17	A-TIRMA G2	1	5	1	2	3.2	49	ReVOLT	7	8	8	2	9.1
18	A-TIRMA G1	1	5	1	2	3.2	50	CS Saucer	8	8	8	2	9.1
19	SailBuoy	1	5	1	2	3.2	51	MUNIN	8	8	8	2	9.1
20	OASIS	1	5	1	2	3.2	52	ASAROME	8	8	8	2	9.1
21	WaveGlider	1	5	1	2	3.2	53	PROPAGATOR 2	8	8	8	3	9.2
22	Lizhbeth	1	5	1	2	3.2	54	PROPAGATOR 1	8	8	8	3	9.2
23	Artemis	1	5	1	2	3.2	55	Rolls Royce ASV 3	8	8	8	4	9.2
24	ACES	1	5	1	2	3.2	56	Delfia-1	8	8	8	5	9.2
25	Swordfish	1	5	1	2	3.2	57	Delfia-1 Star	8	8	8	5	9.2
26	ASV	1	5	1	2	3.2							
27	N-Boat	1	5	1	2	3.2							
28	Proto 1	1	5	1	2	3.2							
29	Proto 2	1	5	1	2	3.2							
30	ASV ROBOAT	1	5	1	2	3.2							
31	WAM-V USV16	1	5	1	2	3.2							
32	VAIMOS	1	5	1	2	3.2							

Project 58, 59, 60 cannot be properly classified since key data is missing.

tem. Moreover, the communication is not cooperative, so the vessel only sends real-time data and receives information which is needed for navigation.

Sailing boats are found in this autonomy level. Those boats can control the direction, but they can not manage the speed. The sail position must be adjusted and the boat can not navigate against wind direction. Tracking algorithms are used to reach the designated point. [60], [63] and [40, 59] (N-Boat) have presented solutions. However, they are not able to navigate in complicated paths. The autonomy devices are implemented, but controllers need to be better arranged. A-Tirma version 1 [10] and 2 [26] manage the position of the sails through a fuzzy logic controller.

Sailing boats are especially chosen for the endurance. The power they use is the wind, which is always available at the sea. The energy required to drive controllers and actuators can be taken from a solar panel or a wind turbine. VAIMOS [6] sailed continuously for 19 hours, completing the whole task, which was expecting to achieve complicated maneuvering. During the test, the lack of obstacle avoidance capability brought VAIMOS close to a collision for two times. ASV Roboat [65] navigated for 27 hours in the Baltic sea before a malfunction to the sail trimmer interrupted the mission. The SailBuoy is able to survive up to 6 months only using the batteries. The SailBuoy has a path following controller, which gives the possibility to follow certain streams or animals.

However, the power the sailing bosts use is unpredictable, and the shape makes the vessel limited in the scope. This is why more electric or gasoline fueled vessels are found in level 3.2. The first documented ASV developed is ARTEMIS [57]. Developed in 1996, it was already capable of waypoint navigation through a fuzzy-logic controller of the rudder. The successive ASV, ACES [46], proposed the same functions with a different hull shape. In the following years, many others ASV with same capabilities have been developed: DELFIM [3], Zarco [20], Swordfish [29], Lizbeth [37], the ASV in [56] and WAM-V USV16 [71].

Alternative solutions in terms of fuel have been proposed by OASIS [35] and Waveglider [36]. The first vessel is entirely covered in solar panels, designed to withstand the harsh ocean environment. The Waveglider integrate a solar panel, which powers the sensors and control system, and a submerged unit, which supply the forward motion through fins and wave motion.

Among those ASVs which achieve Level 3.2, MARV [5] is a fully capable research vessel assembled using only off-the-shelf components. This technology is available to everybody, to successfully create ASVs and experiment new controller techniques. In the military scope, the ASVs are being deployed to patrol, following predefined paths, such as the WAM-V [54]. An attempt to avoid collision has been made by SCOAP [18], integrating a passive AIS signal emitter to alert other vessels of the presence of an uncontrolled vessel.

Level 3.5 has a project called CRW [70]. It is a set of identical ASVs, with an original air propeller, which can be deployed in calm waters (canals, lakes). The swarm is able to cooperate by exchange information. The core of the control system is an Android smart phone.

Level 3.6 of autonomy is achieved by integrating a simple obstacle detectors. USNA sailing boat [50] has the simple waypoint navigation system, but uses an ultrasonic range finder to detect obstacles. However, no reaction has yet been implemented. A similar solution is found on board of the IMOCA 60 sailing boat [62]. The vessel are made to navigate non-stop around the world. The sailor on board must take care of his own needs, this is why a robust autopilot is always integrated. Besides, the AIS system is used to communicate and receive information about the presence of other vessels in the close proximity [16].

Level 4.2 includes the ASVs which has the function of dynamic positioning. Tito Neri [23] is a scaled model (1:30) of a real tugboat. It developed to study the dynamic and platooning\leader following behavior of autonomous ships. Now, it is mainly used for educational purposes.

Level 4.4 is the ASV which has a trajectory controller, such as SeaWASP [7, 45]. Her twin-hull is submerged with the use of ballast water to improve the stability. The controller uses a proportional linear controller to correct the heading and velocity and minimize the tracking error.

Level 4.5 involves the function of cooperation. The Charlie USV is a catamaran which is able to cooperate with a leader vessel. The leader sends GPS reading to the ASV which uses her trajectory tracking controllers to follow. The speed is managed to keep a fixed distance respect to the front vessel.

Level 5.8 has the electric vessel developed by Northrop Grumman [64]. The vessel is able to autonomously navigate and react to obstacles. The stereo vision is used to define the side of the river or the acceptable limits in the harbor. Furthermore, the fixed obstacles are discovered with a color blob technique, while the moving one with motion blobs. The vessel is able to navigate without any prior map and detect obstacles with the array of cameras.

Level 5.17 refers to a updated version of ASV planned by Rolls Royce project [58, 42]. By 2030, an autonomous cargo vessel will be presented. She is able to autonomously navigate, but still requiring full time human remote supervision of the actions and decision making.

Level 7.3 is achieved by iNav-1 [74]. iNav-1 has the capability of path following and heading control. A pod propulsion USV heading control system is designed for it based bipolar fuzzy controller. One thing worth to note is that it is able to cooperate with UAVs for synergetic cruises in maritime supervision.

Level 7.4 is achieved by smart sailing boats, AVALON [33] and MAINAMI [52]. AVALON uses weather data and a digital nautical chart to plan routes with a grid-based A* algorithm. The decisions are then passed to the action subsystem, which translates in actual rudder and sail set up, considering the wind direction. However, the obstacles are not considered. In AVALON, a passive AIS system is applied to send information. MAINAMI communicate with underwater vehicles by means of an acoustic device.

Level 7.5 includes the ROAZ and the follow up ROAZ II [49]. These vessel navigates with a GPS waypoint controller. The surrounding are explored by two cameras, which are able to process the images and define the target position. Once the target is locked, the vessel follows the object at a fixed distance [48].

Level 8.2 includes the project SCOUT, a set of kayaks [21]. The goal is to monitor wide shallow areas and cooperate toward this achievement. The common protocol used to communicate with the remote location gives the ability to these vessels to avoid collisions with each other. This is not a robust approach as of now, since exchange of data between vessels is limited. In the future, if rules change and make mandatory the use of AIS, the simple exchange of information between vessels could avoid the collision.

Level 8.3 is achieved by SEADOO Challenger 2000 [41] and WUT-1 [17, 44]. Cameras, ARPA radar and AIS, together with detailed nautical charts, give the vessel the ability to compute long term path. WUT-1 is able to automatically plan routes according to the navigation objectives and track the preplanned routes. Moreover, WUT-1 can sense the obstacles and determine an anti-collision route with A* algorithm and Artificial Potential Field.

Level 9.1 is a quiet high level. Almost all the vessels which have reached this level are limited to a remote connection, without considering the cooperative communication with other vessels. It is interesting to notice that all the projects or prototypes in this level have been published in recent two years.

The sailing boat ASAROME [55] uses a PD controller for tracking. A 360 camera is applied to detect obstacles. This data is combined with the reading from the underwater sonar and the inertial measurement unit to create a 3D map for a potential-based reactive path-planning.

The CS Saucer is a small circular autonomous vessel [39]. It is equipped with a 2D Lidar to explore and maneuver in unknown terrains. Based on the map made by Lidar, the decision making system can find the path to follow. One drawback of this highly autonomous experiment is the limited usage in agitated sea waters. The prototype has only been tested inside a water basin. For this reason, the vessel is not equipped with a GPS, but relies on IMU for moving.

ReVolt cargo vessel [67, 8] and MUNIN [51] focus on the autonomous vessel which can be aware of the situation around it, and navigate with an occasional supervision. In both cases, the remote control is chosen as a fallback option. Both ReVolt and MUNIN are now ship concepts. For the purpose of testing, the autonomous capabilities of ReVolt, a 1:20 scaled model has been built.

Level 9.2 is achieved by some on-going projects. PropaGator [31, 30, 34] has managed to achieve a really high level of autonomy, by using Lidars, camera vision and cooperation with other autonomous vehicles. PropaGator is able to recognize and avoid obstacles, recognize signs, and communicate with a quad-copter to deploy it and recover it once completed the mission. The only lacking is long term route planning. As of now, the planning is limited to the area explored by the cameras and LiDAR.

Delfia-1 [66] and the follow up Delfia-1 Star [53], also reach Level 9.2. Their shape is designed to make maneuvering applications in crowded environments easier than actual solutions allowing at the same time the possibility to combine multiple Delfia ships in one bigger platform. They have already pass the test of path following, collision avoidance and dynamic positioning. Moreover, they are capable to communicate and cooperate with not only vessels, but also other agents, such as infrastructure operators. The ASVs have a remote controlled option.

Rolls Royce is aiming to achieve the same level by 2035 with a cargo vessel [58, 42]. Their goal is to have an autonomous ocean going vessel, which are able to make decision, take actions and handle exceptions autonomously. The cooperation can be extended to ports and other vessels in the fleet, in order to optimize the overall operations.

4   Trends in ASV research

The information summarized in the previous sections have been combined in order to understand the status and future trends of ASVs in this section. As the development time of those USV usually lasts more than 3 years, in this section, we use 3 years as the class interval.

The first focus is on the number of prototypes developed. Fig. 1 shows a large increase on the number of ASV projects.

As analysis in former section, the autonomy level that most ASVs reached is Level 3 (Figure 2). However, many on-going projects are aiming at high level autonomy vessels which are able to make decision, take actions and handle exceptions autonomously. So far, no ASVs have achieved Level 10 automation.

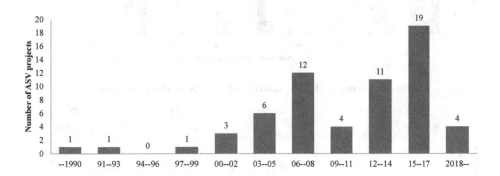

Fig. 1. The number of ASVs developed

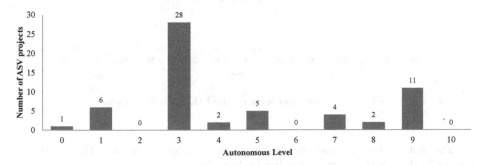

Fig. 2. The number of ASVs in each Autonomy Level

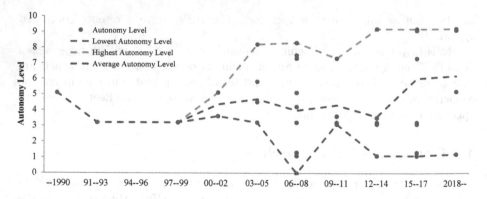

Fig. 3. Trend in the automation of vessels in the past years

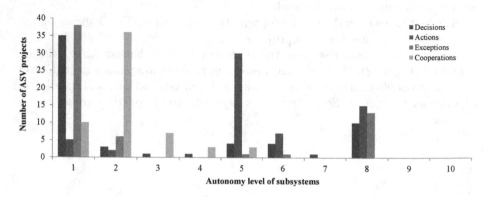

Fig. 4. Trend in the automation of vessels in the past years

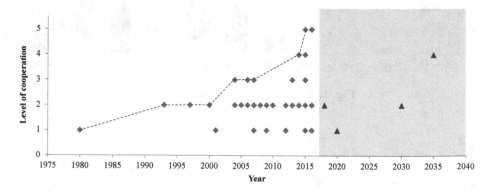

Fig. 5. Cooperation level reached through the years

The automation of the vessels has been increasing through the years. In Figure 3, the range of autonomy levels that the projects achieve become larger because the number increase. The highest level of autonomy that ASVs can achieve increase year by year. The realization of vessels with lower autonomy levels are the basis to develop autonomous vessels with higher autonomy levels. Moreover, vessels with different level of autonomy have different applications.

Looking into the autonomy level of subsystems (Figure 4), the highest autonomy level that the decision making, action taking and exception handling is 8. Thanks to the development of searching algorithms and autopilot, many vessels achieve high autonomy level of the decision making and action taking subsystem. The action taking systems owns the highest level of autonomy with an average 5.4. Then, the decision making system has an average 3.0. The autonomy for the exception handling system are relatively low. Many prototypes with high overall autonomy levels still needs human assistances. For the newly introduced cooperative subsystem, some research groups have already realized the importance. Because the concept of cooperation between agents is a new field to explore, only a limited number of vessels is above Level 2 is found. However, we can still find a rising trend in Figure 5.

From the perspective of dimensions, most of existing ASVs prototypes are scaled models whose length are less than 10 m. Some models are serve as test bench in researching sensor fusion, collision avoidance and other relative software for the full scale autonomous vessels. Moreover, some small dimension prototypes are used for scientific purposes, such as maritime monitoring and oceanographic observation.

5   Conclusions and further research

ASVs have been developed for more than 20 years. In the latest years, it seems that the technology has reached a point where the usage of those vessel could become more extended and integrated in the current environment. Small and big stakeholders are investing on the development of increasingly big autonomous ships. In the literature, many ASV projects have been successfully realized, and as many are still under development. Just a few ASV have reached mass production, since only a niche market is using those devices. In the literature there is a lack on research about different applications and suitable environments for the deployment of ASV.

In this paper, we provide an overview of the existing projects considering their main components, dimensions, scope and deployment year. The automation level that each prototypes achieved are elaborated according to an innovative categorization proposed in our previous work [61]. The analysis about existing research helps to gain knowledge about the emerging concepts and techniques that have been applied in ASV research.

Further comparisons between the existing projects has lead to the agreement that the research on ASVs is rapidly increasing. The autonomy level is following the same trend, proposing new intelligent solutions. The scope of the newly designed autonomous vessels is shifting from small ASVs for scientific researches to bigger cargo crafts. The research of cooperation in ASVs is still at beginning but shows great potential.

References

1. Proteus (watercraft) (2016), https://goo.gl/vuTlSj
2. Alt, C., Wittinghofer, N.: Autonomous Sailing Boats. In: Proceedings of Seminar aus Informatik (SS 2011). Salzburg, Austria (2011)
3. Alves, J., Oliveira, P., Oliveira, R., Pascoal, A., Rufino, M., Sebastiao, L., Silvestre, C.: Vehicle and Mission Control of the DELFIM Autonomous Surface Craft. In: Proceedings of 2006 14th Mediterranean Conference on Control and Automation. pp. 1–6. IEEE, Ancona, Italy (2006)
4. AMS Institute: Roboat (2016), http://www.ams-institute.org/roboat/
5. Azevedo, D., Beltram, S., Del Vecchio, G., Hopner, B.: MARV: Marine Autonomous Research Vessel. Master's thesis, Santa Clara University (2016)
6. Bars, F.L., Jaulin, L.: An Experimental Validation of a Robust Controller with the VAIMOS Autonomous Sailboat. In: Robotic Sailing 2012, pp. 73–84. Springer Berlin Heidelberg (2013)
7. Beck, E., Kirkwood, W., Caress, D., Berk, T., Mahacek, P., Brashem, K., Acain, J., Reddy, V., Kitts, C., Skutnik, J., Wheat, G.: SeaWASP: A Small Waterplane Area Twin Hull Autonomous Platform for Shallow Water Mapping. In: Proceedings of 2008 IEEE/OES Autonomous Underwater Vehicles. pp. 1–7. Woods Hole, MA, USA (2008)
8. Bertram, V.: Towards Unmanned Ships. Presentation (2013), https://goo.gl/YrOgFb
9. Bibuli, M., Caccia, M., Lapierre, L., Bruzzone, G.: Guidance of Unmanned Surface Vehicles: Experiments in Vehicle Following 19(3), 92–102 (2012)
10. Cabrera-Gámez, J., Ramos de Miguel, A., Domínguez-Brito, A.C., Hernández-Sosa, J.D., Isern-González, J., Fernández-Perdomo, E.: An Embedded Low-Power Control System for Autonomous Sailboats, pp. 67–79. Springer International Publishing, Cham (ZG), Switzerland (2014)
11. Caccia, M., Bibuli, M., Bono, R., Bruzzone, G., Bruzzone, G., Spirandelli, E.: Aluminum Hull USV for Coastal Water and Seafloor Monitoring. In: Proceedings of OCEANS 2009-EUROPE. pp. 1–5. Bremen, Germany (2009)
12. Caccia, M., Bibuli, M., Bono, R., Bruzzone, G., Bruzzone, G., Spirandelli, E.: Unmanned Surface Vehicle for Coastal and Protected Waters Applications: the Charlie Project. Marine Technology Society Journal 41(2), 62–71 (2007)
13. Caccia, M., Bono, R., Bruzzone, G., Bruzzone, G., Spirandelli, E., Veruggio, G., Stortini, A.M.: Design and Exploitation of an Autonomous Surface Vessel for the Study of Sea-Air Interactions. In: Proceedings of the 2005 IEEE International Conference on Robotics and Automation. pp. 3582–3587. Shatin, N.T., China (2005)
14. Caccia, M., Bono, R., Bruzzone, G., Spirandelli, E., Veruggio, G., Stortini, A.M., Capodaglio, G.: Sampling Sea Surfaces with SESAMO: An Autonomous Craft for the Study of Sea-air Interactions 12(3), 95–105 (2005)
15. Camilli, L.: Designing Ocean Drones for Maritime Security: The Use of Integrated Sensing Modalities to Enhance Situational Awareness. In: Proceedings of Marine Technology Society and IEEE Oceanic Engineering Society OCEANS 2015 Environmental Intelligence. Washington DC, USA (2015)
16. Campbell, S., Naeem, W., Irwin, G.W.: A Review on Improving the Autonomy of Unmanned Surface Vehicles Through Intelligent Collision Avoidance Manoeuvres. Annual Reviews in Control 36(2), 267–283 (2012)
17. Chen, Z.: Research on Small Unmanned Surface Vehicle Sailing State Obtaining System. Master's thesis, Wuhan University of Technology (2014)

18. Codiga, D.L.: A Marine Autonomous Surface Craft for Long-Duration, Spatially Explicit, Multidisciplinary Water Column Sampling in Coastal and Estuarine Systems. Journal of Atmospheric and Oceanic Technology 32(3), 627–641 (2014)
19. Conte, G., Scaradozzi, D., Mannocchi, D., Raspa, P., Panebianco, L.: Development and Testing of Low-Cost ASV. In: Proceedings of the Twenty-sixth (2016) International Ocean and Polar Engineering Conference. pp. 1–6. International Society of Offshore and Polar Engineers, Rhodes, Greece (2016)
20. Cruz, N., Matos, A., Cunha, S., Silva, S.: Zarco - An Autonomous Craft for Underwater Surveys. In: Proceedings of the 7th Geomatic Week. pp. 1–8. Barcelona, Spain (2007)
21. Curcio, J., Leonard, J., Patrikalakis, A.: SCOUT - A Low Cost Autonomous Surface Platform for Research in Cooperative Autonomy. In: Proceedings of OCEANS 2005 MTS/IEEE. vol. 1, pp. 725–729. Washington, D.C., USA (2005)
22. Delft University of Technology, All algorithms on deck! Working on robotic ships. DELTA 49(6), `https://tudelftroboticsinstitute.nl/news/all-algorithms-deck-working-robotic-ships` (2016)
23. Delft University of Technology, Dynamic Positioning for Tito Neri Tug Boats. `https://www.studeersnel.nl/nl/document/technische-universiteit-delft/mechatronics-in-mt/overige/dp-guide-2017-0228-reader/924363/view?has_flashcards=false` (2017)
24. Demetriou, G.A., Hadjipieri, A., Panayidou, I.E., Papasavva, A., Ioannou, S.: ERON: A PID Controlled Autonomous Surface Vessel. In: Proceedings of 2016 18th Mediterranean Electrotechnical Conference (MELECON). pp. 1–5. Limassol, Cyprus (2016)
25. Demetriou, G.A., Ioannou, S., Hadjipieri, A., cPanayidou, I.E., Papasavva, A., Savva, A.P.: ERON: A Flexible Autonomous Surface Vessel. In: Proceedings of the 24th Mediterranean Conference on Control and Automation (MED). pp. 71–76. Athens, Greece (2016)
26. Domínguez-Brito, A.C., Valle-Fernández, B., Cabrera-Gámez, J., Ramos-de Miguel, A., García, J.C.: A-TIRMA G2: An Oceanic Autonomous Sailboat, pp. 3–13. Springer International Publishing, Cham (ZG), Switzerland (2016)
27. Fernandes, P.C., Marques, M.M., Lobo, V.: Barlavento - Considerations About the Design of an Autonomous Sailboat. In: Robotic Sailing 2016, pp. 19–30. Springer International Publishing, Cham (ZG), Switzerland (2017)
28. Ferreira, H., Martins, A., Dias, A., Almeida, C., Almeida, J.M., Silva, E.P.: ROAZ Autonomous Surface Vehicle Design and Implementation. Robtica Controlo, Automao, Instrumentao 67 (2007)
29. Ferreira, H., Martins, R., Marques, E., Pinto, J., Martins, A., Almeida, J., Sousa, J., Silva, E.P.: SWORDFISH: An Autonomous Surface Vehicle for Network Centric Operations. In: Proceedings of OCEANS 2007 - Europe. pp. 1–6. Aberdeen, Scotland, United Kingdom (2007)
30. Frank, D., Gray, A., Schwartz, E.: PropaGator 2: A Planing Autonomous Surface Vehicle With Azimuth Rim-Driven Thrusters. In: Proceedings of the 14th Annual Early Career Technical Conference. pp. 1–6. Birmingham, AL, USA (2014)
31. Frank, D., Gray, A., Schwartz, E.: PropaGator 2015: UF Autonomous Surface Vehicle. AUVSI Foundations 7th Annual RoboBoat Competition (2015)
32. Ghani, M.H., Hole, L.R., Fer, I., Kourafalou, V.H., Wienders, N., Kang, H., Drushka, K., Peddie, D.: The SailBuoy Remotely-controlled Unmanned Vessel: Measurements of Near Surface Temperature, Salinity and Oxygen Concentration in the Northern Gulf of Mexico. Methods in Oceanography 10, 104–121 (2014)

33. Giger, L., Wismer, S., Boehl, S., Busser, G., Erckens, H., Weber, J., Moser, P., Schwizer, P., Pradalier, C., Yves, R.S.: Design and Construction of the Autonomous Sailing Vessel AVALON. In: Proceedings of The World Robotic Sailing Championship and International Robotic Sailing Conference. pp. 17–22. Matosinhos, Portugal (2009)

34. Gray, A., Shahrestani, N., Frank, D., Schwartz, E.: Propagator 2013: UF Autonomous Surface Vehicle. AUVSI Foundations 6th Annual RoboBoat Competition (2013)

35. Higinbotham, J.R., Hitchener, P.G., Moisan, J.R.: Development of a New Long Duration Solar Powered Autonomous Surface Vehicle. In: Proceedings of OCEANS 2006. pp. 1–6. Singapore (2006)

36. Hine, R., McGillivary, P.: Wave Powered Autonomous Surface Vessels as Components of Ocean Observing Systems. In: Proceedings of 20th Pacific Congress on Marine Science and Technology (PACON 2007). Honolulu, Hawaii (2007)

37. Hitz, G., Pomerleau, F., Garneau, M.E., Pradalier, C., Posch, T., Pernthaler, J., Siegwart, R.Y.: Autonomous Inland Water Monitoring: Design and Application of a Surface Vessel 19(1), 62–72 (2012)

38. Holler, J., Striz, A., Bretney, K., Kavett, K., Bingham, B.: Design, Construction, and Field Testing of an Autonomous Surface Craft for Engineering and Science Education. In: Proceedings of OCEANS 2007. pp. 1–6. Aberdeen, Scotland, United Kingdom (2007)

39. Idland, T.K.: Marine Cybernetics Vessel CS Saucer: Design, construction and control. Master's thesis, NTNU (2015)

40. Júnior, A.G.S., Araújo, A.P.D., Silva, M.V.A., Aroca, R.V., Gonalves, L.M.G.: N-BOAT: An Autonomous Robotic Sailboat. In: Proceedings of 2013 Latin American Robotics Symposium and Competition. pp. 24–29. Arequipa, Peru (2013)

41. Larson, J., Bruch, M., Ebken, J.: Autonomous navigation and obstacle avoidance for Unmanned Surface Vehicles. In: Proceedings of SPIE Defense and Security Symposium. pp. 1–12. International Society for Optics and Photonics, Orlando, FL, USA (2006)

42. Levander, O.: Towards Unmanned Ships. Presentation (2015), https://goo.gl/ENf67f

43. Li, Z., Bachmayer, R.: The Development of a Robust Autonomous Surface Craft for Deployment in Harsh Ocean Environment. In: Proceedings of 2013 OCEANS. pp. 1–7. San Diego, USA (2013)

44. Liu, C., Zheng, H., Negenborn, R.R., Chu, X., Wang, L.: Trajectory Tracking Control for Underactuated Surface Vessels Based on Nonlinear Model Predictive Control. In: Computational Logistics, pp. 166–180. Springer International Publishing, Cham (ZG), Switzerland (2015)

45. Mahacek, P., Berk, T., Casanova, A., Kitts, C., Kirkwood, W., Wheat, G.: Development and Initial Testing of a SWATH Boat for Shallow-water Bathymetry. In: Proceedings of OCEANS 2008. pp. 1–6. Quebec City, QC, Canada (2008)

46. Manley, J.E.: Development of the Autonomous Surface Craft "ACES". In: Proceedings of OCEANS '97. MTS/IEEE Conference Proceedings. vol. 2, pp. 827–832. Halifax, Nova Scotia, Canada (1997)

47. Manley, J.E., Marsh, A., Cornforth, W., Wiseman, C.: Evolution of the Autonomous Surface Craft AutoCat. In: Proceedings of OCEANS 2000 MTS/IEEE Conference and Exhibition. vol. 1, pp. 403–408 (2000)

48. Martins, A., Almeida, J.M., Ferreira, H., Silva, H., Dias, N., Dias, A., Almeida, C., Silva, E.P.: Autonomous Surface Vehicle Docking Manoeuvre with Visual Infor-

mation. In: Proceedings of 2007 IEEE International Conference on Robotics and Automation. pp. 4994–4999. Roma, Italy (2007)

49. Martins, A., Ferreira, H., Almeida, C., Silva, H., Almeida, J.M., Silva, E.: ROAZ and ROAZ II Autonomous Surface Vehicle Design and Implementation. In: Proceedings of International Lifesaving Congress 2007. Porto, Portugal (2007)

50. Miller, P., Beal, B., Capron, C., Gawboy, R., Mallory, P., Ness, C., Petrosik, R., Pryne, C., Murphy, T., Spears, H.: Increasing Performance and Added Capabilities of USNA Sail-Powered Autonomous Surface Vessels (ASV). Tech. rep., DTIC Document (2010)

51. MUNIN: Research in Maritime Autonomous Systems Project Results and Technology Potentials. Tech. rep., Maritime Unmanned Navigation through Intelligence in Networks (2016)

52. Nakatani, T., Hyakudome, T., Sawa, T., Nakano, Y., Watanabe, Y., Fukuda, T., Matsumoto, H., Suga, R., Yoshida, H.: Development of an Autonomous Surface Vehicle for Monitoring Underwater Vehicles. In: Proceedings of OCEANS 2015 - MTS/IEEE Washington. pp. 1–5. Washington, DC, USA (2015)

53. Negenborn R.R., Autonomous Vessel Family of the Waterborne Transport Technology Lab at Delft University of Technology. http://www.mtt.tudelft.nl/, Delft University of Technology, The Netherlands (2017)

54. Pandey, J., Hasegawa, K.: Study on Manoeuverability and Control of an Autonomous Wave Adaptive Modular Vessel (WAM-V) for ocean observation. In: Proceedings of 2015 International Association of Institutes of Navigation World Congress (IAIN). pp. 1–7. Prague, Czech Republic (2015)

55. Plumet, F., Ptrs, C., Romero-Ramirez, M.A., Gas, B., Ieng, S.H.: Toward an Autonomous Sailing Boat 40(2), 397–407 (2015)

56. Prempraneerach, P., Janthong, M., Klanthip, T., Boonyarak, S., Choosui, C., Phothongkum, K., Timpitak, S., Kulvanit, P.: Autonomous Way-point Tracking Navigation of Surveying Surface Vessel with Real-time Positioning System. In: Proceedings of 2015 International Computer Science and Engineering Conference (ICSEC). pp. 1–6. Chiang Mai, Thailand (2015)

57. Rodriguez-Ortiz, C.D.: Automated Bathymetry Mapping Using an Autonomous Surface craft. Master's thesis, Massachusetts Institute of Technology (1996)

58. Rolls-Royce: Remote and Autonomous Ships: The next steps. White paper (2016), https://goo.gl/GJTMaZ

59. Santos, D., Silva Junior, A.G., Negreiros, A., Vilas Boas, J., Alvarez, J., Araujo, A., Aroca, R.V., Gonalves, L.M.G.: Design and Implementation of a Control System for a Sailboat Robot. Robotics 5(1), 1–5 (2016)

60. Sauze, C., Neal, M., others: An Autonomous Sailing Robot for Ocean Observation. In: Proceedings of TAROS-06 : proceedings of Towards Autonomous Robotic Systems 2006. vol. 2006, pp. 190–197. Guildford, United Kingdom (2006)

61. Schiaretti, M., Chen, L., Negenborn, R.R.: Survey on Autonomous Surface Vessels: Part I - A New Detailed Definition of Autonomy Levels. In: Proceedings of 8th International Conference on Computational Logistics, October 18-20, Southampton, UK (2017)

62. Schmidt, D.: Autopilot Anatomy (2016), http://www.sailingworld.com/autopilot-anatomy

63. Sliwka, J., Reilhac, P., Leloup, R., Crepier, P., Roncin, K., Aizier, B., Jaulin, L.: Autonomous Robotic Boat of ENSIETA. In: Proceedings of 2nd International Robotic Sailing Conference. pp. 1–7. Matosinhos, Portugal (2009)

64. Snyder, F.D., Morris, D.D., Haley, P.H., Collins, R.T., Okerholm, A.M.: Autonomous River Navigation. In: Proceedings of SPIE International Symposium - Optics East 2004. pp. 221–232. International Society for Optics and Photonics, Philadelphia (2004)
65. Stelzer, R., Jafarmadar, K.: The Robotic Sailing Boat, ASV Roboat as a Maritime Research Platform. In: Proceedings of 22nd International HISWA Symposium on Yacht Design and Yacht Construction. pp. 1–13. Amsterdam, The Netherlands (2012)
66. TU Delft: TU Delfia-1 in action (2017), https://www.youtube.com/watch?v=yqAfWIkEGUI\&feature=youtu.be
67. Tvete, H.A.: ReVolt: The Unmanned, Zero Emission, Short Sea Ship of the Future. Dnv Gl Strategic Research & Innovation (2015)
68. Tvete, H.A., Engelhardtsen, Ø.: DNV GL's research within Autonomous Systems. Presentation (2014), https://goo.gl/Uz44zJ
69. Ueland, E.S.: Marine Autonomous Exploration using a LiDAR. Master's thesis, NTNU (2016)
70. Valada, A., Velagapudi, P., Kannan, B., Tomaszewski, C., Kantor, G., Scerri, P.: Development of a Low Cost Multi-Robot Autonomous Marine Surface Platform. In: Yoshida, K., Tadokoro, S. (eds.) Field and Service Robotics, pp. 643–658. No. 92 in Springer Tracts in Advanced Robotics, Springer Berlin Heidelberg (2014)
71. Von Ellenrieder, K., Wampler, J.: Unmanned Surface Vessel (USV) Systems for Bridge Inspection. Tech. Rep. BDV27-977-07, Florida Atlantic University (2016)
72. Wang, J., Gu, W., Zhu, J.: Design of an Autonomous Surface Vehicle Used for Marine Environment Monitoring. In: Proceedings of International Conference on Advanced Computer Control. pp. 405–409. Singapore (2009)
73. Wirtensohn, S., Reuter, J., Blaich, M., Schuster, M., Hamburger, O.: Modelling and Identification of a Twin Hull-based Autonomous Surface Craft. In: Proceedings of 18th International Conference on Methods and Models in Automation and Robotics (MMAR 2013). pp. 121–126. Midzyzdroje, Poland (2013)
74. Yan, D., Xiao, C., Wen, Y., et al.: Pod Propulsion Small Surface USV Heading Control Research. In: Proceedings of the 26th International Ocean and Polar Engineering Conference. pp. 630–635. 26 June-2 July, Rhodes, Greece (2016)

Review of Fuzzy Techniques in Maritime Shipping Operations

Jana Ries[1], Rosa G. González-Ramírez[2], Stefan Voß[3]

[1] Portsmouth Business School, University of Portsmouth, Portland Street,
Portsmouth, PO1 3DE, UK
[2] Faculty of Engineering and Applied Sciences, Universidad de Los Andes,
Monsenor Alvaro Portillo 12450, Santiago, Chile
[3] Institute of Information Systems, University of Hamburg, Von-Melle-Park 5,
Hamburg, 20146, Germany

jana.ries@port.ac.uk, rgonzalez@uandes.cl, stefan.voss@uni-hamburg.de

Abstract. Fuzzy Logic has found significant interest in the context of
global shipping networks due to its applicability to uncertain decision
making environments. Its use has been particularly important when solving location and equipment selection problems. While being applicable as
a stand-alone technique, Fuzzy Logic has become increasingly interesting
as an added feature within classic Operational Research techniques. This
paper gives an outline of the methodological relevance of Fuzzy Logic at
a strategic, tactical and operational level for maritime operations. In addition, a general classification of decision problems in maritime logistics
is presented, extending previous classifications in the literature to the
wider context of multiple port networks.

Keywords: Fuzzy Logic, Hybrid techniques, Maritime shipping, Container terminals.

1 Introduction

While the literature on solving decision problems in maritime operations spans
over the diverse field of operational research (Steenken et al. 2004, Stahlbock and
Voß 2008, Böse 2011), Multi-Critieria Decision Making (MCDM) forms an integral part by enabling the simultaneous or sequential consideration of multiple
objectives or a range of criteria. According to Hwang and Yoon (1981), MCDM
techniques can be classified into two main sets, multi-objective decision making
(MODM) and multi-attribute decision making (MADM). The latter are applied
to the ranking, selection or sorting of multi-dimensional alternatives. In maritime shipping, relevant MADM approaches found in the literature are Analytic
Hierarchy Process (AHP) introduced by Saaty (1977), Elimination and Choice
Expressing Reality (ELECTRE), (Benayoun *et al.*, 1966), Techniques for Preference by Similarity to the Ideal Solution (TOPSIS), (Hwang and Yoon, 1981),
and Evidential Reasoning and Fuzzy Logic (Zadeh, 1965). The latter has been

© Springer International Publishing AG 2017
T. Bektaş et al. (Eds.), ICCL 2017, LNCS 10572, pp. 253–269, 2017.
https://doi.org/10.1007/978-3-319-68496-3_17

specifically designed to address imprecision and uncertainty in decision problems. It is based on the use of fuzzy set theory which considers the association of linguistic terms with crisp numerical input. In combination with a rule base, it is referred to as a fuzzy inference system (FIS). In contrast to Fuzzy Logic, traditional MCDM techniques are generally challenged by the inability to address uncertainty with respect to imprecise information which has led to an increasing interest in applying Fuzzy Logic across multiple disciplines.

One of the key reasons for applying Fuzzy Logic in decision making are the existence of fuzziness in the information, rather than randomness in the problem context (Riedewald, 2011). Moreover, the author states that the non-existence of a suitable probability distribution or difficulties in obtaining one, as well as the availability of vague expert information are underpinning the suitability of Fuzzy Logic.

An increasing interest is observed, particularly, in embedding or combining fuzzy set theory into traditional strategies to address real-life uncertainty, e.g. in the problem context of maritime shipping. Hereby, the integration of Fuzzy Logic is distinguished into three concepts, namely classic stand-alone Fuzzy Logic approaches, embedded techniques and hybrid strategies. While stand-alone approaches are predominantly using fuzzy inference systems, embedded fuzzy techniques extend classic operational research strategies by featuring a fuzzy aspect within the problem formulation or the solution approach. Hybrid approaches use the combination of an FIS or embedded fuzzy techniques in combination with traditional non-fuzzy stand-alone approaches.

The goal of this paper is to provide a comprehensive review of decision making stages incorporating Fuzzy Logic to address maritime operations. To our best knowledge, this is the first review of its kind in this sector. The remainder of the paper is organized as follows. A classification of decision problems in maritime oprerations is introduced in Section 2. A review of literature studies that are investigated using a fuzzy philosophy in the context of a single port and a multiple port network are presented in Sections 3 and 4, respectively. Section 5 outlines a classification of proposed solution approaches using Fuzzy Logic and Section 6 outlines concluding remarks.

2   Decision Making in Maritime Operations

Over the years, international trade has significantly increased its volumes supported by national and international efforts from governments and private organizations. Investments in transport infrastructure and technology have also facilitated the exchange of goods in this global environment. However, a significant effort in ensuring competitiveness to allow for ongoing economic growth is required. International trade involves a great number of stakeholders both public and private interacting in global supply chains. The different interactions of stakeholders and the different procedures that need to be undertaken imply very complex procedures and operations at the different echelons of the port supply chain network. This also implies higher levels of uncertainty and variability.

Maritime transport accounts for the highest participation of worldwide foreign trade requiring an efficient maritime shipping network configuration as well as efficient cargo handling at each node of the network. Moreover, maritime ports form strategic nodes within global supply chain networks providing intermodal facilities and hence taking a more active role with respect to transshipments as well as the integration of their hinterland and foreland.

The decision making problems that arise in maritime operations have been classified into two main categories: problems that arise within a single container port and problems that arise within a network of muliple ports and other related terminals (e.g. depots, warehouses, etc.). Furthermore, decisions are also classified based on the decision level and the layout functions of the terminal (seaside, yard, gate). Bierwirth and Meisel (2010) provide a classification of problems at a container terminal focussing on strategic and operational aspects. Figure 1 uses an extended categorisation for the decision level by extending the set of strategic and operational decision problems to tactial ones. The key feature to differentiate between the individual sets of problems is the underlying time horizon. While no integrating links have been identified in the presented problem classification as done by Bierwirth and Meisel (2010), a broader view has been undertaken with the assumption that all problems are somewhat interlinked within a system that operates as integrated as a port. Furthermore, port networks have been considered with regards to decision making within the shipping network (seaside) and the hinterland network (landside).

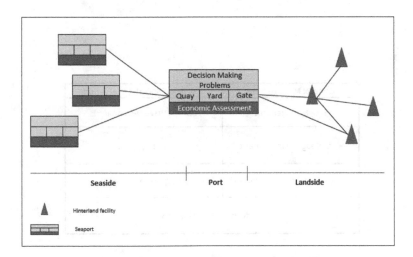

Fig. 1. Multiple Port Network (MPN) structure

Figure 2 illustrates the classification of decision making problems within a single container port or a network of container ports. Management evaluation and assessment tools have been considered in the review. Figure 3 outlines relevant assessment strategies, including maritime-specific considerations.

Decision level	Seaside	Yard	Gate/Landside/Hinterland
Strategic	Choice of Location, Equipment Selection, Layout and Network Design		
Tactical	Tactical Berth Allocation	Tactical Storage Space Allocation	Tactical Gate Capacity Planning
	Ship Routing and Fleet Design	Empty Container Inventory Management	Truck Arrival Forecasting
		Dispatching Policy Design	Rail Transport Planning
			Container Dwell Analysis
Operational	Berth Allocation	Storage Space Allocation and Container Stacking	Gate Management
	Quay Crane Assignment (Crane split)	Block Relocation & Marshalling Problems	
	Quay Crane Scheduling (Crane split)	Transportation Planning	Inter-Terminal Transport Planning and Scheduling
	Stowage Planning	Empty Container Management	
	Resource Planning and Scheduling		

Fig. 2. Decision Making Classification - adapted from Bierwirth and Meisel (2010)

General Management	Maritime Specific Evaluation
Risk Management	Competitiveness Analysis
Knowledge Management	Shipping Analysis
Human Resource Management	Port Development
Performance Evaluation	

Fig. 3. Economic Assessment techniques

3 Fuzzy Decision Making Within a Container Port

This section reviews existing studies in the context of decision making within container ports that use Fuzzy Logic to aid the modelling or solving strategy. The aim is to underpin the diverse applicability of Fuzzy Logic and to identify patterns with regards to the technique being suitable to particular problem structures.

3.1 Seaside Decision Making

At the seaside, fuzzy decision making has been predominantly considered for berth allocation and quay crane management. Hereby, the use of fuzzy techniques was introduced in studies for the berth allocation problem, see Lokuge et al. (2004), Lokuge and Alahakoon (2007), and Zhou et al. (2006). Furthermore, Vukadinovíc and Teodorovíc (1994) address berth allocation problems in the context of river ports introducing a fuzzy strategy to decide the number of operated barges at river ports. In the context of quay crane assignment and scheduling problems, Fuzzy Logic has been applied in selecting suitable equipment (Chao and Lin, 2011), automating quay crane operations (Yasunobu and Hasegawa, 1986; Liu et al., 2005) and the classic quay crane scheduling problem (Chung and Chan, 2013).

Taking an integrating approach, Exposito-Izquierdo et al. (2016) proposed fuzzy optimization models to take interdependencies of seaside decisions such as quay crane scheduling and the berth allocation problem into consideration.

3.2 Yard and Gate Decision Making

Similarly to the seaside operations, decisions in the yard have been addressed in the context of yard equipment and truck scheduling (Ng and Ge, 2006). Moreover, Fuzzy Logic has been applied to container handling (Jin et al., 2004 and Seyed-Hosseini et al., 2009), the management of handling and storage equipment (Homayouni and Tang, 2015), and truck or railyard dispatching (Yu and Zhang 2010, He et al. 2000). Kim et al. (2007) and Ries et al. (2014) apply Fuzzy Logic in the context of real-time decision making for container stacking policies, while Zheng et al. (2015) discuss the container loading problem from a multi-objective point of view. Valdés-González et al. (2014) propose an intelligent system for container stacking based on a Fuzzy Logic model, considering the case of the Port of Valparaiso in Chile.

On a strategic level, Fuzzy Logic has been applied to the selection of the most suitable equipment, i.e. yard cranes (Nooramin et al., 2012) at the gate.

3.3 Economic Assessment

Within a single port, economic assessment studies that employ Fuzzy Logic methodologies can be distinguished into the following General Management areas:

Port Performance and Forecasting

Park and Yeo (2012) and Chiu et al. (2014) propose a framework of evaluation for environmental sustainability. Duru et al. (2010) propose a bivariate long term fuzzy inference system to forecasting dry cargo freight rates. The service requirements of a dedicated container terminal are evaluated by a fuzzy analytic hierarchy process model by Hsu et al. (2015). The performance of container handling operations in the BIK container terminal has been analyzed by Jafari et al. (2013). They employ a Fuzzy TOPSIS approach. Gaonkar et al. (2011) model the decisive factors that affect transportation systems in the form of linguistic variables and perform a subjective operational reliability assessment. The authors extend their work by further proposing two fuzzy reliability models to model the uncertainty in estimating vessel's travel time (Gaonkar et al., 2013).

Risk Assessment

Risk assessment studies in the literature mainly investigate the well-known high level of uncertainty in the context of maritime shipping and its impact on container yard operations (Yang et al., 2009; Ding and Chou, 2012; Gaonkar et al., 2013; John et al., 2014; Mabrouki et al., 2014). However, some studies show a focus on the aspect of safety including terror threats (Yang et al., 2014) and the operational risk of a ship at sea due to, e.g., weather conditions (Balmat et al. 2009, Balmat et al. 2011). Saeidi et al. (2013) propose the application of a fuzzy TOPSIS approach for container terminal risk assessment.

Information Systems and Technology Evaluations

The business intelligence competencies of a port community system (PCS) in the organizations is evaluated by a fuzzy TOPSIS technique that employ fuzzy weights of the criteria and fuzzy judgements of the PCS to compute the evaluation scores and rankings by Ghazanfari et al. (2014). This framework can be used by ports to support decisions related to the selection of the requirements and attributes for implementing a PCS.

Knowledge and Human Resource Management

A different perspective is presented by Ung et al. (2006) who assess the impact of human error in the context of cargo handling in ports. Liang et al. (2012) have studied the integration of knowledge management into port operations.

4   Fuzzy Decision Making in Port Networks

Following up on the overview of studies using Fuzzy Logic for a single port, this section reviews existing literature for port networks that have applied Fuzzy Logic. Fuzzy contributions for decision making at the seaside are mainly associated with tactical and operational decision levels, while fuzzy contributions related to the hinterland are predominantly of strategic nature.

4.1   Seaside Decision Making

The main class of problems that has been addressed using Fuzzy Logic at the strategic level is *port selection*. Chou (2007, 2010), Onut et al. (2011), Yeo et al.

(2014), Wang et al. (2014), Ergin et al. (2015), Zavadskas et al. (2015) address the port selection problem for a set of existing transshipment port locations, container ports, deep water ports and bunkering ports. In an extension to analysing relevant economic criteria, Chou et al. (2010b) demonstrate the flexibility of Fuzzy Logic in a multi-criteria context such as selection problems by considering other criteria such as port facility conditions and volume of containers when evaluating the suitability of a port in an extension to their initial work.

The tactical and operational decisions in which fuzzy methodologies have been employed at the seaside for a MPN can be distinguished into the following key areas:

Empty Container Logistics

Chou (2009), Chou et al. (2010a) and Wang (2007) address the empty container location problem aiming to determine optimal numbers of empty containers at a port or between ports, focussing on the repositioning operations of containers. Tuljak-Suban and Twrdy (2015) propose a fuzzy multicriteria algorithm to evaluate the impact that the global crisis has on the number of excess empty containers at the terminals.

Network Design

Network design has been addressed by Chou (2010) whereby an evaluation of existing transshipment port locations is used to decide upon the planned set-up of a new transshipment port. Wibowo and Deng (2011) propose a decision support system for the ship selection problem, in which cargo shipping tasks are allocated to ships. They propose a rule based approach and the weighting process is modelled as a fuzzy knowledge base.

Ship Fleet Routing

With regards to shipping management, Chuang et al. (2010) investigate ship routing taking into consideration economic and operational parameters, while Wibowo and Deng (2010) consider the case of ship selection studying in particular the setting of criteria weights.

4.2   Hinterland Decision Making

On a strategic level, various decisions have been addressed using the concept of Fuzzy Logic, affecting the hinterland from a MPN perspective. Similarly to the location studies in the context of MPN seaside decisions, the literature shows the relevance of Fuzzy Logic in the selection of dry port and intermodal hub locations by Ka (2011) and Kayikci (2011), respectively. With regards to layout design, the work by Mi and Cheng (2013) investigates the layout of a container centre station by determining the number of lanes at the gate of a railway container centre. Finally, cargo allocation to ports has been investigated by Wanke and Bastos Falcão (2017) who provide an assessment of the cargo allocation patterns to the ports of Brazil. This has several policy implications such as, e.g., investments in the development of logistics corridors.

4.3 Port Performance and Efficiency

The majority of assessment studies take a maritime specific view, including competitiveness analyses of ports and shipping companies, and port development studies in combination with port performance evaluations. Ha et al., (2017) provide a hybrid multi-stakeholder framework for modelling port performance indicators. They define port performance indicators based on the interests and evaluations of several stakeholders of the port using a fuzzy rule-based algorithm and a utility technique. Another topic of interest in the literature is related to the efficiency of a port as discussed by Chao (2017) who provide a multi-stage data envelopment analysis model to evaluate the efficiency of global liner shipping companies. A fuzzy analytical hierarchical process is employed to prioritize the stages. Cho et al. (2007) propose the design of benchmarks for improving container port performance and analyse best practices in this matter. Liu et al. (2009) focus specifically on the aspect of agility in container terminal operations and maritime shipping companies.

In analysing competitiveness and using an evaluative strategy, Ran et al. (2008) and Denisis (2009) investigate the economic strength of container sea shipping, while Yeo and Song (2006) and Celik et al. (2009) investigate the competitiveness of a set of container ports. Within a more generall scope, the competitiveness of Taiwan's free trade ports is analysed by Chen et al. (2016).

Considering a supply chain perspective, Shao et al., (2016) propose a performance evaluation index system for the port supply chain. Their proposal is based on a balanced scorecard framework, and the evaluation model is constructed using a fuzzy-matter-element analysis.

Overall, Fuzzy Logic is shown to be of relevance in particular with regards to context-specific location and selection problems, as well as economic assessment studies.

5 Fuzzy Strategy Classification

In contrast to the previous section, the following classification distinguishes the fuzzy techniques in decision making for maritime shipping into stand-alone approaches, embedded and hybrid designs. The latter two groups make use of a range of operational research methods including meta-heuristics, mathematical programming, queueing theory and statistical techniques.

5.1 Stand-Alone Fuzzy Logic Approaches

In maritime shipping, Fuzzy Logic has been applied in different ways depending on the problem at hand. Vukadinovi and Teodori (1994) introduce a fuzzy strategy to decide on the number of operated barges at river ports. Wibowo and Deng (2011) consider the decision of the type of cargo ship given a particular operational task, while Liu et al. (2005) propose an adaptive control strategy that supports the selection of most suitable quay crane technology. Similarly,

Chou (2007) addresses the selection of transshipment ports from an economic perspective, while Chou (2010) considers the hub location selection problem for shipping liners. All the aforementioned studies focus on selection problems designed to handle equipment and develop strategies based on solving the port selection problem.

5.2   Embedded Fuzzy Logic Strategies

The main driver of AHP is the comparison between two criteria instead of assessing an overall set of criteria combined (Saaty 2000). Analytical Network Processing (ANP) can be seen as an extension of AHP utilizing a network for the consideration of critera, alternatives and goals instead of a hierarchy to integrate dependencies. Drawbacks of AHP include the occurrence of rank reversal, the potential extensive lengths of comparisons needed and the potential limitations of the used preference scale. The latter aspect is partially addressed by Fuzzy AHP (FAHP) which embeds the concept of fuzzy numbers into the assessment of decision maker comparisons, see e.g. Torfi et al. (2010). FAHP has been addressed by various performance evaluation studies including the modelling of green operation performance for ports by Chiu et al. (2014). A comparison of AHP and FAHP is found in Nooramin et al. (2012) on the equipment selection problem for yard cranes. The study showed that given the data provided by decision makers and experts, both approaches did not contradict each other and result in similar conclusions. Onut et al. (2011) apply FANP to the port selection problem based on a range of quantitative and qualitative criteria with the latter being modeled using Fuzzy sets. Ko (2009) applies FAHP to the selection of intermodal transport routes across countries with respect to, for example, interconnections, interoperability and legal frameworks.

TOPSIS belongs to the set of MCDA techniques which aims to identify the best alternative by means of evaluating the (Euclidean) distance to the positive-ideal (or ideal solution) and negative-ideal solutions, also referred to as Nadir point. While the required subjective input is limited, the main required information needed is the set of criteria-specific weights. Similar to FAHP, Fuzzy TOPSIS uses fuzzy numbers to transform performance rankings with the aim to overcome imprecise information. Ghazanfari et al. (2014) use the fuzzy TOPSIS technique to evaluate the business intelligence competencies of PCSs. Saeidi et al. (2013) proposed the application of a fuzzy TOPSIS approach for container terminal risk assessment. The performance of container handling operations in the BIK container terminal by a fuzzy TOPSIS approach is proposed by Jafari et al. (2013).

Heuristic and meta-heuristic strategies are popular concepts when addressing combinatorial optimization problems providing good solutions in reasonable time. In the problem-specific context of maritime shipping, Genetic Algorithms (GA) were found to be a prominent choice. Fuzzy Logic can be incorporated into a GA framework in different ways. Fuzzy control is one approach to the reactive strategy of parameter control during a run of a GA (Chung and Chan,

2013, Homayouni and Tang, 2015). Alternatively, Fuzzy Logic may be incorporated by applying fuzzy set theory to model input parameters dealing with any associated imprecision (Chuang et al., 2010).

Mathematical programming is a set of optimization techniques that are based on the structure of the model. It has been applied to the port allocation problem in combination with fuzzy set theory in a two-stage model addressing the demand split and final port destination (Chou et al. 2010b). The authors further address the empty container allocation problem using a fuzzy inventory model by applying fuzzy set theory to the input parameters, and solving it by means of the Kuhn Tucker conditions (Chou 2009, Chou et al., 2010a). Wang (2006) approaches the empty container allocation problem considering a mathematical programming approach incorporating dynamic, stochastic and fuzzy features. Seyed-Hosseini et al. (2009) propose a fuzzy mathematical programming model for the yard allocation problem. Valdés-González et al. (2014) propose a non-linear optimization problem in combination with a Fuzzy Logic system for the container stacking problem.

Agent-based models apply simulation to a network of interacting entities. In the context of maritime shipping BDI (Beliefs, Desires and Intention) agents have been applied in combination with fuzzy set theory to model fuzzy beliefs. For example, Lokuge et al. (2004) introduce a Adaptive Neuro Fuzzy Inference System (ANFIS) in the context of berth allocation. In an approach to solve the truck dispatching problem, an agent-based model is proposed in combination with a Fuzzy Contract Net Protocol (Fuzzy CNP) by Yu and Zhang (2010).

Mi and Cheng (2013) incorporate fuzzy set theory into the development of a queuing model to address the search for the number of lanes at the door of the domestic railway container centre station.

DELPHI provides a set of techniques to organize the communication process within a group in order to comprehend a complex problem. Wang et al. (2014) apply a combination of Delphi in combination with a fuzzy component that is used for the understanding of key performance indicators (KPI) within ports and Fuzzy TOPSIS to address the selection of bunkering ports for liner shipping companies. Cho et al. (2007) apply DELPHI in combination with FAHP to conduct a performance assessment of ports on the case of the Busan container terminal.

5.3   Hybrid Fuzzy Logic Strategies

Kayikci (2010) apply the combination of Artificial Neural Networks (ANN) together with FAHP to the facility location problem for intermodal freight logistics centres.

Other MCDA techniques that are applied in maritime shipping decision making are ELECTRE and Evidential Reasoning. ELECTRE is a family of MCDA techniques and was first mentioned in Benayoun et al. (1966) although Bernard Ron is widely known as the "father" of ELECTRE. It consists of two main stages, namely the development of outranking relations and an exploitation procedure.

Both stages depend on the problem at hand; sorting, ranking or choosing. Similarly to TOPSIS, ELECTRE requires less subjective information which given the non-required pairwise comparisons enables the consideration of a more extensive set of criteria. In the literature, ELECTRE frameworks incorporating fuzzy set theory can be found. However, this combination has not been applied in maritime shipping. Instead Ka (2011) applied the combination of ELECTRE and FAHP to the dry port location selection.

Factor analysis aims to understand the structure of multiple variables. This has been applied in the evaluation of green operations in a selection of a set of Korean ports together with a FIS in order to identify significant evaluating factors and identify a corresponding ranking of the considered ports, respectively (Park and Yeo, 2012). Similarly, Chao and Lin (2011) develop a decision support system to select quay crane technology by identifying relevant criteria using exploratory factor analysis followed by a FIS to initiate the selection.

A SWOT analysis is used to outline and analyse the Strengths, Weaknesses, Opportunities and Threats for an entity, concept or process. The economic feasibility of short sea shipping is investigated on the basis of a SWOT analysis together with the design of a fuzzy inference system to estimate site-specific costing by Denisis (2009). Liang et al. (2012) apply Fuzzy Logic in combination with Quality Function Deployment to prioritize knowledge management solutions.

6   Concluding Remarks

Fuzzy Logic has received substantial attention in addressing decision making in maritime shipping on the strategic, tactical and operational level. Its use has found particular importance in addressing location or equipment selection problems as well as suitable space selection for yard operations. In addition, it is possible to observe that Fuzzy Logic methodologies have been widely applied in economic assessment contributions such as port performance and efficiency, as well as risk management. From the perspective of a MPN, few contributions are found in which the port supply chain have been analysed under a more systemic vision. Neither inter-terminal transportation problems and truck drayage operations, nor the design and assessment of coordination mechanisms such as Truck appointment systems have been addressed in the literature using fuzzy techniques. Given the dynamic operations and the fact that huge numbers of stakeholders are employed, port performance indicators for landside productivity analysis can be developed using a Fuzzy Logic approach, such as the Fuzzy AHP and agent-based models to capture the interactions of the different stakeholders.

The key emerging research direction that has found increasing interest with the research community in maritime decision making is the increase of integration by developing solving strategies to address problems simultaneously. In practice, container terminal managers do not solve each problem individually and there are important trade-offs and interactions that have to be considered by the decision makers. Based on the papers reviewed, only Exposito-Izquierdo et al. (2016) address an integrated problem of berth allocation and quay crane scheduling implementing a fuzzy element. From the perspective of shipping line companies, some contributions can be found in terms of evaluating the efficiency of operations and empty container repositioning problems. However, in terms of fleet deployment and ship routing and scheduling, no contributions using Fuzzy Logic techniques are found in the literature.

The movement of containers between terminals and typically drayage operations is referred as the inter-terminal transportation problem (Tierney et al., 2014). None of the contributions in the literature has applied Fuzzy Logic techniques, representing a potential area for research as some of the decisions related to assignment of equipment and priorities may have fuzzy components. Other related problems focused on the coordination of truck arrivals at the gate of the port terminals have been also studied in the literature but none has applied Fuzzy Logic techniques in their analysis (Giuliano and Obrien, 2007; Zehendner and Feillet, 2014).

Another research gap that could be identified is related to the container stacking problems which is characterised by a high level of uncertainty which leads to a trade-off between the planning horizon and the risk of disruptions. Import containers, for example, may be assigned variable dwell times which makes it hard to determine the best location to reduce rehandles. Few contributions are found in the literature dealing with this type of problems using Fuzzy Logic.

In the same line of new technologies and the era of digitalization, further analysis can be studied in terms of evaluating the impacts of information systems such as PCS for the electronic data interchange. Furthermore, protocols such as blockchain and the use of sensors and IoT to support the business processes of ports and the exchange of information can be evaluated to estimate benefits and derive recommendations. In this regard, the use of Fuzzy Logic techniques to account for different factors and perspectives can be very useful.

In summary, the literature has shown that while Fuzzy Logic can address a problem in form of a stand-alone approach, it was shown that Fuzzy Logic has gained more importance when being integrated into well-performing operational research techniques within a highly dynamic environment such as port networks.

Being provocative, one can conclude that mainstream combinatorial optimization problem solving and Fuzzy Logic have not yet really found each other. Both sides seem not to utilise the other with appropriate recognition in turn. To overcome this situation is the most important future issue in this realm.

References

1. J.-F. Balmat, L. Frédéric, R. Maifret, and N. Pessel. Maritime risk assessment (marisa), a fuzzy approach to define an individual ship risk factor. *Ocean Engineering*, 36:1278–1286, 2009.
2. J.-F. Balmat, L. Frédéric, R. Maifret, and N. Pessel. A decision-making system to maritime risk assessment. *Ocean Engineering*, 38:171–176, 2011.

3. R. Benayoun, B. Roy, and B. Sussman. Electre: une méthode pour guider le choix en présence des point de vue multiples. Technical report, 1966.
4. C. Bierwirth and F. Meisel. A survey of berth allocation and quay crane scheduling problems in container terminals. *European Journal of Operations Research*, 202:615–627, 2010.
5. J.W. Böse (ed.) Operations research/computer science interfaces series. In *Handbook of terminal planning*. Springer, New York/Heidelberg, 2011.
6. M. Celik, S. Cebi, C. Kahraman, and I.D. Er. Application of axiomatic design and topsis methodologies uner fuzzy environment for proposing competitive strategies on turkish container ports in maritime transportation network. *Expert Systems with Applications*, 36:4541–4557, 2009.
7. S.-L. Chao. Integrating multi-stage data envelopment analysis and a fuzzy analytical hierarchical process to evaluate the efficiency of major global liner shipping companies. *Maritime Policy & Management*, pages 1–16, 2017.
8. S.-L. Chao and Y.-J. Lin. Evaluating advanced quay cranes in container terminals. *Transportation Research Part E: Logistics and Transportation Review*, 47(4): 432–445, 2011.
9. Chun-An Chen, Yi-Hui Chiang, Tzu-Kuang Hsu, and Jung-Wen Hsia. Strategies to increase the competitiveness of Taiwans free trade ports based on the fuzzy importance-performance analysis. *Asian Economic and Financial Review*, 6(11):681, 2016.
10. R.-H. Chiu, L.-H. Lin, and S.-C. Ting. Evaluation of green port factors and performance: A fuzzy AHP analysis. *Mathematical Problems in Engineering*, Article ID 802976, 2014.
11. G.-S. Cho, H.-S. Hwang, and K.-W. Lee. A performance analysis framework for the container terminals by DHP method. In *International Conference on Intelligent Manufacturing and Logistics Systems IML*, Kitakyushu, Japan, 2007.
12. C.-C. Chou. A fuzzy MCDM method for solving marine transshipment container port selection problems. *Applied Mathematics and Computation*, 186:435–444, 2007.
13. C.-C. Chou. Application of FMCDM model to selecting the hub location in the marine transportation: A case study in southeastern Asia. *Mathematical and Computer Modelling*, 51:791–801, 2010.
14. C.C. Chou. A fuzzy backorder inventory model and application to determining the optimal empty-container quantity at a port. *International Journal of Innovative Computing, Innovation and Control*, 5:4825–4824, 2009.
15. C.C. Chou, R.-H. Gou, C.-L. Tsai, C.-P. Tsou, M.-C. ad Wong, and H.-L. Yu. Application of a mixed fuzzy decision making and optimization programming model to the empty container allocation. *Applied Soft Computing*, 10:1071–1079, 2010a.
16. C.C. Chou, F.-T. Kuo, R.-H. Gou, Tsao. C.-L., C.-P. Wong, and M.-C. Tsou. Application of a combined fuzzy multiple criteria decision making and optimization programming model to the container transportation demand split. *Applied Soft Computing*, 10:1080–1086, 2010b.
17. T.-N. Chuang, C.-T. Lin, J.-Y. Kung, and M.-D. Lin. Planning the route of container ships: A fuzzy genetic approach. *Expert Systems with Applications*, 37:2948–2956, 2010.
18. S.H. Chung and F.T.S. Chan. A workload balancing genetic algorithm for the quay crane scheduling problem. *International Journal of Production Research*, 51:4820–4834, 2013.

19. A. Denisis. *An economic feasibility study of short sea shipping including the estimation of externalities with fuzzy logic.* PhD thesis, University of Michigan, 2009.

20. J.F. Ding and Chien-Chang Chou. A fuzzy MCDM model to evaluate investment risk of location selection for container terminals. *WSEAS Transactions on Information Science and Applications,* 9(10):295–304, 2012.

21. O. Duru, E. Bulut, and S. Yoshid. Bivariate long term fuzzy time series forecasting of dry cargo freight rates. *The Asian Journal of Shipping and Logistics,* 26(2):205–223, 2010.

22. Ayfer Ergin, İpek Eker, and Güler Alkan. Selection of container port using electre technique. *Management,* 4(4):268–275, 2015.

23. C. Expósito-Izquiero, E. Lalla-Ruiz, T. Lamata, B. Melián-Batista, and J. M. Moreno-Vega. Fuzzy optimization models for seaside port logistics: berthing and quay crane scheduling. In *Computational Intelligence,* pages 323–343. Springer, 2016.

24. R.S.P. Gaonkar, M. Xie, K.M. Ng and M.S. Habibullah. Subjective operational reliability assessment of maritime transportation system. *Expert Systems with Applications,* 38:13835–13846, 2011.

25. R.S.P. Gaonkar, M. Xie, and X. Fu. Reliability estimation of maritime transportation: A study of two fuzzy reliability models. *Ocean Engineering,* 72:1–10, 2013.

26. M. Ghazanfari, S. Rouhani, and M. Jafari. A fuzzy topsis model to evaluate the business intelligence competencies of port community systems. *Polish Maritime Research,* 21(2):86–96, 2014.

27. G. Giuliano and T. O'Brien. Reducing port-related truck emissions: The terminal gate appointment system at the ports of Los Angeles and Long Beach. *Transportation Research Part D: Transport and Environment,* 12:460–473, 2007.

28. M.-H. Ha, Z. Yang, T. Notteboom, A.K.Y Ng, and M.-W. Heo. Revisiting port performance measurement: A hybrid multi-stakeholder framework for the modelling of port performance indicators. *Transportation Research Part E: Logistics and Transportation Review,* 103:1–16, 2017.

29. S. He, R. Song, and S.S. Chaudhry. Fuzzy dispatching model and genetic algorithms for railyards operations. *European Journal of Operational Research,* 124:307–331, 2000.

30. S. M. Homayouni and S. Hong. A fuzzy genetic algorithm for scheduling of handling/storage equipment in automated container terminals. *International Journal of Engineering and Technology,* 7(6):497–501, 2015.

31. W.-K.K. Hsu, H.-F. Yu, and S.-H.S. Huang. Evaluating the service requirements of dedicated container terminals: a revised ipa model with fuzzy ahp. *Maritime Policy & Management,* 42(8):789–805, 2015.

32. C.L. Hwang and K. Yoon. *Multiple Attribute Decision Making: Methods and Applications.* Springer, New York, 1981.

33. H. Jafari, N. Saeidi, A. Kaabi, E. Noshadi, and H. R. Hallafi. Analysis of performance in container handling operation by using fuzzy TOPSIS method. *International Review of Basic and Applied Sciences,* 1(6):148–155, 2013.

34. C. Jin, X. Liu, and P. Gao. An intelligent simulation method based on artificial neural network for container yard operation. In *Advances in Neural Networks - ISNN 2004, Lecture Notes in Computer Science 3174,* pages 904 – 911, 2004.

35. A. John, D. Paraskevadakis, A. Bury, Z. Yang, R. Riahi, and J. Wang. An integrated fuzzy risk assessment for seaport operations. *Safety Science,* 68:180–194, 2014.

36. B. Ka. Application of fuzzy AHP and ELECTRE to China Dry port location selection. *The Asian Journal of Shipping and Logistics*, 27:331–335, 2011.

37. Y. Kayikci. A conceptual model for intermodal freight logistics centre location decisions. *Procedia-Social and Behavioral Sciences*, 2:6297–6311, 2010.

38. Y.H. Kim, T. Park, and K.R. Ryu. Dynamic weight adjustment for developing a stacking policy for automated container terminals. In *International Conference on Intelligent Manufacturing and Logistics Systems (IML 2007)*, pages 26–28, Kitakyushu, Japan, 2007.

39. H.J. Ko. A dss approach with fuzzy ahp to facilitate international multimodal transportation network. *KMI International Journal of Maritime Affairs and Fisheries*, 1:51–70, 2009.

40. G.S. Liang, J.-F. Ding, and C.-K. Wang. Applying fuzzy quality function deployment to prioritize solutions of knowledge management for an international port in Taiwan. *Knowledge-Based Systems*, 33:83–91, 2012.

41. D. Liu, J. Yi, D. Zhao, and W. Wang. Adaptive sliding mode fuzzy control for a two-dimensional overhead crane. *Mechatronics*, 15(5):505–522, 2005.

42. W. Liu, H. Xu, and X. Zhao. Agile service oriented shipping companies in the container terminal. *Transport*, 24(2):143–153, 2009.

43. P. Lokuge and D. Alahakoon. Improving the adaptability in automated vessel scheduling in container ports using intelligent software agents. *European Journal of Operational Research*, 177:1985–2015, 2007.

44. P. Lokuge, D. Alahakoon, and P. Dissanayake. Collaborative neuro-BDI agents in container terminals. In *18th International Conference on Advanced Information Networking and Application, AINA*, pages 155–158, 2004.

45. C. Mabrouki, F. Bentaleb, and A. Mousrij. A decision support methodology for risk management within a port terminal. *Safety Science*, 63:124–132, 2014.

46. X.-Y. Mi and G. Cheng. Railway container center door lane analysis based on -cut theory. *Procedia - Social and Behavioral Sciences*, 96(6):2425–2430, 2013.

47. W.C. Ng and Y. Ge. Scheduling landside operations of a container terminal using a fuzzy heuristic. *IEEE Industrial Conference on Industrial Informatics*, 2006.

48. A. S. Nooramin, M. Kiani, M. Mansoor, A. R. Jahromi, and J. Sayareh. Comparison of ahp and fahp for selecting yard gantry cranes in marine container terminals. *Journal of the Persian Gulf (Marine Science)*, 3(7):50–70, 2012.

49. S. Onut, U.R. Tuzkaya, and E. Torun. Selecting container port via a fuzzy ANP-based approach: A case study in the Marmara region, Turkey. *Transport Policy*, 18:181–193, 2010.

50. J.-Y. Park and G.-T Yeo. An evaluation of greenness of major Korean ports: A fuzzy set approach. *The Asian Journal of Shipping and Logistics*, 28:67–82, 2012.

51. W. Ran, Z. Xu, and Z. Weihong. Analysis on comprehensive strength of Chinese coastal container shipping company based on genetic fuzzy clustering. In *Proceedings of the IEEE International Conference on Automation and Logistics*, pages 2214–2219, Qingdao, China, 2008.

52. F. Riedewald. *Comparison of deterministic, stochastic and fuzzy logic uncertainty modelling for capacity extension projects of DI/WFI pharmaceutical plant utilities with variable/dynamic demand*. PhD thesis, University College Cork, Ireland, 2011.

53. J. Ries, R.G. González-Ramírez, and P. Miranda. A fuzzy logic model for the container stacking problem at container terminals. In *International Conference in Computational Logistics - ICCL 2014, Lecture Notes in Computer Science 8760*, pages 93–111. Springer.

54. T. Saaty. A scaling method for priorities in hierarchical structures. *Journal of Mathematical Psychology*, 15:234–281, 1977.

55. N. Saeidi, A. Askari, and H. Jafari. Application of a fuzzy topsis approach based on subjective and objective weights in the container terminals risks assessment. *Applied Mathematics in Engineering, Management and Technology*, 1(4):2013, 2013.

56. S.-M. Seyed-Hosseini and K. K. D. Fuzzy container allocation problem in maritime terminal. *Journal of Industrial Engineering and Management*, 2(2):323, 2009.

57. W. Shao, Y. Du, and S. Lu. Performance evaluation of port supply chain based on fuzzy-matter-element analysis. *Journal of Intelligent & Fuzzy Systems*, 31(4):2159–2165, 2016.

58. R. Stahlbock and S. Voß. Operations research at container terminals: a literature update. *OR Spectrum*, 30:1–52, 2008.

59. D. Steenken, S. Voß, and R. Stahlbock. Container terminal operation and operations research - a classification and literature review. *OR Spectrum*, 26:3–49, 2004.

60. K. Tierney, S. Voß, and R. Stahlbock. A mathematical model of inter-terminal transportation. *European Journal of Operational Research*, 235:448–460, 2014.

61. F. Torfi, R.Z. Farahani, and S. Rezapour. Fuzzy AHP to determine the relative weights of evaluation criteria and fuzzy topsis to rank the alternatives. *Applied Soft Computing*, 10:520–528, 2010.

62. D. Tuljak-Suban and E. Twrdy. Fuzzy empty containers excess estimation as an economic indicatorthe case of the north adriatic port system. *Maritime Policy & Management*, 42(8):759–775, 2015.

63. S.T. Ung, V. Williams, H.S. Chen, S. Bonsall, and J. Wang. Human error assessment and management in port operations using fuzzy ahp. *Marine Technology Society Journal*, 40:73–86, 2006.

64. H. Valdés-González, L. Reyes-Bozo, E. Vyhmeister, J. L. Salazar, J. P. Sepúlveda, and M. Mosca-Arestizábal. Container stacking revenue management system: A fuzzy-based strategy for Valparaiso port. *Dyna*, 82(190):38–45, 2015.

65. K. Vukadinović and D. Teodorovíc. A fuzzy approach to the vessel dispatching problem. *European Journal of Operational Research*, 76:155–164, 1994.

66. B. Wang. Research about the fuzzy optimization of repositioning of empty container on sea-bound. *Port Engineering Technology*, 2007.

67. Y. Wang, G.-T. Yeo, and A.K.Y. Ng. Choosing optimal bunkering ports for liner shipping companies: A hybrid fuzzy-delphi-topsis approach. *Transport Policy*, 35:358–365, 2014.

68. P. Wanke and B. B. Falcão. Cargo allocation in Brazilian ports: An analysis through fuzzy logic and social networks. *Journal of Transport Geography*, 60:33–46, 2017.

69. S. Wibowo and H. Deng. A fuzzy screening system for effectively solving maritime shipping problems. Coimbra, Portugal, 2010.

70. S. Wibowo and H. Deng. Intelligent decision support for criteria weighting in multicriteria analysis for evaluating and selecting cargo ships under uncertainty. In *International MultiConference of Engineers and Computer Scientists, IMECS*, Hong Kong, 2011.

71. Z. Yang, A.K.Y. Ng, and J. Wang. A new risk quantification approach in port facility security assessment. *Transportation Research Part A: Policy and Practice*, 59:72–90, 2014.

72. Z.L. Yang, S. Bonsall, and J. Wang. Use of hybrid multiple uncertain attribute decision making techniques in safety management. *Expert Systems with Applications*, 36:1569–1586, 2009.

73. S. Yasunobu and T. Hasegawa. Evaluation of an automatic container crane operation system based on predictive fuzzy control. *Control Theory and Advanced Technology*, 2(3):419–432, 1986.
74. G.-T. Yeo and D.-W. Song. An application of the hierarchical fuzzy process to container port competition: Policy and strategic implications. *Transportation*, 33:409–422, 2006.
75. Gi-Tae Yeo, Adolf KY Ng, Paul Tae-Woo Lee, and Zaili Yang. Modelling port choice in an uncertain environment. *Maritime Policy & Management*, 41(3):251–267, 2014.
76. M. Yu, S. Wang, and C. Yun. A dispatching method for trucks at container terminal by using fuzzy-cnp concept. In *IIEEE International Conference on Logistics Engineering and Intelligent Transportation Systems, LEITS*, pages 1–4, Wuhan, 2010.
77. L.A. Zadeh. Fuzzy sets. *Information and Control*, 8:338–353, 1965.
78. Edmundas Kazimieras Zavadskas, Zenonas Turskis, and Vygantas Bagočius. Multi-criteria selection of a deep-water port in the eastern baltic sea. *Applied Soft Computing*, 26:180–192, 2015.
79. E. Zehendner and D. Feillet. Benefits of a truck appointment system on the service quality of inland transport modes at a multimodal container terminal. *European Journal of Operational Research*, 235:461–469, 2014.
80. J.-N. Zheng, C.-F. Chien, and M. Gen. Multi-objective multi-population biased random-key genetic algorithm for the 3-D container loading problem. *Computers & Industrial Engineering*, pages 80–87, 2015.
81. P. Zhou, Kang H., and Li L. A fuzzy model for scheduling handling equipments handling outbound container in terminal. In *Sixth World Congress on Intelligent Control and Automation*, 2006.

A Relax-and-Fix Algorithm for a Maritime Inventory Routing Problem

Marcelo W. Friske$^{(\boxtimes)}$ and Luciana S. Buriol

Departamento de Informática - Universidade Federal do Rio Grande do Sul,
Porto Alegre, Brazil
{mwfriske,buriol}@inf.ufrgs.br

Abstract. This work presents a relax-and-fix algorithm for solving a class of single product Maritime Inventory Routing Problem. The problem consists in routing and scheduling a heterogeneous fleet of vessels to supply a set of ports, keeping inventory at production and consumption ports between lower and upper limits. Two sets of constraints are proposed both for tightening the problem relaxation and for obtaining better integer solutions. Four MIP-based local searches to improve the solution provided by the relax-and-fix approach are presented. Computational experiments were carried out on instances of the MIRPLIB, showing that our approach is able to solve most instances in a reasonable amount of time, and to find new best-known solutions for two instances. A new dataset has been created by removing the clustered characteristics of ports from the original instances, and the effectiveness of our method was tested in these more general instances.

Keywords: Maritime Inventory Routing Problem, Relax-and-Fix, MIP-Based Local Search

1 Introduction

Maritime transportation is the major mode of transportation used when considering large quantities of goods, mainly bulk products. The Maritime Inventory Routing Problem (MIRP) arises when one has to manage both the scheduling of vessels and the inventories at ports. It can be considered a variant of the Inventory Routing Problem, which combines vehicle routing and inventory management. However, MIRP deals with special features of maritime transportation.

This work considers the single product MIRP model proposed by [12]. Given a finite planning horizon, a fleet of heterogeneous vessels, and a set of ports, one must decide for each vessel which ports will be visited, when they will be visited, and the amount of product that should be loaded or discharged when a vessel operates at each port. In this problem variant, ports are grouped in geographical regions, such that each region has only production (loading) or consumption (discharging) ports. Each port has fixed storage and operating capacities, while production/consumption rates may vary along the planning horizon. The inventory of ports is supplied by vessels, and by simplified spot markets when

T. Bektaş et al. (Eds.), ICCL 2017, LNCS 10572, pp. 270–284, 2017.
https://doi.org/10.1007/978-3-319-68496-3_18

necessary. Vessels can differ by capacity, speed, and cost per sailed kilometer. The problem is classified as deep-sea, the case in which vessels spend most of the time traveling than operating at ports. The objective is to maximize the revenue of delivered products at consumption ports, subtracting travelling, operating, and spot market costs, and respecting inventory bounds of vessels and ports.

There are many opportunities for optimization considering maritime transportation. The reviews [6, 5] present a good overview of works involving optimization of maritime transportation. In [12] a good review on MIRPs models and solution methods is presented, besides proposing a core model with additional features and side constraints. They also proposed a benchmark library for the problem, called MIRPLIB [1].

The work of [4] was one of the pioneers in combining inventory managing and routing of vessels. Besides presenting an arc-flow formulation for the problem of transporting ammonia. For this problem, a path-flow formulation with coupling constraints embedded in a Branch-and-Price algorithm was proposed.

Next, we present some works that deal with deterministic and single product MIRPs. [2] proposed a discrete time fixed-charge network flow model (FCNF) for a short-sea MIRP, with variable consumption and production rates at ports. New valid inequalities generalized from the lot-sizing literature were proposed. Also, branching priorities were used for improving the search on the branch-and-bound algorithm. The FCNF model was capable of providing tight bounds and obtaining optimal solutions faster than the original formulation. [8] proposed a branch-and-price guided search for solving an extended MIRP formulation. The approach has the advantage that its components are not problem-dependent. Six local search schemes were proposed for improving the solution. Experiments have shown that the method can produce high-quality solutions quickly, even being generic. [14] proposed a framework for the inventory routing problem, which can accommodate practical features. A case study on a MIRP was done considering draft limits and minimum transport cargo for each vessel. Cuts, branching strategies, and a large neighborhood search were presented for finding optimal solutions. [9] studied MIRP models with continuous and discrete time formulations, with one or parallel docks. Experiments thereof demonstrated that continuous-time formulations can be more efficient than a discrete time model. [3] worked on a MIRP for transporting feed produced at a factory to salmon farmings in the Norwegian cost. The proposed mathematical model was reformulated for improving branch-and-bound efficiency and tightening the bounds by valid inequalities. Additionally, two matheuristics based on practical aspects of the problem were proposed for obtaining feasible solutions and for improving the current solution. [11] proposed a two-stage algorithm based on Benders decomposition for solving the deep-sea MIRP proposed in [12]. An extended time-space network was used for accommodating practical assumptions on the problem. Improvements on solutions were obtained by MIP-based local searches, branching strategies, valid inequalities, and lazy constraints. The proposed approach provided tight lower bounds and high-quality solutions in a reasonable computational time. [10] presented different matheuristics and hybrid approaches for solving a long-horizon

MIRP. Several computational experiments were performed on a set of MIRPLIB instances, and results provided new best-known values for 26 instances.

We solve a MIRP making use of a Relax-and-Fix (R&F) algorithm. R&F is a matheuristic that splits the problem into intervals or subproblems, solving them sequentially. In the first iteration, only integer variables of the first interval keep the integrality constraints. The remaining variables are relaxed. The model is then solved by a MIP solver for obtaining a partial solution. After solved, all or a part of the integer variables are fixed to their current values, and the integrality constraints are reintroduced to the variables of the next interval, resulting in a new subproblem to be solved. The algorithm iterates until there is no relaxed interval left. This technique can decompose the problem in different manners. When considering a time decomposition, the R&F has similarities with the *rolling horizon heuristic*. An overview of R&F can be found in [13].

The work of [15] applies an extended R&F algorithm on a MIRP variant, known as LNG inventory routing problem. The authors consider a structure called *end-block*, that initially simplifies or ignores part of the model for reducing the number of linear variables to be solved repeatedly.

This work presents a R&F algorithm based on the work of [15] for solving the MIRP variant presented in [12]. A set of constraints is built based on assumptions of [11], while we have proposed another set of constraints based on a assumption. They are used for tightening relaxation bounds and improving the efficiency of the algorithm. Also, four MIP-based local searches are proposed either for improving feasible solutions or removing infeasibilities. Our objective is to provide a more general method for solving MIRP instances with planning horizons up to 60 days. Although not outperforming the results of [11], our method provided new best-known values for two instances. Also, we modified the original instances in order to show that the solution approach remains effective when ports are not grouped in regions.

The remainder of this work is organized as follows. Section 2 presents the MIRP formulation and the additional constraints. In Section 3 we describe the solution method used in our computational experiments, which are presented in Section 4. Finally, Section 5 presents conclusions and future works.

2   Problem Formulation

We use the arc-flow MIRP model from [11], which is presented here for the sake of completeness. Let $\mathcal{V}$ be the set of vessels, $\mathcal{J}$ the set of ports, and $\mathcal{T}$ the set of time periods, where $T = |\mathcal{T}|$. Ports are split in subsets $\mathcal{J}^{\mathrm{P}}$ for production or loading ports ($\Delta_j = 1$), and $\mathcal{J}^{\mathrm{C}}$ for consuming or discharging ports ($\Delta_j = -1$), where $\mathcal{J} = \mathcal{J}^{\mathrm{P}} \cup \mathcal{J}^{\mathrm{C}}$, and $\mathcal{J}^{\mathrm{P}} \cap \mathcal{J}^{\mathrm{C}} = \emptyset$. Ports are grouped in production regions $\mathcal{R}^{\mathrm{P}}$ and discharging regions $\mathcal{R}^{\mathrm{C}}$, such that $\mathcal{R} = \mathcal{R}^{\mathrm{P}} \cup \mathcal{R}^{\mathrm{C}}$. The discrete time model is built under a port-time structure, composed of a set of nodes and a set of directed arcs. Each vessel $v \in \mathcal{V}$ has its own arc set $\mathcal{A}^v$, while the nodes set is shared by all vessels. Regular port-time nodes $n = (j, t) \in \mathcal{N}$ represent a possible operation (loading or discharging) by a vessel at port $j \in \mathcal{J}$

at time $t \in \mathcal{T}$. Node set $\mathcal{N}_{0,T+1}$ is composed by set $\mathcal{N}$, a source node n_0, and a sink node n_{T+1}, which represent the starting and ending positions of each vessel in the system, respectively. Each arc set $\mathcal{A}^v$ is composed by five arc types. A source arc $a = (n_0, (j,t))$ links the source node to the initial vessel position, arriving at port j at time period t. Traveling arcs $a = ((j_1,t_1),(j_2,t_2))$ represent a voyage that departs from port j_1 at time t_1 and arrives at port j_2 at time t_2, such that $j_1 \neq j_2$. Waiting arcs $a = ((j,t),(j,t+1))$ represent that the vessel remains at the same port j at times t and $t+1$. Sink arcs $a = ((j,t),n_{T+1})$ link a regular node to a sink node, for vessels that exit the system at port j at time t. Arc $a = (n_0, n_{T+1})$ links source and sink nodes for unused vessels. We ignore this arc as the instances proposed in [12] consider that all vessels are used.

Binary variable x_a^v is set to 1 if vessel v travels along arc $a \in \mathcal{A}^v$, and binary variable z_{jt}^v is 1 if vessel v operates (discharge or load product) at port j in time t. Continuous variables s_{jt} and s_t^v represent the inventory of port j and vessel v at the end of time period t, respectively. Variables f_{jt}^v represent the amount loaded or discharged at port j in time period t by vessel v. Variable α_{jt} is the amount of product sold to or bought from a spot market by port j at time period t. The single product MIRP can be modeled as follows:

$$\max \sum_{j \in \mathcal{J}^C} \sum_{t \in \mathcal{T}} \sum_{v \in \mathcal{V}} R_{jt} f_{jt}^v - \sum_{v \in \mathcal{V}} \sum_{a \in \mathcal{A}^v} C_a^v x_a^v - \sum_{j \in \mathcal{J}} \sum_{t \in \mathcal{T}} \sum_{v \in \mathcal{V}} (t\epsilon_z) z_{jt}^v - \sum_{j \in \mathcal{J}} \sum_{t \in \mathcal{T}} P_{jt} \alpha_{jt} \quad (1)$$

$$\text{s.t.} \quad \sum_{a \in FS_n^v} x_a^v - \sum_{a \in RS_n^v} x_a^v = \begin{cases} +1 & \text{if } n = n_0, \\ -1 & \text{if } n = n_{T+1}, \\ 0 & \text{if } n \in \mathcal{N}, \end{cases} \forall n \in \mathcal{N}_{0,T+1}, v \in \mathcal{V} \quad (2)$$

$$s_{jt} = s_{j,t-1} + \Delta_j \left(d_{jt} - \sum_{v \in \mathcal{V}} f_{jt}^v - \alpha_{jt} \right), \quad \forall n = (j,t) \in \mathcal{N} \quad (3)$$

$$s_t^v = s_{t-1}^v + \sum_{\{n=(j,t) \in \mathcal{N}\}} \Delta_j f_{jt}^v, \quad \forall t \in \mathcal{T}, v \in \mathcal{V} \quad (4)$$

$$\sum_{v \in \mathcal{V}} z_{jt}^v \leq B_j, \quad \forall n = (j,t) \in \mathcal{N} \quad (5)$$

$$z_{jt}^v \leq \sum_{a \in RS_n^v} x_a^v, \quad \forall n = (j,t) \in \mathcal{N}, v \in \mathcal{V} \quad (6)$$

$$s_t^v \geq Q^v x_a^v, \quad \forall v \in \mathcal{V}, a \in \mathcal{A}_{PC}^v, \quad (7)$$

$$s_t^v \leq Q^v (1 - x_a^v), \quad \forall v \in \mathcal{V}, a \in \mathcal{A}_{CP}^v, \quad (8)$$

$$\sum_{t \in \mathcal{T}} \alpha_{jt} \leq \alpha_j^{\max}, \quad \forall j \in \mathcal{J} \quad (9)$$

$$0 \leq \alpha_{jt} \leq \alpha_{jt}^{\max}, \quad \forall j \in \mathcal{J}, t \in \mathcal{T} \quad (10)$$

$$F_{jt}^{\min} z_{jt}^v \leq f_{jt}^v \leq F_{jt}^{\max} z_{jt}^v, \quad \forall n = (j,t) \in \mathcal{N}, v \in \mathcal{V} \quad (11)$$

$$S_j^{\min} \leq s_{jt} \leq S_j^{\max}, \quad \forall n = (j,t) \in \mathcal{N} \quad (12)$$

$$0 \leq s_t^v \leq Q^v, \quad \forall v \in \mathcal{V}, t \in \mathcal{T} \quad (13)$$

$$x_a^v \in \{0,1\}, \quad \forall v \in \mathcal{V}, a \in A^v; \quad z_{jt}^v \in \{0,1\}, \quad \forall n = (j,t) \in \mathcal{N}, v \in \mathcal{V}. \quad (14)$$

Objective function (1) maximizes the revenue R_{jt} of the unloaded product at discharging ports, subtracting arc costs C_a^v used by each vessel. The third term is an additional value that induces vessels to operate as soon and as few times as possible. The penalization value P_{jt} for using spot markets is accounted in the last term of the equation. Constraints (2) refer to the flow balance of vessels along the nodes, where FS_n^v and RS_n^v refer to the set of outgoing and incoming arcs associated with node $n \in \mathcal{N}_{0,T+1}$ and vessel $v \in \mathcal{V}$, respectively. Constraints (3) define ports inventory balance at the end of each time period, where d_{jt} represents the production/consumption rate of port j in time period t. Constraints (4) refer to the vessels inventory balance at the end of each time period. Constraints (5) limit to B_j (berth limit) the number of vessels that can operate simultaneously at a node. Constraints (6) require that a vessel can only operate at a node if it is actually at that node. Constraints (7) require that the vessels must travel at the maximum capacity when traveling from a loading port to a discharging port or to the sink node, where $\mathcal{A}_{PC}^v = \{a = ((j_1, t), (j_2, t')) \in \mathcal{A}^v : j_1 \in \mathcal{J}^P, j_2 \in \mathcal{J}^C \cup \{n_{T+1}\}\}$. Constraints (8) require that a vessel must be empty when traveling from a discharging port to a loading port or to a sink node, where $\mathcal{A}_{CP}^v = \{a = ((j_1, t), (j_2, t')) \in \mathcal{A}^v : j_1 \in \mathcal{J}^C, j_2 \in \mathcal{J}^P \cup \{n_{T+1}\}\}$. Constraints (10) limit to α_{jt}^{max} the amount of products sold to or bought from spot markets by a port in each time period, and (9) limit to α_j^{max} the cumulative amount for using spot markets. Constraints (11) impose that the amount loaded/discharged by a vessel at a port must lie between F_{jt}^{min} and F_{jt}^{min} in each time period. Constraints (12) assure that ports inventory must lie between lower S_j^{min} and upper S_j^{max} limits in each time period. Constraints (13) limit the vessel inventory to its capacity Q^v. Finally, (14) restricts the variables x_a^v and z_{jt}^v to be binaries.

2.1   Additional Constraints

In this section we consider simplifying assumptions that lead to two sets of constraints for the presented MIRP. They are useful for tightening the lower bound and for accelerating the relax-and-fix approach. We proposed the first set based on the following assumption: considering a small vessel, which capacity Q^v is less or equal to F_{jt}^{max} for some $j \in \mathcal{J}$ and $t \in \mathcal{T}$, then it can fully load or discharge in just one time period at port j. Equation (15) imposes that if a vessel operates at a port in a time period, it must leave the port in the same time period. This assumption allows a vessel to be available for more voyages, avoiding that it waits at a port after finishing its operation.

$$\sum_{a \in FS_{n'}^v} x_a^v = z_{jt}^v > \forall j \in \mathcal{J}, t \in \mathcal{T}, v \in \mathcal{V} : Q^v < F_{jt}^{max} . \tag{15}$$

In Eq. (15), $FS_{n'}^v \subseteq FS_n^v$ is the set of outgoing arcs from node $n = (j, t)$ for vessel v which arrives at a port of different type, or arrives at the sink node.

One may ask if constraints (15) do not cut a possible optimal solution in which a small vessel may split its inventory, operating consecutively at two ports of the same region. However, fractioning a vessel inventory between two or more ports in a region means that a smaller amount will be discharged or loaded at these ports. Therefore, the stocks at ports will reach their lower/upper limits sooner, requiring that another vessel operates at these ports sooner, too. This "premature" visit incurs additional costs and may be avoided by forbidding split inventory of small vessels.

The second set of constraints is based on the "Two-port-with-no-revisit" assumption of [11]. It assumes that if a vessel arrives at a port in some region, then: i) it will visit at most one more port before leaving the region; ii) once it leaves the port, this port will not be revisited by the vessel before leaving the region. [11] developed an augmented time-space network that easily implements this assumption. However, implementing the assumption directly on model (1) requires additional sets of binary variables and side constraints that increase substantially the size of the model, making it more difficult to solve. We then propose the constraints below:

$$\sum_{j\in\mathcal{J}_r}\sum_{t\in\mathcal{T}}\sum_{a\in FS^v_{n\text{intra}}} x^v_a \leq \sum_{j\in\mathcal{J}^r}\sum_{t\in\mathcal{T}}\sum_{a\in RS^v_{n\text{inter}}} x^v_a, \ \forall v\in\mathcal{V}, r\in\mathcal{R}\ . \qquad (16)$$

In Eq. (16), $\mathcal{J}^r$ is the set of ports of a region $r \in \mathcal{R}$, $FS^v_{n\text{intra}}$ is the set of intra-regional arcs of vessel v that depart from node n, and $RS^v_{n\text{inter}}$ is the set of inter-regional arcs of vessel v that arrives at node n. Constraints (16) ensure that the number of selected intra-regional arcs will be less or equal to the number of entering arcs for each region and each vessel. The constraint is partially effective when considering more than one visit to region r of vessel v. This occurs because there may exist a visit that uses no intra-regional arcs (a vessel arrives at some port in the region, operates, and departs to another region), and a second visit that uses more than one intra-regional arc, violating the assumption but not the constraints (16). This occurs because the constraints do not consider each visit of a vessel to a region but the entire time horizon.

3   The Proposed Relax-and-Fix Approach

In the R&F, the planning horizon $\mathcal{T}$ is divided in p intervals, where $\mathcal{I} = \{1, \ldots, p\}$ is the set of all intervals. Each interval $i \in \mathcal{I}$ corresponds to all variables and constraints that have a time index $t \in \{\frac{T}{p}(i-1), \ldots, \frac{T}{p}i\}$, such that $T \bmod p = 0$.

Figure 1 illustrates the first, second, and last iterations of the R&F, considering a network structure for a single vessel, divided in $p = 4$ intervals. At the first iteration ($it = 1$, Fig. 1-(a)), binary variables x^v_a and z^v_{jt} of the interval $i = it$ are restricted to be integer. This interval belongs to the "integer block". The remaining intervals have their integer variables relaxed, belonging to the "relaxed block". The last two intervals ($e = 2$) are omitted from the problem. These intervals belong to the called "end-block" [15], subject to $e \leq p - 2$. A MIP solver is then used for solving the current problem. At iteration $it = 2$ (Fig. 1-(b)), binary variables of interval $i = it - 1$ are fixed with the values obtained in the previous iteration, now belonging to the "fixed block". Original continuous variables of model (1)-(14) are kept unfixed in all iterations. Integrality constraints are reintroduced into the variables of the interval $i = it$. Also, one interval from the end-block turns to belong to the relaxed block. Then, the problem is solved again by the MIP solver. The algorithm continues iterating until $it = p$, i.e. all intervals have been removed from the end-block and integrality constraints are reintroduced to the variables of all intervals (Fig. 1-(c)). At this point, a solution for the original problem is then returned.

According to Fig. 1, arc variables x_a^v have a special treatment in the R&F when they cross two different blocks. For example, let $a = ((j_1, t_1), (j_2, t_2))$ be a travel arc crossing two different blocks. We consider that the block in which time t_2 belongs has dominance over the block in which t_1 belongs. This rule does not apply to the source arcs (that are originally fixed) and sink arcs. Sink arcs are never fixed in the R&F. This occurs because if a sink arc variable is set to 1 and fixed for some vessel, it will not be available in the remaining time horizon, which can lead to an infeasible solution. On the other hand, if sink arcs are fixed to 0, this implies that the vessel remains available in the system when maybe it is no longer necessary, impacting on the objective function value.

In the relax-and-fix strategy, solving each interval up to optimality does not necessarily lead to an optimal solution for the original problem. In this case, we use MIP relative GAP and time limit as stopping criteria in each iteration, as suggested in [15]. Initially, the MIP relative GAP is set to a positive value, which is linearly decreased along the iterations such that in the last iteration the MIP relative GAP is set to 0.0%.

During the R&F iterations, it is possible that the problem becomes infeasible when an interval is fixed and integrality constraints are reintroduced into the next interval. A common approach for avoiding infeasibility is to use an overlap which does not fix part of the integer interval at each iteration [13]. In our case the overlap just reduces the size of the fixed block, leading to more integer variables to be solved along the iterations.

Even using overlap, port-time inventory bounds can be violated. It occurs when no vessel can reach a port at specific times due to the previously fixed routing decisions and the spot market variables are not sufficient to avoid lack or surplus of inventory. To handle this issue, we introduce auxiliary variables $\beta_{jt} \geq 0, j \in \mathcal{J}, t \in \mathcal{T}$. These variables work as an unlimited spot market and are highly penalized in the objective function. Eq. (3) is reformulated:

$$s_{jt} = s_{j,t-1} + \Delta_j \left(d_{jt} - \sum_{v \in V} f_{jt}^v - \alpha_{jt} - \beta_{jt} \right), \ \forall n = (j, t) \in \mathcal{N} \ . \qquad (17)$$

Note that the use of auxiliary variables avoids the solver to stop prematurely, but if a variable $\beta_{jt}, j \in \mathcal{J}, t \in \mathcal{T}$ is positive at the end of R&F, the solution for the original problem remains infeasible.

3.1   Improvement Phase

MIP-based local searches are applied on the solution returned by the R&F algorithm for improving the solution quality, removing possible infeasibilities. MIP-based local search is an effective method which has been used in several works,

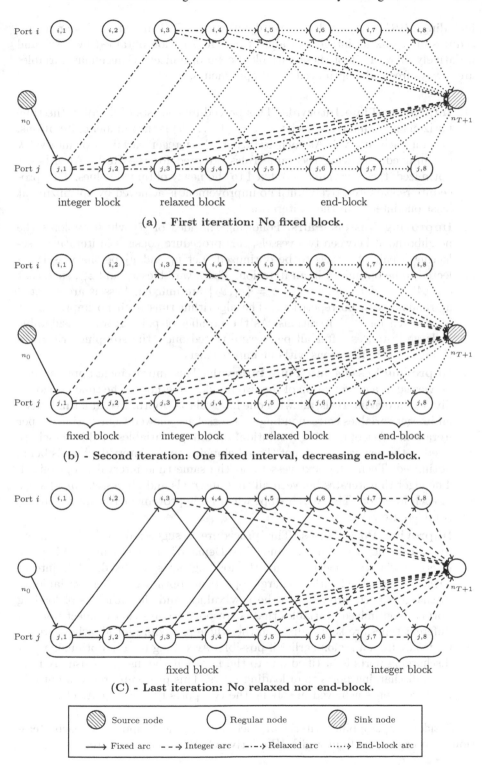

Fig. 1. First, second, and last iteration of relax-and-fix for a network of a single vessel

including MIRPs [14, 7, 8, 11, 3]. We describe four MIP-based local search procedures. They fix all integer variables from the solution obtained by R&F and iteratively allow a set of these variables to be optimized. Continuous variables are always free to be optimized in all approaches.

1. **Improving Time Intervals.** This procedure consists of dividing the time horizon into m intervals, such that $k = \{1, \ldots, m\}$ is the number of iterations, one for each interval. At each iteration, the integer variables of interval k are unfixed, following the same rules adopted for the R&F. After being optimized, theses variables are fixed to the newly obtained values. This procedure repeats iteratively until no improvement is achieved by optimizing at least one interval in the m iterations.

2. **Improving Vessels Pairs.** Following the idea of [7] which explores the neighborhood between two vessels, this procedure consists in iteratively selecting a pair of vessels to be optimized. Let v_1 and v_2 be the vessels selected to be optimized in an iteration. Then, variables x_a^v and z_{jt}^v, such that $a \in \mathcal{A}^v, j \in \mathcal{J}, t \in \mathcal{T}, v \in \mathcal{V} : v = \{v_1, v_2\}$ are unfixed. Vessels are selected at random with no repetitions. The algorithm runs until no improvement is achieved for $\binom{|\mathcal{V}|}{2}$ iterations. As the number of pairs grows considerable in large instances, after all pairs were tested once, the stopping criteria is changed to $|\mathcal{V}|$ iterations without improvement.

3. **Improving Vessels and Time Intervals.** This improvement approach can be viewed as a combination of the two previous methods. The time horizon is divided into m intervals, allowing one interval to be optimized at a time. Also, all integer variables corresponding to a vessel are allowed to be optimized per iteration. After optimizing a solution, all integer variables of this vessel are fixed to the new values, except those belonging to the interval which is being optimized. Then, the next vessel and the same time interval is optimized. The algorithm iterates between all time intervals and all vessels, $m|\mathcal{V}|$ steps in each iteration. The search stops when no improvement is achieved in one complete iteration.

4. **Improving Port Types.** This procedure is suggested by [11] as an extension of the "Fix Supply" and "Fix Demand" proposed in [8]. First, all integer variables associated with the loading ports are fixed, while integer variables associated with discharging ports are optimized. Then, variables of discharging ports are fixed to the new values, and the variables of loading ports are optimized. Variables that correspond to arcs that connect ports of different types are kept unfixed in the whole procedure for allowing a vessel to depart from a region earlier if possible. According to [11], optimizing first discharging ports is justified due to the fact that the instances usually have more discharging ports than loading ports. This procedure repeats until no improvement is achieved in solving the two ports type consecutively.

Besides the stopping criteria of each improvement approach, each iteration/step has a time limit and MIP relative GAP as stopping criteria.

4 Computational Results

This section presents computational results obtained by solving the MIRP model with the algorithms described in Sect. 3 As in [11], we solved the model as a minimization problem, turning the objective function (1) negative. The algorithms were implemented using CPLEX 12.5 C++ API and compiled with the optimization parameter $-O3$. Experiments were carried out on a AMD-FX-8150 computer running at 3.6 GHz on a single core, with 32 GB RAM.

4.1 Benchmark Instances

Computational results were performed on "Group 1" instances available in the MIRPLIB [1]. The instances name present their characteristics. For example, instance "LR2_11_DR2_22_VC3_V6a" means that there exists 2 loading regions (LR), and in each region there is one loading port, two discharging regions (DR), each of them with 2 ports, three vessel classes (VC), and a total of six available vessels (V), at least one for each vessel class. The letter at the end of the name is used for differentiating instances with the same size. Each instance was tested with time horizons of 45 and 60 days, with time periods of one day.

Modified Instances For removing the clustered characteristic of ports, we modified the MIRPLIB instances concerning port coordinates and if necessary, production/consumption rates. Usually, ports are grouped in regions, especially in deep-sea configuration. However, it seems natural that there may exist cases where each region has just one port, or ports in the same region are not necessarily of the same type (loading or discharging). Let x_j and y_j be the coordinates of each port in the original instance. Also, let $\overline{x} = \max_{j \in \mathcal{J}}\{x_j\}$, $\overline{y} = \max_{j \in \mathcal{J}}\{y_j\}$, $\underline{x} = \min_{j \in \mathcal{J}}\{x_j\}$, and $\underline{y} = \min_{j \in \mathcal{J}}\{y_j\}$ be the extreme coordinates of the instance. Then, for each port $j \in \mathcal{J}$ we define the new coordinates at random as follows: $x_j = rand(\underline{x}, \overline{x})$ and $y_j = rand(\underline{y}, \overline{y})$. The seed value used for each instance was $\overline{x}$. The distances between ports and cost of arcs are recalculated according to [12]. Instance "LR2_22_DR2_22_VC3_V10a" turns infeasible due to the new ports positions. For this case, the values of $d_{jt}, j \in \mathcal{J}, t \in \mathcal{T}$ were reduced by 10%. The modified instances are available in the author's web page[1].

4.2 Parameters and Methodology

From initial experiments with parameters that seemed to be promising, we built a methodology for the computational experiments. First, the instances were divided into two sets according to the number of loading regions. Set-1 corresponds to the instances with one loading region (LR1), while set-2 corresponds to the instances with two loading regions (LR2). The difficulty of solving the instances can be evaluated by other characteristics (number of variables/constraints, average port capacity-to-rate ratio $\frac{S_{jt}^{\max}}{d_{jt}}$ [12], among others), but we prefer a first

---

[1] http://inf.ufrgs.br/~mwfriske

simple classification to consider different parameters for each set. Also, we do not distinguish the difficulty considering the time horizon of the same instance, i.e. the parameter for an instance with $T = 45$ will be the same for the correspondent instance with $T = 60$. The exception occurs with the number of intervals p that the time horizon is divided in the R&F. Parameters and possible values tested for each set are described in Table 1.

Table 1. Parameter values used in the computational experiments

Name		Acronym	Value		
			set-1	set-2	
Relax-and-Fix Number of intervals		p	{5,9}		Case $T = 45$
			{6,10}		Case $T = 60$
	Overlap (%)	o	{15,30,50}		
	Time limit for solving each interval (s)	t_{rf}^{it}	{50,100,200}	{100,200,400}	
Local search	Time limit for iteration (s)	t_{ls}^{it}	25	50	Not using β_{jt}
			35	75	
			70	150	Using β_{jt}
			140	300	
	Time limit for the entire local search (s)	t_{ls}^{max}	7200	10800	

According to Table 1, each instance set can have more than one value for each parameter. We first test the smallest value for each parameter, and when necessary they are increased. For example, consider an instance from set-1 with $T = 45$, the first test uses $p = 5$, $o = 15$, $t_{rf}^{it} = 50$. If the solution turns infeasible during a R&F iteration, the overlap is increased from 15 to 30 and the test is restarted. On the other hand, if R&F cannot find an integer solution in some iteration due to the time limit per iteration t_{rf}^{it}, it is increased from 50 to 100. Even with the maximum values of o and t_{rf}^{it}, if no integer solution was found, or solutions remained infeasible, we change the value of p from 5 to 9, and reset the other parameters to the minimum values, increasing them if necessary. If no solution has been found by varying the previous parameters, we added to the model the auxiliary variables β_{jt}, again resetting p, o and t_{rf}^{it} to its minimum values. When using auxiliary variables, t_{ls}^{it} is also increased. If a solution remains infeasible during R&F or at the end of the local search, o, t_{rf}^{it} and t_{ls}^{it} are increased together. At this point, we stopped the tests, even if no feasible solution was found.

The number of intervals in the end-block at starting the R&F algorithm is always set to $p - 2$ in order to solve a minimum number of continuous variables per iteration, saving computational time. The initial optimality GAP is set to 50%. For the local search procedures which divide the planning horizon in m intervals (see items 1 and 3 of Sect. 3.1), we set $m = 3$. For all local search procedures, the optimality GAP is set to 0.1%.

4.3   Lower Bounds

For evaluating the effectiveness of the proposed additional constraints, the lower bounds were computed solving the relaxation of model (1) with and without the additional constraints. We consider the values that were obtained after the solver performed the cuts in the first node of the branch-and-cut tree. Considering the MIRPLIB instances, lower bounds improved on average 46.5% and 6.4% for instances of sets 1 and 2, respectively. This improvement is solely due to the first set of constraints. A reason for improving the bounds is that forcing some vessels to depart from the port to another type of port after the operations avoids the use of waiting arcs, which have no cost. The major effectiveness of the constraints on instances of set-1 may occur because the vessels will be forced to depart in direction to just one region. Then, if a vessel uses fractions of arcs when traveling to another region, as these arcs have similar costs, the relaxation value can be better. On the other hand, since in set-2 one must decide between ports grouped in at least two separated regions, consequently, a fractional solution may use arcs with a large cost difference. When considering the modified instances, the constraints improved the lower bounds in 15.3% for set-1 and 11.3% for set-2. The minor improvement on lower bounds considering instances of set-1 occurs because the ports of the same type are not grouped into regions.

4.4   Relax-and-Fix and Improvement Phase Results

This section presents the results obtained using the relax-and-fix algorithm and the MIP-based local searches. Two combinations of local searches were tested. Combination A uses procedures 1, 2 and 4 from Section 3.1, respectively, while combination B uses procedures 3 and 4, respectively. We present only the results considering the combination B, as it performed better in most of the instances than the combination A. The time limit t_{ls}^{max} of the improvement phase is equally divided between the local searches used in each test. If some local search finishes before reaching the time limit, the remaining time is available for the next local search(es).

Table 2 presents the results of the MIRPLIB and modified instances. Column "Parameters" presents the parameter values, columns "R&F" present the results considering only the R&F algorithm, while columns "LS" present the results concerning the performed local search in the R&F solution. Columns "BKV" present the best-known values of MIRPLIB instances obtained by [11]. Column "Obj" corresponds to the objective value, and column "Time" corresponds to the total processing time in seconds. The processing time of [11] was normalized using the *PassMark Software* [2]. Column "GAP^{BKV}" presents the relative deviation $\left(\frac{Obj-BKV}{-BKV}\right) * 100$, where Obj corresponds to the objective value of our algorithm, while BKV corresponds to the objective value of [11]. Column "GAP^{LB}" corresponds to the relative deviation $\frac{Obj-LB}{-LB}$ from the lower bound LB. The average values do not include instances where the relative deviation is labeled as "-", meaning that no feasible solution was found.

MIRPLIB Instances Results. According to Table 2, the average time for obtaining the corresponding solutions is shorter than the time reported by [11].

---

[2] http://www.cpubenchmark.net/

Table 2. MIRPLIB and modified instance results

Instance	T	MIRPLIB Instances											BKV		Modified instances						R&F		LS		
		β_{j,t}	ρ	o	t_rf^it	t_ls^it	R&F Time	R&F Obj	LS Time	LS Obj	GAP^BKV	Time	Obj	β_{j,t}	ρ	o	t_rf^it	t_ls^it	Time	Obj	Time	Obj	GAP^LB		
LR1.1.DR1.3.VC1.V7a	45		5	15	50	25	55	-13.178	454	-13.272	0,00%	173	-13.272		5	15	50	25	12	-19.547	986	-21.491	5,51%		
LR1.1.DR1.4.VC3.V11a	45		5	15	50	25	159	-10.682	822	-10.910	2,93%	8.362	-11.239		5	15	50	25	65	-22.164	2.556	-24.617	8,02%		
LR1.1.DR1.4.VC3.V12a	45		5	15	50	25	38	-8.540	624	-10.372	3,35%	7.828	-10.732		9	30	50	25	136	-22.263	1.618	-23.062	6,07%		
LR1.1.DR1.4.VC3.V12b	45		5	15	50	25	179	-7.999	1.611	-9.057	0,14%	1.742	-9.069		5	15	50	25	129	-23.883	3.625	-26.842	5,87%		
LR1.1.DR1.4.VC3.V8a	45		9	30	50	25	26	-4.688	86	-5.106	0,00%	4.517	-5.106		5	15	50	25	79	-15.731	2.797	-17.342	13,00%		
LR1.1.DR1.4.VC3.V9a	45		5	15	50	25	29	-5.419	649	-6.629	3,80%	502	-6.891		5	15	100	25	123	-16.196	2.101	-17.324	14,07%		
LR1.2.DR1.3.VC2.V6a	45		5	30	50	25	256	-9.511	1.797	-10.577	5,00%	5.844	-11.134		5	15	50	25	43	-17.896	1.451	-19.597	8,79%		
LR1.2.DR1.3.VC3.V8a	45		5	15	50	25	188	-10.133	1.255	-11.680	2,75%	7.482	-12.010		5	15	100	25	125	-19.138	1.827	-20.568	14,78%		
LR2.11.DR2.22.VC3.V6a	45	•	5	50	400	300	1.610	94.720	5.401	-9.550	1,73%	7.987	-9.718	•	5	15	100	50	171	-14.017	5.410	-15.064	27,22%		
LR2.11.DR2.33.VC4.V11a	45		5	15	100	75	395	565.310	5.475	-13.218	5,70%	8.736	-14.017		9	15	30	50	144	-24.328	5.450	-27.728	21,60%		
LR2.11.DR2.33.VC5.V12a	45		5	15	100	75	435	747.441	5.551	-15.125	17,90%	8.756	-18.423		5	15	100	75	441	925.516	5.852	-22.581	46,39%		
LR2.22.DR2.22.VC3.V10a	45	•	5	50	400	300	2.035	1.374.400	5.436	-21.957	11,43%	8.552	-24.789	•	5	50	400	300	2.041	1.397.820	6.002	-23.326	33,86%		
LR2.22.DR3.333.VC4.V14a	45	•	5	15	100	75	585	1.825.910	6.183	25.843		9.219	-21.952	•	5	15	100	75	597	891.797	5.706	-28.232	41,41%		
LR2.22.DR3.333.VC4.V17a	45	•	5	50	400	300	2.392	6.723.570	9.047	2.033		9.337	-21.713	•	5	15	100	75	756	8.208.870	5.941	62.221	-		
Average							599		3.171		4,56%	6.360							347		3.666		18,97%		
LR1.1.DR1.3.VC1.V7a	60		6	50	50	25	176	-16.326	776	-16.675	0,00%	435	-16.675		6	15	50	25	69	-24.995	1.584	-27.275	6,16%		
LR1.1.DR1.4.VC3.v11a	60		6	15	50	25	214	-11.113	2.312	-11.516	13,13%	6.997	-13.257		6	15	50	25	148	-26.952	3.625	-31.455	7,92%		
LR1.1.DR1.4.VC3.V12a	60		6	15	50	35	190	-10.012	1.584	-11.223	0,41%	7.828	-11.269		6	30	50	35	198	-27.495	3.564	-29.613	2,89%		
LR1.1.DR1.4.VC3.V12b	60		6	15	100	25	481	-8.018	2.960	-9.958	0,94%	8.537	-10.053		6	15	50	25	165	-33.163	3.625	-34.264	6,38%		
LR1.1.DR1.4.VC3.V8a	60		6	15	50	35	115	325.680	865	-4.578	11,81%	7.534	-5.191		6	15	100	25	214	-19.355	2.552	-20.905	17,89%		
LR1.1.DR1.4.VC3.V9a	60		6	15	50	25	178	-6.746	757	-6.904	8,58%	8.120	-7.552		6	15	100	25	172	-18.922	3.701	-21.640	16,99%		
LR1.2.DR1.3.VC2.V6a	60		10	15	30	25	172	-10.514	1.869	-12.639	7,28%	8.135	-13.631		6	15	50	25	165	-22.908	2.377	-25.324	9,85%		
LR1.2.DR1.3.VC3.V8a	60		6	15	200	25	495	-12.857	1.573	-14.329	4,04%	7.871	-14.931		6	15	100	25	277	-23.370	1.827	-25.687	17,35%		
LR2.11.DR2.22.VC3.V6a	60	•	6	15	100	75	245	195.984	5.403	39.102		8.237	-13.351	•	6	15	100	75	432	625.009	5.701	-19.230	27,67%		
LR2.11.DR2.33.VC4.V11a	60	•	6	15	100	75	560	1.523.420	5.702	181.868		8.765	-17.008	•	6	15	100	75	660	504.184	5.551	-32.807	29,46%		
LR2.11.DR2.33.VC5.V12a	60		6	15	100	75	601	906.791	5.702	176.226		8.824	-22.730		6	50	400	300	2.554	2.632.490	7.204	173.385	-		
LR2.22.DR2.22.VC3.V10a	60		6	15	100	75	639	2.685.950	5.823	826.372		8.628	-32.627		6	15	100	75	604	1.514.310	5.787	92.707	-		
LR2.22.DR3.333.VC4.V14a	60	•	6	15	100	75	1.094	7.925.830	6.222	2.218.890		9.352	-26.873	•	6	30	200	150	2.030	2.728.360	5.863	517.543	-		
LR2.22.DR3.333.VC4.V17a	60	•	6	30	200	150	2.134	4.228.370	5.732	1.110.680		9.424	-27.000	•	6	30	200	150	2.526	8.152.140	6.653	3.014.670	-		
Average							521		3.377		5,77%	7.763							730		4.258		14,25%		

The relative gap to the BKV was on average 2.2% for set-1 and 9.2% for set-2 when $T = 45$, and considering instances in which a feasible solution was found. Considering a time horizon of 60 days, the average gap for set-1 was 5.8%, while no feasible solutions were found for set-2. Our algorithm was able to find the same value of BKV for three instances (marked in bold). The local searches improved the objective function on average 11.4% considering only the results that did not use β_{jt} variables in the solutions obtained by the R&F. Moreover, they were able to remove the infeasibilities in five solutions found by the R&F. On the other hand, on average 85.4% of the total time was spent in the improvement phase. The average gap in relation to the lower bound was 37.2% for set-1 and 55.1% for set-2 (only considering feasible results).

Preliminary tests obtained new best-known values for two instances with $T = 45$, presented in Table 3. Column "CPU" presents the computer where the experiments were carried out, where "AMD" corresponds to the previously described computer, while "Intel" corresponds to an Intel Core i5-2300 running at 2.8 GHz, with 16 GB. Both experiments used the combination B of local search procedures. Also, they did not use auxiliary variables β_{jt}.

Table 3. New best-known-values found in preliminary experiments.

Instance	Parameters					R&F + LS			BKV	
	CPU	p	o	t_{rf}^{it}	t_{ls}^{it}	Time (s)	Obj	GAP^{BKV}	Time(s)	Obj
LR1_1_DR1_4_VC3_V11a	Core i5	5	20	50	50	1,578	-11,243	-0.03%	12,009	-11,239
LR1_1_DR1_4_VC3_V12b	AMD	5	15	50	20	1,942	-9,085	-0.17%	1,742	-9,069

Modified Instances Results. Considering the modified instances, the relative gap GAP^{LB} was on average 10.1% for set-1 and 32.5% for set-2, being smaller than the gap in the tests with MIRPLIB instances. This does not necessarily mean that our algorithm is better considering these instances, but the linear relaxations can be better in randomly distributed ports. Also, our algorithm was able to find more feasible solutions for the modified instances than the MIRPLIB instances. But, there are still instances that no feasible solution was found. The average improvement of the objective function with the improvement phase was 9.7%, while the time spent in this phase was on average 87.6%.

5   Conclusion and Future Works

This work presented an extension of a relax-and-fix algorithm for solving a class of Maritime Inventory Routing Problem. Two sets of additional constraints were proposed, either for improving the bounds and for obtaining solutions faster. MIP-based local search procedures were used for improving the solutions and removing infeasibilities. Computational experiments were performed on MIR-PLIB and modified instances. Although it did not obtain feasible solutions for all instances, our algorithm found good solutions in reasonable time, including two best-known values for MIRPLIB instances. As future work, we intend to model MIRP as a fixed charge network flow as in [2], using valid inequalities for improving lower bounds, and using the relax-and-fix as the solution method.

Acknowledgements. The work of the first author was funded by CAPES - Coordenadoria de Aperfeiçoamento de Pessoal de Nível Superior.

References

1. Maritime inventory routing problem library (MIRPLIB), https://mirplib.scl.gatech.edu/, accessed: 2017-04-05
2. Agra, A., Andersson, H., Christiansen, M., Wolsey, L.: A maritime inventory routing problem: Discrete time formulations and valid inequalities. Networks 62(4), 297–314 (2013)
3. Agra, A., Christiansen, M., Ivarsøy, K.S., Solhaug, I.E., Tomasgard, A.: Combined ship routing and inventory management in the salmon farming industry. Annals of Operations Research pp. 1–25 (2016)
4. Christiansen, M.: Decomposition of a Combined Inventory and Time Constrained Ship Routing Problem. Transportation Science 33(1), 3–16 (1999)
5. Christiansen, M., Fagerholt, K., Nygreen, B., Ronen, D.: Ship routing and scheduling in the new millennium. European Journal of Operational Research 228(3), 467–483 (2013)
6. Christiansen, M., Fagerholt, K., Ronen, D.: Ship Routing and Scheduling: Status and Perspectives. Transportation Science 38(1), 1–18 (2004)
7. Goel, V., Furman, K.C., Song, J.H., El-Bakry, A.S.: Large neighborhood search for LNG inventory routing. Journal of Heuristics 18(6), 821–848 (2012)
8. Hewitt, M., Nemhauser, G., Savelsbergh, M., Song, J.H.: A branch-and-price guided search approach to maritime inventory routing. Computers and Operations Research 40(5), 1410–1419 (2013)
9. Jiang, Y., Grossmann, I.E.: Alternative mixed-integer linear programming models of a maritime inventory routing problem. Computers & Chemical Engineering 77, 147–161 (2015)
10. Papageorgiou, D.J., Cheon, M.S., Harwood, S., Trespalacios, F., Nemhauser, G.L., Stewart, H.M.: Recent Progress Using Matheuristics for Strategic Maritime Inventory Routing (2016)
11. Papageorgiou, D.J., Keha, A.B., Nemhauser, G.L., Sokol, J.: Two-stage decomposition algorithms for single product maritime inventory routing. INFORMS Journal on Computing 26(4), 825–847 (2014)
12. Papageorgiou, D.J., Nemhauser, G.L., Sokol, J., Cheon, M.S., Keha, A.B.: MIRPLib - A library of maritime inventory routing problem instances: Survey, core model, and benchmark results. European Journal of Operational Research 235(2), 350–366 (2014)
13. Pochet, Y., Wolsey, L.A.: Production planning by mixed integer programming. Springer Science & Business Media (2006)
14. Song, J.H., Furman, K.C.: A maritime inventory routing problem: Practical approach. Computers & Operations Research 40(3), 657–665 (2013)
15. Uggen, K.T., Fodstad, M., Nørstebø, V.S.: Using and extending fix-and-relax to solve maritime inventory routing problems. TOP 21(2), 355–377 (2013)

Strategic Optimization of Offshore Wind Farm Installation

Stian Backe[1][2](✉) and Dag Haugland[2]

[1] Department of Industrial Economics and Technology Management, Norwegian University of Science and Technology, Trondheim, Norway
[2] Department of Informatics, University of Bergen, Bergen, Norway
stian.backe@ntnu.no

Abstract. This work describes logistical planning of offshore wind farm (OWF) installation through linear programming. A mixed-integer linear programming (MILP) model is developed to analyze cost-effective port and vessel strategies for offshore installation operations. The model seeks to minimize total costs through strategic decisions, that is decisions on port and vessel fleet and mix. Different vessels, ports and weather restrictions over a fixed time horizon are considered in the model. Several deterministic test cases with historic weather data are implemented in AMPL, and run with the CPLEX solver. The results provide valuable insight into economic impact of strategic decisions. Numerical experiments on instances indicate that decision aid could be more reliable if large OWFs are considered in fractionated parts, alternatively by developing heuristics.

Keywords: offshore wind installation, mixed-integer linear programming, fleet optimization

1 Introduction

Renewable energy is a growing industry within the energy sector. The growth is motivated by issues like the challenge of global climate change, the increasing need for energy, and new market opportunities. Harvesting energy from the wind is becoming a developed renewable energy technology. Operating offshore involves greater challenges than onshore, and electricity production from offshore wind farms (OWFs) is today considered expensive.

Offshore construction of a wind farm requires a lot of logistical planning. Vessels and/or barges must transport and install large components in a demanding environment. The challenges include restrictive weather conditions contributing to delays on very costly operations. Farm sites and turbine components are expected to keep growing in size, and wind farm locations are expected to be placed further away from shore. In addition, an increasing number of specialized installation vessels are becoming available on the market. Crucial decisions in planning the installation process include choosing the most cost-effective vessels, figuring out how components should be loaded and installed, and choosing which port to operate from to minimize expenses and delays.

© Springer International Publishing AG 2017
T. Bektaş et al. (Eds.), ICCL 2017, LNCS 10572, pp. 285–299, 2017.
https://doi.org/10.1007/978-3-319-68496-3_19

Operational research models for OWFs are focused on operation and maintenance (O&M) of fully commissioned farms. Some work is also done to support vessel scheduling of OWF installation [6, 7]. To the authors' knowledge, limited published research is focusing on the installation fleet size and mix problem through linear programming. This work seeks to aid decisions for installation fleet size and mix, by means of a mixed-integer linear programming (MILP) model.

Section 2 describes the framework of the model in detail, and its mathematical formulation is given in Section 3. Section 4 presents realistic numerical experiments run with the model, and the paper is concluded in Section 5.

2   Problem Description

The model, to be detailed in the next section, considers the offshore installation stage of a given number of wind turbines.

Each turbine consists of components that can mainly be split into three categories: sub-structures, cables and top-structures. In addition, OWFs consist of one or more sub-stations collecting all the energy generated by the turbines. The options are few on how to perform installation of sub-structures, cables and sub-stations, thus the problem considered concerns installations of top-structures. These structures mainly consist of tower, nacelle, hub and blades. Top-structures for a complete turbine can be partly assembled onshore, and will usually be installed by the same vessel.

All components must be loaded and transported by some vessel to the OWF. Next, the transported components are installed at turbine locations. Before each installation, vessels commonly lower pillars into the seabed (jack-up) to raise their deck above the sea, creating stable platforms where lifting operations can be performed safely given satisfactory weather conditions. After installation is complete, the vessel performs jack-down, and transits to the next turbine or back to port. Depending on the possible onshore assembly of certain components, a number of loading and installation lifts will take place for each turbine.

Vessels can differ in effectiveness and costs, and usually perform several cycles of loading, transportation and installation. The same vessel may load different numbers of turbines on different cycles. Any vessel transit, jack-up/jack-down and installation is restricted by weather conditions.

Chartering vessels is expensive, and there are thus high costs of weather delays. The main decisions we want to support are which vessels and ports to use, how many cycles each vessel performs and how many turbines each vessel loads on each cycle. These decisions will depend on vessel and port costs, transit distances, vessel specifications and weather realizations causing potential delays.

Upon planning the installation of an OWF, the goal is to perform the complete installation with the least amount of costs.

3 Model Formulation

The current section presents the mathematical formulation of the MILP model dealing with the problem presented in Section 2.

Section 3.1 introduces the model framework in terms of input data, and Section 3.2 presents variables representing decisions supported by the model. The objective function is defined in Section 3.3, and Section 3.4 introduces constraints ensuring operation assignment and time tracking. Finally, weather windows are introduced in Section 3.5.

3.1 Model Framework

The model supports decisions on which vessel(s) to use, and which port vessel(s) are to operate from. Vessels are contained in the set V, and ports are contained in the set K.

Offshore operations can be categorized into four tasks: jack-up, installation, jack-down and turbine transit, and they will henceforth be referred to as O_1, O_2, O_3 and O_4, respectively.

Input data in the model represent the following operation durations, which are dependent on vessel and port:

t_v^L: Time needed to load one turbine on vessel $v \in V$,

t_{kv}^K: Time needed for vessel $v \in V$ to transit between port $k \in K$ and farm,

t_v^i: Time to perform operation O_i with vessel $v \in V$, $i = 1, ..., 4$.

The model considers each turbine to be completely installed by exactly one vessel, which means the model does not have to consider each component explicitly. Vessels also represent a defined way of assembling components of one complete turbine, e.g. assemble nacelle, hub and two blades together in one piece. Time consumption for loading and installation is mainly dependent on the number of lifts needed. The assembly of components is therefore reflected through the input data identifying loading time (t_v^L) and installation time (t_v^2). All components are assumed available at potential ports, so the model does not consider possible inventory delays. There are no restrictions on the number of vessels loading at the same port simultaneously.

The transit durations (t_{kv}^K, t_v^4) are not dependent on turbine locations. This is because the model considers transit time to a turbine from port $k \in K$, and transit time from a turbine to its neighbouring turbine, to be equal for all turbines for vessel $v \in V$. Simplifications on the transit times can be defended with arguments that the distance from port to farm is significantly greater than the distance across the farm, and that the turbines installed on one cycle is likely to be neighboring.

Vessel $v \in V$ is limited to carry Y_v turbines per cycle, and limited to perform at most U_v cycles.

The entire OWF must be installed within a given time horizon. The model considers *continuous time*. This means that the length of the time horizon is given as a parameter, which we denote P. The total number of turbines in the OWF is denoted R.

3.2 Decision Variables

Because time is modelled continuously, all variables representing the time at which operations take place are defined separately from the variables concerning operation assignment. The dimensions of the variable vectors are therefore smaller than what is likely to be the case in a discrete-time model.

The following assignment variables are binary:

$$\delta_k = \begin{cases} 1, & \text{if port } k \in K \text{ is in use,} \\ 0, & \text{otherwise,} \end{cases}$$

$$\gamma_v = \begin{cases} 1, & \text{if vessel } v \in V \text{ is used,} \\ 0, & \text{otherwise,} \end{cases}$$

$$x_{kvu} = \begin{cases} 1, & \text{if vessel } v \in V \text{ operates from port } k \in K \\ & \text{on cycle } u = 1, ..., U_v, \\ 0, & \text{otherwise,} \end{cases}$$

$$\theta_{vuy} = \begin{cases} 1, & \text{if vessel } v \in V \text{ installs } y = 1, ..., Y_v \text{ or more turbines} \\ & \text{on cycle } u = 1, ..., U_v, \\ 0, & \text{otherwise.} \end{cases}$$

The variables θ_{vuy} and x_{kvu} are represented in terms of special ordered sets of type 2 (SOS2) [3]. This means that if vessel $v \in V$ installs $y' \leq Y_v$ turbines on cycle $u' = 1, ..., U_v$, that is if $\theta_{vu'y'} = 1$, we have that $\theta_{vu'y} = 1$ for all $y = 1, ..., y'$, and for some $k \in K$, we have that $x_{kvu} = 1$ for all $u = 1, ..., u'$.

Continuous variables are defined to keep track of time:

$q_{vu} \in \mathbb{R}_+$: Time when vessel $v \in V$ starts cycle $u = 1, ..., U_v$,

$e_{vu} \in \mathbb{R}_+$: Time when vessel $v \in V$ ends cycle $u = 0, ..., U_v$,

$s_{vuy}^i \in \mathbb{R}_+$: Time when vessel $v \in V$ starts operation O_i at the yth turbine
   on cycle $u = 1, ..., U_v, \ y = 1, ..., Y_v, \ i = 1, ..., 4$,

$E_v \in \mathbb{R}_+$: Total time vessel $v \in V$ is chartered.

Note that the variables e_{vu} are defined for $u = 0$, where e_{v0} represents the charter start of vessel $v \in V$.

The variables s_{vuy}^4 are defined as the time when vessel $v \in V$ *leaves* turbine y on the uth cycle, which may be a transit to a turbine (if $y < Y_v$ and $\theta_{vu,y+1} = 1$) or to port (if $y = Y_v$ or $\theta_{vu,y+1} = 0$).

3.3 Costs and Objective Function

The following costs relate to ports and vessels:

c_k^K: Cost incurred if port $k \in K$ is used,

c_v^{TC}: Time charter cost per time unit for vessel $v \in V$,

c_v^M: Mobilization cost for starting chartering of vessel $v \in V$.

The goal of the model is to minimize the costs introduced above. Consequently, the objective function is defined in the following way:

$$\min \sum_{k \in K} c_k^K \delta_k + \sum_{v \in V} \left(c_v^M \gamma_v + c_v^{TC} E_v \right). \tag{1}$$

The first sum in (1) measures total port operation costs, while the last sum measures total costs of chartering and mobilizing vessels.

It can be argued that there are more costs related to OWF installation, e.g. fuel and crew costs. However, the charter cost of a jack-up vessel may include several operational costs depending on the contract [4]. The total jack-up vessel charter cost can also be identified as the dominant cost related to jack-up vessels for OWF O&M activities [5]. The terms in (1) are therefore assumed to be sufficient in the context of optimization, where the aim is to support strategic decisions.

3.4 Constraints

The following constraints ensure that all installation operations are assigned to a vessel and a cycle. Further, they make the assignment variables introduced in Section 3.2 consistent with each other:

$$\sum_{v \in V} \sum_{u=1}^{U_v} \sum_{y=1}^{Y_v} \theta_{vuy} = R, \tag{2}$$

$$\theta_{vuy} \leq \gamma_v, \quad v \in V, \ u = 1, ..., U_v, \ y = 1, ..., Y_v, \tag{3}$$

$$x_{kvu} \leq \delta_k, \quad k \in K, \ v \in V, \ u = 1, ..., U_v, \tag{4}$$

$$\sum_{k \in K} x_{kvu} \leq 1, \quad v \in V, u = 1, ..., U_v, \tag{5}$$

$$x_{kvu} \leq x_{kv,u-1}, \quad k \in K, \ v \in V, \ u = 2, ..., U_v, \tag{6}$$

$$\theta_{vu1} \leq \sum_{k \in K} x_{kvu}, \quad v \in V, \ u = 1, ..., U_v, \tag{7}$$

$$\theta_{vuy} \leq \theta_{vu,y-1}, \quad v \in V, \ u = 1, ..., U_v, \ y = 2, ..., Y_v, \tag{8}$$

$$\theta_{vuy} \leq \theta_{v,u-1,1}, \quad v \in V, \ u = 2, ..., U_v, \ y = 1, ..., Y_v. \tag{9}$$

Constraint (2) ensures all turbines are installed by some vessel $v \in V$ on some cycle u.

Constraints (3) make sure that vessels are assigned operations only if they are mobilized, and constraints (4) ensure ports are open if a vessel cycle is initiated there.

Ensuring that each vessel operates from at most one port, constraints (5) and (6) state, respectively, that a vessel cycle can start from at most one port, and that the succeeding cycle, if any, starts from the same port. Constraints (7) say that if vessel $v \in V$ installs at least one turbine on its uth cycle, then it also leaves some port.

Consistently with the SOS2-representation of θ_{vuy}, constraints (8) say that vessel $v \in V$ installs at least $y - 1$ turbines if it installs y turbines or more on a cycle. Likewise, constraints (9) state that if vessel v installs y turbines on its uth cycle, it also installs at least one turbine on cycle $u - 1$.

The next constraints ensure correct time tracking:

$$e_{v,u-1} + t_v^L \sum_{y=1}^{Y_v} \theta_{vuy} \leq q_{vu}, \quad v \in V, \ u = 1, ..., U_v, \tag{10}$$

$$q_{vu} + \sum_{k \in K} t_{kv}^K x_{kvu} \leq s_{vu1}^1, \quad v \in V, \ u = 1, ..., U_v, \tag{11}$$

$$s_{vuy}^{i-1} + t_v^{i-1} \theta_{vuy} \leq s_{vuy}^i, \quad v \in V, \ u = 1, ..., U_v,$$
$$y = 1, ..., Y_v, \ i = 2, ..., 4, \tag{12}$$

$$s_{vu,y-1}^4 + t_v^4 \theta_{vuy} \leq s_{vuy}^1, \quad v \in V, \ u = 1, ..., U_v, \ y = 2, ..., Y_v, \tag{13}$$

$$s_{vuY_v}^4 + \sum_{k \in K} t_{kv}^K x_{kvu} \leq e_{vu}, \quad v \in V, \ u = 1, ..., U_v, \tag{14}$$

$$e_{vu} \leq P, \quad v \in V, \ u = 0, ..., U_v, \tag{15}$$

$$e_{vu} - e_{v0} \leq E_v, \quad v \in V, \ u = 1, ..., U_v. \tag{16}$$

Recall that e_{vu} is defined for all $v \in V$ and $u = 0, ..., U_v$, where e_{v0} represents the charter start of vessel v.

Constraints (10) ensure that vessel $v \in V$ finishes loading before leaving port and starting its uth cycle, and constraints (11) make sure vessel v arrives at the first turbine after the transit from port is complete.

Constraints (12) ensure that vessel $v \in V$ performs operation O_{i-1} before the successive operation O_i at the yth turbine. To connect the time tracking between turbines, constraints (13) make sure vessel v arrives at the yth turbine after the transit from the preceding turbine is complete. All operations are repeated until all loaded turbines are installed on a cycle.

Constraints (14) make sure vessel $v \in V$ returns to port before ending its uth cycle. Constraints (15) ensure all cycles end within the time horizon, and constraints (16) ensure the continuous time variable E_v is no less than the total charter length of vessel v.

3.5 Weather Windows

The model deals with weather restrictions through time intervals, referred to as *weather windows*, in which certain operations are feasible.

The model considers transit, jack-up, jack-down and installation to be weather-restricted, and these operations must be performed within some weather window. The following input data are defined:

W_v^i: Number of weather windows for operation O_i with vessel $v \in V$, $i = 1, ..., 4$,

a_{vn}^i: Start of weather window $n = 1, ..., W_v^i$ for operation O_i with vessel $v \in V$,

   $i = 1, ..., 4$,

b_{vn}^i: End of weather window $n = 1, ..., W_v^i$ for operation O_i with vessel $v \in V$,

   $i = 1, ..., 4$.

Note that the weather windows are only dependent on vessel and operation. Recall from Section 3.1 that vessels also represent a way of assembling components.

Binary decision variables are introduced to identify in which weather window which operation is performed:

$$
N_{vuyn}^i =
\begin{cases}
1, & \text{if vessel } v \in V \text{ performs operation } O_i \text{ at the } y\text{th turbine} \\
   & \text{on cycle } u \text{ in weather window } n = 1, ..., W_v^i,\ u = 1, ..., U_v, \\
   & y = 1, ..., Y_v,\ i = 1, ..., 3, \\
0, & \text{otherwise,}
\end{cases}
$$

$$
N_{vuyn}^4 =
\begin{cases}
1, & \text{if vessel } v \in V \text{ transits to the y}th \text{ turbine on cycle } u \\
   & \text{in weather window } n = 1, ..., W_v^4,\ u = 1, ..., U_v, \\
   & y = 1, .., Y_v + 1, \\
0, & \text{otherwise.}
\end{cases}
$$

Note that the binary variables N_{vuyn}^4 represent the weather windows in which transit *to* the yth turbine for $y = 1, ..., Y_v + 1$ is performed. Thus, the transit to the first turbine to be installed on a cycle is a transit from port to farm. Analogously, the transit to the $(Y_v + 1)$th turbine represents a transit to port.

The binary decision variables above are dependent on the assignment variables introduced in Section 3.2:

$$
\sum_{n=1}^{W_v^4} N_{vuyn}^4 = \theta_{vuy}, \quad v \in V,\ u = 1, ..., U_v,\ y = 1, ..., Y_v, \tag{17}
$$

$$
\sum_{n=1}^{W_v^i} N_{vuyn}^i = \theta_{vuy}, \quad v \in V,\ u = 1, ..., U_v,\ y = 1, ..., Y_v,\ i = 1, ..., 3, \tag{18}
$$

$$
\sum_{n=1}^{W_v^4} N_{vu,Y_v+1,n}^4 = \theta_{vu1}, \quad v \in V,\ u = 1, ..., U_v. \tag{19}
$$

Constraints (17)-(19) make sure assigned operations must happen within exactly one weather window. In particular, constraints (19) state that if vessel $v \in V$ installs at least one turbine on cycle u, then it transits back to port in exactly one weather window.

Transits can be from port to farm, in between turbines or from farm to port, and all transits are subject to the same weather restrictions:

$$\sum_{n=1}^{W_v^4} N_{vu1n}^4 a_{vn}^4 \leq q_{vu}, \ v \in V, \ u = 1, ..., U_v,$$

(20)

$$q_{vu} + \sum_{k \in K} t_{kv}^K x_{kvu} - P(1 - \theta_{vu1}) \leq \sum_{n=1}^{W_v^4} N_{vu1n}^4 b_{vn}^4, \ v \in V, \ u = 1, ..., U_v,$$

(21)

$$\sum_{n=1}^{W_v^4} N_{vu,y+1,n}^4 a_{vn}^4 \leq s_{vuy}^4, \ v \in V, \ u = 1, ..., U_v,$$

$$y = 1, ..., Y_v, \quad (22)$$

$$s_{vu,y-1}^4 + t_v^4 - P(1 - \theta_{vuy}) \leq \sum_{n=1}^{W_v^4} N_{vuyn}^4 b_{vn}^4, \ v \in V, \ u = 1, ..., U_v,$$

$$y = 2, ..., Y_v, \quad (23)$$

$$s_{vuY_v}^4 + \sum_{k \in K} t_{kv}^K x_{kvu} - P(1 - \theta_{vu1}) \leq \sum_{n=1}^{W_v^4} N_{vu,Y_v+1,n}^4 b_{vn}^4, \ v \in V, \ u = 1, ..., U_v.$$

(24)

Constraints (20)-(21) make sure all transits from port to farm are scheduled within the chosen weather window, and constraints (22)-(23) have an analogous function for transits between turbines.

Constraints (24), together with (22) for $y = Y_v$, make sure all transits from farm to port are scheduled within their chosen weather window. Note that constraints (22) for $y = Y_v$ and (24) restrict the transit back to port through the time variable $s_{vuY_v}^4$, because $s_{vuY_v}^4$ equals the time at which vessel $v \in V$ starts its transit back to port on its uth cycle. This is accomplished by constraints (12)-(13).

Constraints concerning operation O_i for $i = 1, .., 3$ are defined in a similar way:

$$\sum_{n=1}^{W_v^i} N_{vuyn}^i a_{vn}^i \leq s_{vuy}^i, \quad v \in V, \ u = 1, ..., U_v,$$
$$y = 1, ..., Y_v, \ i = 1, ..., 3 \qquad (25)$$

$$s_{vuy}^i + t_v^i - P(1 - \theta_{vuy}) \leq \sum_{n=1}^{W_v^i} N_{vuyn}^i b_{vn}^i, \quad v \in V, \ u = 1, ..., U_v,$$
$$y = 1, ..., Y_v, \ i = 1, ..., 3 \qquad (26)$$

Constraints (25)-(26) ensure vessel $v \in V$ executes operation O_i on cycle u within the weather window chosen for the operation.

Note that some constraints, e.g. (26), are only constraining if an operation is assigned to vessel $v \in V$, that is if $\theta_{vuy} = 1$.

4 Numerical Experiments

Several test instances with the model introduced in Section 3 are presented in this section. Instances are inspired by realistic data gathered from relevant literature [1, 8], and the main purpose of these numerical experiments is to test how large instances the model can handle.

The model is implemented in AMPL, and the solver used is CPLEX version 12.5.1. Default values [10] on all the parameters of the solver is used to solve the MILP instances. All experiments where run on a computer with 2 Intel Core2 6600 Duo E6550 processors with a frequency of 2.33 GHz and 3.7 GB memory.

4.1 Test Instances

Cost data for charter rates are mainly inspired by [1], and vessel mobilization cost is assumed to be 5 times the charter cost.

The physical reality behind some vessel $v \in V$, is that transportation and installation operations are performed by two different barges. Involvement of more than one barge in such a collaboration is, however, irrelevant to the model, and consequently, we refer to their combined use as one vessel contained in V.

Henceforth, each vessel under consideration is of either of the following types:

1. The "feed" strategy (FS)
2. The "bunny transit" strategy (BTS)
3. The "unmounted transit" strategy (UTS)

The "feed" strategy (FS) represents two barges that need two towing tugs to be mobilized. One barge only transports (feeds) components from port to farm, and the other barge, located in the wind farm, only performs installations. The

FS can carry up to 10 turbines in 5 parts on each cycle. The FS is vulnerable to wave conditions [1].

The "bunny transit" strategy (BTS) consists of one self-propelled installation vessel performing all operations. The BTS can load up to 4 turbines in 3 parts (in a "bunny-ear" configuration [1, 8]) on each cycle. The BTS is sensitive to installation lifts and transits due to wind forces acting on the partly assembled rotor.

The "unmounted transit" strategy (UTS) is identical to the BTS, except that each turbine is loaded and installed in 5 parts. Therefore, the UTS can carry up to 8 turbines on each cycle. Charter rate is assumed lower than the BTS since each lift requires less crane capacity, and wind restrictions are less strict because of the unmounted components.

Specifications of the three vessels are given in Tab. 1. Time is scaled to working days, where one working day is 12 hours. Loading/installation duration is dependent on the number of lifts, i.e., how components are assembled.

Three ports are defined with increasing distance to farm site and decreasing costs in Tab. 2.

Table 1. Input data for the considered strategies.

Strategy	FS	BTS	UTS
Charter rate [$/day]	144,000	200,000	180,000
Mobilization cost [$]	720,000	1,000,000	900,000
Time, load [day]	0.83	0.5	0.83
Time, setup [day]	0.125	0.083	0.083
Time, install [day]	1.00	0.67	1.00
Time, turbine transit [day]	0.011	0.004	0.004
Turbines per cycle [pcs]	10	4	8
Wind restriction, transit [m/s]	20	15	20
Wind restriction, jack-up/down [m/s]	20	15	20
Wind restriction, install [m/s]	10	8	12
Wave restriction, transit [m]	1.5	3.0	3.0
Wave restriction, jack-up/down [m]	1.5	2.0	2.0
Wave restriction, install [m]	5.0	5.0	5.0

Table 2. Input data for the considered ports.

Port	Fixed cost c_k^K [$]	Transit FS [day]	Transit BTS [day]	Transit UTS [day]
Port 1	1,000,000	2.67	1.08	1.08
Port 2	2,000,000	1.58	0.67	0.67
Port 3	3,000,000	0.42	0.25	0.25

The resolution of weather data is one working day, i.e. vessel $v \in V$ either can or cannot perform a given operation during one entire working day. A weather window for an operation is implemented as a closed time interval, in which wind speed and significant wave height are below their respective maximum values (see Tab. 1), during one or more working days. In all the current instances, historical wind and wave data for an offshore site from the year 2000 are supplied by Metno [9] from the NORA10 reanalysis with a 10 km horizontal resolution.

We assume that the weather restrictions that apply to jack-up operations are identical to those applying to jack-down (see Tab. 1). Hence, $W_v^1 = W_v^3$, and also $a_{vn}^1 = a_{vn}^3$ and $b_{vn}^1 = b_{vn}^3$.

We consider three hypothetical OWFs: 20 turbines to be installed in 1 month (OWF 1), 40 turbines to be installed in 3 months (OWF 2), and 100 turbines to be installed in 5 months (OWF 3).

In the first set of experiments, we let V consist of one vessel of each of the types specified in Tab. 1-2 ($|V| = 3$). In the second set, V consists of two vessels of each type ($|V| = 6$).

4.2 Results

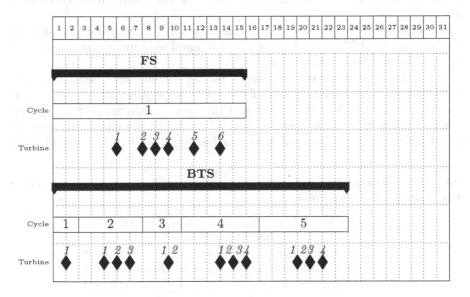

Fig. 1. Gantt chart presenting an optimal installation schedule (Sol. 1.1 in Tab. 3) from OWF 1.

Results from the first set of experiments, with $|V| = 3$, are summarized in Tab. 3.

For OWF 1, with 20 turbines and 1 month time horizon, the CPLEX solver finds the optimal solution in 4 seconds with a total cost of \$ 11,106,600 (see Sol. 1.1 in Tab. 3). The optimal vessel choice is a combination of the BTS and the FS operating from Port 3.

The timing for turbine installations is presented in a Gantt chart (see Fig. 1). The top of the chart represents time, and the duration of each vessel charter period is represented by the black lines. The white boxes with numbers represent cycle durations, and the black milestones, along with the numbers above, represent the start of installation of turbines on a given cycle. Note that most cycles are completed without fully loading the vessels, which is also the case in larger instances.

In OWF 2, we consider 40 turbines and a 3 months time horizon. The CPLEX solver has a harder time finding and/or proving an optimal solution, compared to OWF 1. A feasible solution is obtained within seconds.

After running for 20,000 seconds, an optimal solution is not proven. The best feasible solution obtained is an upper bound to our minimization problem. Because the CPLEX solver is a branch-and-bound algorithm, we also obtain a lower bound to the problem. The difference between these two bounds compared to the best feasible solution is referred to as the *optimality gap*: The maximum potential improvement in the objective function value in the optimal solution. The best upper bound may very well be the optimal solution even though an optimality gap exists, because the potential reduction in costs may not be feasible.

An optimality gap of 12.4 % is obtained in OWF 2 with a combination of the BTS and the UTS operating from Port 3, and the objective cost measures \$ 19,639,480 (see Sol. 2.1 in Tab. 3).

For OWF 3, with 100 turbines and 5 months time horizon, no optimal solution is proven within a time frame of 30,000 seconds. After 30,000 seconds, an optimality gap of 30.5 % is realized, and the total costs measure \$ 47,858,700 (see Sol. 3.1 in Tab. 3). In this solution, all strategies are mobilized operating from Port 3. The FS is chartered longest and assigned most turbine installations.

Table 3. Results from OWF 1,2 and 3. The fourth column represents the total number of turbines installed with vessel $v \in V$.

OWF	Sol.	Objective	Turbines FS BTS UTS			Port	CPU time/Gap
1	1.1	\$ 11,106,600	6	14	0	3	4 s/0.0 %
2	2.1	\$ 19,639,480	0	10	30	3	20,000 s/12.4 %
3	3.1	\$ 47,858,700	38	36	26	3	30,000 s/30.5 %

Results from the second set of experiments, where $|V| = 6$, are summarized in Tab. 4.

The optimal solution for OWF 1 is found after 76 seconds, and total costs are reduced to \$ 10,958,000 (see Sol. 1.2 in Tab. 4). The FS is no longer optimal, and the BTS is duplicated, still operating from Port 3. All vessel operations in the duplicated solution happen within the same weather windows.

If we shorten all weather windows for installation operations for the BTS by one working day, the optimal solution is found after 103 seconds (see Sol. 1.3 in

Tab. 4). The UTS is duplicated with a total project cost increase of 5.4 % from Sol. 1.2. In this case, it proves optimal to operate from Port 1.

If we decrease the charter rate of the UTS to $ 160,000 /day (-11 %) and the mobilisation cost to $ 800,000, the optimal solution is found after 13 seconds, and the total costs are reduced by 5.2 % from Sol. 1.2 (see Sol. 1.4 in Tab. 4). The UTS is duplicated with the same schedule as Sol. 1.3 operating from Port 1.

With the possibility of duplications of identical vessels in OWF 2, the optimality gap reaches 7.2 % after 20,000 seconds, and the total costs sum up to $ 19,204,740 (see Sol. 2.2 in Tab. 4). Note that Sol. 2.2 has a lower objective and a lower optimality gap compared to Sol. 2.1 (see Tab. 3), even though the instance is larger.

Since the FS is not mobilized in OWF 2, we try to simplify the instance by eliminating the FS entirely (we impose $\gamma_{FS} = 0$). In this case, optimality is proven for OWF 2 after 6,000 seconds, and the objective is reduced by 1.0 % compared to Sol. 2.2 (see Sol. 2.3 in Tab. 4).

For OWF 3, a feasible solution is found after 2,200 seconds. After 30,000 seconds, this solution is improved by 4.5 % and has a cost of $ 51,216,768 with an optimality gap of 34.4 % (see Sol. 3.2 in Tab. 4).

In OWF 3, no feasible solution is found after 30,000 seconds for only the FS ($\gamma_{BTS} = \gamma_{UTS} = 0$). By using only the BTS ($\gamma_{FS} = \gamma_{UTS} = 0$ is imposed), the total costs measure $ 55,045,400 with an optimality gap of 39.0 % after 30,000 seconds (see Sol. 3.3 in Tab. 4). For only the UTS ($\gamma_{FS} = \gamma_{BTS} = 0$), the total costs drop below Sol. 3.1 (see Tab. 3) with an objective of $ 44,673,060, and an optimality gap of 6.0 % after 30,000 seconds (see Sol. 3.4 in Tab. 4).

Table 4. Results from OWF 1,2 and 3 with possibility of duplication. The fourth column represents the total number of turbines installed with vessel $v \in V$.

OWF	Sol.	Objective	Turbines						Port	CPU time/Gap
			FS1	FS2	BTS1	BTS2	UTS1	UTS2		
1	1.2	$ 10,958,000	0	0	10	10	0	0	3	76 s/0.0 %
	1.3	$ 11,555,200	0	0	0	0	10	10	1	103 s/0.0 %
	1.4	$ 10,382,400	0	0	0	0	10	10	1	13 s/0.0 %
2	2.2	$ 19,204,740	0	0	14	13	13	0	3	20,000 s/7.2 %
	2.3	$ 19,019,520	-	-	13	13	14	0	3	6,000 s/0.0 %
3	3.2	$ 51,216,768	25	29	5	11	29	0	3	30,000 s/34.4 %
	3.3	$ 55,045,400	-	-	45	55	-	-	3	30,000 s/39.0 %
	3.4	$ 44,673,060	-	-	-	-	54	46	3	30,000 s/6.0 %

4.3   Discussion

Because the model is deterministic, uncertainty is not considered in each instance. The trait of not dealing with uncertainty explicitly is demonstrated to be unfortunate through OWF 1 (see Sol. 1.2-1.4 in Tab. 4). With a small change in uncertain input data concerning weather and costs, the solution output is altered completely in terms of both port and vessel decisions. Conclusions drawn to aid strategic decisions from a single instance are thus rather speculative, even with optimality proven.

The seemingly nice benefit of being able to carry many wind turbines per trip turns out to be of small significance, since most cycles are performed without fully loading the vessels. This may be a consequence of the weather-sensitive installation lifts being the bottlenecks of the process, as concluded by [2].

The suggested port choice for most instances is Port 3 with highest fixed costs and shortest travel distance to the wind farm. The port decision changes from Port 3 to Port 1 in OWF 1 for instances where the UTS is proven the optimal strategy. This is probably due to longer weather windows for the UTS for installation operations, which makes longer transits and lower port handling costs a preferable choice. Potential growth of port handling costs with OWF size is not considered.

The UTS, with the benefit of long weather windows, seems to be a good option for large farms in OWF 3 (see Sol. 3.4 in Tab. 4). However, OWF 3 also show that including more vessel possibilities for the same wind farm does not necessarily produce better solutions (compare Sol. 3.1 in Tab. 3 and Sol. 3.2 in Tab. 4). Thus, our ability to draw conclusions from solutions obtained without proving optimality might be limited, although in some cases (see Sol. 2.2-2.3 in Tab. 4), the proven optimal solution (Sol. 2.3) has the same port and vessel fleet as the solution obtained without proving optimality (Sol. 2.2).

5   Conclusions

The instances in Section 4 can be used to support arguments for which factors are the most critical during the installation of OWFs, and which vessel and port strategy is the preferable choice for a specific OWF. Several instances ought to be implemented for the same OWF to somehow deal with uncertainty.

The framework of the problem in this model calls for drastic simplifications if large instances are to be tackled with an exact solver in a reasonable time frame. Further work can be done on developing heuristic methods to solve instances of the current model, however, proving optimality might still be challenging. Stochastic extensions will further complicate the model, so on a strategic and aggregated level, several scenario analyses may be a better alternative to aid the project decisions considered in this work.

Considering smaller fractions of a large wind farm can be a way of proving optimality with the CPLEX solver. Whether the strategic choices are altered when considering large wind farms in an aggregated versus fractionated manner, depends on how the different input data scale for growing instances, especially the port handling costs.

References

1. Ahn, D., Shin, S. C., Kim, S. Y., Kharoufi, H., & Kim, H. C.: Comparative evaluation of different offshore wind turbine installation vessels for Korean west-south wind farm. International Journal of Naval Architecture and Ocean Engineering, 9(1) (2017) pp. 45–54
2. Barlow, E., Öztürk, D. T., Revie, M., Boulougouris, E., Day, A. H., & Akartunal, K.: Exploring the impact of innovative developments to the installation process for an offshore wind farm. Ocean Engineering, 109 (2015) pp. 623–634
3. Beale, E. M. L., & Tomlin, J. A.: Special facilities in a general mathematical programming system for non-convex problems using ordered sets of variables. J. Lawrence (Ed.), *OR 69: Proceedings of the Fifth International Conference on Operations Research*, Tavistock Publications, London (1970) pp. 447–454
4. Dalgic, Y., Lazakis, I., & Turan, O.: Vessel charter rate estimation for offshore wind O&M activities. Developments in Maritime Transportation and Exploitation of Sea Resources, CRC Press, Boca Raton (2013) pp. 899–907
5. Dalgic, Y., Lazakis, I., Turan, O., & Judah, S.: Investigation of optimum jack-up vessel chartering strategy for offshore wind farm O&M activities. Ocean Engineering, 95 (2015) pp. 106–115
6. Irawan, C. A., Jones, D., & Ouelhadj, D.: Bi-objective optimisation model for installation scheduling in offshore wind farms. Computers & Operations Research, 78(C) (2017) pp. 393–407
7. Scholz-Reiter, B., Lütjen, M., Heger, J., and Schweizer, A.: Planning and control of logistics for offshore wind farms. In *Proceedings of the 12th WSEAS international conference on Mathematical and computational methods in science and engineering*. World Scientific and Engineering Academy and Society (WSEAS) (2010) pp. 242–247
8. Uraz, Emre.: Offshore Wind Turbine Transportation & Installation Analyses Planning Optimal Marine Operations for Offshore Wind Projects. Master's thesis, Gotland University, Department of Wind Energy (2011)
9. Publicly available met-ocean data by Metno from FINO3 offshore location. Uploaded by A. Graham. NORA10 reanalysis with 10 km horizontal resolution from year 2000-2010. *https://rwf.computing.uni.no/download/* (Visited 31-07-2017)
10. Overview of CPLEX Options for AMPL. *http://ampl.com/products/solvers/solvers-we-sell/cplex/options/* (Visited 31-07-2017)

Maritime Load Dependent Lead Times - An Analysis

Julia Pahl[1] and Stefan Voß[2]

[1] SDU Engineering Operations Management, Department of Technology and Innovation, University of Southern Denmark, Campusvej 55, DK-5320 Odense, julp@iti.sdu.dk
[2] Institute of Information Systems, University of Hamburg, Von-Melle-Park 5, D-20146 Hamburg stefan.voss@uni-hamburg.de

Abstract. Traditionally, the maritime sector follows a very conservative approach towards sharing information and adopting *information technology* (IT) to streamline logistic activities. Late arrivals of ships create problems especially with the trend to build large ships leading to peak loads of process steps and increased container lead times. Proposed solutions to fight congestion range from extending port capacities to process optimization of parts of the maritime supply chain. The potential that lies in information sharing and integrated planning using IT has received some attention, but mainly on the operational level concerning timely information sharing. Collaborative planning approaches for the maritime supply chain are scarce. The production industry already implemented planning and information concepts. Problems related to the maritime supply chain have great similarities with those encountered in production. Inspired by supply chain planning systems, we analyze the current state of (collaborative) planning in the maritime transport chain with focus on containers. Regarding the problem of congestion, we particularly emphasize on *load dependent lead times* (LDLT) which are well studied in production.

1 Introduction

Timely transportation at least possible costs is one of the main objectives according to which all actors of the maritime supply chain are measured by the customer. In order to fulfill this goal, an efficient information exchange used for planning and scheduling is required. The industrial production sector has been subject to intensive analysis regarding interacting factors influencing lead times. It is recognized and empirically proven that lead times are dependent on the resource utilization and exponentially increase when utilization passes a certain level (see [11] and the references therein). This can also be measured by *work in process* (WIP) building up in front of workstations. When considering the maritime supply chain, we can see the same dependency which becomes evident in ports with high workloads due to uncertain arrival times of containers and congestion effects of subsequent resources.

Recently, a large amount of work has been attributed to information sharing and related supporting systems (see, e.g., [5]). However, information sharing of maritime supply chain partners is reported to be very conservative and limited to data exchange on cargo and related documentation required by country-specific legislation [6]. Additionally, it focuses on the operative and real-time horizon. Aggregate planning and

T. Bektaş et al. (Eds.), ICCL 2017, LNCS 10572, pp. 300–305, 2017.
https://doi.org/10.1007/978-3-319-68496-3_20

scheduling is rare and has only recently been addressed by researchers and practitioners [1, 2].

As the trend of increased ship sizes will continue, new solutions need to be developed that help to plan and coordinate processes and capacities along the maritime supply chain. Special focus should be on capacity utilization smoothing to ensure reliable lead times and robust transport schedules for customers. Costly capacity expansions requiring space are not always feasible due to restrictions of ports in the vicinity of cities as, e.g., in Europe, so that other solutions should be exploited first.

In this paper, we review the literature in maritime logistics regarding congestion and approaches for advanced (lead time) planning. We focus on container transport due to its discrete features and natural analogies to production.

2   Advanced Planning Approaches in the Maritime Supply Chain

Supply chain management (SCM) emerged from logistics and has been a major management issue in the last decades. It has been stimulated by the developments in information and communication technology (see, e.g., [12]. Despite the fact that the shipping industry is quite conservative, their optimization endeavors lead to more and more tight planning and scheduling, so that disturbances have considerably larger impact at heavy system loads (where systems may relate to terminals, access infrastructure to and from the hinterland etc.). Surprisingly, while SCM in maritime transportation and related concepts to enhance supply chain visibility and orientation are becoming an issue (see also [1]), collaborative planning still seems almost nonexistent (see also [3]). This might be due to its history as a sector with complex networks of fragmented, independent trade partners [7] with different business models. Fierce competition as well as a lack of mutual trust in the maritime sector are frequently stated reasons [14]. This situation seems changing at least on the operational time level with IT pilots aiming at improving information provision. For instance, port community systems have been developed in the 1980s, but are subject to continuous improvement (see, e.g., [5]). However, they do not provide planning functionality, but could serve as a data basis for advanced collaborative planning.

In Figure 1, we adapted the planning modules of the *supply chain planning* (SCP) matrix (see [4] and the references therein) to the maritime case further aligning them to the different phases of transport, i.e., pre-, ocean, and on-carriage [15] extending them to more details on departure and arrival port handling phases. This gives an idea of the areas and modules for *maritime collaborative planning systems* (MCPS). The modules in the SCP matrix underlie a hierarchical planning approach and are linked by vertical and horizontal information flows updated in a rolling horizon fashion and require coordination of planning activities [4].

2.1   Congestion Phenomena and Information Sharing

Maritime supply chain partners depend on reliable information about *estimated times of arrival* (ETAs) of containers handled by their direct up- and downstream partners in order to efficiently plan their capacities, processes, and services. Reasons for congestion

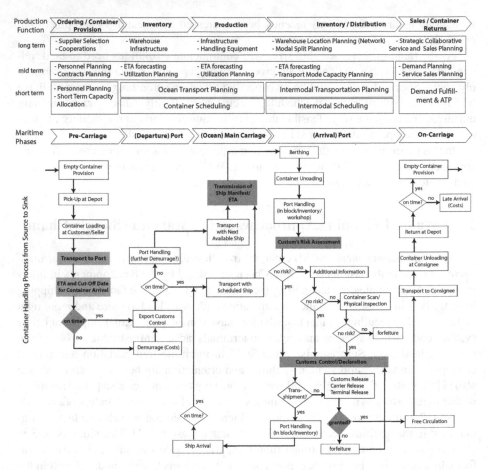

Fig. 1. Analogies in maritime container transport and production planning - process steps and planning functions; own illustration

start with 1) uncertainty of ship and import container ETAs, 2) uncertainty of truck and export container ETAs, and 3) uncertainty of service times of handling equipment and customs.

Innovative IT approaches exist in the form of mobile apps aiming at avoiding congestion on the roads to the port by providing truckers with estimated information on harbor "turn times" (pick-up and delivery) as well as waiting times at the terminal gates (see, e.g., [16]); for more examples see [10]. Apps can also match drivers with empty containers with those needing to pick one up, so that the exchange can be conducted outside the port area.

Especially in the light of increasing ship sizes and related demand peaks, delays of ship arrivals, but also of export containers lead to increases of waiting times. The situation can be improved by short-term provision of sufficient handling equipment and/or long-term capacity extension and related land-side costs [8]. Additionally, the handling of delayed import and transshipment containers becomes more difficult due to export containers congesting the yard and increasing the need for reordering. This decreases port efficiency and increases LDLT as well as costs. Besides, berthing windows for unloading and loading of large vessels extend from 24 to 72 hours not prioritizing unloading [2]. As a result, export containers may loose their hinterland connections or lead to congestion at the port gate due to waiting trucks. Related transport modes depart with unused spaces wasting expensive capacity.

2.2 Collaborative Planning Approaches

There is one reference that directly accounts for MCPS: [1] propose a collaborative SCM system for the maritime logistic chain focusing on three main business processes, i.e., management of 1) orders, 2) demand, and 3) vehicles. These three business processes can be taken into account on a tactical and operational level where demand management contains forecasting and generation of information regarding workloads. Order management is related to coordination, execution, and control of physical and information flows. This is similar to the supply chain processes being one dimension of the SCP matrix (see Figure 1 for the modified version), but differs in the differentiation on orders and demand.

In compliance with other researchers and practitioners, [1] discuss the problem of uncertainty caused by variability on ETAs of supply chain partners as well as related service times also stated in Section 2. The *port river information system project* (PRISE) aims at improving ETA information by providing an IT platform that merges information regarding ship arrivals as well as departures of all partners involved in the dispatching process of ships.[3] Similarly, [2] consider the connection between the arrival of the container and the transport by rail. They reveal that the container-specific ETA is necessary in order to correctly plan a high utilization rate of trains.

The Port of Hamburg recently announced its project "Smart Port Logistics" with several aims, among them optimizing the information flow to manage trade flows in an efficient manner [13]. Related to this, they aim at developing an intelligent IT infrastructure including sensors and (cloud) services.

A major bottleneck of container handling is customs; see Figure 1. Export containers need clearances and release permits to leave the port area [9]. Information on them is given in the ship's manifest before entering the port, but information is not sufficient for risk assessment at customs. Moreover, multiple manual entering of information in related systems increase processing times. Single Window Systems speed up customs processes by providing correct information on cargo [6]; see also [5] for a framework of a port-centric information management system built as a single window system.

3 Conclusions

Information sharing in supply chains is mandatory for the efficient flow of goods. In case of delays, anticipated information can avoid or reduce LDLT and smooth capacity

---

[3]Internet source: https://hhla.de/en/2014/03/it-platform-optimises-harbour-processes.html; Last call: 07.07.2016

utilization if collaborative planning is in place. Industrial production has a long tradition in developing and implementing IT systems for information sharing and process planning. The adoption and/or customization of such systems and related planning approaches can be promising to improve the maritime supply chain. LDLT are due to information distortion in planning and control of the supply chain. We review the maritime supply chain for WIP and related congestion in order to highlight bottlenecks and approaches of collaborative planning. Innovative trends exist to improve its overall efficiency on an operational level. Aggregate planning remains a critical issue. Future research will provide an in-depth-discussion on the applicability of SCP solutions.

References

1. Ascencio, L., Gonzáles-Ramírez, R., Bearzotti, L., Smith, N., Camacho-Vallejo, J.: A collaborative supply chain management system for a maritime port logistics chain. Journal of Applied Research and Technology 12, 444–458 (2014)
2. Elbert, R., Walter, F.: Information flow along the maritime transport chain - a simulation based approach to determined impacts of estimated time of arrival messages on the capacity utilization. In: Tolk, A., Diallo, S., Ryzhov, I., Yilmaz, L., Buckley, S., Miller, J. (eds.) Proceedings of the 2014 Winter Simulation Conference. pp. 1795–1806 (2014)
3. Elbert, R., Walter, F., Grig, R.: Delphi-based planning approach in the maritime transport chain. Journal of Shipping and Ocean Engineering 2, 175–181 (2012)
4. Fleischmann, B., Meyr, H., Wagner, M.: Advanced planning. In: Stadtler, H., Kilger, C. (eds.) Supply Chain Management and Advanced Planning, chap. 4, pp. 81–106. Springer, 5 edn. (2015)
5. Heilig, L., Voß, S.: Port-centric information management in smart ports: A framework and categorization. Tech. rep., Institute of Information Systems, Universtiy of Hamburg (2016)
6. Hesketh, D.: Weaknesses in the supply chain: Who packed the box? World Customs Journal 4(2), 3–20 (2010)
7. Lam, J.: Patterns of maritime supply chains: slot capacity analysis. Journal of Transport Geography 19, 366–374 (2011)
8. McLellan, R.: Bigger vessels: How big is too big? Maritime Policy & Management 24(2), 193–211 (1997)
9. Midoro, R., Pitto, A.: A critical evaluation of strategic alliances in liner shipping. Maritime Policy & Management 27(1), 31–40 (2000)
10. Ockedahl, C.: Trucker apps help drivers save time, reduce port congestion (2016), https://www.trucks.com/2016/05/16/trucker-apps-help-drivers-save-time-reduce-port-congestion/
11. Pahl, J., Voß, S., Woodruff, D.L.: Load dependent lead times - from empirical evidence to mathematical modeling. In: Kotzab, H., Seuring, S., Müller, M., Reiner, G. (eds.) Research Methodologies in Supply Chain Management, pp. 539–554. Physica, Heidelberg (2005)
12. Pahl, J., Voß, S., Woodruff, D.: Production planning with load dependent lead times: an update of research. Annals of Operations Research 153(1), 297–345 (2007)
13. Port of Hamburg: Port of Hamburg – digital gateway to the world. Internet Source: http://www.hamburg-port-authority.de/de/presse/broschueren-und-publikationen/Documents/140401_HPA_Broschuere_spl_web.pdf (2016), last call: 07.08.2016
14. Talley, W.: Maritime transport chains: Carrier, port and shipper choice effects. International Journal of Production Economics 151, 174–179 (2014)

15. Veenstra, A.: Ocean transport and the facilitation of trade. In: Handbook of Ocean Container Transport Logistics Making Global Supply Chains Effective, pp. 429–450. International Series in Operations Research & Management Science 220, Springer (2015)
16. Zampa, M.: Port of Oakland launches smart phone apps for harbor truckers. Internet Source: http://www.portofoakland.com/press-releases/port-oakland-launches-smart-phone-apps-harbor-truckers/ (2016)

Integrating Fleet Deployment into the Liner Shipping Cargo Allocation Problem

Daniel Müller[1], Stefan Guericke[2], and Kevin Tierney[1]

[1] Decision Support & Operations Research Lab, University of Paderborn,
Warburger Straße 100, 33098 Paderborn, Germany
{mueller, tierney}@dsor.de
[2] Stefan Guericke, A.P. Moller Maersk, Copenhagen, Denmark,
stefan.guericke@maersk.com

Abstract Liner carriers change their network on a regular basis, and they are therefore interested in a practical evaluation of the impact these changes have on the cargo flows in their networks. Despite great advancements in the practical applicability of network evaluators in recent years, vessel deployment continues to be considered as an input into the problem, rather than a decision. In this paper, we propose an extension of a state-of-the-art mixed-integer programming model for the LSCAP that incorporates the optimization of vessel count and vessel classes for each service. We perform a computational analysis on liner shipping networks of different sizes and compare our optimized results to fixed deployment scenarios. By integrating fleet deployment decisions into the cargo allocation problem, liner carriers can increase the profitability of their networks by at least 2.8 to 16.9% and greatly enhance their decision making.

Keywords: liner shipping, cargo allocation, fleet deployment

1 Introduction

Seaborne trade plays a critical role in global markets, and is responsible for transporting more than 10 billion tons of goods per year [15]. Furthermore, since the year 2000 the number of containers transported each year has almost tripled [15]. The challenge of designing, adjusting and operating liner shipping networks is thus becoming increasingly difficult to solve with current tools.

Containerized goods are transported in liner shipping networks on cyclical routes called services. Liner shipping companies operate a number of these services to connect different trade regions within their network. Services are generally operated with a certain periodicity (usually weekly or biweekly) such that ports of a service are visited at a fixed time each period. At each port of the service, cargo is loaded, unloaded or transshipped. Furthermore, cargo is transported in varying container types and sizes (*equipment types*).

Liner carriers must regularly make changes to their network, such as adding new services, changing the ports visited on a service, or removing services that are no longer profitable. These network modifications can have far-reaching and

© Springer International Publishing AG 2017
T. Bektaş et al. (Eds.), ICCL 2017, LNCS 10572, pp. 306–320, 2017.
https://doi.org/10.1007/978-3-319-68496-3_21

non-obvious effects on the network, such as changing the capacity or connection time between ports that are not part of the subset of the network being changed. Liner carriers are therefore interested in examining the impact of network changes on the cargo flows of their networks, which has been formulated by the operations research community as the liner shipping cargo allocation problem (LSCAP) (see, e.g., [7]).

The LSCAP targets the strategic and tactical planning horizon of a carrier. It computes the profit-maximal cargo flows on a predefined service network to provide carriers with a holistic view of their network, under the assumption that the cargo flows are deterministic. Models in the literature consider a number of detailed aspects, such as transit time requirements and variable vessel speeds.

Another tactical planning problem in the liner shipping industry is the fleet deployment problem. This problem is solved to determine the number of vessels and the type of vessel (*vessel class*) on a service. The assignment of vessels to services has a direct influence on the capacity of the services and the possible vessel speeds. Currently, these problems are solved independently of each other, with the output of the fleet deployment problem being fed into the LSCAP as fixed numbers of vessels and vessel types. However, the allocation of cargo is dependent on the capacity of the service vessels and the schedule of the services, meaning adjusting the deployment could yield higher profit in the LSCAP for the carrier. Simultaneously optimizing the cargo allocation and deployment offers tactical level guidance to carriers for which types of vessels should go where, and could even be used in a strategic context to determine how many vessels of a particular type should be built or chartered.

We extend the LSCAP model in [7]. The complete model contains the following components: path restricted multicommodity flow, transshipments, complex routes, transit time requirements, leg-based speed optimization and empty container repositioning. We add the assignment of vessel classes to services and the determination of the number of vessels of each service to the model.

With the help of our model, liner carriers can, for example, evaluate whether "upgrading" a service to a bigger vessel class is profitable or not. Furthermore, carriers can evaluate the effects of selecting different vessel classes and numbers of vessels for their services. These decisions influence individual leg speeds and the overall schedule of the service. This, in turn, changes how many containers can be transported, as faster ships can better meet customers' transit time requirements. We show in our computational experiments that considering fleet deployment leads to an increase in profit of several million dollars.

This paper is organized as follows. First, we review the related literature in Section 2. Then, Section 3 presents the cargo allocation problem with fleet deployment and vessel class selection. In Section 4, the model is presented. Section 5 contains the results of our computational experiments. Finally, Section 6 concludes and offers an outlook on future work.

2   Literature Review

There is a wealth of work considering cargo allocation/cargo routing and fleet deployment, however very little that addresses the intersection between these

Table 1. Overview of relevant publications about the fleet deployment problem and the cargo allocation problem[1].

Paper	MCF	TS	TT	TSD	LBSO	ER	VC	VCL
Akyuz and Lee (2014) [1]	✓	✓	✓	✓	-	-	-	-
Karsten et al. (2015) [8]	✓	✓	✓	✓	-	-	-	-
Guericke and Tierney (2015) [7]	✓	✓	✓	(✓)	✓	✓	-	-
Branchini et al. (2015) [2]	-	-	-	-	-	-	(✓)	✓
Wang et al. (2016) [16]	✓	✓	-	(✓)	-	✓	-	-
Gelareh and Meng (2010) [6]	(✓)	-	✓	-	(✓)	(✓)	✓	✓
Meng and Wang (2010) [9]	-	-	-	-	-	-	✓	✓
Wang and Meng (2012) [17]	✓	✓	-	-	-	-	✓	✓
Meng et al. (2013) [10]	✓	✓	-	(✓)	-	-	✓	✓
This article	✓	✓	✓	(✓)	✓	✓	✓	✓

problems. Table 1 presents a summary of relevant work. For details, we refer to [7]. The upper half of the table contains publications about cargo allocation, while the lower half contains fleet deployment publications. The table only refers to publications that consider complex service types. For an extensive overview of other optimization problems in liner shipping, we refer to [4].

2.1 Cargo Allocation

In the work of [1], a column generation approach is used to solve the cargo allocation problem with service levels, which are defined as combinations of vessel capacity and vessel speed. Although in [8] speed optimization is not considered, they extend the previous mentioned literature by including transit times and transshipment durations.

The publication of [7] integrates transit times and transshipment durations as well as speed optimization on individual legs and empty container repositioning. By integrating these requirements and aspects into a single model, [7] provide a high level of realism, making it valuable for liner carriers. Since varying vessel speed results in a non-linear optimization problem, the bunker consumption functions need to be linearized. We refer to [12] for a taxonomy of speed optimization publications, and various formulations of the fuel consumption function.

The integration of contractual cargo and spot cargo is considered in [2]. A mixed-integer programming model is presented that optimizes cargo assignments as well as the deployment and scheduling of vessels. Speed optimization and empty container repositioning are not included in this model.

In the work of [16], a chance-constrained optimization model is presented that considers deterministic and stochastic demand as well as various shipping activities like container loading/unloading, transshipments and waiting times. The model does not include any kind of speed optimization, but it does consider selecting the best vessel class for a specific service.

---

[1] MCF = Multiple cargo flows, TS = Transshipment, TT = Transit times, TSD = Transshipment duration, LBSO = Leg based speed optimization, ER = Empty repositioning, VC = Vessel count, VCL = Vessel class

2.2   Fleet Deployment

The fleet deployment problem is integrated with the optimization of vessel speed and service frequency in [6]. A mixed-integer model considers transit time restrictions and is evaluated on a set of randomly generated instances.

Another chance constrained model to solve the fleet deployment problem is presented by [9]. This model assumes a normal distribution for the cargo demand of each service. Without considering leg-based speed optimization, empty container repositioning or transit times, the mixed-integer programming model is solved on nearly realistic instances.

The model of [17] considers transshipment operations combined with the fleet deployment problem. For this, transshipments are allowed to be carried out multiple times without restrictions. Vessels can either be used from the carrier's fleet or chartered to be deployed on services. The authors assume predetermined vessel speeds for each service leg. In [10], a two-stage stochastic programming model that considers uncertainties in container demand and transshipment options is used to solve the fleet deployment problem.

3   Problem description

Before we describe the details of our mixed-integer programming model we discuss the aspects of the integrated cargo allocation and fleet deployment problem addressed in this paper.

3.1   Cargo allocation problem

Cargo allocation models are used for a strategic or tactical evaluation of a given liner shipping network. By considering possible cargo flows as well as fixed and variable costs, it can determine the profitability of an entire network. Furthermore, liner carriers are able to use the results of this model to refine their service schedules and improve coordination with container terminals.

The solution of the cargo allocation model determines how much cargo from each demand is carried and how that cargo is routed from its origin to its destination. When a single service contains both the origin and destination of a cargo demand, only loading and unloading operations along with the routing within the service need to be determined. For other cargo in which the origin and destination ports are distributed over separate services, both services need to be connected by transshipping the cargo at a shared port. If there is no port present in both services, multiple transshipments will occur until the cargo arrives at its destination port. We allow split cargo flows, but restrict the maximum number of paths the cargo may take.

Figure 1 shows a simple liner shipping network with two services. Both services are connected by the transshipment port Hamburg, such that cargo can be transported from Stavanger to Antwerp or Tillbury.

Cargo demands are associated with a maximum transit time between the demand's origin and destination. The transit time consists of the time cargo spends traveling by ship added to the time it spends in port during transshipment. We take into account the movement time of the containers on and off the ship, but use a constant transshipment time due to the complexity of allowing this to vary.

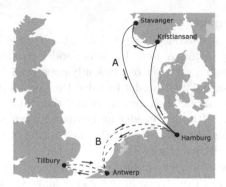

Figure 1. A simple liner shipping network in Northern Europe with two services connecting ports in Germany, Belgium, Denmark and Norway, from [7].

Depending on the overall frequency of the service and the total call time in ports, the remaining time can be spent for sailing between ports. The speed of the vessels is adjusted such that this remaining total sailing time is enough to maintain the periodicity of the service. Since the duration at sea is closely connected to the available time for vessels to move cargo in ports, including speed optimization in the cargo allocation problem is necessary. Additionally, speed optimization reduces bunker fuel consumption, one of the main costs of operating a seagoing vessel [14].

Vessels have a minimum and maximum speed in which the vessel can be operated. Buffer can be added between port visits on a schedule if the sailing time between the ports is longer than the vessel would require even at its minimum speed. Buffer can be used to hedge against uncertainty, although we do not directly consider this in our model.

3.2 Fleet deployment

The assignment of vessels to services is a tactical planning problem in which, typically, an entire shipping season is planned [5]. An assignment consists of the selection of a vessel class for a service as well as the determination of the total number of vessels for a service. Liner carriers use the fleet deployment problem to regularly assess the cost-efficiency of their network structure based on current rates of the charter-market. Dependent on the charter and bunker market, new vessels can be hired or existing off-hired, or own vessels chartered out.

In our model, we integrate the selection of vessel classes for the services and the determination of the number of vessels with the cargo allocation decisions. The goal is to benefit from the close connection between these fleet deployment decisions, the possible leg speeds and cargo moves. This integration also provides a more precise estimation of possible profits [16].

By optimizing the vessel class for each service, we take advantage of the specifications of these classes. In our case, vessel classes are defined by different minimum and maximum speeds as well as differing capacities (called *resource groups*), port call costs and charter costs. Resource groups can be, for example, the maximum weight the vessel can transport, the maximum number of container slots or the maximum number of reefer container plugs. We assume that only a single vessel class can be assigned to a service, which is a reasonable assumption in practice.

4   A mixed-integer programming model

In this section we provide the formal definition of the mixed-integer programming model for the cargo allocation problem with speed optimization and fleet deployment. This model is based on the formulation of [7], which uses a directed graph as a representation of the problem. Nodes represent port calls and arcs represent the legs between ports of a service. The graph includes a layered structure to model multiple visits to the same port in a single service. For more details about the graph formulation we refer to [7]. In addition to adding fleet deployment to the model, we also change the piece-wise linearization of the bunker consumption costs to the more efficient approach of [13].

In the following, we define the relevant index sets of the model. It should be noted that the majority of the index sets are equal to the original formulation. We added two sets to define Cartesian products of other index sets.

Sets

Q	Set of vessel classes
P	Set of ports
S	Set of services
$\mathbb{L}_s$	Set of layers for service s
$P_s \subseteq P \times \mathbb{L}_s$	Set of ports for service s
$L_s \subseteq P_s \times P_s$	Set of legs for service s
R	Set of resources
G	Set of resource groups
$R_g \subseteq G$	Set of resources in resource group g
N	Set of cargo flows
N_p^{OD}	Set of cargo flows whose origin or destination is port p, $N_p^{OD} = \{n \in N \mid o_n = p \vee d_n = p\}$
E	Set of equipment types for empty container balancing
$\Pi = \{0, 1, ...\}$	Set of container paths
N_e	Set of cargo flows and container paths of equipment type $e \in E$, $N_e = \{(n, \pi) \in N \times \Pi \mid e_n = e\}$
$H^N = S \times P \times Q$	Set of the Cartesian product of services, ports and vessel classes
$H^F = N \times \Pi$	Set of the Cartesian product of cargo flows and container paths

We now introduce the parameters of the model. We add parameters for the secant based linearization of the model. It is necessary to determine these secants for each vessel class as the classes have different bunker cost functions.

Parameters

$f_s \in \mathbb{N}_+$	Frequency in days of service s
$\delta^+(s,p,l) \in L_s$	Incoming leg of service s to port p,l
$\delta^-(s,p,l) \in L_s$	Outgoing leg of service s from port p,l
$C_{gq} \in \mathbb{N}_+$	Capacity of vessel type q of resource group g
$k_q^{Min} \in \mathbb{R}_+$	Minimum speed in knots of vessel type q
$k_q^{Max} \in \mathbb{R}_+$	Maximum speed in knots of vessel type q

$a_{rc} \in \mathbb{R}_+$	Utilization of resource r of container c
$o_n \in P$	Origin of cargo flow n
$d_n \in P$	Destination of cargo flow n
$q_n^{Max} \in \mathbb{R}_+$	Maximum quantity of cargo flow n in the planning horizon
$e_n \in E$	Equipment type of cargo flow n
$r_n \in \mathbb{R}_+$	Revenue in US\$ of cargo flow n
$\theta_n \in \mathbb{R}_+$	Maximum transit time of cargo flow n in days

$t_{pq}^E \in \mathbb{R}_+$	Duration in hours to move one container at port p with vessel type q. A move is a loaded or unloaded container
$t_p^{Add} \in \mathbb{R}_+$	Additional constant duration (for pilotage, bunkering etc.) required at port p in hours
$t \in \mathbb{N}_+$	Length of the planning horizon in days
w_s	Weekly volume adjustment parameter, $w_s = \frac{f_s}{t}$
$t_p^F \in \mathbb{R}_+$	Fixed container storage duration in port p in days

$\phi_{pq}^{PC} \in \mathbb{R}_+$	Port call cost in US\$ per call of vessel type q at port p
$\phi_q^D \in \mathbb{R}_+$	Depreciation/time charter cost of vessel type q
$\phi_p^{CH} \in \mathbb{R}_+$	Container handling cost at port p per unit in US\$
$\phi_p^{TS} \in \mathbb{R}_+$	Transshipment cost at port p per unit in US\$
$\phi_e^C \in \mathbb{R}_+$	Depreciation cost for one unit of equipment type $e \in E$
$\phi^P \in \mathbb{R}_+$	Penalty cost for services that have too few vessels deployed

g_{lq}^v	Gradient of secant for bunker consumption approximation of leg $l \in L_S$ for vessel type $q \in Q$
i_{lq}^v	y-intercept of secant for bunker consumption approximation of leg $l \in L_S$ for vessel type $q \in Q$
M_q^{Max}	Max. amount of vessels of vessel type $q \in Q$
M_{kq}^{SMax}	Max. costs to sail leg $k \in L_s$ with vessel type $q \in Q$
M_{spl}^P	Maxiumum port duration for service s, port p,l
M_{sk}^S	Maximum sailing duration for service s, leg k
M_n^C	Maximum duration for all container paths of cargo $n \in N$
ϵ	Small value for adjusting the transshipment indicator variables

Finally, we present the variables of the model. To support vessel class and count decisions, several sets of new variables are required. As discussed previously, the different vessel classes have different consumption functions, leading to different secant sets. Consequently, the variables for leg durations and bunker costs per leg also need a dependency on the vessel class. The main variables that are introduced to reflect the new possible decisions of vessel class selection and setting the vessel count are y_{sq}^V and γ_{sq}. Previously, γ_{sq} was a parameter that was set by the planner beforehand. Now, it can freely range on an integer scale larger than zero. The binary variable y_{sq}^V, however, describes whether a specific vessel is assigned to a service or not.

Variables

y_{sq}^V	Indicates whether vessel type $q \in Q$ is used on service $s \in S$
$\gamma_{sq} \in \mathbb{N}_+$	Vessel count of service $s \in S$ of vessel type $q \in Q$
$b_{skq} \in \mathbb{R}_+$	Bunker cost of leg k of service s for vessel type q
ϕ^F	Fixed cost of all services in the planning horizon
$\alpha_{n\pi} \in \mathbb{R}_+$	The quantity of cargo flow n on container path π over the entire planning horizon
$x_{skn\pi} \in \mathbb{R}_+$	The quantity of cargo flow $n \in N$ for path π on leg $k = (i, l, j, l') \in L_s$ of service s
$x_{ske} \in \mathbb{R}_+$	The amount of flow of equipment type $e \in E$ on leg $k = (i, l, j, l') \in L_s$ of service s
$l_{spln\pi q}$, $u_{spln\pi q} \in \mathbb{R}_+$	The amount of laden containers loaded and unloaded of flow $n \in N$ to and from liner service s at port $(p, l) \in P_s$ on container path π for vessel type $q \in Q$
l_{spleq}, $u_{spleq} \in \mathbb{R}_+$	The amount of empty equipment loaded and unloaded of empty flow $e \in E$ to and from liner service s at port $(p, l) \in P_s$ for vessel type $q \in Q$
$y_{skn\pi}^{CPL} \in \{0, 1\}$	Indicates whether leg k of service s is used to route cargo n on path π
$y_{n\pi}^{CP}$	Indicates whether cargo flow is $n \in N$ is routed on container path $\pi \in \Pi$
$y_{spln\pi}^T \in \{0, 1\}$	Indicates whether cargo n on path π is transshipped at port (p, l) on service s
$\tau_{spln\pi}^{TT} \in \mathbb{R}_+$	The time in days per visit to unload a cargo n on path π at service s port (p, l) for transshipment operations
$\tau_{spln\pi}^{TF} \in \mathbb{R}_+$	The time in days per visit to forward cargo flow n from service s lth call of port p to the succeeding port (and no cargo transshipment is performed)
$\tau_{skn\pi}^{CP} \in \mathbb{R}_+$	The total duration in days to route cargo flow n on path π on service s leg k
τ_s	Round trip time in days of service s
τ_s^V	Total relevant duration of all vessels of service s (number of vessels times the planning duration)
$\tau_{skq}^L \in \mathbb{R}_+$	Duration in days to travel leg k in service s for vessel type q
$\tau_{sk}^S \in \mathbb{R}_+$	Auxiliary variable specifying the duration in days it takes service s to steam leg $k \in L_s$ over the whole planning horizon. $\tau_{s,k}^S \leq t_{s,k}^{SMax}$
$\tau_{spl}^P \in \mathbb{R}_+$	Auxiliary variable giving the duration in days that service s calls port (p, l)
$\tau_{spl}^B \in \mathbb{R}_+$	The additional buffer for service s at port (p, l) in days to hold the round trip time
$\rho_s^{VS} \in \mathbb{R}_+$	Slack variable allowing vessels in service s to steam above maximum speed

We now introduce the objective and constraints of the model.

$$max = \sum_{n \in N} \sum_{\pi \in \Pi} \left(r_n - \phi_{e_n}^C \right) \alpha_{n\pi} - \phi^F - \sum_{s \in S} \phi^P \rho_s^{VS} \tag{1}$$

$$- \sum_{s \in S, (p,l) \in P_s} \sum_{n \in N_p^{OD}} \sum_{\pi \in \Pi} \sum_{q \in Q} \phi_p^{CH} \left(u_{spln\pi q} + l_{spln\pi q} \right) \tag{2}$$

$$- \sum_{s \in S, (p,l) \in P_s} \sum_{n \in N \setminus N_p^{OD}} \sum_{\pi \in \Pi} \sum_{q \in Q} \phi_p^{TS} \left(u_{spln\pi q} + l_{spln\pi q} \right) \tag{3}$$

$$- \sum_{s \in S, (p,l) \in P_s} \sum_{e \in E} \sum_{q \in Q} \phi_p^{TS} \left(u_{spleq} + l_{spleq} \right) \tag{4}$$

$$- \sum_{s \in S} \sum_{k \in L_s} \sum_{q \in Q} b_{skq} \tag{5}$$

The objective function contains terms for revenue (1), container handling costs (2), transshipment costs for laden (3) and empty containers (4) as well as for bunker consumption costs (5). Furthermore, term (1) considers depreciation costs for containers and adds fixed and penalty costs to the objective function. In comparison to the objective function of [7], the dependency on the selected vessel class was added to the terms (2) through (5). The fixed costs term ϕ^F contains costs that are dependent on the selected vessel class, making it a variable in our model. The bunker cost calculation in this model is simplified to the sum of all b_{skq} variables. The constraints of the model are as follows.

$$\sum_{\pi \in \Pi} \alpha_{n\pi} \leq q_n^{Max} \qquad\qquad \forall n \in N \tag{6}$$

$$\sum_{p \in P_s} \sum_{l \in \mathbb{L}_s} \tau_{spl}^P + \sum_{k \in L_s} \tau_{sk}^S - \rho_s^{VS} = \tau_s^V \qquad\qquad \forall s \in S \tag{7}$$

$$\tau_{sk}^S \leq t_{sk}^{SMax} \qquad\qquad \forall s \in S\, k \in L_s \tag{8}$$

$$\tau_{spln\pi}^{TT} \geq \frac{w_s}{2} \tau_{spl}^P + t_p^F - \mathbb{M}_{spl}^P (1 - y_{spln\pi}^T) \qquad \begin{array}{l} \forall s \in S, (p,l) \in P_s, \\ n \in N, \pi \in \Pi \end{array} \tag{9}$$

$$\tau_{spln\pi}^{TF} \geq w_s \tau_{spl}^P - \mathbb{M}_{spl}^P y_{spln\pi}^T \qquad \begin{array}{l} \forall s \in S, (p,l) \in P_s, \\ n \in N, \pi \in \Pi \end{array} \tag{10}$$

$$x_{skn\pi} \leq q_n^{Max} y_{skn\pi}^{CPL} \qquad \begin{array}{l} \forall s \in S, k \in L_s, \\ n \in N, \pi \in \Pi \end{array} \tag{11}$$

$$\tau_{skn\pi}^{CP} \geq \tau_{sk}^S w_s - \mathbb{M}_{sk}^S y_{skn\pi}^{CPL}$$

$$+ \begin{cases} \tau_{siln\pi}^{TT}, & if\, i \neq o_n \wedge i \neq d_n \\ \tau_{sjl'n\pi}^{TT} + \tau_{sjl'n\pi}^{TF}, & if\, j \neq o_n \wedge j \neq d_n \\ \frac{w_s}{2} \tau_{siln\pi}^P, & if\, i = o_n \\ \frac{w_s}{2} \tau_{sjl'n\pi}^P, & if\, j = d_n \\ 0, & otherwise \end{cases} \quad \begin{array}{l} \forall s \in S, \\ k = (i, l, j, l') \in L_s, \\ n \in N, \pi \in \Pi \end{array} \tag{12}$$

$$\alpha_{n\pi} \leq q_n^{Max} y_{n\pi}^{CP} \qquad\qquad \forall n \in N, \pi \in \Pi \tag{13}$$

$$\sum_{s \in S, k \in L_s} \tau_{sknn}^{CP} \le \theta_n + \mathbb{M}_n^C (1 - y_{n\pi}^{CP}) \qquad \forall n \in N, \pi \in \Pi \qquad (14)$$

$$\alpha_{n\pi} \le \alpha_{n\pi+1} \qquad \forall n \in N, \pi \in \{0, ..., |\Pi| - 1\} \qquad (15)$$

Constraints (6) to (15) are unchanged compared to [7] as there are no direct dependencies on the vessel class selection or the determination of the vessel count. Constraints (6) constrain the maximum volume on all container paths of a single cargo flow. The period structure of the services is modeled in the Constraints (7), including the durations at sea and the durations at the ports and an upper bound for the total leg duration is given in Constraints (8). Constraints (9) and (10) are used to calculate the time it takes to transship a container to another service or to simply forward the cargo to the next port of the service. In Constraints (11), cargo flows are allowed if a particular leg is used and restrict the leg capacity to the maximum cargo flow in the planning horizon. Constraints (12) compute the transport duration for cargo flows for all service legs, considering transshipment, forwarding and sea durations as well as port durations. Constraints (13) are used to set the variable $y_{n\pi}^{CP}$ to one if a cargo flow is routed on a container path. In Constraints (14), the maximum transit time is used to bound the sum of all single leg durations. Constraints (15) are symmetry breaking constraints for k-splittable flow problems (see [11]).

$$x_{s\delta+(s,k)n\pi} + \sum_{q \in Q} l_{sknn\pi q} = x_{s\delta-(s,k)n\pi} + \sum_{q \in Q} u_{sknn\pi q} \qquad \begin{array}{l} \forall s \in S, k \in P_s, \\ \pi \in \Pi, n \in N \end{array} \quad (16)$$

$$x_{s\delta+(s,p,l)e} + \sum_{q \in Q} l_{seplq} = x_{s\delta-(s,p,l)e} + \sum_{q \in Q} u_{seplq} \qquad \begin{array}{l} \forall s \in S, (p,l) \in P_s, \\ e \in E \end{array} \quad (17)$$

$$\sum_{z \in H^N} (l_{zn\pi} - u_{zn\pi}) = \begin{cases} \alpha_{n\pi}, & \text{if } p = o_n \\ -\alpha_{n\pi}, & \text{if } p = d_n \\ 0, & \text{otherwise} \end{cases} \qquad \begin{array}{l} \forall p \in P, \\ n \in N, \\ \pi \in \Pi \end{array} \quad (18)$$

$$\sum_{z \in H^N} (l_{ze} - u_{ze}) = \begin{cases} -\sum_{(n,\pi) \in N_e} \alpha_{n\pi}, & \text{if } p = o_n \\ \sum_{(n,\pi) \in N_e} \alpha_{n\pi}, & \text{if } p = d_n \\ 0, & \text{otherwise} \end{cases} \qquad \begin{array}{l} \forall p \in P, \\ e \in E \end{array} \quad (19)$$

$$\sum_{r \in R_g} \sum_{l, n \in H^F} a_{rn} x_{skl} + \sum_{e \in E} \sum_{r \in R_g} a_{re} x_{ske} \le \sum_{q \in Q} C_{gq} y_{sq}^V \qquad \begin{array}{l} \forall s \in S, \\ k \in L_s, \\ g \in G \end{array} \quad (20)$$

$$\tau_r^P = \sum_{q \in Q} \left[\left[\sum_{l \in H^F} (u_{rlq} + l_{rlq}) + \sum_{e \in E} (u_{req} + l_{req}) \right] t_{pq}^E + t_p^{Add} + \tau_r^B \right] \qquad \begin{array}{l} \forall s \in S, \\ (p,l) \in P_s, \\ r \in S \times P_s \end{array} \quad (21)$$

$$\epsilon y_{splnn\pi}^T \le \sum_{q \in Q} u_{splnn\pi q} \le q_n^{Max} y_{splnn\pi}^T \qquad \begin{array}{l} \forall s \in S, (p,l) \in P_s, \\ n \in N, \pi \in \Pi \end{array} \quad (22)$$

$$\epsilon y_{spln\pi}^T \le \sum_{q \in Q} l_{spln\pi q} \le q_n^{Max} y_{spln\pi}^T \qquad \begin{aligned} &\forall s \in S, (p, l) \in P_s, \\ &n \in N, \pi \in \Pi \end{aligned} \qquad (23)$$

$$g_{kq}^v \tau_{skq}^L + i_{kq}^v y_{sq}^V \le b_{skq} \qquad \begin{aligned} &\forall s \in S, k \in L_s, \\ &q \in Q, 0 \le v \le \lambda \end{aligned} \qquad (24)$$

$$b_{skq} \le \mathrm{M}_{kq}^{SMax} \qquad \forall s \in S, k \in L_s, q \in Q \quad (25)$$

$$\tau_{skq}^L \le \mathrm{M}_{sk}^S y_{sq}^V \qquad \forall s \in S, k \in L_s, q \in Q \quad (26)$$

$$\phi^F = \sum_{s \in S} \left(\sum_{(p,l) \in P_s} \sum_{q \in Q} \phi_{pq}^{PC} \frac{t}{f_s} y_{sq}^V + \sum_{q \in Q} \phi_q^D \gamma_{sq} \right) \qquad (27)$$

$$\tau_s = \sum_{q \in Q} \gamma_{sq} f_s \qquad \forall s \in S \quad (28)$$

$$\tau_s^V = \sum_{q \in Q} \gamma_{sq} t \qquad \forall s \in S \quad (29)$$

$$\sum_{q \in Q} y_{sq}^V = 1 \qquad \forall s \in S \quad (30)$$

$$\gamma_{sq} \le \mathrm{M}_q^{Max} y_{sq}^V \qquad \forall s \in S, q \in Q \quad (31)$$

$$t_{sk}^{SMax} = (l_{ij} \frac{t}{f_s}) / (\sum_{q \in Q} 24 k_q^{Min} y_{sq}^V) \qquad \forall s \in S, k \in L_s \quad (32)$$

Constraints (16) through (23) are adjusted to mirror the extension of deployment and duration variables. Constraints (16) and (17) are used to balance the flows of laden and empty containers. Constraints (18) and (19) compute the loading and unloading of laden and empty containers. The capacity limitation on service legs is defined in Constraints (20). It should be noted that the capacity strongly depends on the selected vessel class and therefore needs to be considered for the calculation of the maximum capacity. Constraints (21) computes the port call duration. The indicator variable for transshipments is set in Constraints (22) and (23).

Constraints (24) to (32) are added to the model to include the new linearization approach as well as the fleet deployment decisions. Constraints (27) perform the fixed cost calculation while Constraints (28) compute the round-trip time. Constraints (29) determine the total relevant duration and Constraints (32) the maximum duration of a service. Constraints (24) and (25) are used for the calculation of the bunker costs. The linearization with secants can be seen in Constraints (24) for a given number of secants λ. Constraints (25) are used to restrict the bunker consumption costs for vessel classes that are not used. There are two additional constraints that handle fleet deployment decisions. First, Constraints (30) only allow a single vessel class per service to be selected, and Constraints (31) restrict the number of vessels of a specific class to zero if the class is not selected for a service. If a vessel class is not selected for a particular service, the duration to travel a leg with that specific vessel class is set to zero in Constraints (26).

5   Computational results

Our computational analysis is based on the same instance sets that are used in [7], which consists of data from the public LINER-LIB database. They represent small to medium-sized service networks in three different regions. For each region, there are 30 different network variations. Table 2 provides detailed information about the size of these regions regarding the number of ports, number of legs, cargo flows and available vessel types. While the Baltic and WAF instances represent small feeder networks, the Mediterranean instances portray a medium-sized network. Furthermore, we fixed the number of available container paths for our experiments to one. The analysis of [7] provides more details of the consequences if the number of container paths is increased.

The goal of our analysis is to determine to what extent integrating fleet deployment with cargo allocation can improve the overall profit of a network. For this, we evaluate our instances with dual six-core Intel Xeon X5650 2.67GHz CPUs and 32GB of RAM per instance. We use Gurobi 7.0 with a time limit of 24 hours to solve our model. To evaluate the effects of the proposed model, we fix the fleet deployment to the originally planned vessel assignments. In the following analysis, we refer to these fixed assignments using the term "fixed deployment". The results from our newly proposed model are referred to as "optimized deployment".

Table 3 shows the average runtime in seconds, the average MIP gaps to the optimal solution in percent, and the number of solved instances for optimized and fixed runs over all instance regions.

For the WAF region, there is a single instance for the optimized deployment that was not solved within the timelimit of 24 hours, having a gap of 13.7% to the optimal solution. The last feasible solution in this case was found about 14.5 hours before termination. In the given time frame, none of the Mediterranean instances could be solved to optimality, and only three instances had a gap of less than 20% at the time of termination.

In the fixed deployment, the same WAF instance that could not be solved in the optimized case was solved in less than 13 minutes. Also, only 7 of the 30 Mediterranean instances have an optimality gap of more than 10%.

Although feasible instances have been found in some of the Mediterranean instances, in most cases the MIP gap is too big such that a further analysis of these feasible solutions would not benefit this work. Therefore, the following analysis will only evaluate the results of the Baltic and the WAF instances.

Figure 2 shows scatter plots of performance indicators for fixed and optimized deployments with Baltic instances. Each point represents an instance. The left-

Table 2. LINER-LIB instance information (see [3]).

Instance	Ports	Cargo flows	Legs	Vessel types	min/max services
Baltic	12	22	132	2	1/3
WAF	20	37	380	2	5/10
Mediterranean	39	365	1482	3	1/3

Table 3. Average runtime in seconds, average MIP gaps and number of solved instances for free and fixed runs.

	Optimized			Fixed		
	Avg. time	Gap	Solved	Avg. time	Gap	Solved
Baltic	0.67	0.00	30/30	0.10	0.00	30/30
WAF	3618.06	0.46	29/30	44.92	0.00	30/30
Mediterranean	86400.00	356.81	0/30	58978.33	14.14	10/30

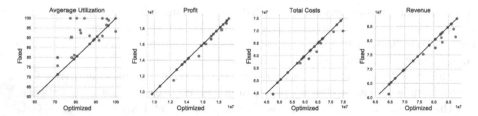

Figure 2. Performance of fixed and optimized deployments with Baltic instances.

most scatter plot shows the average utilization of the vessels as a percentage, the other three display financial indicators in tens of million USD. The performance of the optimized deployments is plotted on the x-axis and the performance of the fixed deployments is plotted on the y-axis. The diagonal line illustrates data points in which the performance of the fixed deployment is equal to the performance of the optimized deployment, while points below the line mean the optimized solution had a higher value than the fixed deployment (and a lower solution value for points above the line).

In the scatter plot showing the average utilization, only three instances have a better utilization in the optimized case for the Baltic region. By repositioning more empty containers, these instances increase the amount of used capacity of the vessels. It can be observed that some instances have a different strategy when to unload cargo, resulting in higher container path durations for their cargo. In these cases, cargo is transported on additional legs compared to the optimized case, increasing the usage of vessel capacity on these legs. In five of all the 53 services of the Baltic region (about 9.4%), the vessel class has been changed to increase the capacity of the service. In most of these cases, the utilization of these services decreased, although the total amount of transported cargo was increased in these instances, leading to higher revenues. The overall additional profit in the Baltic instances is on average about 150,000 USD and ranges from no difference at all to an increase of 1 million USD.

The scatter plots of the fixed and optimized deployment performance with WAF instances are displayed in Figure 3. The structure of this figure is the same as for the Baltic instances, except that the financial indicators are represented in units of 100 million USD.

About 45% of all the services (108 out of 238 services in total) show an adjustment to the deployment. Due to these deployment changes, all WAF instances

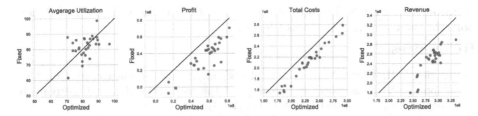

Figure 3. Performance of fixed and optimized deployments with WAF instances.

are able to carry more cargo and generate higher revenues. In many cases, vessel classes with higher capacity are assigned to the services, resulting in less utilization. There are also cases in which smaller vessel classes are selected, which usually leads to higher utilization of the vessels. It can also be observed that in some instances, the number of vessels is increased to take advantage of slow steaming. Despite raising costs by assigning more vessels and transporting more cargo, the overall additional profit is on average about 21 million USD, ranging from 9 million to 46 million USD.

The evaluation of the selected performance indicators (average vessel utilization, profit, total costs and revenue), shows that by optimizing the fleet deployment the profit of a service network can be increased in many cases. Our proposed model allows for increases in the overall capacity of a service network by adding more vessels to a service or by switching vessel classes. Due to the higher capacity, more cargo can be transported.

6   Conclusion and future research

In this paper we integrated fleet deployment decisions into a state-of-the-art cargo allocation model. This extension combines two closely connected problems into a single model, giving liner carriers a decision support tool that enables a practically relevant analysis of their liner shipping service network. By providing the flexibility of optimizing vessel classes of a service as well as the vessel count of a service, services can be further improved regarding the profitability. To demonstrate this, we evaluated instances of two LINER-LIB regions by comparing the previously planned deployment with the results of our optimized deployment. We showed that the integrated optimization of cargo allocation and fleet deployment leads to higher numbers of transported cargo, therefore resulting in overall increases of profits of an average of 150,000 USD in the Baltic instances and an average of 21 million USD for the WAF instances.

Future research can be performed on improving the solution time of this model, as even the relatively small WAF instances take a long time to solve. For this, a column generation approach or a heuristic approach could be implemented. Furthermore, the current model includes assumptions about cargo handling and piloting times that could be relaxed in a stochastic model.

Acknowledgements The authors thank the PC^2 at the University of Paderborn for the use of the Arminius Cluster.

References

1. Akyüz, M.H., Lee, C.Y.: Service level assignment and container routing for liner shipping service networks. Proceedings of the International MultiConference of Engineers and Computer Scientists (2) (2014)
2. Branchini, R.M., Armentano, V.A., Morabito, R.: Routing and fleet deployment in liner shipping with spot voyages. Transportation Research Part C: Emerging Technologies 57, 188–205 (2015)
3. Brouer, B.D., Alvarez, J.F., Plum, Christian E. M., Pisinger, D., Sigurd, M.M.: A base integer programming model and benchmark suite for liner-shipping network design. Transportation Science 48(2), 281–312 (2014)
4. Brouer, B.D., Karsten, C.V., Pisinger, D.: Optimization in liner shipping. 4OR - A Quarterly Journal of Operations Research 15(1), 1–35 (2017)
5. Christiansen, M., Fagerholt, K., Nygreen, B., Ronen, D.: Ship routing and scheduling in the new millennium. European Journal of Operational Research 228(3), 467–483 (2013)
6. Gelareh, S., Meng, Q.: A novel modeling approach for the fleet deployment problem within a short-term planning horizon. Transportation Research Part E: Logistics and Transportation Review 46(1), 76–89 (2010)
7. Guericke, S., Tierney, K.: Liner shipping cargo allocation with service levels and speed optimization. Transportation Research Part E: Logistics and Transportation Review 84, 40–60 (2015)
8. Karsten, C.V., Pisinger, D., Ropke, S., Brouer, B.D.: The time constrained multicommodity network flow problem and its application to liner shipping network design. Transportation Research Part E: Logistics and Transportation Review 76, 122–138 (2015)
9. Meng, Q., Wang, T.: A chance constrained programming model for short-term liner ship fleet planning problems. Marit. Policy Manag. 37(4), 329–346 (2010)
10. Meng, Q., Wang, T., Wang, S.: Multi-period liner ship fleet planning with dependent uncertain container shipment demand. Marit. Policy Manag. 42(1), 43–67 (2013)
11. Petersen, B.: Shortest Path and Vehicle Routing, Ph.D. Thesis. DTU Management Engineering (2011)
12. Psaraftis, H.N., Kontovas, C.A.: Green maritime transportation: Speed and route optimization. In: Psaraftis, H.N. (ed.) Green Transportation Logistics, International Series in OR & MS, vol. 226, pp. 299–349. Springer (2016)
13. Reinhardt, L.B., Plum, C.E., Pisinger, D., Sigurd, M.M., Vial, G.T.: The liner shipping berth scheduling problem with transit times. Transportation Research Part E: Logistics and Transportation Review 86, 116–128 (2016)
14. Stopford, M.: Maritime economics. Routledge, London, 3rd edn. (2009)
15. United Nations Conference on Trade and Development: Review of maritime transport (2016)
16. Wang, H., Zhang, X., Wang, S.: A joint optimization model for liner container cargo assignment problem using state-augmented shipping network framework. Transportation Research Part C: Emerging Technologies 68, 425–446 (2016)
17. Wang, S., Meng, Q.: Liner ship fleet deployment with container transshipment operations. Transportation Research Part E: Logistics and Transportation Review 48(2), 470–484 (2012)

A New Formulation for the Combined Maritime Fleet Deployment and Inventory Management Problem

Bo Dong[1(✉)], Tolga Bektaş[2], Saurabh Chandra[3], Marielle Christiansen[1], and Kjetil Fagerholt[1,4]

[1] Norwegian University of Science and Technology, Trondheim, Norway
`bo.dong,mc,kjetil.fagerholt@ntnu.no`
[2] University of Southampton, Southampton, United Kingdom
`T.Bektas@soton.ac.uk`
[3] Indian Institute of Management Indore, P Madhya Pradesh, India
`saurabh@iimidr.ac.in`
[4] SINTEF Ocean, Trondheim, Norway

Abstract. This paper addresses the fleet deployment problem and in particular the treatment of inventory in the maritime case. A new model based on time-continuous formulation for the combined maritime fleet deployment and inventory management problem in Roll-on Roll-off shipping is presented. Tests based on realistic data from the Ro-Ro business show that the model yields good solutions to the combined problem within reasonable time.

Keywords: Fleet deployment, Maritime inventory routing, Ro-Ro shipping

1 Introduction

In maritime transportation, ships typically operate in one of the three modes: industrial, tramp or liner shipping. In industrial shipping, a shipping company manages the ships and the cargoes to be transported, with the aim of minimizing the transportation costs. In tramp shipping, the ships are assigned to the cargoes (some of which may not be obligatory) under contracts between the shipping company and the cargo owners, with the aim of maximizing profits, similar to a taxi service. In liner shipping, the ships follow a predefined itinerary with given port calls along routes according to a published schedule, similar to a bus service. Christiansen et al. [7] provide a detailed review on ship routing and scheduling for the various operational modes.

Roll-on Roll-off (Ro-Ro) shipping, a segment within liner shipping, is the major mode for the long distance international transportation of automobiles and other types of rolling equipment, as well as cargoes that can be placed on trolleys for loading and unloading. Meanwhile, the involvement of container shipping companies in automobile transportation business provide tough competition to Ro-Ro shipping companies. To improve profitability and strengthen

T. Bektaş et al. (Eds.), ICCL 2017, LNCS 10572, pp. 321–335, 2017.
https://doi.org/10.1007/978-3-319-68496-3_22

the ties with its customers, some Ro-Ro shipping companies may consider to provide vertically integrated logistics services to automobile companies, where a Ro-Ro shipping company is responsible for inventory management at the ports and transportation at sea [5]. The automobile companies share the production and consumption information with the shipping companies, while the shipping companies share the ship schedules with automobile companies on a regular basis.

Fleet deployment can be considered as a tactical planning problem of assigning ships in the fleet to voyages that must be serviced regularly on given geographical routes. The fleet deployment gives which ship will perform which voyage, as well as sailing routes for each ship in the fleet, i.e. each ship is assigned a sequence of voyages to service, probably with ballast sailing between the last port of one voyage and the first port of the next voyage. In most literature, fleet deployment problems were first encountered in container shipping, the largest segment within liner shipping. The models for fleet deployment problems in container shipping usually assume:

1. Each ship is assigned a single route and loop during the planning horizon.
2. Individual ships of the same type are not distinguished.

Perakis and Jaramillo [10, 12] have contributed to develop mathematical models for liner shipping fleet deployment problems. They proposed a linear programming (LP) model for a liner ship fleet deployment problem. The LP model minimizes the total operating costs for a fleet of liner ships over a given planning horizon. The model assigns ships across the routes, determines the number, type and duration of chartering-in ships and owned ships that are laid-up during the planning horizon. In their approach, the ship speed is considered as a parameter in the LP model. Their work was extended by Powell and Perakis [13]. They proposed an integer programming (IP) formulation to optimally assign a fleet of ships for a real liner shipping company. Computational results show substantial savings in total costs in comparison with the manual planning.

In Ro-Ro shipping, ship route planning works under more flexible assumptions. Fagerholt et al. [8] present a mixed-integer programming (MIP) model for fleet deployment in Ro-Ro shipping, and Andersson et al. [3] extend this model for a real fleet deployment problem by including speed as a decision variable.

Inventory management deals with deciding the quantities to transport between the ports along the routes so that the port inventory level of products are kept within given limits. There are a few examples in the literature for maritime inventory routing problems, though mostly in the industrial and tramp shipping (see for example [1, 6, 9, 11, 14–17]). These literature contributions suggest substantial financial savings by combining ship routing and scheduling planning with inventory management in industrial and tramp shipping. Therefore, it can be inferred that the fleet deployment planning in Ro-Ro shipping can achieve better results by integrating inventory management of cargoes at associated production and consumption ports.

In this paper, we propose a new time-continuous formulation for the combined Maritime Fleet Deployment and Inventory Management Problem (MFDIMP), along with computational testings on realistically generated test instances from the Ro-Ro shipping companies. The fleet deployment combined with inventory management in Ro-Ro shipping is rarely dealt with in the literature, but a few studies exist. Chandra et al. [4, 5] propose a time-discrete model for the combined MFDIMP. In deep-sea shipping where the planning horizons can be long, the time-continuous formulation is preferred as it is impractical to use time discretization with large numbers of time periods in a time-discrete model.

The remainder of this paper is organized as follows: In the next section we give a thorough description of the combined MFDIMP. Section 3 presents the mathematical formulation for the problem with a special focus on the modeling of the inventories at ports. A computational study is performed in Section 4, while concluding remarks are given in the final section.

2   Problem Description

We consider a liner shipping company that operates a heterogeneous fleet of ships with different capacities, service speeds and bunker consumption. At the beginning of the planning horizon, all ships in the fleet have unique initial positions, either in a port or somewhere at sea. Moreover, the ships can have different preparation times before they are able to commence new voyages because they must continue their on-going voyages or dry dock (for example, repair) first.

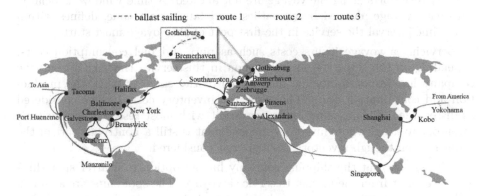

Fig. 1. A three route problem: America to Asia, Asia to Europe, Europe to America, with associated ballast sailings

A route (also called service) is defined as a logistical network used to transport all cargo from their loading ports in one geographical region to unloading ports in another. In general, the shipping company serves several routes. In Fig. 1, three routes are illustrated by solid lines and the ports are shown as dots. Route 1 sails from America to Asia while route 2 connects four Asian ports with five European ports. Similarly, route 3 starts from Europe and sails to America. To maintain regular service, each route must be serviced according to a given frequency, e.g. weekly or bi-weekly. Each sailing along a route is called a voyage. Even though each route should be serviced according to the given frequency, there is some flexibility when each voyage along a route must start, given by a time window. Each voyage (for example voyage number 1 on route 1) must be sailed by a ship and is often called a mandatory voyage. After a ship has completed one voyage on a route, it may serve another voyage on the same route or another route or end its service. To start the next voyage, the ship sails without load (i.e. ballast sailing) to the first port of the next voyage. As an example, a ship may first serve a voyage on route 2 from Yokohama in Asia. This route ends at Gothenburg in Europe. The ship may then continue to serve a voyage on route 3 from Bremerhaven in Europe. In this case, there would be a ballast sailing from Gothenburg to Bremerhaven between the two voyages. The ballast sailing between the two routes in Fig. 1 is illustrated by a dotted line. Different contract terms and product types transported along the various routes may restrict which ships can be assigned to voyages on a particular route, regarding capacity and compatibility.

We assume deterministic sailing times for all ships between successive ports along a route. We also consider deterministic sailing times for each ship between the last port of one route and the first port of another route. It is assumed that the time spent at each port is given regardless of quantities loaded/unloaded as the most important part of the processing time at a port is to enter/leave the port and berth. Waiting at the first port of a voyage is allowed, but waiting times at successive ports along the voyage are not allowed. A time window associated with each voyage, defined by an earliest and latest start time, defines within what time interval the service in the first port of the voyage must start.

Servicing a voyage incurs costs such as port and fuel consumption costs, depending on the ship type. It is common in this service that the automobile company has responsibility for the storage of the cargo at both the production and consumption ports. Therefore, the inventory costs can be considered as disregarded. This assumption is consistent with most research on maritime inventory routing, where inventory management is still a nontrivial part of the problem even though inventory costs are not considered.

We assume that the shipping company has an option to charter spot ships at a given cost from the market to service a voyage. The spot ships are assumed to be ready to service any voyage during the whole planning horizon, and they can start any time within its time window.

We use the term product for the same type of product transported along the same route. Each product has given production rates at its associated loading ports and given consumption rates at its associated unloading ports, which is assumed constant during the planning horizon. Each port has a different production and consumption rate for specified products. At a production port of a product, the shipping company must determine how many units to load of each product transported to its corresponding unloading ports. Each ship is able to carry a number of different products at the same time, and the products need to be carried in dedicated compartments because some of these products cannot be stored together. Similarly, each port has a storage capacity in terms of the maximum number of product it can hold. The size of spot ships for a given product is assumed as the size of the largest ship in the fleet for that product. Cargoes are rarely transshipped in Ro-Ro shipping, so transshipment is disregarded. The aim of this combined MFDIMP is to determine: (a) the ship routes and schedules (i.e. which ship should perform which voyages and in what sequence), (b) the start time of each voyage, (c) which voyages should be serviced by spot ships, and (d) the number of units of each product to be loaded/unloaded at associated ports during each voyage. The problem is to be solved subject to the following constraints: (a) all voyages are serviced within their given time windows, either by a ship in the fleet or by a spot ship, (b) the aggregate inventory limit of all products in a particular port should not exceed the maximum storage limit, and (c) there is no backlogging of demand for any product in any of the ports. The objective is to minimize total costs, which consist of the sailing costs for ships in the fleet and the time charter costs for spot ships, over a given planning horizon.

3   Model Formulation

The number of visits to each route during a given horizon is assumed fixed in Ro-Ro shipping. Thus, we use a time-continuous formulation which considers an ordering of the route visits according to the time of the visit, and introduce an index indicating the visit number to a particular route (i.e., voyage). The ship paths are defined on a network where the nodes correspond to route visits. As far as we know, there exist no studies in the literature which use a similar modeling approach as the one proposed in this paper.

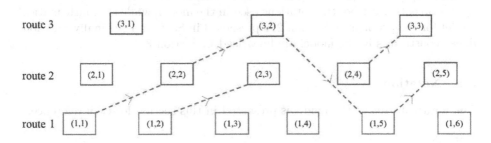

Fig. 2. Illustration of nodes and arcs with three ships: a ship services voyage 1 on route 1, voyage 2 on route 2, voyage 2 on route 3, voyage 5 on route 1 and voyage 5 on route 2; a ship services voyage 2 on route 1, voyage 3 on route 2; a ship services voyage 4 on route 2, voyage 3 on route 3.

We need to explain how nodes and arcs should be interpreted before we start with the modeling. In this model a node represents a given voyage along a route as illustrated in Fig.2. Thus, the pair denoted by (i, m) corresponds to a node in the model, i.e. voyage number m on route number i. Inside each node,

route 2 voyage 2 (2,2)

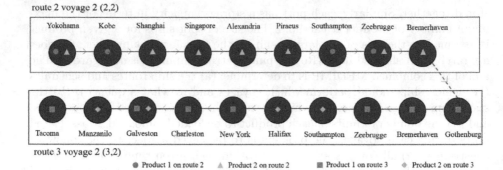

route 3 voyage 2 (3,2)

● Product 1 on route 2   ▲ Product 2 on route 2   ■ Product 1 on route 3   ◆ Product 2 on route 3

Fig. 3. Illustration of structure inside nodes: set of ports along the two routes. In (2,2), a ship loads product 1 and 2 at Yokohama, sails and loads product 1 at Kobe, sails and loads product 2 at Shanghai and Singapore, sails and unloads product 2 at Alexandria and Piraeus, sails and unloads product 1 at Southampton, sails and unloads product 1 and 2 at Zeebrugge, finally arrives at Bremerhaven and unloads product 2. Similarly, a ship carries two types of products from their associated loading ports to unloading ports in (3,2).

all the ports along the route are visited by the ship in sequence as shown in Fig.3. The arc between the nodes is represented by dotted line and denote the ballast sailing. For example in Fig.2 and Fig.3, the arc $\{(2,2)(3,2)\}$ represents the ballast sailing from the last port of voyage number 2 on route 2 to the first port of voyage number 2 on route 3. For a given route of a ship v in Fig.3, the decision variable x_{2232v} is a binary variable that is equal to 1 if the ship performs voyages $(2, 2)$ and $(3, 2)$ in sequence, and 0 otherwise.

Section 3.1 describes the notations used in the model, while the mathematical model for the problem in Section 2 is presented in Section 3.2. Finally, the non-linear constraints in the model are linearized in Section 3.3.

3.1   Notation

The notation used in the model is presented in this section for easy reference.

Sets

$\mathcal{I}$	set of routes, $i \in \mathcal{I}$
$\mathcal{M}$	set of voyages, $m \in \mathcal{M}$
$\mathcal{N}$	set of nodes, i.e. a voyage m along a route i, $(i,m) \in \mathcal{N}$
$\mathcal{N}_v$	set of nodes visited by ship v, $\mathcal{N}_v \subseteq \mathcal{N}$
$\mathcal{A}_v$	set of arcs $(i,m)(j,n)$ that can be serviced by ship v
$\mathcal{V}^R$	set of ships in the fleet, $v \in \mathcal{V}^R$
$\mathcal{V}^A$	set of spot ships, $v \in \mathcal{V}^A$
$\mathcal{V}$	set of ships, $\mathcal{V}^A \cup \mathcal{V}^R = V$
$\mathcal{P}_i$	set of ports along route i, $p \in \mathcal{P}_i$
$\mathcal{K}_i$	set of products transported along route i, $k \in \mathcal{K}_i$

Parameters

M_i	the number of voyages along route i during the planning horizon
P_i	the number of ports along route i
K_i	the number of products transported along route i
C_{iv}^O	cost for ship v sailing from its initial position to the start position of route i
C_{ijv}	cost of performing a voyage along route i and sailing ballast from the last port of route i to the first port of route j with ship v
C_{iv}^R	cost of performing a voyage along route i with ship v
T_{iv}^O	sailing time for ship v from its initial position to the start position of route i
T_{ijv}	sailing time of performing a voyage along route i and sailing ballast from the last port of route i to the first port of route j with ship v
T_{ip}^P	time spent at port p along route i
T_{ip}^R	sailing time on route i from the start position of route i to port p
$\underline{T}_{im}$	the earliest start time of servicing node (i, m)
$\bar{T}_{im}$	the latest start time of servicing node (i, m)
T	the length of the planning horizon
S_{ipk}^O	the initial inventory level of product k at port p along route i at the beginning of the planning horizon
R_{ipk}	production rate of product k at port p along route i, positive if port p is producing the product, and negative if port p is consuming the product
I_{ipk}	1 if port p is a loading port, -1 if port p is a unloading port, and 0 otherwise
$\underline{S}_{ip}$	the minimum inventory level at port p on route i
$\bar{S}_{ip}$	the maximum inventory level at port p on route i
Q_{ikv}	the capacity of the compartment of ship v dedicated for product k along route i
Q_v^C	the total capacity onboard ship v

Variables

x_{imv}^O	1 if ship v sails directly from its initial position to the start position of node (i, m), 0 otherwise
z_v^O	1 if ship v is not used, 0 otherwise
x_{imjnv}	1 if ship v sails directly from node (i, m) to node (j, n) (ship v sails node (i, m) and then ballast sailing to node (j, n) directly afterwards), 0 otherwise
z_{imv}	1 if ship v sails node (i, m) as its last voyage, 0 otherwise
w_{imv}	1 if ship v visits node (i, m), 0 otherwise
t_{im}	the time at which service starts at node (i, m)

s_{impk}	inventory level of product k at port p at the start of service for node (i, m)
s^E_{impk}	inventory level of product k at port p at the end of service for node (i, m)
l_{impkv}	the amount of product k onboard ship v when leaving port p on node (i, m)
q_{impkv}	the amount of product k loaded/unloaded to/from ship v at port p on arrival of node (i, m)

3.2 Mathematical Model

Objective Function. The objective function (1) is to minimize the total transportation costs. It consists of the sailing costs for ships in the fleet (i.e. initial ballast sailing costs, voyage costs and ballast sailing costs between successive voyages) and the time charter costs for spot ships.

$$Minimize \ \sum_{v \in \mathcal{V}} \sum_{(i,m) \in \mathcal{N}_v} C^O_{iv} x^O_{imv} + \sum_{v \in \mathcal{V}^R} \sum_{((i,m),(j,n)) \in \mathcal{A}_v} C_{ijv} x_{imjnv} +$$
$$\sum_{v \in \mathcal{V}} \sum_{(i,m) \in \mathcal{N}_v} C^R_{iv} z_{imv} \tag{1}$$

Routing Constraints. Constraints (2) ensure that ship v either departs from its initial position and sails towards node (i, m), i.e. to serve a voyage, or it is not used.

$$\sum_{(i,m) \in \mathcal{N}_v} x^O_{imv} + z^O_v = 1, \quad v \in \mathcal{V} \tag{2}$$

Constraints (3) and (4) are the flow conservation constraints, ensuring that a ship arriving at a node also leaves that node by either visiting another node or ending its route.

$$\sum_{(j,n) \in \mathcal{N}_v} x_{jnimv} + x^O_{imv} - w_{imv} = 0, \quad v \in \mathcal{V}, (i, m) \in \mathcal{N}_v \tag{3}$$

$$w_{imv} - \sum_{(j,n) \in \mathcal{N}_v} x_{imjnv} - z_{imv} = 0, \quad v \in \mathcal{V}, (i, m) \in \mathcal{N}_v \tag{4}$$

Constraints (5) ensure that ship v either ends after servicing some node or it is not used.

$$\sum_{(i,m) \in \mathcal{N}_v} z_{imv} + z^O_v = 1, \quad v \in \mathcal{V} \tag{5}$$

Voyage Completing Constraints. Constraints (6) ensure that each node is serviced once by either a spot ship or a ship in the fleet.

$$\sum_{v \in \mathcal{V}} w_{imv} = 1, \quad (i, m) \in \mathcal{N} \tag{6}$$

Load Management Constraints. Constraints (7) and (8) relate the quantity on board a ship to the quantity (un)loaded from the ship. Constraints (7) ensure that if ship v sails from port $p-1$ to port p, then the quantity of product k on board at the departure from port p should be equal to the quantity on board at departure from port $p-1$ plus (or minus) the quantity loaded (or unloaded) from p.

$$w_{imv}(l_{im(p-1)kv} + I_{ipk}q_{impkv} - l_{impkv}) = 0,$$
$$v \in \mathcal{V}, (i,m) \in \mathcal{N}_v, p \in \mathcal{P}_i \setminus \{1\}, k \in \mathcal{K}_i \tag{7}$$

We assume that all ships in the fleet start their voyages empty. Constraints (8) relate the quantity on board with the quantity loaded or unloaded at the start position of node (i,m).

$$w_{imv}(I_{i1k}q_{im1kv} - l_{im1kv}) = 0,$$
$$v \in \mathcal{V}, (i,m) \in \mathcal{N}_v, k \in \mathcal{K}_i \tag{8}$$

Similarly, all ships in the fleet are assumed ending their voyages empty.

$$l_{imP_ikv} = 0, \quad v \in \mathcal{V}, (i,m) \in \mathcal{N}_v, k \in \mathcal{K}_i \tag{9}$$

The ship capacity constraints are given by (10) and (11) imposing an upper bound on the quantity on board for a single product and all the products respectively. Constraints (10) also impose a lower bound on the the quantity on board.

$$0 \leq l_{impkv} \leq Q_{ikv}w_{imv}, \quad v \in \mathcal{V}, (i,m) \in \mathcal{N}_v, p \in \mathcal{P}_i, k \in \mathcal{K}_i \tag{10}$$

$$\sum_{k \in \mathcal{K}_i} l_{impkv} \leq Q_v^C w_{imv}, \quad v \in \mathcal{V}, (i,m) \in \mathcal{N}_v, p \in \mathcal{P}_i \tag{11}$$

Constraints (12) impose lower and upper bounds on the quantity loaded or unloaded.

$$0 \leq q_{impkv} \leq Q_{ikv}w_{imv}, \quad v \in \mathcal{V}, (i,m) \in \mathcal{N}_v, p \in \mathcal{P}_i, k \in \mathcal{K}_i \tag{12}$$

Time Constraints. Constraints (13) ensure that if ship v travels from its initial position to node (i,m) to start a voyage at time t, then the service at node (i,m) can only occur after the ship has arrived.

$$t_{im} \geq \sum_{v \in \mathcal{V}} T_{iv}^O x_{imv}^O, \quad (i,m) \in \mathcal{N} \tag{13}$$

Constraints (14) ensure that if ship v sails directly from node (i,m) to node (j,n), then the service at node (j,n) can only start after the start time of service at previous node (i,m) plus the time required to travel from route i to route j.

$$x_{imjnv}(t_{im} + T_{ijv} - t_{jn}) \leq 0, \quad v \in \mathcal{V}^R, ((i,m),(j,n)) \in \mathcal{A}_v \tag{14}$$

Constraints (15) define the time windows for each node.

$$\underline{T}_{im} \leq t_{im} \leq \bar{T}_{im}, \quad (i,m) \in \mathcal{N}_v \tag{15}$$

Inventory Constraints. The inventory constraints are necessary to ensure that the inventory levels are kept within the corresponding bounds and to link the inventory levels to the (un)loading quantities.

Constraints (16) and (17) define the inventory level upon arrival at each port on route i for the first time. Constraints (17) calculate the inventory level of each product at the first port on route i for the first time the route is visited, i.e. first voyage on the route.

$$s_{i1pk} = S_{ipk}^O + R_{ipk}(t_{i1} + T_{ip}^R + \sum_{p'=1}^{p-1} T_{ip'}^P), \quad (i,1) \in \mathcal{N}, p \in \mathcal{P}_i \setminus \{1\}, k \in \mathcal{K}_i \quad (16)$$

$$s_{i11k} = S_{i1k}^O + R_{i1k}t_{i1}, \quad (i,1) \in \mathcal{N}, k \in \mathcal{K}_i \quad (17)$$

The inventory level when service finishes at any port call (i,m,p) can be calculated from the inventory level upon arrival at the port in the call (i,m,p), adjusted for the loaded/unloaded quantity at the port call and the quantity produced/consumed when ships operate at ports as in constraints (18).

$$s_{impk}^E = s_{impk} - I_{ipk} \sum_{v \in \mathcal{V}} q_{impkv} + T_{ip}^P R_{ipk},$$
$$(i,m) \in \mathcal{N}, p \in \mathcal{P}_i, k \in \mathcal{K}_i \quad (18)$$

The inventory level upon arrival at any port call (i,m,p) can be calculated from the inventory level when the service finishes at the port in the call $(i,m-1,p)$, adjusted for the quantity produced/consumed in-between as in constraints (19).

$$s_{impk} = s_{i(m-1)pk}^E + R_{ipk}(t_{im} - t_{i(m-1)} - T_{ip}^P),$$
$$(i,m) \in \mathcal{N} \setminus \{(i,1)\}, p \in \mathcal{P}_i, k \in \mathcal{K}_i \quad (19)$$

The upper and lower bounds on the inventory levels are ensured by constraints (20) – (22). For a loading port, the inventory level increase monotonously before the start of any port operation. Therefore the possible maximum inventory level immediately before any loading port operation cannot exceed the upper bounds on the inventory level. Then the inventory level at the end of any port operation decreases due to the operation at the loading port. Therefore, the possible minimum inventory level immediately after any loading port operation cannot be less than the lower bounds on the inventory level as in (20). (21) describe the similar requirements for unloading ports.

$$\sum_{k \in \mathcal{K}_i} s_{impk} \leq \bar{S}_{ip}, \sum_{k \in \mathcal{K}_i} s_{impk}^E \geq \underline{S}_{ip}, \quad (i,m) \in \mathcal{N}, p \in \mathcal{P}_i^L \quad (20)$$

$$\sum_{k \in \mathcal{K}_i} s_{impk} \geq \underline{S}_{ip}, \sum_{k \in \mathcal{K}_i} s_{impk}^E \leq \bar{S}_{ip}, \quad (i,m) \in \mathcal{N}, p \in \mathcal{P}_i^U \quad (21)$$

Constraints (22) ensure that the inventory level at the end of the planning horizon is within the limits.

$$\underline{S}_{ip} \leq \sum_{k \in \mathcal{K}_i} (s^E_{impk} + R_{ipk}(T - t_{im} - T^R_{ip} - \sum_{p'=1}^{p} T^P_{ip'}) \leq \bar{S}_{ip},$$

$$(i, m) \in \mathcal{N} | m = M_i, p \in \mathcal{P}_i \qquad (22)$$

Binary and Non-negativity Constraints. Constraints (23) – (25) define the variables as binary. The nonnegativity requirements (26) are given for the variables representing the inventory level.

$$x_{imjnv} \in \{0,1\}, \quad v \in \mathcal{V}^R, ((i,m),(j,n)) \in \mathcal{A}_v \qquad (23)$$

$$x^O_{imv}, z_{imv}, w_{imv} \in \{0,1\}, \quad v \in \mathcal{V}, (i,m) \in \mathcal{N}_v \qquad (24)$$

$$z^O_v \in \{0,1\}, \quad v \in \mathcal{V} \qquad (25)$$

$$s_{impk}, s^E_{impk} \geq 0, \quad (i,m) \in \mathcal{N}, p \in \mathcal{P}_i, k \in \mathcal{K}_i \qquad (26)$$

3.3   Linearization

Since constraints (7) are non-linear and cannot be solved by a linear solver, we linearize the constraints (7) by replacing them with the following two sets of constraints (27) and (28), which forces $l_{im(p-1)kv} + I_{ipk}q_{impkv} = l_{impkv}$ when $w_{imv} = 1$.

$$l_{im(p-1)kv} + I_{ipk}q_{impkv} - l_{impkv} \leq Q_{ikv}(1 - w_{imv}),$$
$$v \in \mathcal{V}, (i,m) \in \mathcal{N}_v, p \in \mathcal{P}_i \setminus \{1\}, k \in \mathcal{K}_i \qquad (27)$$

$$l_{im(p-1)kv} + I_{ipk}q_{impkv} - l_{impkv} \geq Q_{ikv}(w_{imv} - 1),$$
$$v \in \mathcal{V}, (i,m) \in \mathcal{N}_v, p \in \mathcal{P}_i \setminus \{1\}, k \in \mathcal{K}_i \qquad (28)$$

Similarly, non-linear constraints (8) can be linearized in (29) and (30).

$$I_{i1k}q_{im1kv} - l_{im1kv} \leq Q_{ikv}(1 - w_{imv}), \quad v \in \mathcal{V}, (i,m) \in \mathcal{N}_v, k \in \mathcal{K}_i \qquad (29)$$

$$I_{i1k}q_{im1kv} - l_{im1kv} \geq Q_{ikv}(w_{imv} - 1), \quad v \in \mathcal{V}, (i,m) \in \mathcal{N}_v, k \in \mathcal{K}_i \qquad (30)$$

Constraints (14) are linearized as constraints (31), following [2].

$$t_{im} - t_{jn} + \max\{\bar{T}_{im} + \sum_{v \in \mathcal{V}^R} T_{ijv} - \underline{T}_{jn}, 0\} \sum_{v \in \mathcal{V}^R} x_{imjnv} \leq \bar{T}_{im} - \underline{T}_{jn},$$

$$((i,m),(j,n)) \in \mathcal{A} \qquad (31)$$

4   Computational Study

The mathematical model described in Section 3 has been implemented in Mosel using Xpress IVE and solved using Xpress 27.01.02. All computational tests are performed on a Windows 8 computer with an Intel i5 core, 2.2 GHz processor and 8 GB RAM. Section 4.1 describes the test instances used, while the performance of the tests using Xpress is presented and discussed in Section 4.2.

4.1   Test Instances

Four sets of test instances have been generated and used in the computational study. The first two sets consist of 6 instances, and the other two sets consist of 8 instances. These test instances are based on reduced versions of a real-sized problem faced by a Ro-Ro shipping company, the first set of instances based on the Asia to Europe route, the second and third set of instances based on the three routes shown in Fig. 1, and the fourth set of instances based on five routes. Table 1 summarizes the test instances developed for the computational study.

Table 1. Test instances. For the number of ships, the number on the left denotes the number of ships in the fleet, while the number on the right is the number of available spot ships.

Instance	Nships	Nroutes	Nports	Nvoyages	NportCalls	Nproduct	Time (days)
9v1r3p2k90d	9/0	1	3	9	27	2	90
9v1r6p2k90d	9/0	1	6	9	54	2	90
9v1r9p2k90d	9/0	1	9	9	81	2	90
7v3r9p6k90d	7/3	3	9	27	81	6	90
10v3r17p6k90d	10/3	3	17	27	162	6	90
10v3r28p6k90d	10/3	3	28	27	225	6	90
10v3r28p11k90d	10/3	3	28	27	225	11	90
10v3r28p11k120d	10/3	3	28	36	300	11	120
10v3r28p11k150d	10/3	3	28	45	375	11	150
10v3r28p11k180d	10/3	3	28	54	450	11	180
18v5r47p17k90d	18/3	5	47	40	341	17	90
18v5r47p17k120d	18/3	5	47	53	451	17	120
18v5r47p17k150d	18/3	5	47	67	572	17	150
18v5r47p17k180d	18/3	5	47	80	682	17	180

The information on routes and ports with respective sailing distances and corresponding costs and sailing times are based on real data. Two ship types are considered, large and small, with capacities of approximately 7100 and 5800 Car Equivalent Units (CEUs), respectively. The cost associated with assigning a voyage to a spot ship is assumed almost three times the variable (i.e. fuel and port) cost of serving the voyage with a large ship from the company's own fleet.

The cost of serving the voyage with a small ship is set to be 20% lower than the cost of serving the voyage with a large ship from the company's own fleet.

The number of voyages on each route during the planning horizon, time windows for starting the voyages, products produced/consumed on a route and production/consumption rate of respective products at each port are estimated by the authors. Inventory management is taken into consideration at both the production and the consumption ports of each product.The number of products to be transported along each route ranges between 2 and 5. The daily production or consumption rates of a product at the respective ports are estimated as a random number between 10 and 100 units of the product.

The typical planning horizon varies from months to a year. Here we consider planning horizons of 90, 120, 150 and 180 days, respectively. The instances are named according to the number of ships in the fleet (v), routes (r), ports (p), products (k) and length of planning horizon (d), for example instance $9v1r3p2k90d$ represent test instance with nine ships, one route, three ports, two products and planning horizon of 90 days. For each test instance, the number of ships, routes, ports, voyages, port calls, products and length of planning horizon (in days) are given.

4.2   Computational Performance

Table 2. Computational results from the MIP model for the test instances.

Instance	ProblemSize		Best Sol.Value	Gap(%)	Spot Ship	Time(s)
	# Constraint	# Variable	(M$)			
$9v1r3p2k90d$	2831	1341	5.09	0.00	0	0.5
$9v1r6p2k90d$	5240	2421	5.29	0.00	0	1.0
$9v1r9p2k90d$	7649	3501	5.49	0.00	0	1.9
$7v3r9p6k90d$	10358	10261	22.21	0.00	3	12.6
$10v3r17p6k90d$	21516	17098	24.51	0.00	3	12.4
$10v3r28p6k90d$	30913	21298	30.70	0.00	3	39.3
$10v3r28p11k90d$	52642	32302	30.70	0.00	3	73.9
$10v3r28p11k120d$	70695	46523	39.09	0.00	3	165.6
$10v3r28p11k150d$	89014	62473	42.98	0.00	3	1599.3
$10v3r28p11k180d$	107599	80152	50.21	0.00	3	1636.2
$18v5r47p17k90d$	118536	84406	40.09	0.00	2	40.2
$18v5r47p17k120d$	158126	124587	52.27	0.00	3	193.9
$18v5r47p17k150d$	201789	175209	68.05	0.50	3	3600.0
$18v5r47p17k180d$	242625	228473	79.70	1.31	3	3600.0

The computational results for solving the MIP model are presented in Table 2. The size of the model for each of the instances is presented in terms of number of constraints and variables. Moreover, Table 2 gives details related to the best MIP solution value (in M$) obtained, and the optimality gap (in %), $Gap =$

$\frac{BestIntegerSolutionValue-BestBound}{BestIntegerSolutionValue} \times 100$, is reported if the model could not be solved to optimality within the time limit which is set to one hour. The actual number of spot ships used is also reported.

The MIP model could be solved to optimality for most small instances within reasonable times except for the two largest ones, $18v5r47p17k150d$ and $18v5r47p17k180d$, for which the feasible integer solutions are found and the gaps are reported are 0.5% and 1.3%, respectively.

Even for the two largest instances, $18v5r47p17k150d$ and $18v5r47p17k180d$, good solutions are obtained within the time limit. It is, however, clear that the computational time increases rapidly with the increase of the number of ships, routes, ports and products. The real problem that can involve up to 19 routes and 60 ships, as well as a larger number of products would result in much longer computational time. Moreover, the computational results also show that the size of the instances as well as the computational time increases dramatically with the increased length of the planning horizon. For budgeting reasons, some Ro-Ro shipping companies could be interested in solving problems with up to one year planning horizons, which would be impossible using only a commercial solver (like Xpress).

5   Concluding Remarks

In this paper, we have presented a planning problem faced by Ro-Ro shipping companies providing integrated logistic services to its customers. We have proposed a new mathematical model, combining inventory management at the ports with the planning of ship routes. This planning problem is called a combined Maritime Fleet Deployment and Inventory Management Problem (MFDIMP).

Test instances are created based on reduced version of a real Ro-Ro shipping company. Out of the 14 test instances, only the two largest instances with 18 ships, 5 routes and planning horizons of 150 and 180 days could not be solved to optimality. The computational results suggest that the time-continuous formulation is likely to perform better than the time-discrete model in [4], particularly for instances with a long planning horizon.

It should be emphasized that even though the results are promising for our test instances, the combined MFDIMP is a very complex problem and instances of realistic size with more ships, routes and longer planning horizon could be even harder or impossible to solve within reasonable computational times by only using a commercial mixed-integer programming solver. Therefore, there are many possible directions for future research. In order to find optimal solutions within reasonable computational times, it would be interesting to study exact solution techniques, for example decomposition approaches. Moreover, the possibility of tightening the formulation and including suitable valid inequalities for the inventory management part of the problem could also be explored. In addition, advanced heuristics could also be developed to obtain near optimal solutions for large realistic instances of the problem.

References

1. Agra, A., Christiansen, M., Delgado, A.: Discrete time and continuous time formulations for a short sea inventory routing problem. Optimization and Engineering 18(1), 269–297 (2017)
2. Agra, A., Christiansen, M., Figueiredo, R., Hvattum, L.M., Poss, M., Requejo, C.: The robust vehicle routing problem with time windows. Computers & Operations Research 40(3), 856–866 (2013)
3. Andersson, H., Fagerholt, K., Hobbesland, K.: Integrated maritime fleet deployment and speed optimization: Case study from roro shipping. Computers & Operations Research 55, 233–240 (2015)
4. Chandra, S., Christiansen, M., Fagerholt, K.: Combined fleet deployment and inventory management in roll-on/roll-off shipping. Transportation Research Part E: Logistics and Transportation Review 92, 43–55 (2016)
5. Chandra, S., Fagerholt, K., Christiansen, M.: Maritime fleet deployment in ro-ro shipping under inventory constraints. Procedia - Social and Behavioral Sciences 189, 362–375 (2015)
6. Christiansen, M., Fagerholt, K.: Ship routing and scheduling in industrial and tramp shipping. In: Toth, P., Vigo, D. (eds.) Vehicle Routing: Problems, Methods, and Applications, chap. 13, pp. 381–408. Society for Industrial and Applied Mathematics Philadelphia (2014)
7. Christiansen, M., Fagerholt, K., Nygreen, B., Ronen, D.: Ship routing and scheduling in the new millennium. European Journal of Operational Research 228(3), 467–483 (2013)
8. Fagerholt, K., Johnsen, T.A.V., Lindstad, H.: Fleet deployment in liner shipping: a case study. Maritime Policy & Management 36(5), 397–409 (2009)
9. Hemmati, A., Hvattum, L.M., Christiansen, M., Laporte, G.: An iterative two-phase hybrid matheuristic for a multi-product short sea inventory-routing problem. European Journal of Operational Research 252(3), 775–788 (2016)
10. Jaramillo, D.I., Perakis, A.N.: Fleet deployment optimization for liner shipping part 2. implementation and results. Maritime Policy & Management 18(4), 235–262 (1991)
11. Papageorgiou, D.J., Nemhauser, G.L., Sokol, J., Cheon, M.S., Keha, A.B.: MIRPLib - A library of maritime inventory routing problem instances: Survey, core model, and benchmark results. European Journal of Operational Research 235(2), 350–366 (2014)
12. Perakis, A.N., Jaramillo, D.I.: Fleet deployment optimization for liner shipping part 1. background, problem formulation and solution approaches. Maritime Policy & Management 18(3), 183–200 (1991)
13. Powell, B.J., Perkins, A.N.: Fleet deployment optimization for liner shipping: an integer programming model. Maritime Policy & Management 24(2), 183–192 (1997)
14. Savelsbergh, M., Song, J.H.: An optimization algorithm for the inventory routing problem with continuous moves. Computers & Operations Research 35(7), 2266–2282 (2008)
15. Siswanto, N., Essam, D., Sarker, R.: Solving the ship inventory routing and scheduling problem with undedicated compartments. Computers & Industrial Engineering 61(2), 289–299 (2011)
16. Song, J.H., Furman, K.C.: A maritime inventory routing problem: Practical approach. Computers & Operations Research 40(3), 657–665 (2013)
17. Stålhane, M., Andersson, H., Christiansen, M., Fagerholt, K.: Vendor managed inventory in tramp shipping. Omega 47, 60–72 (2014)

The Liner Shipping Routing and Scheduling Problem Under Environmental Considerations: The Case of Emission Control Areas

Philip Dithmer[1], Line Reinhardt[2], and Christos A. Kontovas[3]

[1] A.T. Kearney, Copenhagen, Denmark, E-mail: pdithmer@gmail.com
[2] Dept. of Mechanical and Manufacturing Engineering, Aalborg University, Copenhagen, Denmark, E-mail: lbr@m-tech.aau.dk
[3] Dept. of Maritime and Mechanical Engineering, Liverpool John Moores University, United Kingdom, E-mail: C.Kontovas@ljmu.ac.uk

Abstract. This paper deals with the Liner Shipping Routing and Scheduling Problem (LSRSP), which consists of designing the time schedule for a vessel to visit a fixed set of ports while minimizing costs. We extend the classical problem to include the external cost of ship air emissions and we present some results of our work investigating the impact of Emission Control Areas in the routing and scheduling of liner vessels.

Keywords: liner shipping, emissions, emission control areas

1 Introduction

Maritime transportation is essential for the global trade of today. In 2015 the total seaborne trade was almost 10.047 billion tonnes, a remarkable 68 percent increase since 2000. Containerized freight, in particular, has gotten an increased importance on the international seaborne trade market. In addition, the container fleet grew by 240 percent between 2000 and 2014, from 64 millions to 216 millions, measured in deadweight tonnage (UNCTAD 2016, [28]).

Although one would assume that this growth in container shipping has left liner shipping companies in full glory, the recent economic developments have impacted the business significantly and left many industry players struggling. The latest economical crisis hit the liner shipping industry in 2008 and 2009, as reflected by the negative growth of TEUs traded in 2009. Not only did the decreasing demand hit shipping companies on the top line but several other significant complications suddenly hit the industry. Over the recent years shipping companies have been exposed to increased market capacity, declining freight rates and increasing bunker prices, which led shipping operators to focus on cutting costs and improving the efficiency of their operations.

Besides overcapacity, another perilous development for the liner shipping industry has been the fluctuation and, in particular, the step increase of bunker prices. Bunker prices have a huge effect on the overall transportation costs (Stopford (2009, [27]) and Notteboom (2006 and 2009, [16], [17]). Notteboom 2006 argues that the fuel cost can be as much as 50% of total costs. Hence the price

© Springer International Publishing AG 2017
T. Bektaş et al. (Eds.), ICCL 2017, LNCS 10572, pp. 336–350, 2017.
https://doi.org/10.1007/978-3-319-68496-3_23

of bunker fuel is of great concern to the industry. Liner shipping companies have fought to keep bunker consumption down due to the rigorous prices. In 2007 Maersk Line introduced *slow steaming* as a concept to decrease bunker usage. In all its simplicity slow steaming is a question of reducing the speed of the vessels. Maersk Line (2010, [13]) claims that reducing speed by 20% leads to a bunker usage reduction of 40%. Hence slow steaming is seen as a very competitive strategy which is here to stay as indicated by Maersk Line (2010, [13]).

Besides the economic performance, the environmental effects from shipping activities and, especially air pollution, are getting increasing focus in the maritime Operations Research (OR) community (Kontovas 2014, [12]). According to the latest study by the International Maritime Organization (IMO) (IMO, 2014) shipping emitted 796 million tonnes in 2012, which corresponds to around 2.2% of global CO_2 emissions. CO_2 emissions are not the only air pollution front. In areas of dense population pollutants such as SO_x and NO_x can have a high effect on local air quality. For this reason a set of Emission Control Areas, hereafter ECAs, has been introduced. In ECAs vessels are only allowed to use the bunker fuel with lower sulphur content (0.1 % from year 2015). Moreover, a global limit on sulphur in bunker at 3.5 % has been applied in 2015 in order to reduce pollution. In some ECAs the emission of NO_x is also restricted. The bunker with 0.1% sulphur has a significantly higher price than the bunker with 3.5%. Shipping companies have, thus, a desire to decrease the usage of this type of bunker in order to decrease total cost. Discussions on a taxation system on SO_x pollution is considered as a possibility by authorities in the industry.

To that extent, this paper deals with the use of OR tools to design liner shipping routes and schedules in order to minimize the total cost for the ship operator. In particular, we present some results of our work investigating the impact of emission control areas in the routing and scheduling of liner vessels. We here present a model to investigate how the ECAs and the usage of different fuels will impact the sailing speeds and resulting over all emissions and a model to investigate the impact of including the external costs of emissions in order to compare the fuel costs and the emission cost of the two optimization models.

1.1   Literature Review

In the early 1980s Ronen presented the first review of operations research papers on ship routing and scheduling (Ronen, 1983 [25]). Several reviews of the literature available have been published since, Christiansen et al. (2007, [4]) and Christiansen et al. (2013, [5]). The latter points out the increased focus of the literature on bunker consumption optimization and emission minimization. This is due to the increasing bunker prices since 2000 and an extensive focus on the environmental impact. Kjeldsen (2011, [10]) develops an extensive classification method for models and literature for ship routing and scheduling problems in liner shipping. Finally, Meng et al. (2014, [14]) evaluate a significant amount of literature on OR within Liner shipping and conclude that there is a gap between the academic studies and industry practices. Brouer et al. (2014, [2]) present a benchmark suite consisting of relevant data on several important factors in the liner shipping industry. Data on an extensive list of ports is included as well as specifications for different types of vessels.

Network design is a problem that is widely approached in literature. Agarwal and Ergun (2008, [1]) provide a mixed-integer LP that solves the ship scheduling and cargo routing problems with weekly frequency constraints simultaneously. To solve the problem three different algorithms; greedy heuristic, column generation, and two-phase Bender decomposition, are used. This model is slightly updated by Christiansen et al. (2013, [5]). Brouer et el. (2014, [2]) present an integer programming model to solve the Liner Shipping Network Design Problem (LSNDP) and prove that it is *NP-hard*. Routing and scheduling in liner shipping has attracted much attention from researchers. The routing part, mainly consisting of determining the sequence of port visits, is among others treated by Chu et al. (2003, [6]), who develop a mixed-integer programming model for routing container ships and present numerical examples for some Trans-Pacific routes. Plum et al. [19] have solved the problem of optimizing the route of a single service considering flow and transit time. Hsu and Hsieh (2007, [9]) present a two-objective model with the purpose of minimizing costs by choosing optimal route, ship size and sailing frequency. Scheduling of liner shipping services is seen in many different varieties. Wang and Meng (2011, [29]) seek to optimize cost and service level by solving the scheduling and container routing problem simultaneously. The outcome is a nonlinear model which minimizes transshipment and other penalty costs. In 2012, Wang and Meng introduce a mixed-integer nonlinear stochastic model that determines arrival time of a vessel at each port and the sailing speed, somewhat like it is done in this study but with a fixed sequence of port visits (Wang and Meng 2012, [31]). Wang and Meng (2012, [31]) include uncertainties at sea and in ports. Finally, Wang et al. (2014, [33]) design a model that can solve the scheduling problem with port time windows. The authors formulate the problem as a mixed-integer nonlinear nonconvex optimization model and suggest a holistic solution approach. The order of which the ports are visited is fixed and thus further differentiates the model from the investigations made in the report at hand. Yan et al. also give an example of a scheduling with fixed port call sequence (Yan et al. 2009, [34]).

Lowering bunker consumption by optimizing speed and routing has been a popular topic over the past years. Notteboom and Vernimmen (2009, [17]) state that managing bunker consumption gives incentive to reduce speed, but highlight that this incentive is dependent on the bunker price. While reducing speed improves bunker performance it also comes at a cost in terms of transit time and thus also service level as mentioned by Notteboom (2006, [16]). As mentioned above Wang and Meng (2011, [29]) use speed optimization to optimize costs. In another paper from 2011, Wang and Meng optimize sailing speed while considering transshipment and container routing (Wang and Meng 2011, [30]). Additionally, the bunker consumption is calibrated and an outer-approximation method is proposed to model the usage. Psaraftis and Kontovas (2014, [22]) clarify important issues regarding ship speed modeling and incorporate some fundamental parameters that are essential in ship owners' speed decisions. Bunker consumption optimization methods are reviewed by Wang et al. (2013, [32]). The authors discuss different methods of modeling bunker consumption and suggest among others a linear static secant-approximation method closely related to that used in this study.

Emission of CO_2 and SO_x is a topic that has gotten more and more interest from scientists and researchers in the OR field of maritime transportation (Christiansen 2013, [5]). This statement is further supported by Wang et al. (2013, [32]). Psaraftis and Kontovas (2010, [20]) investigates how emission reduction policies can have negative implications due to economic desires. Kontovas (2011, [11]) investigates the reduction of emissions by reducing speed and looking into how the lost time can be made up for by reducing service time in ports and waiting time before berthing. Recent papers include minimization of cost implied by emission regulations, such as the implementation of emission control areas. Kontovas (2014, [12]) conceptualizes the formulation of the "Green Ship Routing and Scheduling Problem" and introduces among others the relationship between bunker consumption and emissions. Moreover, Kontovas presents two ways of incorporating emission minimization in existing formulations of routing and scheduling problems. The method of internalizing external costs of emissions is applied in this study. Fagerholt et al. (2010, [7]) apply speed optimization to reduce emissions using discritized arrival times. Fagerholt et al. (2015, [8]) present a model that minimizes cost for shipping companies by being able to select between different legs between ports that have varying interaction with ECAs. Thus, costs are minimized by determining sailings paths and speeds for vessels along a sequence of ports. This is, to the best of our knowledge, one of the first modeling approaches where ECAs are an actual part of the model, and the paper is furthermore also the most recent in this field.

In this paper we introduce a model that minimizes costs by optimizing the port visit sequence and the time schedule, and hence also speed. In addition, this model will also minimize the external cost of pollution from bunker consumption. Since the cost of emissions is directly proportional to the amount of bunker consumed, emissions are also reduced.

2   Problem definition and mathematical model

The *Liner Shipping Routing and Scheduling Problem* (LSRSP) consists of designing the time schedule for a vessel to visit a fixed set of ports while minimizing costs. A subproblem of the LSRSP is additionally to define the sequence of which the vessel must visit the ports.

The key decisions in an LSRSP model are the following:

1. The order in which the vessel should visit the given set of ports.
2. The vessel's arrival time at each port and the appurtenant speed of the vessel.
3. The roundtrip time and thus the number of vessels needed to ensure a weekly frequency.

Liner shipping operates with a weekly frequency, i.e. each port must be visited once every week. Thus, a set of homogeneous vessels must be assigned to the service to achieve this, however, there exists an upper limit to the number of vessels deployed.

In our model we introduce emission control areas to the LSRSP by minimizing the total cost for the liner shipping company when servicing areas under emission control regulations. The impact of emissions is introduced as described in Kontovas (2014, [12]) by internalizing the external costs of emissions in the model. This means that the impact from emissions will be monetized and, thus, the external cost of emissions will be included in the objective function. The term *external cost* refers to the total societal cost, i.e. this is not necessarily the actual cost that liner shipping companies would be paying if a tax system is implemented. However, in a similar way, by using the tax price instead of the external cost in the model, the results can also reflect how the routing and scheduling of the services will be impacted by a future taxation scheme.

2.1   Model

The model is formulated as a compact model and the emission and bunker costs are combined in an objective optimizing both using the estimated value of the external costs of emissions. The model optimizes the routes and also includes functionality to consider transit time requirement between two ports.

In order to ensure a weekly frequency the number of vessels sailing a service must be the number of weeks it takes to complete a round trip. Moreover, the service duration must be equal to a whole number of weeks. The duration of a service in weeks is indicated by the integer variable Ψ where Ψ_{UP} is the upper limit. Each vessel has a weekly charter rate which is the parameter T_r.

Bunker Consumption and Cost
The cost of bunker is a scalar of the bunker consumption divided into the different bunker types. The consumption of bunker fuel depends on several factors; speed being the most important one.

Let $\mathbf{Z}$ be the set of emission control areas. For tests in later sections the set contains ECA_0 and ECA_1 meaning outside ECA and inside ECA, respectively. The price of bunker is varying with the bunker type required in the different zones.

The consumption of bunker fuel when idle at port is linear, depending mainly on the time spent in port, and thus simple to include in a mathematical model. We assume that any vessel type has an individual constant fuel consumption c^z. For any given time period a_i^z, at port $i \in P$, where P is the set of ports to be visited, the bunker cost is $c^z a_i^z$. Note that a_i^z may be larger than s_i as it includes any idle time for the vessel used at port i.

The relationship between speed and bunker consumption when the vessel is sailing is nonlinear. There are many different analytic formulations presented in the literature, but the most commonly used is the cubic one. With $F(s)$ as the hourly consumption, s_* as the design speed of the vessel, and f_* as the hourly fuel consumption at design speed the cubic law of the speed s is given as

$$F_s^z = \frac{f_*}{s_*^3} \cdot s^3 = \left(\frac{s}{s_*}\right)^3 \cdot f_* \tag{1}$$

Equation (1) is clearly not linear. The method used in our model to linearize this term is an inner approximation with secants. As the speed is distance divided by time, we here have selected to use time as a variable instead of speed s. Let θ_{ij}^z be the time used on sailing from port $i \in P$ to port j in emission zone $z \in Z$ and let N be the set of secants then the bunker consumption is

$$F_{ij}^z = w_{ij}^{nz}\theta_{ij}^z + \delta_{ij}^{nz} \tag{2}$$

For some $n \in N$ where w_{ij}^{nz} and $\delta_{ij}^{n,z}$ is, respectively the slope and intersection of secant $n \in N$ for sailing from port i to port j using bunker type $z \in Z$. For the cost let f^z be the cost of a ton of bunker of type z.

The reader could refer to Vial (2014, [23]) and Wang et al. (2013, [32] for more on the linearization of the fuel consumption formula.

In the objective function we also include the external cost of emissions as described above. The set $\mathbf{E}$ consists of the two emission types considered in this study, SO_x and CO_2. To include costs of the emitted pollutant, the factor $\lambda_{z,e}$ is introduced. This factor determines how much of each pollutant $e \in E$ is emitted per ton of each fuel type in $z \in Z$. Moreover, let $\mu_{z,e}$ be the external cost for emission $e \in E$ when using bunker type $z \in Z$. Thus, the model is constructed in such a way that other emission types, e.g. NO_x can be easily included.

Note that the distance between two ports $i, j \in P$ may now both be inside and outside ECA zones. Therefore the distance parameter d is split such that it describes how long the distance from port i to j is in ECA z. Thus, $\sum_{z \in Z} d_{ij}^z$ is equal to the total distance sailed between i and j.

Objective

In this work, we study and compare two different objectives: In the one objective function we minimize the company costs and in the other we also include the external costs of emissions. We then compare both the emissions produced in these two cases.

The bunker cost objective (without the cost of emissions) can be written using the above notation as follows:

$$OB1: Minimize \sum_{i,j \in P} \sum_{z \in Z} f^z(F_{ij}^z + c^z a_i^z) + T_r\Psi \tag{3}$$

The other model where we minimize the overall costs, including the externalities of the emissions, can be formulated as follows:

$$OB2: Minimize \sum_{i,j \in P} \sum_{z \in Z} (f^z(F_{ij}^z + c^z a_i^z) + \sum_{e \in E} \mu_e^z \lambda_e^z(F_{ij}^z + c^z a_i^z)) + T_r\Psi \tag{4}$$

The model is formulated as follows:

$$OB1 \quad or \quad OB2 \tag{5}$$

Subject to:

$$\sum_{i \in P} x_{ij} + \sum_{k \in P} x_{jk} = 2, \qquad \forall j \in P \tag{6}$$

$$F_{i,j}^z \geq w_{i,j}^{n,z} \cdot \theta_{i,j}^z + \delta_{i,j}^{n,z} - M_2 (1 - x_{i,j}) \qquad \forall i,j \in \mathbf{P}, n \in \mathbf{N}, z \in \mathbf{Z} \tag{7}$$

$$\theta_{i,j}^z \geq \hat{\theta}_{ij}^z x_{i,j} \qquad \forall i,j \in \mathbf{P}, z \in \mathbf{Z} \tag{8}$$

$$\theta_{i,j}^z \leq \bar{\theta}_{ij}^z x_{i,j} \qquad \forall i,j \in \mathbf{P}, z \in \mathbf{Z} \tag{9}$$

$$t_j + M_3 (1 - x_{i,j} + q_j) \geq t_i + a_i^z + s_i + \sum_{z \in \mathbf{Z}} \theta_{i,j}^z \qquad \forall i,j \in \mathbf{P}, z \in \mathbf{Z} \tag{10}$$

$$t_j + M_3 (2 - x_{i,j} - q_j) \geq t_i + a_i^z + s_i + \sum_{z \in \mathbf{Z}} \theta_{i,j}^z - I_w \Psi \qquad \forall i,j \in \mathbf{P}, z \in \mathbf{Z} \tag{11}$$

$$I_w \Psi = \sum_{z \in \mathbf{Z}} \left(\sum_{i,j \in P} \theta_{i,j}^z + \sum_{i \in P} (a_i^z + s_i) \right) \tag{12}$$

$$I_w \Psi \geq t_i, \qquad \forall i \in P \tag{13}$$

$$x_{i,i} = 0 \qquad \forall i \in \mathbf{P} \tag{14}$$

$$p_j + I_w b_j - t_j = 0, \qquad \forall j \in L \tag{15}$$

$$\tau_{ij} \leq r_{ij}, \qquad \forall (i,j) \in R \tag{16}$$

$$\tau_{ij} \geq t_j - t_i - s_i, \qquad \forall (i,j) \in R \tag{17}$$

$$\tau_{ij} \geq t_j - t_i - s_i + I_w \Psi - M_3 u_{ij}, \qquad \forall (i,j) \in R \tag{18}$$

$$t_i - t_j \geq -M_3 u_{ij}, \qquad \forall (i,j) \in R \tag{19}$$

$$t_i - t_j \geq M_3 (1 - u_{ij}) \qquad \forall (i,j) \in R \tag{20}$$

$$\Psi, b_j \leq \Psi_{UP} \tag{21}$$

$$\Psi, b_j \in \mathbb{Z}_0 \tag{22}$$

$$u_{ij}, x_{ij} \in \{0, 1\} \tag{23}$$

$$F_{ij}^z, \theta_{ij}^z, a_i^z, t_i \geq 0 \tag{24}$$

Route selection, speed and bunker requirements

To find the route for the service we introduce the binary variable x_{ij} which is 1 if the vessel sails directly from port i to port j and zero otherwise. Moreover, let the parameter q_i be one for the first port visited on a service and zero otherwise and let M_2 be a large number greater than the fuel needed to sail the longest leg at maximum speed. The parameter $\hat{\theta}_{ij}^z$ is the time needed to sail the distance d_{ij}^z at max speed and the parameter $\bar{\theta}_{ij}^z$ is the time used on traversing the distance d_{ij}^z at minimum speed. Note that these parameters can be calculated in preprocessing. The parameter I_w is the number of hours in a week (168) and M_2 and M_3 are Big-M parameters. Note that $\sum_{z \in Z} \theta_{ij}^z + a_j^z$ is the total time used on sailing from i to j. Since the problem deals with liner shipping, some of the berth times may be locked in order to satisfy locked berth times at ports. A variable t_i is introduced to represent the time the port $i \in P$ is visited and it also can be used to model subtour elimination. The variable t_i is also used to ensure that the transit times are satisfied. Let s_i be a fixed parameter indicating the time needed for loading and unloading in port $i \in P$. The constraints ensuring route selection and round trip are (6), (10), (11), (12) and (13) in the model.

Noe that constraints (10) is active when x_{ij} is selected and p_j is zero while (11) is active when both x_{ij} and p_j are one thus (11) is active for the trip entering the first port on the route. The constraints (8), (9) and (7) are related to bunker consumption and speed limits.

Berth time and transit time restrictions
A berth time may already be booked at a port and in case of a busy port this berth time might be impossible to change. Thus, the company may want to lock the time of the visit at selected ports. Let L be the set of port visits with locked berthing times. Then for a port $i \in L$ there is a parameter p_i which indicates the time the port visit is locked to. Since this time is a time within a week, an integer variable b_i is introduced which indicates the number of whole weeks the vessel has sailed before visiting the port i. To include transit time requirements we let the set R contain the port pairs i to j for which a transit time requirement exists. For each pair $(i, j) \in R$ we have a parameter r_{ij} representing the transit time limit from port i to port j. A variable τ_{ij} is introduced to represent the transit time from i to j in the solution in the model. The constraints ensuring a locked berth time are the constraints (15). The constraints ensuring transit time satisfaction are the constraints (16), (17), (18), (19) and (20) where the variables u_{ij} are used to indicate if port i is visited before j on a roundtrip.

3   Computational Results

The testing of the models $OB1$ and $OB2$ is done on the service illustrated in Figure 1. The visited ports are the following: Antwerp (Belgium), Bremerhaven (Germany), Agadir (Morocco), Casablanca (Morocco), Rotterdam (Netherlands), Gdansk (Poland), Skt. Petersburg (Russia), and Gothenburg (Sweden.) On this service the two ports in Morroco are placed outside the ECA while the remaining ports are located inside an ECA zone.

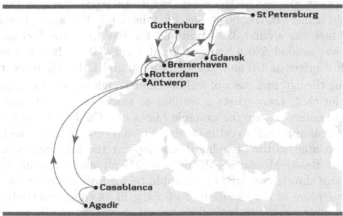

Fig. 1. Illustration of service used for testing the models. Note that the sequence of port visits is not fixed in the problem (Seago Line, [26]).

We utilize our model to investigate two interesting aspects. First, how the ECAs and the usage of different fuels will impact the results. Second, the impact of including the external costs of emissions which is an interesting topic mainly due to the recent discussions on policies to reduce emissions. In the test instance we have only one call in Bremerhaven, however, several port calls to a port can be handled by inserting an additional port visit thus increasing the number of port visits to 9. Here we will not consider the case of several port calls to the same port even though the presented model can handle this as long as the transit times and berth times are attached to a specific port visit.

3.1 Data

The data used for this test are mostly extracted from LINERLIB, see Brouer et al. (2014, [2]), but also modified to include emission control areas. The legs are split into two, one within the ECAs and the other outside them. Distances are taken from Linerlib and partly from the virtual map and geographical information program *Google Earth*©.

The vessel type used for testing is the Panamax 240 vessel from LINERLIB [2]. The specs of the test are as seen in Table 3. As an example we use the instance 8.4.5.10 where the first number is the number of ports in the test instance, in the example it is 8, the second number is the number of locked berth times, in the example it is 4, the third number is the number of transit times between ports on the instance, in the example it is 4 and the last number is the number of secants used in the approximation, in the example it is 10. Transit times can be seen in Table 5 and all transit times are a subset of this set. The transit times have been selected to represent trades origin and destination. The locked berth windows are a fixed weekly arrival time requirement for a port call. Clearly the results for test instances with only one locked berth time will be the same as for the instance with no locked berth time as the schedule can be shifted according to the berth time preserving the same speeds.

Bunker prices are one of the most important parameters as they greatly fluctuate over time. At the beginning of June 2017, the average world price for $BW380$ fuel was around 336 \$/ton and for $BW0.1\%$, the fuel used within the ECAs, was around 580 \$/ton (see Bunkerworld [18]). In our runs we use mid-range fuel prices of 370 and 620 for $BW380$ and $BW0.1\%$ respectively.

Regarding the external costs of emissions, although there is no single acceptable figure for that, there exists a number of works on the estimation of the social costs of emissions; see for example Miola and Cuiffo [15], which presents a methodological approach to estimate the external costs of maritime transport. This is also related to the on-going discussions at the IMO regarding the so-called Market Based Measures (MBM); see [21] for more. Placing a price on GHG emissions through an MBM (this could be for instance a tax on emissions or fuel consumption or the inclusion of shipping in an emissions trading scheme which would force owners to buy allowances that will essentially give them the right to pollute, or actually offset for the damage cause) is still a hot topic at the IMO, and also the European Commission. Given that such an MBM is not in place right now, the values we assume are taken from the Handbook of External Costs of Transport, a report for the DG-MOVE of the European Commission

(Ricardo-AEA (2014), [24]). The external costs of emissions used are presented in Table 1.

Pollutant	τ_e [\$/ton]
CO_2	37
SO_x	12,700

Table 1. External cost τ_e used for testing.

The actual emitted amount of pollutant is given by the parameter $\lambda_{z,e}$. Air emissions are proportional to the fuel consumption of the main and auxiliary engines. To estimate CO_2 emissions one should multiply total bunker consumption by an appropriate empirical emissions factor that depends on the fuel time. SOx emissions depend also on the type of fuel used and in particular on the amount of sulfur present in the fuel. One has to multiply total bunker consumption by the percentage of sulphur present in the fuel and subsequently by the exact factor of 0.02, which is derived from the chemical reaction of sulphur with oxygen. The values for this parameter are presented in Kontovas (2014, [12]) and can be found in Table 2. The reader is also referred to the paper for more information on how to estimate emissions from shipping and the emission factors used.

Bunker type (ECA)	CO_2	SO_x
BW380 (outside)	3.114	0.07
BW0.1% (inside)	3.206	0.002

Table 2. Values of emission factor $\lambda_{z,e}$ used for testing. The unit is [ton].

3.2 Comparison of the Results

OB1 - Without including the emission costs Test results for objective *OB1* are shown in Table 3. We present the operational cost for the sea leg, i.e. the bunker cost and operational running costs. In addition, for illustrative purposes only, the emission costs for CO_2 and SO_x are listed although they are not taken into account in the objective function. For each emission control area the average speed and the distance traveled are stated. Finally, the two final columns show the total active sailing time (not including idling) and the number of vessels deployed for the service. Note that in the following tables, the legs inside the ECA areas are denoted as ECA_1, and that outside the ECA as ECA_0.

ID	Specs	Sailing Cost [\$]	Emissions Cost [\$]			Total Cost [\$]	Avg. speed [nmi/h]		Distance [nmi]			Sailing Time [hours]	# vessels
			CO_2	SO_x	Total		ECA_0	ECA_1	ECA_0	ECA_1	Total		
(8.1)	8.0.0.10	832,486	91,012	333,005	424,017	1,256,478	16.0	13.7	2,434	3,790	6,224	429.0	3
(8.2)	8.0.5.10	1,257,941	178,450	469,101	647,551	1,905,492	18.1	17.3	2,434	5,082	7,516	429.0	3
(8.3)	8.0.8.10	838,815	92,580	340,194	432,774	1,271,559	16.1	13.7	2,434	3,808	6,242	429.0	3
(8.4)	8.4.0.10	881,138	67,165	229,943	297,107	1,178,245	12.8	12.0	2,434	3,790	6,224	505.4	4
(8.5)	8.4.5.10	1,539,336	173,258	413,900	587,158	2,126,494	15.5	15.8	2,434	5,407	7,841	500.4	5
(8.6)	8.4.8.10	1,378,470	180,164	601,350	781,515	2,159,985	20.2	16.6	2,434	4,509	6,943	391.8	4

Table 3. Test results for *OB1*. The emission costs are not included in the objective function for this model.

One important finding is that the average speed, in all cases but for (8.5), is higher outside the ECA (see ECA_0) compared to the one inside the ECA (see ECA_1), which is in line with Psaraftis and Kontovas (2010, [20]). The reason for this is the higher bunker price inside the ECA which induces operators to speed up outside the ECA in order to maintain the schedules. The speed increase inside the ECA for example in cases (8.5) is attributed to the berth and transit time restrictions of the particular cases.

Moreover, the distance traveled outside the ECA stays the same in all cases. This is expected as the vessel will only sail to/from Morocco only once during the service, as sailing back and forth between the continent twice will increase costs tremendously. Interestingly enough, the active sailing time stays the same or increases in all cases as we add more restrictions to the model, see for instance case (8.1) that is without any berth or transit time restrictions. For case (8.6), where both berth and transit time restrictions are applied, the number of vessels increases from three to four, meaning that the round trip time will increase significantly. As the sailing time is low in this case, the vessel must be idling for a long time. Both the sailing and emission costs are very high compared to the other cases. Case (8.5) also has a high sailing cost but here five vessels are deployed and the total actual sailing time is long, meaning that the average speed and emission costs are lower.

Finally, we should note that for case (8.2) and (8.5) the round-trips are very long in terms of distance sailed. This is most likely due to restrictions and this means that the vessel will sail along a complex route.

$OB2$ - **The cost of emission is included** In $OB2$ the external emission costs are included in the objective function, meaning that the vessel will sail in such a way that the sum of both the cost of emissions and the sailing costs will be minimized.

The test results of $OB2$ are listed in Table 4. The columns of this table are the same as described for 3.

ID	Specs	Sailing Cost [$]	Emissions Cost [$]			Total Cost [$]	Avg. speed [nmi/h]		Distance [nmi]			Sailing Time [hours]	# vessels
			CO_2	SO_x	Total		ECA_0	ECA_1	ECA_0	ECA_1	Total		
(8.10)	8.0.0.10	871,833	63,391	190,340	253,731	1,125,564	12.0	12.0	2,434	3,790	6,224	518.667	4
(8.11)	8.0.5.10	1,281,900	179,499	400,560	580,059	1,861,959	15.5	18.7	2,434	5,082	7,516	429.0	3
(8.12)	8.0.8.10	876,078	93,937	228,196	322,133	1,198,211	13.0	15.8	2,434	3,808	6,242	429.0	3
(8.13)	8.4.0.10	890,706	67,321	197,401	264,722	1,155,428	12.0	12.5	2,434	3,790	6,224	507.1	4
(8.14)	8.4.5.10	1,545,079	173,444	396,169	569,613	2,114,692	14.7	16.1	2,434	5,407	7,841	500.4	5
(8.15)	8.4.8.10	1,392,332	180,353	553,467	733,820	2,126,151	19.3	17.0	2,434	4,509	6,943	391.8	4

Table 4. Test results using $OB2$ where external emission costs are included in the objective function.

For all cases, the total costs using objective $OB2$ are lower than those for $OB1$, since in this case we also take into account the monetized social cost of emissions. This is further reflected to the average speed of the vessel. Outside the ECA (see leg ECA_0) the vessels in all cases under objective $OB2$ sail slower than compared to the scenario where the emission costs are not included i.e. under $OB1$. This shows the tremendous impact of the SO_x costs. The optimal solution to the model decreases the speed outside the ECAs to reduce SO_x emissions. It is currently debated in the academic community that the ECAs give incentive to increase speed outside of ECAs and thus emit more emisions outside them. This model also shows that the increased emissions could be reduced by implementing some sort of taxation/monetary cost on the amount of pollutants emitted.

Under $OB2$, in all six cases, the vessels sail the same distance as under $OB1$. This implies that most of the optimization is in terms of speed optimization. The model can also make some changes to the sequence of port visits but the purpose of this will more likely be to shift the arrival times slightly to comply

with restrictions rather than changing the distance sailed or the routing. For the
actual sailing time one can also notice that just one of the six cases is longer under
objective $OB2$. This further supports our assumption that the optimization is
mainly tied to speed adjustments rather than routing. Moreover, it is clear that
Objective $OB2$ decreases speed outside the ECA and increases it inside.

Regarding the computational time, in general the model solves the problem
fairly fast. For the instances tested, using $OB2$ the solver used between ten and
30 seconds to solve the problem. Running times of this magnitude are acceptable
and could be used in practice. This is also a sign that the introduction of the
extra sets, parameters, and variables do not add significant complexity to this
model compared to the $OB1$ model.

4 Discussion

For discussion purposes, we will further analyze the results in instances (8.3)
and (8.12) with specifications 8.0.8.10, which are some scenarios without berth
time restrictions but with transit time restrictions which are shown in Table 5.

Port Pair	Transit time
DEBRV - MAAGA	200
DEBRV - MACAS	200
DEBRV - NLRTM	83
MAAGA - BEANR	240
MAAGA - RULED	240
MACAS - BEANR	240
MACAS - RULED	240
RULED - SEGOT	80

Table 5. Transit time restrictions for cases (8.3) and (8.12).

The order in which the ports are visited and the arrival time of the vessel at
each port are listed in Table 6 under the two objective functions $OB1$ and $OB2$.

	Model [5]			Model [6]	
	Port	Arrival time		Port	Arrival time
Order	UN/LO Port name	t_j [hours]	UN/LO Port name		t_j [hours]
1	DEBRV Bremerhaven	475.074	DEBRV Bremerhaven		472.430
2	NLRTM Rotterdam	0.000	NLRTM Rotterdam		0.00
3	MAAGA Agadir	128.736	MAAGA Agadir		113.694
4	MACAS Casablanca	159.497	MACAS Casablanca		140.916
5	BEANR Antwerp	271.683	BEANR Antwerp		241.986
6	PLGDN Gdansk	337.135	PLGDN Gdansk		317.459
7	RULED St. Petersburg	380.736	RULED St. Petersburg		365.694
8	SEGOT Gothenburg	443.140	SEGOT Gothenburg		436.746

Table 6. Arrival time at each port for test with ID 8.0.2.10 for $OB1$ and $OB2$.

The total cost of the service is the sum of sailing and emissions cost, that
are \$838,815 and \$432,774, respectively for $OB1$, which totals to \$1,271,559. For
$OB2$ these costs are reduced to the sum of \$876,078 and \$322,133, this is a total
of \$1,198,211. There is therefore a cost reduction of \$73,348 or 5.8 %. In addition,
the sailing cost of the latter model is actually increased by roughly \$37,000. On
the other hand, the emission costs have decreased by a total of \$110,642 or

25.6%. This is a significant reduction of emissions cost for the shipping company and shows the environmental benefit of taking the externalities into account.

The distance traveled in both cases is 6,242 nautical miles. The active sailing time is the same, 429 hours, and the number of vessels is also the same as 3 vessels are used in both cases, leading to a total round-trip time of 504 hours. This implies that the reduction in cost comes entirely from speed optimization. It is also clear that the average speed is shifted from being highest outside the ECA for $OB1$ to being higher inside the ECA for $OB2$.

The results are good for the shipping company that seems to reduce the operating expenses, but what effect does it actually have on the amount of pollutants emitted and, thus, to the environment? The actual amount of pollutants emitted in each area is listed in Table 7.

	$OB1$		$OB2$	
ECA	CO$_2$ [ton]	SO$_x$ [ton]	CO$_2$ [ton]	SO$_x$ [ton]
outside	1,154	25.946	750	16.852
inside	1,348	0.841	1,789	1.116
Total	2,502	26.787	2,539	17.968

Table 7. Amount of emitted CO_2 and SO_x for $OB1$ and $OB2$ on test 8.0.8.10.

Based on the results, there is an increase of CO_2 emissions by 1.5%. Although the increase is very small, it is definitely not desired. On the other hand, the SO_x emissions have been reduced from 26.8 tonnes to 18 tonnes, which is a significant reduction of roughly 33%. This means that the implementation of external costs has the desired effect, as SO_x emissions are reduced and speed is decreased outside ECAs. What speaks against it, is the increase of CO_2 emission that we see in the case above. CO_2 emission is not affected by the sulphur content of bunker fuel. Therefore the emission of CO_2 is more reflected by the bunker consumption, and thus the speed of the vessel. Since the distance sailed and the total active sailing time is the same for $OB1$ and $OB2$ in this case, the speed adjustments have been conducted such that the average speed between the two ECAs has been equalized more. This also means that the total amount of consumed bunker fuel must be more or less the same between the two models in this case. For this reason the CO_2 emission does not change significantly.

The decrease of SO_x emission is a result of the decreased average speed outside the ECA. In this area the cheaper bunker with a high content of sulphur is used, and the lower consumption here has a natural impact on the emitted SO_x. A consideration not considered here is that the most cost-efficient direct sail route between two points may change depending on the difference in the bunker price inside and outside an ECA zone and the location of the border of the ECA zones. Finding the most cost-efficient routes depending on bunker prices is discussed in Fagerholt et al. [8]; however, we assume that the routes used are the cost-optimal routes.

5   Conclusion

In this paper we have presented a model for optimizing routes and speeds both with respect to bunker costs and the external costs of emission. We have showed that the emission costs can be reduced significantly by including the emission costs in the routing model, while the bunker cost is only increased slightly. Thus, we conclude that considering the costs of emissions along with bunker cost when planning and scheduling a route is desirable in order to ensure lower emission. This work might be also relevant in the near future with the possible introduction of regulations that will take into account the externalities from ship air emissions, in the form of either a tax or a pollution permit.

References

1. R. Agarwal and O. Ergun. Ship Scheduling and Network Design for Cargo Routing in Liner Shipping. *Transportation Science*, 42(2):175-196, 2008
2. B. Brouer, J. Alvarez, C. Plum, D. Pisinger, M. Sigurd. A Base Integer Programming Model and Benchmark Suite for Liner-Shipping Network Design. *Transportation Science*, 48:281-312, 2014
3. M. Christiansen, K. Fagerholt, and D. Ronen. Ship Routing and Scheduling: Staus and Perspectives. *Transportation Science*, 38(1):1-18, 2004
4. M. Christiansen, K. Fagerholt, B. Nygreen, and D. Ronen. Maritime Transportation. *Handbook in Operations Research and Management Science*, 14:189-284, 2007
5. M. Christiansen, K. Fagerholt, B. Nygreen, and D. Ronen. Ship routing and scheduling in the new millennium. *European Journal of Operational Research*, 228: 467-483, 2013
6. C. Chu, T. Kuo, and J. Shieh. A Mixed Integer Programming Model for Routing Containerships. *Journal of Marine Science and Technology*, 11(2):96-103, 2003
7. K. Fagerholt, G. Laporte, and I. Norstad. Reducing Fuel Emissions by Optimizing Speed on Shipping Routes. *Journal of the Operational Research Society*, 61:523-529, 2010
8. K. Fagerholt, N. Gausel, J. Rakke, and H. Psaraftis. Maritime Routing and Speed Optimization with Emission Control Areas. *Transportation Research Part C*, 52:57-73, 2015
9. C. Hsu and Y. Hsieh. Routing, Ship Size, and Sailing Frequency Decision-Making for a Maritime Hub-and-Spoke Container Network. *Mathematical and Computer Modelling*, 45:899-916, 2007
10. K. Kjeldsen. Classification of Ship Routing and Scheduling Problems in Liner Shipping. *INFOR*, 49(2):139-152, 2011
11. C. Kontovas and H. Psaraftis. Reduction of Emissions along the Maritime Intermodal Container Chain: Operational Models and Policies. *Maritime Policy and Management: The Flagship Journal of International Shipping and Port Search*, 38(4):451-469, 2011
12. C. Kontovas. The Green Ship Routing and Scheduling Probelm (GSRSP): A Conceptual Approach. *Transportation Research Part D*, 31:61-69, 2014
13. Maersk Line. Slow Steaming Here to Stay. *Maersk Line Press Release*, September 2010. Accessed 18/5-2015 (http://www.maersk.com/en/the-maersk-group/press-room/press-release-archive/2010/9/slow-steaming-here-to-stay)
14. Q. Meng, S. Wang, H. Andersson, and K. Thun. Containership Routing and Scheduling in Liner Shipping: Overview and Future Research Directions. *Transportation Science*, 48(2):265-280, 2014

15. A. Miola, C. Ciuffo. Estimating air emissions from ships: Meta-analysis of modelling approaches and available data sources *Atmospheric Environment* Volume 45, Issue 13, 2011, Pages 2242-2251
16. T. Notteboom. The Time Factor in Liner Shipping Services. *Maritime Economics and Logistics*, 8:19-39, 2006
17. T. Notteboom, and B. Vernimmen. The Effect of High Fuel Costs on Liner Service Configuration in Container Shipping. *Journal of Transportation Geography*, 17:325-337, 2009
18. Petromedia Ltd. Bunkerworld Index. Accessed 14/6-2015 (`http://www.bunkerworld.com/prices/`)
19. C. Plum, D Pisinger, D., J.-J Salazar-Gonzalez, M. Sigurd. Document Single liner shipping service design, *Computers and Operations Research* vol 45, 2914, pp. 1-6
20. H. Psaraftis and C. Kontovas. Balancing the Economic and Environmental Performance of Maritime Transportation. *Transportation Research Part D*, 15:458-462, 2010
21. H. Psaraftis and C Kontovas. Speed models for energy-efficient maritime transportation: A taxonomy and survey. *Transportation Research Part C* vol 26, 2013, pp. 331-351
22. H. Psaraftis and C. Kontovas. Ship Speed Optimization: Concepts, Models and Combined Speed-Routing Scenarios. *Transportation Research Part C*, 44:52-69, 2014
23. L. Reinhardt, C. Plum, D. Pisinger, M. Sigurd, G. Vial. The liner shipping berth scheduling problem with transit times. *Transportation Research Part E*, 2016, 86, pp. 116-128
24. Ricardo-AEA Technology (2014), *Update of the Handbook on External costs of Transport: Final report*, DG-MOVE, Harwell.
25. D. Ronen. The Effect of Oil Price on the Optimal Speed of Ships. *Journal of the Operational Research Society*, 33:1035-1040, 1982
26. Seago Line. The Atlantic Sea Route. Accessed 20/3-2015 `http://www.seagoline.com/services/our-network/atlantic/`
27. M. Stopford. Maritime Economics. Routledge, third edition, 2009. ISBN 0203442660
28. UNCTAD. Review of maritime transport 2016, United Nations Conference on Trade and Development. Accessed 20/3-2017 (`http://unctad.org/en/PublicationsLibrary/rmt2016_en.pdf`)
29. S. Wang, and Q. Meng. Schedule Desing and Container Routing in Liner Shipping. *Transportation Research Record*, 2222:25-33, 2011
30. S. Wang, and Q. Meng. Sailing Speed Optimization for Container Ships in a Liner Shipping Network. *Transportation Research Part E*, 48:701-714, 2011
31. S. Wang, and Q. Meng. Liner Ship Route Schedule Design with Sea Contigency Time and Port Time Uncertainty. *Transportation Research Part B*, 46:615-633, 2012
32. S. Wang, Q. Meng, and Z. Liu. Bunker consumption optimization methods in shipping: A critical review and extensions. *Transportation Research Part E: Logistics and Transportation Review*, 53:49-62, 2013
33. S. Wang, A. Alharbi, and P. Davy. Liner ship route schedule design with port time windows. *Transportation Research Part C: Emerging Technologies*, 41:1-17, 2014
34. S. Yan, C. Chen, and S. Lin. Ship Scheduling and Container Shipment Planning for Liner in Short-Term Operations. *Marine Science and Technology*, 14(4):417-435, 2009

A Shortest Path Heuristic for Evaluating the Quality of Stowage Plans in Roll-On Roll-Off Liner Shipping

Jone R. Hansen[1(✉)], Kjetil Fagerholt[1,2], and
Magnus Stålhane[1]

[1] Department of Industrial Economics and Technology Management, Norwegian
University of Science and Technology, Norway: jone.hansen@ntnu.no
[2] SINTEF Ocean, Trondheim, Norway

Abstract. Roll-on Roll-off shipping companies transport rolling cargo, such as cars, trucks and large construction machines. When sailing, this type of cargo must be attached to the deck using chains, to prevent damaging the cargo. For each voyage including multiple port calls where the cargo is loaded/unloaded, an important decision is to decide where to place each vehicle (or unit), such that the time used on shifting is minimized. Shifting means temporarily moving some vehicles to make an entry/exit route for the vehicles that are to be loaded/unloaded at a given port. As the vehicles are securely fastened to the deck, shifting is a time-consuming procedure. We present the stowage plan evaluation problem which is to determine the optimal vehicles to shift at each port call, such that the time spent on shifting is minimized. Given a set of alternative stowage plans for a voyage, the results from the stowage plan evaluation problems are used to determine the best among these stowage plans. We present a shortest path-based heuristic for solving the problem. Computational results show that the solution method is a powerful tool for comparing stowage plans, due to its fast computing times and high success rate, i.e. its ability to determine the better of two stowage plans.

Keywords: Maritime transportation, Stowage, Roll-on Roll-off

1 Introduction

Major improvements to the efficiency of maritime transportation have been made during the last decades due to operations research. However, compared to other segments in maritime transportation, the Roll-on Roll-off (RoRo) shipping segment has received little attention. RoRo vessels transport vehicles and other types of rolling material between different regions of the world according to predefined plans. Lower freight rates provide a challenging reality for the RoRo shipping companies, due to a surplus of tonnage in the world's deep sea fleet. We seek to improve the profitability of the RoRo segment, by introducing a method for evaluating different stowage plans. Better stowage plans may reduce the time used to load and unload vehicles, and hence, the time spent in port.

© Springer International Publishing AG 2017
T. Bektaş et al. (Eds.), ICCL 2017, LNCS 10572, pp. 351–365, 2017.
https://doi.org/10.1007/978-3-319-68496-3_24

The problem addressed in this paper is the stowage plan evaluation problem (SPEP). In RoRo transportation, a feasible stowage plan is not as good as any other feasible stowage plan. A good stowage plan enables seamless loading and unloading of the carried rolling units (hereinafter referred to as vehicles) by using the least amount of time on moving vehicles unnecessarily, which is known as shifting. Shifting means temporarily moving some vehicles to make an entry/exit route for the vehicles that are to be loaded/unloaded at the given port. Given a stowage plan for a voyage, the objective of the SPEP is to minimize the time used on shifting at each port, by identifying the optimal vehicles to shift. The time use for shifting a vehicle is treated as a cost, such that the quality of a stowage plan is determined by its shifting cost, relatively to other stowage plans carrying the same vehicles.

Figure 1 shows the placement of vehicles on a deck, during the deep sea leg between Asia and Europe for a given voyage. Both stowage plans look structured, but there is a major difference in the shifting cost. At the first port call in Europe, all vehicles marked in blue are to be unloaded. In the upper stowage plan in Figure 1, all blue vehicles are placed in the bow of the ship. When arriving at the first port in Europe, two green and several yellow vehicles must be shifted in order to unload all the blue ones. The second stowage plan has all blue vehicles placed close to the ramp, and no shifts are required when unloading the vehicles.

Stowage planning has been widely studied in the context of container shipping, see for example [1, 5, 6]. Minimizing the number of shifts is an important objective, both in container shipping and RoRo transportation. In container shipping, the containers are stacked on top of one another. When dispatching a given container, containers stacked on top of it must be removed, i.e. shifted. Here, which containers to shift at each port call are implicitly given by the stowage plan. In RoRo transportation, which vehicles to shift to enable load-

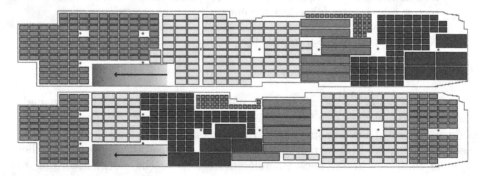

Fig. 1: Two different stowage plans for a given deck and cargo list. The exit ramp is marked with an arrow. Each colored square represents a vehicle and all vehicles with the same color are unloaded at the same port. Unloading sequence: Blue, green, yellow, orange. Thus, the blue vehicles are unloaded at the first unloading port and the orange ones at the last port on the voyage.

ing/unloading of the desired vehicles at each port call, must be determined. The problem of deciding which vehicles to shift at each port (SPEP) is, to the authors' knowledge, new to the OR literature. There are, however, publications dealing with the operational problem of creating stowage plans. Øvstebø et al. [4] consider the RoRo ship stowage problem (RSSP). For a ship set to sail on a given voyage, the problem is to decide which cargoes to carry, how many vehicles to carry from each cargo, and how to stow the vehicles carried during the voyage. They formulate the problem as a mixed-integer programming (MIP) model and present a specially designed heuristic method to solve the problem. For modeling purposes, they divide each deck into several logical lanes, into which the vehicles are lined. The vehicles enter the each deck at stern and are unloaded according to the last in-first out (LIFO) principle. We argue that basing the shifting cost calculations on a LIFO principle is too crude. In practice, vehicles enter the decks using ramps placed somewhere on the deck and take the least inconvenient path from its placement to the ramp when unloaded.

Recently, Hansen et al. [3] presented a mathematical model for the two-dimensional RSSP, a simplification of the RSSP which arises if only one deck is considered. They argue that dividing the decks into lanes, as done in [4], may be too restricting, especially when the cargoes stowed are heterogeneous, i.e. they have different sizes and shapes. The authors propose different objective functions to influence the placement of the vehicles. While promising placement strategies are provided, the shifting cost of the stowage plans is not calculated. Hence, based on the reviewed literature, we identify the need for a method for evaluating and comparing different stowage plans carrying the same cargoes along a voyage.

The purpose of this paper is to present the stowage plan evaluation problem in RoRo transportation. We present a mathematical formulation of the problem and propose a shortest path-based heuristic for solving the problem. Even though a solution to this problem may indicate which vehicles to shift at each port in a practical case, this is not the purpose of this contribution. The problem of deciding which vehicles to shift at each port is easily solved by the port workers, who drive the vehicles on and off the ship. However, the problem is crucial when deciding upon a stowage plan when planning a voyage. The SPEP is then solved for each proposed stowage plan, where the shifting cost is used to determine the best one. The stowage plans could both be provided by planners or a stowage plan generator/heuristic.

The remainder of the paper is structured as follows: We present the problem in Section 2. Section 3 presents a mathematical formulation of the problem. Then, in Section 4, we explain our solution approach. Computational results are presented in Section 5 and concluding remarks are given in Section 6.

2   Problem description

The SPEP considers a RoRo ship carrying a given set of cargoes along a voyage with a predefined set of loading and unloading ports to visit. We take as input a given stowage plan for the voyage, which states the number of cargoes, where to load and unload the cargo, the number of vehicles in each cargo, dimensions of the vehicles, and where each vehicle is placed on the ship. Given this stowage plan, the SPEP is to determine which vehicles to shift at each port call, to enable all vehicles that are to be loaded/unloaded to reach their destination on the deck (if loading) or to exit the ship (if unloading). Thus, the problem is to determine an entry and exit route for each vehicle placed on the deck. An entry route for a given vehicle is defined as the path from the entry/exit ramp to the location it is to be placed on the deck, and vice versa for an exit route. Each possible route is associated with a shifting cost, which depends on both the number of vehicles placed along the route and the vehicle's size. This cost is not necessarily a real cost, but it reflects the cost of time used to move the vehicle. The cost of shifting a vehicle varies, as larger vehicles usually require more effort to move. Objects, such as pillars and ramps, and weight restrictions on the deck limit the possible paths a vehicle can use when entering or exiting the deck. The shifting cost of a stowage plan is given by the cost of shifting all blocking vehicles at each port call, and the objective is to minimize this shifting cost.

Figure 2 presents an example of how the shifting cost is evaluated for different vehicles in different settings, and two loading ports are considered. For the first loading port, the entry route for one vehicle from cargo 2 is shown. The vehicle passes through two vehicles from cargo 1, but the vehicles are not shifted. As these vehicles are loaded in the same port, there always exists a loading sequence where the loaded vehicles do not block each other. In this example, this can be achieved by loading cargo 2 first, and then cargo 1. Thus, the shifting cost should only be accounted for if the blocking vehicle is loaded at a previous port call, or unloaded at a later port call. Note that as each deck is empty at the first loading

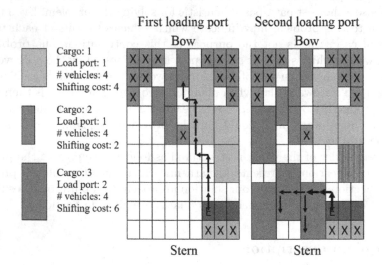

Fig. 2: Possible loading routes for some vehicles at different ports. Entry point is marked with an E. The X's indicate unusable space. Vehicles marked with vertical lines must be shifted.

port, the shifting cost for the first port will always be zero. This also applies to the last port call, as all remaining vehicles are unloaded at this port.

Another important aspect is that each shift is only accounted for once at each port. At the second loading port in Figure 2, two vehicles from cargo 3 use partly the same route, indicated by the arrows. Both vehicles' entry route requires that a vehicle from cargo 1 is shifted, as it is loaded at a previous port. As the vehicle already is shifted to make way for one of the vehicles from cargo 3, e.g. the one furthest to the left, there is no reason to place it back on the deck before the other vehicle from cargo 3 has been placed on the deck. Thus, the shifting cost from the two routes add up to 4, and not 8, which is the sum of the shifting cost for each of the two vehicles.

So to summarize, the SPEP deals with evaluating given stowage plans by determining which vehicles to shift at each port call to minimize the shifting cost of the plan. We consider the stowage plan for a single deck, as we assume that there exists an open path from the entry point of the ship to each deck. Then, when solving for several decks, the total shifting cost is then given by the sum of shifting costs for each deck.

3   Mathematical formulation

Building on the previous work in [3], the SPEP is based on a grid representation of the given deck, where $\mathcal{I}$ is the set of rows and $\mathcal{J}$ the set of columns over a deck, indexed by i and j, respectively. A square (i,j) represents a physical area on the deck where the vehicles may be placed, where square $(1,1)$ is defined as the square located at the stern of the ship's port side. We define the parameter E_{ij} to be 1 if square (i,j) is the entry/exit point on the deck. Let $\mathcal{C}$, indexed by c, be the set of cargoes carried along the voyage. Each cargo c consists of N_c identical vehicles (or units). The set of vehicles $\mathcal{V}_c$ includes all vehicles v from cargo c. The length and width of each vehicle in cargo c, in squares, are given by S_c^L and S_c^W, respectively. Let $\mathcal{P}$ be the set of ports visited along the voyage, indexed by p. Each cargo $c \in \mathcal{C}$ is to be loaded at port P_c^L and unloaded at port P_c^U. We assume a given stowage plan for the voyage is provided, and define parameter P_{ijcvp} to be 1 if vehicle v from cargo c occupies square (i,j) when departing from port p. Further, let P_{ijcvp}^C be 1 if the lower left corner of vehicle v from cargo c is placed in square (i,j) when departing port p. The feasible stowage plan is now given by the parameters P_{ijcvp} and P_{ijcvp}^C.

To represent the SPEP, we present a fixed-charge multicommodity network flow formulation of the problem and define the following additional notation. Let $\mathcal{N}$ be the set of all squares (i,j) and $\mathcal{N}_c \subseteq \mathcal{N} \backslash \mathcal{U}_c$ be the set of squares (i,j) a vehicle from cargo c may use on its entry/exit route. The set $\mathcal{U}_c$ includes all squares that cannot be used by vehicles from cargo c, which typically are squares where pillars and other blocking objects are placed and squares where the weight restrictions are violated. Each cargo c has a graph $\mathcal{G}_c = (\mathcal{N}_c, \mathcal{A}_c)$ associated with it. The set of squares $\mathcal{N}_c$ and the set of arcs $\mathcal{A}_c \subset \mathcal{N}_c \times \mathcal{N}_c$ define the feasible movements for the vehicles in cargo c. Further, the set $\mathcal{C}_p$ includes all cargoes placed on the deck at port p. This set can further be divided into two disjoint sets: C_p^R includes all cargoes placed on the deck at port p, given that the port is either the loading port or the unloading port of cargo c, i.e. $p = P_c^L$ or $p = P_c^U$. Thus, this set includes all cargoes that are to be routed on or off the ship in the given port p. Next, the set C_p^N includes all cargoes placed on the deck at port p, given that the port is neither the loading port nor the unloading port of cargo c, i.e. $p \neq P_c^L$ and $p \neq P_c^U$. If any of these cargoes is shifted at port p, a shifting cost C_c^S is imposed. The shifting cost is based on the vehicle's area, i.e. $C_c^M = S_c^L S_c^W$, as it is usually more time-consuming to move larger vehicles than smaller ones. It is assumed that a shifted vehicle is moved off the deck during the port call and returned to the same location after the loading/unloading.

Let $\mathcal{B}_{ij}$ be the set of all neighboring squares to square (i, j), i.e. $\mathcal{B}_{ij} = \{(i + 1, j), (i-1, j), (i, j+1), (i, j-1)\}$. A vehicle is allowed to move one square forward, backward, left or right from each square (i, j). By allowing sideways movement, some of the proposed entry and exit routes may be infeasible in practice, as most vehicles have a given turning radius and are unable to move sideways. However, it should be emphasized that the stowage plan evaluation is mainly conducted to compare alternative stowage plans and not to actually determine the optimal loading and unloading routes for each vehicle. Hence, it can be argued that this modeling choice is reasonable and sufficient.

We associate with each square $(i, j) \in \mathcal{N}$, cargo c, and port p, an integer number D_{ijcp} representing its supply/demand. If $D_{ijcp} > 0$, square (i, j) is a supply square for cargo c at port p; if $D_{ijcp} < 0$ square (i, j) is a demand square for cargo c at port p with a demand of $-D_{ijcp}$; and if $D_{ijcp} = 0$, square (i, j) is a transshipment square for cargo c at port p. If we are to load four vehicles from cargo 3 at port 4 and the entry point is square $(1,1)$, then we have a supply of four, represented by $D_{1123} = 4$. Further, we have a demand of -1 at the squares where the vehicles are to be stowed, given by the parameter P_{ijcvp}^C for each of the vehicles, i.e. $D_{ijcp} = \sum_{v \in \mathcal{V}_c} -P_{ijcvp}^C$. Similarly, for a cargo's unloading port, the exit square gets a demand of $-N_c$, and $D_{ijcp} = 1$ for all squares where the lower left corner of a vehicle from cargo c is stowed. We define the parameter A_{ijcdvp} to be 1 if a vehicle from cargo c, placed in square (i, j), uses a square where vehicle v from cargo d is placed at port p. If a 2×2 sized vehicle from cargo c temporarily uses square $(1,1)$ for its entry route, this vehicle also uses the squares $(1,2)$, $(2,1)$ and $(2,2)$. If a vehicle v from cargo d is placed in any of these four squares, then $A_{11cdvp} = 1$, which imply that the vehicle v from cargo d must be shifted, if a vehicle from cargo c uses square $(1,1)$.

The arc flow variable f_{ijklcp} represents the flow sent from square (i, j) to a neighboring square (k, l) of cargo c at port p. Finally, binary variables y_{cvp} take value 1 if vehicle v from cargo c is shifted at port p.

The model is solved for every port except the first and the last port along the voyage, since no vehicles are shifted in these ports. Let $\mathcal{P}^S = \mathcal{P} \backslash \{\text{first port, last port}\}$ be the set of ports where shifting may occur. The resulting shifting cost for a voyage is the sum of the shifting costs for each port. We can now formulate the SPEP problem for each $p \in \mathcal{P}^S$ as the following mathematical program:

$$\text{SPEP}(p \in \mathcal{P}^S): \min z_p = \sum_{c \in \mathcal{C}_p^N} \sum_{v \in \mathcal{V}_c} C_c^M y_{cvp} \tag{1}$$

subject to

$$\sum_{(k,l) \in \mathcal{B}_{ij}} f_{ijklcp} - \sum_{(k,l) \in \mathcal{B}_{ij}} f_{klijcp} = D_{ijcp} \quad c \in \mathcal{C}_p^R, (i,j) \in \mathcal{N}_c \tag{2}$$

$$A_{klcdvp} \sum_{(i,j) \in \mathcal{B}_{kl}} f_{ijklcp} \le M_c y_{dvp} \quad\quad c \in \mathcal{C}_p^R, (k,l) \in \mathcal{N}_c, d \in \mathcal{C}_p^N, v \in \mathcal{V}_d \tag{3}$$

$$f_{ijklcp} \ge 0 \quad\quad\quad\quad\quad\quad\quad c \in \mathcal{C}_p^R, ((i,j),(k,l)) \in \mathcal{A}_c \tag{4}$$

$$y_{cvp} \in \{0,1\} \quad\quad\quad\quad\quad\quad c \in \mathcal{C}_p^N, v \in \mathcal{V}_c \tag{5}$$

The objective function (1) is to minimize the cost of shifting vehicles at port p. The flow balance constraints (2) state that the outflow minus inflow must equal the supply/demand of the square i for each cargo c. Constraints (3) are the capacity constraints. If a given vehicle v from cargo d blocks the flow of vehicles from cargo c into square (k,l) at port p, given by A_{klcdvp}, then the blocking vehicle v from cargo d must be shifted to enable flow into the square, i.e. the shifting variable $y_{dvp} = 1$. An upper bound on M_c is given by N_c, i.e. the number of vehicles in cargo c. Constraints (4) and (5) define each variable's domain.

Figure 3a illustrates an optimal solution to the SPEP, obtained by solving model (1)-(5), for an example instance. Here, exit routes for the two vehicles of cargo 1 are to be decided, for a given unloading port. Vehicles from cargoes 2 and 3 must be shifted if routes passing through them are used, as they are to be unloaded at a later port call. The cheapest way to unload the two vehicles from cargo 1 is to shift the marked vehicle from cargo 3. This vehicle has a shifting cost of 9, i.e. the vehicle's area, resulting in a shifting cost of 9 for this port.

4. Shortest path solution method

When determining a stowage plan by using either an exact or a heuristic solution method, the SPEP becomes an important sub-problem that may have to be solved a large number of times to evaluate and compare the shifting costs of alternative stowage plans. Therefore, it can be important to solve the SPEP very quickly. The SPEP model, defined in Section 3, consists of a large number of the continuous flow variables, but relatively few binary variables (one for each vehicle that may be shifted). Due to this, small instances are easily solved by a commercial solver. However, for the large grid resolutions required for solving realistically sized problems, even solving the LP-relaxation of the SPEP model can be too time-consuming for practical use. Thus, we propose a heuristic method based on solving shortest path problems, which can be solved efficiently.

The SPEP deals with deciding which vehicles to shift, considering all cargoes that are to be loaded or unloaded at a given port. Instead of considering all cargoes that are to be loaded/unloaded at a port simultaneously, we consider one vehicle at the time. Thus, for a given vehicle in both its loading and unloading

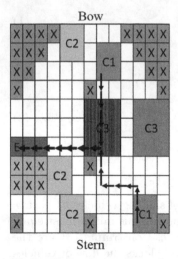

(a) Optimal solution from the
SPEP model

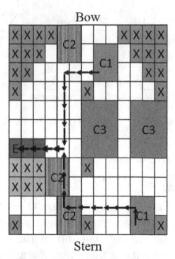

(b) Feasible routes, proposed
by the heuristic in Section 4

Fig. 3: Exit routes for the two vehicles in cargo 1 (C1) are to be decided, for a given unloading port. Vehicles marked with vertical lines are shifted.

port, the problem is to decide which vehicles to shift, such that this vehicle may be loaded/unloaded. The objective is to minimize the shifting cost. This problem is equivalent to finding the cheapest entry/exit path, where the cost of moving from one square to another is dependent on whether we need to shift any vehicles due to the move, i.e. a shortest path problem (SPP).

When using the shortest path approach to solve the example instance in Figure 3b, we evaluate the exit routes for each vehicle individually. This results in a total shifting cost of 12, i.e. three shifted vehicles with an area of four squares. The solution to the left has a shifting cost of 9, as explained in the previous section. It can be shown that the shortest path approach gives an upper bound on the shifting cost for a given port.

The remainder of this section is structured as follows. Section 4.1 describes the procedure of creating the graphs on which the SPPs are solved. Then, in Section 4.2, the procedure of solving a shortest path problem on the graphs are discussed and we present some additional strategies for improving the upper bound on the shifting cost.

4.1 Creating the graphs

For this SPP heuristic, we are not concerned with finding the shortest path in distance, but rather the cheapest path, i.e. the entry/exit route that gives the lowest contribution to the shifting cost. The cheapest paths can be found by solving a one-to-one shortest path problem for each vehicle's loading and unloading port. It is not possible to solve a single one-to-many SPP for each port, where the cheapest path for each entering or exiting vehicle is calculated, as edge costs are dependent on the size of the vehicle traversing the edge. We explain this using a 2×2 sized vehicle and a 4×4 sized vehicle, both initially placed with their lower left corner in square $(1, 3)$, as illustrated in Figure 4. Then, we evaluate the edge cost associated with moving one square to the left for both vehicles. For the smallest vehicle, the edge cost is zero, as moving from square $(1, 3)$ to $(1, 2)$ does not impose any shifts. However, the largest vehicle uses a square where another vehicle is placed. The edge cost equals the cost of shifting the blocking vehicle, which in this case is six, i.e. the vehicle's area.

Since the edge costs depend on the size of the cargo, a graph $\mathcal{G}_{cp} = (\mathcal{N}_c, \mathcal{A}_c)$ must be created for every cargo, for their loading and unloading port $\mathcal{P}_c^{LU} = \{P_c^L, P_c^U\}$. We do not need to create a graph for each vehicle, as all vehicles within a cargo have the same dimensions. Let $\mathcal{N}_c$ be the set of squares (i, j) a vehicle from cargo c may use on its entry/exit route. The set of edges $\mathcal{A}_c$ defines the feasible movements for the vehicles, i.e. maximum four directed outgoing edges per square. We add the edge $((i, j), (k, l))$ to the set of edges $\mathcal{A}_c$, for all $(i, j) \in \mathcal{N}_c$ and $(k, l) \in \mathcal{B}_{ij}$.

Each time an edge is added to the set $\mathcal{A}_c$, the corresponding edge cost C_{ijklcp}^E is calculated. For this edge $((i, j), (k, l))$, let $\mathcal{V}^I$ be the set of vehicles that may be shifted and occupy any of the squares $(\bar{i}, \bar{j})$, $\bar{i} = i..i + S_c^L - 1, \bar{j} = j..j + S_c^W - 1$. Similarly, let $\mathcal{V}^N$ be the set of vehicles that may be shifted and occupies any of the squares $(\bar{k}, \bar{l})$, $\bar{k} = k..k + S_c^L - 1, \bar{l} = l..l + S_c^W - 1$. Then, all vehicles that must be shifted due to the move from (i, j) to (k, l) are given by the set $\mathcal{V}^S = \mathcal{V}^N \backslash \mathcal{V}^I$, i.e. all vehicles that occupy some of the squares in the new position which was not occupying any of the squares in the initial position. The edge cost C_{ijklcp}^E equals the cost of shifting all vehicles in the set $\mathcal{V}^S$.

Evaluating the move shown in Figure 4 for the large 4×4 vehicle, the cost of using edge $((1, 3), (1, 2))$ is six. The use of edge $((1, 3), (1, 2))$ implies that the lower left corner of the vehicle is moved from square $(1,3)$ to $(1,2)$, as shown in Figure 4. Initially, no vehicles that may be shifted are placed in the squares occupied by the vehicle, and the set $\mathcal{V}^I$ is therefore empty. After the move to square $(1,2)$, square $(4,2)$ is used by the moving vehicle. The blue 3×2 vehicle is placed in this square and must be shifted due to the move. Thus, the blue vehicle is added to the set $\mathcal{V}^N$. The set of vehicles to shift due to the move from

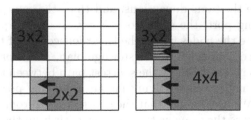

Fig. 4: The cost of moving a vehicle from a square to a neighbor square depends with the size of the moving vehicle.

square $(1,3)$ to $(1,2)$ are now given by the vehicles in the set $\mathcal{V}^S = \mathcal{V}^N \backslash \mathcal{V}^I$, which includes the blue vehicle with a shifting cost of six, giving a edge cost of six. Continuing the example, we now state that a new move from square $(1,2)$ to square $(1,1)$ is free, as the cost of shifting the blue vehicle is already accounted for by the move from square $(1,3)$ to $(1,2)$. For this new move, the blue vehicle initially occupies one of the squares used by the 4×4 vehicle and is added to the set $\mathcal{V}^I$. The blue vehicle is also added to the set $\mathcal{V}^N$, as it uses one or more of the same squares as the 4×4 vehicle after the move to square $(1,1)$. As both sets include the blocking vehicle, the set $\mathcal{V}^S = \mathcal{V}^N \backslash \mathcal{V}^I$ is empty. Thus, no shifting cost is imposed due to this move. One final note regarding this procedure is that vehicles that are to be loaded or unloaded in the same port are never added to the sets $\mathcal{V}^I$ and $\mathcal{V}^N$. As mentioned in Section 2, there always exists a loading/unloading sequence, where none of the loading/unloading vehicles block the other loading/unloading vehicles.

4.2   Shifting cost calculations

Given the graphs created in the previous section, we can now calculate an upper bound on the shifting cost. For each vehicle at its corresponding loading and unloading port, a one-to-one SPP can be solved on the graph created for the cargo the vehicle belongs to. For a given vehicle at its loading port, the loading cost is given by the value of the vehicle's corresponding target node from the SPP solution, where the entry square is the start node. For the vehicle's unloading port, the unloading cost is given by the vehicle's target node, which is the exit square. The sum of the loading and unloading cost for all vehicles in all cargoes gives an upper bound on the shifting cost of the stowage plan. However, this upper bound can be poor, as several of the shifted vehicles may be accounted for more than once. This section presents three strategies which improve both the computational time and the solution quality of the shifting cost evaluation. The *Dijkstra-NoDec* procedure given in [2] is used for solving the SPPs.

4.2.1   Reducing the number of SPPs

In order to speed up the solution procedure, we propose to solve a one-to-many SPP for each cargo's loading and unloading port, instead of many one-to-one SPPs for each vehicle's loading and unloading port. This is possible, as all vehicles in a cargo have the same dimensions, and thus, the same edge costs. When solving for a loading port, the start node is set to entry square on the deck. The target nodes are the nodes where the lower left corner of the vehicles in the cargo are to be placed, provided by the stowage plan. The shortest path for each vehicle in the cargo is now given by the shortest path between the start node and the vehicles target node. When solving for an unloading port, the exact same procedure is used. We use the fact that the shortest path from the exit to a vehicle's location is always the same as the shortest path from the vehicle's location to the exit. So, for an unloading port, we also seek the shortest path from the exit square to each vehicle's location, which can be solved as a one-to-many SPP.

Even though each SPP takes more time to solve, as we now solve one-to-many SPPs, we have reduced the number of SPPs needed to be solved from two times the number of vehicles to two times the number of cargoes, which improves the overall computational time.

4.2.2   Route backtracking

We know that the vehicle's target node gives the cost of loading/unloading a vehicle. However, two or more vehicles may use a loading or unloading route which shifts the same vehicles. If the loading cost of both vehicles A and B are six, this could for example imply that a given vehicle C, with a shifting cost of six, is shifted for both vehicles A and B. We use the fact that each vehicle is only shifted once at each port and backtrack the loading/unloading routes for all vehicles loaded/unloaded in at a port, recording the unique shifted vehicles at each port. A better bound is then given by the sum of the cost of shifting each of the recorded vehicles. In the example above, the bound now becomes six, and not 12, where the latter is the sum of vehicle A and B's loading cost.

4.2.3   Dynamically updating the edge costs

At each port, there are usually several cargoes that are to be loaded or unloaded, and we solve an SPP for each of these, one at the time. By continuously sharing information about which vehicles that are shifted, we can improve the upper bound of the shifting cost. As an example, assume two cargoes are to be loaded at a port. An SPP is solved for the first cargo, and three vehicles must be shifted. When solving the SPP for the second cargo, we can now set the edge costs where these three vehicles are placed to 0, as they must be shifted regardless of the solution for the second cargo. Now, the SPP solution for the second cargo may utilize this and choose alternate routes for the vehicles. The routes may be more expensive when considering only this cargo, but as these vehicles are shifted anyway, the routes contribute less to the overall shifting cost. When imposing this strategy, the order in which we solve the SPPs becomes important. Based on preliminary testing, the cargoes should be ordered based on the area of the vehicles they consist of. Consider a large truck driving from A to B. If we shift the vehicles blocking the truck's route, both the truck and a small car can use this route. This does not apply the other way around. Thus, evaluating the cargoes with the largest vehicles first is both logical and computationally promising.

Dynamically updating the edge costs can also be used to improve the shifting cost estimation within each cargo. We know that as soon as a vehicle has found its shortest path to the entry square, all other vehicles in the cargo could also use this path as part of their route, with no additional cost, as the vehicles have the same size. Thus, each time the shortest path between the start node and a target node has been found during the one-to-many SPP procedure, we force this path to be used by the vehicle placed in the corresponding target node. Then, an edge is added between this target node and the start node, with an edge cost of zero. This means that the vehicles placed at the remaining target nodes could either find the shortest path to the entry square or the shortest path to one of the fixed vehicle's target nodes. This strategy is especially valuable when several vehicles within the same cargo are placed together. Once the shortest path for one of these vehicles to the exit is found, e.g. vehicle A, the other vehicles may move to vehicle A's location, and the shortest path is found. Note that if a vehicle is not placed nearby vehicle A, it can still use the path from vehicle A to the exit as a partial path of its route at no additional cost.

5   Computational study

The mathematical model presented in Section 3 is implemented in Mosel and solved using Xpress-IVE 1.28.12. The SPP heuristic described in Section 5 is coded in Java. All computational experiments have been run on a PC with Intel Core i7-6500U processor and 16 GB of RAM running Windows 10.

5.1   Test instances

Each instance represents a feasible stowage plan for a given deck, cargo list, and grid resolution, where the placement of each vehicle is given. The deck information gives the layout of the deck, location of entry/exit square, and gives the unusable spaces. Four decks are used in this computational study, where decks A and B are fictional, and decks C and D are real deck layouts. Four different grid resolutions are used, i.e. 50×19, 100×38, 150×56, and 200×75. The ratio between the number of rows and columns is based on the length and width of a car equivalent unit (CEU), which has an approximate length-width ratio of 4:1.5. Each stowage plan has a space utilization factor (SUF), i.e. the total area of all vehicles divided by the deck's area. The SUFs used are 0.8 and >0.9. When creating an instance, the vehicles are either randomly placed on the deck (R) or placed in a logical manner (L) according to objective function (3) in [3]. Finally, the cargo list contains information about the number of cargoes, loading and unloading port of each cargo, and each vehicle's size and weight. Two cargo lists are tested for each possible combination of the mentioned aspects.

We identify a test instance by its name Rows-Columns-Deck-SUF-Placing-Cargo List. 150-56-D->0.9-R-2 means an instance with a grid resolution of 150×56 on the real deck D with cargo list number 2, where more than 90% of the deck's area is occupied by vehicles and the vehicles are randomly placed.

For the test instances, we have set the upper limit on computing time to 7,200 seconds for both the solution methods. As a SPEP problem is solved for each port except the first and last port, the computing time is distributed evenly among these ports. Thus, for an instance with six ports, the maximum computing time for each of the ports 2-5 are 1,800 seconds.

5.2   Comparison of SPEP model and SPP heuristic

To compare the performance of SPEP and the SPP heuristic, we have tested both methods on 64 instances. Table 1 presents a summary of the results, where the average results from cargo lists 1 and 2 for each instance are presented. As the SPEP model is solved for every port for each instance, a positive gap may be reported even though the solution time is less than the maximum computation time. The percentage of the gap closed is calculated as $(z_u - z_b)/z_b$ where z_u is the best solution and z_b is the best bound.

In Table 1, we have reported the SPP results from the SPP heuristic using all improvement strategies, denoted SPP_A. To evaluate the effect of the improvement strategies discussed in Section 4.2, we have tested the base heuristic (SPP_B), i.e. without any of the strategies, where the average gap and solution time are 488% and 0.55 seconds, respectively. These results are significantly worse than SPP_A's results and are therefore not reported in the table. For the instances solved to optimality by Xpress, SPP_A found solutions with an average gap of 8.5%. 37 of the 64 instances were solved to optimality by Xpress, using the SPEP model. The SPP heuristic found a solution proved optimal by the SPEP model in two of the 37 instances.

Even for the smallest grid resolution, the SPEP model's computing times are too long for practical use. The SPP heuristic performs significantly better, reducing the average solution times to less than 0.1 seconds, which is acceptable in its intended context, i.e. as a sub-problem when determining a stowage plan. For both methods, grid resolution has the highest impact on solution time.

Table 1: Average gaps and solution times per group of instances. Each group consists of two instances with different cargo lists.

Group of instances	Vehicles logically placed				Vehicles randomly placed			
	SPEP		SPP_A		SPEP		SPP_A	
	Avg. gap(%)	Avg. CPU (s)	Avg. gap(%)	Avg. CPU (s)	Avg. gap(%)	Avg. CPU (s)	Avg. gap(%)	Avg. CPU (s)
50-19-A->90	0.0	12.72	16.4	0.01	0.0	229.82	12.4	0.01
50-19-A-80	0.0	6.22	2.3	0.01	0.0	22.66	5.6	0.01
50-19-B->90	0.0	20.67	9.2	0.01	0.0	408.17	4.6	0.01
50-19-B-80	0.0	46.40	7.7	0.01	0.0	365.21	6.5	0.01
100-38-C->90	3.2	1050.93	6.6	0.03	0.0	397.58	7.7	0.03
100-38-C-80	0.0	299.22	8.1	0.03	0.0	391.90	8.1	0.04
100-38-D->90	8.5	840.57	13.0	0.04	23.6	3077.87	30.1	0.05
100-38-D-80	0.0	341.50	8.2	0.03	13.2	1763.38	17.8	0.05
150-56-C->90	0.0	116.74	8.8	0.08	0.0	877.34	8.5	0.09
150-56-C-80	0.0	95.81	1.8	0.07	4.5	1350.81	9.5	0.10
150-56-D->90	7.4	1224.54	28.3	0.08	75.2	4315.77	97.8	0.12
150-56-D-80	16.0	933.72	29.9	0.09	57.4	4240.85	79.6	0.12
200-75-C->90	15.8	4819.01	25.6	0.18	29.3	3457.04	39.9	0.16
200-75-C-80	6.8	3072.33	6.9	0.16	34.1	3451.87	38.8	0.17
200-75-D->90	58.3	5117.53	54.7	0.20	82.4	4629.67	75.3	0.23
200-75-D-80	22.7	2317.14	29.1	0.22	99.7	4882.36	85.9	0.22
Avg.	8.7	1269.69	16.0	0.08	26.2	2116.39	33.0	0.09

The columns to the left in Table 1 present the results for the instances where the vehicles are placed logically. Considering the SPEP model's results, we see that both the average solution time and the gap are lower when the vehicles are logically placed, than for the randomly generated stowage plans. For the SPP heuristic, we see that the solution times are approximately the same for both placement methods, while the gap is higher when vehicles are randomly placed.

5.3 Comparing stowage plans

We stress that the intended use of the SPP heuristic is to compare stowage plans, not determine the actual shifting cost of a stowage plan. Even though the gaps reported in the previous section were relatively high, this is acceptable as long as they are consistently low/high for all the stowage plans. Thus, the important aspect is that the solutions from the SPP heuristic follow the same trend as the SPEP model's solutions, with respect to the shifting cost evaluated. The quality of the SPP heuristic should be, and is here, determined by its ability to decide which is the better stowage plan, given a set of stowage plans.

To test the quality of the SPP heuristic, the following decision problem is used: Given two stowage plans A and B, which is better? The two stowage plans are evaluated by both the SPEP model and the SPP heuristic, where the better stowage plan is the one with the lowest shifting cost. The SPP heuristic succeeds if it reports the same best stowage plan as the SPEP model. Ten groups of instances are used to test the SPP heuristic's quality. All instances within each group have the same grid resolution, deck, SUF, and cargo list, but the vehicles' placement differs. Each group consists of 50 randomly generated stowage plans. The decision problem is asked for every unique pair of stowage plans out of the 50 plans, resulting in $C(50,2) = 1225$ decision problems. The success rate equals the number of successful evaluations divided by the number of combinations.

Table 2: SPP heuristic's success rate (SR) per group of instances.

Group of instances	SPP_B SR (%), $t = 0.0$	SPP_A SR (%), $t = 0.0$	SR (%), $t = 0.025$	SR (%), $t = 0.05$
50-19-A-80-R-1	62.0	88.9	94.4	97.3
50-19-A-80-R-2	64.5	87.4	92.3	95.7
50-19-A->90-R-1	70.7	91.1	95.7	98.4
50-19-A->90-R-2	78.6	93.8	96.9	98.8
100-38-C-80-R-1	71.5	91.1	96.5	99.2
100-38-C-80-R-2	67.1	86.4	93.7	97.0
100-38-C->90-R-1	53.7	88.3	94.1	97.2
100-38-C->90-R-2	64.8	90.4	95.8	99.0
150-56-C-80-R-1	68.1	91.7	95.0	97.9
150-56-C->90-R-1	64.3	86.5	92.9	96.3
Avg.	66.5	89.6	94.7	97.7

Table 2 presents a summary of the test results. Without any improvement strategies, i.e. SPP_B, we see that the average success rate is 66.5%, which is not much better than random guessing (50%). However, with the improvement strategies (SPP_A), the average success rate improves to 89.6%. The two right-most columns in Table 2, show the success rate when both answers to the decision problem are accepted if relative difference in shifting cost below a certain tolerance value t. The relative difference in shifting cost between stowage plans A and B is given by $|z(A) - z(B)|/\min\{z(A), z(B)\}$. Based on the results, SPP_A will successfully identify the better stowage plan 97.7% of the times on average, given that the two stowage plans have a relative difference in shifting cost greater than 5%. This is certainly an acceptable result for the method's intended use, i.e. as a subroutine in a solution method for generating stowage plans.

6   Concluding remarks

This paper has introduced the stowage plan evaluation problem, which is solved to compare different stowage solutions for a voyage in Roll-on Roll-off liner shipping. We have presented a mathematical formulation describing the problem. To efficiently solve the problem we proposed a shortest path based heuristic.

Our computational tests indicate that the shortest path-based heuristic is a promising method for comparing different stowage plans. The problem of determining the better of two stowage plans was on average successfully solved 9 out of 10 times by the heuristic. In the case where stowage plans with less than 5% difference in shifting cost were considered equally good, the average success rate increased to 98%. In addition to a high average success rate, short computation times were reported for the proposed solution method. These promising results enable the solution method to be used as a subroutine in a stowage plan generator, which is an interesting venue for future research.

References

1. Ambrosino, D., Paolucci, M., Sciomachen, A.: Experimental evaluation of mixed integer programming models for the multi-port master bay plan problem. Flexible Services and Manufacturing Journal 27(2-3), 263–284 (2015)
2. Chen, M., Chowdhury, R.A., Ramachandran, V., Roche, D.L., Tong, L.: Priority queues and Dijkstra's algorithm. Computer Science Department, University of Texas at Austin (2007)
3. Hansen, J.R., Hukkelberg, I., Fagerholt, K., Stålhane, M., Rakke, J.G.: 2d-packing with an application to stowage in roll-on roll-off liner shipping. Lecture Notes in Computer Science 9855, 35–49 (2016)
4. Øvstebø, B.O., Hvattum, L.M., Fagerholt, K.: Optimization of stowage plans for roro ships. Computers & Operations Research 38(10), 1425–1434 (2011)
5. Pacino, D., Delgado, A., Jensen, R.M., Bebbington, T.: Fast generation of near-optimal plans for eco-efficient stowage of large container vessels. Lecture Notes in Computer Science 6971, 286–301 (2011)
6. Parreño, F., Pacino, D., Alvarez-Valdes, R.: A grasp algorithm for the container stowage slot planning problem. Transp. Res. Part E 94, 141–157 (2016)

Optimising and Recognising 2-Stage Delivery Chains with Time Windows

Frank Phillipson[1*], Max Ortega del Vecchyo[12], Bart van Ginkel[12], Dylan Huizing[12], Alex Sangers[1]

[1] TNO, PO Box 96800, 2509 JE The Hague, The Netherlands,
[2] Delft University of Technology, The Netherlands

Abstract. In logistic delivery chains time windows are common. An arrival has to be in a certain time interval, at the expense of waiting time or penalties if the time limits are exceeded. This paper looks at the optimal placement of those time intervals in a specific case of a barge visiting two ports in sequence. For the second port a possible delay or penalty should be incorporated. Next, recognising these penalty structures in data is analysed to if see certain patterns in public travel data indicate that a certain dependency exists.

Keywords: Logistics, Computation Models, 2-Stage Delivery, Data analysis

1 Introduction

Delivery windows are a known phenomenon in time window constrained models for production scheduling and vehicle routing. In [5] an overview can be found of recent literature on the use in production logistics. In the context of a delivery performance model, a delivery window is defined as the difference between the earliest acceptable delivery date and the latest acceptable delivery date. In supply chain management and home delivery in e-commerce the problem of interest is the optimal positioning of the delivery time window to minimise the expected cost of untimely delivery, such as inventory costs and penalties or the estimation of accumulated delivery times with uncertainty [1,5,6,7,8,9,10,12,13].

Delivery windows are also used in Vehicle Routing Problems (VRP). A VRP involves finding a set of routes, starting and ending at a depot, that together cover a set of customers. Each customer has a given demand, and no vehicle can service more customers than its capacity permits. The objective is to minimise the total distance travelled or the number of vehicles used, or a combination of these. A special case of the VRP is when the service at a customer's place must start within a given time window. There are two types of time windows. Time windows are called soft when they can be violated for a penalty cost. They are hard when they cannot be violated, i.e., if a vehicle arrives too early at a

---

* frank.phillipson(at)tno.nl

© Springer International Publishing AG 2017
T. Bektaş et al. (Eds.), ICCL 2017, LNCS 10572, pp. 366–380, 2017.
https://doi.org/10.1007/978-3-319-68496-3_25

customer, it must wait until the time window opens; and it is not allowed to arrive late. In all the cases these time windows are given in advance [11,3,2].

In this work a delivery chain is studied where a barge has to visit two ports. In each port a number of containers is handled. For the planning of the port, the planner of the barge should indicate a time slot in which the barge will arrive. If the barge is too early, it has to wait until the beginning of the slot. If the barge is too late, it has to wait some penalty time. If the barge arrives within the time slot, the handling starts immediately. This means that we introduce a penalty which occurrence is dependent on the arrival time, which duration is dependent on the arrival time in case of early arrival, in combination with a two-stage time window. Within this study, first the optimisation of the choice of the time slots is elaborated in Section 2. The main question here is what the optimal time slots are to be communicated to minimise the total of the penalties. Secondly, in Section 3 the way to recognise the existence of such time slots with penalties in travel data is studied. In practice often not all data and/or the precise process is known. There the question is if we only see the arrival and departure times of a barge (for example from GPS or AIS data) can we predict the underlying process, to be able to predict the arrival time of the barges at some (final) stop.

2   Optimisation

The central case in this paper is a delivery chain where a barge has to visit two ports. In each port a number of containers should be handled. For the planning of the port, the planner of the barge should indicate a time slot in which the barge will arrive. If the barge is too early, it has to wait until the beginning of the slot. If the barge is too late, it has to wait some penalty time. If the barge arrives within the time slot, the handling starts immediately. In this section the optimal choice of the time window is determined.

2.1   Problem description

To formulate the problem, first some notation is defined:

I = Set of ports;
T_i = Transportation time to port $i \in I$, starting at the former location;
H_i = Handling time at port $i \in I$;
W_i = Waiting time at port $i \in I$;
S_i = Start time slot at port $i \in I$;
L = Length time slot;
K, k = Penalty wait time, fixed, stochastic or function depending on context.

The question that arises is what would be the optimal start times S_1 and S_2 of both slots to minimise the sum of the waiting times $(W_1 + W_2)$? Different probability distribution functions are used for the transportation and handling times and, as a consequence, for the arrival time (X) at the port under consideration. The arrival, in each of the ports will be in the interval (A, B) (see Fig. 1); therefore we skip the indices here. We assume that, for each of the two stages, $S \geq A$ and $B \geq S + L$, while losing a part of the time slot will not be smart. Only if $L \geq (B - A)$ this will not hold, but then we have no problem. The arrival will be in one of the three intervals $a = [A, S]$, $b = [S, S + L]$ or $c = [S + L, B]$. For each realisation of the arrival time x we can calculate the waiting time:

$$
\begin{aligned}
A \leq x < S & \qquad W = S - x \\
S \leq x \leq S + L & \qquad W = 0 \\
S + L < x \leq B & \qquad W = K
\end{aligned}
$$

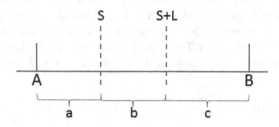

Fig. 1. Process

2.2 First stage

Now the optimal choice for the starting time of the time slots can be derived, by minimising the expected waiting time as a function of S_1. We assume three different options for the penalty: a fixed time, a function of the delay and a random value. At the first port the arrival time X is equal to the transportation time T_1. For various probability distribution functions for T_1 we obtain the optimal value (S) for S_1, the start of the first time slot.

Fixed penalty Given a fixed penalty K, the expected waiting time is given by:

$$
\begin{aligned}
\mathbb{E}[W] &= \mathbb{E}[W \mathbb{1}_{X<S}] + \mathbb{E}[W \mathbb{1}_{S \leq X < S+L}] + \mathbb{E}[W \mathbb{1}_{S+L \leq X}] \\
&= \mathbb{E}[(S - X) \mathbb{1}_{X<S}] + \mathbb{E}[0 \mathbb{1}_{S \leq X < S+L}] + \mathbb{E}[K \mathbb{1}_{S+L \leq X}] \\
&= S\mathbb{E}[\mathbb{1}_{X<S}] - \mathbb{E}[X \mathbb{1}_{X<S}] + 0 + K\mathbb{E}[\mathbb{1}_{S+L \leq X}] \\
&= SF(S) - \int_{-\infty}^{\infty} x \mathbb{1}_{x<S} f(x)dx + K(1 - F(S + L)) \\
&= SF(S) - \int_{-\infty}^{S} x f(x)dx + K(1 - F(S + L)).
\end{aligned}
$$

The expected waiting time is minimised by:

$$\frac{d}{dS}\mathbb{E}[W] = 0$$

resulting in

$$\frac{d}{dS}\mathbb{E}[W] = \frac{d}{dS}SF(S) - \frac{d}{dS}\int_{-\infty}^{S} xf(x)dx + \frac{d}{dS}K(1 - F(S+L))$$

$$= Sf(S) + F(S) - Sf(S) - Kf(S+L) = F(S) - Kf(S+L)$$

So:

$$\frac{d}{dS}\mathbb{E}[W] = 0 \iff F(S) = K \cdot f(S+L)$$

Now any distribution for X can be used. For three examples this will be elaborated.

Uniform distribution If the transportation time and consequently the arrival time X is uniform (A,B): $F(S) = \frac{S-A}{B-A}$ and $f(S) = \frac{1}{B-A}$, so we obtain:

$$\frac{d}{dS}\mathbb{E}[W] = 0 \iff \frac{S-A}{B-A} = K \cdot \frac{1}{B-A} \iff S - A = K \iff S = A + K.$$

Recall that S has a maximum value of $B - L$, thus $S = \min(A + K, B - L)$.

Exponential distribution. If the transportation time and consequently the arrival time X is exponentially distributed (λ) the expected waiting time equals: Exponential: $F(S) = 1 - \exp^{-\lambda S}$ and $f(S) = \lambda\exp^{-\lambda S}$. So we obtain:

$$\frac{d}{dS}\mathbb{E}[W] = 0 \iff 1 - \exp^{-\lambda S} = K\lambda\exp^{-\lambda(S+L)}$$

$$\iff 1 = (K\lambda\exp^{-\lambda L} + 1)\exp^{-\lambda S}$$

$$\iff -\lambda S = \log(\frac{1}{K\lambda\exp^{-\lambda L} + 1})$$

$$\iff S = \frac{1}{\lambda}\log(K\lambda\exp^{-\lambda L} + 1)$$

Normal distribution. If the arrival time is normally (μ, σ) distributed, where $\phi(.)$ denotes the normal probability density function and $\Phi(.)$ the cumulative probability density, the waiting time is minimised by solving for S in:

$$\Phi(S) = K\phi(S + L),$$

which has to be solved numerically.

Penalty as function of delay. Now assume the penalty depends on how late the barge is. Again, $\mathbb{E}[W]$ is calculated, since the only term that changes compared to the situation above is $\mathbb{E}[W\mathbb{1}_{S+L\leq X}]$. The penalty equals $k(X-S-L)$ for some function $k:[0,\infty)\to[0,\infty)$.

$$\mathbb{E}[W\mathbb{1}_{S+L\leq X}] = \mathbb{E}[k(X-S-L)\mathbb{1}_{S+L\leq X}] = \int_{S+L}^{\infty} k(x-S-L)f(x)dx$$

The derivative follows from:[3]

$$\begin{aligned}\frac{d}{dS}\mathbb{E}[W\mathbb{1}_{S+L\leq X}] &= \frac{d}{dS}\int_{S+L}^{\infty} k(x-S-L)f(x)dx \\ &= \int_{S+L}^{\infty} -k'(x-S-L)f(x)dx - k(x-S-L)f(x)|_{x=S+L} \\ &= -\int_{S+L}^{\infty} k'(x-S-L)f(x)dx - k(0)f(S+L) \\ &= -\int_{0}^{\infty} k'(x)f(x+S+L)dx - k(0)f(S+L)\end{aligned}$$

Combining with the steps above results in:

$$\frac{d}{dS}\mathbb{E}(W) = F(S) - \int_{0}^{\infty} k'(x)f(x+S+L)dx - k(0)f(S+L)$$

So

$$\frac{d}{dS}\mathbb{E}(W) = 0 \iff F(S) = \int_{0}^{\infty} k'(x)f(x+S+L)dx + k(0)f(S+L)$$

Note that if k is a constant, this expression reduces to what was found earlier.

Penalty is a random variable, independent of X. The third option concerns a random penalty K, independent of X. Then the last term becomes:

$$\mathbb{E}[W\mathbb{1}_{S+L\leq X}] = \mathbb{E}[K\mathbb{1}_{S+L\leq X}]$$

Since K and X are independent, so are K and $\mathbb{1}_{S+L\leq X}$, the expectations can be multiplied to obtain:

$$\mathbb{E}[W\mathbb{1}_{S+L\leq X}] = \mathbb{E}[K]\mathbb{E}[\mathbb{1}_{S+L\leq X}] = \mathbb{E}[K](1 - F(S+L))$$

$$\frac{d}{dS}\mathbb{E}(W) = 0 \iff F(S) = \mathbb{E}[K]f(S+L)$$

In the case that K is constant this expression reduces to the first case again.

---

[3] Under some regularity assumptions, for instance k must be differentiable on $(0,\infty)$ and continuous on $[0,\infty)$

2.3 Second stage

The first stage resulted in a general formulation that can be used for the second stage, given that the probability distribution of the arrival time at the second port is known. However, the probability distribution function of the arrival time (X) is more complicated, namely the sum of two transportation times, a handling time and possibly a penalty. First the penalty is neglected, later, the propagation of the penalty is studied.

Second time slot without penalty in the first time slot For the second time slot without penalty, the same approach can be taken as in the first stage. First note that here it is assumed that there is no penalty in the first time slot, but obviously there is one in the second (since otherwise nothing would have to be optimised). Now again for the three probability distributions (of each of the stochastic variables, adding up to the arrival time at the second stage) the solution can be derived.

Uniform distribution If the two transportation times and the handling time all follow a uniform distribution, the arrival time has an Irwin-Hall distribution [4]. This distribution converges quickly to the normal distribution. From our experience, even in the case of only three underlying uniform distributions, a normal approximation is usable in practice. If $T_1 \sim uniform(U_1, U_2)$, $T_2 \sim uniform(U_3, U_4)$ and $H_1 \sim uniform(U_5, U_6)$, then by approximation $X \sim Normal(\mu, \sigma)$ where

$$\mu = \frac{1}{2}(U_2 - U_1) + \frac{1}{2}(U_4 - U_3) + \frac{1}{2}(U_6 - U_5),$$

$$\sigma = \sqrt{\frac{(U_2 - U_1)^2}{12} + \frac{(U_4 - U_3)^2}{12} + \frac{(U_6 - U_5)^2}{12}}.$$

Now the method for the normal distribution of the previous stage can be used.

Exponential distribution In the case of exponential handling and transporting times (and assuming independence) the second arrival time has an Erlang$(3, \lambda)$ distribution. This means:

$$F(x) = 1 - \sum_{n=0}^{2} \frac{1}{n!} \exp^{-\lambda x} (\lambda x)^n$$

$$f(x) = \frac{1}{2}\lambda^3 x^2 \exp^{-\lambda x}$$

The formula above reduces the problem to finding S such that:

$$1 - \exp^{-\lambda S} - \lambda S \exp^{-\lambda S} - \frac{1}{2}\lambda^2 S^2 \exp^{-\lambda S} = \frac{1}{2}K\lambda^3 S^2 \exp^{-\lambda(S+L)}$$

$$\Longleftrightarrow \exp^{\lambda S} - 1 - \lambda S - \frac{1}{2}\lambda^2 S^2 = \frac{1}{2}K\lambda^3 S^2 \exp^{-\lambda L}$$

$$\Longleftrightarrow \exp^{\lambda S} = \frac{1}{2}(K\lambda^3 \exp^{-\lambda L} + \lambda^2)S^2 + \lambda S + 1.$$

The latter expression can be solved for S numerically.

Normal distribution If the two transportation times and the handling time are all normally distributed and independent, the arrival time has again a normal distribution. If $T_1 \sim Normal(\mu_1, \sigma_1)$, $T_2 \sim Normal(\mu_2, \sigma_2)$ and $H_1 \sim Normal(\mu_3, \sigma_3)$ then $X \sim Normal(\mu, \sigma)$ where

$$\mu = \mu_1 + \mu_2 + \mu_3,$$

$$\sigma = \sqrt{\sigma_1^2 + \sigma_2^2 + \sigma_3^2}.$$

Now the method for the normal distribution of the previous section can be used.

Propagation of penalty: Second time slot with penalty The challenge now is to derive an expression for the arrival time at the second port, including the fact that there may have been a penalty at the first port. Then the formula presented earlier can be applied to find the expression that has to be solved. We assume T_1, T_2 and H_1 to be independent. The time that is added to this due to not arriving within the time frame, is the penalty P. So P is not only due to arriving late. We see then:

$$P = \begin{cases} S - T_1 & \text{if} & T_1 \leq S \\ 0 & \text{if} \ S < T_1 \leq S + L \\ k & \text{if} & T_1 > S + L \end{cases}$$

Now we are interested in the second arrival time $X = T_1 + P + H + T_2$. Since P and T_1 are dependent of each other and the rest is independent, we will call $X_1 = T_1 + P$ and $X_2 = H + T_2$. The interesting part here is X_1:

$$X_1 = \begin{cases} T_1 + S - T_1 = S & \text{if} & T_1 \leq S \\ T_1 + 0 = T_1 & \text{if} \ S < T_1 \leq S + L \\ T_1 + k & \text{if} & T_1 > S + L \end{cases}$$

Now the cumulative distribution function of X_1 equals:

$$F_{X_1}(x) = \begin{cases} 0 & \text{if} & x < S \\ F_{T_1}(x) & \text{if} & S \leq x \leq S + L \\ F_{T_1}(S + L) & \text{if} \ S + L < x \leq S + L + k \\ F_{T_1}(x - k) & \text{if} & x > S + L + k \end{cases}$$

This is visualised in Fig. 2. The jump in the point S means that the random variable is not absolutely continuous. This is what we expect, since the probability of starting the handling at point S equals $\mathbb{P}(T_1 \leq S) = F_{T_1}(S)$, which is strictly positive. We can describe the 'density' in this way:

$$f_{X_1}(x) = \begin{cases} 0 & \text{if} & x < S \\ \text{mass } F_{T_1}(S) & \text{if} & x = S \\ f_{T_1}(x) & \text{if} & S \leq x \leq S + L \\ 0 & \text{if} \ S + L < x \leq S + L + k \\ f_{T_1}(x - k) & \text{if} & x > S + L + k \end{cases}$$

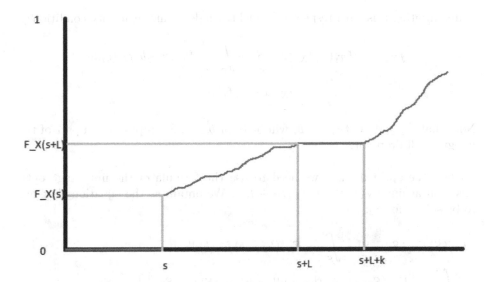

Fig. 2. CDF of time that handling begins

Now we would like to obtain the cumulative density function and the density of the sum of X_1 and X_2.[4]

$$F_X(x) = \mathbb{P}(X_1 + X_2 \leq x) = \int_{b=-\infty}^{\infty} \int_{a=-\infty}^{x-b} f_{X_1,X_2}(b,a)\,\mathrm{d}a\,\mathrm{d}b$$

$$= \int_{b=-\infty}^{\infty} \int_{a=-\infty}^{x-b} f_{X_1}(b) f_{X_2}(a)\,\mathrm{d}a\,\mathrm{d}b = \int_{b=-\infty}^{\infty} \int_{a=-\infty}^{x-b} f_{X_2}(a)\,\mathrm{d}a\, f_{X_1}(b)\,\mathrm{d}b$$

$$= \int_{-\infty}^{\infty} F_{X_2}(x-b) f_{X_1}(b)\,\mathrm{d}b$$

Now, using the description that we found of f_{X_1}, we obtain:

$$F_X(x) = \int_{-\infty}^{\infty} F_{X_2} A(x-b) f_{X_1}(b)\,\mathrm{d}b$$

$$= F_{T_1}(S) F_{X_2}(x-S) + \int_{S}^{S+L} F_{X_2}(x-b) f_{T_1}(b)\,\mathrm{d}b$$

$$+ \int_{S+L+k}^{\infty} F_{X_2}(x-b) f_{T_1}(b-k)\,\mathrm{d}b$$

---

[4] Note that the following computations are strictly speaking ill-defined, since f is not a continuous function. However, it is correct and this way a more intuitive derivation is given. To be precise, one would have to use the Lebesgue-Stieltjes integral to avoid speaking of f. Also note that we use independence of X_1 and X_2 when their joint probability distribution function is written as the product of the marginals.

Differentiating this with respect to x yields (under some regularity conditions):

$$f_X(x) = F_{T_1}(S)f_{X_2}(x - S) + \int_S^{S+L} f_{X_2}(x - b)f_{T_1}(b)db$$

$$+ \int_{S+L+k}^{\infty} f_{X_2}(x - b)f_{T_1}(b - k)db$$

Note that $X_2 \geq 0$, so $f_{X_2}(x - b)$ will be 0 for $b > x$. So in practice, a part of the integral will drop out.

To find the optimal time, we need to use the formula of the first stage optimisation again: $F_X(S_2) = k_2 f_X(S_2 + L_2)$. We obtain as the equation that has to be solved for S_2:

$$F_{T_1}(S)F_{X_2}(S_2 - S) + \int_S^{S+L} F_{X_2}(S_2 - b)f_{T_1}(b)db$$

$$+ \int_{S+L+k}^{\infty} F_{X_2}(S_2 - b)f_{T_1}(b - k)db = k_2 F_{T_1}(S)f_{X_2}(S_2 + L_2 - S)$$

$$+k_2 \int_S^{S+L} f_{X_2}(S_2 + L_2 - b)f_{T_1}(b)db + k_2 \int_{S+L+k}^{\infty} f_{X_2}(S_2 + L_2 - b)f_{T_1}(b - k)db$$

By rearranging a bit, we get:

$$(k_2 f_{X_2}(S_2 + L_2 - S) - F_{X_2}(S_2 - S))F_{T_1}(S)$$

$$= \int_S^{S+L} (F_{X_2}(S_2 - b) - k_2 f_{X-2}(S_2 + L_2 - b))f_{T_1}(b)db$$

$$+ \int_{S+L+k}^{\infty} (F_{X_2}(S_2 - b) - k_2 f_{X_2}(S_2 + L_2 - b))f_{T_1}(b - k)db$$

Note that in any situation with a sum of random variables, the convolution integral appears. This usually cannot be simplified, except for nice situations such as some known sums of random variables. This is the reason for the integrals with two densities in them. The penalty P is of different nature in different cases, this accounts for the multiple integrals. This suggests that there is not much hope of finding nicer expressions.

2.4   Case

As example we look at the following case. As input data we use:

$T_1 = U(180; 234)$
$H_1 = U(50; 150)$
$T_2 = U(120; 156)$
$H_2 = U(50; 150)$
$L = 30$ minutes
$K = 45$ minutes

Now the optimal value of S_1 can be calculated by $S_1^* = \min(A + P, B - L) = \min(180 + 45; 234 - 30) = 204$ resulting in $E(W_1) = 5.33$. The same holds for S_2. First for the case neglecting the penalty at the first port. Minimum value for S_2 can be derived easily $S_2 = 180 + 50 + 120 = 350$, and also the maximum value $S_2 = 234 + 150 + 156 = 540$. The arrival time on port 2 is a sum of three uniform distributed variables. If we assume that the sum of three uniform variables has a normal distribution, then the arrival time on port 2 is normally distributed with $\mu = 350 + 0.5 * (190) = 445$ and $\sigma = \sqrt{\frac{(54)^2}{12} + \frac{(100)^2}{12} + \frac{(36)^2}{12}} = 34.4$. Solving the formula of the first stage for a normal distribution gives $S_2^* = 438$.

These results can be checked by a numerical simulation of 70,000 realisations of trips with these parameters. Figure 3 shows that the minimum delay is reached (indeed) around 204. Furthermore, it can be seen how sensitive the outcome is for a choice of S_1: 10 minutes off, gives 5 minutes extra delay.

Simulating the second stage without penalty results in the outcome as shown in Fig. 4. The optimal value of 438 is confirmed; however, the graph is rather flat around the optimum, and the sensitivity of the delay on the window is low.

From the simulation of the second stage with penalty at the first stage also comes that taking the penalty into account, the optimal S_2* becomes 441, as depicted in Fig. 5.

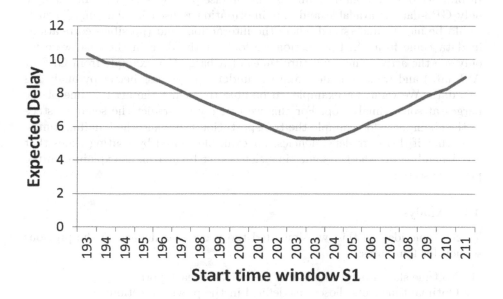

Fig. 3. Simulated optimum S_1.

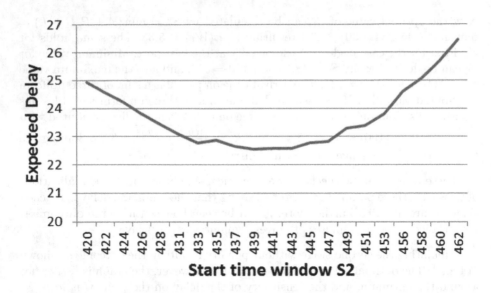

Fig. 4. Simulated optimum S_2 without penalty.

3   Recognizing time windows in data

In practice often not all data and/or the precise process is known. For example only GPS-data is available and this information is used in planning. Then it would be nice to understand where the interactions and (possible) correlations in data come from. In this section we look at the data in the case were we only see the arrival and departure times of a barge (for example from GPS or AIS data) and want to understand the underlying process better by analysing this data. We want, for example, to be able to predict the arrival time of the barges at some (final) stop. For this we can try to predict the separate steps in the chain, here for example the transportation times and the handling times. But what if there are dependencies, for example caused by waiting times that are depending on whether some time slot is met by arrival, as explained in the previous section.

3.1   Analysis

To get some idea on this, we simulated the process as defined in the previous section for four cases:

1. No time slot; a barge is handled on arrival at each port;
2. Optimal time slots chosen; as defined in the previous section;
3. Time slots are chosen around the expected arrival time; the planner puts the time slot symmetrically around the expected arrival time;
4. No optimisation; the planner places the start of the time slot at the earliest arrival time.

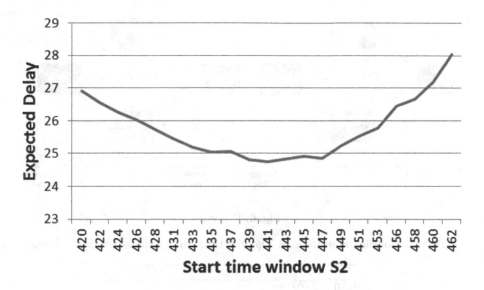

Fig. 5. Simulated optimum S_2 with penalty.

As numerical input we take (in minutes):

$$T_1 = U(180; 234)$$
$$H_1 = U(50; 150)$$
$$T_2 = U(120; 156)$$
$$H_2 = U(50; 150)$$
$$L = 30$$
$$K = 30$$

This gives a minimal lead time of 400 minutes and a maximum lead time of 690 (plus 60 minutes of penalties) minutes. For each of the four cases we simulated 5,000 realisations, were only the arrival and departure times were reported. From these times the two transportation and two handling times were calculated, as depicted in Fig. 6. Again for each of the four cases, the correlation between the four arrival/departure times and the average total lead time were derived. For each correlation value also the p-value was calculated to test whether the correlation is significantly different from zero. The results are presented in Table 1 until Table 5.

Table 1. Correlation in the case 'No time slot'; p-value between brackets.

	T_1	H_1	T_2
H_1	0.028 (0.052)		
T_2	-0.018 (0.201)	0.001 (0.961)	
H_2	0.022 (0.122)	-0.005 (0.750)	-0.001 (0.952)

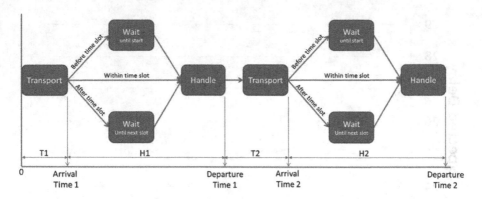

Fig. 6. Process

Table 2. Correlation in the case 'Optimal time slot'; p-value between brackets.

	T_1	H_1	T_2
H_1	-0.210 (0.000)		
T_2	0.004 (0.787)	0.003 (0.850)	
H_2	-0.008 (0.559)	-0.056 (0.000)	-0.005 (0.741)

Table 3. Correlation in the case 'Time slots around the expected arrival time'; p-value between brackets.

	T_1	H_1	T_2
H_1	0.216 (0.000)		
T_2	0.008 (0.562)	-0.012 (0.406)	
H_2	0.047 (0.000)	0.063 (0.000)	-0.009 (0.518)

Table 4. Correlation in the case 'Not optimised'; p-value between brackets.

	T_1	H_1	T_2
H_1	0.382 (0.000)		
T_2	-0.007 (0.635)	-0.011 (0.431)	
H_2	0.171 (0.000)	0.232 (0.000)	0.031 (0.0278)

Table 5. Total process time of the four cases.

Case	Total time
1	545
2	567
3	572
4	581

There are some observations we can make:

1. In the case 'No time slots' there is no correlation between the transportation and handling times.

2. In the case 'No optimisation' there exist: positive correlation between (T_1, H_1), positive correlation between (T_1, H_2) and positive correlation between (H_1, H_2), all by the penalty. There also is a (small but significant) correlation between (T_2, H_2).
3. In the case 'Time slots are chosen around the expected arrival time', the correlations become lower; the effect of the penalty is less than in the not optimised case.
4. In the case 'Optimal time slots chosen', the correlation between (T_1, H_2) disappear (no delay propagation anymore), the two other relations that had a positive correlation (T_1, H_1) and (H_1, H_2) become negative. This means that longer delays do not cause the big penalty anymore, but being early (lower arrival time) leads to small waiting times.

3.2 Limitations

Up to here we assumed that the planning and realisations are independent. However, in practice people are going to react on realisations. For example:

− If a barge is early, the captain can decide to slow down and save fuel. This could lead to a shift in the transportation time distribution and from the optimised case to the 'time slots around expected arrival time' case.
− If a barge had delay in the first part (transportation, penalty and/or handling) the captain could decide to go faster. This again leads to a shift in the transportation time distribution and potentially a decrease in the correlation between (T_1, T_2) and (H_1, T_2).

4 Conclusions

This paper investigated a delivery chain in logistics, where a barge has to visit two ports and was faced by delivery time slots in which the barge has to arrive. We looked at two issues: first, how can the time slot be chosen optimally and secondly, how can time slots with penalty for untimely arrival be recognised in travel data. For the former an optimisation framework was given to derive the optimal time slots at the first and second stage with various options for penalty functions in case of a not timely arrival. For certain distribution functions of the handling and transportation times an explicit expression was derived. Also for the most complicated case, the second stage with propagation of the penalty of the first stage, an expression was derived. For the latter some insight was given to recognise these time slot constructions from correlation values of travel and handling times. Four cases were distinguished where each case showed specific characteristics in the correlation values. The characteristics could, in practice, be compensated by the interaction of humans.

References

1. Agatz, N., Campbell, A., Fleischmann, M., Savelsbergh, M.: Time slot management in attended home delivery. Transportation Science 45(3), 435–449 (2011)

2. Agra, A., Christiansen, M., Figueiredo, R., Hvattum, L.M., Poss, M., Requejo, C.: The robust vehicle routing problem with time windows. Computers & Operations Research 40(3), 856–866 (2013)
3. de Armas, J., Melián-Batista, B., Moreno-Pérez, J.A., Brito, J.: GVNS for a real-world rich vehicle routing problem with time windows. Engineering Applications of Artificial Intelligence 42, 45–56 (2015)
4. Batsyn, M., Kalyagin, V.: An analytical expression for the distribution of the sum of random variables with a mixed uniform density and mass function. In: Models, Algorithms, and Technologies for Network Analysis, pp. 51–63. Springer (2013)
5. Bushuev, M.A., Guiffrida, A.L.: Optimal position of supply chain delivery window: Concepts and general conditions. International Journal of Production Economics 137(2), 226–234 (2012)
6. Garg, D., Narahari, Y., Viswanadham, N.: Achieving sharp deliveries in supply chains through variance pool allocation. European Journal of Operational Research 171(1), 227–254 (2006)
7. Guiffrida, A.L., Nagi, R.: Cost characterizations of supply chain delivery performance. International Journal of Production Economics 102(1), 22–36 (2006)
8. Hernandez, F., Gendreau, M., Potvin, J.Y.: Heuristics for tactical time slot management: a periodic vehicle routing problem view. International Transactions in Operational Research (2017)
9. Safaei, M., Issa, S., Seifert, M., Thoben, K.D., Lang, W.: A method to estimate the accumulated delivery time uncertainty in supply networks. In: Dynamics in Logistics, pp. 337–347. Springer (2013)
10. Safaei, M., Mehrsai, A., Thoben, K.D.: A computational method in analyzing of delivery time uncertainty for highly complex supply networks. Measurement 55, 549–563 (2014)
11. Salani, M., Battarra, M., Gambardella, L.M.: Exact algorithms for the vehicle routing problem with soft time windows. In: Operations Research Proceedings 2014, pp. 481–486. Springer (2016)
12. Tanai, Y., Guiffrida, A.L.: Reducing the cost of untimely supply chain delivery performance for asymmetric Laplace distributed delivery. Applied Mathematical Modelling 39(13), 3758–3770 (2015)
13. Vanany, I., Zailani, S., Pujawan, N.: Supply chain risk management: literature review and future research. In: Strategic Information Systems, IGI Global pp. 16–33 (2009)

Synchromodal Transportation

Framework of Synchromodal Transportation Problems

M.A.M. De Juncker[13], D. Huizing[23], M.R. Ortega del Vecchyo[23], F. Phillipson[3*] and A. Sangers[3]

[1] Eindhoven University of Technology, The Netherlands,
[2] Delft University of Technology, The Netherlands,
[3] TNO, PO Box 96800, 2509 JE The Hague, The Netherlands

Abstract. Problem statements and solution methods in mathematical synchromodal transportation problems depend greatly on a set of model choices for which no rule of thumb exists. In this paper, a framework is introduced with which the model choices in synchromodal transportation problems can be classified, based on literature. This framework should help researchers and developers to find solution methodologies that are commonly used in their problem instance and to grasp characteristics of the models and cases in a compact way, enabling easy classification, comparison and insight in complexity. It is shown that this classification can help steer a modeller towards appropriate solution methods.

Keywords: Synchromodal, Classification, Logistics, Computation Models

1 Introduction

Synchromodal freight transport is a relatively new concept within the logistics sector. Older concepts of logistics are multimodal and intermodal. A transportation network is called a multimodal transport network if the transportation of goods can be made via different modes, where a mode is understood as a means of transportation, such as a barge. In an intermodal transportation network, the goods are transported through a standardised unit of transportation, which we call freight, and in practice is usually a container. Synchromodal freight transport is viewed in this paper as intermodal freight transport with an increased focus on at least one of the following two aspects:

1. Transport planning is done using real-time data, allowing for on-line changes in the planning; [27, 32, 40, 37]
2. Different parties share their real-time information, transportation resources or transportation demands and may even entrust decisions to a central operator or logistics service provider (LSP). In some cases, clients may make an *a-modal* booking, agreeing with an LSP that their goods will be delivered at a set time and place against a set price and leaving it up to the LSP by what modes this is done. [27, 35, 51, 32, 40]

---

* frank.phillipson(at)tno.nl

© Springer International Publishing AG 2017
T. Bektaş et al. (Eds.), ICCL 2017, LNCS 10572, pp. 383–403, 2017.
https://doi.org/10.1007/978-3-319-68496-3_26

Though other important developments exist within intermodal transport [47], synchromodality only concerns synchronising real-time data collection with real-time planning and synchronising the transportation flows and requirements among different parties. The goal of aspect 1 is to increase flexibility and reliability, that is to say, to become able to deal with disturbances in the system more effectively and to more effectively optimise against unknowns. The goal of aspect 2 is to increase efficiency and sustainability, by facilitating *full truck load-consolidation* (FTL-consolidation), in other words, letting one small order wait at a terminal so it can be combined with some other order [49]. Aspect 2 also facilitates smarter *equipment repositioning*, for example, by moving leftover empty containers directly to a nearby terminal where they are needed instead of through a depot [2].

Interest in synchromodality has increased, due to improvements in data technology, an increased focus on the more complicated hinterland transport and the ever-growing need for efficiency. However, synchromodality faces several challenges that keep it from being adopted in practice. The challenges come from several sources. In [32], seven critical success factors of synchromodality are discussed:

1. Network, collaboration and trust
2. Awareness and mental shift
3. Legal and political framework
4. Pricing/cost/service
5. ICT/ITS technologies
6. Sophisticated planning
7. Physical infrastructure

Roughly, it can be argued that the first and second factor are mainly social problems, the third is a political problem, the fourth is a mathematical, social and political problem, the fifth is a technological problem, the sixth is a mathematical problem, and the seventh is a technological and constructional problem.

Each of these factors is currently being addressed by different initiatives. Also in mathematics (applied in logistics) a lot of work has been done that can be used in synchromodality. Mathematical planning problems are often divided into three main categories: strategical, tactical, and operational, so is the case with mathematical synchromodal problems. These problems are related in a pyramidal-like structure in the following sense: tactical problems are usually engaged where a specific strategical instance is given, and operational problems are frequently solved where a strategical and tactical structure are fixed, although sometimes problems in two consecutive levels are solved simultaneously: for instance, in [8], the frequency of a resource is determined along with the flow of freight (that is, part of the schedules to resource and the freight to resources are solved at once). Mathematical synchromodal transportation problems on a tactical or operational level are usually represented via tools from graph theory and optimisation [39]. However, more often than not, the similarities end there: most of the models used to analyse a synchromodal transportation network are targeted to a specific real problem of interest [39], and knowledge and methods of other branches such as statistics, stochastic processes, or systems and control are often used. The models emphasise on what is most important for the given circumstances. Consequently, mathematical synchromodal transportation problems on a tactical or operational level have been engaged with approaches that may differ in many aspects:

- The exhaustiveness of the elements considered varies, e.g. weather or traffic conditions are considered in some models (such as the one presented in [23]) but not all.
- The elements that can be manipulated and controlled may vary, e.g. the departure time of some transportation means may be altered if suitable (as it happens in the model of [8]) or it may be that all transportation schedules are fixed.
- The amount of information relevant to the behaviour of the network may vary, and if a lack of information is considered, the way to model this situation may also vary [31].
- Whether some other stakeholders with authority in the network are in the model, and if so, how their behaviour is modelled.

A model is not necessarily improved by making it increasingly exhaustive. As it happens with most model-making, accuracy comes with a trade-off, in this case, computational power. This computational burden is an intrinsic property of operational synchromodal problems [48] and one that is of the utmost importance given the real-time nature of operational problems: new information is constantly fed and it should be processed on time.

There is no rule of thumb for making the decisions above; also, each of the decisions mentioned above will shape the model, and likely stir its solution methods to a specific direction. Though literature reviews of synchromodal transportation exist [48, 39], no generalised mathematical model for synchromodal transportation problems has been found yet, nor a way of categorising the existing literature by their modelling approaches. The framework for mathematical synchromodal transportation problems on a tactical or operational level presented in this paper aims to capture the essential model-making decisions done in the model built to represent the problem. When no such model is specified, it shows the model-making decisions likely to be done in that case, which makes classification partly subjective. This is done in an attempt to grasp the characteristics of the model/case in a compact way, enabling easy classification and comparison between models and cases, as well as a way to see the complexity of a specific case at a glance. Also, it provides perspective to better relate new problems with previous ones, thus identifying used methodologies for the problem at hand.

In the remainder of this paper, Section 2 gives an overview of the relevant literature. Section 3 introduces the classification framework and Section 4 two shorthand notations for this framework. In Section 5, some examples are provided. Based on these examples, common solution methods are mapped in Section 6 and the relationship with VRP terminology is discussed in Section 7. In Section 8 the examples are used to discuss strengths and weaknesses of the framework.

2   Literature

Synchromodal planning problems exist both in the tactical and operational area. The tactical planning problem is quite extensive. One needs to select and schedule the services to operate, allocate the capacity and equipment, and look at the routing of the goods. Together this is also called *Service Network Design*. The review paper of Crainic [13] gives an extensive review of these problems, their formulations and their solution frameworks. They also give a classification of these problems. In the literature these problems are mostly modelled as *Fixed-Cost Capacitated Multicommodity Network Design Problems*. The paper by Min [29] develops a chance-constrained goal programming model that has multiple aspects in the objective function.

Papers in this area that explicitly deal with synchromodality are [36, 11, 8]. The paper by Puettmann and Stadtler [36] mentions the importance of coordination of plans and operation of independent service providers in an intermodal transportation chain. They present a coordination scheme that will lead to reductions in overall transportation costs. They include stochastic demand in their calculation of the overall costs. Another paper by Caris, Macharis and Janssens [11] also looks at cooperation between inland terminals. In the paper they develop a service network design model for intermodal barge transport and apply it to the hinterland network of the port of Antwerp. They simulate cooperation schemes to attain economies of scale. The paper by Behdani et al. [8] develops a mathematical model for a synchromodal service schedule on a single origin-destination corridor. Taking into account the frequency and capacity of different modalities, it determines the optimal schedule and timing of services for all transport modes. The assignment of containers to services is also determined by the model.

In operational planning problems, problems are regarded that deal with the day-to-day problems in a logistic network. This means that all these problems deal with uncertainty and stochasticity, which makes these problems complex. The decisions depend on the current information and an estimation of the future events. Issues here are:

- reliability of a network: dealing with disruptions [19, 12, 28, 33] and resilience measures [12, 28];
- resource management: empty unit repositioning problems [14, 16, 15] and allocation and positioning of the operating fleet [42–46, 7, 38];
- replanning and online allocation [10, 17, 21].

Papers in the operational area within the synchromodal context are [51, 27, 31]. Zhang and Pel [51] developed a model that captures relevant dynamics in freight transport demand and supply, flexible multimodal routing with transfers and transhipments. It consists of a demand generator (random sampling from historic data), an infrastructure and service network processor (which generates the resource schedule), a schedule-based assignment module (which assigns the demand to resources) and a performance evaluator. The model can be used to compare intermodal and synchromodal transportation from different perspectives: economic, social and environmental. The authors use their model for a case study regarding the Rotterdam hinterland container transport and they show that synchromodality will likely improve service level, capacity utilisation and modal shift, but not reduce delivery cost.

The paper by Mes and Iacob [27] searches for the k-shortest paths through an intermodal network. They present a synchromodal planning algorithm that takes into account time-windows, schedules for trains and barges and closing times of hubs and minimises costs, delays and CO_2 emissions. The k-shortest paths are then presented to a human planner, which can choose the best fitting path for an order by filtering these paths. Their approach consists of offline steps and online steps. In the offline steps, the network is reduced by eliminating paths that are too far from the route. In the online steps an order is assigned to paths, by iterating over the number of main legs. A main leg in this paper is a certain train or barge. The assumption they make is that a cost-efficient route consists of as few legs as possible. The online steps can be done after a disruption to make a new planning.

The paper by Rivera and Mes [31] looks at the problem of selecting services and transfers in a synchromodal network over a multi-period horizon. They take into account the fact that an order can be rerouted at any given moment. The orders become known gradually, but the planner has probabilistic knowledge about their arrival. The objective is to minimise expected costs over the entire horizon. They propose a *Markov Decision Process model* and a heuristic approach based on approximate dynamic programming.

3   Framework identifiers and elements

In this section the framework is introduced. Within the framework *demand* and *resources* are considered. In synchromodal transportation models, demand will likely be containers that need to be shipped from a certain origin to a destination. Resources can for example be: trucks, train and barges. However, the framework allows for a broader interpretation of these terms. In repositioning problems, empty containers can be regarded as resources, where the demand items are bulks of cargo that need to be put in a container.

The framework has two main parts. The first part consists of the *identifiers*; these are specific questions one can answer about the model that depict the general structure of the model. The other is a list of *elements*; these elements are used to depict in more detail what the nature is of the different entities of the synchromodal transportation problem. Note that the notation presented does not include the optimisation objective. Within a specific model there is of course an option to look at different optimisation objectives. This framework is developed in collaboration with multiple parties that study synchromodal systems. However, for certain specific problems one might want to extend the framework. We think this is easily done in the same way as we set up the framework.

3.1   Identifiers

First we will elaborate on the identifiers of the framework. These identifiers are questions about the model. They identify the number of authorities, i.e. how many agents are in control of elements within the model. They will also identify the nature of different elements within the model. The list of elements will be discussed in detail in Section 3.2, but they are used to determine which components in the model are under control, which are fixed, which are dynamic and which are stochastic. For instance, the departure time of a barge may be a control element, but it could also be fixed upfront, or modelled as stochastic. Some of the questions address how the information is shared between different agents and if the optimisation objective is aimed at global optimisation or local optimisation. All the answers on these questions together present an overview of the model, which can then be easily interpreted by others or compared to models from the literature.

The identifiers that describe the behaviour of the model in more detail are discussed below. Note that 'resources' most often refer to transport vehicles and 'demand items' most often refer to freight containers: however, demand items could also be empty containers with no specific destination in equipment repositioning problems. Therefore, a degree of generality is necessary in these identifiers.

1. *Are there other authorities (i.e. agents that make decisions)?*
   Here it is identified if there is one global controller that steers all agents in the network or that there are multiple agents that make decisions on their own.
   - *If there are other authorities, how is their behaviour modelled:* One turn only, Equilibrium *or* Isolated?
     If the previous question is answered with yes, i.e., there are multiple agents that make decisions, one needs to specify how these authorities react to each other. Three different ways for modelling the behaviour of multiple authorities in a synchromodal network are distinguished:
     - *One turn only*: this means that each agent gets a turn to make a decision. After the decision is made, the agent will not switch again. For instance, in the case of three agents A, B and C, agent A will first make a decision, then agent B and then agent C. The modelling ends here, since agent A will not differ from its first decision.
     - *Equilibrium*: the difference between "one turn only" and "equilibrium" is that after each agent has decided, agents can alter their decision with this new knowledge. In the same example: agents A, B and C make a decision, but then agent A changes its decision based on the decisions of B and C. If nobody wants to alter their decision anymore the modelling ends and an equilibrium is reached between the specific agents.
     - *Isolated*: if the behaviour of the multiple authorities is isolated, it means that from the perspective of one of the authorities only limited

information is available about the decisions of the other agents. For instance: agent C needs to make a decision. It is not known what agents A and B have chosen or will choose, but agent C knows historic data on the decisions of agents A and B. Agent C can then use this information to make an educated guess on the behaviour of agents A and B.

2. *Is information within the network: global or local?*
This identifies if the information within the network is available globally or locally. If the information is locally available, it means that only the agents themselves know for example where they are or what their status is at a certain time. If the information is global, the network operator and/or all other agents know all this information as well.

3. *Is the optimisation objective: global or local?*
The same can hold for the optimisation objective. If all agents need to be individually optimised, the optimisation objective is local. If the optimisation objective is global, we want the best alternative for the entire network.

4. *Which elements do you control?*
Since we want to model a decision problem, at least one element of the system must be in control and must take decisions. For example: if one wants to model which containers will be transported by a certain mode in a synchromodal network, we have control over the *demand-to-resource allocation*. If we want to model which trains will depart on which time at certain locations, we have control of the *resource departure time*. An extensive list of elements is given in Section 3.2.
Of course the controllable element can have constraints: for instance, we can influence the departure times of trains, but they cannot depart before a certain time in the morning. This is still a controllable element. We thus consider an element a controllable element if a certain part of it can be controlled.

5. *What is the nature of the other elements* (fixed, dynamic, stochastic *or* irrelevant)*?*
The other elements within the network can also have different behaviour. We distinguish four:

   - *Fixed*: a fixed element does not change within the scope of the problem.
   - *Dynamic*: a dynamic element might change over time or due to a change in the state of the system (e.g. the amount of containers changes the travel time), but this change is known or computable beforehand.
   - *Stochastic*: a stochastic element is not necessarily known beforehand. For instance, it is not known when orders will arrive, but it is a Poisson process. It might also occur that the time the order is placed is known, but the amount of containers for a certain order follows a normal distribution.
   - *Irrelevant*: the list we propose in Section 3.2 is quite extensive. It might occur that for certain problems not all elements are taken into consideration to model the system. Then these elements are irrelevant.

6. *What is the optimisation objective?*

   This identifier is for the optimisation objective. One can look at the exact same system but still want to minimise a different function. One could think of travel times and CO_2 emissions. It is also possible to identify a much more specific optimisation objective. Examples of optimisation objectives are in Section 5.

3.2 Elements

Having defined the identifiers of the framework, now a list of elements is presented, that are expected to exist in most synchromodal transportation problems. They are divided in two parts: *resource elements* and *demand elements*. The resource elements are all elements related to the resources, which are mostly barges, trains and trucks. However, for compactness we also view a terminal as a resource. In the demand elements are all elements related to the demand, which are most of the time freight or empty containers. Most elements mentioned in this list are straightforward, small clarifications are mentioned where necessary.

- Resource elements:
  - *Resource Type*: Different modalities can be modelled as different resource types. Another way to use this element is for owned and subcontracted resources.
  - *Resource Features*: These features can be appointed to the different resource types or can have the same nature for the different types. For instance, it may be that there are barges and trains in the problem, but their schedules are both fixed, thus making the nature of the resource features *fixed* for both resource types.
    * *Resource Origin (RO)*;
    * *Resource Destination (RD)*;
    * *Resource Capacity (RC)*: Indication of how much demand the different resources can handle;
    * *Resource Departure Time (RDT)*;
    * *Resource Travel Time (RTT)*: Time it takes to travel from the origin to the destination (in the case of a moving resource);
    * *Resource Price (RP)*: This can be per barge/train/truck/... or per container.
  - *Terminal Handling time (TH)*: Time it takes to handle the different types of modes at the terminal. This can again be per barge/train/truck/... or per container.
- Demand elements:
  - *Demand Type*: One can also think of different types of demand. For instance, larger and smaller containers or bulk.
  - *Demand-to-Resource allocation (D2R)*: The assignment of the demand to the resources.
  - *Demand Features*:
    * *Demand Origin (DO)*;

∗ *Demand Destination* (*DD*);
∗ *Demand Volume* (*DV*): It might be that different customers have different amount of containers that is being transported. (Note that the demand element in this case will always be 1 container, since each container can have its own assignment.);
∗ *Demand Release Date* (*DRD*): The release date is the date at which the container is available for transportation;
∗ *Demand Due Date* (*DDD*): Latest date that the container should be at its destination, which is not necessarily a hard deadline;
∗ *Demand Penalty* (*DP*): Costs that are incurred when the due date is not met or when the container is transported before the release date (this is sometimes possible with coordination with the customers).

4   Notation

In this section, two types of notation are introduced, which will make it easier to quickly compare different models. Obviously, it is hard to make a compact notation and still incorporate all aspects of a synchromodal system. Therefore, the notation was made as compact as possible and some of the details are left out. When comparing models in detail, it is easier to look at all answers to the identifiers mentioned in Section 3.1. Our six-field notation was built to resemble Kendall's notation for classification of queue types [20] and the notation of theoretic scheduling problems proposed by Graham, Lawler, Lenstra and Rinnooy Kan [18].

4.1   Six-field notation

A synchromodal transportation model can be described by the notation:

$$C|S|D|I|Y|B$$

The letters denote the following things:

− C: controlled elements,
− S: stochastic elements,
− D: dynamic elements,
− I: irrelevant elements,
− Y: system characteristics,
− B: behaviour of other authorities, if any.

The first four entries in the notation can be filled with all elements mentioned in the list in Section 3.2. If any of the elements is not mentioned in these four fields, it is assumed to be fixed. If all unmentioned resource elements should default to stochastic instead, an R can be written in the second field: the same goes for defaulting to controlled, dynamic or irrelevant elements. Analogously, a D can be written in any of the first four fields to set a default for the demand elements.

For the system characteristics, a notation is proposed that gives an answer to questions 1, 2 and 3 of the identifiers. Thus: are there other authorities, is the information global or local and is optimisation global or local? The notation is based on Figure 1 [34]. In a similar way to this figure, the four options for the field *system characteristics* in the notation are:

- *selfish*: information global and optimisation local,
- *social*: information global and optimisation global,
- *cooperative*: information local and optimisation global,
- *limited*: information local and optimisation local.

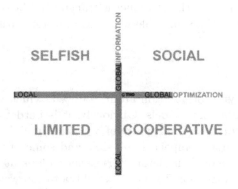

Fig. 1. Different models of a synchromodal network.

The four options for the final field are *one turn only, equilibrium, isolated* and *1*: the first three are explained in Section 3.1, and the final option denotes that there are no other decision-making authorities in the system.

4.2   Two-column notation

Though the proposed six-field notation is a relatively compact way to describe a complex system, it comes with two downsides: it requires a degree of memorisation, and if new natures other than controlled, fixed, stochastic, dynamic or irrelevant are distinguished, there is no place for this in the current notation. These problems are solved by using the two-column notation described in this section, at the cost of compactness.

A synchromodal transportation model can also be described by the notation:

Controlled elements	C, written out
Fixed elements	fixed elements, written out
Stochastic elements	S, written out
Dynamic elements	D, written out
Irrelevant elements	I, written out
System characteristics	Y
Behaviour of other authorities	B

If there are no stochastic elements in a problem, that row can be left out: the same goes for the other natures. If a new nature is distinguished, a row can be easily added for this. In the six-field notation, any unmentioned element was considered fixed, unless an R or D was placed in one of the fields to set the default to that nature. This is again possible here: an R and a D should always be placed in one of the rows to set the default nature of the resource elements and demand elements, respectively.

4.3   On the two notations

In neither notation, the optimisation objective is included: these are considered to be too distinct among different problems to merit classification. As discussed earlier, the two-column notation is much less compact than the six-field notation, but requires less memorisation and lends itself better to change when new natures are distinguished. Our advice is to employ the two-column notation at first, but to switch to the six-field notation when the framework starts gaining familiarity: this familiarity should make the memorisation easier, and this adoption time should suffice to discover any truly important new natures. This paper will largely use the six-field notation for the sake of compactness, seeing how reminders are readily available within this paper.

5   Examples

As discussed earlier, one of the ideas of the framework is that, when starting work on a new problem, one can first classify the assumptions this model would need, then investigate papers that have similar classification. Therefore, a number of classification examples are presented for both existing models and new problems. First, we answer the framework questions for the Kooiman pick-up case [21] in Table 2, and show how this can be written in our compressed notation. Afterwards, Table 3 shows compressed notation of some other problems described in papers, such that the interested reader can study more examples of our framework classification. Then, using Table 4, we examine some real-life cases and classify how we would choose to model these problems. To clarify: these problems do not yet have an explicitly described model, so this classification is based on how we would approach and model these practical problems, but other modellers may make other modelling decisions. Finally, the given examples will be used as input for discussion. In the Kooiman pick-up case [21], a barge makes a round trip along terminals in a fixed schedule to pick up containers to bring back to the main terminal; however, the arrival times of the containers at the terminals are stochastic. At each terminal, a decision has to be made of how many containers to load onto the barge, and a guess has to be made of how much capacity will be needed for later terminals, all while minimising the amount of late containers. The actual time of residing at the terminal is disregarded. We refer to Table 2 for the answering of the framework questions. We refer to Table 1 for a reminder of the framework element abbreviations.

R: unmentioned resource elements	D: unmentioned demand elements
RO: resource origin	DO: demand origin
RD: resource destination	DD: demand destination
RC: resource capacity	DV: demand volume
RDT: resource departure time	DRD: demand release date
RTT: resource travel time	DDD: demand due date
RP: resource price	DP: demand penalty
TH: terminal handling time	D2R: demand-to-resource allocation

Table 1. Abbreviations of the framework elements used in the compressed notation.

Other authorities	No
Information global/local	Global
Optimisation global/local	Global
Resource elements	Resource type: barges
	Controlled resource elements: none
	Resource features: fixed, except TH (irrelevant)
Demand elements	Demand type: freight containers
	Controlled demand elements: $D2R$
	Demand features: fixed, except DRD (stochastic)
Optimisation objective	Maximal percentage of containers that travel by
	barge instead of truck

Table 2. The framework applied on the Kooiman pick-up case [21].

Note that only barges are taken into consideration as resources, not trucks. It would have been possible to describe trucks as resources as well, but we have chosen to classify these as part of the lateness penalty, because there is no decision-making in how the trucks are used. Also, it may seem strange to speak of global or local information and optimisation when there are no other decision-making authorities. The information is considered global, because the only decision-making authority knows 'everything' that happens in the network; the optimisation is considered global, because the decision-maker wants to optimise the performance over all demand in the network put together, not over some individual piece or pieces of freight.

Using the six-field notation, most of Table 2 can be summarised as follows:

$$D2R|DRD| \cdot |TH|social|1$$

It could also be represented in the two-column notation, as follows:

Controlled elements	Demand-to-resource allocation
Fixed elements	R, D
Stochastic elements	Demand release date
Irrelevant elements	Terminal handling time
System characteristics	social
Behaviour of other authorities	1

Here, the row for dynamic elements can be left out because the problem has no dynamic elements, and R and D are written in the row for fixed elements to indicate that any unmentioned resource element and any unmentioned demand element is fixed by default.

Only the optimisation objective and type specifications are lost in this process. In Table 3, we apply the framework to more problems from academic papers. In this table, we include the optimisation objective to illustrate the wide range of optimisation possibilities. It is not actually necessary to describe the optimisation objective when using the compressed problem notation. In some cases, especially practical problem descriptions, optimisation objectives may not yet be explicitly known. Therefore, Table 4 leaves them out. In that table we review some practical problem descriptions and apply the framework to them.

Behdani [8]: $D2R, RDT \mid \cdot \mid \cdot \mid \cdot \mid social \mid 1$ Objective: minimal transportation costs and waiting penalties
Kooiman [21]: $D2R \mid DRD \mid \cdot \mid TH \mid social \mid 1$ Objective: maximal percentage of containers by barge instead of truck
Le Li [24]: $D2R \mid \cdot \mid DV \mid RDT, DRD, DDD \mid cooperative \mid equilibrium$ Objective: with self-optimising subnetworks, total minimal cost in union
Lin [26]: $D2R \mid \cdot \mid RC \mid RP \mid social \mid 1$ Objective: minimal total quality loss of perishable goods
Mes [27]: $D2R \mid \cdot \mid RP \mid RC \mid social \mid 1$ Objective: best modality paths against different balances of objectives
Nabais [30]: $D2R \mid \cdot \mid RC, RTT, RP, DV, DP \mid TH \mid social \mid 1$ Objective: sustainable transport modality split that retains client satisfaction
van Riessen [37]: $D2R, RDT \mid \cdot \mid RC, RTT, RP, TH, DP \mid \cdot \mid social \mid 1$ Objective: minimise transport and transfer cost, penalty for late delivery and cost of use of owned transportation
Rivera [31]: $D2R \mid D \mid R \mid \cdot \mid social \mid 1$ Objective: minimal expected transportation costs
Theys [41]: $RP, D2R, DP \mid \cdot \mid \cdot \mid RDT, DRD, DDD \mid selfish \mid equilibrium$ Objective: fairest allocation of individual costs
Xu [50]: $D2R, RC \mid RP, DV, DP \mid \cdot \mid RDT, RTT, TH, DRD, DDD \mid social \mid 1$ Objective: maximised expected profit during tactical planning
Zhang [51]: $D2R \mid D \mid \cdot \mid \cdot \mid social \mid 1$ Objective: maximised balance of governmental goals

Table 3. Selected papers in the synchromodal framework.

Lean and Green Synchromodal [1]: $D2R \mid \cdot \mid \cdot \mid \cdot \mid selfish \mid 1$
Rotterdam – Moerdijk – Tilburg [3]: $D2R \mid RTT, TH \mid \cdot \mid \cdot \mid social \mid 1$
Synchromodaily [4]: $D2R, RDT \mid D \mid \cdot \mid \cdot \mid social \mid 1$
Synchromodal Control Tower [5]: $D2R, RC, DV \mid RP, RTT, TH \mid \cdot \mid \cdot \mid social \mid 1$
Synchromodale Cool Port control [6]: $D2R, RDT \mid RTT \mid DDD, DP \mid \cdot \mid social \mid 1$

Table 4. Selected use cases in the synchromodal framework.

Another example we reviewed is the modelling of an agent-centric synchromodal network. Here all agents want to be at their destination as fast as possible, but everyone does share the information about where they are and where they are going with everybody else in the network. Table 5 shows the answer on the questions of the framework. In the short notation this problem is:

$$D2R|D| \cdot |DP|selfish|equilibrium$$

Other authorities	Yes
Information global/local	Global
Optimisation global/local	Local
Resource elements	Resource type: barges, trains and trucks
	Controlled resource elements: none
	Resource features: fixed
Demand elements	Demand type: containers
	Controlled demand elements: $D2R$
	Demand features: stochastic, except DP (irrelevant)
Optimisation objective	Minimise travel times

Table 5. The framework for an agent-centric synchromodal network.

6   Solution method mapping

In the previous section, a number of papers on synchromodal transport problems and solution methods were studied. Some of the choices in solution methods are similar between papers and can be partially recognised from their framework notation. Here, we group the papers on solution method with remarks on complexity issues and insightful framework similarities:

- *Shortest path algorithms*: In [27], $D2R$ is to be performed under the absence of capacity constraints. Mes et al. rightfully note that, in the absence of capacity constraints, the best modality paths can be found simply by using shortest path algorithms, which are known to run in polynomial time in the input size. Whenever capacity is included, this brings computational difficulties, as dividing flow over capacitated arcs is related to the NP-hard multi-knapsack problem. In [51], this is handled by a sequential shortest path algorithm: whenever a demand item comes in, assign it to the cheapest path with remaining capacity and repeat this until everything is assigned. Though this, too, is an efficient method, one can imagine it yielding sub-optimal results, especially under the stochastic release dates. However, if $D2R$ is the only control element, a sequential shortest path algorithm is a recognised as a computationally efficient option: in the absence of capacity constraints, stochastic elements and control-based dynamic elements, it is likely to yield the optimal solution.
- *Two-stage stochastic programming*: In [50], $D2R$ must again be performed. RC is technically a control element as well, but the challenge lies mainly in the $D2R$ control. Now, the stochasticity is dealt with by means of two-stage stochastic programming. The studied model may lend itself well to stochastic programming because no intermediary nodes are recognised between the one origin and the set of destinations. Even so, Xu et al. propose a meta-heuristic to deal with the computational intensity incurred by large sets of freight types, destinations, transportation modes or scenarios.

- *Approximate dynamic programming*: In [21] and [31], Markov Decision Process models are presented but argued to be too computationally expensive. Instead, they solve $D2R$ with stochastic elements by making tentative decisions, simulating the potential results of this decision and their incurred costs, then taking the tentative decision with the lowest simulated expected cost. This is recognised as a computationally reasonable alternative to solving $D2R$ with stochastic elements.
- *Systems and control theory*: In [24], a cooperative $D2R$ equilibrium problem is studied rather than a social problem without other authorities. In [26] and [30], $D2R$ is performed while dynamic elements play an important role. Finding a good equilibrium with the other authorities, or settling on a good equilibrium between the control elements and the dynamic parameters that depend on control, is understandably modelled using systems and control theory. In two out of these three papers, Model Predictive Control is employed. However, the similarities between these three papers could also be explained by their shared authors.
- *Multi-control integer linear programming*: In both [8] and [37], not only $D2R$ is controlled, but RDT as well, as a form of partial resource schedule control. Both papers resort to using integer linear programs to find an optimal solution. As many of the variables in these programs are indexed on three sets, these methods are expected to scale poorly to larger instances. Efficient solution methods to problems where not only $D2R$ is controlled but the resource schedules as well, appears to be an open problem: though the Vehicle Routing Problem (VRP) comes to mind, Section 7 will address the challenges that synchromodality introduce to the VRP.
- *Game theory*: In [41], fair pricing must be determined in a system with selfish decision-makers. Understandably, steering this selfish behaviour is attempted by using game theory. Theys et al. note that the proposed techniques work for limited systems, but that moderately advanced synchromodal systems require advanced game-theoretical techniques.

One could put this the other way round and wonder, given a problem classification, what solution methods could be suitable and what complexity issues arise. To this, we give the following answer. Selfish problems have been investigated with game theory, but only moderately advanced synchromodal systems already seem to require advanced game theory. Cooperative problems have been studied using Model Predictive Control, for which commercial solvers exist. Social $D2R$ problems could be solved using sequential shortest path algorithms. These are efficient methods, but only optimal under the absence of capacity constraints, stochasticity and control-based dynamic elements. Under the presence of capacity constraints, $D2R$ problems are likely to be NP-hard due to their similarity to the multi-knapsack problem. To solve $D2R$ with stochastic elements, two-stage stochastic programming and Markov Decision Processes have been examined, but proposed to be computationally too expensive. Approximate Dynamic Programming and Xu's meta-heuristic are proposed as efficient alternatives. To solve $D2R$ with dynamic elements, Model Predictive Control and other systems and control theory techniques are proposed. To solve social $D2R$ and RDT simultaneously, only large-scale integer linear programs have been proposed in the examined literature.

This is far from a complete mapping from framework classification to solution method. Components that are not described by the framework may be critical to the viability of a solution method, like the absence of intermediary locations in [50] facilitating two-stage stochastic programming. However, we believe that worthwhile relationships have been and can be drawn between framework classifications and potential solution methods.

7   Relationship to VRP terminology

When optimising the transport of freight using several vehicles, thus simultaneously determining $D2R$ and resource schedules, the Vehicle Routing Problem (VRP) immediately comes to mind. The VRP is a widely studied transport problem. In a sense, a framework for the classification of different VRP variants exists in the form of consensus: the Capacitated Vehicle Routing Problem (CVRP), the Vehicle Routing Problem with Pickup and Delivery (VRPPD), the Vehicle Routing Problem with Time Windows (VRPTW), subvariants and combinations of these variants are well-known and their definitions largely agreed upon [22, 25]. However, none of the papers investigated in Section 5 seem to involve themselves explicitly with VRP models. This can be explained and recognised by applying the developed framework on VRP variants.

The VRP, in its most classical sense, is the problem of minimising transport costs when dispatching m vehicles from some depot node to service all other nodes exactly once. A synchromodal version of this is quite imaginable. The real-time flexibility aspect of synchromodality would mean that re-evaluations may occur where the vehicles 'start' at their current destination, but must still return to the depot, and the already visited nodes are taken out of the problem. The information sharing aspect of synchromodality can be assumed to already be part of the problem: the resources and demands can be assumed to be pooled from several parties and put under the control of a central operator. Under these minor assumptions, the synchromodal VRP lends itself to the following classification:

$$D2R, RD| \cdot | \cdot |RC, RDT, RTT, TH, DV, DRD, DDD, DP|social|1$$

The decision-maker must simultaneously decide which service nodes are visited by which vehicle and in which order. Time and capacity constraints are not present and all related elements are irrelevant. Only the total 'price' of these routes is minimised: though this price may equal the travel time, the actual element of time does not influence the decision space, as long as release time, due times and time windows are absent. When adding vehicle capacities, the

RC and DV become fixed rather than irrelevant, so the synchromodal CVRP is denoted by

$$D2R, RD| \cdot | \cdot |RDT, RTT, TH, DRD, DDD, DP|social|1$$

When time windows are added, the RDT becomes a control element and the RTT, DRD, DDD, DP and sometimes the TH becomes relevant. Note that soft and hard time windows are not necessarily classified differently: the demand penalty could be an arbitrarily high constant to simulate hard deadlines, but soft due dates may also come with fixed penalties that are not arbitrarily high. As such, the synchromodal Capacitated Vehicle Routing Problem with Time Windows (CVRPTW) could be classified as, depending on whether or not terminal handling times are observed,

$$D2R, RD, RDT| \cdot | \cdot |TH|social|1 \quad \text{or} \quad D2R, RD, RDT| \cdot | \cdot | \cdot |social|1$$

If separate pickup and delivery locations are specified, this would still mean that each demand item has a fixed DO and DD, so the Capacitated Vehicle Routing Problem with Time Windows and Pickup and Delivery (CVRPTWPD) would be classified the same way as the CVRPTW.

One of the most important differences between synchromodal VRP variants and the problems examined in Section 5 are laid bare by the framework notation: all synchromodal VRP variants have the resource destination as a control element, while none of the studied papers do. In fact, having the RD as a control element is largely synonymous with having the responsibility of routing.

While this definitely helps in recognising the absence of vehicle routing in the studied papers, it does not yet explain it. The following explanations for the absence of vehicle routing in the studied papers are proposed:

- Papers with more control elements than just $D2R$ tend to resort to using large ILP's, making inclusion of the RD as a control element computationally challenging;
- In many of the papers, the routes were already predetermined in a strategical/tactical phase, and only the day-by-day assignment remained as a problem on the operational level, possibly due to this computational intensity and the real-world implications of planning vehicles routes;
- Most Multiple Travelling Salesman Problem (mTSP)-based models, including most VRP variants, do not lend themselves to the concept of intermodality, thus synchromodality: while intermodal transport encourages that different vehicles take care of different parts of a container's journey, most mTSP-based models encourage that the entire voyage of one container is taken care of by one vehicle only [9].

We conclude that the class of synchromodal transport problems differs significantly from the classical VRP variants: as such, they require a classification scheme of their own.

8 Discussion

The examples in Section 5 show some strengths and limitations of the classification framework, which are discussed in this section.

One of the goals of this framework was to offer guidance when tackling a new problem: as an example, if the problem from the Synchromodaily [4] case is modelled in a non-stochastic way, we can now see that it may be worthwhile to study the solution method presented by Behdani [8], because they then have a very similar compressed framework classification: in particular, the Synchromodaily case involves the same control elements. If such a record is kept of papers and models, this could greatly improve the efficiency of developments in synchromodal transport. This would fulfil the second goal of the framework: to collect literature on synchromodal transportation within a meaningful order.

The final goal of this framework was to expose and compare relationships between seemingly different problems: for example, we can now see that the problems described by Le Li [24] and Theys [41] have similarities, in that they investigate negotiation between parties and do not focus on timeliness of deliveries. Similarly, we can see that the model assumption Mes [27] makes in disregarding resource capacity, is an uncommon decision. In Section 6, it was argued that such similarities and dissimilarities can help explain the effectiveness of certain solution methods.

In the Synchromodaily case [4], our interpretation of the problem implies that the demand features are stochastic. However, the problem could also be approached in a deterministic way, depending on choices that the modeller and contractor make based on the scope of the problem, the requirements on the solution and the available information. This shows the most important limitation of the classification framework: what classification to assign to a problem or model remains dependent on modelling choices, as well as interpretation of problem descriptions. Even without the framework, however, modelling choices will always introduce subjective elements into how a real-world problem is solved. This framework can be used to consistently communicate these underlying model assumptions.

A second limitation of the framework is that, because of the large amount of elements described in it, two similar problems are relatively unlikely to fall in the exact same space in the framework because of their minor differences. Therefore, one should not only look for problems with the exact same classification, but also problems with a classification that is only slightly different. In a more general sense, solution methods may apply to far more than one of these very specific framework classes. If two problems have the exact same controlled elements, it is imaginable that their models and solution methodologies may largely apply to the other. As a point of future research, it could be interesting to further investigate which classification similarities are likely to imply solution similarities, which may also be a stepping stone towards a general solution methodology.

As a final limitation, the compressed notation does not reveal that the paper by Lin [26] and the 'Synchromodale Cool Port control' [6] case both focus on perishable goods. This shared focus is not only cosmetic: mathematically, it may imply objective functions and constraints not focused on in other cases. To combat this limitation, we advise anyone using the framework to offer both a compressed and an extended description of their problem or model.

References

1. Lean and green synchromodal. www.synchromodaliteit.nl/case/lean-and-green-barge/, accessed: 2017-02-27
2. Ontwikkeling van een synchromodale planningstool. http://www.synchromodaliteit.nl/case/ontwikkeling-van-een-synchromodale-planningstool/, accessed: 2017-01-04
3. Rotterdam – Moerdijk – Tilburg; een pilot met synchromodaal vervoer. www.synchromodaliteit.nl/case/rotterdam-moerdijk-tilburg-een-pilot-met-synchromodaal-vervoer/, accessed: 2017-02-27
4. Synchromodaily. www.synchromodaliteit.nl/case/synchromodaily/, accessed: 2017-02-27
5. Synchromodal control tower. www.synchromodaliteit.nl/case/synchromodale-control-tower/, accessed: 2017-02-27
6. Synchromodale cool port control. www.synchromodaliteit.nl/case/synchromodale-cool-port-control/, accessed: 2017-02-27
7. Bandeira, D., Becker, J., Borenstein, D.: A DSS for integrated distribution of empty and full containers. Decision Support Systems 47(4), 383–397 (2009)
8. Behdani, B., Fan, Y., Wiegmans, B., Zuidwijk, R.: Multimodal schedule design for synchromodal freight transport systems. European Journal of Transport & Infrastructure Research 16(3), 424–444 (2016)
9. Bektas, T.: The multiple traveling salesman problem: an overview of formulations and solution procedures. Omega 34(3), 209–219 (2006)
10. Bock, S.: Real-time control of freight forwarder transportation networks by integrating multimodal transport chains. European Journal of Operational Research 200(3), 733–746 (2010)
11. Caris, A., Macharis, C., Janssens, G.: Corridor network design in hinterland transportation systems. Flexible Services and Manufacturing Journal 24(3), 294–319 (2012)
12. Chen, L., Miller-Hooks, E.: Resilience: an indicator of recovery capability in intermodal freight transport. Transportation Science 46(1), 109–123 (2012)
13. Crainic, T.: Service network design in freight transportation. European Journal of Operational Research 122(2), 272–288 (2000)
14. Crainic, T., Gendreau, M., Dejax, P.: Dynamic and stochastic models for the allocation of empty containers. Operations Research 41(1), 102–126 (1993)
15. Di Francesco, M., Lai, M., Zuddas, P.: Maritime repositioning of empty containers under uncertain port disruptions. Computers & Industrial Engineering 64(3), 827–837 (2013)

16. Erera, A., Morales, J., Savelsbergh, M.: Global intermodal tank container management for the chemical industry. Transportation Research Part E: Logistics and Transportation Review 41(6), 551–566 (2005)
17. Goel, A.: The value of in-transit visibility for supply chains with multiple modes of transport. International Journal of Logistics: Research and Applications 13(6), 475–492 (2010)
18. Graham, R., Lawler, E., Lenstra, J., Rinnooy Kan, A.: Optimization and approximation in deterministic sequencing and scheduling: a survey. Annals of Discrete Mathematics 5, 287–326 (1979)
19. Huang, M., Hu, X., Zhang, L.: A decision method for disruption management problems in intermodal freight transport. In: Intelligent Decision Technologies, pp. 13–21. Springer (2011)
20. Kendall, D.: Stochastic processes occurring in the theory of queues and their analysis by the method of the imbedded markov chain. The Annals of Mathematical Statistics pp. 338–354 (1953)
21. Kooiman, K., Phillipson, F., Sangers, A.: Planning inland container shipping: a stochastic assignment problem. 23rd International Conference on Analytical and Stochastic Modelling Techniques and Applications (2016)
22. Laporte, G.: The vehicle routing problem: An overview of exact and approximate algorithms. European Journal of Operational Research 59(3), 345–358 (1992)
23. Li, L.: Coordinated Model Predictive Control of Synchromodal Freight Transport Systems. Ph.D. thesis, Delft University of Technology TRAIL thesis series (2016)
24. Li, L., Negenborn, R.R., De Schutter, B.: Distributed model predictive control for cooperative synchromodal freight transport. Transport. Res. Part E (2016), http://www.sciencedirect.com/science/article/pii/S1366554515303069
25. Lin, C., Choy, K.L., Ho, G.T., Chung, S.H., Lam, H.: Survey of green vehicle routing problem: past and future trends. Expert Systems with Applications 41(4), 1118–1138 (2014)
26. Lin, X., Negenborn, R.R., Lodewijks, G.: Towards quality-aware control of perishable goods in synchromodal transport networks. IFAC-PapersOnLine 49(16), 132–137 (2016)
27. Mes, M., Iacob, M.: Synchromodal transport planning at a logistics service provider. In: Logistics and Supply Chain Innovation, pp. 23–36. Springer (2016)
28. Miller-Hooks, E., Zhang, X., Faturechi, R.: Measuring and maximizing resilience of freight transportation networks. Computers & Operations Research 39(7), 1633–1643 (2012)
29. Min, H.: International intermodal choices via chance-constrained goal programming. Transportation Research Part A: General 25(6), 351–362 (1991)
30. Nabais, J.L., Negenborn, R.R., Benitez, R.B.C., Botto, M.A.: A constrained MPC heuristic to achieve a desired transport modal split at intermodal hubs. In: Intelligent Transportation Systems-(ITSC), 2013 16th International IEEE Conference on. pp. 714–719. IEEE (2013)
31. Pérez Rivera, A., Mes, M.: Service and transfer selection for freights in a synchromodal network. Lecture Notes in Computer Science 9855, 227–242 (2016)
32. Pfoser, S., Treiblmaier, H., Schauer, O.: Critical success factors of synchromodality: Results from a case study and literature review. Transportation Research Procedia 14, 1463–1471 (2016)
33. Phillipson, F.: Creating timetables in case for disturbances in simulation of railroad traffic. In: Proceedings of the 45th International Conference on Computers & Industrial Engineering (CIE45). pp. 1–8 (2015)

34. Phillipson, F.: A thought on optimisation, complexity and self-organisation in synchromodal logistics. Tech. rep., TNO, The Netherlands (2017)
35. Pleszko, J.: Multi-variant configurations of supply chains in the context of synchromodal transport. LogForum 8(4) (2012)
36. Puettmann, C., Stadtler, H.: A collaborative planning approach for intermodal freight transportation. OR Spectrum 32(3), 809–830 (2010)
37. Riessen, B.V., Negenborn, R.R., Dekker, R., Lodewijks, G.: Service network design for an intermodal container network with flexible due dates/times and the possibility of using subcontracted transport. International Journal of Shipping and Transport Logistics 7(4), 457–478 (2015)
38. Song, D., Dong, J.: Cargo routing and empty container repositioning in multiple shipping service routes. Transportation Research Part B: Methodological 46(10), 1556–1575 (2012)
39. SteadieSeifi, M., Dellaert, N.P., Nuijten, W., Van Woensel, T., Raoufi, R.: Multimodal freight transportation planning: A literature review. European Journal of Operational Research 233(1), 1–15 (2014)
40. Tavasszy, L., Behdani, B., Konings, R.: Intermodality and synchromodality. SSRN.com (2015)
41. Theys, C., Dullaert, W., Notteboom, T.: Analyzing cooperative networks in intermodal transportation: a game-theoretic approach. In: Nectar Logistics and Freight Cluster Meeting, Delft, The Netherlands. pp. 1–37 (2008)
42. Topaloglu, H.: A parallelizable dynamic fleet management model with random travel times. European Journal of Operational Research 175(2), 782–805 (2006)
43. Topaloglu, H.: A parallelizable and approximate dynamic programming-based dynamic fleet management model with random travel times and multiple vehicle types. In: Dynamic Fleet Management, pp. 65–93. Springer (2007)
44. Topaloglu, H., Powell, W.: A distributed decision-making structure for dynamic resource allocation using nonlinear functional approximations. Operations Research 53(2), 281–297 (2005)
45. Topaloglu, H., Powell, W.: Dynamic-programming approximations for stochastic time-staged integer multicommodity-flow problems. INFORMS Journal on Computing 18(1), 31–42 (2006)
46. Topaloglu, H., Powell, W.: Sensitivity analysis of a dynamic fleet management model using approximate dynamic programming. Operations Research 55(2), 319–331 (2007)
47. Van Binsbergen, A., Konings, R., Tavasszy, L., Van Duin, J.: Innovations in intermodal freight transport: lessons from europe. In: Papers of the 93th annual meeting of the Transportation Research Board, Washington (USA), Jan 12-16, 2014; revised paper. TRB (2014)
48. Van Riessen, B., Negenborn, R.R., Dekker, R.: Synchromodal container transportation: An overview of current topics and research opportunities. Computational Logistics 9335, 386–397 (2015)
49. Vinke, P.: Dynamic consolidation decisions in a synchromodal environment: Improving the synchromodal control tower. Master's thesis, University of Twente (2016)
50. Xu, Y., Cao, C., Jia, B., Zang, G.: Model and algorithm for container allocation problem with random freight demands in synchromodal transportation. Mathematical Problems in Engineering 2015 (2015)
51. Zhang, M., Pel, A.: Synchromodal hinterland freight transport: model study for the port of Rotterdam. Journal of Transport Geography 52, 1–10 (2016)

Scheduling Drayage Operations in Synchromodal Transport

Arturo E. Pérez Rivera and Martijn R.K. Mes

Department of Industrial Engineering and Business Information Systems
University of Twente, P.O. Box 217, 7500 AE Enschede, The Netherlands
{a.e.perezrivera,m.r.k.mes}@utwente.nl

Abstract. We study the problem of scheduling drayage operations in synchromodal transport. Besides the usual decisions to time the pick-up and delivery of containers, and to route the vehicles that transport them, synchromodal transport includes the assignment of terminals for empty and loaded containers. The challenge consists of simultaneously deciding on these three aspects while considering various resource and timing restrictions. We model the problem using mixed-integer linear programming (MILP) and design a matheuristic to solve it. Our algorithm iteratively confines the solution space of the MILP using several adaptations, and based on the incumbent solutions, guides the subsequent iterations and solutions. We test our algorithm under different problem configurations and provide insights into their relation to the three aspects of scheduling drayage operations in synchromodal transport.

Keywords: Drayage operations, synchromodal transport, matheuristic

1 Introduction

During the last years, intermodal transport has received increased attention from academic, industrial, and governmental stakeholders due to potential reductions in cost and environmental impact [10]. To achieve such benefits, these stakeholders have proposed new forms of organizing intermodal transport. One of these new initiatives is synchromodality, which aims to improve the efficiency and sustainability of intermodal transport through flexibility in the choice of mode and in the design of transport plans [12]. However, the potential benefits of any new form of intermodal transport depend to a great extent on the proper planning of drayage operations, also known as pre- and end-haulage or first and last-mile trucking. Drayage operations, which account for 40% of the total transport costs in an intermodal transport chain [5], are the first step where the synchromodal flexibility in transport mode can be taken advantage of. In this paper, we study the scheduling of drayage operations of intermodal transport considering terminal assignment (i.e., long-haul mode) decisions.

Drayage operations in intermodal transport include delivery and pick-up requests of either empty or loaded containers, to and from a terminal where long-haul modes arrive and depart. These operations occur, for example, at a Logistic

© Springer International Publishing AG 2017
T. Bektaş et al. (Eds.), ICCL 2017, LNCS 10572, pp. 404–419, 2017.
https://doi.org/10.1007/978-3-319-68496-3_27

Service Provider (LSP) handling both import and export containers. The planner scheduling drayage operations must decide upon the time to fulfill each request and the route of the vehicles that will carry out all requests. In synchromodality, the planner must also decide to which terminal to bring a loaded container and to which terminal or customer to bring an empty container. All these decisions must be made simultaneously, considering constraints such as time-windows for requests, terminals, containers, trucks, and decoupling of requests for the delivery of an empty container and the subsequent pickup of a loaded one (and vice versa). Furthermore, re-scheduling the requests is allowed as new information becomes known (e.g., real-time information about requests, delays, etc.). In such a dynamic environment, making assignment, timing, and routing decisions together is difficult [5, 15]. Nonetheless, scheduling drayage operations with an integrated approach can bring significant savings [1].

In this paper, we develop an integrated approach to make assignment, timing, and routing decisions of drayage operations dynamically. First, we categorize the drayage requests in synchromodality and analyze their relations. With our categorization, we identify challenges and opportunities for scheduling methods. Second, we formulate the problem as a Mixed-Integer Linear Programming (MILP) model based on our categorization of requests. Third, we present several adaptations to the MILP model and design a heuristic algorithm around them to schedule drayage operations and update the schedule as new requests arrive.

2   Literature Review

We briefly review the literature about scheduling drayage operations in intermodal transport. We examine the characteristics of the proposed models and study their applicability to our problem. We finalize by stating our contribution.

Most studies about scheduling drayage operations use mathematical programming. This technique allows researchers to model various problem characteristics at the price of high computational complexity. For this reason, researchers consider one problem characteristic at a time. For example, studies that consider more than one terminal, such as [11] and [1], assume a homogenous fleet. Studies that consider a flexible origin or destination for some requests, such as [2] and [6], consider only one terminal. Studies that do not assume a homogenous fleet, such as [8], avoid other constraints such as request time-windows. All in all, mathematical programming can relate various problem attributes to optimal decisions but requires further developments to handle the actual scheduling.

There is a variety of approaches available to solve the actual scheduling of drayage operations. There are sequential approaches, such as [2] and [11], that pair delivery and pickup customers before the routing. There are also integrated approaches, such as [1,6,13,16], which handle paring (i.e, scheduling) and routing decisions simultaneously. Particularly, these integrated approaches show that a combination of parts of the mathematical problems with other heuristics perform well in solving the problem. Finally, the majority of approaches focuses on "one plan" per day with no re-planning, except for [5], which re-schedules when the problem conditions change, and for [7], which re-schedules when new orders arrive, or when real-time information regarding traffic or position of trucks gives rise to this. Naturally, dynamic re-scheduling is another attribute of drayage operations that increases the complexity of the problem.

Although drayage operations contribute significantly to the total costs of intermodal transport [9], research on these operations has been limited in modeling considerations and solution approaches [3]. The need for dynamic scheduling methods for intermodal routing that take into account multiple attributes of the problem has been recognized [3]. For these reasons, our contribution to the literature is two-fold: (i) we model many attributes of the scheduling of drayage operations in synchromodal transport as an integrated MILP with various adaptations, and (ii) we develop a dynamic matheuristic to solve the model.

3   Problem Description

We study the problem of scheduling drayage requests in a synchromodal network with the objective of minimizing routing and terminal (i.e., long-haul mode) assignment costs. There are three simultaneous decisions: (i) timing the execution of requests, (ii) routing the vehicles that carry out the requests, and (iii) assigning long-haul terminals (or customers) to the requests. These decisions are subject to the characteristics of the requests, available trucks, available containers, and terminals. Requests are characterized by customer location, type of truck (e.g., driver clearance, chasis, trailer, etc.), type of container (e.g., size, security, refrigeration, etc.), time-window, service (i.e., loading, unloading) time, and decoupling allowance. Trucks are characterized by start and end location, type, maximum working time, setup cost, and variable cost. Containers are characterized by location, type, and amount. Terminals are characterized by location, time-window, and an assignment cost that represents costs for using a certain long-haul mode, container storage, etc.

The terminal assignment cost and the various request attributes in synchromodality enrich the common drayage operations in intermodal transport. To analyze this enrichment, we classify the requests into pre-haulage and end-haulage. In a pre-haulage request, an empty container is brought to a customer location and subsequently (after loading) brought to one of the long-haul terminals. In an end-haulage request, a loaded container is brought to a customer location and subsequently (after unloading) brought to a terminal for storage or to another customer who has a container-compatible pre-haulage request. Some of these requests allow *decoupling*, which means that a truck delivering an empty (or loaded) container does not need to wait for it to be loaded (or unloaded) and that another truck can pick up the loaded (empty) container later on. We refer to all possible pre- and end-haulage requests as *jobs* in the remainder of the paper. We now elaborate on the job configurations.

In drayage operations, there are various job configurations as seen in Fig. 1. These configurations arise due to different contractual agreements, types of freight, types of resources, etc. In the complete job configurations of the end-

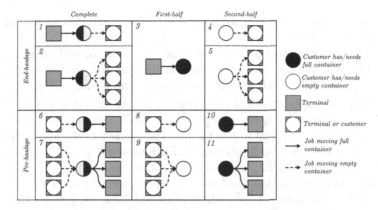

Fig. 1. Possible job configurations in synchromodal transport

haulage, the origin is a fixed terminal, but the destination can be either a given terminal (or customer) or one of multiple terminals (or customers), as seen in Types 1 and 2, respectively. If decoupling is allowed, one can divide the end-haulage job configurations into first- and second-half, as seen in Types 3, 4, and 5. In the complete job configurations of the pre-haulage, the origin can be a given terminal (or customer) and the destination a given terminal, or the origin can be one of multiple terminals (or customers) and the destination one of multiple terminals, as seen in Types 6 and 7, respectively. Once more, if decoupling is allowed, the pre-haulage configurations can be divided into first- and second-half, as seen in Types 8, 9, 10, and 11. Due to the full-truckload and multi-resource nature of the job configurations, some challenges and opportunities arise. For example, executing some job configurations after each other (e.g., Type 3 followed by Type 10) will require an *empty movement* of a truck, i.e., truck moving without a container. In another example, executing some job configurations after each other (e.g., Type 1 followed by Type 6) can allow the truck to skip the visit to a terminal (e.g., supersede the use of an empty container at a terminal). In such opportunities, some job configurations can be merged to reduce the decision complexity as also proposed by [8]. Using this job categorization, we formulate an MILP model that captures the challenges and opportunities in drayage operations in the following section. In the remainder of this paper, when we talk about job *types*, we refer to the configurations seen in Fig. 1.

4   MILP formulation

Using the previous categorization of jobs, we construct two directed graphs $\mathcal{G} = (\mathcal{V}, \mathcal{A})$ and $\mathcal{G}' = (\mathcal{V}, \mathcal{A}')$, which have the same nodes $\mathcal{V}$ but different arcs $\mathcal{A}$ and $\mathcal{A}'$. Nodes $\mathcal{V}$ represent all locations related to jobs and trucks: $\mathcal{V} = \mathcal{V}^{\mathrm{R}} \cup \mathcal{V}^{\mathrm{D}} \cup \mathcal{V}^{\mathrm{B}} \cup \mathcal{V}^{\mathrm{F}}$. Specifically, $\mathcal{V}^{\mathrm{R}}$ contains all job locations (i.e., request locations), $\mathcal{V}^{\mathrm{D}}$ all terminal locations, $\mathcal{V}^{\mathrm{B}}$ all beginning location of trucks and $\mathcal{V}^{\mathrm{F}}$ their finishing location. All nodes in $\mathcal{V}$ are indexed with i and j. Arcs A and $\mathcal{A}'$ are built to distinguish the assignment and the routing decisions, respectively. Arcs in A include all *job-arcs* between two nodes (connections as in Fig. 1). Job-arcs are connections between nodes that comply with all resource and long-haul mode constraints. We define $\delta^-(r) = \{j : (j, r) \in \mathcal{A}\}$ and $\delta^+(r) = \{j : (r, j) \in \mathcal{A}\}$ as the sets of nodes that form job-arcs that are incoming to, and outgoing from, node $r \in \mathcal{V}^R$, respectively. Arcs in $\mathcal{A}'$ include all *routing-arcs*. These arcs follow a similar logic as in the VRP with time-windows formulation of [4].

In $\mathcal{V}^R$, each job is represented as a single node. We index nodes in $\mathcal{V}^R$ with r. In $\mathcal{V}^D$, each terminal $d \in \mathcal{U}^D$ is represented as N_d identical nodes, in order to keep track of arrival times in the model. The set $\mathcal{U}^D$ is the set with unique terminal nodes. We index both sets with d. Each node $i \in \mathcal{V}^R \cup \mathcal{V}^D$ has a service time S_i (i.e., time for loading, unloading, coupling, or decoupling a container), as well as a time-window described by an earliest arrival time E_i and a latest arrival time L_i. For nodes $r \in \mathcal{V}^R$, which represent jobs, D_r gets a value of one if decoupling is allowed and zero otherwise. Traveling time between nodes i and j is denoted with $T_{i,j}$. Note that, for the identical nodes of each terminal, all time parameters are the same and traveling times between them are zero. Note also that two jobs can be at the same location, and thus traveling time between them is also zero. However, service times and time-windows can be different, depending on the job type.

To carry out all jobs, there is a fleet of heterogeneous trucks $\mathcal{K}$. The trucks that can carry out job $r \in \mathcal{V}^R$ are represented with $\widetilde{K}(r) \subseteq \mathcal{K}$. Each truck begins its route in node $B_k \in \mathcal{V}^B$ and finishes its route in node $F_k \in \mathcal{V}^F$. All trucks have a maximum working time T_k^K. Truck movements are modeled using the binary variable $x_{i,j,k}$, which gets a value of 1 if node j is visited immediately after node i by truck k, and 0 otherwise. Note that truck movements can either be to carry out a request (i.e., truck has an empty or loaded container) or to reposition the truck (i.e., no container). To model time in the movements of trucks, we use the auxiliary variable w_i, which represents the time at which the chosen truck arrives at node i. Note that w_i does not depend on k since each job can be done by only one truck and we duplicate the terminal nodes such that each node is again visited by only one truck.

The goal is to perform all jobs, within their time-window, while minimizing routing and terminal assignment costs. To model the routing costs, we introduce (i) a fixed cost C_k^F for using truck $k \in K$ and (ii) a variable cost $C_{i,j,k}^V$ for its movement over arc $(i, j) \in \mathcal{A}'$. To model the terminal assignment costs, we introduce a cost $C_{r,d}^D$ for assigning terminal $d \in \mathcal{V}^D$ to job $r \in \mathcal{V}^C$. Using the parameters and variables above, the optimization goal can be achieved solving the mathematical program shown in (1).

$$\min z = \sum_{k \in \mathcal{K}} \left(C_k^F \cdot \sum_{j \in \delta'^+(B_k)} x_{B_k,j,k} \right) + \sum_{k \in \mathcal{K}} \sum_{(i,j) \in \mathcal{A}'} C_{i,j,k}^V \cdot x_{i,j,k} \tag{1a}$$

$$+ \sum_{k \in \mathcal{K}} \sum_{r \in \mathcal{V}^R} \sum_{d \in \delta^+(r) \cup \mathcal{V}^D} C_{i,j}^D \cdot x_{r,d,k}$$

s.t.

$$\sum_{k \in \widetilde{K}(r)} \sum_{j \in \delta^+(r)} x_{r,j,k} = 1, \ \forall \, r \in \mathcal{V}^R \, | \delta^+(r) \neq \emptyset \tag{1b}$$

$$\sum_{k \in \widetilde{\mathcal{K}}(r)} \sum_{j \in \delta^-(r)} x_{j,r,k} = 1, \ \forall\, r \in \mathcal{V}^{\mathrm{R}} \,|\, \delta^-(r) \neq \emptyset \tag{1c}$$

$$(1 - D_r) \left(\sum_{j \in \delta^+(r)} x_{r,j,k} - \sum_{j \in \delta^-(r)} x_{j,r,k} \right) = 0,$$
$$\forall\, r \in \mathcal{V}^{\mathrm{R}} \,\big|\, \delta^+(r) \neq \emptyset \text{ and } \delta^-(r) \neq \emptyset, k \in \widetilde{K}(r) \tag{1d}$$

$$\sum_{k \in \mathcal{K}} \sum_{j \in \delta'^+(r)} x_{r,j,k} = 1, \ \forall\, r \in \mathcal{V}^{\mathrm{R}} \tag{1e}$$

$$\sum_{k \in \mathcal{K}} \sum_{j \in \delta'^+(d)} x_{d,j,k} \leq 1, \ \forall\, d \in \mathcal{V}^{\mathrm{D}} \tag{1f}$$

$$\sum_{j \in \delta'^+(i)} x_{i,j,k} - \sum_{j \in \delta'^-(i)} x_{j,i,k} = 0, \ \forall\, i \in \mathcal{V}^{\mathrm{C}} \cup \mathcal{V}^{\mathrm{D}}, k \in \mathcal{K} \tag{1g}$$

$$E_i \leq w_i \leq L_i, \ \forall\, i \in \mathcal{V} \tag{1h}$$

$$\sum_{k \in \mathcal{K}} (x_{i,j,k} \cdot (w_i + S_i + T_{i,j} - w_j)) \leq 0, \ \forall\, i,j \in \mathcal{V} \tag{1i}$$

$$\sum_{k \in \mathcal{K}} (x_{B_k,j,k} \cdot T_{B_k,j}) \leq w_j, \ \forall\, j \in \mathcal{V} \tag{1j}$$

$$x_{i,F_k,k} \cdot \left(w_i + S_i + T_{i,F_k} - T_k^{\mathrm{K}} \right) \leq 0, \ \forall\, i \in \delta'^-(F_k), k \in \mathcal{K} \tag{1k}$$

$$\sum_{(i,j) \in \mathcal{A}'} x_{i,j,k} - M_k^{\mathrm{A}} \cdot \sum_{j \in \delta'^+(B_k)} x_{B_k,j,k} \leq 0, \ \forall\, k \in \mathcal{K} \tag{1l}$$

$$\sum_{j \in \delta'^+(B_k)} x_{B_k,j,k} \leq M_k^{\mathrm{K}}, \ \forall\, k \in \mathcal{K} \tag{1m}$$

$$\sum_{i \in \delta'^-(F_k)} x_{i,F_k,k} - \sum_{j \in \delta'^+(B_k)} x_{B_k,j,k} = 0, \ \forall\, k \in \mathcal{K} \tag{1n}$$

$$x_{i,j,k} = 0, \ \forall\, i \in \mathcal{V}^{\mathrm{B}} \setminus \{B_k\}, j \in \mathcal{V}^{\mathrm{R}} \cup \mathcal{V}^{\mathrm{D}}, k \in \mathcal{K} \tag{1o}$$

$$x_{i,j,k} = 0, \ \forall\, i \in \mathcal{V}^{\mathrm{R}} \cup \mathcal{V}^{\mathrm{D}}, j \in \mathcal{V}^{\mathrm{F}} \setminus \{F_k\}, k \in \mathcal{K} \tag{1p}$$

$$w_i \in \mathbb{R}, \ \forall\, i \in \mathcal{V} \tag{1q}$$

$$x_{i,j,k} \in \{0,1\}, \ \forall\, i,j \in \mathcal{V}, k \in \mathcal{K} \tag{1r}$$

The objective is to minimize the total costs z as shown in (1a). Constraints (1b) state that only one incoming job-arc can be used for job r. Note that it is possible that job r does not require incoming job-arcs (e.g., Type 10), and thus $\delta^+(r) = \emptyset$. Similarly, (1c) ensure that only one outgoing job-arc can be used for job r. For jobs that have both incoming and outgoing job-arcs (i.e., Types 1, 2, 6, and 7), (1d) ensure that the same vehicle does both the incoming and outgoing job-arc if decoupling is not allowed for job r. Constraints (1e) ensure that all jobs $r \in \mathcal{V}^{\mathrm{R}}$ are carried out by one truck only. Constraints (1f) ensure that all terminal nodes $d \in \mathcal{V}^{\mathrm{D}}$ are visited at most once. Remind that a terminal has duplicate nodes for keeping track of time, meaning that the same terminal might be visited multiple times (e.g., for different jobs) but each time to a different duplicated node. Constraints (1g) ensure flow conservation, meaning that all nodes that are exited must be entered as well. The time-windows of jobs, terminals, and truck locations are enforced in (1h). Constraints (1i) and (1j) keep track of the time variables. The maximum working time of trucks is guaranteed by (1k). Constraints (1l) and (1m) establish that each truck can only depart once from its starting location if it is used for doing jobs. In (1l), M_k^A works as a "big-M" parameter that can be initialized, for example, with $M_k^A = |\mathcal{V}^R| + |\mathcal{V}^D| + 1$. However, it can also be used to *restrict* the number of routing-arcs that vehicle k can traverse, as we will explain in Section 5. In a similar way, the auxiliary parameter M_k^K can be used to restrict the use of vehicle k by setting $M_k^K = 0$. Initially, we set $M_k^K = 1, \forall k \in K$. Constraints (1n) state that each truck must end at its ending location if it has departed from its beginning location. Since the nodes $\mathcal{V}^B$ and $\mathcal{V}^F$ are used for modeling beginning and ending locations of trucks (i.e., not for carrying out jobs), we have to ensure that trucks do not visit them in any case, as shown in (1o) and (1p). Finally, Constraints (1q) and (1r) establish the domains of the variables.

Although the formulation above is not linear due to (1i) and (1k), we can linearize it by substituting these two with (2a) and (2b). An explanation on the logic behind these constraints can be found in [2].

$$w_i + S_i + T_{i,j}^T - (L_i + S_i + T_{i,j} - E_j) \cdot \left(1 - \sum_{k \in \mathcal{K}} x_{i,j,k}\right) \leq w_j \; \forall \, i, j \in \mathcal{V} \qquad (2a)$$

$$w_i + S_i + T_{i,F_k} - (L_i + S_i + T_{i,F_k}) \cdot (1 - x_{i,F_k,k}) \leq L_{F_k}, \; \forall \, i \in \delta^{'-}(F_k), k \in \mathcal{K} \quad (2b)$$

Our MILP formulation models the jobs as arcs that need to be traversed by the trucks. Another option to represent jobs in drayage operations is to model them as nodes. Modeling jobs as nodes reduces the size of the graph if some of the nodes are fixed beforehand [1]. However, flexible jobs (such as ours with the terminal assignment) cannot be collapsed into a single-node [13] and the gains of an integrated approach are harder to obtain when modeling jobs as nodes [1]. Although modeling jobs as arcs come with the price of a larger graph, there are other opportunities to improve the formulation through valid inequalities and pre-processing, as we describe in the following section.

4.1   Valid Inequalities and Pre-Processing

Due to the full-truckload nature of our problem, all jobs deal with at most one terminal either as the origin or the destination of a container. This means that a truck carrying out jobs will never visit more than two terminals consecutively. Since we model the requests and terminals as separate nodes, this means that not all arcs between terminal nodes will be traversed. An arc between two terminal nodes will only be traversed when delivering a container to the first one, and picking up a container from the second one. Thus, we can use a bound M^{DE} on them as shown in (3).

$$\sum_{k \in \mathcal{K}} \sum_{i \in \mathcal{V}^D} \sum_{j \in \mathcal{V}^D} x_{i,j,k} \leq M^{DE} \qquad (3a)$$

$$M^{DE} = \sum_{r \in \mathcal{V}^R} \sum_{d \in \mathcal{U}^D} B_{r,d} \left| B_{r,d} = \begin{cases} 1 & \text{if } d \in \delta^-(r) \\ 0 & \text{otherwise} \end{cases} \right. \qquad (3b)$$

In addition to the bound on the number of arcs between all terminal nodes $\mathcal{V}^D$, we can bound the traversed arcs between replicated nodes of a terminal using a similar logic. We define the set $\mathcal{V}_d^{DR} \subseteq \mathcal{V}^D$ as the set containing all duplicated nodes of terminal $d \in \mathcal{U}^D$. We put a bound M_d^{DI} for each unique terminal node $d \in \mathcal{U}^D$ as shown in (4).

$$\sum_{k \in \mathcal{K}} \sum_{i \in \mathcal{V}_d^{DR}} \sum_{j \in \mathcal{V}_d^{DR}} x_{i,j,k} \leq M_d^{DI}, \ \forall\, d \in \mathcal{U}^D \tag{4a}$$

$$M_d^{DI} = \sum_{r \in \mathcal{V}^R} \sum_{i \in \mathcal{V}_d^{DR}} B_{r,i} \left| B_{r,i} = \begin{cases} 1 & \text{if } i \in \delta^-(r) \\ 0 & \text{otherwise} \end{cases} \right., \ \forall\, d \in \mathcal{U}^D \tag{4b}$$

Taking advantage that our problem deals with jobs that have at most one origin and at most one destination, we can compute a minimum traveling distance and traveling time to fulfill all jobs by choosing the origin and destination with the shortest distance and time, respectively. Using this information, we can calculate the minimum number M^{LK} of trucks needed (since trucks have a maximum working time) and a lower bound on the routing costs M^{LC}. Furthermore, using a constructive heuristic (e.g., the one we benchmark to in Sect. 6), we can find upper bounds M^{UK} and M^{UC} for the number of trucks needed and the routing costs, respectively. Thus, we can limit the number of trucks as shown in (5) and the routing costs as shown in (6).

$$M^{LK} \leq \sum_{k \in K} \sum_{j \in \delta'+(B_k)} x_{B_k,j,k} \leq M^{UK} \tag{5}$$

$$M^{LC} \leq \sum_{k \in K} \left(C_k^F \cdot \sum_{j \in \delta'+(B_k)} x_{B_k,j,k} \right) + \sum_{k \in K} \sum_{(i,j) \in \mathcal{A}'} C_{i,j,k}^{\mathcal{V}} \cdot x_{i,j,k} \leq M^{UC} \tag{6}$$

The last adaptation we introduce is the pre-processing of time-windows. In our model, there are duplicated nodes (i.e., same location, service time, and time-window) for each terminal to keep track of time. However, each duplicated terminal node can only be used for one job. Since we duplicate a terminal for each job that might use that terminal, we can use the time-window of the job to reduce the time-window of the duplicated node for that terminal. As an example, consider Fig. 2. In this figure, we see a job of Type 1 that requires a full container from terminal d and delivers an empty container to terminal d'. In order to carry out this job within its time-window $[E_r, L_r]$, the full container must be put on a truck and

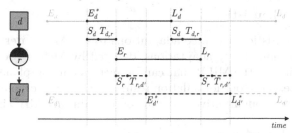

Fig. 2. Example of pre-processing of time-windows for a job Type 1

travel from terminal d anywhere between $[E_r - (S_d + T_{d,r}), L_r - (S_d + T_{d,r})]$. Similarly, after unloading the container, the empty container can arrive to terminal d' anywhere between $[E_r + (S_r + T_{r,d'}), L_r + (S_r + T_{r,d'})]$. We can repeat this logic with all jobs, their associated (possible) terminals, and the duplicated nodes for those terminals.

The benefit of the aforementioned enhancements of the MILP is twofold. First, the valid inequalities tighten the feasible solution. Second, the time-window pre-processing breaks the symmetry in MILP solutions introduced by the duplicated terminal nodes. However, these modifications are sufficient to solve only small problems. In the following section, we elaborate on further adaptations of the MILP that can allow it to be applied to larger problems.

5   Matheuristics

In our problem, MILP solvers are able to find a good feasible solution fast, but struggle on improving it further or in proving its optimality. In this section, we design three adaptations to the MILP that are aimed to help a solver find good feasible solutions faster. Furthermore, we design two matheuristics: (i) a static matheuristic to solve a single instance of the problem using Math-Heuristic Operators (MHOs), and (ii) a dynamic matheuristic to solve a re-planning instance of the problem using Fixing Criteria (FCs), as shown in the pseudo-code of Algorithms 1 and 2, respectively. We now elaborate on the MHOs, FCs, and parts of each algorithm.

Algorithm 1 Static Matheuristic	**Algorithm 2** Dynamic Matheuristic
Require: Graph $\mathcal{G}$ and associated parameters	**Require:** Re-planning trigger and current schedule
1: Initialize best solution	1: Determine current state
2: **while** Stopping criterion not met **do**	2: Fix trucks with FCs (10) and (11)
3: Get MHOs (7), (8), and (9)	3: Determine re-planning jobs
4: Build adapted MILP	4: Build $\mathcal{G}$ and associated parameters
5: Solve adapted MILP	5: Run Algorithm 1
6: **if** Current solution $\leq$ Best solution **then**	6: **return** Solution
7: Best solution = Current Solution	
8: **end if**	
9: **end while**	
10: **return** Best solution	

5.1   Static Matheuristic

Our static matheuristic uses three adaptations to the MILP, iteratively and in a local-search fashion. These adaptations, denoted by MHOs, are basically additional constraints in the MILP that can be seen as cutting planes that reduce the feasible space. Since our formulation results in a lot of arcs, our MHOs focus on fixing those arcs in an intuitive way. We now explain each MHO in more detail.

MHO 1: For N^{M1} random jobs $r \in \mathcal{V}^R$, we limit the number of feasible job-arcs to at most two, i.e., $|\delta^-(r)| \leq 2$ and $|\delta^+(r)| \leq 2$. These arcs are from (or to) the two closest locations (i.e., shortest traveling time). In other words, all remaining job-arcs are cut out, as shown in (7).

$$x_{j,r,k} = 0, \forall k \in \mathcal{K}, j \in \delta^-(r) \setminus \{i, i'\} \,\bigg|\, i = \underset{j \in \delta^-(r)}{\arg\min} \, T_{j,r} \text{ and } i' = \underset{j \in \delta^-(r) \setminus \{i\}}{\arg\min} \, T_{j,r} \quad (7a)$$

$$x_{r,j,k} = 0, \forall k \in \mathcal{K}, j \in \delta^+(r) \setminus \{i, i'\} \,\bigg|\, i = \underset{j \in \delta^+(r)}{\arg\min} \, T_{r,j} \text{ and } i' = \underset{j \in \delta^+(r) \setminus \{i\}}{\arg\min} \, T_{r,j} \quad (7b)$$

MHO 2: For N^{M2} times, the arc between a job r of Type 2 and a job r' of Type 7 with the minimum traveling time is fixed. Remind that the arc is feasible when $r \in \delta^-(r')$ and $r' \in \delta^+(r)$, and thus the fixing of a pair of jobs r and r' can be done as shown in (8).

$$\sum_{k \in \mathcal{K}} x_{r,r',k} = 1 \,\bigg|\, r = \underset{j \in \delta^-(r')}{\arg\min} \, T_{j,r'} \quad (8)$$

MHO 3: For N^{M3} random jobs $r \in \mathcal{V}^{\mathrm{R}}$, we fix the feasible job-arcs from (or to) the closest location (i.e., shortest traveling time), as shown in (9).

$$\sum_{k \in \mathcal{K}} x_{i,r,k} = 1 \,\bigg|\, i = \underset{j \in \delta^-(r)}{\arg\min} \, T_{j,r} \quad \text{and} \quad \sum_{k \in \mathcal{K}} x_{r,i,k} = 1 \,\bigg|\, i = \underset{j \in \delta^+(r)}{\arg\min} \, T_{r,j} \quad (9)$$

Assigning a value to the parameters $N^{\mathrm{M*}}$ requires tuning (see Sect. 6.2). In general, the larger the value of $N^{\mathrm{M*}}$ the smaller the problem becomes for the solver, but the higher the chance of ruling out the global optimum.

5.2   Dynamic Matheuristic

Our dynamic matheuristic builds upon the static and is used for re-planning situations (e.g., new jobs arrived, delays, etc.). Jobs sequences that are being executed during the re-planning trigger are completed (i.e., no preemption). For jobs that have not been started yet, we have the option to use the previous plan or to re-plan them. In the first option, we fix jobs in current truck routes using two Fixing Criteria (FC). The idea of these criteria is to identify good routes from the current schedule that can be kept in the new plan. In the second option, we use the static matheuristic to build a new schedule. The fixing of a route means that the routes (i.e., job sequences) will be preserved, but the time at which and the truck by which they are executed is left flexible. This time flexibility allows new jobs to be added to the trucks already being used and also to handle delays.

FC 1: We fix N^{F1} routes k^{C} from the current schedule x^{C} with the largest number of jobs. We define $\mathcal{F}^1(k^{\mathrm{C}})$ as the set of arcs (i,j) that fulfill this criteria, as shown in (10), and fix the routes by $\sum_{k \in \mathcal{K}} x_{i,j,k} = 1, \forall (i,j) \in \mathcal{F}^1(k^{\mathrm{C}})$.

$$\mathcal{F}^1(k^{\mathrm{C}}) = \left\{ (i,j) \in \mathcal{A} : x_{i,j,k^{\mathrm{C}}}^{\mathrm{C}} = 1, k^{\mathrm{C}} = \underset{k' \in \mathcal{K} | \sum_{j \in \mathcal{V}} x_{B_k,j,k}^{\mathrm{C}} = 1}{\arg\max} \sum_{i \in \mathcal{V}^{\mathrm{R}}} x_{i,j,k}^{\mathrm{C}} \right\} \quad (10)$$

FC 2: We fix N^{F2} routes with the shortest traveling time, similar to FC 1. We define $\mathcal{F}^2(k^{\mathrm{C}})$ as the set of arcs (i,j) that fulfill this criteria, as shown in (11).

$$\mathcal{F}^2(k^{\mathrm{C}}) = \left\{ (i,j) \in \mathcal{A} : x^{\mathrm{C}}_{i,j,k^{\mathrm{C}}} = 1, k^{\mathrm{C}} = \underset{k' \in \mathcal{K} | \sum_{j \in \mathcal{V}} x^{\mathrm{C}}_{B_k,j,k} = 1}{\arg\min} \sum_{(i,j) \in \mathcal{A}'} x^{\mathrm{C}}_{i,j,k} T_{i,j} \right\} \quad (11)$$

Just as in the static matheuristic, the best value of the parameters $N^{\mathrm{F*}}$ depends on circumstances such as the current schedule, the instance $\mathcal{G}$, and the re-planning trigger. In the following, we present a brief proof-of-concept of the algorithms just described.

6   Numerical Experiments

We test our solution approach in two numerical experiments. First, we examine the benefits that our adaptations have in solving the MILP. Second, we test the gains of using our dynamic matheuristic compared to a benchmark heuristic. Our goal is to explore our approach and gain insights for further research.

6.1   Experimental Setup

We design 32 problem instances containing 25 jobs each. The location, time-window, and service time for each job is obtained from the first 25 customers of the Solomon instances for the VRPTW [14]. We use the first eight instances of four categories in [14]: C1, C2, R1, and R2, where C stands for clustered locations, R for random locations, 1 for short time-windows, and 2 for long-time windows. For each instance, there are 25 homogeneous trucks to guarantee there is a feasible solution. For each truck, the fixed cost is 1000 and the traveling time and variable cost is equal to the Euclidean distance between two locations.

The job configurations for all instances are shown in Table 1. These job configurations are based on the average drayage operations of a Dutch LSP in the Eastern part of The Netherlands. This LSP has three terminals that we use as follows. Terminal 1 is located in the same location as the Depot in the corresponding Solomon instance and has a terminal assignment cost of 500. Terminal 2 and Terminal 3 are located at $(60,60)$ and $(10,10)$, which are points along the diagonal in the Euclidean space that are close to the most distant customers from the geographical center of each of the Solomon instances. The assignment costs vary per instance, and are defined as $500 - 2\beta$, where β is the length of the diagonal formed by the extremes of the corresponding Solomon instance. The rationale is to make the distant terminals worth "assigning" if a job is within half of the diagonal. The time-window of each terminal is twice the time-window of the depot in the corresponding Solomon instance. The maximum working time for each truck is equal to the length of the time-window of each terminal. Terminal 1 is the beginning and finishing location of nine trucks, and Terminals 2 and 3 of eight trucks each.

Table 1. Job configuration for all instances

Characteristic	Job Type										
	1	2	3	4	5	6	7	8	9	10	11
Number of jobs	2	3	2	2	2	2	4	3	3	1	1
Jobs decoupling D_r	1	1	-	-	-	1	1	1	-	-	-

In both the static and dynamic experiments, we compare to the use of a benchmark heuristic that follows the logic from [2]. First, each job of Type 2 is paired with a job of Type 7 that incurs the minimum variable cost considering all constraints. Note that the origin of the full container of Type 2 is known, thus the pairing occurs in the destination of the empty container of Type 2 with the source of the empty container of Type 7. Subsequently, the closest terminal is assigned to the full container of Type 7. The paired jobs are sorted in non-decreasing route distance and scheduled using a cheapest insertion method. This method schedules the paired jobs in the position of the route that yields the lowest routing cost. All remaining jobs are then scheduled with a similar cheapest insertion method. For the jobs that have a flexible source or destination of a container, all combinations of sources and destinations are examined and the position with the cheapest routing and terminal assignment cost is chosen. To use this heuristic dynamically, the job sequences that are being executed during the re-planning trigger are fixed (i.e., no preemption of the current schedule). Jobs that have not been started and that are not in a non-preemptive sequence are re-scheduled with the steps described before. We now describe each experiment in detail and present their results.

6.2 Static Experiments

In the static experiments, we test the effect that the Valid Inequalities (VIs), Time-Window Pre-Processing (TWPP), and the three Math-Heuristic Operators (MHOs) have on the total costs. For each of the eight instances in categories C1, C2, R1, and R2, we test the MILP without any modification, the MILP with the VIs, the MILP with the TWPP, and the MILP with the VIs, TWPP, and each of the MHOs. We use CPLEX 12.6.3 (via the C API) with a limit of 300 seconds and a warm-start given by the solution of the Benchmark Heuristic (BH). For MHO 1 and 3, we perform nine iterations; and at each iteration, we choose seven random jobs in MHO 1 and one random job in MHO 3. MHO 2 has no randomness, so we perform only three iterations and we fix 1, 2, and 3 jobs respectively. The "random" settings are arbitrary, since we just test their usefulness rather than tuning them. We show the aggregated results in Table 2.

In Table 2, four interesting observations arise. First, the VIs do not improve the solution of the MILP but the TWPP does. Second, the best solutions in the clustered (C) instances are achieved by MHO 3, and in the random (R) instances by MHO 1. It is reasonable that MHO 1 achieves better solutions in R instances than C ones because this operator increases the chance of assigning the closest

Table 2. Total costs for various MILP adaptations

Instances	BH	MILP	VIs	TWPP	MHO 1	MHO 2	MHO 3
C1	77,960	77,926	77,960	76,924	76,829	77,926	75,189
C2	52,904	52,882	52,904	52,049	51,841	52,078	50,802
R1	111,087	111,078	110,904	107,649	107,254	107,647	107,736
R2	50,500	50,435	50,500	50,497	50,255	50,500	50,378

origin and destination to each job in a network with more disperse locations. Third, MHO 2 has worse solutions than the other MHOs. It seems that choosing a job as the origin/destination of an empty container (i.e., logic of the BH) is not better than allowing a job or a terminal to be origin and destination, as MHO 1 and 3 allow. Fourth, in instances C1, C2, and R1, our adaptations to the MILP result in savings (from the BH) between 3-4%, but in instances R2 there are no noticeable savings. It seems that in R2, which has long time-windows and longer traveling times, the cheapest insertion and job-pairing nature of the BH results in good solutions.

6.3 Dynamic Experiments

In the dynamic experiments, we test the effect of the Fixing Criteria FC 1 and FC 2. In addition, we test a no-fixing criteria FC 0 meaning that all non-preemptive jobs can be re-scheduled. The problem instances are similar to the static experiments. We consider five stages for re-scheduling after the initial planning of the first 25 jobs of each Solomon instance (i.e., the static setup). These five stages are uniformly distributed within the first half of the trucks and terminals maximum working time (i.e., half a day). At each stage, five new jobs are revealed, which correspond to the next five jobs in each Solomon instance, and whose time-window is increased proportionally to the stage to guarantee they occur after they are revealed. Non-preemptiveness applies to all jobs scheduled in a truck before the next stop at a terminal. For the static

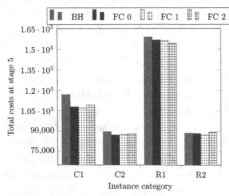

Fig. 3. Comparison FCs at last stage

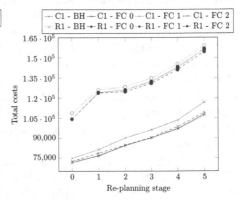

Fig. 4. Performance of best FC per stage

matheuristic within the dynamic matheuristic, we use MHO 3 for C instances and MHO 1 for R instances. We define the number of truck routes to fix for FC1 and FC2 as a percentage of the available truck routes: $N^{F*} = (0.1, 0.5)$. The results are shown in Fig. 3 and 4.

In Fig. 3, we observe that in the last re-planning stage (i.e., costs over the entire day), our dynamic matheuristic achieves significant savings compared to the BH in instances C1, C2 and R1 (around 8%, 3%, and 3% respectively). The winning FC, however, seems to vary per instance type. It is reasonable that fixing routes with the largest number of jobs (i.e., FC 1) is good in C1 since these instances contain closely located jobs with tight time-windows. Furthermore, it seems also reasonable that in instances with disperse located jobs such as R1, fixing routes with good traveling times (i.e., FC 2) is better. We focus on these two instance categories in Fig. 4. For R1 we observe that FCs 0 and 1 have similar performance and that FC 2 starts differentiating more from the other FCs and the BH towards the last stages. For C1 we observe similarly that FCs 0 and 1 have comparable performance, and that the gap to the BH seems to widen towards the last stages.

6.4   Discussion

In the static experiments, we observe that the MHOs help obtaining a better MILP solution than the VIs and the TWPP. We observe also that the performance of the MHO depends on the problem settings. In the dynamic experiments, we observe that the dynamic matheuristic outperforms the BH but the performance of the FCs therein depends again on the problem settings. Although these experiments serve as a proof-of-concept and give an indication of the gains to be expected, they have three limitations. First, we do not tune the parameters with respect to the problem setting. As described in the results, our MHOs and FCs have implicit distance and time effects on the solution and thus require tuning. Second, we do not adapt the algorithms towards previous iterations or stages. Our MHOs and FCs are analogous to neighborhood operators in local search heuristics, and thus mechanisms that adapt them can be beneficial to further guide the algorithm to better solutions. Third, we limit the computational time of the matheuristics and use a heuristic for the warm-start. The interaction of these two methods and the solver has a larger effect on some problems than others. We observed that for some instance categories, the solver was able to find improvements at every stage, but in some others failed to find a different solution than the heuristic within the allowed time. These limitations in our study, however, give rise to new research questions, specially in the combination of exact and heuristic approaches, i.e., matheuristics: how to tune the parameters, how to adapt the algorithm that uses the parameters after each iteration, and how to handle the interaction between solver and solution are examples of promising research lines.

Even though we analyze one trigger for re-scheduling, i.e., fixed intervals, it is important to note there can be other triggers such as change in the status of trucks, traffic data, or cancellation of customer requests [7,15]. Different triggers for re-scheduling may require different FCs. For example, fixing routes with the shortest traveling time from the previous schedule may not be the best option if the trigger for disruption was a delay due to increased traffic. Furthermore, the interaction between the real-time aspect of synchromodality and the re-scheduling trigger needs to be considered. When the time required for re-planning (e.g., computation time of the matheuristic) is larger than the effect of a trigger (e.g., delay) it can be that re-planning is not even necessary. Overall, these re-scheduling aspects in synchromodality need to be investigated and tackled within a dynamic solution approach.

7   Conclusion

We developed a MILP and a matheuristic to schedule drayage operations in synchromodal transport. Timing, routing, and long-haul terminal assignment decisions are integrated and simultaneously considered. Dynamic scheduling is done as new information is revealed throughout the day.

Through numerical experiments, we studied the performance of our adaptations to the MILP model and fixing criteria in the matheuristic. Overall, we observed that the gains of our approach are dependent on problem attributes such as customer dispersion, time-window lengths, and dynamic re-planning. Further research in the relation between these characteristics and our matheuristics is needed. The proper handling of such relations is essential for scheduling drayage operations in synchromodal transport.

Acknowledgment: This research has been partially funded by the Dutch Institute for Advanced Logistics, DINALOG, under the project SynchromodalIT.

References

1. Braekers, K., Caris, A., Janssens, G.: Integrated planning of loaded and empty container movements. OR Spectrum 35(2), 457–478 (2013), dx.doi.org/10.1007/s00291-012-0284-5
2. Caris, A., Janssens, G.: A local search heuristic for the pre- and end-haulage of intermodal container terminals. Computers & Operations Research 36(10), 2763 – 2772 (2009), dx.doi.org/10.1016/j.cor.2008.12.007
3. Caris, A., Macharis, C., Janssens, G.K.: Decision support in intermodal transport: A new research agenda. Computers in Industry 64(2), 105 – 112 (2013), dx.doi.org/10.1016/j.compind.2012.12.001, decision Support for Intermodal Transport
4. Cordeau, J.F., Laporte, G., Savelsbergh, M.W., Vigo, D.: Vehicle Routing. In: Barnhart, C., Laporte, G. (eds.) Transportation, Handbooks in Operations Research and Management Science, vol. 14, chap. 6, pp. 367 – 428. Elsevier (2007), dx.doi.org/10.1016/S0927-0507(06)14006-2
5. Escudero, A., Muñuzuri, J., Guadix, J., Arango, C.: Dynamic approach to solve the daily drayage problem with transit time uncertainty. Computers in Industry 64(2), 165 – 175 (2013), dx.doi.org/10.1016/j.compind.2012.11.006, decision Support for Intermodal Transport

6. Francis, P., Zhang, G., Smilowitz, K.: Improved modeling and solution methods for the multi-resource routing problem. European Journal of Operational Research 180(3), 1045 – 1059 (2007), dx.doi.org/10.1016/j.ejor.2006.03.054

7. Heilig, L., Lalla-Ruiz, E., Voß, S.: port-io: an integrative mobile cloud platform for real-time inter-terminal truck routing optimization. Flexible Services and Manufacturing Journal (Jan 2017), dx.doi.org/10.1007/s10696-017-9280-z

8. Imai, A., Nishimura, E., Current, J.: A Lagrangian relaxation-based heuristic for the vehicle routing with full container load. European Journal of Operational Research 176(1), 87 – 105 (2007), dx.doi.org/10.1016/j.ejor.2005.06.044

9. Konings, J.: Intermodal barge transport: network design, nodes and competitiveness. PhD thesis, TU Delft, Delft University of Technology (2009), http://repository.tudelft.nl/view/ir/uuid%3Aff6f5f10-2acc-43fb-9474-5317b0988bdd/

10. del Mar Agamez-Arias, A., Moyano-Fuentes, J.: Intermodal transport in freight distribution: a literature review. Transport Reviews 0(0), 1–26 (2017), dx.doi.org/10.1080/01441647.2017.1297868

11. Nossack, J., Pesch, E.: A truck scheduling problem arising in intermodal container transportation. European Journal of Operational Research 230(3), 666 – 680 (2013), dx.doi.org/10.1016/j.ejor.2013.04.042

12. Riessen, B., Negenborn, R.R., Dekker, R.: Synchromodal container transportation: An overview of current topics and research opportunities. In: Corman, F., Voß, S., Negenborn, R.R. (eds.) Proceedings ICCL 2015, Delft, The Netherlands, pp. 386–397. Lecture Notes in Computer Science, Springer (2015), dx.doi.org/10.1007/978-3-319-24264-4_27

13. Smilowitz, K.: Multi-resource routing with flexible tasks: an application in drayage operations. IIE Transactions 38(7), 577–590 (2006), dx.doi.org/10.1080/07408170500436898

14. Solomon, M.M.: Algorithms for the vehicle routing and scheduling problems with time window constraints. Operations Research 35(2), 254–265 (1987), http://www.jstor.org/stable/170697

15. Ulmer, M.W., Heilig, L., Voß, S.: On the value and challenge of real-time information in dynamic dispatching of service vehicles. Business & Information Systems Engineering 59(3), 161–171 (Jun 2017), dx.doi.org/10.1007/s12599-017-0468-2

16. Wang, X., Regan, A.C.: Local truckload pickup and delivery with hard time window constraints. Transportation Research Part B: Methodological 36(2), 97 – 112 (2002), dx.doi.org/10.1016/S0965-8564(00)00037-9

Survey on Characteristics and Challenges of Synchromodal Transportation in Global Cold Chains

Wenjing Guo[1,*], Wouter Beelaerts van Blokland[1], Gabriel Lodewijks[2]

[1] Delft University of Technology, Delft, The Netherlands
[2] University of New South Wales, Sydney, Australia
W.Guo-2@tudelft.nl, W.W.A.BeelaertsvanBlokland@tudelft.nl,
g.lodewijks@unsw.edu.au

Abstract. Transportation of perishables such as fruits and vegetables with short shelf life in international, long distance and cooled condition, plays a key role in global cold chains. Compared with truck transportation, intermodal transportation largely reduces logistics cost and emissions, however, has less flexibility for disturbances. Another aspect is that truck transportation occupies the largest share in inland transportation, which causes traffic congestion and environmental pollutions. Synchromodal transportation is a known method to study the effectiveness, efficiency and sustainability of transportation by using real-time information. However, limited articles can be found about the cold chain perspective, an integral analysis is missing. Our objective is to thoroughly analyze the characteristics and challenges of synchromodal transportation in global cold chains. The critical successful factors are analyzed at first. After that, we survey on planning problems in strategic, tactical and operational level, respectively. Finally, we conclude by suggesting further research directions.

Keywords: Global cold chains, Flexibility, Environmental impact, Synchromodal transportation, Real-time switching

1   Introduction

In this paper, we define global cold chains in perishable products with short shelf life, such as fruits and vegetables, either fresh produces or processed products. It consists of farmers, wholesalers, processors, exporters, transporters, importers, retailers and consumers [3,13,34]. As perishable products show continuous quality changes throughout the global chain, international, long distance and temperature controlled transportation is essential [4,38].

With the increasing volume of containers in global trade, intermodal transportation has been developed for integrated transport in the last decades [35]. The International Transport Forum defined intermodal transportation as: Multimodal transport of goods, in one and the same intermodal transport unit by successive modes of transport without handling of goods themselves when changing modes [14]. Compared with truck transportation, intermodal transportation can largely reduce logistics cost and emissions, however, has less flexibility for disturbances [37]. The capacity sharing of ser-

© Springer International Publishing AG 2017
T. Bektaş et al. (Eds.), ICCL 2017, LNCS 10572, pp. 420–434, 2017.
https://doi.org/10.1007/978-3-319-68496-3_28

vices among different shippers contributes to cost reduction, and the utilization of barge and train brings about less emissions. However, in global cold chains, outside temperature might vary widely during the transportation from origin to destination. In order to maintain certain temperature, flexible energy consumption is required [4]. In addition, even under optimal temperature, the quality of perishable products is still degrading with time [34,38,39]. The impact of disturbances (such as service delay and traffic congestion) for perishable products in intermodal transportation, is therefore, more critical than truck transportation. Dynamic and real-time intermodal transportation plan is needed. However, current intermodal transportation planning models tend to be static and offline, resulting in less flexibility for disturbances [6,10,11,37].

Another aspect is that truck transportation still occupies the largest share in inland transportation, which causes transportation congestion and environment pollutions. The main reason is that truck exhausts more emissions than barge and train. According to the statistics, in 2014 about 75.4% of total freight transportation in European union countries were transported via road, around 18% via rail, and 6.6% via inland waterways. The Netherlands has better performance, with 56.1%, 4.9%, and 39% respectively [15]. Recently, global cold chains are confronted with increasing consumer demands on sustainability [8,34]. Sustainability commonly refers to how the needs of the present human generation can be met without compromising the ability of future generations to meet their needs [9]. In terms of sustainable transportation, it generally relates to less emissions. Increasing the utilization of barge and train in inland transportation can reduce emissions on one side. On the other side, the transport models become more complex due to the increasing number of transfers.

Synchromodal transportation is a potential method for global cold chains to reach better performance in long distance transportation [17], first proposed by Tavasszy in 2010 [24]. It refers to creating the effective, efficient and sustainable transportation plan for all orders by using real-time information [35]. Under synchromodality, the mode combinations for orders can be changed before or during the transportation in case of disturbances. The capacity of barge and train will be better used in inland transportation for reducing logistics cost and emissions. The main objectives of synchromodal transportation focus on reducing logistics cost, emissions and improving reliability [19]. Therefore, this new transport concept has benefits on both economy, society and environment aspect. Compared with intermodal transportation, synchromodal transportation has several advantages, as shown in Figure 1. Firstly, it aims at horizontal collaboration as well as vertical collaboration. Horizontal collaboration can promote information sharing among different carriers, avoiding vicious competition. Secondly, the mode booking pattern is mode-free booking rather than mode booking in advance. The shippers only specify origin and destination position, time window, volume and lead time, leaving the choice of mode combinations to logistics service providers. Thirdly, instead of one OD pair planning, synchromodal transportation refers to network-wide planning, which includes all the orders and services arrived before planning horizon. Most importantly, it focuses on real-time switching in case of disturbances to guarantee service efficiency, operational effectiveness and less environmental impact [30,35,40].

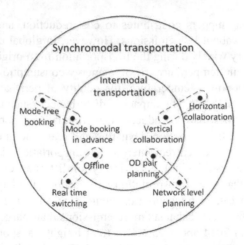

Fig. 1. Synchromodal transportation versus intermodal transportation

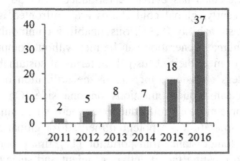

Fig. 2. Publication trends of synchromodal transportation

However, as a new concept, limited articles have been published about synchromodal transportation, especially for global cold chains. By 2016, totally 77 articles of synchromodal transportation are found using research databases, such as Web of Science, Science direct, and Emerald. Nevertheless, this research area has an increasing trend, as illustrated in Figure 2. Due to the perishability of agri-food, the transportation models are more complex than non-perishables [2,38], and only 3 papers researched synchromodal transportation involving perishable products [17,31,32]. And none of them provide an integral analysis about the characteristics and challenges of synchromodal transportation in global cold chains. The objective of this paper, is therefore, to thoroughly analyze it.

The structure of this paper is shown as follows. In Section 2, the critical successful factors are illustrated. After that, we analyze the planning problems in strategic, tactical and operational level respectively. Strategic infrastructure network design problem is described in Section 3, while Section 4 analyzes the tactical service network design problem. Operational intermodal routing choice problem is discussed in Section 5. At each level, the characteristics and challenges are discussed. We conclude our work by suggesting further research in Section 6.

2   Critical Successful Factors

Although synchromodal transportation is an interested idea, it is hard to realize in practice. Until now, only several successful pilot studies are known in the Netherlands. Almost all the case studies exist in literatures are based on the European Gateway Services network, which includes Rotterdam port and at least 20 hinterland terminals in Europe [35]. Critical successful factors analysis is an effective method to identify the key enablers of synchromodality [21]. In order to achieve an integral analysis of synchromodal transportation in global cold chains, the critical successful factors are analyzed at first.

According to the literature review, we find that synchromodal transportation includes eight factors, as shown in Table 1. Legal and political issues and physical infrastructure investment are decided by governments, such as tax incentives for sustainable logistics and new hub construction. In terms of shippers' mode booking pattern, the benefits of synchromodality, like cost receiving and environmental friendly, can promote customers' mind shift. Advanced information technology and horizontal collaboration are foundation, while service-based pricing strategy plays as an incentive. Integrated planning is the core of synchromodal transportation, which will be further discussed in strategic, tactical and operational level respectively. Real-time switching is the highest requirement which responses to dynamic demands and varying disturbances. As the first three factors are determined by government or high level organizations, next, we further analyze the last five factors.

Table 1. Critical successful factors of synchromodal transportation

Reference	Behdani (2014)	Tavasszy (2015)	Putz (2015)	Riessen (2015)	Singh (2016)	Pfoser (2016)
Legal and political issues			●		●	
Physical infrastructure			●		●	
Mind shift		●	●	●		
Information technology		●	●		●	
Horizontal collaboration	●	●	●		●	
Service-based pricing strategy	●		●	●		
Integrated planning	●	●	●	●	●	
Real-time switching	●	●		●		

2.1 Information Technology

Information technology mainly refers to information sharing, track and trace, and communication technology [27]. Regarding global cold chains, radio frequency identification is a critical technology for monitoring environment data of reefer containers, such as temperature and moisture. Real-time position of services and reefer containers can be attained by using global positioning systems. Information and communications technology can promote information sharing and communication among different operators. In summary, advanced information technology is the foundation of synchromodal transportation in global cold chains.

2.2 Horizontal Collaboration

Horizontal collaboration is another basic factor in realizing synchromodal transportation. It refers to the collaboration relationship between actors in the same level, whereas vertical collaboration refers to different level. For example, the relationship among different carriers belongs to horizontal collaboration, while carriers and shippers build vertical collaboration. For switching flexibility among different services, horizontal collaboration among carriers turns out to be essential. Shippers also establish horizontal cooperation to achieve lower cost by the capacity sharing of services. The collaboration contract between them used to be long term, static and offline. However, due to the dynamic characteristic of global agri-food market, dynamic and online contract become more suitable. What is more, considering the private safety of different actors, totally information sharing is unpractical. Real-time decisions based on limited information are still challenging. Agent-based modelling is an effective method for analyzing dynamic collaboration owing to its real-time, adaptive features [12].

2.3 Pricing Strategy

In terms of pricing strategy, synchromodal transportation shows distinct characteristics with intermodal transportation [35]. Intermodal transportation adopts mode-based pricing strategy, the price is determined by the mode used. Mode combination is decided before the transportation, thus the price is fixed. With respect to synchromodal transportation, the mode booking pattern is mode-free booking. The mode combinations would be changed before or during transport in case of disturbances, such as service delay. The mode-based pricing strategy is thus unsuitable for synchromodal transportation. The pricing strategy in synchromodal transportation should be differentiate with respect to different mode combinations. Even for the identical mode combination, the price can be different according to the spare capacity of services. Considering the credits of customers, different price for different credits is an effective motivation. With regard to agri-food, received quality can further influence product's price. Based on the above analysis, we can predict that the pricing strategy of synchromodal transportation is still challenging and thus deserves further research.

2.4   Integrated Planning

An effective planning model is the core of synchromodal transportation. While inter-modal transportation focus on one OD pair planning, synchromodal transportation aims at integrated planning at a network level. Under synchromodality, all the services belong to different carriers are assumed to be a large resource pool and all the arriving orders will be allocated simultaneously. Due to the complexity of planning models, most researches focus on centralized planning of synchromodal transportation. However, the entities in global cold chains are often geographically distributed. It is thus very difficult to apply a central coordinator to manage the whole system [12]. Moreover, when the computation size becomes large enough, distributed system promotes better computation performance. In order to improve operational efficiency, service effectiveness and reduce environmental impact, the key performance indicators of synchromodal transportation are logistics cost, agri-food quality and emissions. Therefore, an integrated model combining the logistics model with the agri-food quality decay model and the emission model is required for transport planning.

2.5   Real-Time Switching

With the development of information technology, real-time information becomes available for intermodal operators. Due to the occurrences of variety disturbances during transportation, such as service delay, real-time switching is essential for improving the service reliability. An integrated planning model is the prerequisite of real-time switching [36]. With respect to agri-food, the characteristics of perishable and short shelf life also requires real-time switching in case of disturbances [17]. Otherwise, the quality may decay to an unacceptable level for customers. In order to realize real-time switching, researchers have proposed different methods, like rolling horizon strategy, model predictive control, decision tree and decomposition algorithm. In rolling horizon strategy [1], orders arrive continuously in different planning horizons. The planning horizon is rolled forward to include more known information. Decisions are made at the deadline of the orders. Regarding model predictive control approach [17], it is an effective method to obtain an ideal output by controlling the inputs. For instance, in order to keep banana's shelf life, both the container's temperature and mode choice will be controlled by the system operators in real-time. As for decision tree [36], it can be used in a decision support system for instantaneously allocating incoming orders to suitable services, without the requirement of continuous planning updates. Decomposition algorithm attempts to solve the original problem by solving a number of smaller problems [18]. As real-time switching requires short response of disturbances, the computation efficiency indicates significant means.

2.6   Discussion

According to the discussions above, we know that under government support, based on advanced information technology and horizontal collaboration as well as attracted pricing strategy, the synchromodal transportation can be realized in global cold chains by combining real-time switching with effective planning models. However, synchromodal transportation planning models are more complex than intermodal transportation. Considering the perishability of agri-food, both the objectives and constraints will be different. Next, we will further analyze the characteristics and challenges of synchromodal transportation in global cold chains in strategic, tactical and operational level respectively.

3   Strategic Infrastructure Network Design

Strategic level focuses on long term decisions. The infrastructure network design problem in synchromodal transportation refers to investment decisions on hub locations [6,29]. Under synchromodal transportation, different shippers' containers are bundled together in hubs for large container flow. To reduce total transport cost, the allocation of hubs depends on the service demands in different areas. The connection between hubs can be road, rail or inland waterway. Under the same OD pair, different corridors refers to different modes. Regarding global cold chains, due to the short shelf life and low temperature requirements of perishable products, the location of processing factory is also an important strategic decision. Considering the logistics performance of global cold chains, different locations of processing factory will result in different transport mode combinations choice. For example, the pineapples from Ghana to the Netherlands can be cutting in Ghana and then transport to the Netherlands by aircraft, or transport to the Netherlands by barge at first and then cutting in the Netherlands, as shown in Figure 3 [34].

The infrastructure network design problem mainly depends on the availability of infrastructure, transport assets, the adequacy of cargo flow in a specific corridor and the shelf life of perishable agri-food [6,34]. Typically, this problem can be described by using mixed-integer linear programming models which include both binary decision variables and continuous decision variables. Binary decision variables is related to that whether the hub or processing factory is used or not, while continuous decision variables illustrate bundled flow [4].

The objective of the network design used to be simply focus on cost. As agri-food quality deeply affects customers satisfaction degree, it should be considered as another important objective. With respect to environmental impact, proper network design maximizes the utilization of green modes which produce less emissions. Thus, for global cold chains, the objectives of infrastructure network design should include both logistics cost, products' quality and emissions.

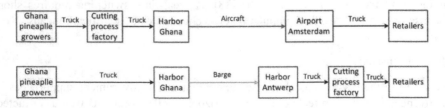

Fig. 3. Transportation of Pineapples from Ghana to the Netherlands

4   Tactical Service Network Design

Tactical level focuses on middle term decisions. It optimally utilizes the given infrastructure by choosing services and associated transportation modes, allocating their capacities to orders, and planning their itineraries and frequency. Service network design (SND) is the major problem in tactical level. It mainly gives decisions on choosing the transportation services and modes for forecasted customer demands, and the frequency and capacity of each mode on certain corridor [29]. Here, a service is characterized by its origin, destination and intermediate terminals, its transportation mode, route and its service capacity. Likewise, a mode is characterized by its loading capacity, speed and price [29], which means that different services may have a same mode. As synchromodal transportation aims at integrated planning, both self-operated or outsourced transportation need to be considered to minimize transport cost [25].

In order to improve operational efficiency, service effectiveness and sustainability, the objectives of SND problem of synchromodal transportation for perishables include logistics cost, products quality and emissions. The availability and capacity of infrastructure networks or inland terminals are the primary resource constraints [6]. In intermodal transport planning, dynamic service network design problem is closest to the synchromodal planning problems. It involves the selection of transportation services and modes for freights, where at least one feature of the network varies over time [26]. Except time-varying network, the demands of synchromodal transportation is also dynamic. Orders arrive in sequence rather than in advance before the planning horizon. According to the perishable and dynamic characteristics of global cold chains, we analyze the challenges exist in six aspects of SND problem given in Table 2.

Table 2. Service network design problem

Reference	Riessen et al. (2015)	Rivera et al. (2016)	Li et al. (2016)
Mode	Rail, Truck, Barge	Rail, Truck, Barge	Rail, Truck, Barge
Objectives	Cost	Cost	Cost
Centralised /Distributed	Centralised	Centralised	Distributed
Transfer cost	Yes	No	Yes
Self-operation/ Outsource	Both	Self-operation	Both
Static/Dynamic	Static	Dynamic	Dynamic

4.1 Distinct aspects

For global cold chain, transportation distance tends to be very long. As agri-food is distinct from other products, temperature controlled transportation is essential. Compared with sea transport, rail transport is more faster than sea transport. Compared with air transport, the cost of rail transport is 50% less than air transport. This means that the rail transport is optimally suited for perishable products which need to be at the final destination as quick as possible, but not at any cost. However, for perishable products with high value and short lead time, air transport is a better choice. Both Riessen [25], Rivera [26] and Li [16] only consider mode combinations of truck, barge and train.

As agri-food is perishable and reefer containers exhaust extra emissions, the objectives of transportation should include the reduction of cost, emissions, and improving service reliability. Both Riessen [25], Rivera [26] and Li [16] only view cost as objective.

Compared with centralized planning systems, decentralized systems are more practical. Farms, processing factories and retail stores tend to be generically distributed. Information sharing is crucial for centralized planning. However, it is difficult to realize among different entities, especially for stakeholders with competitive relationship. Li [16] proposed a distributed service network design approach, however, this approach is applied in general supply chain.

4.2 General aspects

Transfers brings more chance to the utilization of barge and train, which result in less emissions and cost. However, it also takes additional cost and time in terminals. Thus, transfer cost should be calculated in transport cost, like Riessen [25] and Li [16].

Outsourced logistics refers to horizontal collaboration between different carriers. Self-operated logistics is calculated on fixed cost. In contrast, outsourced logistics is based on container volumes. In terms of service capacity, the capacity of self-operated logistics can be completely used, while the capacity of outsourced logistics depends on spare capacity [25].

SND problem can be further divided in static and dynamic groups [29]. Riessen [25] proposed a static SND model, temperature and travel time are assumed as static parameters, and all the orders arrived before the planning horizon. However, time-varying network is more practical, because transport conditions normally change with time, and orders tends to be arriving in sequence. In addition, Li [16] proposed a dynamic SND model in synchromodal transportation based on a model predictive control approach.

4.3 Discussion

Synchromodal transportation service network design problem in global cold chains is a challenging problem owing to its dynamic, long distance, multi-objective and distributed features. To our best knowledge, only Riessen [25], Rivera [26] and Li [16] proposed SND model for synchromodal transportation. But none of them considered the characteristics of global cold chain. Therefore, there still have lots of chances for further research of dynamic SND problem for global cold chains.

5   Operational Intermodal Routing Choice Problem

Operational level deals with dynamical problems that are not explicitly addressed at strategic and tactical levels [29]. In the operational level, the mainly issue is the determination of the best choice of services and the associated transportation modes, best itineraries and allocation of resources to demands [29]. Nevertheless, the intermodal routing choice decision is designed for orders in this level, while for services in tactical level. The demand is the actual demand rather than the forecasted demand, and the resource constraints are the time windows rather than availability and capacity of infrastructure and services. Within the constraints of tactical service design (which determines the routes, frequency, and capacity of each modality), the operational level considers the details of transport orders and resources, then the orders to different intermodal transport services are assigned.

The operational intermodal routing choice (OIRC) problem refers to the selection of mode combinations for arriving orders. Based on different characteristics, researchers proposed different titles for the OIRC problem, such as international intermodal choices [20], intermodal route selection [28], international intermodal routing [5,10], intermodal freight routing problem [11], container transportation planning problem [37], operational service schedules [6], and selection of transport mode combination [19]. Although this problem has been investigated so many years, limited publications can be found in literatures. The mainly reasons are the complexity of computation, and the dynamic feature of both demand and supply. Other reasons include the unattainable of information, the competition relationship instead of cooperation relationship among operators.

Compared with intermodal transportation, the operational intermodal routing choice problem in synchromodal transportation has several new characteristics. Firstly, the routing choice decisions are made at network level and in real-time. Secondly, the inland transportation modes are mainly barge and train. Truck is only used for the first and last mile transportation or for urgent demands.

For global cold chain, operation routing choice problem faces several new challenges. According to the perishable and dynamic characteristics of global cold chains, we analyze the challenges exist in eight aspects of operational intermodal routing choice problem, as shown in Table 3.

Table 3. Operational intermodal routing choice problem

Reference	International/ Inland	Multi-objective	Time window	Time-varying network	Centralized/ Distributed	Multi-pattern	Transfer	Real-time/ Dynamic
Mes (2016)	Inland	Cost, Time, Emissions	Yes	No	Centralized	No	Yes	Real-time, Dynamic
Riessen (2016)	Inland	Cost	Yes	No	Centralized	Yes	Yes	Real-time, Dynamic
Riessen (2015)	Inland	Cost	Yes	No	Centralized	Yes	Yes	Offline, Static
Behdani (2014)	Inland	Cost, Time	Yes	No	Centralized	No	No	Offline, Static
Cho (2012)	International	Cost, Time	No	No	Centralized	No	Yes	Offline, Static
Chang (2008)	International	Cost, Time	Yes	No	Centralized	Yes	Yes	Offline, Static
Ziliaskopoulos (2000)	-	Time	No	Yes	Centralized	No	Yes	Offline, Static
Bookbinder (1998)	International	Cost, Time	No	No	Centralized	No	Yes	Offline, Static
Barnhart (1993)	National	Cost	No	No	Centralized	Yes	Yes	Offline, Static
Min (1991)	International	Cost, Time, Risk	No	No	Centralized	No	Yes	Offline Static

5.1   Distinct aspects

Typically, global transportation can be divided into international and national/inland transport [35]. The literatures that researched on international transportation normally regard truck as the only transport mode in inland transportation [7,10,11,20]. With the development of hinterland terminal, researchers begin to focus on the combinations of truck, train and barge in inland transportation [6,19,37].

Due to the perishable and dynamic characteristics of agri-food, the objectives of OIRC problem consists of reducing logistics cost, preserving product quality and reducing emissions. This problem thus belongs to multi-objective planning problem. Multi-objective planning is more complex than single objective planning. One method is to assign different weights for different objectives, and then summarizes these objectives as a single objective [10]. Another method is to solve all the single objective respectively while others are assigned as constrains. Pareto optimum solutions can be attained by optimisation and composition method[11].

Time constraints can be described either implicitly or explicitly. Time window [6] explicitly represents time constrains, while total transport time limitation [7] is implicitly. The time windows of terminals, services and orders both have important influences on route decision. For agri-food, total transport time limitation is critical because of the perishable characteristic.

Time-varying network has developed fast recently. Transport cost, transport time and environment temperature normally change with time [41]. Time expanded network is an extended graph based on time and space information. Under time expanded network, the shortest path with time windows is easy to find [18].

According to Table 3, we can find that both of these literatures proposed centralized model. As computation size increases, distributed model promotes better performance than centralized model [12,16]. Furthermore, the stakeholders of global cold chain tends be to distributed worldwide, distributed model is more practical.

5.2   General aspects

As for the multi-pattern aspect, it refers to the demand patterns of customer. Different patterns correspond to different information about origination, destination, container volume and time windows. Only Riessen [37], Chang [10] and Barnhart [5] considered multiple demand patterns in the intermodal routing choice model.

With the increasing of transfer number, the OIRC model becomes NP-hard problem [19]. An effective algorithm is significant for computational efficiency. Researchers proposed different algorithms recently, like decision tree [36], k-shortest algorithm [19], rolling horizon [18] and decomposition algorithm [10].

Typically, intermodal routing choice problem is static and offline [5,7,10,11,20]. The planning horizon used to be one day. The intermodal planning system assume all the information of shippers and carriers are accessed before the planning horizon [5]. However, in practice, it is difficult to achieve or predict all the information before planning [6]. Thus, dynamic/real-time routing choice is critical in synchromodal transportation [36].

5.3   Discussion

Based on above analysis, we conclude that OIRC problem for global cold chains is still challenging. To our best knowledge, none of these literatures consider both the aspects of dynamic/real-time, distributed/peer-to peer, transfer and time-varying network. What's more, none of them consider the characteristics of global cold chain. As OIRC problem in synchormodal transportation is NP-hard problem, only sub-optimal algorithm can obtained by using heuristic algorithms. As a result, how to improve the computation efficiency and effectiveness simultaneously deserve further research.

6   Conclusion

Temperature controlled transportation of perishables plays a key role in global cold chains. Synchromodal transportation is an effective method, which characterized by flexibility, reliability and sustainability. However, limited articles have published about the cold chain perspective, an integral analysis is missing.

In order to analyze the characteristic and challenges of synchromodal transportation in global cold chains, we have discussed the critical successful factors at first. We found that information technology and horizontal collaboration are the foundation factors, while service-based pricing strategy plays as an incentive. Integrated planning model is essential, and real-time switching is the most challenging factor.

After that, we have further discussed the planning problems in three different levels. Strategic infrastructure network design problem refers to hub location and processing factories location. Tactical service network design problem decides mode routes and the frequency of services. Operational intermodal routing choice problem aims at real-time matching different orders with different mode combinations. While infrastructure network design problem and service network design problem focus on infrastructures and services, respectively, operation intermodal routing choice problem researches on the decision of orders.

In our future work, we will focus on the operational intermodal routing choice problem under synchromodality. We call it mode matching problem in our project. First, we will research on dynamic/real-time mode matching problem. Rolling horizon framework and decision tree are potential tools. Second, the multi-hop transfer will be considered to improve matching rate. Since the problem is NP-hard problem, heuristics algorithm will be used. After that, we prefer to focus on distributed/peer-to-peer mode matching. Agent-based modelling tends to be an effective method. Finally, considering the practical factors, time-vary travel time and temperature deserve further research. Time-expanded network will be used based on time, temperature and location information.

Acknowledgments. This research is financially supported by the China Scholarship Council under Grant 201606950003.

References

1. Agatz, N. A. H., Erera, A. L., Wang, X. (2011). Dynamic ride-sharing: A simulation study in metro Atlanta. Transportation Research Part B: Methodological, 45(9), 1450-1464.
2. Ahumada, O., & Villalobos, J. R. (2011). A tactical model for planning the production and distribution of fresh produce. Annals of Operations Research, 190(1), 339-358.
3. Akhtar, P., Tse, Y. K., Khan, Z., & Rao-Nicholson, R. (2016). Data-driven and adaptive leadership contributing to sustainability: global agri-food supply chains connected with emerging markets. International Journal of Production Economics, 181, 392-401.
4. Akkerman, R., Farahani, P., & Grunow, M. (2010). Quality, safety and sustainability in food distribution: a review of quantitative operations management approaches and challenges. Or Spectrum, 32(4), 863-904.
5. Barnhart, C., & Ratliff, H. D. (1993). Modeling intermodal routing. Journal of Business logistics, 14(1), 205.
6. Behdani, B., Fan, Y., Wiegmans, B., & Zuidwijk, R. (2014). Multimodal schedule design for synchromodal freight transport systems.
7. Bookbinder, J. H., & Fox, N. S. (1998). Intermodal routing of Canada–Mexico shipments under NAFTA. Transportation Research Part E: Logistics and Transportation Review, 34(4), 289-303.
8. Bortolini, M., Faccio, M., Ferrari, E., Gamberi, M., & Pilati, F. (2016). Fresh food sustainable distribution: cost, delivery time and carbon footprint three-objective optimization. Journal of Food Engineering, 174, 56-67.
9. Brundtland, G. H., & Khalid, M. (1987). Our common future. New York.
10. Chang, T.-S. (2008). Best routes selection in international intermodal networks. Computers & operations research, 35(9), 2877-2891.
11. Cho, J. H., Kim, H. S., & Choi, H. R. (2012). An intermodal transport network planning algorithm using dynamic programming—a case study: from Busan to Rotterdam in intermodal freight routing. Applied Intelligence, 36(3), 529-541.
12. Di Febbraro, A., Sacco, N., & Saeednia, M. (2016). An agent-based framework for cooperative planning of intermodal freight transport chains. Transportation Research Part C: Emerging Technologies, 64, 72-85.
13. Doukidis, G. I., Matopoulos, A., Vlachopoulou, M., Manthou, V., & Manos, B. (2007). A conceptual framework for supply chain collaboration: empirical evidence from the agrifood industry. Supply Chain Management: An International Journal, 12(3), 177-186.
14. European Commission. Illustrated glossary for transport statistics. Belgium. 2009.
15. EUROSTAT. http://ec.europa.eu/eurostat/data/database. 2016
16. Li, L., Negenborn, R. R., & De Schutter, B. (2016). Distributed model predictive control for cooperative synchromodal freight transport. Transportation Research Part E: Logistics and Transportation Review.
17. Lin, X., Negenborn, R. R., & Lodewijks, G. (2016). Towards Quality-aware Control of Perishable Goods in Synchromodal Transport Networks. IFAC, 49(16), 132-137.
18. Masoud, N., & Jayakrishnan, R. (2017). A decomposition algorithm to solve the multi-hop Peer-to-Peer ride-matching problem. Transportation Research Part B: Methodological, 99.
19. Mes, M. R., & Iacob, M.-E. (2016). Synchromodal transport planning at a logistics service provider Logistics and Supply Chain Innovation (pp. 23-36): Springer.
20. Min, H. (1991). International intermodal choices via chance-constrained goal programming. Transportation Research Part A: General, 25(6), 351-362.
21. Pfoser, S., Schauer, O. (2016). Critical Success Factors of Synchromodality: Results from a Case Study and Literature Review. Transportation Research Procedia, 14, 1463-1471.

22. Pieters, R., van Beek, P., Glöckner, H.-H., Omta, O., & Weijers, S. (2017). Innovative Approaches to Improve Sustainability of Physical Distribution in Dutch Agrifood Supply Chains Efficiency in Sustainable Supply Chain (pp. 31-52): Springer.
23. Putz, L.-M., Haider, C., Haller, A., & Schauer, O. (2015). Identifying Key Enablers for Synchromodal Transport Chains in Central Europe. Paper presented at the Proceedings of the WCTRS SIGA2 2015 Conference, Antwerpen, Belgien.
24. Reis, V. (2015). Should we keep on renaming a+ 35-year-old baby? Journal of Transport Geography, 46, 173-179.
25. Riessen, B. V., Negenborn, Lodewijks, G. (2015). Service network design for an intermodal container network with flexible transit times and the possibility of using subcontracted transport. International Journal of Shipping and Transport Logistics, 7(4), 457-478.
26. Rivera, A. P., & Mes, M. (2016). Service and transfer selection for freights in a synchromodal network. International Conference on Computational Logistics.
27. Singh, P., van Sinderen, M., & Wieringa, R. (2016). Synchromodal Transport: Prerequisites, Activities and Effects. Paper presented at the ILS Conference.
28. Southworth, F., & Peterson, B. E. (2000). Intermodal and international freight network modeling. Transportation Research Part C: Emerging Technologies, 8(1), 147-166.
29. SteadieSeifi, M., Dellaert, N. P., Raoufi, R. (2014). Multimodal freight transportation planning: A literature review. European Journal of Operational Research, 233(1), 1-15.
30. Tavasszy, L. A., Behdani, B., & Konings, R. (2015). Intermodality and synchromodality.
31. Van Der Burg, M. (2012). Synchromodal transport for the horticulture industry: Erasmus University.
32. Van Der Vorst, J. G., Ossevoort, R., De Keizer, M., Van Woensel, T., Verdouw, C. N., Van Willegen, R. (2016). DAVINC3I: Towards Collaborative Responsive Logistics Networks in Floriculture Logistics and Supply Chain Innovation (pp. 37-53): Springer.
33. Van Der Vorst, J. G., Peeters, L., & Bloemhof, J. M. (2013). Sustainability assessment framework for food supply chain logistics: empirical findings from dutch food industry. Proceedings in Food System Dynamics, 480-491.
34. Van Der Vorst, J. G., Tromp, S.-O., & Zee, D.-J. v. d. (2009). Simulation modelling for food supply chain redesign; integrated decision making on product quality, sustainability and logistics. International Journal of Production Research, 47(23), 6611-6631.
35. Van Riessen, B., Negenborn, R. R., & Dekker, R. (2015). Synchromodal container transportation: an overview of current topics and research opportunities. Paper presented at the International Conference on Computational Logistics.
36. Van Riessen, B., Negenborn, R. R., & Dekker, R. (2016). Real-time container transport planning with decision trees based on offline obtained optimal solutions. Decision Support Systems, 89, 1-16.
37. Van Riessen, B., Negenborn, R. R., Lodewijks, G., & Dekker, R. (2015). Impact and relevance of transit disturbances on planning in intermodal container networks using disturbance cost analysis. Maritime Economics & Logistics, 17(4), 440-463.
38. Yu, M., & Nagurney, A. (2013). Competitive food supply chain networks with application to fresh produce. European Journal of Operational Research, 224(2), 273-282.
39. Zhang, G., Habenicht, W., W. E. (2003). Improving the structure of deep frozen and chilled food chain with tabu search procedure. Journal of Food Engineering, 60(1), 67-79.
40. Zhang, M., & Pel, A. (2016). Synchromodal hinterland freight transport: model study for the port of Rotterdam. Journal of Transport Geography, 52, 1-10.
41. Ziliaskopoulos, A., & Wardell, W. (2000). An intermodal optimum path algorithm for multimodal networks with dynamic arc travel times and switching delays. European Journal of Operational Research, 125(3), 486-502.

Transportation, Logistics and Supply Chain Planning

Stochastic Programming for Global Supply Chain Planning Under Uncertainty: An Outline

Yingjie Fan[1,3], Frank Schwartz[1], Stefan Voß[1], and David L. Woodruff[2]

[1] IWI, University of Hamburg, 20146 Hamburg, Germany,
{fan.yingjie, frank.schwartz, stefan.voss}@uni-hamburg.de,
[2] University of California, Davis, CA 95616, USA,
dlwoodruff@ucdavis.edu,
[3] Xuzhou University of Technology, Xuzhou 221008, Jiangsu, China

Abstract. When supply chain networks become more complex through the application of modern trends such as outsourcing and global marketing, supply chains become more uncertain. Supply chain planning under uncertainty is a challenge for decision makers. Without considering uncertainties in supply chain planning, global supply chains may suffer enormous economic costs. When probability distributions for uncertain parameters can be estimated, stochastic programming can be used for capturing the characteristics of uncertainties and generating flexible production and transportation plans for global supply chains. This paper presents an outline on how to use stochastic programming for decision support under uncertainty. This includes a high level exposition of how to quantify uncertainties, develop stochastic programming models, generate representative scenarios, apply algorithms for model solving, undertake experimental design and present computational results. Through exemplifying supply chain planning and decision making under uncertainty by using stochastic programming, this paper aims to provide a valuable reference for future research in this area.

Keywords: stochastic programming, supply chain planning, decision making, uncertainty

1 Introduction

With larger and more complex networks, global supply chains (SCs) become more uncertain and unpredictable. Without effective risk mitigation strategies, SCs are vulnerable in uncertain environments. In this paper, uncertainty means that some of the problem data can be represented as random variables. When supply chain (SC) uncertainties can be quantified by random variables, stochastic programming can be used for providing flexible SC plans which helps to mitigate negative impacts from uncertainties in environments with stochastic disruption risks. For a SC where decisions are made or plans are revised periodically with updated information, stochastic programming can be used for

T. Bektaş et al. (Eds.), ICCL 2017, LNCS 10572, pp. 437–451, 2017.
https://doi.org/10.1007/978-3-319-68496-3_29

SC decision support in a rolling horizon approach. The aim of stochastic programming is to find an optimal decision in problems involving uncertain data. The treatment of uncertainties depends on the moment when the information becomes available (Birge and Louveaux, 1997).

Although research in the area of SC management is increasing, there is a clear research gap in quantitative analyses for global SC uncertainties, especially for SC disruption risks. In order to boost research in this domain, based on the authors' recent research (Fan et al., 2016, 2017a,b), this paper reviews how to use stochastic programming for supply chain planning under uncertain environments. This introduction addresses the issues:

- how to build stochastic programming models for global SCs under uncertainties,
- how to solve a related model,
- how to design computational experiments, and
- how to analyze and present computational results.

SC uncertainties may include, e.g., customer demand fluctuations, disruption risks at SC partner companies as well as transportation delays. In order to include uncertainties in the process of SC plan generation, these uncertainties should be quantified in advance. Based on historical records analytics, customer demand can be expressed with probability distribution functions. For disruption risks and transportation delays, the lasting time of negative impacts and the point in time of occurrence can be characterized according to historical records as well as real time information. With quantified SC risks, a mathematical model can be developed for a global SC.

The rest of this paper is organized as follows: Stochastic programming and other methods for decision support in uncertain environments are reviewed and compared in Section 2. A two-stage stochastic programming model can be developed by incorporating uncertainties in the second stage. The basic model and the principles for setting up stages are introduced in Section 3. *PySP*, an open-source framework for modeling and solving stochastic programs with a Progressive Hedging Algorithm (*PHA*), can be used for solving the model. Both the algorithm as well as user-defined parameters of the algorithm are explained in Section 4. When the number of possible realizations for uncertainties (scenarios) of a model is large, only a limited number of realizations and therefore only a subset of all possible scenarios is taken into consideration in the computational analyses. These scenarios are called *representative scenarios*. In this case, a *representative scenario* generation method is needed. Different scenario generation methods and their applicable scales are presented in Section 5. In computational experiments, benchmark solutions can be calculated for comparison. Different benchmarks are provided in Section 6. After solving a stochastic programming model, a solution can be evaluated through simulating the solution with a large number of scenarios generated with Monte Carlo sampling for simulating possible realizations. A flowchart is presented to illustrate how to design computational experiments. This paper ends with the conclusions in Section 7.

2   Literature Review

Usually most natural and man-made catastrophes cannot be precisely and accurately predicted, especially with a comparatively long prediction lead time. However, by utilizing big data analytics and other advanced prediction techniques, the probability distribution of occurrence and/or the severity can be predicted for an increasing number of catastrophes, e.g., extreme weathers (Fan et al., 2015). A range of approaches is available for making use of imperfect prediction information for decision support, (e.g., stochastic programming, robust optimization, metaheuristics and simulation-optimization approaches. These approaches are briefly sketched in this section.

When uncertainties can be quantified by random variables, stochastic programming can be used for capturing the essence of uncertainties. *PHA* proposed by Rockafellar and Wets (1991) is a scenario-based decomposition technique for solving stochastic programming problems. In a stochastic programming model, random variables can take on numerous values. It may not be possible and reasonable to take all those values into consideration for solving the model. In many cases, characteristics of uncertainties can be captured by specifying a reasonable number of *representative scenarios* (Løkketangen and Woodruff, 1996). *Out-of-sample* simulation is used for evaluating the quality of solutions generated from *representative scenarios*.

When the prediction information is only known in the form of interval values without the probability distribution of random data, a robust optimization can be implemented. A robustness approach aims at finding solutions that hedge against the worst contingency that may arise (Goren and Sabuncuoglu, 2008; Yu, 1997). The *minmax* criterion can be used for quantifying robustness of a decision.

Approximate solutions of optimization problems can be efficiently produced by using metaheuristics. Metaheuristics benefit from different random-search and parallel paradigms, but they frequently assume that the problem inputs, the objective function, and the set of constraints are deterministic (Caserta and Voß, 2010; Juan et al., 2015).

The computing time for solving large-scale models for real-world problems, such as transportation, production, finance and telecommunication problems, is comparatively long. In order to obtain high-quality solutions for large-scale stochastic problems with a short computing time, simulation-optimization approaches have attracted an increasing number of researchers' attentions (Gosavi, 2015; Juan et al., 2015). Although an optimal solution might not be produced in this way, obtaining an approximate solution for an accurate model of a real system is more meaningful than obtaining the optimal solution for an oversimplified model.

In Fan et al. (2016, 2017a,b), stochastic programming is used for global SCs in environments with stochastic disruption risks. Medium-scale stochastic programming models are investigated in the first two papers and a large-scale stochastic programming model is developed in the latter. The large-scale model is solved by running *PySP* on a High-Performance Computing (HPC) cluster.

Stochastic programming is also used by Haugen et al. (2001), Veliz et al. (2015) and Gade et al. (2016) for lot-sizing and forest planning problems.

In the sequel we explain how to use stochastic programming for SC planning in environments with stochastic disruption risks. A *PHA* according to Rockafellar and Wets (1991) is employed for solving stochastic programming models. Monte Carlo simulation is applied for generating *out-of-sample* scenarios for evaluating the quality of solutions.

3   A Basic Two-Stage Stochastic Programming Model

Two-stage stochastic programming models are widely applied for decision support in uncertain environments. The decision maker takes some action in the first stage in the presence of uncertainties about future realizations. *Recourse decisions* can then be made in the second stage after uncertainties are disclosed.

For a SC, plans for the coming time period (the first-stage decision) are made without perfect information for future realizations. The first-stage decision should be ideal for all those possible realizations. When uncertainties are revealed, additional decisions (*recourse decisions*) can be taken. A *recourse decision* may concern SC plans for the subsequent time period with the knowledge of uncertainties for the coming time period or emergency plans when disruptive events arise. A *recourse decision* depends on the realization of the uncertainty. For a two-stage stochastic programming model for a SC, the overall objective is to minimize the cost of the first-stage decision plus the expected costs over the uncertain scenarios.

Let us focus on two-stage stochastic programming models for global SCs. In order to explain the basic model, the following notation is used:

$\mathcal{S}$	:	The set of possible scenarios
s	:	An individual scenario, $s \in \mathcal{S}$
x	:	The first-stage decision variable
y_s	:	The second-stage decision variable in scenario $s \in \mathcal{S}$
c	:	The first-stage cost coefficient
f_s	:	The second-stage cost coefficient in scenario $s \in \mathcal{S}$
R_s	:	The probability of occurrence of scenario $s \in \mathcal{S}$, $\sum_{s \in \mathcal{S}} R_s = 1$
$\mathcal{Q}_s$	:	The set of constraints in scenario $s \in \mathcal{S}$
T_s^{bang}	:	The point in time of occurrence of a disruptive event in scenario $s \in \mathcal{S}$
T_s^{dur}	:	The duration of negative impacts once a disruption arises in scenario $s \in \mathcal{S}$

Note that x, y_s, c and f_s are vectors. The basic model can be mathematically described as follows (Birge and Louveaux, 1997; Kall and Wallace, 1994):

$$\min_{x,y_s} c \cdot x + \sum_{s \in \mathcal{S}} (R_s \cdot f_s \cdot y_s) \qquad (1)$$

$$\text{subject to: } (x, y_s) \in \mathcal{Q}_s \quad \forall s \in \mathcal{S}$$

Each scenario represents a possible realization in the future. The first-stage decision variable, x, is unified for all scenarios. The second-stage variable, y_s, is scenario-specific with the associated cost coefficient f_s. Problem (1) is the well-known extensive form of a two-stage stochastic program.

In order to develop a quantitative analysis of catastrophic disruptions as a stochastic programming problem, each scenario s can be characterized by three parameters: the probability of occurrence (R_s), the point in time of occurrence (T_s^{bang}) and the duration of negative impacts (T_s^{dur}). Parameters for each scenario $s \in S$ of our investigation are included both in the cost coefficient vector and in the constraints (see (2) and (3)). In this paper, a scenario with a disruption is called a disruptive scenario. A scenario without a disruption is called a non-disruptive scenario.

$$f_s \leftarrow \left(T_s^{bang}, T_s^{dur}\right) \tag{2}$$

$$\mathcal{Q}_s \leftarrow \left(T_s^{bang}, T_s^{dur}\right) \tag{3}$$

The overall probability of all disruptive scenarios for a time-span is assumed to be predictable according to the historical records. The point in time of occurrence (T_s^{bang}) can be assumed to be uniformly distributed within a time-span. The duration of negative impacts (T_s^{dur}) depends on the severity of a disruption and the flexibility of a SC and is assumed to be exponentially distributed.

When specifying the stages, according to the statements above, the first-stage decision is identical for all future realizations and the second-stage decisions depend on the particular realizations. For a two-stage stochastic programming model, the principle of setting up stages is that the first stage is scenario-independent and the second stage is scenario-dependent. Based on this principle, two approaches of setting up stages for our stochastic programming models are introduced:

1. **According to the time line**
   This approach fits for predictable disasters. According to the description in Fan et al. (2017b), probability predictions for predictable disasters are available a certain period of time in advance. Updated predictions become available before the occurrence of a disaster. With periodically updated predictions for disruptions, stages for stochastic programming models can be set up according to the time line. In this case, decisions are periodically updated according to a rolling horizon scheme.

2. **According to uncertainty related and unrelated costs**
   This approach fits for disasters which we call half-predictable disasters. In Fan et al. (2017b), half-predictable disasters are those for which a probability of occurrence can be estimated a proper period of time in advance. The point in time of occurrence of a half-predictable disaster cannot be predicted in advance. In this situation, stages should be set up in a way that uncertainty related costs are assigned to the second stage and costs that are not related to uncertainty are assigned to the first stage.

Algorithm 1: Progressive Hedging Algorithm (PHA)

1   $k \leftarrow 0$

2   **for** $s \in \mathcal{S}$ **do**

3     $x_s^{(k)} \leftarrow \operatorname{argmin}_{x, y_s} \left(c \cdot x + f_s \cdot y_s \right) : (x, y_s) \in \mathcal{Q}_s$

4   $\bar{x}^{(k)} \leftarrow \sum_{s \in \mathcal{S}} R_s \cdot x_s^{(k)}$

5   **for** $s \in \mathcal{S}$ **do**

6     $w_s^{(k)} \leftarrow \rho \left(x_s^{(k)} - \bar{x}^{(k)} \right)$

7   $k \leftarrow k + 1$

8   **for** $s \in \mathcal{S}$ **do**

9     $x_s^{(k)} \leftarrow \operatorname{argmin}_{x, y_s} \left(c \cdot x + w_s^{(k-1)} x + \rho/2 \left\| x - \bar{x}^{(k-1)} \right\|^2 + f_s \cdot y_s \right) : (x, y_s) \in$
    $\mathcal{Q}_s$

10   $\bar{x}^{(k)} \leftarrow \sum_{s \in \mathcal{S}} R_s \cdot x_s^{(k)}$

11   **for** $s \in \mathcal{S}$ **do**

12     $w_s^{(k)} \leftarrow w_s^{(k-1)} + \rho \left(x_s^{(k)} - \bar{x}^{(k)} \right)$

13   $g^{(k)} \leftarrow \sum_{x \in \mathcal{S}} R_s \cdot \left\| x_s^{(k)} - \bar{x}^{(k)} \right\|$

14   **if** $g^{(k)} \leq \epsilon$ **then**

15   terminate.

16   **else**

17   **if** $k = K$ **then**

18   terminate and implement a local search to find an identical feasible
      solution for x.

19   **else**

20   go to 7

---

4   Progressive Hedging Algorithm and PySP

In this section, the *PHA* proposed by Rockafellar and Wets (1991) as well as
PySP are introduced. *PHA* is implemented for solving stochastic problems in
different areas, i.e., Haugen et al. (2001), Watson and Woodruff (2011), Veliz
et al. (2015) and Gade et al. (2016). In these papers, *PHA* is proven to be an
effective method for solving stochastic programming models.

For the optimization problem in Section 3, the basic *PHA* can be stated in
Algorithm 1, taking a penalty factor $\rho > 0$, a termination threshold ϵ, and a
maximum number of iterations K as input parameters.

PHA is embedded in *PySP*, an open-source framework for modeling and solving stochastic programs in Python. In this framework, the *runph* script provides
a command-line interface to solve stochastic programming models with *PHA*.

When *PySP* is implemented for solving stochastic programming models, the
maximum number of iterations K and the value of ρ are user-defined parameters.
Effective methods for determining element-specific $\rho(i)$ values based on problem-
specific data are developed in Watson and Woodruff (2011). For independent

integer variables, we have:

$$\rho\left(i\right) \leftarrow \frac{c\left(i\right)}{x^{max} + x^{min} + 1} \tag{4}$$

For independent continuous variables, $\rho(i)$ is calculated by:

$$\rho\left(i\right) \leftarrow \frac{c\left(i\right)}{max\left(\left(\sum_{s \in \mathcal{S}} R_s \cdot |x_s^{(0)} - \bar{x}^{(0)}|\right), 1\right)} \tag{5}$$

Element-specific $\rho\left(i\right)$ values are implemented for stochastic programming models in Fan et al. (2016, 2017a,b).

The intention of solving a stochastic programming model with *PySP* is to find a good quality feasible solution, rather than obtaining a provably optimal solution. In particular, it may not be possible to find an optimal solution and prove optimality for a stochastic programming model for a global SC. For SC planning problems, feasible and good quality solutions generated within a reasonable time frame are meaningful and valuable in practice.

5   Scenario Generation

For two-stage stochastic programming models with a small number of possible realizations, the list of all possible realizations can be incorporated in the solution process for stochastic programming problems. For problem instances with a large number of possible realizations for the second stage, it is more efficient to include a certain number of representative possible realizations (*in-sample* scenarios) than to incorporate all possible realizations in the solution process. When different *representative scenarios* are used, the solutions are probably different. In this section, methods for generating *representative scenarios* for capturing characteristics of uncertainties are investigated.

For a stochastic programming model with multiple uncertain parameters, *representative scenarios* are composed by uncertain parameters' *representative values*. The probability for each scenario is deduced from probabilities of *representative values*. Three methods for generating *representative values* for uncertain parameters are presented in this section. In order to exemplify these methods, the duration T^{dur} in Fan et al. (2016) is taken as an example. T^{dur} is the duration of negative impacts for a global SC in case of a disruption which is assumed to be exponentially distributed and uncorrelated with other uncertain parameters (see Fig. 1). Uncertainties are assumed to be uncorrelated for low frequency and high impact SC disruptions because the probability for the occurrence of more than one disruption at the same time period is extremely low. It is possible to explore SCs with complicated multiple intercorrelated uncertainties with Monte Carlo sampling which will be introduced in this section.

Different methods are implemented for generating *representative values* for the uncertain parameter T^{dur}. For scenario s, the value of T^{dur} is indicated by T_s^{dur}. In Fig. 2–5, the values of $T_s^{dur}(s \in \mathcal{S})$ generated with different methods

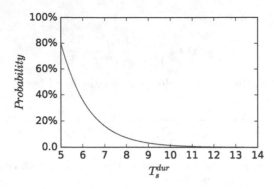

Fig. 1. Probability distribution

are presented. T_s^{bang} ($s \in \mathcal{S}$) in the basic model in Section 3 can be calculated with the same methods.

1. **Selecting equal probability values**
   By splitting the probability distribution of an uncertain parameter into a number of equal probability segments, the medians of these segments can be selected as *representative values*. The median is the value that splits the probability distribution into two portions whose areas are identical. Representative values selected in this way have the same probability.

   Fig. 2 shows 5 and 10 *representative values*, which are generated with this method for T^{dur}. The probabilities for *representative values*, in case of $T_{Num}^{dur} = 5$ and $T_{Num}^{dur} = 10$, are 20% and 10%, respectively. However, this method need not work for generating discrete *representative values*.

2. **Selecting representative values and calculating probabilities**
   For a discrete parameter, *representative values* can be selected at first. In order to calculate the probability of these *representative values*, the probability distribution is split into segments in a way that each *representative value* is the median or close to the median of a segment. The overall probability of a segment is the probability of the *representative value* in this segment.

   Fig. 3 gives examples of *representative values* and probabilities generated with this method when T_{Num}^{dur} is 5 and 10. In order to assure that each *representative value* is the median of a segment, in Fig. 3 *representative values* and segments are alternately selected from the left side to the right side one by one. The right frontier of the previous segment is the left frontier of the next segment. This method is implemented in Fan et al. (2016).

3. **Monte Carlo sampling**
   An easy way for generating *representative values* for uncertain parameters is to use Monte Carlo sampling. With an uncertain parameter's probability distribution function as the input, *representative values* can be generated by using statistical functions of *SciPy*, which is a collection of mathematical algorithms and functions built in *Python*. Representative values generated with

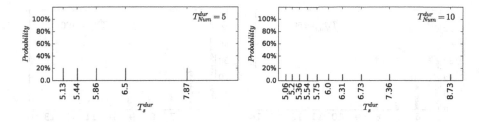

Fig. 2. *Representative values* with equal probability

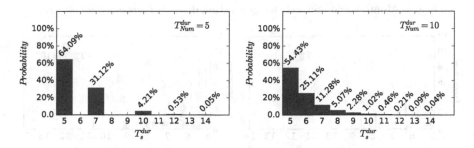

Fig. 3. Discrete *representative values* and their probabilities

Monte Carlo sampling have equal probability. With probability distribution functions, Monte Carlo sampling can also be used for generating *representative values* for multi-dimensional correlated random variables which makes it possible to explore SC planning problems with intercorrelated and real world uncertainties (Joy et al., 1996; Touran and Wiser, 1992).

Representative values and their frequencies generated with Monte Carlo sampling for uncertain parameters are shown in Fig. 4 and Fig. 5. Monte Carlo sampling also fits for uncertain parameters with a large number of dimensions, e.g., the customer demand for each production at each seller in each time period (Fan et al., 2017b).

In order to test the quality of a solution for a stochastic programming model, a number of *out-of-sample* scenarios is required for simulating possible realizations. When Monte Carlo sampling is adopted, it is more accurate to simulate the reality with a larger number of *out-of-sample* scenarios (see Fig. 6). For instance, 500 or 1000 scenarios may be generated with Monte Carlo sampling for simulating possible realizations.

6   Benchmarks

As mentioned in Section 4, the intention of solving stochastic programming models for global SCs is to obtain high quality feasible solutions. Instead of proving optimality, we demonstrate the quality of solutions from stochastic programming

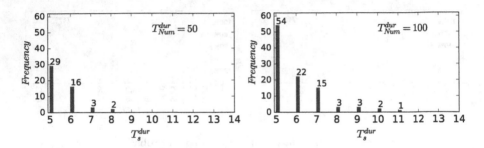

Fig. 4. Monte Carlo methods for generating discrete *representative values*

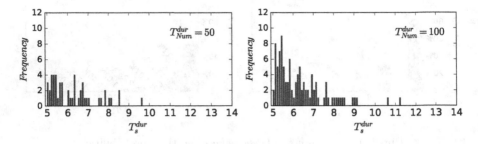

Fig. 5. Monte Carlo methods for generating *representative values*

through comparing with different benchmark solutions. In our previous research, solutions for stochastic programming models generated with *PySP* based on *representative scenarios* are always superior to benchmark solutions. In this section, we describe decision makers with four different attitudes to deal with risk, which are pessimistic, moderate, optimistic and rational attitudes. In the following, the assumptions for these attitudes are introduced (Fan et al., 2017b):

1. **Pessimistic (*pess*)**
   Decision makers with pessimistic attitudes prepare for the worst possible catastrophe, which is characterized by the longest duration and the earli-

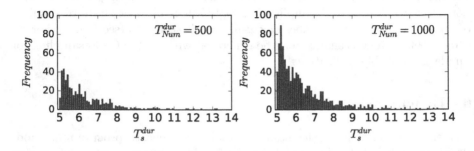

Fig. 6. Monte Carlo methods for generating a large set of *out-of-sample* values

est time of occurrence. f^{pess} and Q^{pess} indicate the parameter set and the constraints set for the worst possible catastrophe.

2. **Moderate (mod)**
Decision makers with moderate attitudes believe that a moderate catastrophe will happen. The moderate catastrophe has the mean duration and the mean occurrence time. f^{mod} and Q^{mod} indicate the parameter set and the constraints set for the moderate catastrophe.

3. **Optimistic (opt)**
Decision makers with optimistic attitudes believe that catastrophes will never happen. They anticipate catastrophes in no way. For this type of decision makers, disruptions appear to be totally unpredictable in the first stage. f^{opt} and Q^{opt} indicate the parameter set and the constraints set for a case without the occurrence of any catastrophe.

4. **Rational (sp)**
Decision makers with rational attitudes are aware of the fact that catastrophes may be of different severities. Probability distributions of their time of occurrence and duration are incorporated in a stochastic programming model for decision support.

In addition, the expected value of *wait-and-see* (*ws*) solutions for each problem instance represents a lower bound. The *ws* solution represents an ideal situation that all uncertainty will be resolved before decisions have to be made. For the sake of a compact presentation, we treat *ws* as an additional element for the set of attitudes. We use a set $\mathcal{U} = \{pess, mod, opt, sp, ws\}$ to indicate solutions introduced above.

A large set of *out-of-sample* scenarios is generated with Monte Carlo sampling for simulating possible realizations (see Section 5). Solutions by solving a stochastic programming model (*SP* solutions) and solutions for decision makers with different attitudes are tested with these scenarios. Ω indicates the set of *out-of-sample* scenarios. g_ω indicates the parameter set for each scenario $\omega \in \Omega$. The size of Ω is N. The expected value of *ws* solutions is calculated by (6). The expected values of solutions for decision makers with different attitudes are deduced from (8).

1. **Expected value of *wait-and-see* solutions**
A *ws* solution is generated until an observation of the uncertainty is made (Madansky, 1960). The expected value of *ws* solutions for *representative scenarios* can be obtained by:

$$EV_{ws} = \frac{1}{N} \sum_{\omega \in \Omega} \left[\min_{x, y_\omega} \left(c \cdot x + g_\omega \cdot y_\omega \right) \right] \qquad (6)$$

As mentioned in Section 5, scenarios generated with Monte Carlo sampling have the same probability. Thus, the probability for each scenario is $\frac{1}{N}$.

2. **Expected value of solutions for decision makers with different attitudes**

The *pess*, *mod* and *opt* solutions are obtained by solving the model in (1) with a single scenario. f^{pess}, f^{mod} and f^{opt} are the second-stage parameters. Then the stochastic programming model in (1) is transformed into a deterministic model in (7). x_u^* indicates the first-stage optimal solution for a decision maker with an attitude $u \in \{pess, mod, opt\}$.

$$
x_u^* \leftarrow \min_{x,y} (c \cdot x + f^u \cdot y)
$$
$$
s.t. \quad (x,y) \in Q^u, \quad \forall u \in \{pess, mod, opt\} \tag{7}
$$

Note that the *SP* solution, which is indicated by x_{sp}^*, is not included in (7). x_{sp}^* is deduced by solving the stochastic programming model in (1). The expected value of a solution for a decision maker with an attitude $u \in \{pess, mod, opt, sp\}$ is calculated by:

$$
EV_u = c \cdot x_u^* + \frac{1}{N} \min_{y_\omega} \sum_{\omega \in \Omega} (g_\omega \cdot y_\omega)
$$
$$
s.t. \quad (x_u^*, y_\omega) \in \mathcal{Q}_\omega, \quad \forall u \in \{pess, mod, opt, sp\}, \omega \in \Omega. \tag{8}
$$

GAP_u indicates the gap between the expected value of a solution x_u^* and the expected value of *ws* solutions. It shows the quality of a solution: The smaller GAP_u, the better the solution. GAP_u is calculated by:

$$
GAP_u = \frac{EV_u - EV_{ws}}{EV_{ws}} \tag{9}
$$

In Fig. 7, a flowchart is presented for explaining processes of computational experiments. The following abbreviations are used:

Param(s)	:	Parameter(s)
Probs	:	Probability distribution functions
SimScen	:	Scenarios for simulating possible realizations (*out-of-sample*)
RepScen	:	Representative scenarios for the stochastic programming model (*in-sample*)
DET Model	:	Deterministic model, which is the *SP* model with a single scenario

Incorporating probability distribution functions of uncertain parameters as input, *representative scenarios* ($s \in \mathcal{S}$) and scenarios for simulating possible realizations ($\omega \in \Omega$) can be generated with a *RepScen* Generator and a *SimScen* Generator, respectively. Scenario generation methods for *RepScen* Generators depend on the characteristics of uncertain parameters (see Section 5). Monte Carlo sampling can be used for *SimScen* Generators. For problem instances with a medium-scale of possible realizations, the full list of all possible realizations can be included in set Ω (Fan et al., 2014).

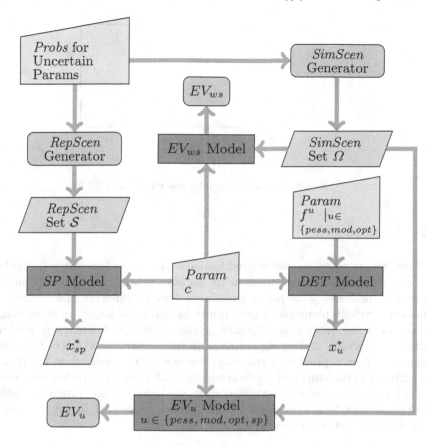

Fig. 7. A flowchart for computational experiments

With *representative scenarios* and the first-stage parameter set c as input, a solution x_{sp}^* for the stochastic programming model can be obtained by using *PySP*. With parameter set f^u and c as input, the first-stage optimal solutions x_u^* for decision makers with attitude $u \in \{pess, mod, opt\}$ are obtained by solving deterministic models (see (7)).

To evaluate the quality of a solution, each solution $x_u^* \mid u \in \{pess, mod, opt, sp\}$ is tested with a large number of scenarios ($\omega \in \Omega$) through an evaluation model. $EV_u \mid u \in \{pess, mod, opt, sp\}$ is calculated according to (8). EV_{ws} is calculated by solving (6). An identical first-stage solution for ws solutions is not required. In order to compare the quality of different solutions, final results can be presented with box plots (see Fig. 8). Another way is calculating GAP_u according to (9) and presenting the obtained values in a table.

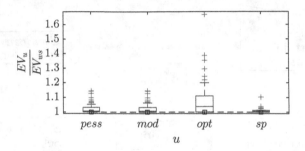

Fig. 8. Presenting results; see Fan et al. (2017a)

7   Conclusion

When we try to realize automated business processes, Industry 4.0, the 5G era or autonomous logistics, autonomous decision making under uncertainty is an essential problem. This paper introduced how to generate and evaluate flexible supply chain plans under uncertainty by using stochastic programming. The framework for supply chain planning problems presented here is a general framework for decision making regarding problems under uncertainty. This paper is meaningful as it provides a valuable reference for the research in the domain of supply chain planning and decision making under uncertainty. For the next step, it is important to develop an autonomous decision making system by combining the framework for supply chain planning with a framework for big data analytics for demand and risk prediction.

Acknowledgements

The author Yingjie Fan acknowledges financial support from the Universtät Hamburg Equal Opportunity Fund.

Bibliography

J. R. Birge and F. V. Louveaux. *Introduction to Stochastic Programming.* Springer, New York, 1997.

M. Caserta and S. Voß. Metaheuristics: Intelligent problem solving. In V. Maniezzo, T. Stützle, and S. Voß, editors, *Matheuristics: Hybridizing Metaheuristics and Mathematical Programming*, pages 1–38. Springer US, 2010.

Y. Fan, F. Schwartz, and S. Voß. Flexible supply chain design under stochastic catastrophic risks. In W. Kersten, T. Blecker, and C. Ringle, editors, *Next Generation Supply Chains*, pages 379–406, Berlin, 2014. Epubli.

Y. Fan, L. Heilig, and S. Voß. Supply chain risk management in the era of big data. *Lecture Notes in Computer Science*, 9186:283–294, 2015.

Y. Fan, F. Schwartz, S. Voß, and D. L. Woodruff. Stochastic programming for flexible global supply chain planning. *Flexible Services and Manufacturing Journal*, pages 1–33, 2016. 10.1007/s10696-016-9261-7.

Y. Fan, F. Schwartz, and S. Voß. Flexible supply chain planning based on variable transportation modes. *International Journal of Production Economics*, 183: 654–666, 2017a.

Y. Fan, F. Schwartz, S. Voß, and D. L. Woodruff. Impacts of catastrophe insurance policies on global supply chain operational planning. Institute of Information Systems, University of Hamburg, 2017b.

D. Gade, G. Hackebeil, S. M. Ryan, J.-P. Watson, R. J.-B. Wets, and D. L. Woodruff. Obtaining lower bounds from the progressive hedging algorithm for stochastic mixed-integer programs. *Mathematical Programming*, 157(1): 47–67, 2016.

S. Goren and I. Sabuncuoglu. Robustness and stability measures for scheduling: single-machine environment. *IIE Transactions*, 40(1):66–83, 2008.

A. Gosavi. *Simulation-Based Optimization*. Springer, Berlin, 2nd edition, 2015.

K. K. Haugen, A. Løkketangen, and D. L. Woodruff. Progressive hedging as a meta-heuristic applied to stochastic lot-sizing. *European Journal of Operational Research*, 132(1):116–122, 2001.

C. Joy, P. P. Boyle, and K. S. Tan. Quasi-Monte Carlo methods in numerical finance. *Management Science*, 42(6):926–938, 1996.

A. A. Juan, J. Faulin, S. E. Grasman, M. Rabe, and G. Figueira. A review of simheuristics: Extending metaheuristics to deal with stochastic combinatorial optimization problems. *Operations Research Perspectives*, 2:62–72, 2015.

P. Kall and S. Wallace. *Stochastic Programming*. Wiley, Chichester, 1994.

A. Løkketangen and D. L. Woodruff. Progressive hedging and tabu search applied to mixed integer (0, 1) multistage stochastic programming. *Journal of Heuristics*, 2(2):111–128, 1996.

A. Madansky. Inequalities for stochastic linear programming problems. *Management Science*, 6(2):197–204, 1960.

R. T. Rockafellar and R. J.-B. Wets. Scenarios and policy aggregation in optimization under uncertainty. *Mathematics of Operations Research*, 16(1): 119–147, 1991.

A. Touran and E. P. Wiser. Monte Carlo technique with correlated random variables. *Journal of Construction Engineering and Management*, 118(2):258–272, 1992.

F. B. Veliz, J.-P. Watson, A. Weintraub, R. J.-B. Wets, and D. L. Woodruff. Stochastic optimization models in forest planning: a progressive hedging solution approach. *Annals of Operations Research*, 232(1):259–274, 2015.

J.-P. Watson and D. L. Woodruff. Progressive hedging innovations for a class of stochastic mixed-integer resource allocation problems. *Computational Management Science*, 8(4):355–370, 2011.

G. Yu. Robust economic order quantity models. *European Journal of Operational Research*, 100(3):482–493, 1997.

Towards the Physical Internet Paradigm: a Model for Transportation Planning in Complex Road Networks with Empty Return Optimization

Claudia Caballini[a], Massimo Paolucci[a], Simona Sacone[a], and Evrim Ursavas[b]

[a]DIBRIS-Department of Informatics, BioEngineering, Robotics
and Systems Engineering, University of Genova, ITALY
{claudia.caballini,massimo.paolucci,simona.sacone}@unige.it
[b] Department of Operations, University of Groningen, THE NETHERLANDS
e.ursavas@rug.nl

Abstract. The Physical Internet paradigm is redsigning the logic of moving goods around the planet, with the goal of making logistics more effective, sustainable and efficient. In this paper a road transportation-network devoted to the PI paradigm is designed, modeled and implemented. The problem deals with groupage transportation, including consolidation and deconsolidation centers in the network nodes where goods are loaded/unloaded in/out from containers. The goal is to serve the demand of some shipment orders belonging to different areas with the final goal of minimizing total costs, exploiting trucks capacity and reducing empty trips. A mixed-integer linear programming (MILP) model is presented and an experimental analysis is provided. The results obtained have shown the effectiveness of the approach proposed.

Keywords: Physical Internet, Road Network, Empty truck return, MIP optimization, Groupage, Social sustainability

1 Introduction

The current logistic system is affected by numerous inefficiencies by disconnecting flows, creating empty movements and producing unuseful storage of goods. [1], [2] and [3] list several symptoms of inefficiency and unsustainability of the current logistic and transportation system, among which we can report the following ones:

- logistic networks are highly fragmented and mostly dedicated to specific organizations or supply chains, which translates in a disconnection of flows.
- Even if transport means share the same road infrastructure, they are dedicated to specific logistics networks and they often travel partially full.
- Empty trips (i.e. travelling without a payload) are not an exception but the norm. Vehicles and containers often travel empty or have to travel additional distances to reach the load to be transported on their way back.

© Springer International Publishing AG 2017
T. Bektaş et al. (Eds.), ICCL 2017, LNCS 10572, pp. 452–467, 2017.
https://doi.org/10.1007/978-3-319-68496-3_30

- Working conditions of truckers are difficult. Being the road transport still highly used to cover long distances, many drivers are forced to spend many hours and days on roads, thus sacrificing their family and social life, and undergoing more easily health and road accidents (in the United States, more than 50 % of truck incidents in the last years are attributable to tiredness and lack of sleep). The serious and chronic problem of high driver turnover rate, with enormous associated costs encountered by the trucking industry, is also pointed out in [6], where the authors consider the strategic design of a relay network that may potentially help to alleviate this problem by providing a network that facilitates an assignment of drivers to their home bases. In such a network, a certain number of relay point locations (i.e. road-road transit points) are determined, as well as the route for each truckload on the network.
- Goods often remain unused, stored where there is no need and not available where they should be.

To improve the way things are travelling and stored around the world, a new way of making logistics has been proposed: the Physical Internet (PI) ([1] - [5]).

The idea of Physical Internet is envisioned to completely change the way of producing and transporting goods around the planet. PI would mimic the way information is packaged, distributed and stored in the virtual world to improve real world logistics ([1]-[4]). Accordingly, representing the virtual data transmission, freight travels from hub to hub in an open network rather than from origin to destination directly. Cargo is routed automatically and, at each segment, is bundled for gaining efficiency.

The literature regarding PI is still scarce. Yang et al. [5] proposed a nonlinear optimization model and a simulated annealing heuristic to investigate inventory management problems for fast-moving consumer goods in the PI, where goods are stored and distributed in an interconnected and open network of hubs. In [7], Sallez et al. focused on the informational context of modular, reusable and smart containers, called PI-containers, specifically dedicated to the PI network. PI can also help enhancing the way things are transported in local areas and cities, as properly highlighted in [8].

Moreover, PI can help reducing the number of empty trips performed by vehicles; in the literature, some interesting contribution on empty transport resources in road transportation are provided, for instance, by Dejax and Cranic [9], Caballini et al. [10], and Schulte et al. [11].

In this paper, groupage activities are considered to exploit truck capacities. In [12], a distributed architecture planning of transportation activities is presented with the goal of better utilizing transport resources by grouping several orders of transport. Wasner and Zapfel [13] tackles the problem of optimally design a depot and hub transportation networks for parcel service providers. For enhancing groupage and collaborative transportation, Vanovermeire and Sorensen [14] proposed a model that integrates a cost allocation method into the optimization of the synchronized consolidation of transportation orders.

The goal of the present paper is to define and model a road network where groupage is encouraged and different road alternatives are permitted, with the final goal of minimizing total costs, exploting truck capacities and minimizing empty return trips.

In this way, negative externalities related to driver conditions are reduced, in terms of better social impacts and exploitation of driving hour rules (which also translates in a better optimization of mandatory breaks).

The remaining of the paper is organized as follows. Section 2 provides a detailed description of the problem, whereas in section 3 the mathematical model is formalized. Section 4 shows the results obtained by running an experimental analysis, and, finally, section 5 discloses some conclusions and presents future research ideas.

2   Problem Description

In the present section, the problem under study is described. The aim is to satisfy some order demands by utilizing groupage technique and providing different road mode alternatives with the final goal of minimizing total costs and total penalty incurred for late order deliver. Moreover, empty trips are also minimized and truck capacity exploited at best.

Figure 1 provides a general sketch of the problem considered: a certain number of orders has to be delivered and each order refers to a transportation demand betweend different areas (for instance, as shown in Figure 1, the origin and destination nodes of order i are located respectively in area 1 and area 2). Moreover, each order is characterized by a feasible topological path, that represents the path formed by an acceptable sequence of nodes: from the source node to the consolidation/deconsolidation node of the source area, to eventually some road-road transit nodes - if the mid-distance road mode is chosen-, to the consolidation/deconsolidation node of the destination area, up to the final destination node. This means, for instance, that the path from a consolidation/deconsolidation node of a certain area to another consolidation/deconsolidation node of the same area is not allowed.

As shown in Figure 1, three different types of nodes are considered: (i) *Origin-Destination (OD)* nodes represent the nodes where boxes/parcels have to be collected or delivered (indicated with blue circles in Fig. 1. Note that each node can be at the same time origin and destination of different orders); (ii) *Consolidation/ Deconsolidation (CD)* nodes, where containers are staffed or stripped with boxes; and (iii) *Road-Road (RR) transit* nodes, in which trailers bringing containers changes their tractor/driver on the different segments of the mid-road transport route (note that each transport route has been assumed to be around 250 km to allow a driver to go back to its origin in a working day of 8 hours).

Moreover, three types of transport modes are considered: (i) *Long-distance road transport*, which refers to long travelling roads that connect one area with another one; (ii) *Mid-distance rode transport* that considers the distance covered by trucks between road-road transit centers and (iii) *Short-distance road trans-port*, which refers to local transportation carried out by vans in local areas to pick up and deliver boxes.

The first and last mile transport to/from consolidation/deconsolidation centers is performed with the short-distance road transport, while the distance between consolidation centers may be covered by using long-distance or mid-distance road transport.

Long and mid-distance road transports are modeled with resources (i.e. trucks) flowing into the network (so allowing minimizing empty trips), while the short-distance road transport is managed with a daily aggregated capacity, in terms of number of vans per each node CD, as it will be better explained in in the next section.

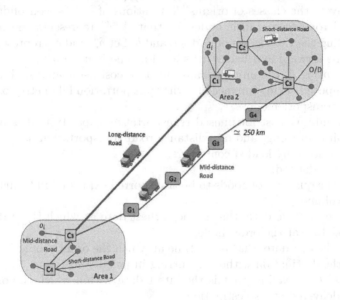

Fig. 1: General representation of the problem

3   Mathematical Formulation

In this section, the problem described above is detailed and stated as a mathematical program.

The problem can be described considering a transportation network whose topology is represented by a directed graph $G = (N, A)$, where N is the set of nodes associated with different locations (i.e., customers, road-road exchange points, consolidation/deconsolidation centers), and A is the set of arcs connecting such locations. The problem consists in serving a set O of transportation orders exploiting the different transportation means available on such network, with the aim of minimizing the overall transportation cost and the total penalty incurred for late order delivery.

In order to formalize the model, the following notation is introduced:

- $N^O \subset N$ and $N^D \subset N$ are respectively the set of origin and destination nodes associated with transportation demand; note that in general $N^O \cap D^D \neq \varnothing$ as a same location can be both origin and destination of orders;
- L the set of local areas where the origins and destinations of orders are located;
- N^I is the set of intermediate nodes defined as $N^I = N \setminus (N^O \cup N^D)$, where $N^I = N^C \cup N^G$, being N^C the set of consolidation/deconsolidation centres and N^G the set of road-road interchange points;
- $A = \cup_{l \in AC} A^l$, with $AC = \{(O,C),(C,G),(G,G)\}$, where O, C, G denotes respectively the classes of origins/destinations of orders, consolidation centres and road-road transit nodes, so that $A^{(a,b)}$ represents the set of arcs connecting the two classes of nodes a and b. Let δ_n^+ and δ_n^- represent respectively the forward and backward star of a generic node n.
- $C_{nm}, (n,m) \in A$, the unitary transportation cost associated with arc (n,m) and computed taking into account the transportation kilometre cost and the type of transport mode;
- C^E, the unitary cost for unused transportation capacity that is introduced to penalize the long- and mid-distance road transportation associated with empty or not fully loaded containers;
- $\forall i \in O$ are defined:
  - Q_i, the quantity of goods to be transported expressed in terms of weight or volume;
  - S_i, the release date, that is the earliest date at which the order can be picked up at the order node;
  - D_i, the due date, that is the time at which the order should be delivered at the destination without incurring in penalty costs;
  - DD_i, the deadline that is the latest date within which the order must be delivered at its destination;
  - C_i^D, the unitary tardiness cost for delivering the order i late respect to its due date;
  - $o_i \in N^O$, $d_i \in N^D$, respectively the origin and destination nodes for order i;
  - $l_i^O, l_i^D \in L$, the local areas to which the origin and destination of order i respectively belong.
  - $A_r^{TR} = \{((n,t),(m,t+T_{n,m}^r)),((m,t),(n,t+T_{n,m}^r)) : t = 1,...,H-T_{n,m}^r\}$, the set of transportation arcs between node n and m in the planning horizon;
  - $A_r^I = \{((n,t),(n,t+1)),((m,t),(m,t+1)) : t = 1,...,H-1\}$, the set of arcs modeling inactivity of the transportation resource, and f_r a final fictitious flow sink node.

A unique transportation mode is associated with each arc. In particular, each arc has a transportation capacity that is considered as an aggregated capacity for short-distance road transportation, i.e., for arcs $(n, m) \in A^{(O,C)}$, whereas associated with specific resources for road long-distance and mid-distance transportation, i.e., $(n, m) \in A \setminus A^{(O,C)}$. Then, the overall set of road transportation resources that are explicitly considered is denoted by R, and the subset of resources of a given mode available for the transport on arc $(n, m) \in A$ is denoted as $R_{n,m} \subseteq R$. Each resource $r \in R$ is hence assumed associated with a single pair of nodes n and m, i.e., it can be used to perform transportation activities between such two nodes.

For each resource r, a maximum transportation capacity C_r^{max} is set. For $r \in R$ a fixed cost C_r^R is paid if the resource is used for transport activities. The travel time needed by a resource $r \in R$ to cover an arc $(n, m) \in A$ is denoted as $T_{n,m}^r$. It is also assumed that the time $T_{n,m}^r$ includes the service time in node m needed for loading and unloading boxes in consolidation/deconsolidation centers (i.e., stuffing and stripping containers) and for changing tractors in road-road transit points.

For each order $i \in O$, a transportation sub-network can be defined as $G_i = (N_i, A_i)$, consisting of the set of feasible paths in G from o_i to d_i.

The planning considers a time horizon H subdivided into a set P of time periods, with $P = \{1 \ldots H\}$. Therefore, associated with each order, a time-space flow network $G_i^T = (N_i^T, A_i^T)$ is defined. The set N_i^T includes time-space nodes denoted with the pair (n, t) where $n \in N_i$ and $t \in P$; in particular, the flow from a node (n, t) represents a part of the quantity of goods of an order departing on period t from location n. Then, $N_i^T = \{(n, t) : n \in N_i, t \in P, t \geq T^{min}(o_i, n)\}$ where $T^{min}(o_i, n)$ is the minimum time for reaching n from the origin o_i in graph G_i. Note that for $n = o_i$, $T^{min}(o_i, o_i) = S_i$. For each order $i \in O$, a set of nodes $N_i^{TO} \subseteq N_i^T$ is defined as $N_i^{TO} = \{(o_i, t) : S_i \leq t \leq LS_i\}$, where LS_i is the latest start of order i, i.e., $LS_i = DD_i - T^{min}(o_i, d_i)$. A positive flow contribution equal to Q_i enters the time-space flow network G_i^T at node (o_i, S_i).

The set A_i^T includes directed arcs between pairs of time-space nodes, which in particular model either transportation between different locations or inventory at the same location. More specifically, if an arc $(n, m) \in A_i$ is included in the space network and if $r \in R_{n,m}$ is a resource available for that arc, then an arc $((n, t), (m, t + T_{n,m}^r)) \in A_i^T$. Note that the duration of the considered time periods must be determined in order to allow a consistent circulation of the resources whose capacity is explicitly modeled, i.e., the resources of medium and long-distance road transportation. Differently, the local collection/delivery of goods within an area is modeled as a daily activity. The set A_i^T also includes the set of inventory arcs $A_i^I = \{((n, t), (n, t + 1)), \forall (n, t) \in N_i^T\}$ connecting the same physical location for a succession of time periods. A unitary inventory cost C_n^I is associated with each inventory arc in A_i^I related to node n.

The space-time flow network for an order i is completed introducing a fictitious final sink node f_i that is connected with all the space-time nodes $(d_i, t), t = S_i + T^{min}(o_i, d_i), \cdots, DD_i$, associated with the destination for i. Finally, an outgoing flow equal to Q_i leaves the fictitious node f_i.

Each transportation arc in the networks $G_i^T, \forall i \in O$, is associated with a shipment. A shipment represents a transportation activity executed with a specific transportation resource between a pair of locations, characterized by a starting time from the location of origin and by an arrival time at the location of destination. Each transportation resource provides a transportation capacity to an arc. A shipment is identified by a tuple (r, t, n, m) specifying that a transportation, performed by resource r, departs at time t from location n directed to location m. The availability of a transportation resource in a location may depend on the routing of the resource in the transportation network. In general, the set of transportation arcs of a network G_i^T can be denoted as $A_i^{TR} = A_i^T \setminus A_i^I$, also being $A_i^{TR} = \cup_{r \in R} A_{ir}^T$, where for each $r \in R$, A_{ir}^T is the subset of arcs $((n, t), (m, t + T_{n,m}^r)) \in A_i^{TR}$. Note that when a set A_{ir}^T is specified, then also the related arc $(n, m) \in A_i$ is univocally determined, since a resource is assigned to a single arc in the networks associated with an order. The overall set of transportation arcs for a resource r associated with the shipments for all the orders in O, i.e., included in any space-time flow network $G_i^T, i \in O$, is denoted as $A_r^{TO} = \cup_{i \in O} A_i^{TR}$.

Figure 2 shows a generic scheme of the space-time network above outlined.

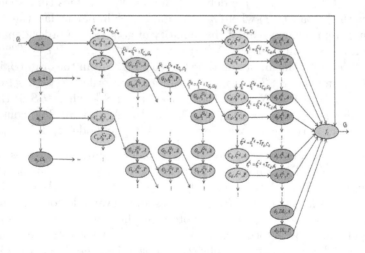

Fig. 2: The space-time network.

In the network G_i^T the following decision variables are defined:

- $x_{ira} \geq 0$, $\forall i \in O$, $r \in R_{n,m}$, $a = ((n, t), (m, t + T_{n,m}^r)) \in A_{ir}^T$, is a transportation flow variable specifying the positive quantity of order i transported by resource r departing at time t from location n and reaching location m at $t + T^r_{n,m}$.

- $s_{ia} \geq 0$, $\forall i \in O$, $a = ((n,t),(n,t+1)) \in A^I_i$, is an inventory flow variable variable specifying the positive quantity of order i in inventory at location n from time t to time $t+1$.
- $w_{it} \geq 0$, $\forall i \in O$, $t = S_i + T^{min}(o_i, d_i), \cdots, DD_i$, is a flow variable specifying the positive quantity of order i arrived at destination d_i at time t which flow to the fictitious final sink node f_i.
- y_{ra}, $r \in R_{n,m}$, $a = ((n,t),(m,t+T^r_{n,m})) \in A^{TO}_r$, is a binary variable such that $y_{ra} = 1$ if a shipment using resource r departs at time t from location n directed to location m.
- $y^n_r \geq 0, y^m_r \geq 0, r \in R_{n,m}$, are two flow variables associated with the final location of the resource r in the network G^R_r.
- $u_{ra} \geq 0$, $r \in R_{n,m}$, $a = ((n,t),(m,t+T^r_{n,m})) \in A^{TO}_r$, is a real variable representing the unused transportation capacity of resource r during the shipment between nodes n and m departing at time t.
- z_r, $\forall r \in R$, is a binary variable such that $z_r = 1$ if resource r is used in a transportation activity. $v_i \forall i \in O$ is a flow variables representing the boxes for order i which are not served.

The availability of a transportation resource in R is managed as follows:

- the short-distance road transportation between the demand origins and the consolidation centers, as well as the deliveries between the consolidation centers and the order destinations, is assumed to be provided by fleets of small trucks (i.e. vans or similar vehicles) that, at the planning level, are modeled considering a daily transport capacity disregarding their detailed routing.
- differently from the short-distance road resources, the mid- and long-distance ones are modeled taking into account the dynamics of resources during time. In particular, the availability of the resources for such a road transportation is modeled through the binary variables y_{ra}, whose value is ruled by the flow in a space-time resource network defined to represent the routing (flow) of the resource r. In particular, for each $r \in R$ a resource network $G^R_r = (N^R_r, A^R_r)$ is introduced. The set of arcs of G^R_r is defined as:

$$A^R_r = A^{TR}_r \cup A^I_r \cup \{((n,H), f_r), ((m,H), f_r)\} \tag{1}$$

The set of nodes of G^R_r is given by:

$$N^R_r = \{(n,t) : (n,t) \in \cup_{i \in O} N^T_i, \delta_{(n,t)} \cap A^{TO}_r \neq \varnothing\} \cup \{f_r\} \tag{2}$$

i.e., they correspond to the nodes in the space-time networks for the orders that are incident to a transportation arc associated with resource r, plus the fictitious sink node f_r.

The planning of the transportation activities in order to serve the orders in O over the network G can be formulated as a set of network flow problems on the networks $G_i^T, i \in O$ with capacity coupling constraints on the transportation resource $r \in R$, whose availability is in turn modeled as a flow in the resource networks $G_r^R, r \in R$.

The mathematical problem formulation follows.

Problem.

$$min \quad Z = \sum_{i \in O} \sum_{(n,m) \in A_i} \sum_{r \in R_{nm}} \sum_{a \in A_{ir}^T} C_{nm} x_{ira} +$$

$$\sum_{i \in O} \sum_{r \in A_i^I} C_a^I s_{ia} + \sum_{r \in R^G} C_r^G z_r^G +$$

$$\sum_{i \in O} \sum_{t=D_{i+1}\cdots,DD_i} C_i^D (t - D_i) w_{it} + C^E \sum_{r \in R} \sum_{a \in A_r^{TO}} u_{ra} + \sum_{i \in O} m v_i \quad (3)$$

subject to

$$\sum_{(o_i,m) \in A_i} \sum_{a \in \delta_{(o_i,S_i)}^+ \cap A_{ir}^T} x_{i0a} + \sum_{a \in \delta_{(o_i,S_i)}^+ \cap A_i^I} s_{ia} + v_i = Q_i \qquad \forall i \in O \quad (4)$$

$$\sum_{(n,m) \in A_i} \sum_{r \in R_{n,m}} \sum_{a \in \delta_{(n,t)}^+ \cap A_{ir}^T} x_{ira} + \sum_{a \in \delta_{(n,t)}^+ \cap A_i^I} s_{ia}$$

$$- \sum_{(k,n) \in A_i} \sum_{r \in R_{k,n}} \sum_{a \in \delta_{(n,t)}^- \cap A_{ir}^T} x_{ira} - \sum_{a \in \delta_{(n,t)}^- \cap A_i^I} s_{ia} = 0$$

$$\forall i \in O \qquad \forall n \in N_i \setminus \{o_i, d_i\}, (n,t) \in N_i^T \quad (5)$$

$$w_{it} - \sum_{(k,d_i) \in A_i} \sum_{r \in R_{kd_i}} \sum_{a \in \delta_{(d_i,t)}^- \cap A_{ir}^T} x_{ira} = 0 \qquad \forall i \in O \qquad \forall (d_i, t) \in N_i^T \quad (6)$$

$$\sum_{i=S_i+T^{min}(o_i,d_i),\cdots,DD_i} w_{it} + v_i = Q_i \qquad \forall i \in O \quad (7)$$

$$\sum_{i \in O_{l(n)}} \sum_{a \in A_i^T : dep(a)=(o_i,t)} x_{i0a} \leq C_n^{max} \qquad \forall n \in N^C \qquad \forall t \in P \quad (8)$$

$$\sum_{i:a \in A_{ir}^T} x_{ira} + u_{ra} = C_r^{max} y_{ra} \qquad \forall r \in R \qquad \forall a \in A_r^{TO} \quad (9)$$

$$\sum_{a \in \delta_{(n,t_0)}^+} y_{ra} = z_r \qquad \forall r \in R \quad (10)$$

$$\sum_{a \in \delta_n^+} y_{ra} - \sum_{a \in \delta_n^-} y_{ra} = 0 \qquad \forall r \in R \qquad \forall n \in N_r^R \setminus \{(n, t_0)\} \qquad (11)$$

$$y_r^n - \sum_{a \in \delta_{(n, T_r^f)}^-} y_{ar} = 0 \qquad \forall r \in R \qquad (12)$$

$$y_r^m - \sum_{a \in \delta_{(m, T_r^f)}^-} y_{ar} = 0 \qquad \forall r \in R \qquad (13)$$

$$y_r^n + y_r^m = 1 \qquad \forall r \in R \qquad (14)$$

$$x_{ira} \geq 0 \quad \forall i \in O \quad \forall r \in R_{n,m} \quad \forall a = ((n, t), (m, t + T_{n,m}^r)) \in A_{ir}^T \qquad (15)$$

$$s_{ia} \geq 0 \quad \forall i \in O \quad \forall a = ((n, t), (n, t + 1)) \in A_i^I \qquad (16)$$

$$w_{it} \geq 0 \quad \forall i \in O \quad \forall t = S_i + T^{min}(o_i, d_i), \cdots, DD_i \qquad (17)$$

$$y_{ra} \in (0, 1) \quad \forall r \in R_{n,m} \quad \forall a = ((n, t), (m, t + T_{n,m}^r)) \in A_r^{TO} \qquad (18)$$

$$y_r^n \geq 0 \quad \forall r \in R_{n,m} \qquad (19)$$

$$y_r^m \geq 0 \quad \forall r \in R_{n,m} \qquad (20)$$

$$u_{ra} \geq 0 \quad \forall r \in R_{n,m} \quad \forall a = ((n, t), (m, t + T_{n,m}^r)) \in A_r^{TO} \qquad (21)$$

$$z_r \in (0, 1) \quad \forall r \in R \qquad (22)$$

The resulting problem is a Mixed-Integer Linear Program (MILP) in which the objective function (3) is the sum of six different terms: the transportation cost (associated with the flow in transportation arcs of the G_i^T networks) related to the whole demand, the inventory cost (associated with the flow in the inventory arcs of the G_i^T networks) due when goods have to remain in the same location for one or more time periods, the fixed cost related to the use of transportation resources, the tardiness cost paid for the orders whose final delivery exceeds the related deadlines, the sum of the penalties due to not full truck trips on long- and mid-distance travels, and the cost for non-served orders, where m is a large penalization parameter.

The flow conservation in the networks G_i^T is guaranteed by constraints (4)-(7). Constraints (4) state that, for each order $i \in O$, the forward flow from the origin node i_i at the release time S_i has to be equal to the quantity of goods to be transported. Constraints (5) guarantee the flow conservation for a generic node in N_i^T different both from the origin and the destination of the order. Constraints (6) model the flow conservation for the destination nodes, whereas (7) impose that the flow exiting from the final fictitious sink nodes for each networks G_i^T equals the quantity of goods for the orders. In order not to violate the transportation capacity, constraints (8) and (9) are introduced. Such constraints, in particular, link the flow on the transportation arcs of the G_i^T networks with the availability of the long-distance road resources for such arcs, defining also the value of the unused capacity as slack variables u_{ra}.

Constraints (10)-(14) model the flow conservation for each resource network G_r^R. Constraints (10) define the entering flow in each resource network, so modeling the initial availability of the related resources in the node $v_0 = (n, t_0)$, where $(n, t_0) \in N_r^R$, being t_0 the fist time period in the planning horizon in which r can depart from a node for transporting an order in any network G_i^T. Hence, (10) also define the forward flow from nodes (n, t_0) in each networks G_r^R. Constraints (11) are the flow conservation for the generic nodes in the networks G_r^R. Constraints (12) and (13) give the flow conservation for the nodes associated with the two locations n and m, between which the resource r can travel, in correspondence with the last time period, denoted as T_r^f, in which a transport can end in the networks $G_i^T, i \in O$. Then these two sets of constraints define the flows on the arcs linking such final nodes (n, T_r^f) and (m, T_r^f) with the final fictitious node f_r in each network G_r^R, i.e., the value of the variables y_r^n and y_r^m. Constraints (14) impose the flow conservation for the fictitious node f_r. Finally, Constraints (15)- (22) define the decision variables of the problem.

4   Experimental Analysis

An experimental analysis has been carried out to validate the efficacy of the mathematical problem here proposed. The model has been implemented in Visual Studio 2015 C ♯ using Cplex 12.7 as MILP solver. All the computations have been executed using a laptop with the following features: Intel R core TM i7 CPU M430 2,7 GHz with 16 GB of RAM.

An instance generator has been implemented to randomly generate instance features. In the following, an instance having the following features is analyzed: 30 orders over 3 areas; between 20 and 160 boxes per each order; 16 origin-destination nodes (OD); 3 consolidation/deconsolidation nodes (CD), one per each area; 25 road-road transit exchange nodes (RR).

The capacity of each container (for mid- and long-distance transport) and van (for local transport) has been set equal to 440 and 320 boxes, respectively. The number of resources for mid and long-distance road transport has been set to 122. Besides, the planning horizon has been fixed to 30 days and the time step to half a day (morning and afternoon).

Figure 3 displays the nodes distribution over the three areas generated.

The characteristics related to orders and parameters used in the experimental analysis are shown in Tables 1 and 2, respectively.

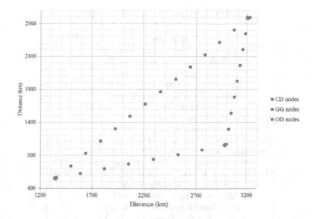

Fig. 3: The space-time network for a transportation resource.

Table 1: Data related to orders

Order ID	Quantity	Release	Duedate	Deadline	Origin node	Origin area	Destination node	Destination area
0	119	5	9	18	8	0	18	2
1	144	2	7	14	20	2	6	0
2	90	5	8	16	4	0	11	1
3	140	7	11	22	17	2	7	0
4	124	7	9	18	11	1	8	0
5	52	2	7	14	7	0	19	2
6	123	2	5	10	16	2	13	1
7	94	7	9	18	10	0	12	1
8	154	8	10	20	5	0	14	1
9	24	6	8	16	16	2	14	1
10	53	6	10	20	20	2	6	0
11	45	5	8	16	19	2	12	1
12	29	7	9	18	13	1	5	0
13	63	5	8	16	16	2	11	1
14	77	4	8	16	18	2	4	0
15	38	6	8	16	8	0	15	1
16	156	0	5	10	18	2	8	0
17	128	10	12	24	13	1	5	0
18	86	10	12	24	12	1	5	0
19	50	6	8	16	17	2	15	1
20	148	6	8	16	13	1	18	2
21	53	3	8	16	4	0	19	2
22	98	3	6	12	10	0	13	1
23	89	3	6	11	19	2	13	1
24	91	5	8	16	14	1	19	2
25	66	1	4	8	5	0	13	1
26	152	3	6	12	7	0	14	1
27	132	8	10	20	15	1	6	0
28	125	5	8	16	19	2	11	1
29	26	6	8	16	14	1	20	2

Table 3 provides the objective function value and its composition. It can be noticed that, in this case, each order is fully served.

Table 2: Problem parameters

Parameter	Value
Long-Distance Truck Speed (km/h)	70
Long-Distance Truck Speed (km/h)	30
Planning Horizon (days)	21
Long-Distance Capacity (boxes)	440
Short-Distance Capacity (boxes)	320
Maximum Number of Long-Distance Trucks	2
Unitary Long-Distance Road Cost (/km x box)	1,2
Unitary Mid-Distance Road Cost (/km x box)	0,8
Unitary Short-Distance Road Cost (/km x box)	1,4
Inventory cost at Node type OD (/day x box)	0,1
Inventory cost at Node type CD (/day x box)	0,08
Inventory cost at Node type GG (/day x box)	0,08
Tardiness Cost (/day x box)	0,2
Mid Road Fixed Cost (/truck)	30
Long Road Fixed Cost (/truck)	15
Cost of Not Full Transport (/box)	50

Table 3: Global instance results obtained

Objective function value	6034716.12
Total transportation cost	5271924.64
Total inventory cost	41051.48
Total tardiness cost	1940
Cost for not full trucks	719800
Total quantity not served	0
Number of not served orders	0

Tables 4 and 5 show the results obtained, respectively, for order ♯ 2 and order ♯ 16; in both tables the following data are provided: arc type, starting node ID and type, starting time both in terms of day and period of the day (i.e. morning if the value is equal to 0 and afternoon if it is 1), travel time, ending node ID and type, ending time both in terms of day and period of the day (i.e. morning if the value is equal to 0 and afternoon if it is 1), resource used and quantity transported.

In case of order ♯ 2, the mid-distance road transport is used (as a matter of fact, RR nodes are encountered), whereas in the latter, i.e. for order ♯ 16, long-distance road mode is chosen as the optimal way of transport between the consolidation and deconsolidation nodes. Moreover, in the "Resource" column, column, a value equal to −1 indicates local resources that are managed at an aggregate level.

Table 6 provides a detailed picture of the path covered, in each half day, by resource (i.e., truck) ♯ 50, which is used -for instance- to serve order ♯ 2. It can be observed that, as it should be, this truck goes back and forth between RR node ♯ 21 and RR node ♯ 22 (written in red color in Figure 6).

Besides, in order to provide the evidence that groupage transportation is executed and promoted by the model, Table 7 shows that orders ♯ 2, 7 and 8 are transported on the same truck (i.e. resource ♯ 50) in day ♯ 12.

Table 4: Results obtained for order ♯ 2

Order ID	Arc type	Start node ID	Start node type	Start time (day)	Start time 0=morn 1=after	Travel time (days)	End node ID	End node type	End time (day)	End time 0=morn 1=after	Res.	Quant. transp.
2	RoadLocal	4	OD	11	0	0.104	0	CD	11	0	-1	90
2	RoadMid	0	CD	11	1	0.443	21	RR	12	0	6	90
2	RoadMid	21	RR	12	0	0.434	22	RR	12	1	50	90
2	RoadMid	22	RR	12	1	0.434	23	RR	13	0	55	90
2	RoadMid	23	RR	13	0	0.434	24	RR	13	1	58	90
2	RoadMid	24	RR	13	1	0.434	25	RR	14	0	63	90
2	RoadMid	25	RR	14	0	0.434	26	RR	14	1	68	90
2	RoadMid	26	RR	14	1	0.434	27	RR	15	0	71	90
2	RoadMid	27	RR	15	0	0.420	1	CD	15	0	14	90
2	RoadLocal	1	CD	15	1	0.057	11	OD	15	0	-1	90

Table 5: Results obtained for order ♯ 16

Order ID	Arc type	Start node ID	Start node type	Start time (day)	Start time 0=morn 1=after	Travel time (days)	End node ID	End node type	End time (day)	End time 0=morn 1=after	Res.	Quant. transp.
16	RoadLocal	18	OD	0	0	0.03773	2	CD	0	0	-1	156
16	RoadLong	2	CD	0	0	5.51080	0	CD	6	0	2	156
16	RoadLocal	0	CD	6	0	0.11219	8	OD	6	-1	-1	156

Finally, from a computational viewpoint, the above described instance has been solved in a computational time equal to 30 minute, reaching a gap of 5% from the optimum value. The number of variables and linear constraints that have been generated are respectively 56715 (of which 24154 are binary variables) and 53863.

5 Conclusion

In the present paper, a model devoted to represent a road transportation network in a Physical Internet environment has been provided. The aim is to minimize total costs, exploiting trucks capacity and reducing empty truck trips, by using groupage transportation and including consolidation and deconsolidation centers in the network nodes, as well as road-road transit exchange points where trucks can exchange containers. A MILP model has been designed, formulated and implemented and preliminary results obtained on an instance of 30 orders have shown the effectiveness of the proposed approach.

Future research will be devoted to make a more extensive experimental and computational analysis, to develop a proper heuristic in order to manage bigger problem instances and to extend the problem formulation to the intermodal case, considering also rail transportation as an alternative mode.

Table 6: Results obtained for mid-distance road resource ♯ 50 at day ♯ 12 - groupage transportation

Resource ID	Start Node Type	Start Time (Day)	Start Time (M/A)	End Node Type	End Time (Day)	End Time (M/A)
50	21	0	0	21	0	1
50	21	0	1	21	1	0
50	21	1	0	21	1	1
50	21	1	1	21	2	0
50	21	2	0	21	2	1
50	21	2	1	21	3	0
50	21	3	0	21	3	1
50	21	3	1	21	4	0
50	21	4	0	21	4	1
50	21	4	1	21	5	0
50	21	5	0	21	5	1
50	21	5	1	21	6	0
50	21	6	0	21	6	1
50	21	6	1	21	7	0
50	21	7	0	21	7	1
50	21	7	1	21	8	0
50	21	8	0	21	8	1
50	21	8	1	21	9	0
50	21	9	0	21	9	1
50	21	9	1	21	10	0
50	21	10	0	21	10	1
50	21	10	1	21	11	0
50	21	11	0	21	11	1
50	21	11	1	21	12	0
50	21	12	0	22	12	1
50	22	12	1	22	13	0
50	22	13	0	22	13	1
50	22	13	1	22	14	0
50	22	14	0	22	14	1
50	22	14	1	21	15	0
50	21	15	0	21	15	1
50	21	15	1	21	16	0
50	21	16	0	21	16	1
50	21	16	1	21	17	0
50	21	17	0	21	17	1
50	21	17	1	21	18	0
50	21	18	0	21	18	1
50	21	18	1	21	19	0
50	21	19	0	21	19	1
50	21	19	1	21	20	0
50	21	20	0	21	20	1
50	21	20	1	21	21	0
50	21	21	0	21	21	1
50	21	21	1	21	22	0
50	21	22	0	21	22	1
50	21	22	1	21	23	0
50	21	23	0	21	23	1
50	21	23	1	21	24	0
50	21	24	0	21	24	1

Table 7: Results obtained for mid-distance road resource ♯ 50 at day ♯ 12 - groupage transportation

Order ID	Arc type	Start node ID	Start node type	Start time (day)	Start time 0=morn 1=after	Travel time (days)	End node ID	End node type	End time (day)	End time 0=morn 1=after	Res.	Quant. transp.
2	RoadMid	21	RR	12	0	0.43431	22	RR	12	1	50	90
7	RoadMid	21	RR	12	0	0.43431	22	RR	12	1	50	62
8	RoadMid	21	RR	12	0	0.43431	22	RR	12	1	50	154

References

1. Ballot, E., Montreuil, B., Thivierge, C.: Functional Design of Physical Internet Facilities:a Road-Rail Hub. Progress in Material Handling Research 2012. MHIA, Charlotte, NC, U.S.A. (2012).
2. Meller, R., Montreuil, B., Thivierge, C., Montreuil, Z.: Functional Design of Physical Internet Facilities: A Road-Based Transit Center. Progress in Material Handling Research 2012. MHIA, Charlotte, NC, U.S.A. (2012).
3. Montreuil, B.: Toward a Physical Internet: meeting the global logistics sustainability grand challenge. Logistics Research. 3 (2), 71-87 (2011).
4. Cranic, T.G., Montreuil, B.: Physical Internet Enabled Interconnected City Logistics. Working paper. CIRRELT 2015-13 (2015).
5. Yang, Y., Pan, S., Ballot, E.: A model to take advantage of Physical Internet for vendor inventory management. IFAC-PapersOnLine. 48 (3),1990-1995 (2015).
6. Uster, H., Kewcharoenwong, P.: Strategic design and analysis of a Relay network in truckload transportation. Transportation Science,45,4,505523, (2011).
7. Sallez, Y., Montreuil, B., Ballot, E.: On the activeness of intelligent Physical Internet containers. In: Studies in Computational Intelligence. 594, 259-269 (2015).
8. Crainic, T.G., Montreuil, B.: Physical Internet Enabled Hyperconnected City Logistics. Transportation Research Procedia. 12, 383-398, (2016).
9. Dejax, P. J., Crainic, T. G.: Survey papera review of empty flows and fleet management models in freight transportation. Transportation science, 21(4), 227-248, (1987).
10. Caballini, C., Rebecchi, I., Sacone, S.: Combining multiple trips in a port environment for empty movements minimization. Transportation Research Procedia, 10, 694-703, (2015).
11. Schulte, F., Lalla-Ruiz, E., Gonzlez-Ramrez, R. G., Vo, S.,: Reducing port-related empty truck emissions: a mathematical approach for truck appointments with collaboration. Transportation Research Part E: Logistics and Transportation Review, (2017).
12. Memon, M.A., Archimede, B.: A Multi-Agent Distributed Framework for Collaborative Transportation Planning. IFAC Proceedings Volumes. 46 (9), 1370-1375, (2013).
13. Wasner, M., Zapfel, G.: An integrated multi-depot hub-location vehicle routing model for network planning of parcel service. International Journal of Production Economics 90, 403419, (2004).
14. Vanovermeire, C., Sorensen, K.: Integration of the cost allocation in the optimization of collaborative bundling. Transportation Research Part E: Logistics and Transportation Review. 72, 125143, (2014).

Simulating Storage Policies for an Automated Grid-Based Warehouse System

Michaela Beckschäfer, Simon Malberg, Kevin Tierney, and Christoph Weskamp

Decision Support & Operations Research Lab, University of Paderborn,
Warburger Straße 100, 33098 Paderborn, Germany
{beckschaefer,tierney,weskamp}@dsor.de, malberg@mail.upb.de

Abstract Robotic fulfillment systems are becoming commonplace at warehouses across the world. High-density, grid-based storage systems in particular, such as the AutoStore system, are being used in a variety of contexts, but very little literature exists to guide decision makers in picking the right policies for operating such a system. Storage policies can have a large effect on the efficiency and storage capacity of robotic fulfillment systems. We therefore introduce a discrete event simulation for grid-based storage and examine input storage policies under a couple of storage scenarios. Our simulation provides decision makers with an easy way of testing policies before implementing them in a real system, and shows that selecting the correct policy can lead to up to a 7% input performance improvement, and 60% better box utilization.

Keywords: robotic fulfillment, grid-based storage, simulation

1 Introduction

Warehouses are becoming increasingly automated. Several types of automation have been present in warehouses for several decades or more, such as conveyor belts, sorting units and specialized vehicles. However, more complex forms of automation are steadily taking hold. In particular, automated picking systems are becoming more and more common, as these systems can increase warehouse efficiency, lower costs, and make the working environment more comfortable for human employees.

In its more basic form, manual, or *pickers-to-parts*, order fulfillment in a warehouse involves several steps[1]. First, one or more orders are selected for fulfillment. Second, the products required to fulfill the order are picked from the warehouse; in a manual system, this involves an employee walking or driving through the warehouse and locating the necessary products. Third, customization may be performed on some products. Fourth, the employee consolidates the products for each order into one or more boxes and sends them to be stored until they can be shipped to customers.

---

[1] We limit the scope of this paper to systems that retrieve goods in small quantities (i.e., not pallets).

© Springer International Publishing AG 2017
T. Bektaş et al. (Eds.), ICCL 2017, LNCS 10572, pp. 468–482, 2017.
https://doi.org/10.1007/978-3-319-68496-3_31

Automated picking systems generally replace the second step in the above process, and is called *parts-to-pickers*. Instead of a person gathering the items necessary for an order, robots do it instead. A variety of options exist to do this, including rack carrying robots from Amazon Robotics (formerly Kiva Systems) [1], the "shuttle-based" conveyor system CycloneCarrier [5] from Swisslog, the Tornado [22] "case storage system" also from Swisslog, and the grid-based robotic retrieval system AutoStore [2]. While rack carrying and automated conveyor systems place an emphasis on retrieval efficiency, grid-based systems focus on maximizing the use of available warehouse space for storing goods.

The operations research (OR) literature explores a number of aspects of fulfillment systems, including some automated ones (see [6] for an overview). While some automated systems share similar optimization and decision support challenges, the different types of systems for the most part form unique ecosystems, requiring customized algorithms for effective use. Grid-based storage in particular has seen little attention in the literature, despite containing a number of interesting OR problems.

In this paper, we create a simulation of an automated grid-based storage system similar to AutoStore and evaluate different policies for storing goods in the system. The novel components of this paper are as follows:

1. A discrete event simulation for an automated grid-based storage system[2]
2. Two heuristics for placing products into the storage grid
3. An experimental evaluation of the strategies with business insights.

We examine two simple policies for storing goods in the system in two cases. In the first, bins can only be used for a single type of product, whereas in the second a divider can be placed in a bin and two types of products can be stored. Our results show that dividers do not provide significant productivity gains unless there is a very high likelihood that the products will be ordered together, and that the choosing a good input policy can provide up to 5% higher output efficiency.

This paper is structured as follows. We first describe the setting of automated grid-based storage in Section 2, followed by an overview of the related literature in Section 3. We formalize our simulation in Section 4 and show computational results in Section 5. Finally, we conclude and discuss future work in Section 6.

2   Automated Grid-based Storage

In grid-based storage systems, products are stored in bins that are stacked on top of each other and laid out into a grid of rows and columns. Figure 1 shows a sample system with four robots. In existing systems, such as the AutoStore system, bins in a system are homogeneous, but they can be divided to store different products in one bin (see Figure 2). Robots store and retrieve bins by

---

[2] We note that the AutoStore system has a simulation available for certain users of the system, but the simulation is not public and its capabilities are unknown.

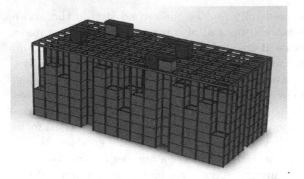

Figure 2: A bin with a single separator, and locations for additional separators.

Figure 1: A visualization of the grid-based storage system AutoStore.

traveling on top of the grid. The robots lift and transport bins to work stations, located to the sides of the grid (or, in special cases, in a tunnel through the grid). Ports are visible in Figure 1 as empty stacks on the sides of the grid. In principle, ports can be used for either input or output, however, in practice, they are often either used exclusively for one or the other. When workers are done processing a box, the robots bring it from the work station back to a free location. Work stations are the places where pickers can store the products in the bins. When the system receives an order, the robots start working. The robots in a system are all based on the same hardware, however systems generally partition robots into sorting and transport robots. If a requested bin is not on the top level, the sorting robots must re-sort the bins. They lift all bins that are blocking the requested bin and move them to nearby locations. After sorting, the transport robots can grab the bin and bring it to the work station where pickers can take a product out of the bin to satisfy an order.

The layout of the warehouse is block storage, but the system still deals with dynamic storage in contrast to other systems using block storage [13]. Pickers do not have to walk through the warehouse because the robots transport the bins with the products to them. This leads to a more efficient process of picking because the travel time in a manual picking system takes about 50% of the entire picking time [21]. The ports can have a queue for bins so that pickers do not have to wait for the next bin.

Grid-based storage systems can be tuned with policies or optimization models in a number of ways. Multiple robots can coordinate to retrieve or store bins faster, more ports can be added for faster picking, and even the grid can be extended after a system is already built. Therefore, it is possible for a company to start with a small warehouse and extend it iteratively. The layout is flexible and the grid can be built around pillars and other static obstacles.

A technical implementation of the robot-based warehouse system is the product AutoStore. This system is space efficient and cost-saving [2]. Aisles are not necessary and the system uses 40-60% less space than conventional systems [2].

3 Literature Review

Automated warehouse systems have been the focus of much research in the past, however grid-based storage systems are nearly completely missing from the operations research literature. We provide an overview of various approaches for storage systems which are discussed in the literature, followed by a subjective comparison of grid-based storage to other robotic fulfillment systems.

3.1 Previous research

There are several surveys in the area of warehouse systems. A literature review on typical decision problems in design and control of manual order-picking processes is given in [6]. The authors focus on optimal layout design, storage assignment methods, routing methods, order batching and zoning. The papers [10] and [11] present an overview on warehouse operations and provide a bridge between academic and practical contexts. They include warehouse design, performance evaluation, practical case studies and computational support tools. The authors of [18] focus on static scheduling and design problems, and [9] includes simulation- and travel-time-based models. An up-to-date overview of robotized handling systems is provided by [3], in which it is noted that there is currently only one paper that discusses operations research topics in grid-based storage.

Grid-based storage Storage policies were first evaluated for grid-based storage in [26]. The authors introduce a semi-open queuing model for estimating the performance of such a system. The provided models optimize the length to width ratio of the storage area and the stack height relating to the storage strategy. The authors investigate whether storing only a single type of product in a stack can provide performance gains versus multiple products in the same stack.

Rack-carrying storage systems In rack-carrying storage systems, robots bring shelves with bins to a work station where employees fulfill orders. This warehouse system is especially suitable for companies that distribute a large amount of small products. The system allows for the sorting of inventory and adapting the warehouse layout in a short period of time. The authors of [14] tackle the performance of such systems. They develop four queuing network models to estimate performance and robot utilization under various system parameters.

Compact systems without storage and retrieval machines A system with no usage of cranes or storage and retrieval machines is described in [25]. The system works with shuttles that move in x and y direction. A lift is used for the movement in z direction. Each product is on a shuttle and is accessible individually. In [25], a mixed-integer nonlinear model is provided to optimize the dimensions of the system. Furthermore, they compare several values of the cube compact storage system with traditional systems. The authors of [17] give approaches for considering multiple retrieval loads simultaneously. They develop an optimal method for two loads and a heuristic solution for three or more loads.

Compact systems with storage and retrieval machines Another approach for cube compact storage system is using a crane or a storage and retrieval machine. The storage and retrieval machine is for horizontal and vertical movements and a conveying mechanism for depth movements. In [24], optimal rack dimensions are determined by minimizing the expected cycle time using different storage policies. An analysis of the system performance and the optimal dimensions of the systems are discussed in [7]. The authors minimize the travel time for a random storage strategy by calculating the optimal ratio between the three dimensions. Similar research is presented in [8]. The authors introduce a methodology which minimizes the service response time by developing two separate models, one that minimizes the expected travel time and one that minimizes the maximum travel time between points.

The authors of [4] develop a travel-time model for storage and retrieval machines with respect to the speed profiles of real-world applications. The paper [23] extends the travel-time model of [4] by adding acceleration and deceleration rates. The paper [19] focuses on a flow-rack automated storage and retrieval system. In this warehouse system, there are two machines used: one for storage and the other for retrieval. The authors develop closed form travel-time expressions and compare them with exact models.

3.2   Comparison of existing storage systems

We provide a subjective overview of the previously discussed storage systems in Table 1. In manual storage systems, the racks need lots of space because they cannot be as high as in the automated systems, unless aisles are made wider so that pickers can use ladders or forklifts. Case storage systems also need lots of space because of the cranes. Rack-carrying and shuttle-based storage systems need less space because the aisles can be small when using robots. In grid-based storage systems aisles are not necessary and thus the warehouse is very compact.

The access time for one or more products in manual storage systems is very high. The reason for this is that pickers must walk through the warehouse to collect products and then walk back to their work stations. In grid-based storage systems, the bin with the requested product could be in the bottom level of the grid and this leads to very long access times as well. However, the throughput for most products is higher because different robots can work simultaneously. Sorting robots re-sort the bins to retrieve a bin in the bottom level while transport robots deliver bins with other products to work stations. The access time for the three remaining systems is short because robots or cranes can easily reach the requested products or shelves.

In the four automated storage systems the physical activity of pickers is low. In contrast to manual storage systems, pickers do not have to walk through the

Table 1: Comparison of different storage systems

Criteria Systems	Required space	Access time	Physical activity	Search area
Manual storage systems	-	-	-	-
Rack-carrying storage systems	o	+	+	o
Shuttle-based storage systems	o	+	+	+
Case storage systems	o	+	+	+
Grid-based storage systems	+	o	+	+

warehouse because robots or cranes transport the products between the work stations and the storage yards.

The criterion "search area" describes the size of the area in which pickers have to find the products. The search area in manual storage systems is huge because pickers first have to find the right shelf and then extract the requested product from it. When using rack-carrying storage systems, robots transport the shelves to the work stations and pickers only have to find the product in the shelf. The other three systems are superior regarding the search area because robots or cranes transports the bins, boxes or products to work stations. One bin or box often contains just one or two different products, which leads to a shorter duration for finding the requested product.

4 Discrete event simulation framework

In this section we specify the structure and the behavior of our simulation framework. Moreover, we give an overview of the operating principles of the developed storage policies for a grid-based warehouse system.

Simulation overview Discrete event simulation (DES) is a well-established modelling technique in operations research and has been successfully applied as a decision support tool in the field for various logistics applications, such as transportation planning and inventory planning [20]. Grid-based storage systems can be modeled in several ways. Using a mathematical model would allow us to identify optimal settings for the system, however the multitude of path finding and storage strategy decisions would result in an enormously sized model even for a small system. Second, queuing networks, such as in [14], require simplifying assumptions that a DES does not require, especially in regards to the movement of the robots. Hence, we have identified DES as an appropriate modelling technique for simulating and analyzing a grid-based warehouse system. The main purpose of our simulation model is to support decision makers in terms of identifying viable storage policies according to several key performance indicators, such as the number of products input/output and the overall storage utilization.

Due to the complexity of warehouse operations, we focus our simulation on a single 8-hour shift of storage operations. This allows us to avoid having to create heuristics or policies for, e.g., inventory ordering/stocking strategies, order fulfillment prioritization, etc. This limited simulation time naturally results in some challenges, such as the lack of a "burn-in" period.

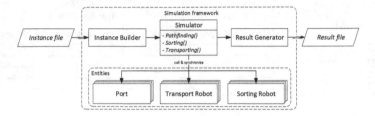

Figure 3: Architecture of the simulation framework

We propose a discrete event simulation framework based on common design patterns. In Figure 3 we present a conceptual architecture of our simulation framework[3]. An instance file contains warehouse layout data, the sequence of input and output orders, and the initial assignment of products to bins. The instance builder initializes the simulation model at time 0 (i.e., start of the planning horizon). Next, the simulator provides a main routine to execute the simulation and communicates with the coordinator that controls the process of performing events and synchronizes the activities of the main entities (i.e., ports, transport robots and sorting robots). Lastly, a result generator consolidates statistical information about the system and generates a result file.

Formalization In the following, we specify the simulation's behavior in more detail. Typically, a DES comprises a system state, a simulation clock, an event list as well as a termination condition [15]. Changes to the system state occur at discrete points in time and are handled by the simulation clock. In our case, the system state S represents (*i*) the remaining orders, (*ii*) the positions of all bins in the system, (*iii*) the types and quantities of products stored in each bin, (*iv*) the buffer/working space available at each input/output port, (*v*) the position of all robots, and (*vi*) which bin, if any, a robot is currently carrying. Since we only intend to simulate a single working shift, we do not consider the battery charge of robots and instead simply assume that they are all charged and available for the entire planning horizon. The event list handles all pending events (i.e., activities that are performed by an entity and modify the system state) and schedules the execution of the next event. An overview of our events is given in Table 2.

Algorithm 1 provides the main loop of the simulation that drives all further activity using the parameters given in Table 3. The loop checks if input and output ports are busy, meaning that the port is currently servicing a particular order. If the port is not busy, an order is pulled from the queue. We assume the orders are sorted before they are passed into the system. The sorting could be determined based on any number of business criteria. Bins are then requested for each product, ensuring that a specified amount of product is located in the grid, or, in the case of an input order, enough capacity for the product is found.

---

[3] To guarantee high adaptability of the simulation, we do not use a commercial simulation package. We instead create a custom implementation of the DES in C#.

Table 2: Overview of events in the DES.

Entity	Event	Description
Port	Select-bin$(p, o, \overleftarrow{\pi})$	This method determines which bin should be retrieved from port p according to the order o and the request policy $\overleftarrow{\pi}$.
	Request-bin(p, b, o)	Requests that bin b be brought to port p to (partially) fulfill order o.
	Process-bin(p, b, o)	All products from order o are removed from bin b; assumes the bin is in the buffer of port p.
	Replace-bin$(p, b, \overrightarrow{\pi})$	Puts bin b from port p back into the warehouse according to replacement policy $\overrightarrow{\pi}$.
Robot	Transport-bin(r, b, t)	Assign a new transportation task to an available transport robot r to transport bin b to target position t.
	Move(r, x, y)	Moves a robot up, down, left or right one unit on the grid if the destination is not blocked.
	Take-bin(r, b)	A bin b is lifted from the top of a stack into robot r's transport unit.
	Release-bin(r, b)	Places a bin b on top of robot r's current stack if the stack is not full.
	Sort-to-top(r, b)	Requests that a sort robot r moves the bin b to the top of its stack.

Table 3: Simulation input parameters.

Parameter	Description
B	Set of bins
I, O	Sequence of input and output orders, respectively, consisting of (u, k) of product type u with amount k
R^T, R^S	Set of sorting and transport robots, respectively
P^I, P^O	Set of input and output ports, respectively
$\overleftarrow{\pi}, \overrightarrow{\pi}$	Bin retrieval and replacement policies, respectively
t^x, t^y	Time required for a robot to travel in the x and y directions, respectively
t^l	Time required to lift a bin a single unit in the z direction
T	Maximum time of the planning horizon

The *Select-Bin* (line 9) method uses a policy to determine which bin should be retrieved, such as the closest empty bin or closest bin with the same product type in it. The Request-bin(p, b, o) event is carried out if the buffer of port p is not yet full. If bin b is not at the top of its stack, a Sort-To-Top(b) event is generated and the next available sorting robot will move bin b to the highest position in the stack. Once the bin is in this position a Transport-Bin(r, b, t) event is created. This event waits for a transport robot r to be available and then sends it to bring bin b to the target position t using the Take-Bin(r, b), Move, and Release-Bin(r, b) primitives. Finally, on line 12, if a bin contains other products relevant to the current order the amount of needed product is updated.

When a bin b arrives in a port's buffer, it is processed by an employee. We model this with the Process-bin(b) event. For an output order, this event removes the specified product from the bin, and in the case of an input order, places the specified amount of product into the bin. If the order o is now completed, the port marks itself as no longer busy. The Replace-bin$(b, \overrightarrow{\pi})$ event is then immediately placed into the event list. The event calls for a transport robot to take the bin back to a location determined using the output policy $\overrightarrow{\pi}$.

Algorithm 1 Event generation for input and output ports.

```
 1: function PORT-IO(S, P^O, P^I, I, O, T, ⃖π)
 2:     for (P', L) ∈ {(P^O, O), (P^I, I)} do
 3:         for p ∈ P' do
 4:             if ¬BUSY(p) then
 5:                 o ← DEQUEUE(L)
 6:                 SET-BUSY(p, o)
 7:                 for (u, k) ∈ o do
 8:                     while k > 0 do
 9:                         b ← Select-Bin(p, u, k, ⃖π)
10:                         REQUEST-BIN(p, b, o)
11:                         k ← k − Capacity(b, u)
12:                         for (u', k') ∈ o where u' ∈ Bin-Products(b) do
13:                             k' ← k' − Capacity(b, u')
14:     if TIME() > T then end simulation
```

4.1   Robot navigation and coordination

In a busy warehouse, the robots are all operating at the same time traveling around the grid and placing bins in the way of other robots. The simulation thus requires a path finding mechanism for robots to plan their routes through the grid. We note that our case is normally somewhat simpler than other automated robot settings, such as in [16], as robot movement does not block entire aisles.

On the basis of a start and a target position for a given robot, our path finding procedure calculates a route through the grid for the robot. We allow each robot to individually plan its path using the A* algorithm [12]. If positions are not blocked by obstacles (i.e., other robots or bins on top of the grid), robots can move horizontally or vertically but not diagonally. Without going into detail, when a path is planned, the grid spaces along the path must be reserved at the times that the robot will traverse them to avoid collisions. A sequence of MOVE events is then generated and added to the event list.

4.2   Avoiding deadlock

Due to the block layout, the majority of bins are buried within the grid's stacks. When a bin beneath the top layer is requested, a SORT-TO-TOP event is generated and serviced by a sorting robot. A sequence of MOVE events are first scheduled to move the sorting robot to the stack that should be sorted. Then, the sorting robot needs to burrow into the stack and find the requested bin. Since each robot can only store one bin in its transportation unit at a time, all removed bins must be placed on top of other stacks. Thus, bins may be placed on top of the grid, which could result in robots being walled-in or one part of the grid becoming disconnected from another. To avoid deadlocks, we constrain the stacks that can be used for sorting (see Figure 4). The basic idea is to create a corridor of size two around the stack being sorted. Then, every four bins a row in the "wall" must be left free for robots to pass through. Once a requested box has been placed on top of another stack, it is authorized for transportation to the corresponding output station. The sorting process terminates as soon as all removed bins are put back in the original stack.

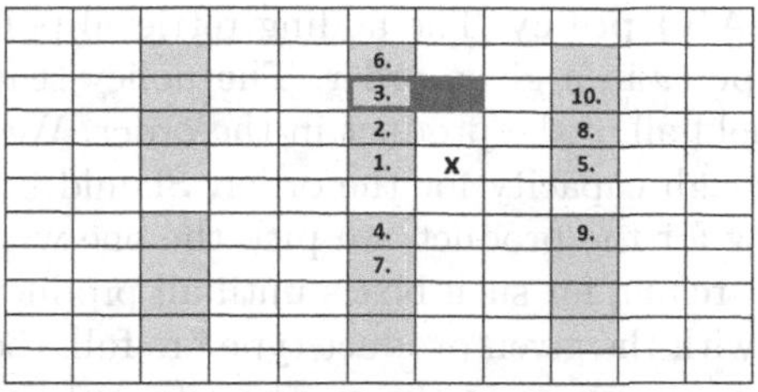

Figure 4: Example of the bin placement constraint when sorting a stack. The stack marked with an "x" is to be re-sorted. Bins may only be placed on the gray cells, an example placement sequence is given by the numbered cells, and a sorting robot with its lifting unit is shown in red.

4.3   Storage policies

The efficient operation of the storage system hinges on the choices for the storage policies $\overleftarrow{\pi}$ and $\overrightarrow{\pi}$. Our focus in this paper is on the insertion of goods into the system, meaning we suggest several alternatives for $\overleftarrow{\pi}$ for input orders. For $\overrightarrow{\pi}$, we use the following simple heuristic. Whenever a bin must be placed back in the grid from a port, place it in the nearest available location. For this, we define a weighted Manhattan distance metric

$$\text{DISTANCE}(x, y, z, x', y') := |x - x'| + |y - y'| + \alpha z,$$

where x and y indicate the position of the bin to be retrieved, and z the number of bins on top of the bin to be retrieved. The position of the port is given by x', y', and α is a penalty factor for having to dig down into a stack. Note that since ports do not have a z component, we leave that out of the distance calculation.

We assume that either all bins have a divider in them or none of them do, and simulate both cases to see if dividing bins is beneficial to any of the policies we propose. We assume that input orders are associated with a single product type, or that they are associated with product types that have been randomly selected. The reason for this is that input orders of multiple items would have to be first sorted by humans in a buffer, and we do not simulate this aspect of the problem. It is therefore possible that in an actual system with a marshalling area higher input rates could be achieved, especially for systems with dividers in the bins.

Empty retrieval (ER) policy Given an input order, this policy selects the next available bin that is completely empty, or has a completely empty half. The main advantage of this policy is that it distributes goods widely across the grid. This can be beneficial in an AutoStore-like system, as output ports are usually distributed across the grid, and with multiple bins containing a particular product it is less likely that a product is completely stored deep down in a stack. A drawback, however, is that in systems with many different types of products, there might not be any available empty bins.

Adding retrieval (AR) policy The adding retrieval policy seeks a bin with the same product type as in a given order. The policy searches for a bin with enough capacity to hold all of the product in the order. We arbitrarily take one of the boxes with enough capacity for the order. Should no box be found with enough spare capacity for the product, we pick the one with the most capacity available and keep searching for such boxes until all product has been placed in the grid. If all boxes with the given product type are full, the nearest empty box (or empty box half) is chosen as in the empty retrieval policy. If we fill a box half completely and there is still product available, we request a new box rather than put the same product in the other half.

5   Computational Evaluation

We carry out computational experiments to demonstrate that our simulation framework effectively supports a decision maker regarding the planning of a storage policy. In our investigations we compare an empty retrieval policy (ER) with an adding retrieval policy (AR). Moreover, we consider adding and empty retrieval policies in which all bins contain a single separator (AR2 and ER2, respectively). First, we specify our test scenarios. Afterwards, we give an overview of the design of the computational experiments and present the results of our investigation.

Settings of test scenarios We base the parameters of the simulation on the AutoStore system and use data from an industrial collaborator to generate input and output orders. We generate four test scenarios to evaluate the presented storage policies. We run each scenario five times, varying the order list, giving us a total of 20 instances. Table 4 represents the key properties of our scenarios. The storage utilization (i.e., 50%), the number of ports (i.e., 2 input and 6 output ports) and the height of the system (i.e., 13 bins) are the same for all scenarios. To get different sized scenarios, the number of bins and product types, as well as the number of sorting and transport robots are varied. We set the parameter α to 5 for all experiments.

Table 4: Test scenarios for the computational experiments.

Properties	Tiny	Small	Medium	Large
Size (LxW)	20x20	30x30	40x40	60x60
Bins	4987	11481	20571	46545
Sorting robots	6	8	10	12
Transport robots	4	5	6	8
Product types	1000	1500	2000	4000

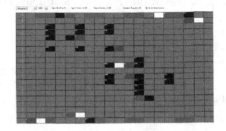

Figure 5: Visualization of a simulation state of the tiny scenario.

Figure 5 displays the system state of an example warehouse observed from a bird's-eye view. Ports are located on the top and bottom edge of the grid. Ports for handling input orders are colored green, whereas ports for handling output orders are colored red. If a bin is positioned on top of the grid, it is colored black and the ID of the bin is displayed. Sorting robots are colored blue and transport robots are colored red. The white portion of a robot shows the transportation unit. As can be seen, equal numbers of robots are available in both orientations (Left-Right and Right-Left). Since robots cannot turn around, this is important for ensuring all parts of the grid can be accessed.

Analysis We address the following research questions:

1. How do different storage policies influence the overall input and output performance of the warehouse system as well as the average utilization of the bins?
2. How does varying the level of product types impact the performance of the system?
3. How does varying the number of product types per input order influence the performance of the system?

In Figure 6, we present the input and output performance as well as the average utilization of the bins for different storage policies for each test scenario. The results reveal that the relative differences for the input and output performance between all policies hold relatively constant for varying scenario sizes. On average, the input performance of the ER2 policy performs best while the AR2 policy leads to the lowest input performance. This effect occurs because empty boxes can be acquired more quickly by the input ports than boxes that are partially filled. Moreover, ER policies obviously require less boxes than AR policies and so lead to significantly higher input performance.

In terms of output performance, the results show that the ER1 strategy outperforms the other strategies. In the case of the large scenario, applying the ER1 policy leads to an average performance improvement of ca. 7%, which could have a significant impact on the revenue of a company over the course of a fiscal year. We believe the reason behind this to be that orders are satisfied without requiring multiple bins when multiple units of a product are requested. In the AR2 case, the amount of products stored in each bin is lower than in the AR1 case, leading to reduced performance, even though the retrieval time of individual bins is potentially lowered.

Figure 7 shows the output performance of the policies when we vary the number of product types on the large scenario. When the number of product types is low, all policies perform better because the distance of bins to the output ports is lower and the bin utilization is higher. Especially the policies ER2 and AR2 show better performance with low numbers of product types because less bins have to be transported to the stations. However, the probability that products are ordered together (at random) decreases with rising number of product types. This can be seen in Figure 8, in which the number of bins

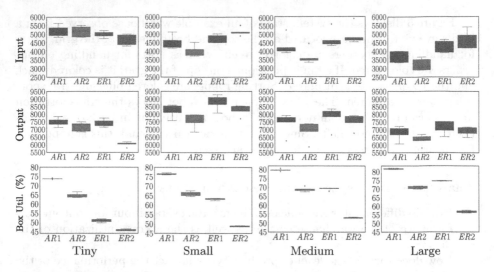

Figure 6: Input and output performance (number of items) and box utilization (%) over the entire 8-hour planning horizon for all four scenario sizes.

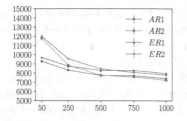

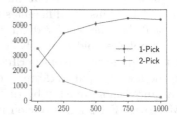

Figure 7: Output performance when varying the number of product types for the large scenario.

Figure 8: Number of bins satisfying one/two products in a single order (1-pick/2-pick) for the AR2 policy for varying numbers of product types for the large scenario.

satisfying two products from the same order declines drastically for AR2. This shows that for the ER2 and AR2 strategies to work, the products must be very likely to be ordered together. Alternatively, the products could be different pieces of a single product that can be ordered separately or together, for example a car part and the matching screws for mounting the component. We intend to investigate this further in future work.

Moreover, we investigate how different policies perform if the number of product types per input order varies. Figure 9 represents the input and output performance for the ER2 policy in case of only one product type per input order (ER2-1) and six product types per input order (ER2-6). The results reveal that the input performance of ER2 can be significantly increased if the number of products per order is raised. This effect occurs because empty boxes can be filled more quickly. However, the output performance remains relatively constant.

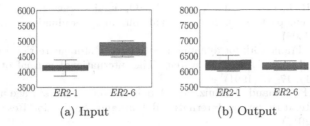

(a) Input   (b) Output

Figure 9: Input and output performance (in number of products) for input orders with one or with six product types for the ER2 strategy.

6   Conclusion

We presented a novel discrete event simulation for automated grid-based storage systems and evaluated simple policies for inputting products into the system. Although our simulation period is relatively short, an encouraging result is that relatively simple strategies are sufficient for raising the input efficiency of the system. This raises hope that more advanced policies could have an even larger effect. However, somewhat disconcertingly, storing products together is difficult to do unless there is significant domain knowledge available about which items are often ordered together. For future work, we intend to try to match items based on past orders. A challenge is that for businesses with a high product turnover rate, sufficient historical data may not be directly available. Another open question is how grid-based storage compares to other robotic fulfillment systems, such as rack-carrying systems, when given a similar set of products and input/output orders.

Acknowledgments We thank Max Wissing for the visualizations of the grid-based storage system.

References

1. Amazon Robotics: www.amazonrobotics.com (2017), last access: 31.05.2017
2. AutoStore: www.autostoresystem.com (2017), last access: 15.05.2017
3. Azadeh, K., de Koster, M., Roy, D.: Robotized warehouse systems: Developments and research opportunities. Social Science Research Network (2017)
4. Chang, D.T., Wen, U.P., Lin, J.T.: The impact of acceleration/deceleration on travel-time models for automated storage/retrieval systems. IIE Transactions 27(1), 108–111 (1995)
5. CycloneCarrier: www.swisslog.com/CycloneCarrier (2017), last access: 06.06.2017
6. De Koster, R., Le-Duc, T., Roodbergen, K.J.: Design and control of warehouse order picking: A literature review. European Journal of Operational Research 182(2), 481–501 (2007)

7. De Koster, R.B., Le-Duc, T., Yugang, Y.: Optimal storage rack design for a 3-dimensional compact as/rs. International journal of production research 46(6), 1495–1514 (2008)
8. Egbelu, P.J.: Framework for dynamic positioning of storage/retrieval machines in an automated storage/retrieval system. The international journal of production research 29(1), 17–37 (1991)
9. Gagliardi, J.P., Renaud, J., Ruiz, A.: Models for automated storage and retrieval systems: a literature review. International Journal of Production Research 50(24), 7110–7125 (2012)
10. Gu, J., Goetschalckx, M., McGinnis, L.F.: Research on warehouse operation: A comprehensive review. European journal of operational research 177(1), 1–21 (2007)
11. Gu, J., Goetschalckx, M., McGinnis, L.F.: Research on warehouse design and performance evaluation: A comprehensive review. European Journal of Operational Research 203(3), 539–549 (2010)
12. Hart, P.E., Nilsson, N.J., Raphael, B.: A formal basis for the heuristic determination of minimum cost paths. IEEE transactions on Systems Science and Cybernetics 4(2), 100–107 (1968)
13. Hompel, M., Schmidt, T.: Warehouse Management: Automatisierung und Organisation von Lager-und Kommissioniersystemen. Springer-Verlag (2013)
14. Lamballais, T., Roy, D., De Koster, M.: Estimating performance in a robotic mobile fulfillment system. European Journal of Operational Research 256(3), 976–990 (2017)
15. Law, A.: Simulation Modeling and Analysis. McGraw-Hill, 5th edn. (2014)
16. Merschformmann, M., Xie, L., Erdmann, D.: Path planning for robotic mobile fulllment systems (2017)
17. Mirzaei, M., De Koster, R.B., Zaerpour, N.: Modelling load retrievals in puzzle-based storage systems. International Journal of Production Research pp. 1–13 (2017)
18. Roodbergen, K.J., Vis, I.F.: A survey of literature on automated storage and retrieval systems. European journal of operational research 194(2), 343–362 (2009)
19. Sari, Z., Saygin, C., Ghouali, N.: Travel-time models for flow-rack automated storage and retrieval systems. The International Journal of Advanced Manufacturing Technology 25(9), 979–987 (2005)
20. Sari, Z., Saygin, C., Ghouali, N.: The application of discrete event simulation and system dynamics in the logistics and supply chain context. Decision Support Systems 52(4), 802–815 (2012)
21. Tompkins, J.A., White, J.A., Bozer, Y.A., Tanchoco, J.M.A.: Facilities planning. John Wiley & Sons (2010)
22. Tornado: www.swisslog.com/tornado (2017), last access: 06.06.2017
23. Wen, U., Chang, D., Chen, S.: The impact of acceleration/deceleration on travel-time models in class-based automated S/R systems. IIE Trans. 33, 599–608 (2001)
24. Yu, Y., De Koster, M.: Designing an optimal turnover-based storage rack for a 3d compact automated storage and retrieval system. International Journal of Production Research 47(6), 1551–1571 (2009)
25. Zaerpour, N., Yu, Y., de Koster, R.B.: Small is beautiful: A framework for evaluating and optimizing live-cube compact storage systems. Transportation Science (2015)
26. Zou, B., de Koster, M., Xu, X.: Evaluating dedicated and shared storage policies in robot-based compact storage and retrieval systems. Social Science Research Network (2016)

Quality-Aware Modeling and Optimal Scheduling for Perishable Good Distribution Networks: The Case of Banana Logistics

Xiao. Lin[1], Rudy R. Negenborn[1], Mark B. Duinkerken[1],
and Gabriel. Lodewijks[2]

[1] Department of Maritime & Transport Technology
Delft University of Technology, Delft, The Netherlands
x.lin@tudelft.nl
[2] School of Aviation, University of New South Wales
NSW 2052, Sydney, Australia

Abstract. Modern technologies have enabled approaches to estimate freshness of perishable products during production and distribution. Nevertheless, the loss of perishable goods is still high due to the deteriorating nature and inefficiencies in supply chains. This research focuses on improving the scheduling of banana logistics using real-time quality information. Bananas are typically shipped from tropical production sites to other places in the world. With temperature controlled reefer containers and sensor technologies, bananas can be monitored during transport and situations like early ripening can be predicted. In order to minimize spoilage, we propose a mathematical model for scheduling logistics activities with the consideration of both the biological process and the logistics procedure of bananas. Results of simulation experiments indicate that the method could reduce spoilage using real-time monitoring and scheduling.

Keywords: Perishable goods logistics, banana supply chain, green-life, ripeness, quality-aware modeling.

1 Introduction

Each year, approximately 45% of fruits and vegetables produced for human consumption are lost worldwide according to Food & Agriculture Organization [3]. The wastage happens at all stages of supply chains, namely farming, post-harvest, processing, distribution, and consumption, due to the perishing nature of fresh products and inefficiencies in supply chains.

The advancing of modern technologies such as sensing and communication provides new insights on perishable goods supply chain planning and potential solutions to reduce the wastage due to perishing feature of agricultural products and inefficiencies of logistics activities [5]. For example, Jedermann et al. [4] study the impact of banana quality change on an international banana supply chain. They conclude that remote quality monitoring has high potential in improving

© Springer International Publishing AG 2017
T. Bektaş et al. (Eds.), ICCL 2017, LNCS 10572, pp. 483–497, 2017.
https://doi.org/10.1007/978-3-319-68496-3_32

supervision of transport processes to reduce losses in a banana supply chain. Furthermore, techniques of ripening bananas in reefer containers can be made available with remote monitoring and supervision.

Transport and logistics planning for perishable goods has received growing attention from research. By considering quality information along supply chains, decision makers can have better control over the influence of perishability. Nevertheless, limited research explicitly considers perishability matters in planning and decision making processes [2]. For example, Rong et al. [11] study a multi-echelon supply chain using a network flow model. Their approach reflects the impacts of quality information on logistics planning decisions by showing a clear relationship between an increased cooling cost and prolonged shelf life. They incorporate product deterioration by duplicating nodes for products of different quality levels at each location. Similarly, Yu and Nagurney [13] develop a food supply chain model based on network flow. They capture quality decay by assigning multipliers to arcs in the network. However, since network models aggregate products as flows in their formulations, they limit the complexity of the quality models considered. This is because quality decreasing and decisions in distribution of products are two different events in a perishable goods supply chain. Although quality aspect and logistics aspect can affect each other, they should not be considered in such way that one is dependent on the other [6].

The aforementioned approaches may have limited potential in addressing quality attributes in a more realistic way, which could be one of the reasons why Ahumada and Villalobos [1] observe a lack of planning models addressing realistic shelf life features in the different echelons of supply chains. In reality, perishable goods differ in their depreciation natures. Pahl and Voss [9] observed 3 basic types of product quality depreciation in general: perishability, by which perishable goods lose all the value after a certain time period; discrete/continuous deterioration, describing a decreasing of value in stages or continuously. In our previous work, we have proposed a quality-aware modeling method in [6] and applied this method for starch potato post-harvest scheduling [7]. In that research, starch content in potatoes, considered as product quality, follows a continuous deterioration described by a kinetic model. It is demonstrated that the quality-aware modeling method has the potential of incorporating more realistic quality features, which can better assist decision making processes in supply chain planing.

In this paper, we take a first step to consider real-time quality information made available in logistics activities of a banana supply chain. As one of the most traded fruit in the world (18.7 million tons exported worldwide in 2011 [10]), bananas suffer from spoilage due to the perishing nature [12]. In order to increase the efficiency of logistics activities in banana supply chains and reduce loss, we propose a scheduling method based on an extension of the quality-aware modeling approach. We focus on a part of an international banana supply chain, from a warehouse at a port to distribution centers: supply chain planners need to make decisions on which container of bananas to be moved to which location at what time, and which bananas to go through a ripening process for how much

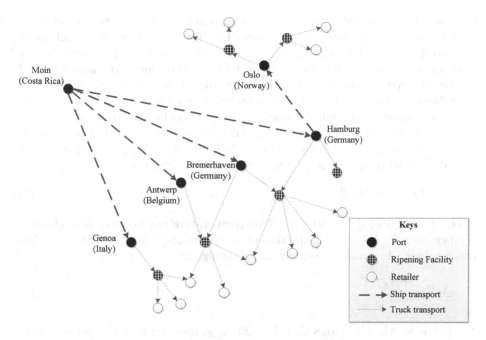

Fig. 1: A banana distribution network (adapted from [8]).

time. Different from the previous study on potato post-harvest scheduling in [7], in a banana supply chain, the logistics activities need to be considered in more detail. For instance, supply chain planners need to make schedules to fulfill the demand from retailers, and bananas' quality changing process is more complex and has a direct impact on acceptance of retailers.

The remainder of this paper is organized as follows. Section 2 analyzes the logistics process of banana supply chains as well as the physiological features of bananas. A scheduling method based on a quality-aware model is then proposed. Subsequently, simulation experiments are conducted in Section 3. We compare results with the proposed method with a current one. Section 4 concludes the paper and provides directions for future research.

2   Scheduling with quality information for a banana logistics system

In this section, we firstly formalize our problem. Then assumptions considered in this study are listed. Next, the quality-aware model is developed for scheduling in a banana logistics system.

2.1   Problem statement and assumptions

Figure 1 shows a banana distribution network in Europe. Bananas grown in tropical countries are shipped to several ports in Europe. They are then transported by truck to local ripening facilities and afterwards to wholesalers and retailers. In a ripening facility, bananas stay 4-8 days to get ethylene treatment to be ripened. In today's banana supply chain, the latest quality information is only available when bananas reach certain check points. If bananas are found with bad quality at a check point, they should be discarded, or a secondary customer who is willing to receive them should be contacted. If real-time information would be available, adjustments could be made in time to avoid such situations.

The quality change of bananas can be divided into two periods: the green-life period and the ripe period. The relationship between the length of the green-life period t^{GP} and temperature T is derived from [4] as follows:

$$t^{\mathrm{GP}}(T) = 159.86e^{-0.124T}. \tag{1}$$

When $T = 13.5°C$, $t^{\mathrm{GP}} = 30$ days. This temperature can be used as a reference temperature T_0, so that a reduction of green-life Δg^{T_0} is 1 day. When T has other values, Δg^T varies based on the following rate:

$$\Delta g^T = \frac{t^{\mathrm{GP}}(T_0)}{t^{\mathrm{GP}}(T)}. \tag{2}$$

For instance, when $T = 16.8°C$, $t^{\mathrm{GP}} = 20$ days, meaning that the bananas have their green-life decreasing 1.5 times as fast as when considering T_0. Therefore, $\Delta g^{16.8} = 1.5\Delta g^{T_0}$. For bananas in the ripe period, we consider an indicator of ripeness r, which increases after bananas have gone through the ripening process. The ripeness is checked at retailers when making the decision of whether to accept the bananas.

The objective of this paper is to propose a scheduling method for banana supply chains, based on the quality-aware modeling approach. The scheduling method makes decisions on distribution and ripening of bananas with the consideration of quality information, aiming at reducing losses in banana supply chains, which could be useful for banana trading companies or logistics service providers. We state the following general assumptions in the modeling:

- Bananas have homogeneous quality within each container.
- The time bananas can remain green does not affect the time needed for ripening.
- Information regarding the quality of bananas is predictable and available.
- Demand from retailers is known in advance.
- Bananas that ripen early are considered spoiled and thus discarded.

Next, we present the quality-aware model for the banana logistics.

2.2 Quality-aware modeling for banana logistics

We consider a container of bananas as a minimum controllable unit $m \in \mathcal{M}$, with $\mathcal{M}$ being the collection of considered containers. Each container goes through different stages $i \in \mathcal{N}$ as it is transported in the supply chain over a discrete

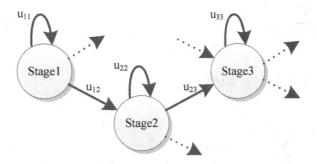

Fig. 2: A typical example of the logistics representation. Each node represents a stage that a container could be at; each arc represents a possible transition from one stage to another.

time horizon $\mathcal{K} = \{1, 2, \dots\}$. Container m can be at a certain stage i (e.g., at a port) at time step $k \in \mathcal{K}$ (denoted by $l_{mi}(k) = 1$, otherwise $l_{mi}(k) = 0$); and if a decision at time step k is made to move this container to another stage j (e.g., loaded on a truck), $u_{mij}(k) = 1$ and $l_{mj}(k+1) = 1$. The collections of stages (nodes) and transitions (arcs) form a graph $\mathcal{G} = \{\mathcal{N}, \mathcal{E}\}$, as shown in Figure 2. Note that a unit m can stay at a stage i over multiple time steps ($u_{mij}(k) = 1$, $i = j$). The collections of origin stages (where containers start from) and destination stages (where containers should end up) are denoted by $\mathcal{O}$ and $\mathcal{D}$, respectively. Variables related to each unit m are linked by three types of constraints, namely logistics, demand from retailers, and quality constraints. Using the introduced notation, we next provide all the constraints of the model followed by their motivations:

$$\sum_{j \in S(i) \cup \{i\}} u_{mij}(k) = l_{mi}(k), \qquad \forall m \in \mathcal{M}, i \in \mathcal{N}, k \in \mathcal{K} \quad (3)$$

$$\sum_{i \in P(j) \cup \{j\}} u_{mij}(k) = l_{mj}(k+1), \qquad \forall m \in \mathcal{M}, j \in \mathcal{N}, k \in \mathcal{K} \quad (4)$$

$$\sum_{i \in \mathcal{N}} l_{mi}(k) = 1, \qquad \forall m \in \mathcal{M}, k \in \mathcal{K} \quad (5)$$

$$\sum_{j \in S(i) \cup \{i\}} \left(t_{mi}^{\text{lead}} u_{mij}(k) \right) - a_{mj}(k) - Q u_{mjj}(k+1) \leq 0, \qquad (6)$$

$$\forall m \in \mathcal{M}, i \in \mathcal{N}, k \in \mathcal{K}$$

$$a_{mj}(k) = \sum_{\tau=1}^{k} \sum_{i \in P(j) \cup \{j\}} u_{mij}(\tau), \qquad \forall m \in \mathcal{M}, j \in \mathcal{N}, k \in \mathcal{K} \quad (7)$$

$$\sum_{m \in \mathcal{M}} \sum_{j \in P(i) \cup \{i\}} u_{mji}(k) \leq C_i^{\text{node}}(k+1), \qquad \forall i \in \mathcal{N}, k \in \mathcal{K} \quad (8)$$

$$\sum_{m \in \mathcal{M}} \sum_{j \in S(i)} u_{mij}(k) \leq C_i^{\text{arc}}(k), \qquad \forall i \in \mathcal{N}, k \in \mathcal{K} \quad (9)$$

$$s_i(k) = \sum_{m \in \mathcal{M}} \sum_{j \in P(i)} u_{mij}(k), \qquad \forall i \in \mathcal{D}, k \in \mathcal{K} \tag{10}$$

$$\sum_{\tau=0}^{l_w-1} f_i^\tau(k) + f_i^C(k) = d_i(k), \qquad \forall i \in \mathcal{D}, k \in \mathcal{K} \tag{11}$$

$$s_i(k) = \sum_{\tau=0}^{\min(l_w-1,k-1)} f_i^\tau(k-\tau), \qquad \forall i \in \mathcal{D}, k \in \mathcal{K} \tag{12}$$

$$g_m(k+1) = g_m(k) - \Delta g_m^T(k), \qquad \forall m \in \mathcal{M}, k \in \mathcal{K} \tag{13}$$

$$r_m(k+1) = r_m(k) + \Delta r_m(k), \qquad \forall m \in \mathcal{M}, k \in \mathcal{K} \tag{14}$$

$$\Delta r_m(k) \leq Q d_m^{\mathrm{ripe}}(k), \qquad \forall m \in \mathcal{M}, k \in \mathcal{K} \tag{15}$$

$$Q \Delta r_m(k) \geq d_m^{\mathrm{ripe}}(k), \qquad \forall m \in \mathcal{M}, k \in \mathcal{K} \tag{16}$$

$$\Delta r_m(k) \leq 1 + Q \sum_{j \in N_{\mathrm{RF}}} \sum_{i \in P(i)} u_{mij}(k), \qquad \forall m \in \mathcal{M}, k \in \mathcal{K} \tag{17}$$

$$\sum_{i=P(j)} u_{mij}(k) \leq Q g_m(k), \qquad \forall m \in \mathcal{M}, j \in N_{\mathrm{RF}}, k \in \mathcal{K} \tag{18}$$

$$\sum_{k \in \mathcal{K}} d_m^{\mathrm{ethy}}(k) \leq 1, \qquad \forall m \in \mathcal{M} \tag{19}$$

$$\sum_{j \in N_{\mathrm{RF}}} \sum_{i \in P(j)} u_{mij}(k) \geq d_m^{\mathrm{ethy}}(k+1), \qquad \forall m \in \mathcal{M}, k \in \mathcal{K} \tag{20}$$

$$Q(d_m^{\mathrm{ethy}}(k) - 1) \leq g_m(k+1), \qquad \forall m \in \mathcal{M}, k \in \mathcal{K} \tag{21}$$

$$d_m^{\mathrm{ripe}}(k+1) = d_m^{\mathrm{ripe}}(k) + d_m^{\mathrm{ethy}}(k), \qquad \forall m \in \mathcal{M}, k \in \mathcal{K} \tag{22}$$

$$Q(1 - \sum_{j \in \mathcal{D}} \sum_{i \in P(j)} u_{mij}(k)) \geq r_m(k+1) - r^{\mathrm{high}}, \qquad \forall m \in \mathcal{M}, k \in \mathcal{K} \tag{23}$$

$$Q(1 - \sum_{j \in \mathcal{D}} \sum_{i \in P(j)} u_{mij}(k)) \geq r^{\mathrm{low}} - r_m(k+1), \qquad \forall m \in \mathcal{M}, k \in \mathcal{K}. \tag{24}$$

Logistics. Constraints (3)-(9) belong to the aspects related to the logistics. Constraints (3) and (4) denote that when changing stages, containers follow the directed arcs. In the constraints, $P(i)$ and $S(i)$ are the collections of predecessor and successor nodes of node i excluding i itself. Constraint (5) ensures that each container can only be at one of the stages for each time step. Constraint (6) ensures that a lead time t_{mi}^{lead} is given to container m when it enters a node i and can only move out after the lead time is reached. Here (also for the rest of the constraints) Q is a big number. In (7), $a_{mj}(k)$ is a counter that calculates the number of time steps for which container m has stayed in node j up to time step k. Constraint (8) limits the number of containers at node i at time step k, and (9) limits the number of containers moving from node i to any other successive nodes.

Demand from retailers. Constraints (10)-(12) belong to this aspect. Logistics planners need to fulfill retailers' demand by sending them ripe bananas from ripening facilities. Constraint (10) explains the relation between number of containers received by wholesaler $i \in \mathcal{D}$ and decisions of the logistics planners. Constraint (11) specifies how demand from retailer $i \in \mathcal{D}$ at time step k can be responded in different ways: $f_i^\tau(k)$ represents the number of containers that fulfills the demand with a τ days' delay ($0 \leq \tau \leq l_{\text{w}} - 1$), and $f_i^C(k)$ denotes the number of containers in the demand $d_i(k)$ that cannot be fulfilled. Constraint (12) links fulfillments of demand f_i^τ to supply $s_i(k)$. Note that a supply of container on day k can respond to the demand from day $k - l_{\text{w}+1}$ to day k.

Quality. Constraints (13)-(24) belong to the aspect of quality. Constraint (13) describes the decreasing of green-life period $g_m(k)$ of bananas in container m in days, with $\Delta g_m^T(k)$ derived from (2). Constraint (14) describes quality change of bananas after ripening. Variable $r_m(k)$ represents ripeness of bananas. Integer decision variable $\Delta r_m(k)$ represents the increasing of ripeness, which can be one of the values from $\{0, 1, 2\}$ for each day, each container. When bananas are not ripe, $\Delta r_m(k) = 0$, which is described by (15). When bananas are in ripening facilities, $\Delta r_m(k)$ can be 1 or 2 depending on how fast they need to be ripened but cannot be 0, limited by (16). After moving out of ripening facilities $\Delta r_m(k) = 1$ in a static environment, ensured by (17). Constraint (18) enforces that only containers with unripe bananas ($g_m(k) \geq 0$) can be moved to a ripening facility $j \in \mathcal{N}_{\text{RF}}$. Constraint (19) makes sure that each container m can go through ripening process no more than once. Constraint (20) indicates that the decisions to start ripening can only be made when container m is in a ripening facility. Constraint (21) ensures that containers holding ripe bananas cannot go through ripening process. In Constraint (22), an indicator d_m^{ripe} becomes 1 from 0 at time step k when bananas in container m go through an ethylene treatment at time step k ($d_m^{\text{ripe}}(k) = 1$). Wholesalers need bananas within a certain ripeness range, which is ensured by (23) and (24) with a maximum and minimum acceptable range of ripeness r^{high} and r^{low}.

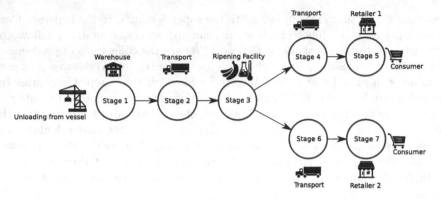

Fig. 3: Considered supply chain.

2.3   Scheduling objective

We consider an objective function over a finite time period ($\mathcal{K} = \{1, \ldots, N_\mathrm{s}\}$) as follows:

$$
J = \sum_{k=1}^{N_\mathrm{s}} \sum_{i \in \mathcal{D}} s_i(k)\alpha - \sum_{k=1}^{N_\mathrm{s}} \sum_{m \in \mathcal{M}} \sum_{(i,j) \in \mathcal{E}} u_{mij}(k)\beta_{ij}
$$
$$
- \sum_{k=1}^{N_\mathrm{s}} \sum_{i \in \mathcal{D}} \sum_{\tau=0}^{min(l_\mathrm{w}-1,k-1)} (f_i^\tau(k-\tau)\gamma\tau) - \sum_{k=1}^{N_\mathrm{s}} \sum_{i \in \mathcal{D}} f_i^\mathrm{C}(k)\delta,
\tag{25}
$$

in which α is the price for delivering a container to a wholesaler; β_{ij} is the cost for a container to transit from stage i to stage j (e.g., cost for transport); γ is the penalty for delaying an order of a container by 1 day; δ is the penalty for not fulfilling a demand of a container.

In summary, the quality-aware model considers three aspects. First, it considers the decisions in logistics activities including movements of the containers (3)–(9). Secondly, demand-supply coupling is considered in Constraints (10)–(12). Thirdly, we consider bananas' two-period quality changing process (13)–(14), and how quality affects decision making in logistics (18)–(24). The objective function considers income for selling bananas to retailers, transition costs, and penalties for delays and lost sales. The combination of the objective function and the constraints forms a mixed-integer linear programming (MILP) problem: max J, subject to Constraints (3)-(24). The decision variables are $u_{mij}(k)$, $f_i^\tau(k)$, $f_i^\mathrm{C}(k)$, $\Delta r_m(k)$, and $d_m^{\mathrm{ethy}}(k)$, for all $k \in \{1, 2, \ldots, N_\mathrm{s}\}$.

3   Simulation experiments

In this section, simulation experiments are carried out to illustrate the potential of the proposed scheduling method. In the experiments, we consider a typical

Table 1: Scenario settings

Variable	Value
M	5
N	7
N_p	16
l_w	3
t^{lead}	$t_3^{\text{lead}} = 4, t_6^{\text{lead}} = 2$
C_3^{node}	2
$d_i(k)$	$d_5(7) = 3, d_5(10) = 3, d_5(14) = 1$ $d_7(1) = 1, d_7(8) = 1$
$\Delta g_m(k), \Delta r_m(k)$	1
$g_m(1)$	$[7, 3, 2, 8, 10]$
$r_5^{\text{high}}, r_7^{\text{high}}$	12, 11
$r_5^{\text{low}}, r_7^{\text{low}}$	8, 7
α	10
β	0
γ	1
δ	5

supply chain shown in Figure 3. There are seven stages that each container with bananas could be located in. Stage 1 represents the container being stored in the warehouse at the port of destination. Stage 2 represents the transportation from the port to a ripening facility by truck. Stage 3 is when the container being at the ripening facility. Stage 4 and 6 are the container being transported to different retailers (denoted by stage 5 and 7).

In order to illustrate the performance of the proposed scheduling method, we perform two experiments: one inspired by the current handling procedures, the other based on our proposed future scheduling method. In the current case experiment, quality information is only available at certain check points. The ripening facilities identify early ripened bananas upon their arrival and discard the containers that do not meet the requirement; the retailers examine the ripeness of bananas upon arrival and make decisions on accepting or rejecting bananas; reefer containers are moved according to a pre-defined sequence.

3.1   Scenario setup

The details of a typical scenario setting are shown in Table 1. We assume that five of the reefer containers are assigned to a particular ripening facility. The lead times for the transport from the port to the ripening facility (Stage 2) and from the ripening facility to the two retailers (Stage 4 and 6) are 1, 1, and 2, respectively. The capacity of the ripening facility is two containers. The demand of retailer 1 and retailer 2 falls on different days given in the table. We consider the temperature in containers to be static, but the initial remaining green-life can vary among containers, and quality requirements of the retailers can also

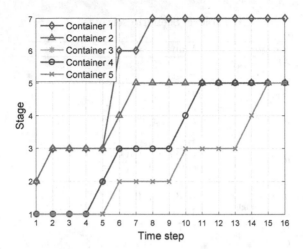

Fig. 4: Movements of each container over time in the current case experiment.

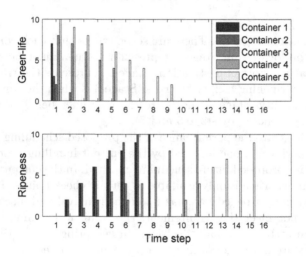

Fig. 5: Quality of each container over time in the current case experiment.
(Only positive green-life is shown.)

differ as shown in the table. Fulfilling a container of bananas with the right quality brings 10,000 EUR, while each day's delay of an order costs the supply chain planner 1,000 EUR. Canceling the order results in a penalty of 5,000 EUR. We assume that the ripening facilities and transport companies are contracted, so that transporting and ripening costs are fixed. The experiments are carried out using Matlab 2015b, on a desktop with Intel Core 2 CPU Q8400, 4GB RAM, and Windows 7-64bit. The optimization problems are solved using the CPLEX

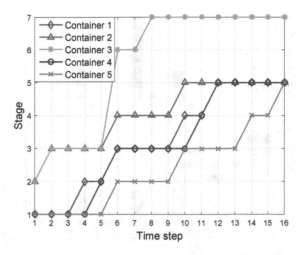

Fig. 6: Movements of each container over time by the proposed method.

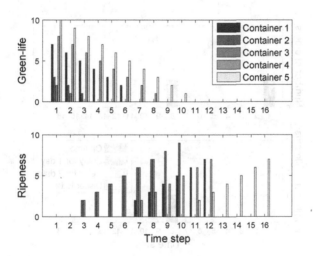

Fig. 7: Quality of each container over time with the proposed method. (Only positive green-life is shown.)

(v12.5.1) MILP solver. Next, we compare the results given by the current case experiment and the experiment with the proposed method.

3.2   Results and discussion

Solving the MILP problem takes only a few seconds. The results are shown in Figures 4-11. Figure 4 shows the scheduled container movements over time for the current case experiment. From the figure we can see that container 1 and

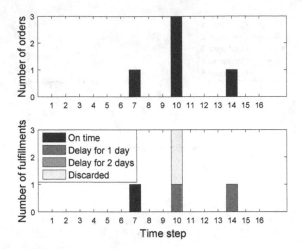

Fig. 8: Fulfillments of Retailer 1 in the current case experiment.

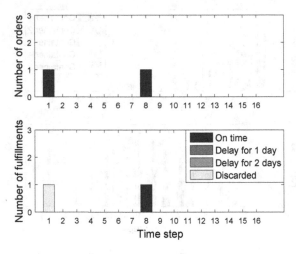

Fig. 9: Fulfillments of Retailer 2 in the current case experiment.

2 are given priority to move to the ripening facility while container 3, 4, and 5 await for the call. Note that container 3 (overlaps with Container 4) no longer moves forward after reaching the ripening facility (stage 3) at time step 6. The reason is shown in Figure 5: the green-life of bananas in container 3 is the lowest amongst the five containers. However, the ripening facility only becomes aware of this on time step 6 and has to discard the bananas.

For the future case experiment, using the proposed method, Figure 6 shows the scheduled movements according to the optimization. Considering the qual-

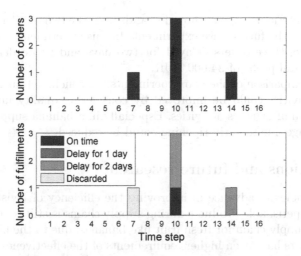

Fig. 10: Fulfillments of Retailer 1 with the proposed method.

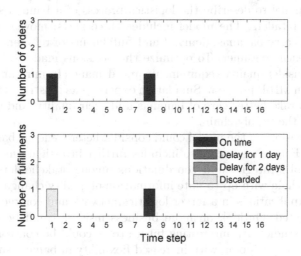

Fig. 11: Fulfillments of Retailer 2 with the proposed method.

ity conditions, container 2 and 3 receive the priority to be transported to the ripening facility before early ripening takes place (see Figure 7). This method saves the bananas in container 3 from being discarded.

Figure 8 and Figure 9 show how demands from the two retailers are fulfilled (or discarded) in the current case experiment. In this experiment, two orders are fulfilled on time, two orders delayed for a day, and three orders are not fulfilled, resulting in a total profit of 23,000 EUR.

Figure 10 and Figure 11 show how demands from the two retailers are fulfilled (or discarded) in the future case experiment. In this experiment, two orders are fulfilled on time, three orders delayed for two days and two orders discarded, resulting in a total profit of 34,000 EUR.

From the comparison of the two experiments, we conclude that the efficiency of logistics activities could be improved by considering quality information in the optimization of logistics activities. Especially in a banana supply chain, the potential wastage due to early ripening could be reduced.

4   Conclusions and future research

Although technologies advance in improving the efficiency of logistics systems, the wastage of perishable products during supply chains is still concerning. Particularly, in a supply chain for fresh fruit like bananas, due to the high perishing nature, customers have even higher requirements of the effectiveness of logistics. Therefore, it could be beneficial to take perishability into consideration when making plans for logistics activities. This research focuses on a banana supply chain. Based on descriptions of remaining green-life and ripeness, we propose a quality-aware model to describe the logistics process of a banana supply chain from a port to retailers. The model includes three parts: movements of reefer containers that carry bananas, demand and fulfillments of retailers, and quality of bananas in each container. To optimize the decisions made by supply chain planners, we consider quality requirements and demands from retailers as objectives, forming an MILP problem. Simulation experiments illustrate that decisions can be made to take better care of bananas and their quality, and could reduce wastage during the supply chain.

Further extensions of the model could consider heterogeneous banana quality in a container. Future research also includes further investigations on adopting real-time control strategies and coordinations among stakeholders within the banana supply chain with up-to-date information of quality change and logistics disturbances. Applications in a larger logistics network and complexity analysis can be investigated. Outlook on more business insights could be gained from real-world case studies. An interesting future topic could be controlled ripening in containers during shipping with increased flexibility in banana supply chains.

Acknowledgment

This research is supported by the China Scholarship Council under Grant 2014-06950004: "Controlled cool logistics: Real-time coordination for fresher products".

References

1. Ahumada, O., Villalobos, J.R.: Application of planning models in the agri-food supply chain: A review. European Journal of Operational Research 196(1), 1–20 (2009)

2. Amorim, P., Meyr, H., Almeder, C., Almada-Lobo, B.: Managing perishability in production-distribution planning: a discussion and review. Flexible Services and Manufacturing Journal 25(3), 389–413 (2013)
3. FAO: Global food losses and food waste: Extent, causes and prevention. Rome, Italy (2011)
4. Jedermann, R., Praeger, U., Geyer, M., Lang, W.: Remote quality monitoring in the banana chain. Philosophical Transactions of the Royal Society of London A: Mathematical, Physical and Engineering Sciences 372(2017), 20130303 (2014)
5. Lin, X., Negenborn, R.R., Lodewijks, G.: Survey on operational perishables quality control and logistics. In: Proceedings of the 6th International Conference on Computational Logistics. pp. 398–421. Delft, The Netherlands (2015)
6. Lin, X., Negenborn, R.R., Lodewijks, G.: Towards quality-aware control of perishable goods in synchromodal transport networks. In: Proceedings of the 5th IFAC Conference on Sensing, Control and Automation Technologies for Agriculture. pp. 132–137. Seattle, Washington (2016)
7. Lin, X., Negenborn, R.R., Lodewijks, G.: Predictive quality-aware control for scheduling of potato starch production. Technical report, Delft University of Technology (2017)
8. Lütjen, M., Dittmer, P., Veigt, M.: Quality driven distribution of intelligent containers in cold chain logistics networks. Production Engineering 7(2-3), 291–297 (2013)
9. Pahl, J., Voß, S.: Integrating deterioration and lifetime constraints in production and supply chain planning: A survey. European Journal of Operational Research 238(3), 654–674 (2014)
10. Potts, J., Lynch, M., Wilkings, A., Huppé, G., Cunningham, M., Voora, V.: The state of sustainability initiatives review 2014: Standards and the green economy. International Institute for Sustainable Development (IISD) and the International Institute for Environment and Development (IIED) 332 (2014)
11. Rong, A., Akkerman, R., Grunow, M.: An optimization approach for managing fresh food quality throughout the supply chain. International Journal of Production Economics 131(1), 421–429 (2011)
12. Ventour, L.: The food we waste, vol. 237. WRAP Banbury/Oxon (2008)
13. Yu, M., Nagurney, A.: Competitive food supply chain networks with application to fresh produce. European Journal of Operational Research 224(2), 273–282 (2013)

Cost-Efficient Allocation of Bikes to Stations in Bike Sharing Systems

Patrick Vogel[1], Jan Fabian Ehmke[2], and Dirk Christian Mattfeld[1]

[1] Technische Universität Braunschweig, Decision Support Group, 38106 Braunschweig, Germany
[2] Otto-von-Guericke University Magdeburg, Management Science Group, 39106 Magdeburg, Germany, jan.ehmke@ovgu.de

Abstract. In Bike Sharing Systems, spatio-temporal variation of rentals leads to imbalances in the distribution of bikes causing full or empty stations in the course of a day. Providing a sufficient number of bikes and bike racks is crucial for the viability of these systems. Introducing the notion of service network design, we aim to show the usefulness of tactical planning for bike sharing systems. We design a bike sharing service network considering the suitable aggregation of operational data as well as the anticipation of operational decisions. In particular, we present a mixed-integer programming formulation aiming at cost-efficient allocation of bikes to stations given a predefined service level for different scenarios of bike demand. The scenarios are considered as realizations of typical bike flows between stations in terms of time-dependent origin / destination matrices. Operational relocation decisions are anticipated by a dynamic transportation model. The proposed methodology is exemplified based on two years of operational data from Vienna's "Citybike Wien". Computational experiments show how target fill levels vary according to the different scenarios of bike demand. Furthermore, spatio-temporal characteristics of relocation services are derived, which can support operators of bike sharing systems in the planning of relocation services.

Keywords: Service Network Design, Shared Mobility, Relocation.

1 Bike Sharing Systems

Emerging metropolitan areas need efficient and sustainable mobility services in order to ensure their attractiveness, quality of life, and economic power. Municipalities have begun to implement innovative shared mobility systems in order to accommodate the mobility needs of their citizens. The number of implemented Bike Sharing Systems (BSS) is impressive; in Europe, about 400 BSS have been introduced in the last ten years (Büttner and Petersen 2011), and markets in America and Asia are catching up (Shaheen et al. 2010).

BSS provide an individual but likewise public means of transportation for inner city trips (Midgley 2011). They are characterized by a high density of service facilities in heavily populated areas, e.g., with an average distance of 300 meters between bike stations (Büttner and Petersen 2011). Short bike rentals are often free of charge, and revenue is indirectly generated from a license to advertise on street furniture. Rental, return and maintenance processes are automated, enabling fast and easy access as well as one-

© Springer International Publishing AG 2017
T. Bektaş et al. (Eds.), ICCL 2017, LNCS 10572, pp. 498–512, 2017.
https://doi.org/10.1007/978-3-319-68496-3_33

way use and short rental times through unattended stations. Every trip is recorded for tracking and billing purposes.

Efficient and reliable design, management and operation of BSS is challenging. Demand for bike rentals varies strongly, following typical traffic patterns in the course of day and week caused by commuter, leisure or tourist trips. Furthermore, one-way rentals can intensify imbalances in the distribution of bikes. Due to limited capacity at stations, rentals are impossible at empty stations, and returns are impossible at full stations. Hence, BSS operators aim to ensure a service level which is self-stipulated or stipulated by municipalities. For instance, a tendering for the Arlington BSS requests that "stations shall not be full of bicycles for more than 60 minutes during the hours of 8am – 6pm and 180 minutes during the hours of 6pm – 8am" (Metrobike 2009).

Bike imbalances can be handled by means of strategic, tactical or operational planning. On the strategic level, decisions on the number, location and size of stations have to be made. Acquiring a high number of bike racks at stations increases the probability of successful returns. On the tactical level, bike fill levels at stations need to be determined in order to compensate varying bike demand in the course of day. High fill levels can increase the probability of successful rentals and can decrease the probability of successful returns at particular stations, for example. On the operational level, relocation of bikes from commonly full to commonly empty stations can help maintaining the service level. Planning levels are interdependent: reasonable sizing of stations and fill levels of bikes may reduce relocation efforts, whereas high relocation efforts may compensate insufficient sizing and fill levels.

In this paper, we propose an integrated approach of intelligent data analysis and mathematical optimization supporting service network design (SND) in BSS. The presented mathematical mixed-integer program (MIP) determines optimal target fill levels at bike sharing stations by minimizing the expected costs of relocation. The MIP guarantees a given service level for different scenarios of bike demand for a mid-term planning horizon. Scenarios are defined through bike flows that are represented by time-dependent origin / destination (OD) matrices. The required information is derived from the aggregation of recorded customer trips in combination with well-known traffic modeling approaches.

A brief literature overview is presented in Sect. 2. We discuss our approach and present the MIP in Sect. 3. A case study including two years of trip data from Vienna's BSS "Citybike Wien" is shown in Sect. 4, and the paper is concluded in Sect. 5.

2   Recent Literature

Compared to work on strategic and operational planning, literature on tactical planning of shared mobility systems is rather scarce. The following studies differ in whether they include anticipation of operational decisions, especially the relocation operations. We begin with the work that does not anticipate operational decisions.

George and Xia (2011) model shared mobility systems by means of a closed queuing network. Their objective is to maximize profit and to determine the optimal fleet size and allocation of rental vehicles. Cepolina and Farina (2012) determine the fleet size and vehicle allocation for a car sharing system with electric vehicles. Costs for user waiting times and system operation (vehicle purchasing and running costs) are minimized by an algorithm based on Simulated Annealing. Dynamic user-based relocation is assumed to be achieved at no additional cost. Raviv and Kolka (2013) also use queuing models. With the help of a user dissatisfaction function, the optimal fill level at bike sharing stations is determined. Schuijbroek et al. (2013) minimize the costs of relocation and incorporate service level requirements at stations by means of a cluster-first route-second heuristic. They focus on the static case ignoring varying user demand. The service level is precalculated for each station without anticipation of the routing decisions. Finally, Shu et al. (2013) use a network flow model to determine the initial allocation of bikes at stations in order to maximize bike flows and successful trips within the network on a weekly basis. In a separate optimization model, they assess the impact of relocations on the number of required bikes in the system.

To the best of the authors' knowledge, only the following studies anticipate relocation operations in tactical planning. Correia and Antunes (2012) present multi-periodic MIP formulations to maximize the profit of a car sharing system considering the revenue of trips, costs of depot and vehicle maintenance as well as costs of vehicle relocation. They determine the number and the location of stations as well as the number of vehicles at each station in each period of daily operation. They consider static relocation at the end of the day to reset the system to the initial fill level. The validity of the MIP approach is investigated by a simulation model (Jorge et al. 2012). Sayarshad et al. (2012) introduce a dynamic LP formulation to maximize profit in BSS. Relocation, maintenance, capital and holding costs of bikes as well as penalty costs for lost demand are deducted from the revenue generated by trips. Unutilized bikes can be relocated in every period of daily operation. Boyaci et al. (2015) present a MIP formulation for tactical planning of car sharing systems. Here, the revenue of the system is maximized considering station sizes, fill levels and dynamic relocation. Due to the large number of relocation variables, an imaginary hub station is introduced. Relocation is considered only between bike stations and the hub station. This simplification significantly reduces the number of relocation variables.

In the following, we adapt existing optimization approaches of SND and focus on the adequate anticipation of relocation tours. We also present a new approach to aggregate operational data as input for SND.

3   Service Network Design Model

SND requires the aggregation of operational data and the anticipation of operational decisions. In this section, for data aggregation, an information model is proposed, which represents typical bike flows for different scenarios of bike demand by time-dependent OD matrices (Sect. 3.1). In Sect. 3.2, an MIP formulation is presented, aiming at cost-efficient allocation of bikes to stations while maintaining a predefined service level for different scenarios of bike demand. We determine the total number of bikes in the system, optimal target fill levels of stations, and expected relocation operations. Target fill levels ensure the provision of service depending on the time of the day for a given scenario, e.g., high bike demand on a working day in the main season. The anticipation of relocation operations yields the expected costs of relocation services to compensate insufficient fill levels.

3.1   An Information Model for Generation of Typical Bike Flows

BSS automatically record extensive amounts of trip data. Recorded trip data represent individual observations of customer behavior and are therefore not suited as input for tactical planning. Thus, we propose a combined approach of traffic modeling and intelligent data analysis to derive an information model that represents trip purposes and typical bike flows. We detail how this information model can be used to generate bike flows for SND.

Generation of Typical Bike Flows. To fully explore spatio-temporal characteristics of bike trips, we apply the Urban Transportation Planning Systems (UTPS) process (Johnston 2004). The UTPS process is a common approach to model trips in urban areas. Extending this idea with approaches from intelligent data analysis, we derive trip purposes from an extensive amount of trip data recorded by BSS. Then, with the temporal distribution at hand, the spatial distribution of trips between groups of stations with similar temporal activity are determined.

We construct *temporal activity clusters* by cluster analysis as detailed in Vogel et al. (2011). A temporal activity cluster yields the typical proportion of rentals and returns for each hour of the day. As a result of cluster analysis, each station is characterized by its assigned temporal activity cluster. Then, the spatial distribution of trips between stations can be derived from the associated temporal activity clusters as follows:

- The *inter-cluster distribution* describes trip distribution patterns between stations of individual activity clusters. They are specified by the proportion of trips between individual temporal activity clusters for a given hour of the day. For instance, in the morning, the majority of trips is directed from "residential" to "working" clusters, whereas the opposite is true for afternoon hours.
- The *intra-cluster distribution* specifies how trips are distributed from a particular station to all stations contained within a cluster. We approximate this distribution based on the distance between stations and the resulting trip duration. The distribution of trip durations can be derived empirically from recorded trip data.

With the temporal and spatial distributions at hand, the information model can be formalized as follows:

- The BSS consists of a set bike stations $N = \{s_1, ..., s_n\}$.
- The planning horizon comprises $T = \{0, ..., t_{max}\}$ periods, e.g., 24 hourly periods representing a typical working day.
- The total activity of a station s_i is denoted by the absolute number of daily rentals B_i^- and daily returns B_i^+.

- The set of temporal activity clusters is $C = \{c_1, \ldots, c_z\}$.

The clustering $\gamma: N \to C$ assigns each station $s_i \in N$ to a temporal activity cluster $c_j \in C$ defining the trip purposes at the station. Trip purposes are represented by the temporal rental activity $\beta^-_{c_j,t} \in [0,1] \ \forall t \in T, c_j \in C$. The temporal activity expresses the relative hourly activity and thus summarizes to 1 over the course of the day for each cluster, i.e., $\sum_{t \in T} \beta^-_{c_j,t} = 1 \ \forall c_j \in C$. The same holds for returns $\beta^+_{c_j,t} \in [0,1] \forall t \in T, c_j \in C$ with $\sum_{t \in T} \beta^+_{c_j,t} = 1 \ \forall c_j \in C$.

The spatial trip distribution is given according to the inter-cluster distribution $\kappa: C \times C \times T \to [0,1]$ and intra-cluster distribution $\lambda: N \times N \to [0,1]$:

- The inter-cluster distribution expresses the fraction of flows between clusters per time period. The fraction of inter-cluster flows summarizes to 1 from a particular cluster c_i in a specific time period t to all clusters c_j by means of $\sum_{c_j \in C} \kappa_{c_i c_j,t} = 1 \ \forall c_i \in C, t \in T$.
- The intra-cluster distribution expresses the fraction of flows from station s_i to station s_k depending on the assigned cluster. The fraction of intra-cluster flows summarizes to 1 based on flows s_i to all stations s_k of the particular cluster by means of $\sum_{s_k \in c_j} \lambda_{s_i s_k} = 1 \ \forall C_j \in C, s_i \in N$.

With these notation in mind, we can describe the temporal and spatial distribution of bike rentals as follows:

1. *Temporal distribution:* We determine the hourly activity at stations $B^-_{i,t}$ by distributing the number of rentals at stations to the time periods provided by the temporal rental activity: $B^-_{s_i,t} = B^-_{s_i} \cdot \beta^-_{\gamma(s_i),t} \ \forall s_i \in N, t \in T$.
2. *Spatial distribution:*
   a. Inter-cluster distribution: We determine the bike flows $f^-_{s_i c_j,t}: N \times C \times T \to \mathbb{R}^+$ from each station to each cluster by distributing the hourly rentals to the clusters: $f^-_{s_i c_j,t} = B^-_{s_i,t} \cdot \kappa_{\gamma(s_i)c_j,t} \ \forall s_i \in N, c_j \in C, t \in T$.
   b. Intra-cluster distribution: We determine the bike flows $f^-_{s_i s_j,t}: N \times N \times T \to \mathbb{R}^+$ from each station s_i to each station s_j by distributing the bike flows to the clusters among the stations belonging to the clusters: $f^-_{s_i s_j,t} = f^-_{s_i \gamma(s_j),t} \cdot \lambda_{s_i s_j} \ \forall s_i, s_j \in N, t \in T$.

The distribution of bike returns can be modeled analogously. In the end, rental and return flows are averaged. Output of the information model are time-dependent, real-valued bike flows $f_{s_i s_j,t}$, which represent the expected bike flow between origin station s_i and destination station s_j in hour t.

The above information model provides typical bike flows for each pair of stations in each time period in terms of *real-valued* metrics. However, realistic anticipation of relocation operations requires *integer-valued* bike flows. We transform the real-valued bike flows into integer bike flows by scaling and transformation as follows:

- In the *scaling step*, the real valued bike flows $f_{s_i s_j, t}$ are multiplied such that they equal the desired number of bike flows d in relation to the total number of observed bike flows o with $f'_{s_i s_j, t} = mult \cdot f_{s_i s_j, t} \forall s_i, s_j \in N, t \in T, mult = {}^d/_o$.

- In the *transformation step*, the flows are rounded according to a threshold τ for rounding up and down such that the total number of rounded flows amounts to the desired number of flows: $\sum_{s_i \in N} \sum_{s_j \in N} \sum_{t \in T} Round\left(\tau, f'_{s_i s_j, t}\right) = d$ with $Round\left(\tau, f'_{s_i s_j, t}\right)$: If $f'_{s_i s_j, t} - \left\lfloor f'_{s_i s_j, t}\right\rfloor < \tau$ then $\left\lfloor f'_{s_i s_j, t}\right\rfloor$ else $\lceil f'_{s_i s_j, t}\rceil$.

A binary search is applied to determine τ yielding the desired number of bike flows. Finally, the information model can generate integer-valued, time-dependent OD matrices of bike flows as required for SND optimization.

3.2 MIP Formulation for Service Network Design

The following optimization model is based on the work of Crainic (2000) on SND in freight transportation. We propose a MIP formulation which determines optimal target fill levels at stations in the course of the day, ensuring the fulfillment of demand scenarios according to a predefined service level. The objective is to obtain fill levels at minimal expected costs of system operation. Resulting target fill levels and relocation services may serve as input for the optimization of relocation tours on the operational level.

Within the scope of tactical planning, anticipation of operational decisions is required to avoid suboptimal decisions on fill levels. Our optimization model is based on a relaxation of relocation operations. We refrain from a detailed modeling of routing as known from traditional computationally challenging SND models (Crainic 2000) or inventory routing models (Campbell et al. 1998), but we anticipate relocation operations by means of a dynamic transportation model (Bookbinder and Sethi 1980) yielding the required demand for relocation services. To this end, we use a binary variable allowing constraints on the frequency and the capacity of relocation services by consolidating relocations.

A relocation service is described by pickup and return station, time period, and the number of relocated bikes. Relocation services represent the design decision for implementing a service between two stations in each period at each day of system operation. They are modeled by binary variables $RS_{s_i s_j, t}$. The number of relocated bikes for a particular service is modeled by continuous variables $R_{s_i s_j, t}$. Note that this is an approximation of relocation operations, which cannot replace detailed optimization from an operational perspective by means of vehicle routing procedures.

Let N be a set of rental stations and T the set of time periods in a day. The total number of bikes in the system is given by b. The number of bikes can be adjusted if needed. The typical demand for bikes and bike racks is depicted by bike flows $f_{s_i s_j, t}$ between stations s_i and s_j in time period t. The fulfillment of demand at stations depends on the given design and configuration of system infrastructure, i.e., the number of bike racks br_{s_i} for returns ("size" of a station) and the number of allocated bikes at each station and period $B_{s_i,t}$ for rentals. The objective is to minimize the total costs for relocation services, whereas ch_t denotes the average handling costs of one relocated bike in time period t and $ct_{s_i s_j}$ the average transportation costs of one relocated bike between stations s_i and s_j. While optimizing, the availability of rental and return resources for time-dependent "safety buffers" of bikes $sb_{s_i,t}$ and bike racks $sbr_{s_i,t}$ is maintained. Based on time-dependent OD matrices, the information model provides a scenario of bike flows $f_{s_i s_j,t}$ that serve as input for the following optimization model:

$$\text{Minimize} \quad \sum_{t=0}^{t_{max}} \sum_{s_i=1}^{n} \sum_{s_j=1}^{n} \left(ch_t \cdot R_{s_i s_j,t} + ct_{s_i s_j} \cdot RS_{s_i s_j,t} \right) \quad (1)$$

subject to

$$l \cdot RS_{s_i s_j,t} \geq R_{s_i s_j,t} \ \forall s_i, s_j \in N, t \in T \ (2)$$

$$B_{s_i,t+1} = B_{s_i,t} + \sum_{s_j=1}^{n} \left(f_{s_j s_i,t} - f_{s_i s_j,t} + R_{s_j s_i,t} - R_{s_i s_j,t} \right) \ \forall s_i \in N, t \in T \backslash t_{max} \quad (3)$$

$$B_{s_i,t} - \sum_{s_j=1}^{n} f_{s_i s_j,t} + \sum_{s_j=1}^{n} f_{s_j s_i,t} - \sum_{s_j=1}^{n} R_{s_i s_j,t} \geq sb_{s_i,t} \ \forall s_i \in N, t \in T \quad (4)$$

$$br_{s_i} - B_{s_i,t} - \sum_{s_j=1}^{n} f_{s_j s_i,t} + \sum_{s_j=1}^{n} f_{s_i s_j,t} - \sum_{s_j=1}^{n} R_{s_j s_i,t} \geq sbr_{s_i,t} \ \forall s_i \in N, t \in T \quad (5)$$

$$R_{s_i s_j,0} = 0 \ \forall s_i, s_j \in N \quad (6)$$

$$B_{s_i,0} = B_{s_i,t_{max}} \ \forall s_i \in N \quad (7)$$

$$\sum_{s_i=1}^{n} B_{s_i,t} = b \ \forall t \in T \quad (8)$$

$$B_{s_i,t}, R_{s_i s_j,t} \geq 0 \ \forall s_i, s_j \in N, t \in T \quad (9)$$

In the objective function (1), the costs for anticipated relocation services are minimized, comprising handling costs for each individual bike $R_{s_i s_j,t}$ and setup costs for operating the particular relocation service $RS_{s_i s_j,t}$ between two stations. Handling costs can vary depending on the time of the day, e.g., there are higher costs at night due to surcharges for the staff. Transportation costs are assumed to be constant. Depending on the given infrastructure configuration, potentially missing bikes or bike racks are compensated by relocation of bikes $R_{s_i s_j,t}$ between stations for each period of the day. Constraint (2) ensures that a relocation service does not exceed a predefined capacity given by the lot size l. Equation (3) ensures flow conservation, i.e., the number of bikes at a station in the next period is a result of the current number of bikes plus returns from customers (f) and relocation services (R) minus customer rentals and relocation pickups. We assume that a particular relocation service is realized within one time period, but if relocation services take longer, (2) has to be adjusted by setting $R_{s_j s_i, t-1}$ as well as the range of the index t.

The availability of resources is maintained by constraints (4) and (5). On the one hand, it is guaranteed that a sufficient number of bikes (4) is present at every station and period, i.e., the number of bikes minus customer rentals plus costumer returns and relocation pickups is always larger than a given bike safety buffer $sb_{s_i, t}$. On the other hand, the number of free bike racks (bikes racks minus allocated bikes, customer and relocation returns plus customer rentals) is always larger than the bike rack safety buffer $sbr_{s_i, t}$ (5). These two constraints ensure that rented bikes and used bike racks are not available for relocation in the particular period, and all demand is satisfied. Relocation services are not allowed in the first period (6), and the initial fill level is restored at the end of the day (7). Equation (8) ensures that all existing bikes need to be allocated. Decision variables must be non-negative (9). The above constraints enable particular safety buffers for bike and bike racks depending on the time of day. For instance, in periods with a high rental activity and a low return activity at a station, the bike safety buffer can be set to a high value while the safety buffer can be kept low for bike racks. Reasonable values for safety buffers can be determined by analyzing the demand variation based on observed trip data.

Modeling the availability of resources as shown in constraints (4) and (5) is a rather optimistic approach, since customer rentals and returns are interchanged simultaneously. An alternative approach would handle bikes and bike racks as separate resources. However, this could result in a too pessimistic modeling, since recently returned bikes could not be used by the next customer in the same time period any more.

4 Service Network Design for "Citybike Wien"

In the following case study, the presented models are applied to an existing BSS in order to demonstrate the usefulness of SND and the interplay of information and optimization models. The information model is parameterized with trip data recorded by Vienna's "Citybike Wien". Two demand scenarios are generated (Sect. 4.1). For each scenario, results of SND are discussed along spatio-temporal dimensions (Sect. 4.2).

4.1 Generation of Typical Bike Flows for Service Network Design

Citybike Wien provided trip data for the years 2008 and 2009. The operational dataset comprises approx. 750'000 data records for a BSS of 59 stations with a total of 1253 bike racks and 627 bikes. In order to employ a tactical planning perspective and to reflect the typical usage of the system, we restrict our analysis to summer trips only (April to October), accounting for 72% of all trips. In the summer season, 1569 trips occur per day or 2.5 trips per bike and day on average, respectively. The data analysis tool RAPIDMINER (http://rapid-i.com/) has been used for generation, documentation and implementation of the information model. The transformation and the scaling of flows has been implemented in JAVA.

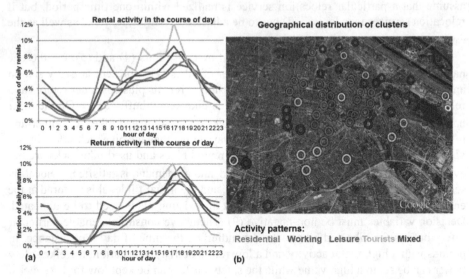

Fig. 1. Rental and return activity clusters **(a)** and geographical distribution of clusters **(b)**

Temporal Distribution of Trips. In order to determine temporal activity clusters of stations, the hourly rental and return activity for each station is calculated, i.e., the fraction of daily rentals and returns, respectively. This leads to a data set of 59 stations with 48 attributes representing the temporal activity. Cluster analysis groups the 59 stations to five activity clusters. Cluster centroids represent the main trip purposes at stations that were assigned to the particular cluster. Figure 1 shows the obtained rental activities $\beta_{C,t}^-$ and return activities $\beta_{C,t}^+$ as well as the geographical distribution of clusters in the city of Vienna:

- Stations within the *working* cluster are characterized by commuter trips showing a return activity peak in the morning and a rental activity peak in the late afternoon. These stations are located in the city center, having a high number of working places and points of interest as well as a low proportion of residents.
- The *residential* cluster shows the opposite activity of commuter trips with dominating rental activity in the morning and return activity in the afternoon. These stations are located at the periphery, which has more residential buildings.
- The *leisure* cluster shows activities similar to the residential cluster, but stands out due to different nighttime activities likely resulting from leisure trips. These activities are probably caused by popular nightlife districts.
- The *tourist* cluster is distinguished by a significant proportion of daytime rental and return activity, but almost no nighttime activity. Stations are close to popular tourist attractions in the west (castle Schoenbrunn), east (Prater carnival) and the city center (St. Stephan's Cathedral). Note that Citybike Wien's "tourist card" is also handed

out next to the city center station, which may explain the distinguished activity of this particular station.

- The *mixed* cluster represents stations that cannot be distinguished according to their main trip purposes and thus reflects a more average rental and return activity on working days. This observation is also underlined by the location of these stations, which is often between stations of other clusters.

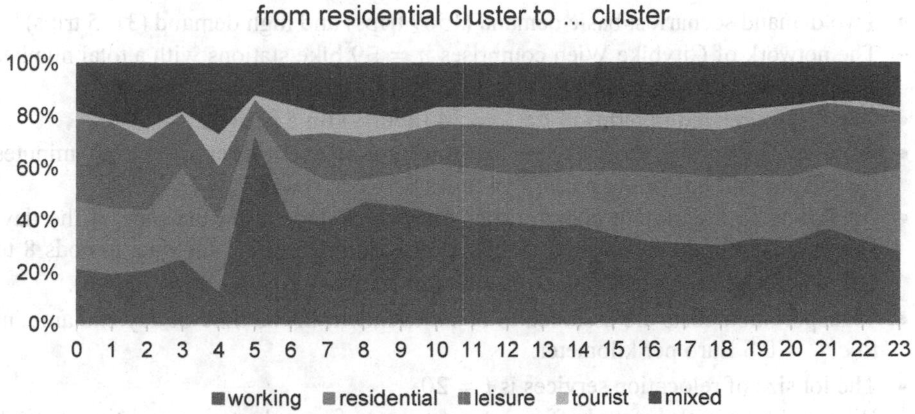

Fig. 2. Inter-cluster distribution between the residential cluster and other clusters

Spatial Distribution of Trips. Based on the temporal activity clusters, the spatial distribution of trips between temporal activity clusters is computed considering the different trip purposes (working, residential, leisure, tourist, mixed). We exemplify the results for the time-dependent inter-cluster distribution $\kappa_{CC,t}$ for stations of the residential cluster (cf. Fig. 2). In the morning hours, more than 40% of trips starting at the residential cluster terminate at the working cluster reflecting commuter trips. Note that the peak in hour 5 with of proportion of 70% commuter trips might be overrepresented, since this is the hour with the lowest overall usage. In the afternoon hours, the proportion of trips from the residential cluster to working cluster declines. In contrast, the proportion of trips to the residential and leisure cluster increases. Trips to the leisure cluster dominate during night time. In sum, the inter-cluster distribution follows the general mobility behavior in Citybike Wien.

Generation and Validation of Bike Flows. Bike flows are generated providing 24 time-dependent OD matrices for all 59 stations. The OD matrices contain a total of 1569 daily trips performed with 627 bikes. The information model distributes these trips to $59 \times 59 \times 24 = 83544$ OD pairs. By scaling and transformation, different demand scenarios can be generated. We use the original data set (1569 trips, 2.5 trips per bike) as the basic demand scenario and create a second scenario, the high demand scenario, with twice the demand (3138 trips, 5 trips per bike).

4.2   Service Network Design for Different Demand Scenarios

We first describe the experimental setup with particular focus on the parameters and the computational solution environment. Then, we optimize the SND for the basic demand scenario and compare the results to SND for the high demand scenario.

Experimental Setup. The experimental setup for SND is as follows:

- Two demand scenarios: basic demand (1569 trips) and high demand (3135 trips)
- The network of Citybike Wien comprises $n = 59$ bike stations with a total number of 1253 bike racks and a total of $b = 627$ bikes (~50% average fill level).
- Time is discretized in terms of $t_{max} = 24$ (hourly) time periods.
- We assume that relocation services take one hour on average (approx. 15-20 minutes for loading and unloading plus travel times between stations).
- According to the system operator, handling costs depend on the time of the day. Daytime handling costs are set to $ch_{day} = 4$ Euro (in effect for time periods 8 to 17), while night time handling costs are more expensive ($ch_{night} = 7$ Euro).
- Transportation costs are assumed to be independent of the time of day and amount to $ct_{ij} = 0.5$ Euro per kilometer.
- The lot size of relocation services is $l = 20$.
- Bike and bike rack safety buffers are set to zero for each station and time period, ensuring that fill levels are non-negative and do not exceed station capacities.

The MIP model described in Section 3 is implemented in IBM ILOG OPL and solved with CPLEX 12.5 on an INTEL Core i5 processor at 3.2 GHz and 8 GB RAM running Windows 7 64 Bit. Both demand scenarios are given 30 minutes run time. CPLEX returns solutions with a gap of 1-2%. Although these gaps are very small, the optimal solution could still not be obtained after an increased run time of 24 hours. Note that this instance, compared to other BSS, is a small instance with a total of $59 \times 59 \times 24 = 83544$ binary relocation service variables. For bigger instances, a heuristic approach would be needed due to the sheer number of binary variables.

Key Figures of the Service Network. In order to demonstrate the benefit of optimized fill levels, we compare the costs of relocation required for the "optimal" fill levels to manually preset "naïve" fill levels. As often suggested by practitioners, we set the naïve fill levels for all stations to 50% in the hour of the lowest demand (hour 5). Table 1 summarizes these figures in terms of the number of relocated bikes, the number of relocation services, average number of relocated bikes per service as well as total and relative costs of relocation. The relative costs of relocation can be interpreted as the "usage fee" per trip required to compensate relocation costs.

For the basic demand scenario, naïve fill levels result in 130 relocated bikes with 42 relocation services. Each relocation service carries 3.09 bikes on average. Total costs for relocation services amount to 584 Euros. A "usage fee" of 0.37 Euros per trip would thus be required to compensate relocation costs. In contrast to the naïve fill levels, optimal fill levels result in significantly lower relocation costs (17%), namely 496 Euros

(119 relocated bikes with 32 relocation services). For the high demand scenario, the benefit of optimal fill levels becomes even more significant. Naïve fill levels result in 1345 Euros relocation cost (282 relocated bikes with 70 relocation services), whereas a saving of 44% is achieved with optimal fill levels. It is of note that doubling the demand does not result in doubled relocation services and costs. With doubled demand, the relative costs of relocation decrease slightly. Due to consolidation of relocation services, service capacities can be utilized better, and only few additional relocation services are required. Furthermore, adapted fill levels compensate increased demand to a certain extent.

Table 1. Key Figures of Relocation Services

Demand scenario	Relocated bikes	Relocation services	Relocated bikes per service	Total relocation costs	Relative relocation costs
basic (naïve)	130	42	3.09	584	0.37
basic (optimal)	119	32	3.71	496	0.32
high (naïve)	282	70	4.02	1345	0.42
high (optimal)	215	46	4.67	932	0.30

Characteristics of Fill Levels. We present and evaluate the optimized fill levels for the two demand scenarios and the morning and afternoon peak hours. They are depicted in Fig. 3 by means of box plots of fill levels per cluster and hour of day.

The *basic demand scenario* reflects the demand for a typical working day. In the morning peak hour, stations belonging to the working cluster require a low fill level of about 18% on average, and stations of the other clusters require a high fill level of about 60% and 70% on average. In the afternoon peak hour, stations of the working cluster require higher fill levels than stations of the residential clusters. Fill levels at working cluster stations are almost 50% on average and almost 40% at residential cluster stations. Striking is the high variance of fill levels of the working and residential cluster compared to the morning peak. For the working, residential and leisure cluster stations, capacity is sufficient to reserve bikes or bike racks for the demand of the upcoming time periods. Regarding mixed cluster stations, the high variance occurs due to diverse trip purposes. Tourist stations seem to serve as "buffer" stations being (almost) full or (almost) empty because the demand in general is rather low.

For the high demand scenario, average fill levels are more distinct, and the variance within individual clusters is lower. Generally, the system seems to be more used to capacity which is reflected by the more distinct fill levels with smaller variance. In the morning peak hour, the higher demand induces more returns at working cluster stations and more rentals at residential cluster stations. Thus, more bike rack capacity is required at working cluster stations and more bike capacity is needed at residential cluster stations. As a result, fill levels at working cluster stations are 8% on average and 95% at residential cluster stations. In the afternoon peak hour, fill levels at stations of the working and residential clusters are more distinct than in the basic demand scenario for the same reason. Missing bike capacity is compensated by means of the leisure cluster stations, which show lower fill levels in the morning and afternoon.

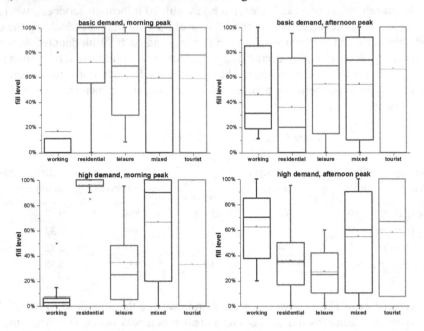

Fig. 3. Boxplots of fill levels per cluster for peak hours in two demand scenarios

Characteristics of Relocation Services. Characteristics of relocation services can aid the system operator in preparing and implementing relocation services. We present spatio-temporal characteristics of relocation services resulting from SND. In particular, Fig. 4 shows the total number of bikes that are expected to be picked up and returned by relocation services at each station, arranged by cluster assignment for the basic and high demand scenarios. We can clearly identify stations that require relocation pickups and relocation returns, respectively, or stations that can compensate demand without relocation. For the basic demand scenario, relocation demand ranges between 20 relocation pickups and 14 relocation returns, i.e., the first station in the working cluster requires 14 bikes to be returned by relocation services, whereas the last station in the residential cluster expects 20 bikes to be picked up by relocation services. Stations that require relocation returns mainly belong to the working cluster, and stations requiring relocation pickups mainly belong to the residential cluster. Stations of the leisure and mixed clusters need both relocation pickups and relocation returns, but they are also often able to balance pickups and returns properly without relocation services.

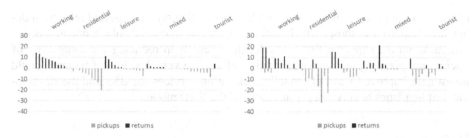

Fig. 4. Total number of returned (positive) and picked up (negative) bikes by relocation for the basic demand scenario (left) and high demand scenario (right)

Regarding the high demand scenario, the presented order of stations is the same as in the low demand scenario. Higher demand causes increasing relocation demand, ranging from 32 relocation pickups to 21 relocation returns. A comparison of the two demand scenarios shows that the tendency of a station requiring either relocation returns, relocation pickups or no relocation remains the same for 66% of the stations when demand increases. For 7% of the stations, the required relocation efforts decrease, and for 22%, the type of relocation service changes from pickups to returns or vice versa.

Optimization with SND shows that stations either require relocation pickups or returns. Especially the "direction" of relocation may support the planning of relocation operations. Furthermore, SND can give indications on the priority of relocation operations at stations. Stations requiring a high number of relocation pickups or returns may be visited once a day. Stations with a medium number of relocation pickups or returns may need relocation only on certain days of the week. The remaining stations may be serviced occasionally. For this case study, SND highlights that there are three stations in the high demand scenario that require both relocation pickups and relocation returns. This implies insufficient capacity, because these stations cannot compensate demand variation throughout the day. Implications for the operational level are that these stations require relocation services more than once a day. Implications for the strategic level are that the size of the station should be extended, if possible.

Overall, our tactical approach can provide target fill levels for operational planning. Characteristics of relocation services can aid the operator in the planning of relocation tours. SND provides information on the expected relocation demand at stations and shows which stations might play a crucial role in operations.

5   Conclusions and Future Research

In this paper, we have proposed an integrated approach of intelligent data analysis and mathematical optimization for SND in BSS. The optimization model determines the optimal fill level at stations minimizing the expected costs of relocation services while ensuring a predefined service level. Computational experiments show that SND helps determining reasonable fill levels and relocation services. The benefit of this tactical approach is that determined fill levels may serve as target fill levels for operational planning. Furthermore, characteristics of relocation services can aid the operator in the planning of relocation tours. SND provides information on the expected relocation demand at stations and shows which stations might play a crucial role in operations. Information on the expected flows of relocations can help reducing the complexity of operational planning tasks such as routing of service vehicles. Future research could investigate improved ways of modeling relocation services for BSS and the development of heuristics to solve larger instances of the SND model.

References

1. Bookbinder JH, Sethi SP (1980) The dynamic transportation problem: A survey. Naval Research Logistics Quarterly 27:65–87.
2. Boyaci B, Zografos KG, Geroliminis N (2015) An optimization framework for the development of efficient one-way car-sharing systems. European Journal of Operational Research 240:718–733.
3. Büttner J, Petersen T (2011) Optimising Bike Sharing in European Cities – A Handbook.
4. Campbell A, Clarke L, Kleywegt A, Savelsbergh M (1998) The inventory routing problem. Fleet management and logistics. Springer, pp 95–113.
5. Cepolina EM, Farina A (2012) A new shared vehicle system for urban areas. Transportation Research Part C: Emerging Technologies 21:230–243.
6. Correia GHA, Antunes AP (2012) Optimization approach to depot location and trip selection in one-way carsharing systems. Transportation Research Part E: Logistics and Transportation Review 48:233 – 247.
7. Crainic TG (2000) Service network design in freight transportation. European Journal of Operational Research 122:272–288.
8. George DK, Xia CH (2011) Fleet-sizing and service availability for a vehicle rental system via closed queueing networks. European Journal of Operational Research 211:198–207.
9. Johnston RA (2004) The Urban Transportation Planning Process. The geography of urban transportation, The Guilford Press.
10. Jorge D, Correia G, Barnhart C (2012) Testing the validity of the MIP approach for locating carsharing stations in one-way systems. Procedia-Social and Behavioral Sciences 54:138–148.
11. Metrobike (2009). Invitation to Bid Number 59. Request for Proposals for the operation of the Arlington Bike-sharing Program. http://www.metrobike.net/resources/Arlington%20Bike-sharing%20RFP.pdf.
12. Midgley P (2011) Bicycle-sharing schemes: enhancing sustainable mobility in urban areas. United Nations Department of Economic and Social Affairs.
13. Raviv T, Kolka O (2013) Optimal inventory management of a bike-sharing station. IIE Transactions 45:1077–1093.
14. Sayarshad H, Tavassoli S, Zhao F (2012) A multi-periodic optimization formulation for bike planning and bike utilization. Applied Mathematical Modelling 36:4944 – 4951.
15. Schuijbroek J, Hampshire R, van Hoeve W-J (2013) Inventory Rebalancing and Vehicle Routing in Bike Sharing Systems. European Journal of Operational Research 257(3):992 – 1004.
16. Shaheen SA, Guzman S, Zhang H (2010) Bikesharing in Europe, the Americas, and Asia. Transportation Research Record: Journal of the Transportation Research Board 2143:159–167.
17. Shu J, Chou MC, Liu Q, Teo C-P, Wang I-L (2013) Models for effective deployment and redistribution of bicycles within public bicycle-sharing systems. Operations Research 61:1346–1359.
18. Vogel P, Greiser T, Mattfeld, DC (2011) Understanding Bike-Sharing Systems using Data Mining: Exploring Activity Patterns. In: Procedia-Social and Behavioral Sciences 20:514–523.

A Dynamic Network Flow Model for Interdependent Infrastructure and Supply Chain Networks with Uncertain Asset Operability

Nils Goldbeck[1*], Panagiotis Angeloudis[1] and Washington Y Ochieng[1]

[1] Centre for Transport Studies (CTS), Imperial College London, UK
* Corresponding author: n.goldbeck14@imperial.ac.uk

Abstract. In globally integrated supply chain networks, initially local disruptions can quickly escalate to major problems due to complex interdependencies and cascading failure. This paper is particularly concerned with the role of infrastructure failure causing or exacerbating such cascading effects in supply chain networks. To improve the understanding of infrastructure and supply chain interdependency, we propose a novel modelling approach that captures the dynamics of both asset operability and network flows. The method uses a Markov process to generate operability scenarios and a multistage stochastic linear program to assign dynamic flows and optimise network capacities. The model takes into account different mechanisms of cascading failure, namely failure propagation, delay of recovery and unavailability of production inputs. A numeric example demonstrates how the method can be used to assess and optimises the resilience of a global supply chain against multiple hazards and infrastructure failure.

Keywords: supply chain resilience, interdependency, network flow modelling

1   Introduction

The problem of managing disruptions in supply chains and ensuring business continuity is growing in complexity as supply chains are becoming ever more global and integrated. Numerous incidents in recent years have demonstrated the vulnerability of supply chains to cascading failure. In many cases, the disruptions were either caused or exacerbated by the failure of infrastructure systems. For example, in 2000 power fluctuations in the electricity grid caused a fire in the plant of a sub-supplier of the mobile phone manufacturer Ericsson. The fire was quickly extinguished, but it affected a clean room for the production of radio frequency chips and, eventually, resulted in a business interruption for Ericsson that lasted for months and cost $200 million [1]. After the 2011 earthquake in Japan, production at all of Toyota's assembly plants stopped completely for two weeks even though most of these plants did not suffer direct damage from the earthquake. The problem was the unavailability of parts sourced from the affected Tohoku region [2]. When Hurricane Sandy hit the US East Coast in 2012, the liquid fuel supply chain broke down due to a combination of extensive power outages and direct damage to terminals, pipelines, refineries and other infrastructure assets [3].

© Springer International Publishing AG 2017
T. Bektaş et al. (Eds.), ICCL 2017, LNCS 10572, pp. 513–528, 2017.
https://doi.org/10.1007/978-3-319-68496-3_34

In future, the risk of supply chain disruptions due to infrastructure failure is bound to become even more problematic as climate change is expected to put more stress on many critical infrastructure networks [4, 5].

Simulation and optimisation tools, such as network flow models, can support the planning of strategies to improve the resilience of supply chains. However, existing network flow models do not fully capture the uncertainty associated with the reliance on infrastructure systems and the risk of cascading failure. This paper proposes a novel stochastic programming approach for modelling supply chains and their dependencies on infrastructure systems. The model optimises the capacities of a supply chain network based on operability scenarios generated with a Markov model for individual assets in the supply chain and interdependent infrastructure networks. The novelty of the proposed method lies in the modelling of dependency relations both on the asset operability level and on the network flow level.

The paper is structured as follows. Section 2 reviews the most relevant existing models for disruption management in supply chains. Section 3 gives an overview of the proposed modelling approach. Section 4 describes the scenario tree generation algorithm. Section 5 presents the stochastic programming model. Finally, Section 6 demonstrates the practical application of the method with a numerical example.

2   Literature review

Various modelling methods have been developed to improve the analytical understanding of what makes a supply chain resilient, including network optimisation models [6], system dynamics models [7], agent-based simulation models [8], queuing models [9] and game theory models [10]. Comprehensive reviews of such models are provided by [11–13]. Regarding future research priorities, these reviews highlight the importance of addressing time-related aspects in more detail [11], and state that models based on stochastic modelling and optimisation theory are most likely to make significant contributions to the methodology [13].

Network flow theory [14] provides the methods to analyse infrastructure and supply chain networks with respect to the nature of their core purpose, the transportation of people, goods, energy, and information. Numerous network flow models have been developed for the specific purpose of minimising the risk of disruptions in supply chains [15]. Many models use stochastic programming methods to capture uncertainty aspects, for example, capacity uncertainty [16], demand uncertainty [17], unreliable suppliers [18], and the random failure of various elements of the logistics network [19].

The network flow model proposed by Glockner and Nemhauser [16] is of particular relevance to this paper because it addresses both dynamic and uncertainty aspects. It uses a linear multi-stage stochastic programming method that captures the evolution of capacity uncertainty over time with a scenario tree. Each node in the scenario tree has a separate set of flow variables. The leaves of the scenario tree correspond to the scenarios, and the optimal flow assignment is found by minimising the expected costs over all scenarios. The method is capable of modelling flows that span over more than one time step, thereby allowing a certain degree of anticipation.

The method developed in this paper builds upon the model formulated by Glockner and Nemhauser and extends it in several ways. First, we add inventory holding to the model, because inventory optimisation is an important way of improving the resilience of a supply chain. Second, we add a network design aspect to the model by also optimising network capacities. Third, we add interdependency to the model. Interdependency can affect both the scenario tree generation and the flow assignment. We refer to the former with operability interdependency and to the later with flow interdependency. The following sections will review techniques to model these interdependencies.

2.1   Scenario tree generation with operability interdependency

A widely used approach to generate scenario trees for multi-stage stochastic programs is to sample from a stochastic process. A difficulty when using sampling methods to generate scenario trees for stochastic programs is to achieve a good representation of the underlying probability distribution while keeping the number of scenarios small enough to solve the optimisation problem. Clustering and moment matching are useful methods for efficient scenario tree generation [20]. Stability testing can be used to ensure the quality of the scenario tree generation method [21].

For reliability engineering applications, a standard method to model failure and repair processes are discrete-time Markov chains [22]. The flexibility of Markov chain modelling allows capturing dependencies in many different ways, according to the requirements of the modelling task. For example, Rahnamay-Naeini and Hayat [23] use binary variables to express the susceptibility of a system to further failures. However, this method only models the total number of failures in a system, not where they occur. Son et al. [24] propose a decomposition approach that can model the availability of individual sub-systems and expresses dependencies in terms of voting logics. A limitation of this method is that only deterministic dependencies can be modelled.

2.2   Network flow assignment with flow interdependency

The literature on interdependent infrastructure systems contains several methods for modelling coupled flows in different networks. For example, Lee II et al. [25] model the flows in the public transport, power and telecommunication networks in New York City in a disruption scenario similar to the attacks on 11 September 2001. The model uses a minimum cost flow assignment method. Dependencies between the different networks are modelled with binary coupling variables. These coupling variables reduce the capacity of a dependent network component if the demand at the connected node cannot be fully met.

Holden et al. [26] also use minimum cost flow assignment but propose an alternative method for the coupling of flows across networks. The model constraints the production rates at supply nodes to be proportional to the consumption rates at nodes that deliver the required input resources. Whether this proportional coupling or the binary coupling proposed by Lee II et al. is more realistic depends on the nature of the dependency relation. The most flexible model would arguably be a combination of both coupling methods. However, the use of binary coupling variables comes with a higher computational cost.

Another key difference between the various flow assignment models is how they capture the dynamics of flows. Lee II et al. [25] use a static model that optimises the network configuration at one point in time after the disruption occurs. Holden et al. [26] analyse the dynamics of network flows over ten days by carrying out a minimum cost flow assignment separately for each day. Glockner and Nemhauser [16] integrate the flow assignment for all time steps into one single optimisation problem. The advantage of integrating the flow assignment for the entire simulation period is that flows can be modelled which span over more than one time step. However, the disadvantage is that the integrated flow assignment tends to allow too much anticipation, which can only be mitigated by a suitable branching structure of the scenario tree. In terms of computational requirements, the step-wise dynamic flow assignment leads to more manageable problem sizes that scale linearly with the length of the simulation period and the number of scenarios.

3   Model overview

We model an interdependent infrastructure and supply chain network as a directed graph $G = (V, H, E, D)$. The node set V contains production plants, suppliers, warehouses, transhipment hubs, infrastructure systems and demand nodes. The node set H contains hazard nodes, for example the risk that a specific flooding event occurs. The link set E contains links over which goods are transported and services are delivered. The link set D contains dependency links.

In contrast to Glockner and Nemhauser, we do not consider the network capacities themselves as random but instead the operability of each network component over time. The operability expresses how much of a component's nominal capacity is available at a given time. This separation between nominal and available capacity allows us to add the nominal capacities as decision variables to the optimisation problem.

The two main steps in our methodology are scenario tree generation and network flow assignment, as depicted in **Fig. 1**. In the first step, scenarios for the operability of network components are created using a Markov process. In the second step, a linear stochastic program is solved to calculate the optimal flow assignment for each scenario as well as the optimal component capacities considering all scenarios.

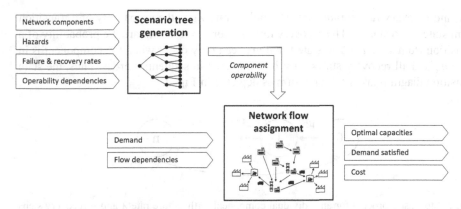

Fig. 1. Overview of model inputs and outputs

Interdependency effects play a role both in the generation of operability scenarios and in the flow assignment. Hence, we define two types of dependency links:

- **Operability dependencies:** An operability dependency $(j, k) \in D$, where $j \in V \cup H \cup E$ and $k \in V \cup E$, means that an operability loss at j can affect the operability of k, for example due to co-location.

- **Flow dependencies:** A flow dependency $(j, k) \in D$, where $j \in V$ and $k \in V$, means that the production of a certain commodity at k requires the input of a commodity provided by j.

The following two sections present the two steps of the proposed method in detail and explain how the two types of dependency are formulated in mathematical terms.

4   Scenario tree generation

The primary sources of uncertainty in our model are the hazard nodes, which represent specific hazard events that may occur at a given time with a given probability. Furthermore, there is uncertainty about the direct impact of these hazard events on the supply chain and infrastructure components, the propagation of failure due to dependencies and the speed of recovery. A scenario in our model is a unique realisation of the operability variables $x_k^t \in [0,1]$ for all network components $k \in V \cup E$ over time steps $t = 0, \dots T$. The following sections describe how a Markov process is used to generate operability scenarios and how these scenarios are then combined to form a scenario tree.

4.1   Markov process modelling failure and repair of a single component

Let $\{X_k^t, t = 0, \dots, T\}$ be a Markov process describing the operability of an individual supply chain component $k \in V \cup E$. The state space of this Markov process is $X_k = \{0,1, \dots, n_k\}$, where n_k is the normal state, 0 is the failure state, and the rest are intermediate recovery states. The transition probabilities are given in terms of failure rate and recovery rate parameters. The failure rate λ_k is the probability of a transition from state n_k to state 0. The recovery rates μ_k^i for $i = 1, \dots, n_k$ are the probability of a transition from state $i - 1$ to state i. Failures can only occur when the component is in state n_k and all recovery states must be completed in sequential order. Thus, the state transition diagram takes a cyclic form as depicted in **Fig. 2**.

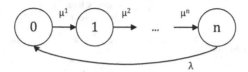

Fig. 2. Stochastic process for an individual component with failure rate λ and n recovery steps with recovery rates $\mu^1, \dots, \mu^n$

The duration of each individual recovery stage follows a geometric distribution. The total recovery time R_k^i until component k reaches recovery state i is the sum of i independent geometric random variables [27]:

$$P(R_k^i = t) = \sum_{u=1}^{i} \mu_k^u (1 - \mu_k^u)^{t-1} \prod_{v=1, j \neq u}^{i} \left(\frac{\mu_k^v}{\mu_k^v - \mu_k^u} \right) \tag{1}$$

Fig. 3 depicts the probability distributions of the recovery times for an example with three recovery stages. The distribution for full recovery exhibits the skewness characteristics typical for the recovery times of many repairable systems [28–30].

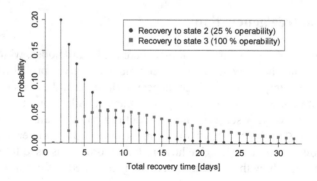

Fig. 3. Probability mass function for the recovery times of a three-stage recovery process with expected individual durations of 1, 5 and 10 days

The expected recovery time is the sum of the mean durations of each recovery stage:

$$E[R_k^i] = \sum_{u=1}^{i} \frac{1}{\mu_k^u} \tag{2}$$

The operability function $\psi_k: X_k \to [0,1]$ maps the Markov state X_k^t to the operability value x_k^t. The average operability of a component can be calculated as the weighted mean of the operability levels:

$$E[x_k^t] = \frac{\frac{1}{\lambda_k} \psi_k(n_k) + \sum_{i=1}^{n_k} \frac{1}{\mu_k^i} \psi_k(i-1)}{\frac{1}{\lambda_k} + \sum_{i=1}^{n_k} \frac{1}{\mu_k^i}} \tag{3}$$

4.2   Operability dependencies

Introducing operability dependencies to the model means coupling the Markov processes for the individual supply chain components. In the previous section, the failure rates λ_k and the recovery rates μ_k^i were fixed. In this section, each component's failure and recovery rates are affected by the inoperability of other components that it depends on. In other words, the failure and recovery rates are now defined as functions of the operability vector x^t for the entire supply chain.

Let $\bar{\lambda}_k$ and $\bar{\mu}_k^i$ denote the intrinsic (or independent) failure and recovery rates of component k. The effect of an operability dependency $(j,k) \in D$ is quantified by four parameters: the failure propagation slope parameter $\alpha_{j,k}^F$ and intercept parameter $\beta_{j,k}^F$, and the recovery delay slope parameter $\alpha_{j,k}^R$ and intercept parameter $\beta_{j,k}^R$. The effective failure and recovery rates are calculated as follows:

$$\lambda_k(x^t) = \bar{\lambda}_k + \sum_{j \in V \cup H \cup E: (j,k) \in D} \left(\alpha_{j,k}^F \left(1 - x_j^t\right) + \mathrm{sgn}\left(1 - x_j^t\right)\beta_{j,k}^F \right) \qquad \text{for } k \in V \cup E \tag{4}$$

$$\mu_k^i(x^t) = \bar{\mu}_k^i + \sum_{j \in V \cup H \cup E: (j,k) \in D} \left(\alpha_{j,k}^R \left(1 - x_j^t\right) + \mathrm{sgn}\left(1 - x_j^t\right)\beta_{j,k}^R \right) \qquad \begin{matrix} \text{for } k \in V \cup E \\ i = 1, \dots, n_k \end{matrix} \tag{5}$$

Equations (4) and (5) mean that the effect of a dependency from j to k is zero if the operability of j is one. Otherwise, the dependency increases the failure rate of k by $\alpha_{j,k}^F \left(1 - x_j^t\right) + \beta_{j,k}^F$ and the recovery rate by $\alpha_{j,k}^R \left(1 - x_j^t\right) + \beta_{j,k}^R$.

In the case that a dependency link originates at a hazard node, the hazard node is treated as a component with operability 0 if the hazard event is currently active and with operability 1 otherwise.

Rahnamay-Naeini and Hayat [23] point out that the coupling of individual Markov chains does not necessarily result in a process that fulfils the Markov property. In our case, however, we can show that the coupling of Markov chains does create a new Markov process. The state space of this process is the Cartesian product of the states of all individual Markov chains $X = \prod_{k \in V \cup E} X_k$ and is therefore very large. We can calculate the transition probabilities for this overall Markov process and show that it depends on the state in the previous time step but not on earlier time steps:

$$\Pr(X^{t+1}|X^t) = \prod_{\substack{k \in F: \\ X_k^t = n_k \wedge X_k^{t+1} = 0}} \lambda_k(\psi(X^t)) \prod_{\substack{k \in F: \\ X_k^t = n_k \wedge X_k^{t+1} = n_k}} \left(1 - \lambda_k(\psi(X^t))\right) \quad (6)$$

$$\prod_{\substack{k \in F, \ i=1,\dots,n_k: \\ X_k^t = i-1 \wedge X_k^{t+1} = i}} \mu_k^i(\psi(X^t)) \prod_{\substack{k \in F, \ i=1,\dots,n_k: \\ X_k^t = i-1 \wedge X_k^{t+1} = i-1}} \left(1 - \mu_k^i(\psi(X^t))\right)$$

$$\prod_{\substack{k \in F: \\ X_k^{t+1} - X_k^t \neq -n_k \wedge X_k^{t+1} - X_k^t \neq 1}} 0$$

The function $\psi: X^t \to x^t$ in equation (6) is the operability function for the entire system, which maps the vector of Markov states to a vector of operability values.

4.3   Components with deterministic operability

A limitation of modelling interdependency by changing the transition probabilities in the Markov process is that it takes one time step to transmit the dependency effect via a dependency link. In reality, some interdependency effects are more immediate. For example, a component could depend on a number of sub-components and become inoperable as soon as any sub-component fails. To take this into account, we introduce components with deterministic operability to the model. The operability of these components is a function of the operability of components that they depend upon. For example, to model a component k as a series or parallel systems the following deterministic operability functions can be used:

Parallel system: $$x_k^t = \max_{j \in V \cup H \cup E:(j,k) \in D}(x_j^t) \quad (7)$$

Series system: $$x_k^t = \min_{j \in V \cup H \cup E:(j,k) \in D}(x_j^t) \quad (8)$$

The deterministic operability functions are included in the system operability function $\psi: X^t \to x^t$. Components with deterministic operability can depend on components with stochastic operability and vice versa, as long as there are no cycles in the dependency links connecting components with deterministic operability.

4.4   Sampling and scenario tree generation

With the model of stochastic failure and recovery for some components and deterministic operability functions for others, we can now sample the operability for all components of the entire infrastructure and supply chain network for a simulation period $t = 0, \dots, T$. For each hazard node $h \in H$, we create n samples with h set as active. Additionally, we create n samples with no hazard event set as active. This results in a set of

$(|H| + 1)n$ samples. The probability of each sample is $\frac{1}{n}$ times the probability of the active hazard event. If necessary, the sampling could be extended to include the simultaneous occurrence of different hazard events. For simplicity, we assume here that the probability of joint occurrence is negligible and that the probability of no hazard event occurring is one minus the sum of the probabilities of all hazard events.

The scenario tree is created from the operability samples by grouping together for each time step $t = 0, \dots, T$ the samples with identical operability values for t and all previous time steps. Each of these groups represents a node in the scenario tree indexed by $s = 1, \dots, S_t$. A scenario tree node is uniquely identified by the tuple (t, s) and this will be used to index the scenario-specific variables, e.g. $x_k^{t,s}$ is the operability of component k at time t and scenario node s.

For $t = 0$, the scenario tree only contains the root node, so $S_0 = 1$. The number of scenario tree nodes at the last step S_T is equal to the number of unique operability samples. The probability $P_{t,s}$ of each scenario tree node is the sum of the respective sample probabilities and $\sum_{s=1}^{S_t} P_{t,s} = 1$ for $t = 0, \dots T$.

5   Dynamic network flow model with uncertain capacity

In this section, we present the multistage stochastic linear program that is used to calculate the optimal nominal capacities and network flows. This step takes the scenario tree generated in the previous section as an input.

There are two types of decision variables in the optimisation problem. First, the nominal link flow capacities $\bar{f}_{i,j}$, production capacities $\bar{g}_i$, and storage capacities $\bar{h}_i$. Second, the scenario-specific variables $f_{i,j}^{t,s}$ for link flows, $g_i^{t,s}$ for production rates, $h_i^{t,s}$ for inventory levels, $u_i^{t,s}$ for consumption rates, and $s_i^{t,s}$ for unmet demand.

The commodity demand is denoted with $\breve{u}_i^t$. The parameters $\hat{f}_{i,j}$, $\hat{g}_i$, and $\hat{h}_i$ specify upper limits for the component capacities. Furthermore, each of the decision variables (with the exception of consumption rates) has a cost parameter. The cost parameters $c_{i,j}^{\mathrm{fcap}}$, c_i^{gcap}, and c_i^{hcap} are the fixed costs of providing the flow, production and holding capacities for the entire duration of the simulation period. The cost parameters $c_{i,j}^{\mathrm{f}}$, c_i^{g}, and c_i^{h} are the variable costs that occur for the usage of flow, production and holding capacities. The parameters c_i^{s} are the penalty cost for not meeting the demand.

The multistage stochastic linear program is then formulated as follows:

$$\min \sum_{(i,j)\in E} c_{i,j}^{\text{fcap}} \bar{f}_{i,j} + \sum_{i\in V} c_i^{\text{gcap}} \bar{g}_i + \sum_{i\in V} c_i^{\text{hcap}} \bar{h}_i$$

$$+ \sum_{t=0}^{T} \sum_{s=1}^{S_t} P_{t,s} \left(\sum_{(i,j)\in E} c_{i,j}^{\text{f}} f_{i,j}^t + \sum_{i\in V} c_i^{\text{g}} g_i^t + \sum_{i\in V} c_i^{\text{h}} h_i^t + \sum_{i\in V} c_i^{\text{s}} s_i^t \right) \tag{9}$$

subject to

$$\bar{f}_{i,j}, \bar{g}_i, \bar{h}_i, f_{i,j}^{t,s}, g_i^{t,s}, h_i^{t,s}, u_i^{t,s}, s_i^{t,s} \geq 0 \qquad \begin{array}{l} i \in V, (i,j) \in E, \\ t = 0, \dots, T, s = 1, \dots, S_t \end{array} \tag{10}$$

$$\bar{f}_{i,j} \leq \hat{f}_{i,j} \qquad (i,j) \in E \tag{11}$$

$$\bar{g}_i \leq \hat{g}_i \qquad i \in V \tag{12}$$

$$\bar{h}_i \leq \hat{h}_i \qquad i \in V \tag{13}$$

$$f_{i,j}^{t,s} \leq x_{i,j}^{t,s} \bar{f}_{i,j} \qquad (i,j) \in E, t = 0, \dots, T, s = 1, \dots, S_t \tag{14}$$

$$g_i^{t,s} \leq x_i^{t,s} \bar{g}_i \qquad i \in V, t = 0, \dots, T, s = 1, \dots, S_t \tag{15}$$

$$h_i^{t,s} \leq x_i^{t,s} \bar{h}_i \qquad i \in V, t = 0, \dots, T, s = 1, \dots, S_t \tag{16}$$

$$s_i^{t,s} = \breve{u}_i^t - u_i^{t,s} \qquad i \in V, t = 0, \dots, T, s = 1, \dots, S_t \tag{17}$$

$$\sum_{j\in V:(j,i)\in E} f_{j,i}^{\tau(t,s,t-t_{j,i})} - \sum_{j\in V:(i,j)\in E} f_{i,j}^{t,s}$$

$$+ h_i^{t,s} - h_i^{\tau(t,s,t-1)} + g_i^{t,s} - u_i^{t,s} \qquad i \in V, t = 0, \dots, T, s = 1, \dots, S_t \tag{18}$$

$$- \sum_{j\in V:(i,j)\in D} \alpha_{i,j}^{\text{P}} g_j^{t,s} = 0$$

The objective function (9) comprises the cost of providing the capacities, and for each scenario, the scenario probability multiplied with the respective transportation costs, production costs, inventory costs and the penalties for unmet demand. The constraints (11) - (13) set upper bounds for the capacity decision variables. For each scenario, the constraints (14) - (16) ensure that the actual flows, production rates and inventory levels do not exceed the capacity multiplied by the scenario-specific operability of the respective component. Constraint (17) sets the slack variable for unmet demand equal to the difference between demand and supply.

Equation (18) expresses the conservation of flow constraints for each node. It comprises net flow, inventory change, production, consumption, and supply to a dependent node. The parameter $t_{j,i}$ is the duration for the transit of link (j,i). To take into account this flow over time, the function $\tau: (t_2, s_2, t_1) \to (t_1, s_1)$ is defined. For time step t_2, scenario tree node s_2 and time step $t_1 \leq t_2$, $\tau(t_2, s_2, t_1)$ returns the tuple (t_1, s_1) that is the scenario tree node at time t_1 which belongs to the path to scenario tree node (t_2, s_2).

The last term of the conservation of flow constraint (18) models the interdependency of network flows. The parameter $\alpha_{i,j}^{\text{P}}$ of a flow dependency $(i,j) \in D$ defines how many units of a commodity at node i have to be provided for each unit of a commodity produced at the dependent node j. Thus, the model assumes a linear production function.

6   Numerical example

To demonstrate the modelling method proposed in this paper, we use an example supply chain from the dataset published by Willems [31]. The dataset contains 38 real-world examples of multi-echelon supply chains from different industries. For each supply chain, the data provided includes the topology of the supply chain, the cost and duration of each stage, and demand data.

6.1   Problem configuration

The supply chain number 3 from the dataset was chosen to test our model because the size of this example will allow the demonstration of various interesting aspects of the methodology. The supply chain consists of 4 distribution or demand nodes, 4 manufacturing plants, 5 component suppliers and 4 transportation links.

The dataset is primarily intended to provide a testbed for models that optimise inventory under demand uncertainty. Since the aim of our study is to analyse the resilience of supply chains under the uncertainty of disruptive events and interdependencies with infrastructure networks, we extend the example with some hypothetical hazard nodes, infrastructure nodes and dependency relations. This is for demonstration purposes only and was not validated with real-world data.

Considering the topology of the supply chain (**Fig. 4**), we can assume that it stretches over three separate geographic regions. For each region, we add one hazard node: an earthquake occurs with probability 0.001 in region A, a flood event occurs with probability 0.033 in region B, and a storm occurs with probability 0.050 in region C.

We assume that the transport links connecting these regions are air freight links and we add three airports to the model as examples of critical transportation infrastructure. Furthermore, we add one node that represents the electricity supply and another node that represents the telecommunication services in region A.

The flow dependencies in **Fig. 4** show the combination of parts and intermediate products in the manufacturing processes. For example, the node *Manuf_1 (prod)* has three incoming flow dependencies, meaning that it requires parts 1, 2 and 3 as production inputs. All flows are normalised to a common unit measure, and we set the $\alpha^P_{i,j}$ parameter to 1 for each flow dependency.

The operability dependencies determine the magnitude and impact of the hazard events, as well as the probabilities of failure propagation. The parameters for these dependencies are given in **Table 2** in the appendix.

The time step length given in the original dataset is one business day. The average length of the entire supply chain is 77 business days. The duration of the simulation is set to 210 time steps. The first 80 time steps are the warm-up phase, in which the demand is zero. For the remaining 130 days (or half a year) the demand is set by sampling from a normal distribution with the parameters taken from the original dataset. The time of occurrence for the hazard modes is normalised to $t = 100$. The operability levels and recovery rates for the simulation of component failure and repair are presented in **Table 3** in the appendix. The cost parameters in Willems [31] are not disaggregated into fixed and variable cost. Thus, we assume here a fix cost ratio of 0.5.

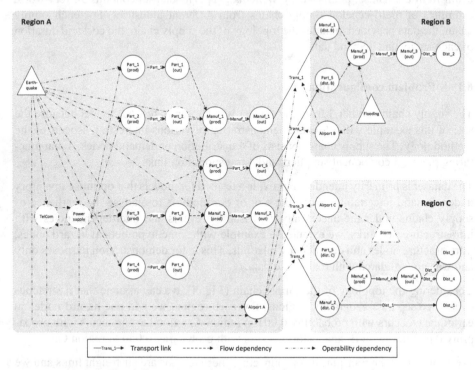

Fig. 4. Example supply chain and infrastructure network

6.2   Results

For each of the three hazard events, 300 operability scenarios were sampled. The interior-point method of the Gurobi optimisation software was used to solve the linear program. After presolving, the linear program had about 10^7 nonzeros and the computation time was about 40 minutes.

Fig. 5 shows a clear correlation between the average inoperability and the total unmet demand. However, the correlation is different for each hazard mode. **Fig. 6** depicts the performance of the supply chain network over time in terms of the proportion of demand that can be satisfied. This plot shows that the final consumers will experience the most severe disruptions between 15 and 45 days after the trigger event. While on average over all scenarios the supply chain can always satisfy more than 70 % of demand, the performance can drop to around 10 % in the most extreme cases. After about 85 days the supply chain has fully recovered in most scenarios, although some repercussions are possible up to 100 days after the trigger event.

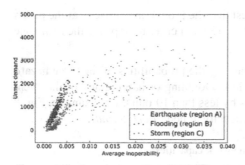

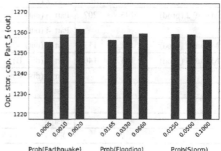

Fig. 5. Average inoperability and unmet demand for 901 scenarios

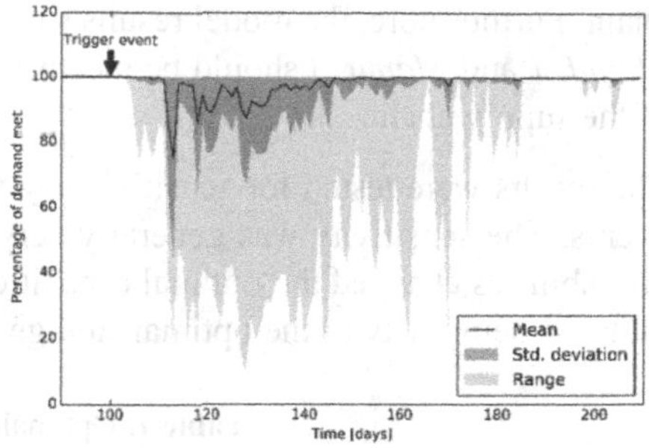

Fig. 6. Loss of supply chain performance over time

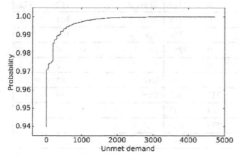

Fig. 7. Cumulative distribution function for unmet demand (expected value: 11.7)

Fig. 8. Sensitivity of optimal storage capacity at *Part_5 (out)*

While in some scenarios the total unmet demand can amount to nearly 5,000 units, the expected value over all scenarios is only 11.7 units. This is largely due to the full-operability scenario that has a probability of 94 % and in which the demand is fully met. Further insights into the probability distribution of the supply chain performance can be gained from plotting the cumulative distribution function for unmet demand (**Fig. 7**). The analysis suggests that with a probability of 99 % unmet demand will be less than 350 units. On the other hand, the plot also shows the long tail of the distributions with a probability of 0.04 % that the unmet demand will be greater than 2,000 units.

The optimal network capacities are presented in **Table 1**. For comparison, the optimal values for a separate simulation run with no hazard events are included. The largest differences between the two simulation runs are the optimal storage capacities. The simulation suggests that if no hazard events were considered, the supply chain should operate in a just-in-time configuration with storage only at the distribution centres to provide for the fluctuations in demand. On the other hand, when the three hazard events and the interdependencies with infrastructure systems are taken into account the model suggests that storage capacity should be provided at various parts throughout the supply chain. Furthermore, the model results suggest that the production capacity at the plants *Manuf_1* and *Manuf_3* should be increased by 13 % in order to improve the resilience of the supply chain.

The results were tested for sensitivity by varying the probabilities of the three hazard events. The sensitivity was generally very low. Doubling or halving any of the event probabilities changed the optimal capacities by less than 10 units. For example, **Fig. 8** plots the sensitivity of the optimal storage capacity at node *Part_5 (out)*.

Table 1. Optimal network capacities

Node	Op. prod. cap.		Node	Op. stor. cap.		Link	Op. flow cap.	
	Without hazards	*With hazards*		*Without hazards*	*With hazards*		*Without hazards*	*With hazards*
Manuf_1 (prod)	152	173	Part_1 (out)	0	2216	Trans_1	155	176
			Part_2 (out)	0	2719	Trans_2	152	173
Manuf_2 (prod)	195	207	Part_3 (out)	0	2719	Tarns_3	144	139
			Part_4 (out)	0	2360	Trans_4	198	303
Manuf_3 (prod)	152	173	Part_5 (out)	0	1259	Dist_1	76	79
Manuf_4 (prod)	144	140	Part_5 (dist. B)	0	6	Dist_2	152	173
			Part_5 (dist. C)	0	159	Dist_3	85	77
			Dist_1	221	812	Dist_4	59	62
			Dist_2	744	1643			
			Dist_3	203	687			
			Dist_4	165	610			

7   Conclusion

The main contributions of this paper can be summarised as follows. Firstly, the proposed method extends an existing network flow model to include inventory holding, the coupling of flows across interdependent networks, and capacity optimisation. Secondly, we combine the network flow model with a novel stochastic simulation method for the generation of operability scenarios for interdependent network assets. Key features of this methodology are that it considers interdependency both at the level of asset operability and at the level of network flows, that it captures dynamic aspects of network flows and supply chain performance in greater detail than previously existing models, and that it addresses the issues of uncertainty and anticipation.

It has to be noted, however, that the model depends on the assumption that the uncertainty can be captured by a finite scenario tree and that all decisions are taken based on full knowledge of that scenario tree. The maximal size of the scenario tree is limited by the computational memory requirements for solving the resulting linear program. Thus, for large problem instances, a trade-off exists between reducing the number of scenarios or reducing the number of time steps. An opportunity for further research is to develop a clustering method that reduces the number of operability scenarios while maintaining representativeness.

References

1. Norrman A, Jansson U (2004) Ericsson's proactive supply chain risk management approach after a serious sub-supplier accident. Int J Phys Distrib Logist Manag 34:434-456.

2. Matsuo H (2015) Implications of the Tohoku earthquake for Toyota's coordination mechanism: Supply chain disruption of automotive semiconductors. Int J Prod Econ 161:217–227.

3. The City of New York (2013) A Stronger, More Resilient New York. http://www.nyc.gov/html/sirr/html/report/report.shtml. Accessed 11 May 2017

4. Koetse MJ, Rietveld P (2009) The impact of climate change and weather on transport: An overview of empirical findings. Transp Res Part D Transp Environ 14:205–221.

5. van Vliet MTH, Yearsley JR, Ludwig F, Vögele S, Lettenmaier DP, Kabat P (2012) Vulnerability of US and European electricity supply to climate change. Nat Clim Chang 2:676–681.

6. Geunes J, Pardalos PM (2003) Network Optimization in Supply Chain Management and Financial Engineering: An Annotated Bibliography. Networks 42:66–84.

7. Wilson MC (2007) The impact of transportation disruptions on supply chain performance. Transp Res Part E Logist Transp Rev 43:295–320.

8. Geng L, Xiao R, Xu X (2014) Research on MAS-Based Supply Chain Resilience and Its Self-Organized Criticality. Discret Dyn Nat Soc 2014:1–14.

9. Gillen D, Hasheminia H (2016) Measuring reliability of transportation networks using snapshots of movements in the network – An analytical and empirical study. Transp Res Part B Methodol 93:808–824.

10. Nagurney A, Daniele P, Shukla S (2016) A supply chain network game theory model of cybersecurity investments with nonlinear budget constraints. Ann Oper Res 248:405–427.

11. Heckmann I, Comes T, Nickel S (2015) A critical review on supply chain risk - Definition, measure and modeling. Omega 52:119:132.

12. Tukamuhabwa BR, Stevenson M, Busby J, Zorzini M (2015) Supply chain resilience: definition, review and theoretical foundations for further study. Int J Prod Res 53:5592–523.

13. Kamalahmadi M, Mellat Parast M (2016) A review of the literature on the principles of enterprise and supply chain resilience: Major findings and directions for future research. Int J Prod Econ 171:116–133.

14. Ahuja RK, Magnanti TL, Orlin JB (1993) Network Flows: Theory, Algorithms, and Applications. Prentice Hall

15. Snyder L V, Scaparra MP, Daskin MS, Church RL (2006) Planning for Disruptions in Supply Chain Networks. TutORials Oper Res INFORMS 234–257.

16. Glockner GD, Nemhauser GL (2000) A dynamic network flow problem with uncertain arc capacities: Formulation and problem structure. Oper Res 48:233–242.

17. Tsiakis P, Shah N, Pantelides CC (2001) Design of Multi-echelon Supply Chain Networks under Demand Uncertainty. Ind Eng Chem Res 40:3585–3604. doi: 10.1021/ie0100030

18. Lu M, Huang S, Shen ZJM (2011) Product substitution and dual sourcing under random supply failures. Transp Res Part B Methodol 45:1251–1265.

19. Salehi Sadghiani N, Torabi SA, Sahebjamnia N (2015) Retail supply chain network design under operational and disruption risks. Transp Res Part E Logist Transp Rev 75:95–114.

20. Xu D, Chen Z, Yang L (2012) Scenario tree generation approaches using K-means and LP moment matching methods. J Comput Appl Math 236:4561–4579.

21. King A, Wallace S (2012) Modeling with Stochastic Programming. Springer

22. Rausand M, Høyland A (2004) System reliability theory: models, statistical methods, and applications, 2nd ed. John Wiley & Sons

23. Rahnamay-Naeini M, Hayat MM (2016) Cascading Failures in Interdependent Infrastructures: An Interdependent Markov-Chain Approach. IEEE Trans Smart Grid 7:1997–2006.

24. Son KS, Kim DH, Kim CH, Kang HG (2016) Study on the systematic approach of Markov modeling for dependability analysis of complex fault-tolerant features with voting logics. Reliab Eng Syst Saf 150:44–57.

25. Lee II EE, Mitchell JE, Wallace WA (2007) Restoration of Services in Interdependent Infrastructure Systems: A Network Flows Approach. IEEE Trans Syst Man, Cybern Part C Appl Rev 37:1303–1317.

26. Holden R, Val D V., Burkhard R, Nodwell S (2013) A network flow model for interdependent infrastructures at the local scale. Saf Sci 53:51–60.

27. Sen A, Balakrishnan N (1999) Convolution of geometrics and a reliability problem. Stat Probab Lett 43:421–426.

28. Cadwallader LC (2012) Review of Maintenance and Repair Times for Components in Technological Facilities Components in Technological Facilities. https://inldigitallibrary.inl.gov/sites/sti/sti/5554588.pdf. Accessed 11 May 2017

29. Pukite J, Pukite P (1998) Modeling for Reliability Analysis: Markov Modeling for Reliability, Maintainability, Safety, and Supportability Analyses of Complex Systems. Wiley

30. Smith DJ (2011) Reliability, Maintainability and Risk: Practical Methods for Engineers, 8th ed. Butterworth-Heinemann

31. Willems SP (2008) Real-World Multiechelon Supply Chains Used for Inventory Optimization. Manuf Serv Oper Manag 10:19–23.

Appendix

Table 2. Operability dependency parameters

From	To	Failure propagation		Recovery delay	
		$\alpha_{j,k}^{F}$	$\beta_{j,k}^{F}$	$\alpha_{j,k}^{R}$	$\beta_{j,k}^{R}$
Earthquake	Power supply	0.50	-	-	-
Earthquake	TelCom	0.10	-	-	-
Earthquake	Airport_A, Part_1, Part_2, Part_3, Part_4, Part_5, Manuf_1, Manuf_2	0.25	-	-	-
Flooding	Airport_B	0.50	-	-	-
Flooding	Manuf_3	0.25	-	-	-
Storm	Airport_C	0.75	-	-	-
Storm	Manuf_4	0.10	-	-	-
Power supply	TelCom	0.75	-	-	-
Power supply	Airport_A, Part_1, Part_2, Part_3, Part_4, Part_5, Manuf_1, Manuf_2	0.50	-	-	-
TelCom	Power supply, Airport_A	-	-	0.50	-

Table 3. Operability level and recovery time parameters

Component	Operability levels	Recovery rates
Manuf_1, Manuf_2, Manuf_3, Manuf_4	[0.00, 0.25, 0.90, 1.00]	[0.50, 0.25, 0.33]
Parts_1, Parts_2, Parts_3, Parts_4, Parts_5	[0.00, 0.50, 1.00]	[0.50, 0.33]
Airport A, Airport B, Airport C	[0.00, 0.67, 1.00]	[1.00, 0.50]
Electricity network	[0.00, 0.50, 1.00]	[1.00, 0.50]
TelCom	[0.00, 0.25, 1.00]	[1.00, 0.67]

Establishing Outsourcing and Supply Chain Plans for Prefabricated Construction Projects Under Uncertain Productivity

Pei-Yuan Hsu[1]*, Marco Aurisicchio[1], Panagiotis Angeloudis[2]

[1] Dyson School of Design Engineering, Imperial College London, Exhibition Road, South Kensington SW7 2AZ, London, UK
[2] Department of Civil and Environmental Engineering, Imperial College London, Exhibition Road, South Kensington SW7 2AZ, London, UK
p.hsu15@imperial.ac.uk

Abstract. In prefabricated construction projects, unlike onsite assembly construction projects, structural components are produced in a factory environment. Thus, similarly to the manufacturing industries, the productivity of building components can fluctuate owing to human errors and machine malfunctions. Since the site demand must always be met, manufacturing is at times outsourced to supplement uncertainties in production. Furthermore, a storage facility between the factory and the construction site becomes indispensable to deal with components that are large in size, yielding a three-tier supply chain that is absent in traditional construction. The objective of this research is to determine the most appropriate production plan and the optimal outsourcing quantities for multi-prefabricated components produced in a manufacturing environment subject to uncertainties in productivity. A workflow including a two-stage stochastic programming model and a mixed-integer linear programming model is established to resolve the above issues. The most favourable schemes for dispatching components and the variation of inventory are also determined. A large infrastructure built through the prefabrication method was selected as a case study to validate the models.

Keywords: Logistic, Manufactured construction, Outsourcing manufacturing.

1 Introduction

In conventional onsite assembly construction projects, raw materials are dispatched by suppliers to construction sites following the orders placed by contractors [33]. In this context, the supply-demand relationship is straightforward, as there are only two decisions to be made: when to purchase new materials and how many materials to purchase. It should also be noted that orders are typically based on a predetermined construction schedule [35], and raw materials on the supply end are always ready to be sent over to the site [5].

In recent years, the construction sector is undergoing a shift from the onsite assembly to the prefabricated construction method. In prefabricated construction projects, building materials are initially shipped to the manufacturing facility, where they are transformed into structural components following a rigorous production sequence [23]. The completed components are then transported to sites for assembling. Moreover, the logistics of prefabricated construction includes aspects that distinguish it from generic

© Springer International Publishing AG 2017
T. Bektaş et al. (Eds.), ICCL 2017, LNCS 10572, pp. 529–543, 2017.
https://doi.org/10.1007/978-3-319-68496-3_35

supply chains [13]. For instance, prefabricated structural components are usually tailor-made and project-specific, so their total production quantity usually matches exactly the demand from the construction site. Consequently, the inventory will reach zero when a project ends. Also, these components are often large and cumbersome, necessitating extra caution when carrying them across public road networks [27]. Since many construction sites are located in urban settings with limited storage space, inventory management within warehouse becomes more prominent. However, previous studies to establish optimal supply chain configurations can only be partially used to inform the definition of a new logistics model for prefabricated construction projects as additional features have to be considered.

Since prefabricated construction has the characteristics of both manufacturing and traditional construction, the production rate of structural components can be affected by factors such as workers' productivity fluctuation and machine or equipment downtime [6]. Hence, manufacturing is at times outsourced to overcome production insufficiencies brought about by productivity uncertainty [32]. However, to meet the demand from a construction site and minimise the total cost, a favourable scheme for self-production and outsourcing should be identified well before the start of construction works. To the best of our knowledge, the optimal production plan for prefabricated construction projects under uncertain productivity has never been proposed.

This research has two main aims. The first is to define a production scheme including the best outsourcing quantities for multi-prefabricated components and the most appropriate duration of self-production when facing uncertain productivity. The second aim is to identify the most favourable schemes for dispatching components manufactured by self-production and outsourcing, while disclosing the variation of inventory in the three tiers of the supply chain: prefabrication factory, warehouse and construction site.

In this research the above issues are addressed by defining a workflow composed of a two-stage stochastic programming model and a mixed-integer linear programming (MILP) model. The results of the workflow could serve as the basis to support decision making by managers of prefabricated construction projects who require to make a holistic plan encompassing self-production, outsourcing, inventory and transportation.

2 Background

This section provides an overview of current research to quantify productivity fluctuation and the strategies to outsource manufacturing. Furthermore, methods to determine the optimal configuration for a multiple-tier supply chain are also reviewed.

2.1 Productivity uncertainty in manufacturing facilities

In a manufacturing factory, the productivity within a finite time horizon can generally be expressed as a bell-shaped curve indicating how frequently a production level can be reached [7,8]. If the target productivity is located on the right side of the curve, which can be fairly common, in most situations the production rate would fall below expectations. Under this context, if the demand is to be met, outsourcing of production is often inevitable.

2.2 Identifying the optimal outsourcing scheme

In manufacturing research, many studies have been conducted to identify and understand outsourcing strategies. Ross and Westerman [34], for example, stated that a firm should establish a holistic outsourcing plan to minimise the total investment cost at the preparation stage. Outsourcing a proportion of production can lower the total operational cost as a result of the efficiency improvement due to parallel manufacturing [1,9]. Alvarez and Stenbacka [3] also identified that partial outsourcing is the most profitable strategy to take under high market uncertainty. Real option theory has been extensively adopted to establish an executable plan for outsourcing. For example, it has been employed to determine whether or not to use outsourcing and revealing the most favourable timing for initiating the outsourcing when a market demand is uncertain [3,22,30,32]. Construction companies engaging in prefabricated construction often need time before a factory is fully equipped and its personnel sufficiently experienced. Thus, the uncertainty lies in the self-productivity of structural components, rather than in the demands at the planning stage. Under this context, the point of an outsourcing plan is to determine the best quantity to order from an outsourcing manufacturer under fluctuating self-production.

2.3 Solving production planning problems

Many previous production planning studies focused on determining the best production quantity and schedule under demand uncertainty [18]. The methods applied for solving the problems were mathematical programming models which can give optimal or near optimal solutions [19,31].

Different types of modelling techniques have been proposed such as stochastic programming, fuzzy set theory, robust optimisation and dynamic stochastic programming [16]. Among them, the two-stage stochastic programming has been commonly adopted, because it can capture different types of uncertainties effectively [17]. Ierapetritou and Pistikopoulos [20] sought the optimal production quantities under fluctuating customer demands by a two-stage stochastic programming with an objective function for minimising the total operational cost and the expected penalty cost incurred by unmet customer demand. Two-stage stochastic programming has also been employed to deal with production planning problems of multi-products, in multi-periods and multi-sites under demand uncertainty [26,27]. Mirzapour Al-e-Hashem et al. [29] implemented a multi-objective stochastic programming model for minimising the total operational cost and its variance while maximising the labour productivity. In their research the demand and labour productivity are both fluctuating and presented as pre-defined distributions. Because of the computational complexity, the model was solved by a hybrid algorithm that is a combination of several mathematical methods, and numerical examples were implemented to demonstrate the validity of the model.

Thus, it is feasible to apply a two-stage stochastic programming model to solve the problem of outsourcing with fixed demand and uncertain self-productivity. This is because they share a common objective: pursuing the most economical production, either pulling by uncertain demand as in previous studies or pushing by uncertain productivity as in the case of this research.

2.4 Integrating supply chains across the organisational boundary

Construction components manufactured through self-production and outsourcing need to be delivered to the site following an appropriate scheme for minimising the transportation and inventory costs while fulfilling the site demand. Under this circumstance, an integrated supply chain configuration between the factory, the warehouse, the construction site and the outsourcing manufacturer needs to be proposed. Chandra and Fisher [11] pointed out that in supply chain design, the activities in different echelons should be considered simultaneously to achieve high overall efficiency. Coelho and Laporte [12] suggested that decisions in production planning, shipment and inventory management should be modelled in a single problem statement. Under this context, a model and its optimal solution can serve as the foundation for tactical decision making.

The idea of a supply chain integrating all stakeholders has been realised by many researchers. Lei et al. [24], for example, developed a model which considered production, inventory, and distribution synchronously. In their study, the most appropriate operation schedule pursued is the one that is capable of satisfying all the customers' demands. Elimam and Dodin [15] combined the production and distribution chains into one integrated supply chain, and identified the optimal supply chain configuration.

A recent review by Díaz-Madroñero et al. [14] summarised the research trends in studying supply chain integration. A common assumption adopted in previous studies is that the customer demand must be satisfied at all times. Another tendency is that most of the integrated supply chain design problems are modelled using mixed-integer linear programming (MILP), which has also been adopted in this research. At this point it is worth noting that prefabricated construction supply chains have certain unique features that set them apart from conventional construction and generic logistic operations. These are reflected in the design of the model presented in this paper.

3 Methodology

This section introduces the assumptions behind the mathematical models, the structure of the models and the background to the case study used to test the models.

3.1 Assumptions

The assumptions applied in the model to represent the logistics operations in the case studied are outlined below. A complete list of indices, parameters and variables is provided in the Appendix. According to the data collected from the cooperating construction company, the schedule engineers organised a detailed weekly assembly plan for the whole construction period *(TW weeks)* before the manufacturing process started. The exact weekly demand quantities D_{ti} ($i \in I$, where I is the set of component types; $t \in T$, where $T=1\ldots TW$) for each type of structural components are known. Thus, the total quantity (TN_i) needed for each type of structural component in the whole project is also revealed at the design stage and is used as the basis for cost estimation.

The manufacturing factory for producing prefabricated concrete components is owned by the construction company. Nevertheless, the weekly production level is uncertain owing to factors such workers' productivity fluctuation and machine or equipment downtime. Thus, there exists different scenarios of total self-production quantity SP_{si} ($s \in S$, where S is the set of scenarios) for each type of component i. This research assumes that all the self-production scenarios are independent and their probabilities of happening are denoted as P_s. The scenario generation process is explained in the next section.

Since the productivity in the factory is uncertain, there exists a possibility that the demand cannot be met by self-production. Thus, two types of outsourcing manufacturing are adopted. The first type is the planned outsourcing which places orders to another prefabrication company in advance, and the total quantity of planned outsourcing (q_i) is estimated based on the most likely inadequacy of self-production. The cost of adopting planned outsourcing for each type of structural component is $q_i \cdot PC_i$, where PC_i represents the price for purchasing one unit of component i from the outsourcing company in advance. The second type is the emergency outsourcing. Since the self-production rate is fluctuating, there exists certain extreme occasions in which, even with backup from planned-outsourcing, the site demand still cannot be satisfied. Under these circumstances, emergency orders are sent to the outsourcing manufacturer and the price of adopting such measure would be higher than the planned outsourcing one. The emergency outsourcing cost is scenario specific and it is expressed as $Max\{TN_i - SP_{si} - q_i, 0\} \cdot EC_i$, where EC_i is the price for buying one unit of component i from the outsourcing company in an urgent situation. On the other hand, if the sum of self-production and planned-outsourcing exceeds the site demand, an extra cost is needed to dispose of redundant components. The redundancy disposing cost is illustrated as $Max\{SP_{si} + q_i - TN_i, 0\} \cdot RC_i$, where RC_i is the cost to dispose of one unit of redundant product i. It should be emphasised that in each self-production scenario, the occurrence of component insufficiency and redundancy are mutually exclusive.

This research also includes inventory management considerations. The inventory levels for each type of component i at the factory, warehouse and site in week t are denoted as n_{ti}^F, n_{ti}^W and n_{ti}^S, respectively. The weekly inventory cost of each type of component is composed of the inventory costs within the factory ($n_{ti}^F \cdot VOL_i \cdot FIC$), warehouse ($n_{ti}^W \cdot VOL_i \cdot WIC$) and site ($n_{ti}^S \cdot VOL_i \cdot SIC$), where FIC, WIC and SIC are the weekly unitary storage costs in the factory, warehouse and site, respectively, and VOL_i is the volume of prefabricated component i. The sum of the weekly inventory cost of each component in all places gives the total inventory cost (IC). It is worth noting that, since most modular products are tailor-made for a project with exact quantity, n_{ti}^F, n_{ti}^W and n_{ti}^S are expected to be exhausted by the end of the project. Moreover, assumptions have been made that the total volumes of inventory cannot exceed their respective storage capacities in factory ($FCAP$), warehouse ($WCAP$) and site ($SCAP$) at all time.

As for the transportation process, there are two sector of transportation; one is from the factory to the warehouse, while the other one is from the warehouse to the site. The overall transportation cost (TC) is the sum of the costs for moving components in these two sectors. In this research, we assumed that all prefabricated components are transported from the warehouse to the construction site according to the weekly demand on a just-in-time basis. The number of trucks needed for moving one type of component from the warehouse to the site is calculated by dividing the weekly transportation quantity (t_{ti}^W) by the quantity of product that can be loaded onto a single truck (NL_i^W) running on this route. The weekly transportation cost from the warehouse to the site for a certain type of component then is determined as: $(t_{ti}^W / NL_i^W) \cdot CWS \cdot DWS$, where DWS is the distance in between and CWS the unitary transportation cost. The transportation cost for moving components from the factory to the warehouse is calculated in the same manner using the corresponding variables and parameters: the weekly transporting quantities of one type of components (t_{ti}^F), truck loading quantity (NL_i^F), moving distance (DFW) and unitary transportation cost (CFW). Another assumption is that, all the finished outsourcing components are delivered to the site directly and the weekly delivery quantities $(o_{ti}^P$ and o_{ti}^E, where P and E stand for planned and emergency, respectively) of each type of components are decided based on both the fluctuating self-production rate and the demand on site.

3.2 Two-stage stochastic programming model for pursuing the optimal outsourcing

This research uses a two-stage stochastic programming model to define the most favourable planned outsourcing quantity for each type of prefabricated component under uncertain productivity. In the first stage of the model, an optimal planned-outsourcing quantity is decided, and in the second stage, the difference between the demand on site and the sum of planned-outsourcing and self-production quantity is taken as the cause of penalty.

Objective function:

The goal of the model is to minimise the objective function (1), which is the sum of the planned outsourcing cost and the expected value of the penalty cost, i.e., the expected cost of using emergency outsourcing or disposing of the redundant components when all possible self-production scenarios are considered.

Minimise:
$$\sum_{i \in I} q_i \cdot PC_i + \sum_{s \in S} \sum_{i \in I} [Max\{TN_i - SP_{si} - q_i, 0\} \cdot EC_i + Max\{SP_{si} + q_i - TN_i, 0\} \cdot RC_i] \cdot P_s \tag{1}$$

Subject to:
$$q_i \geq 0 \ \forall i \in I \tag{2}$$

Constraint (2) states that the planned outsourcing quantity for all types of product must not be negative. The output of the model, the optimaly planned outsourcing quantity (q_i), will be used as a parameter (TPQ_i) in the mixed-integer linear programming (MILP) model described in the next section.

3.3 MILP model for establishing the transportation and inventory scheme

A MILP model was developed to determine the following items:
1. The most favourable weekly transportation quantities of each type of self-production components between factory, warehouse and construction site.
2. The variation of inventory levels in the factory, warehouse and site.
3. The time and quantities of outsourcing components that should be sent to the site by the outsourcing company.

Objective function:

The goal is to minimise the objective function (3), which is the sum of the costs to store (IC) and transport (TC) all types of components.

Minimise:

$$IC + TC \tag{3}$$

$$IC = \sum_{t \in T} \sum_{i \in I} (n_{ti}^F \cdot ICF + n_{ti}^W \cdot ICW + n_{ti}^{FS} \cdot ICS) \cdot VOL_i \tag{3.1}$$

$$TC = \sum_{t \in T} \sum_{i \in I} (\frac{t_{ti}^F}{NL_i^F} \cdot DFW \cdot CFW + \frac{t_{ti}^W}{NL_i^W} \cdot DWS \cdot CWS) \tag{3.2}$$

Equation (3.1) calculates IC, which includes the costs of the inventories within the factory, warehouse and construction sites. Equations (3.2) calculates TC for moving the products from the factory to the warehouse and from the warehouse to the construction site in two terms, respectively.

Subject to:

$$\sum_{t \in T} o_{ti}^P = TPQ_i \quad \forall \, i \in I \tag{4.1}$$

$$n_{ti}^F = n_{t-1,i}^F + ESP_{ti} - t_{ti}^F \quad \forall \, t \in T, i \in I \tag{4.2}$$

$$n_{ti}^W = n_{t-1,i}^W + t_{ti}^F - t_{ti}^W \quad \forall \, t \in T, i \in I \tag{4.3}$$

$$n_{ti}^S = n_{t-1,i}^S + t_{ti}^W + o_{ti}^P + o_{ti}^E - D_{ti} \quad \forall \, t \in T, i \in I \tag{4.4}$$

$$n_{0,i}^F = n_{0,i}^W = n_{0,i}^S = 0 \quad \forall \, t \in T, i \in I \tag{4.5}$$

$$\sum_{i \in I} n_{ti}^F \cdot Vol_i \leq FCAP, \sum_{i \in I} n_{ti}^W \cdot Vol_i \leq WCAP, \sum_{i \in I} n_{ti}^S \cdot Vol_i \leq SCAP \quad \forall \, t \in T \tag{4.6}$$

$$\sum_{t \in T} D_{ti} = \sum_{t \in T} ESP_{ti} + o_{ti}^P + o_{ti}^E \quad \forall \, i \in I \tag{4.7}$$

$$\sum_{t \in T} t_{ti}^F = \sum_{t \in T} t_{ti}^W = \sum_{t \in T} ESP_{ti} \quad \forall \, i \in I \tag{4.8}$$

$$o_{ti}^P, o_{ti}^E \geq 0 \quad \forall \, t \in T, \forall \, i \in I \tag{4.9}$$

$$n_{ti}^F, n_{ti}^W, n_{ti}^S \geq 0 \quad \forall \, t \in T, i \in I \tag{4.10}$$

$$t_{ti}^F, t_{ti}^W \geq 0 \quad \forall \, t \in T, j \in I \tag{4.11}$$

Constraint (4.1) ensures that the total quantity of planned outsourcing delivered does not exceed its limit. Constraint (4.2) represents the balance of inventory in the factory, constraint (4.3) is the balance in the warehouse, while constraints (4.4) handles the balance in the construction site. Constraint (4.5) states that there is nothing in storage in the beginning at the factory, warehouse and site. Constraint (4.6) makes sure that the sums of the volumes of all the stored components in factory, warehouse and site do not exceed their respective storage capacities at all times. Constraint (4.7) assures that the demand on site must be met. Constraint (4.8) ensures that all the components produced in the factory will be shipped to the warehouse and all the above components will also be transported to the construction sites. Constraints (4.9), (4.10) and (4.11) assure the non-negativity of the quantities of planned and emergency outsourcing delivered weekly, the inventory at the factory, warehouse and construction site, as well as the quantities of components transported weekly from the factory to warehouse and from the warehouse to the site, respectively, for every type of product and at all times.

3.4 Background to the case study

This research used the case of a wastewater treatment facility, built in northern England, to test the models. The facility involved use of two types of prefabricated concrete components: walkways and beams. The values of the manufacturing, transportation, inventory and construction parameters used in the models were obtained from the cooperating construction company. The cost data were estimated based on information obtained from civil engineering websites (e.g. http://decastltd.com/ products/ and http://www.anchorconcrete.com/price_list.html) and the literature [13,23].

4 Results and discussion

Using a wastewater treatment facility case study, this section presents the outputs of the two programming models, which were implemented in IBM ILOG CPLEX Studio (version 12.6), an optimisation software package employing the OPL mathematical modelling language. The CPLEX Optimizer is used to solve the problems studied. The models were executed on a personal computer (i7-4790, 8G RAM) with the computational time of 5 minutes for the two-stage stochastic model and 2 minutes for the MILP model. Exact solutions were outputted by both models.

4.1 The workflow

Figure 1 presents a flow chart which, employing the two models described above, aims at obtaining the following information:
1. The optimal duration for self-production in a construction project, i.e., the best time, prior to assembly at the construction site, to start the production of prefabricated components.
2. The best planned and emergency outsourcing quantities for each type of components.
3. The most favourable transportation and inventory schemes for self-produced components.
4. The most favourable dispatch plan for outsourced components that can match up with the above schemes.

As shown in Figure 1, the process starts by representing uncertainty in productivity through a bell-shaped probability distribution [7], which is discretised using a 3-point estimation [21]. Based on this, possible self-production scenarios at the factory over a finite time horizon are generated. Then the two-stage stochastic programming model is implemented to find out the best planned-outsourcing quantity by considering all the possible self-production scenarios simultaneously. Afterwards, the MILP model is adopted to reveal the optimal transportation scheme and inventory variations, along with the dispatch plan for outsourcing. This whole process can be individually carried out for each possible option of self-production duration. For each option, the total cost, which includes the costs of factory overhead, self-production, transportation, inventory, planned outsourcing, and the penalty for emergency outsourcing or disposal of redundant components, is calculated. The optimal self-production duration is determined as the one with the lowest total cost.

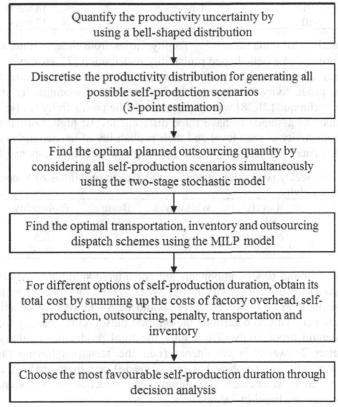

Fig. 1. The workflow.

4.2 Generation of the production scenarios in the factory

In the case study, the detailed design of the prefabricated components was handed over to the construction company 7 weeks before the construction start date, and the duration of the construction work was fixed at 17 weeks. Thus, the construction company had at most 24 weeks for producing all the components demanded by the project. But it also had the opportunity to opt for a shorter self-production duration while increasing the outsourcing quantity. In this context, 8 distinct options for self-production duration are established, each with a different manufacturing period before the construction starts (see Table 1).

Table 1. Options for self-production duration.

Option No.	Length of in-advance preparation	Total self-production duration
I	7 week	24 week
II	6 week	23 week
III	5 week	22 week
IV	4 week	21 week
V	3 week	20 week
VI	2 week	19 week
VII	1 week	18 week
VIII	0 week	17 week

The productivity of a manufacturing facility varies from time to time, and generally, can be expressed as a bell-shaped probability distribution [7]. However, prefabricated components are produced in discrete integer numbers making it more appropriate to present the productivity distribution in a discrete form. For simplicity, the three-point estimation technique [21,28] was employed, i.e., the productivity for the prefabricated components was assumed to have three different levels: high, normal and low. The weekly productivity at each level and their probability of happening were established based on the data obtained from the cooperating construction company (Table 2).

Table 2. The weekly production quantities and their probabilities of happening for the 3 levels of productivity.

Levels	Walkway	Beam	Probability
High	15	10	0.25
Normal	12	8	0.5
Low	9	6	0.25

When walkway and beam components are considered simultaneously there are $3^2=9$ possible scenarios of productivity in one week. Thus, for option I with a total self-production duration of 24 weeks, there should be 9^{24} kinds of production scenarios. This research is trying to determine the optimal outsourcing quantity for components under uncertain productivity. Thus, only the total production quantity that can be realised after 24 weeks is considered (i.e., the scenarios having the same total production quantity are combined as one scenario), and there are only 2401 kinds of production quantity scenarios in this option. The production quantity scenarios for each of the 8 options are listed in Table 3.

Table 3. Production quantity scenarios for the 8 self-production duration options.

Option No.	Duration	Number of Scenarios
I	24 Week	2401
II	23 Week	2209
III	22 Week	2025
IV	21 Week	1849
V	20 Week	1681
VI	19 Week	1521
VII	18 Week	1369
VIII	17 Week	1225

4.3 Output of the two-stage stochastic programming model

Following the flow chart shown in Figure 1, the total production scenarios generated in section 4.2 were used as input to the two-stage stochastic programming model, which was executed for each of the 8 options of self-production duration while taking all the self-production quantity scenarios in that option into consideration simultaneously. The outputs are the optimal planned outsourcing quantities for both the walkway and the beam along with the costs of planned outsourcing and the lowest expected penalties incurred by the emergency outsourcing and the disposal of redundant components, see Table 4.

Table 4. The planned outsourcing quantities, costs and the penalty for the 8 options.

Option No.	Optimal planned outsourcing quantity		Planned outsourcing cost (£)	Expected total penalty (£)
	Walkway	Beam		
I	72	46	246,000	46,750
II	84	54	288,000	45,883
III	96	62	330,000	44,997
IV	108	70	372,000	44,092
V	120	78	414,000	43,165
VI	132	86	456,000	42,216
VII	144	94	498,000	41,243
VIII	156	102	540,000	40,243

4.4 Output of the MILP model

The planned-outsourcing quantities were used as input to the MILP model established in section 3.3 to determine a holistic distribution scheme and reveal the variation of inventory that would yield the lowest transportation and inventory costs while taking both self-production and outsourcing into consideration. It is noteworthy that here the three level weekly productivity (see Table 2) was turned into an expected value to represent the most likely weekly productivity of the self-production.

The outputs included the optimal weekly transportation quantity between the factory, the warehouse and the site, as well as the weekly variations of the inventories at these three locations. Moreover, a dispatch plan for delivering outsourcing components to the site was outlined. For illustration purpose, all the schemes recommended by the model for option IV (4 weeks in-advance preparation plus 17 weeks of construction works) are presented in Table 5.

Table 5. Detailed distribution schemes for option IV.

Week	-4		-3		-2		-1		1		2		3		4		5		6		7		8		9		10		11		12		13		14		15		16		17	
Component	w	b	w	b	w	b	w	b	w	b	w	b	w	b	w	b	w	b	w	b	w	b	w	b	w	b	w	b	w	b	w	b	w	b	w	b	w	b	w	b	w	b
Production	12	8	12	8	12	8	12	8	12	8	12	8	12	8	12	8	12	8	12	8	12	8	12	8	12	8	12	8	12	8	12	8	12	8	12	8	12	8	12	8
Tran. (F-W)	0	4	4	12	12	8	12	8	12	8	12	8	12	8	20	4	21	10	15	10	12	8	12	8	12	8	12	8	12	8	12	8	12	8	12	8	12	8	12	8
Inv. (F)	12	4	20	0	20	0	20	0	20	0	20	0	20	0	12	4	3	2	0	0	0	0	0	0	0	0	0	0	0	0	0	0	0	0	0	0	0	0	0	0
Tran. (W-S)	0	0	0	0	0	0	0	0	21	14	21	14	21	14	21	14	21	14	15	10	12	8	12	8	12	8	12	8	12	8	12	8	12	8	12	8	12	8	12	8
Inv. (W)	0	4	4	16	16	24	28	32	19	26	10	20	1	14	0	4	0	0	0	0	0	0	0	0	0	0	0	0	0	0	0	0	0	0	0	0	0	0	0	0
Plan-Out	0	0	0	0	0	0	0	0	0	0	0	0	0	0	0	0	6	4	9	6	9	6	9	6	9	6	9	6	9	6	9	6	9	6	9	6	4	9	6	12 8
Eme-Out	0	0	0	0	0	0	0	0	0	0	0	0	0	0	0	0	0	0	0	0	0	0	0	0	0	0	0	0	0	0	0	0	0	0	0	0	2	0	0	0
Demand	0	0	0	0	0	0	0	0	21	14	21	14	21	14	21	14	21	14	21	14	21	14	21	14	21	14	21	14	21	14	21	14	21	14	21	14	21	14	24	16
Inv. (S)	0	0	0	0	0	0	0	0	0	0	0	0	0	0	0	0	0	0	0	0	0	0	0	0	0	0	0	0	0	0	0	0	0	0	0	0	0	0	0	0

The model also yielded the various costs for transportation and inventory. The results for the 8 options are listed in Table 6. It should be noted that the model suggested not to have inventory on the site for all options.

Table 6. Various costs (in £) for transportation and inventory for 8 self-production options

Option No.	Inventory costs			Transportation costs		Total
	Factory	Warehouse	Site	Factory to warehouse	Warehouse to site	
I	297	1696	0	23,520	21,504	47,017
II	249	1182	0	22,540	20,608	44,579
III	203	764	0	21,560	19,712	42,239
IV	157	436	0	20,580	18,816	39,989
V	109	202	0	19,600	17,920	37,831
VI	63	64	0	18,620	17,024	35,771
VII	21	8	0	17,640	16,128	33,797
VIII	0	0	0	16,660	15,232	31,892

4.5 Determining the best self-production duration

The total cost for performing each of the 8 options had to be estimated to select an optimal self-production duration. The cost of self-production can be calculated as the expected weekly productivity times the unit production cost. The factory fix cost is obtained by timing the weekly factory overhead with the total self-production duration. The costs for transportation and storage are given by the MILP model. The cost for outsourcing and penalty (including emergency outsourcing and disposal of redundant components) is revealed by the two-stage stochastic programming model. The results are given in Table 7, which shows that option IV has the lowest total cost (highlighted with a framed box). Table 7 also reveals that if the self-production duration is too long (e.g. Option I), the factory fix cost and inventory cost would be relatively higher. On the other hand, if the duration is too short such as in option VIII, the cost of using outsourcing becomes more expensive. Thus, there exists a balance point between self-production and outsourcing, at which the total cost is the lowest.

Table 7. The costs (in £) of the eight options of self-production duration

Costs / Options	Self-production	Factory fix cost	Transp. cost	Inv. cost	Planned-outsourcing	Penalty	Total
I	672,000	261,600	45,024	1993	246,000	46,750	1,273,367
II	644,000	250,700	43,148	1431	288,000	45,883	1,273,162
III	616,000	239,800	41,272	967	330,000	44,997	1,273,036
IV	588,000	228,900	39,396	593	372,000	44,092	1,272,981
V	560,000	218,000	37,520	311	414,000	43,165	1,272,996
VI	532,000	207,100	35,644	127	456,000	42,216	1,273,087
VII	504,000	196,200	33,768	29	498,000	41,243	1,273,240
VIII	476,000	185,300	31,892	0	540,000	40,243	1,273,435

4.4 Discussion

Prefabricated construction projects have several features that distinguish their logistic operations from those of onsite assembly projects. In prefabricated construction, building materials are sent to a factory and turned into structural components following a rigorous production sequence. To match the assembly schedule on site, the production of components in the factory has to start prior to the construction work and continue till the end of the project.

For this reason, the detailed design of components must be finished at a much earlier stage than that required in onsite assembly projects, making accuracy and timeliness the two most critical requirements for the design of components in prefabricated construction projects. This situation has become one of the major reasons to constrain many projects from adopting the prefabricated method [2,10]. However, late design release is very frequent in the construction industry [4]. In our case study, the design team handed in the design 7 weeks before the start of construction rather than the 24 weeks initially agreed making the outsourcing of manufacturing unavoidable. To make things more complicated, the productivity in the factory was uncertain due to factors such as human errors and equipment failure. Hence, the actual production quantity could not be precisely determined. The fluctuating productivity could result in insufficiency or redundancy of components after an order is sent off to the outsourcing company, and further incurring the penalties like the arrangement of emergency outsourcing or disposition of redundancy. The managers of prefabricated projects thus face two major questions: 1) when should the production in a factory start? and 2) what quantity of components should be acquired from an outsourcing company, so that the total cost can be minimised? These questions are absent in conventional construction projects but are believed to be critical to the growing field of prefabricated construction.

In this study, the optimal quantity of planned outsourcing is calculated using a two-stage stochastic programming model, which takes into account the uncertainty of productivity. The best schemes for dispatching components produced by self-production and outsourcing along with the variation of inventory are disclosed by a MILP model. As an optimisation strategy for inventory management, the MILP model, implemented in this study, suggests not to have any inventory on the site anytime. Not to store finished components on the site is conceivable due to the higher inventory cost at the site, e.g. extra precaution must be taken to protect finished components from the harsh open environment. By adopting this configuration, components need to be delivered to the site on a just-in-time basis, which can be regarded as a realisation of the lean concept in the construction industry. Additionally, the MILP model adopts a three-tier logistic structure, which includes two sectors of transportation and three locations for storage. The three-tier logistic structure is usually missing in conventional onsite assembly projects. Finally, the total costs for different options of self-production duration are calculated, and the optimal duration is determined as the one with the lowest total cost. It is worth noting that there exists a balance point in the self-production duration as revealed in Table 7. This balance is incurred because long self-production duration would incur high factory overhead and inventory costs. On the one hand, high outsourcing cost would arise from short duration.

The model outputs could serve as the basis for decision-making by managers of prefabricated construction projects who are required to make a holistic plan encompassing self-production, outsourcing, inventory and transportation. Future research can use real options theory to calculate the optimal option price for reserving the right to use emergency outsourcing.

Acknowledgement

The authors acknowledge the support of the Taiwan Top University Strategic Alliance-Imperial PhD scholarship and Emma Rigler, Anthony English and Russell Smith from Laing O'Rourke.

References

1.   Aksin, O. Z., de Vericourt, F., & Karaesmen, F. (2008) Call center outsourcing contract analysis and choice. Management Science, 54(2), 354–368.
2.   Alazzaz, F. & Whyte, A. (2015) A review of current barriers (real and perceived) to off-site construction. "21st IIER International Conference", 11 April 2015, Australia, 27-31.
3.   Alvarez, L. H. R., & Stenbacka, R. (2007) Partial outsourcing: A real options perspective. International Journal of Industrial Organization, 25(1), 91–102.
4.   Assaf, S. A. and Al-Hejji, S. (2006) Causes of delay in large construction projects. International journal of project management, 24(4), 349
5.   Azambuja, M. & O'Brien, W. J. (2008) Construction supply chain modelling: Issues and perspectives. In: O'Brien, W.J., Formoso, C. T., Vrijhoef, R., & London, K.A. (eds.) Construction supply chain management handbook. Boca Raton, CRC Press.
6.   Azhar, S., Lukkad, M.Y. & Ahmad, I. (2013) An investigation of critical factors and constraints for selecting modular construction over conventional stick-built technique, International Journal of Construction Education and Research, 9(3) 203-225.
7.   Baily, M. N., Hulten, C., Campbell, D., Bresnahan, T., & Caves, R. E. (1992). Productivity dynamics in manufacturing plants. Brookings papers on economic activity. Microeconomics, 1992, 187-267
8.   Bartelsman, E. J., and Phoebus J. D. (1992) Productivity Dynamics: U. S. Manufacturing Plants, 1972-1986. Discussion Paper CES 92-1. Center for Economic Studies, Bureau of the Census. February.
9.   Barthelemy, J. (2001) The hidden costs of IT outsourcing. MIT Sloan Management Review, 42(3), 60–69.
10. Blismas, N. G., Pendlebury, M., Gibb, A. and Pasquire, C. (2005) Constraints to the use of off-site production on construction projects. "Architectural engineering and design management", 1(3), 153-162.
11. Chandra, P., & Fisher, M. L. (1994). Coordination of production and distribution planning. European Journal of Operational Research, 72(3), 503-517
12. Coelho, L. C., & Laporte, G. (2014) Optimal joint replenishment, delivery and inventory management policies for perishable products. Computers & Operations Research, 47, 42-52
13. De La Torre, M.L. (1994). A review and analysis of modular construction practice. MS thesis, Lehigh University.
14. Díaz-Madroñero, M., Peidro, D., & Mula, J. (2015) A review of tactical optimization models for integrated production and transport routing planning decisions. Computers & Industrial Engineering, 88, 518-535
15. Elimam, A. A., & Dodin, B. (2013) Project scheduling in optimizing integrated supply chain operations. European Journal of Operational Research, 224(3), 530-541
16. Felfel, H., Ayadi, O., & Masmoudi, F. (2015) A multi-site supply chain planning using multi-stage stochastic programming. In: Multiphysics Modelling and Simulation for Systems Design and Monitoring. Springer International Publishing.
17. Garcia-Herreros, P., Wassick, J. M., & Grossmann, I. E. (2014). Design of resilient supply chains with risk of facility disruptions. Industrial & Engineering Chemistry Research, 53(44), 17240-17251
18. Holt, C. C., Modigliani, F., & Simon, H. A. (1955) A linear decision rule for production and employment scheduling. Management Science, 2(1), 1-30
19. Hsu, P. Y., Aurisicchio, M., and Angeloudis, P. (2017). "Supply Chain Design For Modular Construction Projects." In: LC3 2017 Volume II – Proceedings of the 25th Annual Conference of the International Group for Lean Construction (IGLC), Walsh, K., Sacks, R., Brilakis, I. (eds.), Heraklion, Greece, 805–812
20. Ierapetritou, M. G., & Pistikopoulos, E. N. (1996) Batch plant design and operations under uncertainty. Industrial & Engineering Chemistry Research, 35(3), 772-787
21. Keefer, D. L., & Bodily, S. E. (1983) Three-point approximations for continuous random variables. Management 43 Science, 29(5), 595-609.
22. Kogut, B., Kulatilaka, N. (1994) Operating flexibility, global manufacturing, and the option value of a multinational network. Management Science 40, 123–139.
23. Lawson, M., Ogden, R., & Goodier, C. (2014) Introduction to planning of modular buildings. In: Lawson, M. (ed.) Design in modular construction. Boca Raton, CRC Press.
24. Lei, L., Liu, S., Ruszczynski, A., & Park, S. (2006) On the integrated production, inventory, and distribution routing problem. IIE Transactions, 38(11), 955-970
25. Leung, S. C. H., Tsang, S. O., Ng, W. L., & Wu, Y. (2007) A robust optimization model for multi-site production planning problem in an uncertain environment. European journal of operational research, 181(1), 224-238.
26. Leung, S. C. H., Wu, Y., Lai, K.K. (2006) A stochastic programming approach for multi-site aggregate production planning. Journal of the Operational Research Society 57, 123–132

27. Li, Z., Shen, G.Q. & Xue, X. (2014) Critical review of the research on the management of prefabricated construction. Habitat International, 43, 240-249.
28. Liu, M. (2013) Program Evaluation and Review Technique (PERT) in Construction Risk Analysis. In Applied 52 Mechanics and Materials (Vol. 357, pp. 2334-2337). Trans Tech Publications.
29. Mirzapour Al-e-Hashem, S. M. J., Baboli, A., Sadjadi, S. J., & Aryanezhad, M. B. (2011) A multi-objective stochastic production-distribution planning problem in an uncertain environment considering risk and workers productivity. Mathematical Problems in Engineering, 2011
30. Moon, Y. (2010). Efforts and efficiency in partial outsourcing and investment timing strategy under market uncertainty. Computers & Industrial Engineering, 59(1), 24-33.
31. Nam, S. J. and Logendran, R. (1992) Aggregate production planning—a survey of models and methodologies. European Journal of Operational Research, 61(3), 255–272
32. Nembhard, H., Shi, L., & Aktan, M. (2003). A real options design for product outsourcing. The Engineering Economist, 48(3), 199–217.
33. Pryke, S. (2009). Introduction. In: Pryke, S. (ed.) Construction Supply Chain Management: Concepts and Case Studies. Oxford, Wiley-Blackwell.
34. Ross, J. W., & Westerman, G. (2004) Preparing for utility computing: The role of IT architecture and relationship management. IBM Systems Journal, 43(1), 5–19.
35. Vrijhoef, R., & Koskela, L. (2000) The four roles of supply chain management in construction. European Journal of Purchasing & supply management, 6(3), 169-178.

Appendix

(Two-stage stochastic programming model) Indices:
i Product types; $i \in I$, I is the set of product types
s Self-production scenarios ; $s \in S$, S in the set of scenarios

Parameters
P_s The probability that scenario s occurs
SP_{si} The total self-production quantity for product i in scenario s
TN_i The total demand quantity for product i for the whole construction project
PC_i The planned outsourcing cost for one unit of product i
EC_i The emergency outsourcing cost for one unit of product i
RC_i The cost of disposing of one unit of redundant product i

Decision variables
q_i The planned outsourcing quantity for product i

(Mixed-integer linear programming model) Indices
t Working weeks for the project; $t \in T$, $T = \{1, 2, ..., TW\}$
i Product types; $i \in I$, I is the set of product types

Parameters
TW The total working duration for the project in weeks
D_{ti} The demand for product i in week t
TPQ_i The total quantity of planned outsourcing of product i
VOL_i Volume of product i in m^3
ESP_{ti} The expected self-production quantity for product i in week t
FIC Inventory cost per m^3 per day in factory
WIC Inventory cost per m^3 per day in warehouse
SIC Inventory cost per m^3 per day at construction site
$FCAP$ Maximum inventory capacity in factory in m^3
$WCAP$ Maximum inventory capacity in warehouse in m^3
$SCAP$ Maximum inventory capacity at construction site   m^3
DFW Distance between factory and warehouse in km
DWS Distance between warehouse and site in km
CFW Transportation cost from factory to warehouse per truck per km
CWS Transportation cost from warehouse to site per truck per km
NL_i^F Quantity of product i that can be loaded onto a truck from factory to warehouse
NL_i^W Quantity of product i that can be loaded onto a truck from warehouse to site

Decision variables
t_{ti}^F Transportation quantity of product i from factory to warehouse on week t
t_{ti}^W Transportation quantity of product i from warehouse to site on week t
n_{ti}^F Quantity of inventory of product i in factory on week t
n_{ti}^W Quantity of inventory of product i in warehouse on week t
n_{ti}^S Quantity of inventory of product i at site on week t
o_{ti}^P The planned outsourcing product i be delivered to site on week t
o_{ti}^E The emergency outsourcing for product i be delivered to site on week t

Agent-Based Simulation to Assess the Performance of Intersections with Pre-Signals: Comparison with Roundabouts

António A.C. Vieira, Luís M.S. Dias, Guilherme, A.B. Pereira, José A. Oliveira

University of Minho, Campus Gualtar, 4710-057, Braga, Portugal,
University of Minho, Portugal
{antonio.vieira, lsd,gui,zan}@dps.uminho.pt

Abstract. Solving traffic congestion problems in intersections is a complex logistic problem that usually consists in building infrastructures, such as bridges, tunnels, or roundabouts, which represent the costliest solutions. Concerning the case of roundabouts, many parameters influence its performance, e.g. geometry and size. Thus, other less costlier solutions should be pondered. This paper introduces a low-cost approach to traffic intersections, by using pre-signals; and conducts simulation experiments to verify if this approach could be used to improve the performance of traffic intersections. In this sense, an agent-based traffic simulation model was developed that applies the object modelling paradigm of Simio to model the individual behaviour of vehicles. The simulation experiments results indicate that the flow of vehicles can be increased up to 20%, reducing the average queue sizes and crossing time per vehicle and saving the fuel consumed up to 64%.

1   Introduction

Since the motor vehicle became the main means of transport, many traffic congestion problems can be witnessed. To overcome them, usually two types of solutions are used: optimization approaches for the duration of traffic light phases, or physical-changes (Heng and Perugu, 2009), such as the expansion of the intersection, or the construction of tunnels, bridges or roundabouts, representing a more onerous type of solution (Treiber and Helbing, 2001).

In a previous work, Vieira et al. (2014b) presented the pre-signals concept as a low-cost technique to improve the performance of an intersection and compared an intersection implementing this concept with a regular intersection. The concept consists on implementing an additional traffic-light on each lane, located prior to the main traffic-light of each lane. To implement them, it is necessary to provide some dozens of meters on the approaches of the intersection, working as "launch pads". The achieved results indicated that the best values to use for the green signal on intersections with pre-signals (different from the best green signal duration on normal intersections) and the best distance to keep between a pre-signals and its main traffic-light: 20 seconds of green signal, at about 40 meters of distance to the pre-signals, are enough to allow

© Springer International Publishing AG 2017
T. Bektaş et al. (Eds.), ICCL 2017, LNCS 10572, pp. 544–556, 2017.
https://doi.org/10.1007/978-3-319-68496-3_36

maximum flow and minimize queue sizes and waiting time per vehicle. These values will be used in the work presented in this paper.

This paper presents a discrete-event simulation model, developed to compare the performance of intersection with pre-signals and roundabouts. It was developed in Simio, a recently developed object oriented discrete simulation tool that also supports the agent modelling approach and other approaches, such as processes and events.

Simulation enables the visualization of the results from modifications made to a system, without making experiments in the real world. To address this kind of traffic-related problems, usually traffic simulation packages, such as VISSIM are used. However, to the best of the knowledge of the authors, these traffic simulation packages lack the ability of modelling concepts not standardized, such as the one here proposed. As such, discrete-event simulation was used for this work.

Next section reviews the literature on this topic. Section 3 is dedicated to the data gathering and validation processes. In section 4, the main tasks conducted to develop the simulation model will be covered and section 5 is related to the simulation experiments conducted. Conclusions are discussed in the last section.

2   Literature Review

Despite only having been first documented in 1991 in the UK (Oakes et al., 1994), pre-signals were already in use in several European cities (Wu and Hounsell, 1998). Its implementation is becoming significant in some cities of the United Kingdom and, in fact, until 1993, only in London, 14 pre-signals were implemented and a further 20 to 25 pre-signals were planned for the coming years (Wu and Hounsell, 1998).

The implementation of pre-signals can have many goals. One of these is "to give buses priority access into a bus advance area of the main junction stop line so as to avoid the traffic queue and reduce bus delay at the signal controlled junction" (Wu and Hounsell, 1998). Conversely, in Xie and Ma (2012) pre-signals were used to avoid losses of capacity on the lanes that cannot discharge completely during its green phases, due to the existence of turning lanes. More recently, Xuan et al. (2011) were pioneers on the utilization of pre-signals to increase the capacity of a traffic intersection. In their study the approaches receives "2 green sub-phases: one for protected left turns only, and the other exclusively for through movements and right turns" (Xuan et al., 2011). In Zhou and Zhuang (2013), this idea was seized and the authors proposed "an integrated model for lane assignment and signal timing optimization at tandem intersections". The model aimed to minimize the average delay that vehicles experienced in the pre-signal and main signal.

Currently there are not many studies that use Simio for modelling traffic related problems. A possible justification for this is that most of the studies that use simulation in problems related to traffic, use packages of micro simulation tools like VISSIM or AIMSUN. However, to test the applicability of new proposed concepts such as the one proposed in this paper, to the best of the knowledge of the authors, these simulation packages reveal to be inadequate, since they are prepared to model only certain infrastructures types. Therefore, for this study, a discrete event simulation software was used. The number of commercial tool options can be very high, thus simulation tool comparison becomes a very important task.

In Hlupic and Paul (1999), a set of simulation tools were compared, distinguishing between users of software for educational purposes and users in industry. In his turn, Hlupic (2000) developed a survey of academic and industrial users on the use of simulation software, to discover how the users are satisfied with the simulation software they use and how this software could be further improved. In Dias et al. (2007), Pereira et al. (2011) and Dias et al. (2016) a comparison of tools based on popularity on the internet, scientific publications, WSC (Winter Simulation Conference), social networks and other sources, was established. According to the authors, popularity should not be used as the only comparison indicator, otherwise new tools, better than existing ones, would never get market place. However, a positive correlation may exist between popularity and quality, since the best tools have a higher chance of being more popular. According to this ranking, the most popular tool is Arena, whilst the classification of the "newcomer" Simio is noteworthy. Vieira et al. (2014a) and Oueida et al. (2016) compared both tools taking into consideration several factors.

Simio was created in 2007 from the same developers of Arena and is based on intelligent objects (Sturrock and Pegden, 2010, Pegden, 2007, Pegden and Sturrock, 2008). In this tool, a vehicle, a costumer or any other agent of a system are examples of possible objects and, combining several of these, one can represent the components of the system in analysis. In other words, the user can use realistic representations of the objects that compose the real system being modelled and, thereafter, at a lower level, define additional logic to the model, through the development of processes for instance. Thus, in Simio the model logic and animation are built in a single step (Pegden and Sturrock, 2008, Pegden, 2007), making the modelling process very intuitive with the addition of a full built-in 3D animation.

3   Data Collection and Validation

In this section, some of the data that was gathered and entered into the developed model will be presented and explained. It should be noted that, some of these data had already been explained in Vieira et al. (2014b), namely those related to the intersection with pre-signals. To build a model capable of representing the real system, the following data related traffic situations was gathered through literature collected and analysed:

- Cycle times of the traffic lights: Pan et al. (2010) stated that when the signal cycle length is around 100 seconds, the waiting time of vehicles is minimal.
- Safety distances kept while driving: Drivers that travel at a speed next to 50 km/h maintain a safety distance of about 16 meters (Luo et al., 2011).
- Space occupied by a vehicle in a queue: The analysed studies indicate that a stopped vehicle occupies a distance between 7.6 meters and 7.9 meters (Bonneson, 1992, Messer and Fambro, 1997, Zhu, 2008, Herman et al., 1971)
- Start-up acceleration: Zhu (2008) analysed several studies regarding this matter. The author developed a polynomial acceleration model characterized by expression (1). Since in Simio it is not possible to implement the acceleration of entities, it was necessary to use the correspondent velocity expression (2).

$$a = 2{,}46 - 0{,}24t + 0{,}006t^2 \tag{1}$$

$$v = 2{,}66 + 2{,}46t - 0{,}12t^2 + 0{,}002t^3 \tag{2}$$

- Time the drivers on the first position of a queue take to react to a traffic light signal change to green: Some authors considered that the first vehicle of a queue normally wastes 2 seconds to initiate the start-up acceleration process after the traffic light changes to green (Bonneson, 1992, Messer and Fambro, 1997); others, considered the wasted time lies between 1.5 and 2 seconds (Bonneson, 1992, George and Heroy, 1966).
- Time spent, by the drivers on the remaining positions of a queue, to react to a traffic light signal change to green: According to Bonneson (1992), these values correspond to 1 second per vehicle, 1.22 seconds or 1.3 seconds.
- Reaction time of drivers on roundabouts: It is difficult to find in the literature and to measure in the filed the reaction time that drivers take to start accelerating, from a resting position, in a roundabout queue. This is because drivers are constantly trying to access a gap in the roundabout and many times they do not completely stop, which influences their start-up accelerating process. This does not happen, for instance, in signalized intersection, since drivers must wait for a red light that they do not know when it is going to change. Thus, the reaction time of drivers in the queues of signalized intersection was used. As already stated, these values can go from 1 to 1.3 seconds for the vehicles in the first position of the queue, to 1.5 to 2 seconds for the remaining positions. These values were incorporated in Simio, adjusting them to have the reaction time of drivers being dependent on their distance to the one on the first position of the queue, as authors agree. Moreover, since the reaction time of drivers in roundabouts is lower than on signalized intersections, these values were calibrated. Thus, in this model, the first vehicle of the queue on the signalized intersection took considerable more time than the vehicle on the same position of the queue of the roundabout. Concerning the reaction time of the vehicles on the remaining positions, their values decrease until an average of 1 second. After that, the average value is maintained.
- Velocity while circulating inside the roundabout: Skrodenis et al. (2011) stated that speeds of vehicles, circulating inside roundabouts, of diameter varying between 16 to 45 meters, should be around 16-30 km/h. Furthermore, the speed of vehicles entering and circulating roundabouts tends to be higher for bigger roundabouts (Brilon, 2005). Based on this and on numerous calibrations to the simulation model, it was considered that the vehicles could accelerate to a maximum speed of 30 km/h in roundabouts of similar size. For smaller roundabouts, the vehicles will only be able to speed up until 25 km/h. While circulating on roundabouts of 60 meters of diameter the vehicles will be able to speed up until 35 km/h and on roundabouts of 80 meters the vehicles will be able to speed up until 40 km/h. Thus, these speed differences also have an influence on the space gap required by the drivers to access the roundabouts of different sizes.
- Space gap to access the roundabout: While circulating a roundabout, the velocity of a vehicle affects the required space, or time, for a second vehicle to access the same roundabout. Since these values were modelled based on data collected from the literature, the authors empirically calibrated the required space gap, in order to

minimize the occasions on which a vehicle decides to access a roundabout and, because of that, another vehicle, circulating on the roundabout, had to slowdown, since the available gap was too small for the other vehicle to access the roundabout. Thus, the space required for a vehicle, to access the roundabout was 17 meters for the roundabout of around 10 meters of radius, 22 meters for the roundabout with around 20 meters of radius, 33 meters for the roundabout of a radius of around 30 meters and 47 meters for the roundabout with around 40 meters of radius.

- Discharge rate of a queue: Bonneson (1992) concluded that this takes place at a rate of approximately 1 vehicle per 2 seconds. Other authors considered lower values like 1.97 (Lee and Chen, 1986) or 1.92 seconds (Zegeer, 1986).
- Instant speed when crossing the stop line of an intersection: Bonneson (1992) stated that the velocity of each vehicle increases until the fourth or fifth vehicle. From that number, the velocity of the vehicles tends to stabilize.
- Fuel consumption and emission rates: Some of the models that estimate consumption rates and emissions include those based on the instant velocity of vehicles. Tong et al. (2000) established a formula for the fuel consumption of diesel vehicles in order of the instantaneous vehicle speed, whilst Chan et al. (2004) used a formula to estimate "the fuel consumption of petrol vehicles as a function of the instantaneous vehicle speed". Notwithstanding, there are models that consider other factors, such as the model proposed by Akçelik and Besley (2003), which considers the acceleration of the vehicle, its mass, instant speed, among other parameters. Akçelik (1983) also provided a model that expresses fuel consumption as a function of cruising, idling and stop-start manoeuvers. In its turn, Guo and Zhang (2014) indicated the formula currently being used by some traffic micro simulation tools (c.f. VISSIM, TRANSYT, and SYNCHRO).

Apart from formulas that estimate the consumption and emission rates, Coelho et al. presented the emission factor of HC, NOx, CO_2 and CO for several vehicle speed powers (2006). In its turn, Tong et al. collected data related to vehicle speed, emission, and fuel consumption from four types of vehicles while they travel on different driving modes (i.e., idle, acceleration, cruise and deceleration) (2000). The authors presented the results in g/km, g/sec and g/kg fuel. Even though, there are more recent works that provide similar data, like the one Lau et al. (2011) conducted. These authors studied the CO, NO and HC emission rates, as well as the fuel consumption rates from four LPG taxis of different years, driven under urban traffic conditions. Notwithstanding, the data used in this study was the one collected by Tong et al. (2000), since it considers the time the drivers spend on each of the four driving modes. Thus, is consists on a simple, yet efficient, way to model the main consume patterns. The data provided by the authors and used on this study is presented in Table 1. Despite its age, to the best of the knowledge of the authors, this reference was the only one we could find meeting the previously stated established requirements. Nowadays, all these values should be inferior, albeit at the same proportion.

Table 1. Modal emission and fuel consumption rates (Tong et al., 2000)

	Driving mode	Modal emission rate (mg/sec)			Fuel Consumption
		CO	HC	NOx	
Passenger Car	Acceleration	9.54	0.69	0.62	62.62
	Cruising	9.15	0.49	0.77	39.1
	Deceleration	9.96	0.58	0.69	28.11
	Idling	2.99	0.36	0.14	18.11
Petrol Van	Acceleration	15.14	1.85	1.96	67.29
	Cruising	14.52	1.70	1.81	52.14
	Deceleration	17.30	1.91	2.33	52.16
	Idling	8.39	1.88	0.81	12.71
Diesel Van	Acceleration	2.71	0.65	0.91	62.02
	Cruising	2.64	0.54	0.79	52.47
	Deceleration	2.67	0.65	0.89	56.01
	Idling	1.33	0.22	0.44	18.52

4   Model Development

To provide greater realism to the model, 3D models of road segments, traffic lights, vehicles and safety cancels were downloaded from Google Warehouse. Some sample videos of the model in execution were recorded and can be watched online at the following address: http://pessoais.dps.uminho.pt/lsd/pre_semaforos/. Fig. 1 illustrates the developed simulation model modelling a roundabout. In signalized intersection, signal cycles are processed on a counter clockwise direction, through the regular repetition of green, yellow and red lights.

Fig. 1. 3D view of the modelled roundabout

The main processes of the model of the signalized intersection were already described in a previous paper (Vieira et al., 2014b). To access the roundabouts, each vehicle is dynamically executing several processes. In one of those processes, each entity is actively deciding – agent modelling - if it can enter or not the roundabout, by analysing the distance to the closest cars at his left, on the roundabout. This decision depends on the size of the roundabout, since for smaller roundabouts the vehicle may have to analyse the number of vehicles traveling the roundabout and approaching its entry lane and even the two previous entry lanes; conversely, for bigger roundabouts, each vehicle may only need to evaluate part of the roundabout between its entry lane and the previous one. Apart from this, the characteristics of the drivers also influences the decision of entering the roundabout, since more cautious drivers require a bigger gap than less cautious do. This process is also responsible for modelling these and other decisions related to the entry of in the roundabout, as well as the acceleration of vehicles that decide to enter the roundabout. Moreover, this process is also responsible for adjusting the speed of vehicles circulating inside the roundabout, depending on the size of the roundabout.

To model the behaviour of the vehicles, both on an intersection with traffic lights or on roundabouts, it was necessary to create many processes, functions, states among others, on the Simio software, to model all the traffic situations, e.g. to maintain a safety distance between vehicles. Nonetheless, in this paper, only some of the processes will be illustrated. Fig. 2 shows the process responsible for updating the fuel and emissions rates of the vehicles. To accurately calculate these rates, the 4 distinct operating modes of the vehicles (i.e. idle, acceleration, cruise and deceleration) had to be correctly defined.

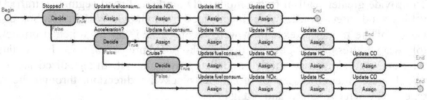

Fig. 2. Process to update consumption and emissions

5   Simulation Experiments

In this section, a comparison between the results obtained by modelling an intersection with pre-signals and roundabouts will be established. For the present work, the authors considered the following properties, or parameters, for the conducted simulation experiments:

- the frequency with which the vehicles arrive to the system,
- the radius of the roundabout,
- the balancing of the roundabout,
- the different driving behaviour pattern;
- and the type of intersection, i.e., roundabout or intersection with pre-signals.

As KPI (Key Performance Indicators), the following were defined:

- KPI1: The average flow of vehicles in vehicles/hour. This KPI is the inverse of the time interval between passages of vehicles through the intersection;

- KPI2: Average crossing time per vehicle in seconds. This KPI is calculated considering the elapsed time when a vehicle is created and when it travels an additional distance of 150 meters after having crossed the intersection;
- KPI3: The average number of vehicles on the queues. This KPI is measured every minute;
- KPI4 to KPI7: The average total fuel consumed per vehicle in milligrams and the average total emissions of vehicles in milligrams (CO, HC and NOx). KPI 4 to KPI 7 respectively refer to fuel consumed, CO, HC and NOx emissions. These KPI start being accounted when vehicles are created and they are updated every minute. When a vehicle crosses the intersection, these KPI are recorded;
- KPI8: the average number of stops per vehicle.

Moreover, the values 4, 8, 13 and 50 seconds were considered, respectively, for the time interval that defines the creation of vehicles, i.e., the intensities very high, high, medium and low. Based on previous results (Vieira et al., 2014b), a warm-period of 360 seconds was used, along with a simulation time of 2 hours and 6 replications.

Regarding the roundabouts that were modelled, it was considered that only 50% of the drivers that are trying to access a roundabout, do it, when they notice a vehicle, circulating in the roundabout signalizes its exit in the next lane. This also covers situation in which the driver circulating inside the roundabout does not signalize its intention to leave in the next exit, forcing the vehicle that is trying to access the roundabout to wait. It should be noted that this percentage can be adjusted. In addition, vehicles do not choose the exit of a roundabout in equal proportions, i.e., these exit lanes have different weights on the overall capacity of the roundabout. Considering this, different weights were assigned to the 4 lanes of the modelled roundabouts – respectively 40%, 30%, 20% and 10%.

Fig. 3 shows the values obtained for the flow of vehicles of 2 types of roundabouts, under very high traffic conditions. The 2 compared roundabouts consist on an optimistic one and the one that was modelled with the purpose of conducting the simulation experiments for this study. The difference between these types of roundabouts is that the former does not consider what was exposed, regarding the weights of the exits of roundabouts and the different driving behaviour, and the latter considers.

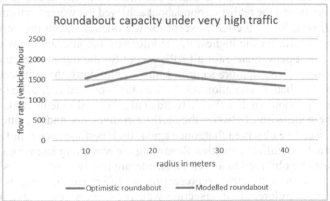

Fig. 3. Flow rates of roundabouts modelled with different sizes

As can be seen, regardless of the type of roundabout the best size to be used would be around 40 meters of diameter, which was also found by Oketch et al. (2004). It can also be noted that the different weights assigned to the roundabout and the different driving behaviour impact the overall performance of the system. Table 2 summarizes the results to be discussed.

Table 2. Comparing all the modelled intersections

Traffic intensities	Intersection type	KPI1	KPI2	KPI3	KPI4	KPI5	KPI6	KPI7	KPI8
Very high	Roundabout	1 686	9,19	63,63	16,71	2,72	0,25	0,16	32,63
	Pre-signals	2 106	7,15	67,89	8,97	1,68	0,17	0,09	5,12
High	Roundabout	1 650	4,5	26,57	8,62	1,51	0,12	0,1	14,91
	Pre-signals	1 801	1,49	9,35	3,01	0,62	0,04	0,05	0,9
Medium	Roundabout	1 108	1,1	0,15	2,69	0,61	0,03	0,05	0,39
	Pre-signals	1 109	1,44	5,61	2,9	0,61	0,04	0,05	0,82
Low	Roundabout	289	1,07	0,01	2,63	0,6	0,03	0,05	0,19
	Pre-signals	288	1,42	1,5	2,84	0,6	0,04	0,05	0,75

As the simulation experiments results illustrate, for low and medium traffic intensities, both modelled roundabouts obtained the best results for all the KPI, aside from the average flow of vehicles, when compared to the remaining three modelled intersections. Thus, on these traffic intensities, roundabouts achieved a better performance than the modelled intersection with pre-signals, as has been previously observed (Fouladvand et al., 2003, Skrodenis et al., 2011). These observations can be explained by the fact that, on a roundabout, the vehicles only wait for a gap to access the roundabout, while on an intersection the vehicles must wait for the traffic-light to turn to green. Thus, the vehicles on the roundabout could stop less times and consequently form shorter queues, consume less fuel and emit less polluting gases. Conversely, as the traffic conditions become more saturated, the available gaps on the roundabout become less frequent.

Focusing the analysis on the high and very high intensities, it is possible to note that what was observed in the low and medium intensities no longer applies. The only KPI that still got better results in these traffic conditions was the queue size. In fact, it is possible to verify that the realistic roundabout achieved the worse performance in these traffic conditions, for all the KPI, except for the queues size in the very high traffic intensity. In its turn, for the highest traffic intensity, the intersection with pre-signals achieved the best performance for all KPI, except for the queues size and the average number of stops. Thus, on more saturated traffic conditions, the intersection with pre-signals presented better simulation results than the modelled roundabouts, which is in accordance to previous studies (Fouladvand et al., 2003, Skrodenis et al., 2011).

Focusing the comparison between the realistic roundabout and the intersection with pre-signals, it can be observed that, once again, their performance is not differentiated in low and medium traffic intensities. Regarding the remaining intensities, significative differences can be observed in all KPI. Considering this flow of vehicles KPI, it could be increased from 8 to 20%, representing a difference of roughly 150 to 420 vehicles/hour. Therefore, the intersection with pre-signals could have more vehicles crossing it at the same time, which culminated in significative reduced queues and crossing time per vehicle. In its turn, vehicles stop considerably less times to cross the intersection. This is explained by the fact that in most situations vehicles can cross the intersection with just one stop, rather than having to repeatedly stop and start while trying to reach the roundabout and attempting to access it. This culminates with significative differences in the fuel and emissions per vehicle. In fact, vehicles modelled in the intersection with pre-signals spent less 54 to 65% of fuel than the ones modelled in the roundabout.

6   Conclusions

The resolution of traffic congestion problems usually implies the construction of expensive infrastructures such as bridges, tunnels and roundabouts. This paper presented a low-cost solution for this problem that consists on using an additional set of traffic-lights situated some meters away from these, working as pre-signals and acting as "launch-pads" for vehicles in intersection lanes. Thus, a simulation model was developed to evaluate the proposed alternative. In a previous study, this new concept had already been compared to regular signalized intersection with good results (Vieira et al., 2014b). Thus, the second objective of this paper was to compare this new concept to the performance of roundabouts, one of the more expensive type of solutions that is usually adopted, since it involves the construction of an infrastructure and usually much space available.

The first set of conducted simulation experiments focused on evaluating the size of the roundabouts in its performance. It was found that the best size is a diameter of 40 meters. Thereafter, the human factor in the driving behaviour and the unbalancing of the roundabout were considered in its performance. Thus, a realistic roundabout – considering its unbalancing and the driving behaviour – and an optimistic roundabout were compared. The main conclusions from this analysis were that the human factor had more negative impact in the performance than the balancing did. In addition, in the highest traffic intensities, the flow of vehicles decreased 8 to 15% when the optimistic roundabout was compared to the realistic one. It was also found that the unbalancing of roundabouts and the human driving style can decrease the waiting time per vehicle in 3 minutes, the queue size in up to 90% and the number of stops per vehicle in up to 88%, culminating in an increase in the fuel consumption in up to 63%.

The second set of experiments focused the analysis on the roundabouts and on the intersection with pre-signals. The results were accordingly to previous studies, stating that on low traffic volumes the modelled roundabouts presented better results, while on high intensities the signalized intersection presented better results (Fouladvand et al., 2003, Skrodenis et al., 2011). Focusing the comparison on the highest traffic intensities and comparing the realistic roundabout to the intersection with pre-signals, it was possible to note an increase in the flow of vehicles from 8 to 20%, representing a difference of roughly 150 to 420 vehicles/hour. This was accomplished while still reducing the queues and crossing time per vehicle, which culminated in the vehicles modelled in the intersection with pre-signals spending less 54 to 65% of fuel than the ones modelled in the roundabout.

Regardless of the positive simulation results achieved, it is still imperial to evaluate the safety of this kind of solution. For future development: (1) it would be interesting to adapt the developed traffic model to handle intersections and roundabouts with multi lanes on the approaches, as well as inside the roundabout; (2) illustrate the behaviour of intersections with pre-signals in a context of proximity with other intersections; (3) since agents are being modelled, it would be interesting to model different types of drivers – accelerate more or less, needs more or less space to enter the roundabout, among others; (4) compare the proposed solution to other types of infrastructures, such as bridges and tunnels.

References

AKÇELIK, R. 1983. Progress in Fuel Consumption Modelling for Urban Traffic Management. Australian Road Research Board.

AKÇELIK, R. & BESLEY, M. 2003. Operating cost, fuel consumption, and emission models in aaSIDRA and aaMOTION. 25th Conference of Australian Institutes of Transport Research (CAITR 2003).

BONNESON, J. A. 1992. Modeling Queued Driver Behavior at Signalized Junctions. Transportation Research Record, No 1365, pp. 99–107.

BRILON, W. 2005. Roundabouts: A state of the art in Germany. National Roundabout Conference, Vail, Colorado, vol. 16.

CHAN, T. L., NING, Z., LEUNG, C. W., CHEUNG, C. S., HUNG, W. T. & DONG, G. 2004. On-road remote sensing of petrol vehicle emissions measurement and emission factors estimation in Hong Kong. Atmospheric Environment, 38, 2055-2066.

COELHO, M. C., FARIAS, T. L. & ROUPHAIL, N. M. 2006. Effect of roundabout operations on pollutant emissions. Transportation Research Part D: Transport and Environment, 11, 333-343.

DIAS, L., PEREIRA, G. & RODRIGUES, G. 2007. A Shortlist of the Most Popular Discrete Simulation Tools. Simulation News Europe, 17, 33-36.

DIAS, L., PEREIRA, G., VIK, P. & OLIVEIRA, J. A. 2011. Discrete simulation tools ranking: a commercial software packages comparison based on popularity. Industrial Simulation Conference. Venice, Italy, 6-8 June: Eurosis.

DIAS, L. M. S., VIEIRA, A. A. C., PEREIRA, G. A. B. & OLIVEIRA, J. A. 2016. Discrete Simulation Software Ranking – a Top list of the Worldwide most Popular and Used Tools. Proceedings of the 2016 Winter Simulation Conference.

FOULADVAND, M. E., SADJADI, Z. & SHAEBANI, M. R. 2003. Characteristics of vehicular traffic flow at a roundabout. Physical Review E 70.4 (2004): 046132.

GEORGE, E. T. & HEROY, F. M. 1966. Starting Response of Traffic at Signalized Intersections. Traffic Engineering 36.1Q, pp. 39-43.

GUO, R. & ZHANG, Y. 2014. Exploration of correlation between environmental factors and mobility at signalized intersections. Transportation Research Part D: Transport and Environment, 32, 24-34.

HENG, W. & PERUGU, H. C. 2009. Oversaturation inherence and traffic diversion effect at urban intersections through simulation. Jiaotong Yunshu Xitong

Gongcheng Yu Xinxi/ Journal of Transportation Systems Engineering and Information Technology, 9, 72-82.

HERMAN, R., LAM, T. & ROTHERY, R. W. 1971. The Starting Characteristics of Automobile Platoons. Proc., 5th International Symposium on the Theory of Traffic Flow and Transportation, American Elsevier Publishing Co., New York, pp. 1-17.

HLUPIC, V. 2000. Simulation software: an Operational Research Society survey of academic and industrial users. Proceedings of the 32nd Winter Simulation Conference (pp. 1676-1683 vol. 2). Society for Computer Simulation International.

HLUPIC, V. & PAUL, R. 1999. Guidelines for selection of manufacturing simulation software. *IIE Transactions*, 31, 21-29.

LAU, J., HUNG, W. T. & CHEUNG, C. S. 2011. On-board gaseous emissions of LPG taxis and estimation of taxi fleet emissions. *Science of The Total Environment*, 409, 5292-5300.

LEE, J. & CHEN, R. L. 1986. Entering Headway at Signalized Intersections in a Small Metropolitan Area. Transportation Research Record (1091).

LUO, Q., XUN, L., CAO, Z. & HUANG, Y. 2011. Simulation analysis and study on car-following safety distance model based on braking process of leading vehicle. 9th World Congress on Intelligent Control and Automation (WCICA). pp. 740-743. IEEE.

MESSER, C. J. & FAMBRO, D. B. 1997. *Effects of Signal Phasing and Length of Left Turn Bay on Capacity*, No. 644. 1977.

OAKES, J., THELLMANN, A. M. & KELLY, I. T. 1994. Innovative bus priority measures. Proceedings of Seminar J, Traffic Management and Road Safety, 22nd PTRC European Transport Summer Annual Meeting, University of WARWICK, U.K., vol.381, pp.301-312.

OKETCH, T., MIKE DELSEY, AND DOUG ROBERTSON. 2004. Evaluation of Performance of Modern Roundabouts Using Paramics Microsimulation Model. TAC Conference.

OUEIDA, S., CHAR, P. A., KADRY, S. & IONESCU, S. 2016. Simulation Models for Enhancing the Health Care Systems. *FAIMA Business & Management Journal*, 4, 5.

PAN, M., DONG, S., SUN, J. & LI, K. 2010. Microscopic Simulation Research on Signal Cycle Length of Mixed Traffic Considering Violation. International Conference on Intelligent Computation Technology and Automation (ICICTA). Vol. 2, pp. 674-678.

PEGDEN, C. D. 2007. Simio: A new simulation system based on intelligent objects. Proceedings of the 39th Winter Simulation Conference: 40 years! The best is yet to come, pp. 2293-2300, IEEE Press.

PEGDEN, C. D. & STURROCK, D. T. 2008. Introduction to Simio. 2008 Winter Simulation Conference, pp 29-38, IEEE.

SKRODENIS, E., VINGRYS, S. & PASHKEVICH, M. 2011. Lithuanian experience of implementation of roundabouts: the research of accidents, operation and efficiency. The 8th International Conference "Environmental Engineering": Selected papers. Ed. by D. Čygas, KD Froehner, pp.   980-985.

STURROCK, D. T. & PEGDEN, C. D. 2010. Recent innovations in Simio. *Proceedings - Winter Simulation Conference, pp. 52-62.* Proceedings - Winter Simulation Conference, pp. 52-62.

TONG, H. Y., HUNG, W. T. & CHEUNG, C. S. 2000. On-Road Motor Vehicle Emissions and Fuel Consumption in Urban Driving Conditions. *Journal of the Air & Waste Management Association,* 50, 543-554.

TREIBER, M. & HELBING, D. 2001. Microsimulations of Freeway Traffic Including Control Measures. *at - Automatisierungstechnik,* 49, 478.

VIEIRA, A., DIAS, L., PEREIRA, G. & OLIVEIRA, J. 2014a. Comparison of Simio and Arena simulation tools. *ISC.* University of Skovde, Skovde, Sweden.

VIEIRA, A., DIAS, L., PEREIRA, G. & OLIVEIRA, J. 2014b. Micro Simulation to Evaluate the Impact of Introducing Pre-Signals in Traffic Intersections. University of Minho at Guimarães - Portugal: International Conference on Computational Science and its Application, pp. 722-745, Springer International Publishing.

WU, J. & HOUNSELL, N. 1998. Bus Priority Using pre-signals. *Transportation Research Part A: Policy and Practice,* 32, 563-583.

XIE, H. & MA, W. 2012. Simulation-based study on a pre-signal control system at isolated intersection with separate left turn phase. 9th IEEE International Conference on Networking, Sensing and Control (ICNSC), pp. 103-106.

XUAN, Y., DAGANZO, C. F. & CASSIDY, M. J. 2011. Increasing the capacity of signalized intersections with separate left turn phases. *Transportation Research Part B: Methodological,* 45, 769-781.

ZEGEER, J. D. 1986. Field Validation of Intersection Capacity Factor. Transportation Research Record 1091, pp.67-77.

ZHOU, Y. & ZHUANG, H. 2013. The optimization of lane assignment and signal timing at the tandem intersection with pre-signal. *Journal of Advanced Transportation, 48(4), pp. 362-376.*

ZHU, H. 2008. *Normal Acceleration Characteristics of the Leading Vehicle in a Queue at Signalized Intersections on Arterial Streets*, Doctoral dissertation. Oregon State University.

Efficient Local Search Heuristics for Packing Irregular Shapes in Two-Dimensional Heterogeneous Bins

Ranga P. Abeysooriya[✉], Julia A. Bennell, and Antonio Martinez-Sykora

Business School, University of Southampton, SO17 1BJ, Southampton, UK
{rpa1v13,J.A.Bennell,A.Martinez-Sykora}@soton.ac.uk

Abstract. In this paper we proposed a local search heuristic and a genetic algorithm to solve the two-dimensional irregular multiple bin-size bin packing problem. The problem consists of placing a set of pieces represented as 2D polygons in rectangular bins with different dimensions such that the total area of bins used is minimized. Most packing algorithms available in the literature for 2D irregular bin packing consider single size bins only. However, for many industries the material can be supplied in a number of standard size sheets, for example, metal, foam, plastic and timber sheets. For this problem, the cut plans must decide the set of standard size stock sheets as well as which pieces to cut from each bin and how to arrange them in order to minimise waste material. Moreover, the literature constrains the orientation of pieces to a single or finite set of angles. This is often an artificial constraint that makes the solution space easier to navigate. In this paper we do not restrict the orientation of the pieces. We show that the local search heuristic and the genetic algorithm can address all of these decisions and obtain good solutions, with the local search performing better. We also discuss the affect of different groups of stock sheet sizes.

Keywords: Irregular shapes, Multiple bin size bin packing, Jostle Algorithm

1 Introduction

The two dimensional bin packing problem consists of placing a set of pieces, usually represented as rectangles or polygons, in one or several stock sheets (bins) in such a way the total waste generated is minimized. This problem arises in several industries where metal, foam, wood, plastic, paper or leather need to be cut. Depending on the industrial application this problem has several variants described by the properties of both the pieces to be placed and the bins. In this paper we address the problem where the pieces to be cut are irregular and may have concavities. Pieces can be placed in any orientation within rectangular bins that have a variety of different dimensions (heterogeneous bin sizes). We assume that there are a limited number of bin types and there are enough bins of each type to place all the demanded pieces in any set of bins. In this paper we denote

© Springer International Publishing AG 2017
T. Bektaş et al. (Eds.), ICCL 2017, LNCS 10572, pp. 557–571, 2017.
https://doi.org/10.1007/978-3-319-68496-3_37

this problem as the two-dimensional irregular shape multiple bin size bin packing problem (2D-IMBSBPP) and propose a local search heuristic, called jostle, and a genetic algorithm to find efficient solutions.

Most of the publications in the literature that consider heterogeneous bins are focused on packing rectangular pieces. Pisinger and Sigurad [19] consider a variable bin cost when solving this problem. They propose a MILP model which is then solved by column generation. The model is intractable for large instances and difficult to solve even for small instances. Ortmann et al. [18] propose a two-phase approach. During the first phase they use first-fit decreasing with the largest bins first. A second phase repacks bins into smaller bins. The two phase algorithm is implemented with different bin sizes and aims to minimise the total area of the occupied bins. Wei et al. [21] propose a tabu search that uses a sequential packing heuristic, a local search, and a post-improvement procedure to reduce the total area of used bins in a feasible solution. Alvarez-Valdes et al. [2] implement meta-heuristic algorithms with variable bin costs which are not proportional to the size of the bin. The objective is to minimize the cost of the occupied bins, and the authors employ a greedy randomized adaptive search procedure with path re-linking strategies to combine the best solutions obtained in the iterative process. In order to compare their results with Ortmann et al. [18]'s, they modify the objective function to maximize the overall utilization of the occupied bins.

The vast majority of research publications considering the packing of 2D irregular shapes address the 2D strip packing problem, also known as the nesting problem. Instead of placing pieces into bins the aim is to place all the pieces into a strip with fixed width and infinite length in such a way the total required length is minimized. However, recent publications of packing algorithms for irregular pieces consider the bin packing problem with homogeneous bins, see [14], [20], [16] and [1]. However, in many situations bins are readily available to purchase as rectangular sheets in different standard sizes. In these industries companies usually handle several bin sizes in order to satisfy customer demand. The aim of the companies is not only to reduce the waste generated in the cutting process, but also charge a competitive price to the customers, which usually depends on the area of material needed to meet the demand. There are several publications considering heterogeneous irregular bins, see [4] and [5], who solve an applied problem which arises in the leather industry. In these publications the pieces are approximated by grid squares or pixels rather than polygons. While this simplifies the geometry, solutions suffer from inaccuracy in shape representation.

It is important to highlight that in this paper we use the direct representations of the pieces as polygons and do not restrict the rotation of pieces to a predefined set of angles. Han et al. [13] and Martinez-Sykora et al. [15] considered free rotation for the 2D irregular bin packing problem with guillotine cuts, solving an application derived from the glass industry. More recently, Martinez-Sykora et al. [16] and Abeysooriya et al. [1] considered free rotation for the problem with homogeneous bins and also report results with restricted and fixed rotations. For comparison purposes, we also address the problem where a finite set of rotations are allowed.

The main contribution of this paper is to efficiently solve the 2D-IMBSBPP considering continuous rotation of pieces by using an adaptation of the jostle procedure. Jostle was first proposed by Dowsland et al. [10] for the strip packing problem and then used in [1] in bin packing problems with homogeneous bins. One of the most important properties of the jostle procedure is that it explores efficient solutions with a relatively low computational effort, compared with other available algorithms. The jostle procedure works over the sequence of pieces that represents the order pieces are inserted in the layout. The constructive heuristic iterates between packing from one end of the strip and then the other end taking the sequence from the last iteration. The results presented in this paper show a considerable improvement when using a heterogeneous set of bin sizes, which demonstrates the efficiency of the algorithms presented.

The paper is organized as follows. In Section 2 we describe the problem and we discuss the measure of performance used to evaluate the quality of feasible solutions. Section 3 explains the jostle algorithms and the genetic algorithm to solve 2D-IMBSBPP. Computational tests are presented in Section 4. Finally, in Section 5 we present the conclusions of the paper.

2   Problem Description

Let N' be the number of rectangular bin types (stock sheets) and let L_k and W_k be, respectively, the length and the width of bin type $k \in \{1, \ldots, N'\}$. Let $P = \{p_1, \ldots, p_n\}$ be the set of pieces to be cut from the bins, where n is the number of pieces. We assume that all the pieces may have a different shape.

A solution $s = \{B_k^s | \ k = 1, \ldots, N'\}$ is represented by a set of bins of each type used in the solution, where each single bin $b_{jk}^s(P_{jk}, O_{jk}, X_{jk}, Y_{jk}) \in B_k^s$ is determined by the subset of pieces placed in the bin (P_{jk}), the set of orientations used for each piece (O_{jk}) and the X and Y coordinates of the reference point of each piece. A solution s is a feasible solution if all the pieces are placed, i.e, $\bigcup_{k=1}^{N'} \bigcup_{j| \ b_{jk} \in B_k^s} \overline{P}_{jk} = P$, there is no overlapping between each pair of pieces placed in the same bin and no piece exceeds the bins dimensions.

Initially we consider an unlimited number of bins of each type k. We denote by N_k^s the number of occupied bins of type k in solution s.

The position of the pieces into the bins is given by the coordinates of the reference point, which we assume it is the bottom-left corner point of the enclosing rectangle whose edges are orthogonal to the edges of the bin.

The aim is to minimize the waste generated when placing all the demand pieces. However, this measure could lead to many ties. In order to guide the search, we propose a second measure, which is the standard deviation of absolute bin waste, where a larger standard deviation indicates the potential to empty poorly packed bins.

2.1   Evaluation function of a solution

We use two measurements to evaluate the quality of a complete solution s.
  1) The overall utilization U_s is defined as;

$$U_s = \frac{\sum_{i=1}^{n} Area(p_i)}{\sum_{k=1}^{N'} W_k L_k N_k^s}$$

where $Area(p_i)$ denote the area of the ith piece. Since $\sum_{i=1}^{n} Area(p_i)$ is constant then maximizing the utilization is equivalent to minimize to total area of bins used in s. In this paper the aim is to maximize U_s.
  2) The standard deviation of absolute bin waste of the occupied bins (σ_s). This measurement is used during the algorithm to break ties when two solutions have the same overall utilization. A low σ_s value shares the waste among the bins with low variance and balances individual bin utility. A higher σ_s leads to a higher variation in bin space utilization. We encourage this type of solution during the search process of the algorithm to move the few pieces packed inside a large bin (i.e, a lower utilized bin) to another occupied bin.

3   Packing procedure

In this section we introduce two heuristic algorithms to solve 2D-IMBSBPP. The first algorithm is an iterated jostle approach with random assignment of bins (IJRAB), and the second is a hybrid genetic algorithm with iterated jostle (HGAIJ). Jostle iteratively applies a fast constructive procedure and searches over the sequence of pieces. Jostle was first used to solve strip packing problems in [10]. In [1], this idea was extended to the bin packing problem by placing bins consecutively simulating a strip, and adding the constraint that no piece can be placed across the boundary of two bins. However, with heterogeneous bin sizes the available width depends on the bin type and, therefore, may change from one part of the strip to another.

Most of the state of the art algorithms to solve the strip packing problem with irregular pieces works with infeasible solutions. The main idea, first proposed in [6], is to fix the strip length, randomly place the pieces within the strip and then solve the overlapping problem. Once a feasible solution is found, the strip length is reduced and the search starts again. While effective at finding good solutions, it is slow. The heterogeneous bin packing problem, requires finding feasible solutions for different bin combinations. Hence, fast constructive approaches like jostle that work with feasible solutions are a more reasonable option.

3.1   Iterated Jostling approach with Random Assignment of Bins (IJRAB)

IJRAB is an iterative procedure that uses a constructive algorithm (CA) within a local search. The fast constructive procedure allows us to build a feasible solution given a permutation of bins and pieces. The local search works over the sequence of pieces and bins.

Layout construction The constructive algorithm (CA) is based on placing the pieces sequentially, according to a given placement rule. We first select a set of bins which are placed concurrently in a given order, in such a way the bottom edge of a bins are aligned, as is depicted in Figure 1. Given the different bin dimensions, the strip width is set to be the same as the widest bin. Note that there will be areas of the strip where pieces cannot be placed, shown by shaded areas in Figure 1. Finally, the strategy to place the pieces is inspired by the TOPOS algorithm proposed in [17] and improved by Bennell and Song [9]. Therefore, for a given order of bins and a given order of pieces with a given orientation we use this fast CA to build a solution.

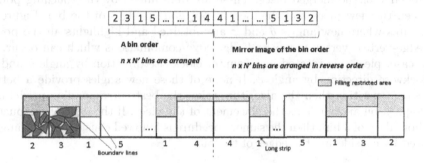

Fig. 1. Packing Layout

In the following description of the CA we assume we have a given ordered combination of bin types and a given permutation of all the pieces.

First we setup the strip of bins. Let $\tau^{(t)} \in \mathbb{N}^{n \times N'}$ be a vector with values corresponding to the bin types used in the solution in the given order. This vector represents $n \times N'$ bins in order to guarantee that all the pieces can be placed. Since jostle packs from both ends of the strip alternately, we arrange the $n \times N'$ bins on the strip and arrange another $n \times N'$ bins following the mirror order as illustrated in Figure 1.

Then, for each piece, we determine the placement position and orientation. Assuming a given orientation, the CA generates non-overlapping placement positions following the improved TOPOS approach that was adapted for bin packing by Abeysooriya et al. [1]. This approach uses the no-fit polygon (NFP) and inner-fit polygon (IFP), see [8], to identify all feasible touching positions between pieces. New pieces are inserted in the layout in a touching position with pieces already placed. Once a position and orientation is selected, the new piece is merged with the already placed pieces. Any space between pieces that could be used to place another piece is a hole and is recorded into a list of holes. At each piece insertion, the partial solution is represented by a merged polygon, for each occupied bin, and a list of holes. When placing the next piece, we first try the holes, sorted by non-increasing area. If the piece does not fit in any of the holes, then we try placing the piece on the boundary of the merged polygons starting with the first bin. If this fails, the new piece is placed in a new bin.

The above assumes a fixed orientation, whereas we are permitted to use any orientation. The placement angle of a piece is determined by an angle tuning strategy. First we identify the candidate placements by finding the best placement position for each of the pre-assigned angles, which are $o_i = 0, 90, 180, 270$. Then we pick the position and orientation angle from these candidates according to the *Maximum Utilization (MU)* placement policy described below. Note that up to this point, this is also the method CA applies if the rotation of pieces is restricted to a predefined set of angles. When the rotation is not restricted, we try alternative angles by rotating the piece so that one of its edges are concurrent to the edge of the merged piece. These are determined by the touching points between the new piece and the merged polygon or edges of the bin. Figure 2, illustrates where new angles θ and φ are obtained and highlights all the possible edge-vertex, vertex-vertex and edge-edge combinations which can occur. In each case, piece p is rotated in a counter-clockwise direction by angle θ and in a clockwise direction by angle ϕ. If none of these new angles provide a better placement position then the algorithm takes the best corresponding predefined angle position and angle as the placement of the piece. If the next piece touches the boundary of a bin, then the same procedure is followed considering the angles created by considering the edges of the bin.

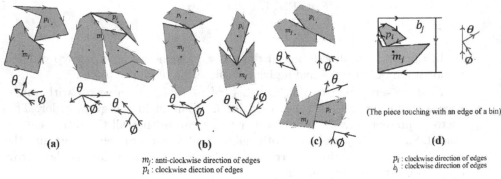

(The piece touching with an edge of a bin)

(a)   (b)   (c)   (d)

m_j: anti-clockwise direction of edges p_i : clockwise direction of edges
p_i : clockwise diection of edges b_j : clockwise direction of edges

If direction of edges direct away from the touching point, the piece is rotated counter-clockwise direction by angle θ
If direction of edges direct towards the touching point, the piece is rotated clockwise direction by angle $\emptyset$

Fig. 2. Angle Tuning

The algorithm uses the *Maximum Utilization (MU)* placement policy as proposed in [1] since their results show it is more efficient than the bottom-left and minimum length placement rules. The MU rule places the next piece in the position that maximises the area utilisation of the convex hull of the layout in the first bin the piece fits. Let m_l be the merged polygon of the placed pieces in the lth bin in the order. For each feasible position, the area utilisation is calculated as $(CHull(m_l) + Area(p_i))/CHull(m_l + p_i)$, where $CHull(m_l)$ denotes the convex hull area of the placed pieces m_l, $Area(p_i)$ denotes area of the new piece and $CHull(m_l + p_i)$ denotes area of the convex hull of both m_l and p_i once placed in a feasible position. The placement position corresponds to the maximum area utilisation is selected as the placement position for the new piece.

Solution improvement phase - Jostle The improvement mechanism works over the sequence of bins and pieces. IJRAB starts with a solution generated by the CA using an arbitrary order of pieces and an arbitrary order of bins and packs the pieces from the left end of the bin strip towards the right along the strip. Given this solution, all the pieces are re-ordered according to the right-most x-coordinates position of the pieces continuing to the left-most. Following this order, pieces are packed starting at the right-most position of the strip building the packing layout from right to left. The idea is to shake pieces from left to right and right to left along the bin order, so that each jostle iteration generates a new sequence of the pieces. This approach has been proven to be more efficient than a multi-start approach randomizing over the sequence of pieces (see [1]).

Abeysooriya et al. [1] points out that jostle gets stuck in local optima and suggests an iterated jostle approach where they apply a kick, analogous to iterated local search. We design two types of kick, which are applied after a predefined number of jostle cycles with no improvement. The first kick is called *piece kick*, applied to the current locally optimal solution, where a random piece is removed and reinserted in a random position in the sequence (used in [7] and [1]). The second kick is the *Bin kick*, applied to the best solution found so far, where a random bin is selected from the occupied bins of this solution and is replaced with a random bin selected from the other bin types. The corresponding change is applied to the mirror bin position of the bin order as well, so that the same bin configuration is retained at both ends of the strip. We denote K_p as the number of jostle cycles with no improvement before performing a *piece kick*, and K_b as the number of piece kicks performed with no improvement before performing a *bin kick*.

Algorithm 1 provides the steps of the IJRAB algorithm. We use $P^{(L,t)}$ to denote the piece order used at the tth iteration of the algorithm, which packs pieces from left to right. Similarly, $P^{(R,t)}$ denotes the piece order, which packs pieces from right to left at the tth iteration. We use $\tau^{(L,t)}$ to denote bin order at t^{th} iteration where the bin arrangement is considered from left to right when placing pieces. The bin arrangement $\tau^{(R,t)}$ is the mirror arrangement of $\tau^{(L,t)}$. As explained before, a certain bin order is considered at a time. Depending on the best solution found so far (see Algorithm 1), the leading bin order τ^* is updated.

The algorithm terminates after a given maximum computation time. At each local optima leading to a bin kick, we apply post processing to improve the best solution found within each bin configuration (see line 25). We propose the following post processing strategies.

- Strategy 1 (S1): Attempt to repack pieces in the least utilized bin into the smallest possible bin.

Algorithm 1: IJRAB

1 Set number of iterations $t = 1$;
2 Set $P^{(L,t)}$ as a random permutation of the pieces;
3 Set $\tau^{(L,t)}$ as a random order of bins;
4 Initialize best utilization and best standard deviation $U^* = 0$, $\sigma^* = 0$;
5 Initialize counters for piece kicks and bin kicks $q_p = 0$; $q_b = 0$;
6 **while** *termination condition is not met* **do**
7 | Generate solution layout, s_L, from $P^{(L,t)}$ and $\tau^{(L,t)}$;
8 | Evaluate U_{s_L} and σ_{s_L};
9 | Derive $P^{(R,t)}$ from the solution;
10 | Generate solution layout, s_R, from $P^{(R,t)}$ and $\tau^{(R,t)}$;
11 | Evaluate U_{s_R} and σ_{s_R};
12 | Set s the best solution between s_L and s_R taking into account utilization (U) and breaking ties with the standard deviation (σ);
13 | **if** $U^s > U^*$ *OR* $(U^s = U^*$ *AND* $\sigma^s > \sigma^*)$ **then**
14 | | Set $U^* = U^s$, $\sigma^* = \sigma^s$; Reset $q_p = 0$;
15 | **else**
16 | | $q_p = q_p + 1$;
17 | **end**
18 | **if** $q_b < K_b$ **then**
19 | | **if** $q_p > K_p$ **then**
20 | | | Apply piece kick. Change the position of one piece in the current solution piece sequence;
21 | | | $q_b = q_b + 1$;
22 | | | Reset $q_p = 0$;
23 | | **end**
24 | **else**
25 | | Apply post processing to the best solution;
26 | | Apply bin kick. Return to the best solution found so far and change one bin type;
27 | | Reset $q_b = 0$, $q_p = 0$;
28 | **end**
29 | $t = t + 1$;
30 **end**

- Strategy 2 (S2): Attempt to repack pieces in each of occupied bins into the smallest possible bin.

For the experimental investigation we compare the effectiveness of each post processing strategy based on the solution quality and computational time. Specifically we run the following three variants:

- *IJRAB*: Implement Algorithm 1 with no post processing.
- *IJRAB-A2*: Implement Algorithm 1 applying S1 for the best solution found at each bin configuration.
- *IJRAB-A3*: Implement Algorithm 1 applying S2 for the best solution found at each bin configuration.

3.2   GA/Jostle approach (HGAIJ)

Our second computational method combines a Genetic Algorithm (GA) and the Iterated Jostle (IJ). GAs have been successfully implemented for the single bin size bin packing problem with rectangular pieces (SBSBPP) in [12], multiple bin size bin packing problem (MBSBPP) with rectangular pieces in [3], and irregular pieces packing problems with irregular bins in [4].

A solution is encoded as a chromosome by a permutation of bins followed by a permutation of pieces. This is decoded using the CA to produce the packing layout and evaluate the fitness, U_s. The coding structure of HGAIJ is illustrated in Figure 3 along with the decoded solution, which packs 16 pieces into four types (sizes) of input bins. In order to guarantee all the pieces can be packed, the length of bin permutation is $n \times N'$. Note that when we use the jostle operation the strip is twice as long to include the mirror bin order.

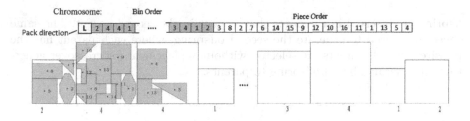

Fig. 3. Representation of solutions

The initial population contains S solutions generated by applying the *CA* to S random permutations of bins and pieces. Each piece permutation contains all the pieces to be packed. For each generation, we execute the main loop in Algorithm 2. A *pool* of solutions is populated at each iteration of the main-loop. This contains solutions of the current population (parents) as well as the new solutions (offspring) created by the crossover and mutation operators. The selection mechanism selects S solutions from the pool to enter the next generation.

Crossover: Crossover creates two offspring from two parent chromosomes using two type of crossover operator. We use the *uniform crossover*, see [11] for the bin part of the chromosome. The operator first constructs a random binary mask. Using the mask, the first child inherits the genes (in the bin order) of the first parent if there is a "1" in the mask and from the second parent if there is a "0" in the mask. The second child is formed in a similar way by reversing the role of mask. Step 1 in figure 4 shows an example of the crossover operator for the bin part of the chromosome.

The second crossover operator changes the piece permutation. Given a randomly selected point in the permutation the genes before this point are copied from the first parent to the first offspring as illustrated in step 2 of figure 4. The second parent's piece permutation is then scanned and the missing genes in the

---

Algorithm 2: General structure of HGAIJ

---

1 Initialization;
2 Main loop: Generations;
3 $GenN = 1$;
4 **while** $GenN < MaxGen$ **do**
5 | Populate the pool;
6 | - crossover;
7 | - mutation;
8 | - generate offspring solutions using the constructive algorithm CA;
9 | - improve offspring solutions by *jostling with piece kicks*;
10 | Sort the pool according to solution quality;
11 | Select solutions for nest population;
12 | $GenN = GenN + 1$;
13 **end**

---

offspring are inserted in the order they appear in the second parent. The same procedure is used to generate the second offspring, where each parent has the opposite role. All parents are selected without replacement for crossover generating an equal number of offspring to parents.

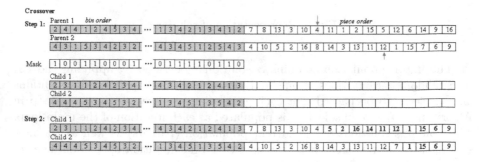

Fig. 4. Crossover operation

Mutation: The purpose of mutation is to provide greater diversity within the population and inhibit premature convergence. Each offspring will be mutated with probability P_{mu}. If an offspring is selected for mutation, then randomly select two points in the part of the bin permutation that contains pieces and reverse the order of bins between these two points. Note that this mutation generates a major change in the corresponding solution as bin spaces of the layout change dramatically.

Improving offspring solutions by jostling with piece kicks: In this step, the child chromosomes are improved with the help of the iterated jostle procedure (with piece kicks) discussed in Section 3.1. Initially, we applied IJ to all offspring, however the computation time was too long. In our final experiments we only apply IJ to the fittest solution.

Selection for the next population: The next population is selected from the pool that currently contains both the parent and offspring solutions. The selection strategy aims to ensure both quality and diversity of the next population using *elitist* and *tournament* selection methods. Solution quality is measured by utilisation, U_s. For diversity we define the distance $(dist)$ of a solution, x, from the best solution in the population, y, where the best solution has the largest U_s:

$$dist(x) = |x_1 - y_1| + |x_2 - y_2| + \ldots\ldots + |x_{Nx} - y_{Nx}|$$

where x_i denotes the area of the ith bin located in the bin permutation of the chromosome for solution x, y_i denotes the area of the ith bin located in the bin permutation of the chromosome with best U. In the case that chromosomes x and y have a different number of used bins $(N_x \neq N_y)$, then the distance is calculated up to $\min\{N_x, N_y\}$.

The selection process sorts the chromosomes in the pool in descending order of their U_s value. We compare the bin permutation of chromosomes that have the same U_s value. Those with identical occupied bin permutations are compared by their $dist$ value. Since we wish to maintain diversity in the population, we retain only one of these chromosomes, keeping the one with the largest value of $dist$. Given the sorted list of offspring and parents, the elitist selection scheme copies γ of the best chromosomes in pool to the new population. The population is made up to S by tournament selection, where it randomly selects two chromosomes and selects the best by U_s breaking ties by σ_s.

Based on different computational test we performed we found the following best set of parameters. For the GA, S is set to 16, $\gamma = 2$ and $P_{mu} = 0.025$. For IJ within the GA, $K_p = 4$ and the search terminates after 12 cycles. Similarly, for IJRAB approach we found that $K_p = 4$ and $K_b = 3$ produce better results.

4 Computational Experiments

The algorithms described above were coded in Visual C++ 2012 as a sequential program. All experiments were carried out using an Intel 2.60 GHz processor and 4GB RAM. The algorithms do not contain parallel processing and therefore can be run using a single processor.

The data instances are taken from the benchmark nesting instances published on ESICUP (EURO Special Interest Group on Cutting and Packing) website. We used 14 irregular shape instances representing both convex and non-convex polygons. Since these are defined for strip packing problems, we define a set of bin sizes. In this case, for each instance, we identify parameter d_{max} as the maximum length or width among the pieces in their initial orientation. Using d_{max} we generate nine different bin sizes and define four subsets of bin sizes;

Table 1. Instances

Instance	No.of Pieces	Instance	No.of Pieces
Shapes2	28	2×Jakobs2	50
3×Dighe1	48	Poly3a	45
3×Dighe2	30	Poly3b	45
Poly4a	60	Poly4b	60
3×Fu	36	Poly5a	75
2×Han	46	Poly5b	75
2×Jakobs1	50	Shapes	43

Table 2. Bin Configurations

Configuration	No. of Bin types	Input bin sizes	Bin type ID
SB	5	$0.5d_{max}$, $0.75d_{max}$, $1.0d_{max}$, $1.25d_{max}$,$1.5d_{max}$	1,2,3,4,5
MB	5	$1.0d_{max}$, $1.25d_{max}$, $1.5d_{max}$, $1.75d_{max}$,$2.0d_{max}$	3,4,5,6,7
LB	5	$1.5d_{max}$, $1.75d_{max}$, $2.0d_{max}$, $2.25d_{max}$,$2.5d_{max}$	5,6,7,8,9
Mix	9	$0.5d_{max}$, $0.75d_{max}$, $1.0d_{max}$, $1.25d_{max}$,$1.5d_{max}$	1,2,3,4,5
		$1.75d_{max}$, $2.0d_{max}$, $2.25d_{max}$, $2.5d_{max}$	6,7,8,9

small (SB), medium (MB), large (LB) and mixed, which contains all nine bin sizes, as illustrated in tables 1 and 2.

We test IJRAB and HGAIJ using the 14 data instances combined with each set of bin sizes and run our experiments for variants where we restrict the allowed rotation angles (RR) and also allow unrestricted rotation (UR) of the pieces. For RR the permitted angles of orientation are $0, 90, 180, 270$ degrees. Since there are random elements in the algorithm, we run each algorithm test for 10 trials and report the average. Previous research into the irregular bin packing problem have only used homogeneous bins, hence there are no benchmark results. In order to validate our search mechanism, we compare with the best result from repeated runs of the constructive algorithm with random permutations of bins and pieces (CA (Rnd)). The termination condition for all algorithms is 800 seconds.

In Table 3 we compare the different implementations of IJRAB for RR and UR. For each bin configuration report the average U_s, percentage improvement over IJRAB-A1, and the average number of jostle cycles performed in the 800 seconds (Avg. cycles). We can observe that *IJRAB-A3* performs better, although the difference between *IJRAB-A2* and *IJRAB-A3* for Mix, LB and MB bin size configurations is small. For SB, since bins will contain very few pieces the bin allocation is more critical, hence there being greater value in trying to reduce the size of all bins.

In Table 4 we compare the two algorithms, IJRAB-A3 and HGAIJ along with CA (Rnd). CA (Rnd) performs least well, as expected. Although the performance gap is less than 5% showing that the CA is optimising well. IJRAB performs better than HGAIJ. This may be because a change in the bin or piece permutation can lead to a significant change in the decoded solution, hence the crossover operators are not able to retain good parts of the solution.

Table 3. Performance comparison of IJRAB algorithms for different bin configurations

Bin Config.		Restricted Rotation of pieces			Unrestricted Rotation of pieces		
		IJRAB-A1	IJRAB-A2	IJRAB-A3	IJRAB-A1	IJRAB-A2	IJRAB-A3
Mix	Avg. U	0.692	**0.700**	**0.703**	0.699	**0.706**	**0.708**
	Impv %	0%	**1.16%**	**1.59%**	0%	**1.00%**	**1.29%**
	Avg. cycles	*1202.2*	*1156.5*	*1123.4*	*802.0*	*764.9*	*744.1*
LB	Avg. U	0.667	**0.687**	**0.689**	0.680	**0.695**	**0.696**
	Impv %	0%	**3.00%**	**3.30%**	0%	**2.21%**	**2.35%**
	Avg. cycles	*1117.3*	*1072.4*	*1041.7*	*717.4*	*695.6*	*660.7*
MB	Avg. U	0.671	**0.684**	**0.686**	0.684	**0.692**	**0.693**
	Impv %	0%	**1.94%**	**2.24%**	0%	**1.17%**	**1.32%**
	Avg. cycles	*1275.9*	*1215.8*	*1176.4*	*814.7*	*789.8*	*776.7*
SB	Avg. U	0.656	**0.662**	**0.677**	0.668	**0.675**	**0.685**
	Impv %	0%	**0.91%**	**3.20%**	0%	**1.05%**	**2.54%**
	Avg. cycles	*1584.2*	*1506.6*	*1365.2*	*956.9*	*909.1*	*862.1*

Table 4. Performance comparison of IJRAB and HGAIJ methods

Bins Config.	Restricted Rot. *Avg. U*			Unrestricted Rot. *Avg. U*		
	CA (Rand)	IJRAB	HGAIJ	CA(Rand)	IJRAB	HGAIJ
Mix.	0.678	**0.703**	0.693	0.682	**0.708**	0.699
Impr. %	-	3.69%	2.21%	-	3.81%	2.49%
LB	0.665	**0.689**	0.686	0.675	**0.696**	0.690
Impr. %	-	3.61%	3.16%	-	3.11%	2.22%
MB	0.663	**0.686**	0.681	0.671	**0.693**	0.687
Impr. %	-	3.47%	2.71%	-	3.28%	2.38%
SB	0.650	**0.677**	0.659	0.657	**0.685**	0.666
Impr. %	-	4.15%	1.38%	-	4.26%	1.37%

5   Concluding Remarks and future work

In this paper, we develop solutions methods for the two dimensional bin packing problem with irregular pieces and multiple bins sizes, also known as 2D-
IMBSBPP, where the objective is to maximize the overall utilisation of bins.
This problem is practical in several material cutting industries yet new to the
research literature.

We demonstrate that the iterated jostle algorithm outperforms an adapted
genetic algorithm and simple repeated random construction. Our results also
show that a greater selection of bins provides more efficient packing and, when
restricting the subset of bins, large bins are more useful. Moreover, for smaller
bins, the bin selection is more important than with larger bins.

Our algorithms support the objectives of efficient material use and material
procurement decisions. Being able to solve bin packing over heterogeneous bins
means that retaining and re-using residual material becomes possible within
the cutting planning system. We note that other costs in addition to material
waste affect production cost. Our method is also robust to implement different
objective functions such as including set-up and inventory costs.

References

[1] Abeysooriya, R. P., Bennell, J. A., and Martinez-Sykora, A. (2015). Jostle heuristic for 2D-Irregular shaped Packing Problems with Free Rotation. *27th European Conference on Operational Research.*

[2] Alvarez-Valdes, R., Parreño, F., and Tamarit, J. M. (2013). A GRASP/Path Relinking algorithm for two- and three-dimensional multiple bin-size bin packing problems. *Computers & Operations Research,* 40:3081–3090.

[3] Babu, A. R. and Babu, N. R. (1999). Effective nesting of rectangular parts in multiple rectangular sheets using genetic and heuristic algorithms. *International Journal of Production Research,* 37(7):1625–1643.

[4] Babu, A. R. and Babu, N. R. (2001). A generic approach for nesting of 2-D parts in 2-D sheets using genetic and heuristic algorithms. *Computer-Aided Design,* 33(12):879–891.

[5] Baldacci, R., Boschetti, M. A., Ganovelli, M., and Maniezzo, V. (2014). Algorithms for nesting with defects. *Discrete Applied Mathematics,* 163, Part 1:17–33.

[6] Bennell, J. A. and Dowsland, K. A. (2001). Hybridising Tabu Search with Optimisation Techniques for Irregular Stock Cutting. *Management Science,* 47(8):1160–1172.

[7] Bennell, J. A. and Oliveira, J. F. (2009). A Tutorial in Irregular Shape Packing Problems. *The Journal of the Operational Research Society,* 60:s93–s105.

[8] Bennell, J. A. and Song, X. (2008). A comprehensive and robust procedure for obtaining the nofit polygon using Minkowski sums. *Computers & Operations Research,* 35(1):267–281.

[9] Bennell, J. A. and Song, X. (2010). A beam search implementation for the irregular shape packing problem. *Journal of Heuristics,* 16(2):167–188.

[10] Dowsland, K. A., Dowsland, W. B., and Bennell, J. A. (1998). Jostling for position: local improvement for irregular cutting patterns. *Journal of the Operational Research Society,* 49(6):647–658.

[11] Falkenauer, E. (1999). The worth of the uniform [uniform crossover]. In *Proceedings of the 1999 Congress on Evolutionary Computation-CEC99 (Cat. No. 99TH8406),* volume 1, page 782 Vol. 1.

[12] Gonçalves, J. F. and Resende, M. G. C. (2013). A biased random key genetic algorithm for 2D and 3D bin packing problems. *International Journal of Production Economics,* 145(2):500–510.

[13] Han, W., Bennell, J. A., Zhao, X., and Song, X. (2013). Construction heuristics for two-dimensional irregular shape bin packing with guillotine constraints. *European Journal of Operational Research,* 230(3):495–504.

[14] Lopez-Camacho, E., Ochoa, G., Terashima-Marin, H., and Burke, E. K. (2013). An effective heuristic for the two-dimensional irregular bin packing problem. *Annals of Operations Research,* 206(1):241–264.

[15] Martinez-Sykora, A., Alvarez-Valdes, R., Bennell, J., and Tamarit, J. M. (2015). Constructive procedures to solve 2-dimensional bin packing problems with irregular pieces and guillotine cuts. *Omega,* 52:15–32.

[16] Martinez-Sykora, A., Alvarez-Valdes, R., Bennell, J. A., Ruiz, R., and Tamarit, J. M. (2017). Matheuristics for the irregular bin packing problem with free rotations. *European Journal of Operational Research,* 258(2):440–455.

[17] Oliveira, J. F., Gomes, A. M., and Ferreira, J. S. (2000). TOPOS – A new constructive algorithm for nesting problems. *OR-Spektrum,* 22(2):263–284.

[18] Ortmann, F. G., Ntene, N., and van Vuuren, J. H. (2010). New and improved level heuristics for the rectangular strip packing and variable-sized bin packing problems. *European Journal of Operational Research,* 203(2):306–315.

[19] Pisinger, D. and Sigurd, M. (2005). The two-dimensional bin packing problem with variable bin sizes and costs. *Discrete Optimization*, 2(2):154–167.

[20] Song, X. and Bennell, J. A. (2014). Column generation and sequential heuristic procedure for solving an irregular shape cutting stock problem. *Journal of the Operational Research Society*, 65(7):1037–1052.

[21] Wei, L., Oon, W., Zhu, W., and Lim, A. (2013). A goal-driven approach to the 2D bin packing and variable-sized bin packing problems. *European Journal of Operational Research*, 224:110–121.

Reducing Airport Emissions with Coordinated Pushback Processes: A Case Study

Branko Bubalo, Frederik Schulte, and Stefan Voß

Institute of Information Systems, University of Hamburg, Germany
{branko.bubalo,frederik.schulte,stefan.voss@uni-hamburg.de}

Abstract. Empirical research has shown that airside ground operations imply a significant percentage of overall airport-related emissions. Among those operations, taxiing is one of the most emission-intensive processes, directly related to the initial pushback process that has a significant impact on the taxiing duration of departing flights. Possible approaches for an effective management of pushbacks at an airport are simulation and optimization models. Airside operations at major airports involve a complex interplay of many operations and parties and therefore need to be planned in a coordinated fashion. Yet, existing approaches have not been applied in a comprehensive planning environment for airside operations. In this work, we develop an algorithm-based relocation approach for pushback vehicles that enables an effective minimization of delays and emissions during the taxiing process. As a result alternative sequences of departing flights are evaluated against each other to find the ones with least total emissions and delay. These algorithms are applied in a simulation environment and evaluated against real-world cases. Preliminary results demonstrate that we are able to solve the underlying pushback routing problem in appropriate computational times for dynamic decision support needed at airports.

1 Introduction

Airport emissions have recently received plenty of attention by regulators, airport operators, and researchers aiming to foster environmental sustainability that is threatened by emissions and delays caused in the aviation industry. Apart from the reduction of noise and gaseous emissions like carbon dioxide (CO_2), other emissions like, e.g., oxides of nitrogen (NO_x) need to be considered as well. Currently, the (German) automobile industry is troubled by intense public debates. This industry failed to reduce NO_x emitted by diesel motors according to the permitted threshold values. Regarding airports, empirical research has shown that airside ground operations form the biggest share of overall airport-related emissions [2,6,22]. Among those ground operations, aircraft that are taxiing, i.e., traveling to the runways from the aircraft parking position or vice versa, are the largest contributors to pollution. At some airports, over 40% of ground-based aircraft emissions are related to taxiing [2]. Therefore, various approaches to reduce taxiing times and emissions have recently been introduced [18,23]. These

© Springer International Publishing AG 2017
T. Bektaş et al. (Eds.), ICCL 2017, LNCS 10572, pp. 572–586, 2017.
https://doi.org/10.1007/978-3-319-68496-3_38

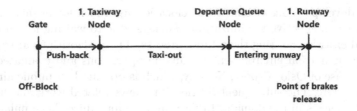

Fig. 1. Relation of pushback and taxiing process

studies have focused on the development of alternative engine power settings or pushback frequencies to control the taxiing duration, but did not consider approaches to grant the availability of pushback vehicles in a holistic planning model for airside operations. The taxiing time of departing flights is directly related to the initiating pushback processes [19]. Possible approaches to tackle this problem are simulation and optimization models for an effective management of pushbacks as a resource at the airport. Promising relocation models and adoptions of the vehicle routing problem (VRP) [17] have been proposed for related problems in different domains [16]. Airside operations at major airports involve a complex interplay of many operations and parties [20] and thus need to be planned and optimized in a coordinated fashion, especially as air traffic growth will lead to increasing demand, quicker aircraft turnarounds and requests for available pushback vehicles in higher frequencies. Yet, existing approaches have not been applied in a comprehensive planning environment for airside operations. They rather take pushback availability for granted in taxiing planning [18]. However, we regard this view as too narrow.

With the constant increase in air traffic, airports are facing capacity problems. This can be due to bottlenecks on each and every level of airport operations. Optimization methods for specific airport processes are increasingly utilized by many large airports. However, many processes occur in parallel and make more complex optimization models necessary, which can consider multiple parallel processes simultaneously [21]. This general observation also holds in the regarded case of the pushback control problem considering taxiing emissions as Fig. 1 illustrates. A pushback vehicle pushes an aircraft into a taxiway and initiates the taxiing process. Hence, the pushback defines when an aircraft starts the taxi-out phase and enters the departure queue. However, with an increasing amount of aircraft in queue the taxiing time and delay of an aircraft grows non-linearly—an effect that is explained in the general theory of load-dependent lead times [14] and has been confirmed for the taxiing process in aviation [19]. In line with the increased delay, evitable costs for fuel burn and emissions result from a too large departure queue of aircraft. To address the issue of bad timing in pushback control, we propose to plan taxiing in order to minimize delay and emissions and to schedule pushbacks on that basis. For this approach pushback vehicles need to be relocated according to the position of aircraft scheduled for taxiing. In this work, we develop an algorithm-based relocation approach for pushback vehicles that enables an effective minimization of delays, due to waiting for an available truck, and emissions during the taxiing process. These algorithms are applied in a realistic simulation environment for airside operations and evaluated for the real-world case of Oslo Airport, Norway, which is operated by public airport operator AVINOR. The subsequent Section 2 reviews related work and highlights current challenges in the domain. In Section 3 we introduce the simulation used for the emission evaluation. Section 4 proposes several vehicle routing models for the pushback relocation, a metaheuristic for quick solutions within the dynamic airport environment, and quantitative results for instances available in literature [17]. Section 5 elaborates on the promising conceptual integration of the simulation and the routing model, before Section 6 draws conclusions and discusses future work.

2   Related Work

Research related to this study falls into three basic categories: (I.) Estimation of airport ground emissions, especially taxiing emissions, (II.) general work on airside operations including taxiing and pushback processes as well as (III.) routing of airport vehicles. In describing the System for assessing Aviations Global Emissions (SAGE), Kim et al. [10] lay the fundamentals for modeling emission inventories related to aircraft fuel burn. Setting the focus on take-off activities, Zhu et al. [25] demonstrate the local air quality impacts at the Los Angeles International Airport. Following these studies, Koudis et al. [11] show that reduced thrust takeoff operations can reduce fuel consumption and pollutant emissions in the studied case of London Heathrow airport. Moreover, several authors examine taxiing emissions in detail. Nikoleries et al. [13] as well as Khadilkar and Balakrishnan [9] apply different approaches to estimate taxiing emissions. Yang et al. [24] extend these findings by predicting the market potential and environmental benefits of deploying electric taxis in Nanjing, China. With a focus on airside operations, Atkin et al. [1] address the pushback time allocation problem at London Heathrow airport. Stergianos et al. [21] follow up in this direction by analyzing the effect of pushback delays on the routing and scheduling problem of aircraft, while Mori [12] applies a reinforcement learning approach to obtain optimal pushback times facing uncertainties at busy airports. Similarly, Balakrishna et al. [3] use reinforcement learning algorithms for predicting aircraft taxi-out times. Related to routing problems at an airport, Guépet et al. [7] provide a mixed-integer programming formulation for the aircraft ground routing problem. Summarizing, the literature review reveals promising approaches in all three categories mentioned initially. Nevertheless, the integration of various interconnected problems at an airport appears to remain an important challenge for future research, and that applies also for the considered problems of pushback routing and taxiing.

3   Simulation Model

In order to analyze the dependencies between pushback control and aircraft taxiing, we have built a simulation model for the practical case of Oslo airport. The
simulation model captures the queuing behavior of aircraft during the taxiing
process and thus allows us to analyze different schedules of pushback control
with respect to taxiing delay, i.e. lead times, fuel burn (costs), and emissions.
We have constructed the simulation model based on real-world input data. The
link-and-node network model is a representation of Oslo airport and its terminal maneuvering airspace (TMA) on a design peak day in the year 2017. This
means, all arrival and departure routes within the terminal area, and all runways, taxiways, and parking stands which are expected to be installed by 2017
are included in the model, even infrastructure that was still under construction
during the preparation of this study. For our taxiing times and delay calculations
we made use of the Airport & Airspace Simulation Model (SIMMOD) version
4.7.9 that is developed by the U.S. Federal Aviation Administration. We have
run the simulation engine on a 64-bit Windows 10 machine with 8 GB RAM and
an Intel Core i5-3337U 1.8 GHz processor. A run of 100 iterations took less than
seven minutes, of which pure calculation time (without additional time required
for user input in cases when gridlocks occur in the simulation) is estimated at
less than three minutes.

   Based on documents from the airport, we were able to build a model which
behaves sufficiently realistic and which shows similar characteristics as the
real airport. We included the flight schedule, the aircraft type mix, the air and
ground movements into our model which was continuously approved by feedback
talks and discussion with local experts. Arrivals in the schedule are linked to the
respective departure in the schedule to model the full aircraft turnaround. The
taxiing of aircraft on the apron is modeled by the SIMMOD logic, which directs
aircraft to take the quickest path from the runway exits to the gates after landing
or from the gates to the runway departure queues prior departure. An important
prerequisite in the simulation is the programming of traffic rules at taxiway
crossings and largers tarmac areas to prevent collision conflicts. When aircraft
share certain single lane taxiways in both directions this could lead to head-on
situations, where the simulation needs rules of how to prioritize aircraft to pass
such bottlenecks. Otherwise it could happen that aircraft around bottlenecks
and hotspots gridlock, i.e., they indefinitely block each other. The simulation
is unable to solve gridlock situations automatically, it is only able to predict
potential conflict situations and let aircraft wait at predefined nodes until they
can pass one or many taxiway segments unhindered. We solved many gridlock
problems by including additional traffic rules at intersections and at certain
taxiways, but we stopped, when more than 50% of all iterations were gridlock
free.

   Oslo airport operates two independent parallel runways. The runways are
operated under mixed mode, which means departures and arrivals are served in
sequence on both runways during the same hours of day. This type of operation
offers more capacity for the airport, as long as air traffic control (ATC) permits

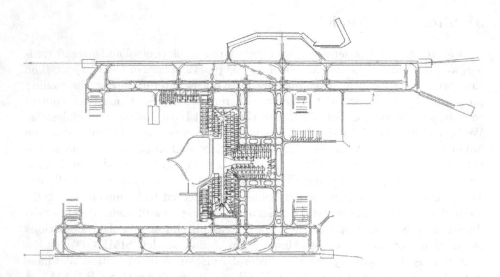

Fig. 2. A simulation model for Oslo airport

departures to be put between two consecutive arrivals or vice versa. If the gaps between two flights are becoming narrow, long queues can form at the departure queues, where aircraft wait for approval to enter the runway to start the take-off roll.

In our model we defined six different concourses, i.e., groups of gates which are located near to each other at different terminals. We have defined concourses for gates and parking stands around taxiway Kilo and taxiway Lima, one East and one West of the new North pier, one remote concourse for mail flights and one concourse with a few stands for heavy cargo aircraft as shown in Figure 2. The main purpose why we run simulations is its output in form of taxiing durations and delays for each flight when traveling from the gates to the runways, while crossing the airfield and paths of other aircraft. From the SIMMOD output we can extract an extensive amount of useful data for further computational experiments. The taxiing phase from and to the runways can be broken down in segments, by pushback, taxi-out, taxi-in, departure queue arrival, departure queue departure, runway exit times, etc.

In order to calculate emissions, such as hydrocarbon (HC), carbon monoxide (CO), NO_x and CO_2 for each aircraft for a particular airport, we need the amount of burned fuel as a basis for further emission estimations [22]. The process to calculate emissions for this study was conducted as follows:

1. Step: We take the time records (e.g., pushback times and departure ground delay) from SIMMOD.

2. Step: Calculate fuel burn during the taxiing (in kilograms per second) from off-block time at the gate to the time (point) of brakes release at the runway departure queue, before the aircraft turns into the runway and starts its take-off run.
3. Step: Calculate HC, CO and NO_x from fuel flow quantity (in grams per kilogram fuel).
4. Step: Multiply emission by the number of engines per aircraft.
5. Step: Calculate CO_2 emissions from fuel flow by applying factor 3.157 (kilogram CO_2 per kilogram fuel) [8].

This sequence of calculation steps is repeated after each iteration. We have run first 20, later up to 100, iterations. Due to the complex interactions of aircraft on the modeled airfield of Oslo airport we experienced several gridlock problems, where aircraft block each other on the apron and the situation could not be solved by the SIMMOD logic. In such cases queuing aircraft accumulate quickly and block other aircraft on taxiways in the area. When threshold values for very long waiting times of blocked aircraft are reached, the simulation will stop. We analyzed only simulation runs that were gridlock-free, which means that all scheduled flights during the day were simulated. The design peak day schedule from June 14, 2013 had 776 flights. To make the model and its results more realistic and robust, we included random factors in form of probability distributions into the model, mainly for actual departures occurring within a 15-minute time window after the scheduled departure time, for landing and take-off roll distance and for arriving aircraft choosing a particular gate at a defined concourse. In this study, growth above the amount of traffic in the design peak day schedule is neglected.

We intentionally include aircraft delay experienced along the taxiway path from the beginning of the pushback process at the gate until the exiting of the departure queue at the runway. Thus, we want to increase traffic and minimize total taxiing time (by changing the pushback sequence). In this study, we only examine the effect of randomly re-sequencing flights within a 15-minute time window. This gives us an indication of the minimal and maximal externalities (delay and emissions) and their respective flight and pushback sequence. The pushback begins at the scheduled departure time plus a random time between 0 and 15 minutes, assuming a uniform distribution. In this study the pushback duration has been set at 180 seconds for all gates, except for self maneuvering aircraft stands, where a pushback truck is not needed. In subsequent studies we want to model the pushback procedures more gate specific.

We take the taxiing times from the simulation and apply the factors shown in Table 1. At first, we calculate the amount of burned fuel during the taxiing out phase for different aircraft types. We observe that more than 60% of the aircraft flying into OSL are Boeing 737 type aircrafts. Table 1 gives us the factors for fuel flow in kilograms per second at idle engine conditions, which means the engine thrust is set between 0% and 7% (in case of turbo prop aircaft, e.g. DHC8, DHC6 or SF340) of the maximum. This number must then be multiplied by the number of engines. The amounts of gaseous emissions (in grams) correspond to the amount of fuel burned (in kilograms), thus we can now apply the factors for HC, CO, or NO_x from Table 1. The last emission type we want to quantify is CO_2. As presented in Step 5, we derive the amount of CO_2 (in kilograms) by multiplying the total fuel burned during taxi-out (in kilograms) times 3.157 [8]. Table 2 gives us an overview of the calculated quantities for nine different

Table 1. Oslo airport aircraft mix and engine emission factors

Aircraft type	Percentage of flights	Engine identification	Number of engines	HC emission index (g/kg) at idle condition	CO emission index (g/kg) at idle condition	NO_x emission index (g/kg) at idle condition	Fuel burn (kg/sec) at idle condition
	%	-	-	g/kg	g/kg	g/kg	kg/sec
737	38,4%	JT8D-9	2	3,12	14,1	2,9	0,132
737300	25,8%	CFM56-3-B1	2	2,28	34,4	3,9	0,114
A320	9,6%	CFM56-5-A1	2	1,40	17,6	4,0	0,101
DHC8	8,0%	PW123	2	3,10	48,3	3,1	0,043
737500	6,8%	CFM56-3-B1	2	2,28	34,4	3,9	0,114
SF340	4,0%	CT7-9B	2	3,52	27,7	1,7	0,019
F10062	2,4%	TAY Mk620-15	2	3,40	24,1	2,5	0,110
720	1,4%	JT3D-3B	4	112,00	98,0	2,5	0,135
757PW	1,0%	PW2037	2	1,92	22,4	4,1	0,152
DHC6	0,9%	PT6A-67	2	3,10	48,3	1,8	0,019
747400	0,4%	PW4056	4	1,92	21,9	4,8	0,208
747SP	0,4%	JT9D-7	4	36,50	84,1	3,1	0,210
767300	0,3%	PW4060	2	1,66	20,3	4,9	0,213
MD82	0,3%	JT8D-217	2	3,33	12,3	3,7	0,137
A300	0,1%	CF6-5C2	2	2,72	24,0	3,4	0,163

iterations. The taxiing out durations vary between 2937 and 3048 minutes (or around 50 hours) per day, of which about 7% are waiting times (delay). This results directly in between 40.12 and 42.01 tons of burned fuel for all daily departures. Not surprisingly CO_2 emissions have the highest amounts of all emissions, with between 126.7 and 132.6 tons for all 382 daily departing flights. Amounts of HC are calculated between 252.2 and 327.1 kilograms, amounts of CO between 1032.3 and 1119.6 kilograms and amounts of NO_x between 134.3 and 140.99 kilograms. We have ranked the iterations by total externalities, delay and emissions (Table 2). Our results seem to be of the same order of magnitude compared to similar studies, such as [22]. From all run iterations, iteration 13 performs best with regard to total externalities. We ranked the iterations by each category, and then by overall performance. Iteration 13 reveals 382 daily departures, which need 2938 minutes of taxi-out time. On average aircraft taxi-out to one of the two parallel runways approximately 8 minutes, of which around 3 minutes are pushback time. It should be noted that the simulation represents a "perfect" environment, i.e., weather effects were not taken into account and we assume that aircraft always travel the maximum allowed speed limit, which may be 5, 10 or 15 knots etc., depending on the type and location of the taxiway. Aircraft are usually placed at a gate close to the landing runway or directed to a runway close to the parking stand in case of arrivals. This procedure, that is administered by ATC, shall minimize the number of aircraft traveling around the whole airfield. We followed the same approach when the simulation was programmed, particularly in such cases, when the information was not given in the original schedule from Oslo airport.

Table 2. Results from the computations ranked by lowest to highest total emissions

Rank	Iter-ation	Taxi time	Taxi fuel burn	HC	CO	NO_x	CO_2	Ground delay	Depar-tures
		min.	tons	kg	kg	kg	tons	min.	-
1	13	2937,8	40,1	252,1	1032,3	134,3	126,6	209	382
2	1	2937,4	40,3	284,2	1079,8	135,1	127,2	280	381
3	17	2964,3	40,4	294,0	1082,5	134,3	127,5	277	381
4	14	2943,7	40,9	287,8	1088,5	137,6	129,1	311	382
5	18	2981,4	40,9	323,4	1100,7	135,7	129,2	357	382
6	5	3033,1	41,0	284,0	1062,3	136,6	129,5	304	382
7	2	2999	41,0	301,7	1090,9	136,4	129,5	337	382
8	12	2978,3	41,3	327,1	1119,6	138,4	130,6	245	382
9	9	3048,3	42,0	279,4	1108,6	140,9	132,6	293	381

4   Dynamic Vehicle Routing Model

The pushback relocation problem described in the introduction has been modeled as skill vehicle routing problem (skill VRP) to reflect different qualifications of pushback vehicles to serve aircraft types. Next, we introduce two ways to model a skill pushback routing problem (Section 4.1) and present a large neighborhood search (LNS) metaheuristic for the dynamic application (Section 4.2) as well as results for benchmark instances from literature (Section 4.3).

4.1   A Skill VRP Formulation for Pushback Vehicles

This skill VRP is a variant of the site-dependent VRP; see, e.g., Cordeau and Laporte [4]. Following Schwarze and Voß [17], we adopt the skill VRP formulation to the pushback routing and control introduced in the beginning. Assuming $G = (N, A)$ as a directed graph, with $|N| = n$ and $|A| = m$. Let each node $j, j \neq 1$, represent a service requirement by an aircraft, and s_j denote the skill level required by node j for the associated pushback service by a specific aircraft. On the other hand, node 1 denotes the depot. We assume a set P of available pushback vehicles, each one operating at a certain skill level, were s_p denotes the skill level of pushback vehicle $p \in P$. Furthermore, we suppose that the service requirement at node j can be operated by any pusback vehicle having a skill level of at least s_j, for $j \in N \setminus \{1\}$, and S denotes the set of skills given by the union of the skill requirements sets at the nodes and the skill sets associated with the pushback vehicles, i.e., $S = s_i : i \in N \cup s_p : p \in P$. Given non-negative skill-dependent traveling costs c_{ij}^p for each $(i, j) \in A$ and pushback vehicle $p \in P$, we study the problem of defining the tour vehicles, each one starting and ending at node 1, in such a way that each service requirement of the considered aircraft is fulfilled by exactly one pushback vehicle, and the skill level constraints are satisfied. Moreover, we define c_{ij}^p as the time needed by p to traverse edge (i, j) and $a_i, b_i \geq 0$ as the lower and upper bounds of the time window for node i. Finally, let the operation time $o_i \geq 0$ be the time needed to carry out the service at i and M be a large number. For each $(i, j) \in A$ and $p \in P$ with $s_p \geq \max\{s_i, s_j\}$ denote

$$
x_{ij}^p = \begin{cases} 1 \text{ if } (i, j) \in A \text{ is in the tour of vehicle } p, \\ 0 \text{ otherwise} \end{cases}
$$

and

$$
z_k^p = \begin{cases} 1 \text{ if } k \in N \setminus \{1\} \text{ is served by vehicle } p, \\ 0 \text{ otherwise.} \end{cases}
$$

Moreover, let y_{ij} be a non-negative flow variable for each $(i, j) \in A$ and $w_i^p \geq 0$ the time when the vehicle starts a service at node $i \in N \setminus \{1\}$. The problem is then given as

$$
\min \sum_{(i,j) \in A} \sum_{p: s_p \geq \max\{s_i, s_j\}} c_{ij}^p x_{ij}^p \tag{1}
$$

$$
\sum_{i \in N} \sum_{p: s_p \geq \max\{s_i, s_j\}} x_{ij}^p = 1 \quad \forall j \neq 1 \tag{2}
$$

$$
\sum_{i \in N: s_p \geq s_i} x_{ij}^p = \sum_{i \in N: s_p \geq s_i} x_{ji}^p \quad \forall j \neq 1, p : s_p \geq s_j \tag{3}
$$

$$
\sum_{i \in N} y_{1i} = n - 1 \tag{4}
$$

$$
\sum_{i \in N} y_{ij} - \sum_{i \in N} y_{ji} = 1 \quad \forall j \neq 1 \tag{5}
$$

$$y_{ij} \leq (n-1) \sum_{p:s_p \geq \max\{s_i, s_j\}} x_{ij}^p \quad (i,j) \in A \tag{6}$$

$$w_i^p + o_i + c_{ij} - w_j^p \leq M(1 - x_{ij}^p) \quad \forall (i,j) \in A :\neq 1; p : s_p \geq \max\{s_i, s_j\} \tag{7}$$

$$a_i z_k^p \leq w_k^p \leq b_k z_k^p \quad \forall k \neq 1, p : s_p \geq s_j \tag{8}$$

$$w_k^p \geq 0 \quad \forall k \neq 1, p : s_p \geq s_j \tag{9}$$

$$x_{ij}^p \in \{0,1\} \quad (i,j) \in A, p : s_p \geq \max\{s_i, s_j\} \tag{10}$$

$$y_{ij} \geq 0 \quad (i,j) \in A \tag{11}$$

$$z_k^p \in \{0,1\} \quad \forall k \neq 1, p : s_p \geq s_j \tag{12}$$

The objective function (1) minimizes the total routing costs for the pushback vehicles. Constraints (2) and (3) grant that each node is served by an appropriate vehicle and establish tours for the vehicles. The flow constraints (4) and (5) in combination with constraints (6), linking the decision variables, break potential subtours. Constraints (7) and (8) enforce time windows, while constraints (9) – (12) are standard restrictions on the decision variables.

4.2 A Large Neighborhood Search Algorithm

An initial CPLEX implementation of the introduced mathematical program for the problem lead to impractical computational times, even for small instances. For planning in the dynamic environment of an airport computationally efficient algorithms for the defined pushback routing problem are desirable. We have therefore developed a LNS algorithm for the problem. LNS algorithms have been successfully applied to VRPs with time windows [15]. The core idea of an LNS heuristic is a large neighborhood that enables the algorithm to explore the solution space easily, even if the instance is tightly constrained. This is usually much harder with small neighborhoods [15]. Let U be the set of feasible solutions for the pushback routing problem, then $u \in U$ is a single solution and $N(u)$ be the neighborhood of solution u, defined as the set of solutions that can be reached by applying the *destroy* and *repair* methods typical for LNS. The function $d(\cdot)$ is the destroy method, while $r(\cdot)$ is the repair method. That means, $d(u)$ returns a modified version of u that is partly destroyed. In the case skill VRP for pushback vehicles, the destroy method removes a percentage of random gates, i.e., nodes of the VRP. The method $r(\cdot)$ repairs partly destroyed solutions, i.e., it returns a feasible solution constructed of the destroyed one. In our case, the repair method applies a greedy heuristic that gradually selects gates with the lowest cost and adds them to the solution.

Algorithm 1 An LNS algorithm for the pushback routing problem

---

1: $u \leftarrow$ feasible solution
2: $u^b \leftarrow initialize(u)$
3: **repeat**
4:      $u^t \leftarrow r(d(u))$
5:      **if** $accept(u^t, u)$ **then**
6:         $u \leftarrow u^t$
7:      **end if**
8:      **if** $c(u^t) < c(u^b)$ **then**
9:         $u^b \leftarrow u^t$
10:    **end if**
11: **until** stop criterion
12: **return** u^b

The LNS procedure is illustrated in Algorithm 1. The algorithm uses three variables. u^b is the best solution, u is the current solution, and u^t is a temporary solution that can either become the current solution or get discarded. The algorithm starts by initializing the global best solution u^b using a feasible solution u. This solution enters a loop in which the destroy method $(d(\cdot))$ and then the repair method $(r(\cdot))$ are repeatedly applied to obtain new solutions u^t. Then this solution is evaluated based on some criterion; we have used cost-improving solutions as a default criterion. If it is accepted, the current solution is updated. The accept function can be implemented in different ways. Next x^t is evaluated, comparing its costs $c(u^t)$ to the costs of the best solution $c(u^b)$. The value $c(u)$ obviously corresponds to the objective function value of the model. If costs can be reduced, u^b is updated. After that, the termination condition—a time limit in our case—is verified. Finally, the best solution found is returned.

4.3   Computational Results

The numerical experiments have been executed on a computer equipped with an AMD Opteron Processor 6272 2,1 GHz and 128 GB of RAM under Windows Server 2012. We use the instances introduced by Schwarze and Voß [17] that assume an airport with 17 gates and 6 pushback vehicles. The skills of the vehicles are $s_1 = s_2 = s_3 = s_4 = 2$ and $s_5 = s_6 = 3$. At each node (gate) there is a single aircraft that requires a pushback service with a certain skill level. We have three aircraft that require skill 1, seven requiring skill 2 and another seven requiring skill 3. The time windows start between time units 0 and 100 and have a constant length of 25 time units.

We have conducted the scenarios assuming *skill levels* and *skill sets* for the pushback vehicles. That means, vehicles with skill levels have downwards compatible skills and can serve all aircraft with skill levels less than or equal to their own skill, and vehicles with skill sets have to exactly match the skill requirements. Table 3 and Table 4 display the results for both scenarios. The preliminary results demonstrate that we are able to solve all considered instances under three seconds with the implemented LNS. Though the instances are relatively small, this confirms that the LNS provides solutions in adequate computational time for the dynamic application. Instances of the described problem reflect a decentralized organization at airports where different companies operate different fleets of of pushback vehicles. Moreover, the implementation of skill sets or skill levels has no significant impact on the computational times, and computational times are consistently low for different initial solutions.

<table>
<tr><td colspan="5">**Table 3.** Results for skill levels</td></tr>
<tr><td># Routes</td><td>Jobs</td><td>Time</td><td>Costs</td></tr>
<tr><td>1</td><td>9</td><td>17</td><td>2,65</td><td>328,44</td></tr>
<tr><td>2</td><td>9</td><td>17</td><td>2,61</td><td>512,64</td></tr>
<tr><td>3</td><td>8</td><td>17</td><td>2,58</td><td>873,69</td></tr>
<tr><td>4</td><td>9</td><td>17</td><td>2,59</td><td>382,47</td></tr>
<tr><td>5</td><td>8</td><td>17</td><td>2,49</td><td>719,19</td></tr>
</table>

Table 3. Results for skill levels

#	Routes	Jobs	Time	Costs
1	9	17	2,65	328,44
2	9	17	2,61	512,64
3	8	17	2,58	873,69
4	9	17	2,59	382,47
5	8	17	2,49	719,19

Table 4. Results for skill sets

#	Routes	Jobs	Time	Costs
1	9	17	2,69	480,71
2	9	17	2,76	567,23
3	8	17	2,33	1297,27
4	10	17	2,48	590,23
5	8	17	2,34	982,21

5   Conceptual Integration

In order to leverage the fuel, cost, and emission saving potential in taxiing, the pushback routing and control model has to be linked to the queuing model for the taxiing process. Fig. 3 sketches the integration of the respective models presented in Section 3 and Section 4. First, the simulation model built in Simmod is used to determine load-dependent emission curves. These curves basically model aircraft taxiing times based on the number of aircraft in the taxiing process—a concept known as load-dependent lead times in production planning [14]. With the information from the simulation model, this model is extended to capture emissions as well. Next, the flight schedule is iteratively improved to minimize costs and emissions based on the queuing situation modeled using the load-dependent performance curves. This schedule is then given to the pushback routing and control model (skill VRP) in order to implement the flight schedule for the pushback processes, i.e., define the time windows for the routing problem. In the case of dynamic changes, this process is repeated. Finally, the simulation model evaluates how the plan is actually conducted, again considering costs, emissions, and delays. The implicit management strategies used are changes in the flight sequence and thresholds for the taxiing queue. The final evaluation step considers costs and emissions, while emissions are weighted using various emission price levels discussed in literature [5]. This means that delays or waiting times are implicitly considered in terms costs caused by them.

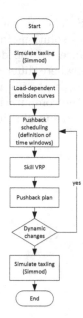

Fig. 3. Conceptual integration flow chart

6   Conclusion

Current research has emphasized the importance of the taxiing process for the overall aircraft emissions. Several studies appeared to capture and mitigate taxiing emissions. However, most approaches have not taken into account the interconnection of airport processes such as the pushback process. In this work, we have developed a simulation model for taxiing lead times and related costs as well as emissions. Furthermore, we have presented a pushback control and routing model based on skill VRP formulation, and implemented a LNS algorithm for fast solutions in the dynamic airport environment. We have also shown how the simulation model and the routing model can be integrated to fully leverage the cost and emission saving potential. Nevertheless, the presented results only refer to small benchmark results available in literature. Future work will therefore cover extensive numerical experiments with real-world data and comprehensive quantitative analysis of the integration of both the simulation and the routing model.

References

1. Jason AD Atkin, Geert De Maere, Edmund K Burke, and John S Greenwood. Addressing the pushback time allocation problem at Heathrow airport. *Transportation Science*, 47(4):584–602, 2012.
2. British Airports Authority. Heathrow Air Quality Strategy 2011–2020. Technical report, 2011.

3. Poornima Balakrishna, Rajesh Ganesan, and Lance Sherry. Accuracy of reinforcement learning algorithms for predicting aircraft taxi-out times: A case-study of Tampa Bay departures. *Transportation Research Part C: Emerging Technologies*, 18(6):950–962, 2010.

4. Jean-François Cordeau and Gilbert Laporte. A tabu search algorithm for the site dependent vehicle routing problem with time windows. *INFOR: Information Systems and Operational Research*, 39(3):292–298, 2001.

5. Ottmar Edenhofer, Michael Jakob, Felix Creutzig, Christian Flachsland, Sabine Fuss, Martin Kowarsch, Kai Lessmann, Linus Mattauch, Jan Siegmeier, and Jan Christoph Steckel. Closing the emission price gap. *Global Environmental Change*, 31:132 – 143, 2015.

6. Selcuk Ekici, Gorkem Yalin, Onder Altuntas, and T. Hikmet Karakoc. Calculation of HC, CO and NO x from civil aviation in Turkey in 2012. *International Journal of Environment and Pollution*, 53(3):232–244, 2013.

7. Julien Guépet, Olivier Briant, Jean-Philippe Gayon, and Rodrigo Acuna-Agost. The aircraft ground routing problem: Analysis of industry punctuality indicators in a sustainable perspective. *European Journal of Operational Research*, 248(3):827–839, 2016.

8. Christian N Jardine. Calculating the carbon dioxide emissions of flights: Final report by the Environmental Change Institute. Technical report, Environmental Change Institute, 2009.

9. Harshad Khadilkar and Hamsa Balakrishnan. Estimation of aircraft taxi fuel burn using flight data recorder archives. *Transportation Research Part D: Transport and Environment*, 17(7):532–537, 2012.

10. Brian Y Kim, Gregg G Fleming, Joosung J Lee, Ian A Waitz, John-Paul Clarke, Sathya Balasubramanian, Andrew Malwitz, Kelly Klima, Maryalice Locke, Curtis A Holsclaw, et al. System for assessing aviations global emissions (sage), part 1: Model description and inventory results. *Transportation Research Part D: Transport and Environment*, 12(5):325–346, 2007.

11. George S Koudis, Simon J Hu, Arnab Majumdar, Roderic Jones, and Marc EJ Stettler. Airport emissions reductions from reduced thrust takeoff operations. *Transportation Research Part D: Transport and Environment*, 52:15–28, 2017.

12. Ryota Mori. Optimal pushback time with existing uncertainties at busy airport. In *Proceedings of 29th Congress of the ICAS, St. Petersburg*, 2014.

13. Tasos Nikoleris, Gautam Gupta, and Matthew Kistler. Detailed estimation of fuel consumption and emissions during aircraft taxi operations at dallas/fort worth international airport. *Transportation Research Part D: Transport and Environment*, 16(4):302–308, 2011.

14. Julia Pahl, Stefan Voß, and David L Woodruff. Production planning with load dependent lead times: an update of research. *Annals of Operations Research*, 153(1):297–345, 2007.

15. David Pisinger and Stefan Ropke. Large neighborhood search. In *Handbook of metaheuristics*, pages 399–419. Springer, 2010.

16. Frederik Schulte. Allocation, routing, and sharing of empty transport resources: An overview on problems and methods. *Working Paper, Institute of Information Systems, University of Hamburg, Hamburg*, 2017.

17. Silvia Schwarze and Stefan Voß. A Bicriteria Skill Vehicle Routing Problem with Time Windows and an Application to Pushback Operations at Airports. In Jan Dethloff, Hans-Dietrich Haasis, Herbert Kopfer, Herbert Kotzab, and Jörn Schönberger, editors, *Logistics Management*, Lecture Notes in Logistics, pages 289–300. Springer, 2015.

18. Ioannis Simaiakis and Hamsa Balakrishnan. Queuing models of airport departure processes for emissions reduction. In *AIAA Guidance, Navigation and Control Conference and Exhibit*, 2009.
19. Ioannis Simaiakis and Hamsa Balakrishnan. Impact of congestion on taxi times, fuel burn, and emissions at major airports. *Transportation Research Record: Journal of the Transportation Research Board*, 2184(1):22–30, 2010.
20. L. Douglas Smith, Jan F. Ehmke, Dirk C. Mattfeld, Raimund Waning, and Laura Hellmann. Strategic Decision Support for Airside Operations at Commercial Airports. In *Computational Logistics*, pages 132–150. Springer, 2014.
21. Christofas Stergianos, Jason Atkin, Patrick Schittekat, Tomas Eric Nordlander, Chris Gerada, and Herve Morvan. The effects of pushback delays on airport ground movement. *Journal of Applied Operational Research*, 7(2):68–79, 2015.
22. Morten Winther, Uffe Kousgaard, Thomas Ellermann, Andreas Massling, Jacob Klenø Nøjgaard, and Matthias Ketzel. Emissions of NOx particle mass and particle numbers from aircraft main engines, APU's and handling equipment at Copenhagen Airport. *Atmospheric Environment*, 100:218–229, 2015.
23. Richard Wollenheit and Thorsten Mühlhausen. Operational and environmental assessment of electric taxi based on fast-time simulation. *Transportation Research Record: Journal of the Transportation Research Board*, 2336(1):36–42, 2013.
24. Jie Yang, Jing Dong, Zhenhong Lin, and Liang Hu. Predicting market potential and environmental benefits of deploying electric taxis in nanjing, china. *Transportation Research Part D: Transport and Environment*, 49:68–81, 2016.
25. Yifang Zhu, Elinor Fanning, Rong Chun Yu, Qunfang Zhang, and John R Froines. Aircraft emissions and local air quality impacts from takeoff activities at a large international airport. *Atmospheric Environment*, 45(36):6526–6533, 2011.

Author Index

Printed in the United States
By Bookmasters

Printed in the United States
By Bookmasters